The DEVIL REACHED TOWARD *The* SKY

ALSO BY GARRETT M. GRAFF

D-DAY The Oral History: The Turning Point of WWII By the People Who Were There

UFO: The Inside Story of the US Government's Search for Alien Life Here—and Out There

Watergate: A New History

The Only Plane in the Sky: An Oral History of 9/11

Raven Rock: The Story of the U.S. Government's Secret Plan to Save Itself—While the Rest of Us Die

The Threat Matrix: The FBI at War

The First Campaign: Globalization, the Web, and the Race for the White House

Dawn of the Code War: America's Battle Against Russia, China, and the Rising Global Cyber Threat
(with John P. Carlin)

GARRETT M. GRAFF

NEW YORK TIMES BESTSELLING AUTHOR
AND PULITZER PRIZE FINALIST

The DEVIL REACHED TOWARD *The* SKY

THE MAKING & UNLEASHING
OF THE ATOMIC BOMB
BY THE PEOPLE WHO WERE THERE

monoray

First published in the United States in 2025 by Avid Reader, an imprint of
Simon & Schuster, Inc.,
1230 Avenue of the Americas,
New York, NY 10020

First published in Great Britain in 2025 by Monoray, an imprint of
Octopus Publishing Group Ltd
Carmelite House
50 Victoria Embankment
London EC4Y 0DZ
www.octopusbooks.co.uk

An Hachette UK Company
www.hachette.co.uk

The authorized representative in the EEA is Hachette Ireland,
8 Castlecourt Centre, Dublin 15, D15 XTP3, Ireland (email: info@hbgi.ie)

Interior design by Kyle Kabel

Hardback ISBN 978-1-80096-339-9
Trade paperback ISBN 978-1-80096-346-7
eISBN 978-1-80096-348-1

A CIP catalogue record for this book is available from the British Library.

Printed and bound in Great Britain.

1 3 5 7 9 10 8 6 4 2

This FSC® label means that materials used for
the product have been responsibly sourced.

FSC www.fsc.org MIX Paper | Supporting responsible forestry FSC® C104740

To Donna and Paul—
with love and gratitude for how
you make my writing possible

"Science is made by men, a self-evident fact that is far too often forgotten."

—Werner Heisenberg

"It is a profound and necessary truth that the deep things in science are not found because they are useful; they are found because it was possible to find them."

—J. Robert Oppenheimer

CONTENTS

PART III Making the Bomb

PART IV Readying the Bomb

PART V Unleashing the Bomb

AUTHOR'S NOTE

To watch the bombers come off the production line at Ford Motor Company's Willow Run was to be awed, hour by passing hour, with the unbeatable industrial war machine America developed to win World War II. Willow Run opened just two months before the attack on Pearl Harbor in 1941, before America was in the war but as officials and leaders came to understand that it wouldn't be long before the country was called to combat. It stretched across nearly seven million square feet, each of which had been carefully organized and custom-built to make bombers with all the precision and speed that Henry Ford's automobile factories were known for. There were eleven major assembly lines and sixty-nine smaller ones, each stage of manufacturing and construction joining together like streams into an ever-larger and onrushing river that poured bombers out faster than anyone had ever imagined possible. Throughout the factory floor, it was often women, working a prescribed fifty-four-hour week, who put together the 300,000 rivets required for each bomber; one of those workers at Willow Run, Rose Will Monroe, would be among the women forever immortalized as "Rosie the Riveter."

The result of this carefully choreographed industrial ballet was that a new bomber rolled out of the plant every sixty-three minutes, the start of a long journey to the front lines of Europe and the Pacific. And Willow Run was just one plant making one kind of bomber. All told, the United States manufactured about 50,000 bombers for action in World War II—some 18,000 B-24s, as well as about 12,700 B-17s, nearly 10,000 B-25s, 5,200 B-26s, and, toward the war's end, nearly 4,000 B-29s. Those 50,000 planes took to the skies filled with crews of brave—and often scared—young men (and, at home, female army pilots knowns as WASPs), dashingly and romantically dressed in leather jackets and scarves that would make them instant fashion icons. The romance, though, mostly existed only in one's imagination: The life expectancy of these aircrews in combat was often short. From 1942 onward, their bombs rained down with an almost unending and inescapable ferocity on Axis positions, ships, and equipment, including some 656,400 tons of bombs on Japanese targets in the Pacific and, with the help of the Royal Air Force, some 2.7 million tons of bombs on Europe. Entire cities, like Dresden and Tokyo, burned in single nights. Many of these aerial angels of death were adorned with playful names, mascots, and painted pinup girls. But in the end, history remembers the name of just two of those 50,000 planes: the *Enola Gay* and *Bockscar*.

We remember those two planes not because of how many bombs they dropped, but because of how few. One mission each, one bomb each, dropped on two different cities, three days apart in the final week of the final theater of the war. Those bombs, too, had names now also forever etched in history: "Fat Man" and "Little Boy." Globally, World War II killed upward of sixty million people—the National World War II Museum estimates the toll at 15 million combatants and 45 million civilians—and it was a war filled with horrors that continue to echo across history: the Bataan Death March, the Tokyo firebombings, the siege of Stalingrad, and the six million Jewish victims dead in Europe from the Holocaust. But the atomic bombs—weapons that killed a hundred thousand people faster than a human could react to the flash of the explosion—are not mere history. They announced the beginning of a new postwar atomic era that remains present and threatening to our daily life eight decades later.

The making of those two bombs stands as one of humanity's most monumental achievements—a project conducted completely in secrecy, under immense time pressure, that delivered to the earth a never-before-seen source of tremendous energy. It was a technology that would transform the politics and geopolitics of our world. As the head of the US science effort Vannevar Bush concluded, "The merging of efforts of science, engineering, technology, industry, labor, finance, and the military brought about the atomic bomb. In scale relative to the scale of its time, the building of the Pyramids offers a possible comparison."

While World War II was *fought* in places like Guadalcanal, El Alamein, and Bastogne, in the skies over Britain, Germany, and Japan, and in the seas of the North Atlantic, Midway, and Leyte Gulf, the war was *won* in factories like Willow Run and in laboratories at Bletchley Park, MIT, Los Alamos, and the University of Chicago, where inventions like radar, the proximity fuse, and the atomic bomb were created and advances made in meteorology, computers, and physics. Robert Furman, an engineer on the Manhattan Project, reflected decades later, "Although World War II was a big military operation—with perhaps eleven million men and women in uniform before it was over—it was equally a scientists' and mathematicians' war."

It is one of the great ironies of World War II that the weapon that would end the war with Japan was rooted firmly in the rise of the Third Reich. The story of the building of those atomic bombs began long before World War II, as teams of physicists in the US and Europe raced to unlock the secrets of the atom in the 1920s and 1930s—a small group of visionary scientists, who understood the massive destructive potential of their discoveries long before any government or military did. It was Hitler's purge and persecution of Jews that led to a flood of refugee talent departing Europe and, specifically, a group of groundbreaking physicists who had been busy inventing a new atomic science decamping for schools in the US, putting them in the right places at the right times to participate in something called the Manhattan Project. Together they formed perhaps the most talented group of scientists who have ever come together for a single purpose in world history. Having fled fascism and seen its evils up close, many also knew the esteemed scientists—led by the giant Werner Heisenberg—who would be working on the same questions in Nazi Germany, and were terrified by the consequences if Adolf Hitler unlocked the bomb's mysteries first. They woke each day in an all-out fearful race to preserve freedom and democracy.

* * *

Set on a stage as large as World War II, it's easy to lose sight that all of this—the brutality of war, the puzzle of grand strategy, the mystery of science, the advance of technology—was being lived through the individual lives and experiences of scientists, soldiers, sailors, and civilians. This oral history of the road to the atomic bomb and its first (and thus far, only) horrifying use on the cities of Hiroshima and Nagasaki, two cities specially "saved" by US war planners from earlier bombing missions to better demonstrate the monstrosity of the split atom, is meant to capture that human-level experience.

Today, the Manhattan Project stands as instant shorthand for ambition, audacity, and daring—when Covid hit in 2020, US officials immediately turned to the moniker to capture the race to build a vaccine, and more recently there have been calls by Congress for a "Manhattan Project–style" effort around artificial intelligence, semiconductor chips, and other pressing scientific challenges. And yet what continues to capture our fascination with "the" Manhattan Project is that there has never been an effort like it before or since. There is no doubt that its short three-year life from 1942 to 1945 forever transformed warfare and the world. As project director General Leslie Groves wrote, "There has never been an improvement in weapons comparable in degree and in sudden impact to the atomic bomb. In the case of other developments, such as explosives, the airplane, the tank, long-range artillery, armor-clad warships, submarines, and even rifles, it took years, if not decades and centuries, after their first use for their revolutionary influence upon warfare to be felt. In the case of the atomic bomb it took only a few hours."

The project was indeed every bit as audacious as popular memory now imagines—a crash wartime effort spread across a dozen key locations around the country, with whole new cities and facilities carved out of mountains and deserts to employ hundreds of thousands of people, scientists and engineers discovering new elements and fundamental rules of the universe and inventing new technologies in a matter of just weeks and months in the hope of building a bomb more powerful than any before out of materials that at the start of the war existed only in microscopic amounts, and all of it, from the cities to the science to the people, classified and cloaked in silence and mystery so total that the spouses of the key participants only learned the reality of the effort when it was announced on the radio by President Truman on August 6, 1945. Much of the crew of the *Enola Gay* learned the word "atom" only as the bomb was being loaded aboard. As its pilot, Col. Paul W. Tibbets, reflected, "The atom bomb was probably the best-kept military secret since a handful of Greek soldiers got inside the gates of Troy in the belly of a wooden horse."

This is not meant to be a comprehensive history of the war with Japan nor a technical explanation of nuclear fission or the atomic bomb—great books by Stephane Groueff, Lansing Lamont, Richard Rhodes, and others have already trod that ground—nor is it meant to be a detailed character study of the fascinating personalities who assembled under the umbrella of the Manhattan Project, again well-trod ground by writers like Kai Bird and Martin J. Sherwin in their magisterial biography of J. Robert Oppenheimer, *American Prometheus*. I have in certain instances streamlined the nuclear science and the twists and turns engaged in the development of the atomic bombs, skipping over certain tangential experiments, dead ends, cul-de-sacs, and red herrings to focus primarily on the main (and ultimately successful) projects.* Instead, this is the story of the daring square-dancing, pottery-buying, graphite-dust-covered, mutton-eating, poker-playing men and women who made the bombs a reality and the adventurous lives they lived against the backdrop of one of the grandest stages and highest-stakes projects in world history.

Many of these events unfolded simultaneously or near simultaneously across the 1930s and 1940s, but in order to keep the narrative straight, I have generally tended to keep geographic or thematic comments together as these parallel stories unfurl.

To assemble this oral history, I mined more than a hundred books and dozens of archives on multiple continents that contain thousands of personal memories. Altogether, the preliminary draft stretched to more than 1.4 million words of quotations, reports, testimony, and firsthand accounts, ranging from large-scale oral history projects, science memoirs, Nobel Prize lectures, and recollections from military reunions, to government reports and letters from bomb survivors in Hiroshima and Nagasaki, as well as the 1,000-page transcript of the Atomic Energy Commission's infamous 1954 security hearing focused on J. Robert Oppenheimer. Despite the eighty-year remove from the events that follow, parts of this story continue to emerge—sections of the Oppenheimer hearing were finally declassified only in 2014, and the first news reports from Nagasaki by American journalist George Weller, lost to history for decades, were uncovered only in the early 2000s.† Throughout,

* The truth about the much-feared German bomb effort is interesting itself: Germany never came close to an atomic weapon, in part because of the raging anti-Semitism that kept the Third Reich from enlisting the help of Jewish scientists. There is a fascinating book to be written—one I've long hoped to do myself—about the US hunt for atomic intelligence in Europe, but it's a story I largely keep outside this book, in the interest of streamlining the story herein. Similarly, the Russian and Japanese efforts to make a working device, neither of which advanced far during the war, also sit outside this book.

† Unlike any other oral history project I've done, not all of the testimonies herein were given voluntarily—as one witness in the Oppenheimer hearing noted, "I would like the record to show that I am appearing here by military orders, and not on my own volition."

I have edited quotations and memories for clarity and concision, clarifying antecedents and fixing verb tenses, standardized and Westernized spelling and names, and clarified certain misremembered details for historical accuracy.

A full guide to the quote sourcing is included at the back of the book, allowing interested readers to understand how I've woven together the roughly 500 voices included in this book into a grand symphony to tell a fresh story of the Manhattan Project and the end of the war with Japan. Many of the underlying sources and first-person memoirs that I've drawn upon are wonderful and fascinating reads on their own, although most are long out of print. But taken together, their memories create a vast tapestry larger and more all-encompassing than any one of the first-person testimonies could witness at the time on their own and, in this new context, even richer in their implications.

For the most part, I've chosen to identify individuals by the name and position they held during the period they're discussing. However, I have generally not provided specific titles and affiliations for the few dozen core scientists of the Manhattan Project that you will come to know in the pages ahead. They shifted repeatedly and often in short order during the course of the multidecade story, flipping from one university to another one year to the next, and in the war, from one lab to another depending even on the month. Similarly, among the military, wartime promotions or unit transfers were frequent, and for some figures, like Colonel Tibbets and other members of the B-29 crews of that 509th Composite Group, I've generally chosen the rank they held at the time of the bombings in August 1945 for consistency in identification. For most workers in the sprawling Manhattan Project labs and factories, I've generally identified them by occupation rather than precise hierarchy or job title.

* * *

Pregnant throughout this book is the debate that the US, Japan, the world, historians, and military strategists remain locked in today, a debate that will never be fully settled, about the morality and necessity of the use of the atomic bombs and the total war that engulfed the Pacific in the final months of the conflict in 1945. *Was Japan ready to surrender soon anyway? Was the second bomb used on Nagasaki necessary at all? Did the atomic bombs save more lives than they took in the cold calculation of war—and, if so, does that make their use against large civilian populations any more acceptable? How much of the US calculus on using the bomb was less about Japan than about Russia and the coming conflict of the Cold War?*

Of course, by the time the atom bomb arrived, the war in Europe was over, but the conclusion of the war with Japan appeared still distant. Since 1942, the US and its allies had marched steadily up the islands of the Pacific, drawing ever closer to Japan, reversing its imperial ambitions, and dismantling its fearsome navy one battle, one torpedo, and one bomb at a time. Every inch of scores of Pacific islands—with names like Tarawa, Peleliu, Iwo Jima, and Okinawa, now forever evocative of heroism—was paid for in American blood. It's easy to forget how costly those final stages of the Pacific campaign were—and how, in the summer of 1945, the war appeared as if it would stretch not just weeks or months, but a year or more ahead. In fact, during just the first three months of Harry Truman's presidency, the US suffered roughly *half* the casualties that it had in the Pacific since Pearl Harbor. The cost of the war in Japan was no less; entire cities were being burned in single fiery bombing missions, and as the US naval blockade tightened on a country that imported vast energy and food resources, some 200,000 Japanese civilians were starving to death each month.

World War II was a conflict that shattered the lines of morality and the traditional divides in warfare between civilians and combatants; as James D. Hornfischer, one of the premier modern scholars of the conflict, wrote, "The question of morality in warfare is vexing. Is there a moral way to kill someone? Is a bullet preferable to starvation, starvation to incineration?" The ebb and flow of that debate surely has influenced some of the memories captured by the participants over the years; many of the memories of the 509th Composite Group, the Army Air Force unit that delivered the bombs to Japan, and others were gathered after history took a strong turn against the bombing in the 1980s and 1990s, and controversy erupted over the display of the *Enola Gay* at the Smithsonian Institution.

We will as a society surely never satisfy the what-ifs and could-have-beens, though recent scholarship by historians like Evan Thomas in his book *Road to Surrender* has made a convincing case that hard-liners in the Japanese government were not anywhere close to surrender even after the second bomb; in fact, a military coup unfolded in the Imperial Palace the night before the surrender was announced, with troops rushing unsuccessfully to uncover and destroy the emperor's recorded announcement.

Regardless of the ultimate moral calculation to use atomic weapons, the result of those twin bombings in August 1945 was so horrific that the world has sought to avoid ever using these terrible weapons again. Even so, the US, the Soviet Union, and a dozen other countries pursued building tens of thousands of weapons many times more powerful than those dropped on Japan. Today, several thousand nuclear weapons remain on constant alert, hidden in missile silos and submarines beneath the ocean, ready to annihilate most life on our planet in thirty minutes or fewer at the personal order of the US or Russian president. Eighty years into the nuclear age, there is still no check or balance nor second opinion necessary to issue this world-ending order by these two presidents. Any study of modern postwar history makes clear that we have avoided global nuclear war since as much by luck as by skill.

The bombings of Hiroshima and Nagasaki now belong almost entirely to history. Captain Charles D. "Don" Albury, the last surviving crew member to see both bombings, died in May 2009. But the quest to ensure our world's safety and remove these awful weapons from our planet continues to this day, a quest particularly inspired and driven by the survivors of the bombings in Hiroshima and Nagasaki, known as "Hibakusha." In 2024, Nihon Hidankyo, the Japan Confederation of A- and H-Bomb Sufferers Organizations, won the Nobel Peace Prize for their ongoing work to ensure that they are the last to suffer the consequences of an atomic or thermonuclear bomb.

On August 12, three days after the second atomic bomb was dropped on Nagasaki, while all of the Pacific Theater waited anxiously for word that Japan was prepared to finally surrender, a B-29 radio operator named Richard Nelson sat down on the lush Marianas island of Tinian to write his parents. He had an update he wanted to share: "We finally named our airplane. Colonel Tibbets named it after his mother. It is called *Enola Gay*." Then, he added a second thought before signing his letter, "all my love, Rich." "Perhaps," he wrote, "by the time this gets there, you will also have heard of our ship."

Indeed, by the time the letter arrived in Los Angeles, California, they had—and it's a name, one of two, that the world will never forget even long after the last witnesses of that day pass.

Foreword

DAWN AT TRINITY

The "gadget" sits at the Trinity test site.

Laura Fermi, *spouse of physicist Enrico Fermi*: Early in July men had started to disappear from the mesa and the word "Trinity" had floated with insistence in the air. By July 15, nobody who was anybody was left in Los Alamos—wives excepted, of course.

Otto R. Frisch, *physicist, British delegation to the Manhattan Project*: We all went in cars and buses to the test site, code-named "Trinity" in the desert near Alamogordo, also known as *El Jornado del Muerte*, Spanish for the Journey of Death.

William L. Laurence, ***reporter,*** **The New York Times:** I had been with the Atomic Bomb Project a little over two months. I had visited all the secret plants, which at that time no one mentioned by name—Oak Ridge, Hanford, Los Alamos; the Martian laboratories at Columbia, Chicago, and California universities. I had seen things no human eye had ever seen before, things that no one had ever thought possible. I had watched men work with heaps of Uranium-235 and plutonium great enough to blow any city off the map. I had prepared scores of reports on what I had seen—every one of them marked "Top Secret" and locked in a special top-secret safe.*

Otto R. Frisch: A steel tower, about a hundred feet tall, had been constructed to carry the explosive device. When it finally arrived and was being hoisted to the top I was standing there with George Kistiakowsky—our top expert on explosives—at the bottom of the tower. "How far," I asked him, "do we have to be for safety in case it went off?" "Oh," he said, "probably about ten miles." "So on that case," I said, "we might as well stay and watch the fun."

William L. Laurence: The bomb was set on a structural steel tower one hundred feet high. Ten miles away to the southwest was the base camp. This was H.Q. for the scientific high command, of which Professor Kenneth T. Bainbridge of Harvard University was field commander. Here were erected barracks to serve as living-quarters for the scientists, a mess hall, a commissary, a post exchange, and other buildings. Here the vanguard of the atomists, headed by Professor J. R. Oppenheimer of the University of California, scientific director of the Atomic Bomb Project, lived like soldiers at the front, supervising the enormously complicated details involved in the epoch-making tests.

Here early that Sunday afternoon had gathered Major General Leslie R. Groves, commander-in-chief of the Atomic Bomb Project; Brigadier-General T. F. Farrell, hero of World War I, General Groves's deputy; Professor Enrico Fermi, Nobel Prize winner and one of the leaders in the project; President James Bryant Conant of Harvard; Dr. Vannevar Bush, director of the Office of Scientific Research and Development; Dean Richard C. Tolman of the

* Laurence, a science writer at the *Times*, was recruited in the spring of 1945 by the Manhattan Project to write the official announcements and press releases about the creation of the atomic bomb. He spent the summer of 1945 on loan to the Manhattan Project, then returned to the *Times*.

California Institute of Technology; Professor R. F. Bacher of Cornell; Colonel Stafford L. Warren, University of Rochester radiologist; and about a hundred and fifty other leaders in the atomic bomb program.

Maj. Gen. Leslie Groves, *director, Manhattan Project*: After arriving at the Alamogordo base camp on July 15, a brief review of the situation with Oppenheimer revealed that we might be in trouble. The bomb had been assembled and placed at the top of its hundred-foot-high steel tower, but the weather was distinctly unfavorable.

The bomb is loaded atop the test tower.

Kenneth T. Bainbridge, *director, Trinity Test Site*: The weather prognosis was poor.

Maj. Gen. Leslie Groves: The weather that evening was quite blustery and misty, with some rain.

William L. Laurence: Base Camp was a dry, abandoned reservoir, about 500 feet square, surrounded by a mound of earth about eight feet high. Within this mound bulldozers dug a series of slit trenches, each about three feet deep, seven feet wide, and twenty-five feet long. Three other posts had been established, south, north, and west of Zero, each at a distance of 10,000 yards. These were known, respectively, as S-10, N-10, and W-10. Here the shelters were much more elaborate—wooden structures, their walls reinforced by cement, buried under a massive layer of earth. S-10 was the control center. Here Professor Oppenheimer, as scientific commander-in-chief, and his field commander, Professor Bainbridge, issued orders and synchronized the activities of the other sites.

Maj. Gen. Leslie Groves: There was an air of excitement at the camp that I did not like, for this was a time when calm deliberation was most essential. Many of Oppenheimer's advisers at the base camp were urging that the test be postponed for at least twenty-four hours. I felt that no sound decision could ever be reached amidst such confusion, so I took Oppenheimer into an office that had been set up for him in the base camp, where we could discuss matters quietly and calmly.

Edward Teller, *theoretical physicist, Los Alamos Lab*: Rain—in the desert in July!

Maj. Gen. Leslie Groves: I had become a bit annoyed with Fermi when he suddenly offered to take wagers from his fellow scientists on whether or not the bomb would ignite the atmosphere, and if so, whether it would merely destroy New Mexico or destroy the world. He had also said that after all it wouldn't make any difference whether the bomb went off or not because it would still have been a well worthwhile scientific experiment. For if it did fail to go off, we would have proved that an atomic explosion was not possible. Afterward, I realized that his talk had served to smooth down the frayed nerves and ease the tension of the people at the base camp, and I have always thought that this was his conscious purpose. Certainly, he himself showed no signs of tension that I could see.

Kenneth T. Bainbridge: The first possible time for the detonation of the real bomb had been set for 2 a.m. July 16, and the Arming Party was scheduled to arrive at Point Zero—the tower supporting the bomb—before 11 p.m. July 15. At that hour, Don Hornig would connect the cables to the bomb and detach the detonating unit used in rehearsals.

Berlyn Brixner, ***optical engineer and photographer, Los Alamos Lab*****:** July 16, 1945, came.

Maj. Gen. Leslie Groves: Oppenheimer and I agreed to meet again at 1 a.m., and to review the situation then. I urged Oppenheimer to go to bed and to get some sleep, or at least to take a rest, and I set the example by doing so myself. Oppenheimer did not accept my advice and remained awake—I imagine constantly worrying.

Boyce McDaniel, ***physicist, Los Alamos Lab*****:** When I heard of the delay, I went back to the barracks to try to catch a little nap. That was a fruitless endeavor. To sleep during the excitement was impossible. I finally arose and went outside to check on the weather. It was still drizzly and overcast. I could hear one of the observation planes above the clouds trying to locate the site.

Brig. Gen. Thomas F. Farrell, ***chief of field operations, Manhattan Project*****:** For some hectic two hours preceding the blast, General Groves stayed with the Director, walking with him and steadying his tense excitement. Every time the Director would be about to explode because of some untoward happening, General Groves would take him off and walk with him in the rain, counselling with him and reassuring him that everything would be all right.

Maj. Gen. Leslie Groves: About 1 a.m., Oppenheimer and I went over the situation again, and decided to leave the base camp, which was ten miles from the bomb, and go up to the control dugout, which was about five miles away.

Brig. Gen. Thomas F. Farrell: The scene inside the shelter was dramatic beyond words. In and around the shelter were some twenty-odd people concerned with last minute arrangements prior to firing the shot. The shelter was cluttered with a great variety of instruments and radios.

Kenneth T. Bainbridge: When the time came to go to Point Zero, I drove Joe McKibben and Kistiakowsky in my car; I had selected them to be in the Arming Party. On the way in, I stopped at S-10 and locked the main sequence timing switches. Pocketing the key I returned to the car and continued to Point Zero.

Maj. Gen. Leslie Groves: While the weather did not improve appreciably, neither did it worsen. It was cloudy with light rain and high humidity; very few stars were visible. Every five or ten minutes, Oppenheimer and I would leave the dugout and go outside and discuss the weather. I was devoting myself during this period to shielding Oppenheimer from the excitement swirling about us, so that he could consider the situation as calmly as possible, for the decisions to be taken had to be governed largely by his appraisal of the technical factors involved.

Berlyn Brixner: By 3:00 a.m. we were at our camera stations preparing to photograph the explosion.

Maj. Gen. Leslie Groves: As the hour approached, we had to postpone the test—first for an hour and then later for thirty minutes more—so that the explosion was actually three and one half hours behind the original schedule.

Edward Teller: The night seemed long and became even longer when the test was postponed.

Maj. Gen. Leslie Groves: I was extremely anxious to have the test carried off on schedule. Every day's delay in the test might well mean the delay of a day in ending the war.

Kenneth T. Bainbridge: Finally, just before 4:45 a.m., [Chief Meteorologist Jack] Hubbard gave me a complete weather report and a prediction that at 5:30 a.m. the weather at Point Zero would be possible but not ideal. I called Oppenheimer and General Farrell to get their agreement that 5:30 a.m. would be T = 0.

Rudolf Peierls, *physicist, British Mission to the Manhattan Project*: Finally, the news came through that the test would proceed.

Berlyn Brixner: By 5:00 the weather was clearing, and shortly thereafter the countdown started.

Otto R. Frisch: Now it would be only minutes before the explosion took place.

Maj. Gen. Leslie Groves: Once the decision was made to go ahead, no additional orders were needed. At thirty minutes before the zero hour, the five men who had been guarding the bomb to make certain that no one tampered with it left their point of observation at the foot of the tower.

Kenneth T. Bainbridge: After turning on the lights, I returned to my car and drove to S-10 arriving about 5:00 a.m. I unlocked the master switches and McKibben started the timing sequence at -20 minutes, 5:09:45 a.m. At -45 seconds a more precise automatic timer took over. At the final seconds another circuit sent out electronically-timed signals for the still more precise pulses needed by many special instruments.

Maj. Gen. Leslie Groves: Leaving Oppenheimer at the dugout, I returned to the base camp.

William L. Laurence: At our observation post on Compania Hill the atmosphere had grown tenser as the zero hour approached. We had spent the first part of our stay eating an early morning picnic breakfast that we had taken along with us. It had grown cold in the desert, and many of us, lightly clad, shivered. We knew there were two specially equipped B-29 Superfortresses high overhead to make observations and recordings in the upper atmosphere, but we could neither see nor hear them.

Otto R. Frisch: We sat around through the night, waiting for the weather to clear up. For some hours I dozed in the car, waking up whenever the loudspeaker said something. In between it was playing dance music.

Maj. Gen. Leslie Groves: Our preparations were simple. Everyone was told to lie face down on the ground, with his feet toward the blast, to close his eyes, and to cover his eyes with his hands as the countdown approached zero. As soon as they became aware of the flash they could turn over and sit or stand up, covering their eyes with the smoked glass with which each had been supplied.

Rudolf Peierls: We had been given pieces of dark glass through which to look at the spectacle.

Boyce McDaniel: Finally at t-minus-ten minutes, all of us at the base site crouched on the ground behind an earthen barricade watching the light glowing on top of the tower.

Otto R. Frisch: The very first trace of dawn was in the sky.

Edward Teller: Just a shade of pink had appeared.

Brig. Gen. Thomas F. Farrell: As the time interval grew smaller and changed from minutes to seconds, the tension increased by leaps and bounds. We were reaching into the unknown and we did not know what might come of it.

Joseph L. McKibben, *group leader, Manhattan Project*: Sam Allison was the announcer on the radio and gave the countdown. He had a wonderfully senatorial voice. When I turned on the automatic timer at minus 45 seconds, a bell chimed every second to assist in the countdown.

Berlyn Brixner: I removed the waterproof covers from the Mitchell and other cameras on the roof of my bunker, sat down behind the Mitchell, and listened on the intercom to the countdown from the timing station at S-10. I shivered partly from thoughts about the expected explosion and partly from the wet cold desert air. Then, at minus 30 seconds the cameras began to run.

Maj. Gen. Leslie Groves: The quiet grew more intense. I, myself, was on the ground between Bush and Conant.

Val L. Fitch, *technician, Special Engineer Detachment, Los Alamos*: About half a minute before the scheduled moment of detonation my boss, Ernest Titterton, a member of the British Mission to Los Alamos, suggested that since there was nothing more for me to do I might as well go outside the bunker to get a good view. This I did, taking with me the two-by-four-inch piece of nearly opaque glass which someone had handed me earlier.

Edward Teller: We all were lying on the ground, supposedly with our backs turned to the explosion. But I had decided to disobey that instruction and instead looked straight at the bomb. I was wearing the welder's glasses that we had been given so that the light from the bomb would not damage our eyes. But because I wanted to face the explosion, I had decided to add some extra protection. I put on dark glasses under the welder's glasses, rubbed some ointment on my face to prevent sunburn from the radiation, and pulled on thick gloves to press the welding glasses to my face to prevent light from entering at the sides.

Boyce McDaniel: I remember thinking, "This is a very dramatic moment. I must concentrate on it so that I can remember it." I looked around me at the leaders of the program and at my friends. I remember especially I. I. Rabi, Fermi, and Bacher, each staring intently into the darkness.

William L. Laurence: Suddenly, at 5.29.50, as we stood huddled around our radio, we heard a voice ringing through the darkness, sounding as though it had come from above the clouds: "Zero minus ten seconds!" A green flare flashed out through the clouds, descended slowly, opened, grew dim, and vanished into the darkness.

Otto R. Frisch: I sat on the ground in case the explosion blew me over, plugged my ears with my fingers, and looked in the direction away from the explosion as I listened to the end of the count.

Edward Teller: We all listened anxiously as the broadcast of the final countdown started; but, for whatever reason, the transmission ended at minus five seconds.

Brig. Gen. Thomas F. Farrell: Dr. Oppenheimer, on whom had rested a very heavy burden, grew tenser as the last seconds ticked off. He scarcely breathed.

Maj. Gen. Leslie Groves: As I lay there, in the final seconds, I thought only of what I would do if, when the countdown got to zero, nothing happened.

Kenneth T. Bainbridge: My personal nightmare was knowing that if the bomb didn't go off or hang-fired, I, as head of the test, would have to go to the tower first and seek to find out what had gone wrong.

Edward Teller: For the last five seconds, we all lay there, quietly waiting for what seemed an eternity.

Otto R. Frisch: . . . *Five* . . .

J. Robert Oppenheimer, *Director, Los Alamos Lab*: Years of hard and loyal work culminated on July 16, 1945.

Otto R. Frisch: . . . *Four* . . .

George B. Kistiakowsky, *Director, X Division (Explosives), Los Alamos Lab*: The Trinity test was the climax of our work.

Otto R. Frisch: . . . *Three* . . .

William L. Laurence: Silence reigned over the desert.

Otto R. Frisch: . . . *Two* . . .

Rudolf Peierls: The big moment came.

PART I

EXPLORING *the* ATOM

51 BC–AD 1941

"Atoms were talking to us"

PARTICLES UNSEEN

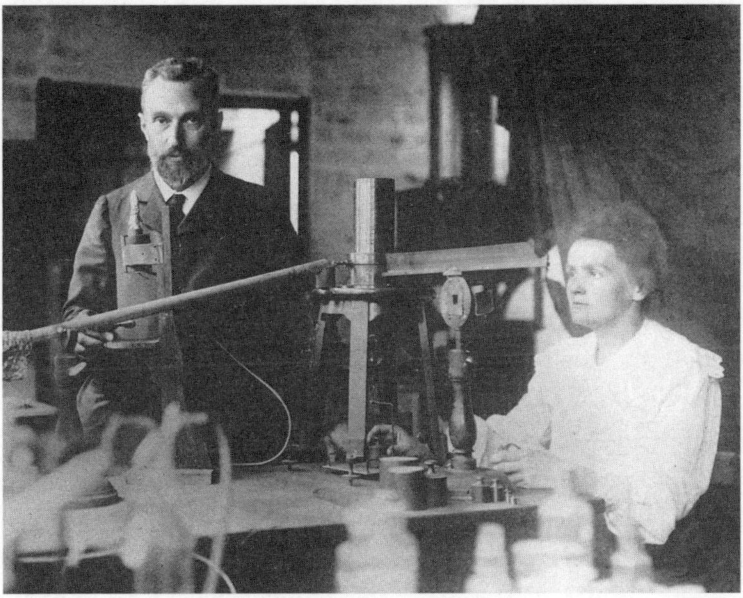

Pierre and Marie Curie helped launch the atomic age.

The journey toward the atomic bomb dates back nearly as far as recorded science, as ancient thinkers strove to understand the building blocks and rules of the world around us. That our world was made of tiny particles was posited in Ancient Greece, when the philosopher Democritus first came to believe that the world was made of "atoms." His moniker comes from the Greek word atomos, *which means "uncuttable" or "indivisible." Nothing, he imagined, could be smaller. The quest to understand atoms would unfurl for centuries and generations after and only really take off at the start of the twentieth century. In fact, nearly all of modern physics—from the theory of relativity to quantum physics—has unfolded in just about a single human lifetime.*

Albert Einstein: In the beginning—if there was such a thing—God created Newton's laws of motion together with the necessary masses and forces. This is all; everything beyond this follows from the development of appropriate mathematical methods by means of deduction.

Lucretius, *Roman philosopher*: Besides, the clothes hung-out along the shore, / When in they take the clinging moisture, prove / That Nature lifts from over all the sea / Unnumbered particles. / When tiny salt eats into great sea cliffs, / You cannot see the process of the loss / At any given moment. Nature's work / Is done by means of particles unseen.

Diogenes Laërtius, *Greek biographer, writing circa AD 225*: Democritus' opinions are these: The first principles of the universe are atoms and empty space; everything else is merely thought to exist.

Sir Isaac Newton, *English physicist, writing in 1704*: All these things being considered, it seems probable to me, that God in the Beginning form'd matter in solid, massy, hard, impenetrable, moveable Particles, of such Sizes and Figures, and with such other Properties, and in such Proportion to Space, as most conduced to the end for which he form'd them; and these primitive Particles being Solids, are incomparably harder than any porous Bodies compounded of them; even so very hard as never to wear or break in pieces: no ordinary Power being able to divide what God himself made one in the first Creation.

Ruggero Giuseppe Boscovich, *Italian physicist, writing in 1764*: If the matter is worked back to the genuine & simplest natural principles, it will be found that everything depends on the composition of the forces with which the particles of matter act upon one another; & from these very forces, as a matter of fact, all phenomena of Nature take their origin.

John Dalton, *English chemist and physicist, writing in 1810*: Matter, though divisible in an extreme degree, is nevertheless not infinitely divisible. That is, there must be some point beyond which we cannot go in the division of matter. I have chosen the word "atom" to signify these ultimate particles. I have chosen the word atom to signify these ultimate particles in preference to particle, molecule, or any other diminutive term, because I conceive it is much more expressive; it includes in itself the notion of indivisible.

Lise Meitner: Though I may try to tell you something of the development of physics since the beginning of the twentieth century, I naturally cannot give you a connected or comprehensive report. I can only pick out a few things which I especially remember, and which form as it were a magic musical accompaniment to my life.

Otto R. Frisch: Incredible though it may seem, at the turn of the century many respectable scientists did not believe in atoms.

C. P. Snow: Modern physics began with the discovery of the particles of which atoms are made: first electrons, then protons, and neutrons. These discoveries began to be made in the last years of the nineteenth century.

Emilio Segrè: In 1895, a German physicist, Wilhelm Röntgen, found that cathode rays produce a type of radiation when they hit a solid object. He called them X-rays: X for unknown, for these highly penetrating rays were unlike anything then known.

Wilhelm Röntgen: Of what nature the rays are is not entirely clear to me. I had not spoken to anyone about my work. To my wife I mentioned merely that I was doing something of which people, when they found out about it, would say, "*Der Röntgen ist wohl verrückt geworden.*" [Röntgen has really gone crazy.] I mailed the [preliminary paper], and then the devil was to pay!

Emilio Segrè: His paper was unbelievable—but with it he also sent x-ray photographs of hands, which provided evidence that could not easily be dismissed. Upon reading Röntgen's paper, many scientists ran to their laboratories, brought out their spark coils, and set about finding out whether they could see the x-rays. They did. By January 1896, news of the discovery of x-rays had created a tremendous commotion all over the world. In 1901 Röntgen received the first Nobel Prize for physics.

Pierre Curie: Antoine Becquerel discovered in 1896 the special radiating properties of uranium and its compounds.

Otto Hahn: For more than 100 years, uranium—discovered by M. H. Klaproth in 1789—had had a quiet existence as a somewhat rare, but not particularly interesting element. It was distinguished from all the other elements in one particular respect: it occupied the highest place in the table of the elements. As yet, however, that did not have any particular significance.

Pierre Curie: Uranium emits very weak rays which leave an impression on photographic plates. These rays pass through black paper and metals; they make air electrically conductive. The radiation does not vary with time, and the cause of its production is unknown.

Otto Hahn: The echo of Becquerel's fundamental observations on the radioactivity of uranium in scientific circles was at first fairly weak. Two years later, however, they acquired an exceptional importance when the Curies succeeded in separating from uranium minerals two active substances, polonium and radium.

Pierre Curie: In making measurements, Marie found that certain of these were more active than they should have been. She then made the assumption that these substances contained radioactive chemical elements which were as yet unknown. We first found a highly radioactive substance which we called polonium, and then—in collaboration with [Gustave] Bémont—a second highly radioactive substance which we called radium.

Marie Curie: All the elements emitting such radiation I have termed radioactive, and the new property of matter revealed in this emission has thus received the name radioactivity. From that time onward numerous scientists devoted themselves to the study of radioactivity.

Otto R. Frisch: It felt that atoms were talking to us, but in a code we couldn't decipher.

Ernest Rutherford, *writing in 1904*: If it were ever found possible to control at will the rate of disintegration of the radio-elements, an enormous amount of energy could be obtained from a small quantity of matter.

Abraham Pais: The birth of quantum theory (1900) and relativity theory (1905) marked the beginning of an era in which the very foundations of physical theory were found to be in need of revision. Two men led the way toward the new theoretical concepts: Max Karl Ernst Ludwig Planck, professor at the University of Berlin, possessed—perhaps obsessed—by the search for the universal function of frequency and temperature, and Albert Einstein, technical expert at the Swiss patent office in Bern.

I. I. Rabi: In 1905, Einstein enunciated the Theory of Special Relativity from a general consideration of the nature of clocks, the measurement of time, and the remarkable consistency of the velocity of light as measured on different systems moving relatively to one another. As a straightforward deduction from this theory, he enunciated the equivalence of mass and energy.

Albert Einstein: $E = MC^2$. Energy equals mass times the speed of light, squared.

Glenn Seaborg, *chemist, UC-Berkeley*: The speed of light is a very large number; the speed of light squared is a ridiculously large number. So a very small amount of mass converts to a relatively large amount of energy.

Max Planck: Einstein's work on relativity probably exceeds in audacity everything that has been achieved so far in speculative science and even in epistemology; non-Euclidean geometry is child's play by comparison.

Otto R. Frisch: A few papers were published which extended Einstein's reasoning, but it took another eight years before the floodgates were opened by a young Danish physicist, Niels Bohr, through his proposed model of the atom. You must have seen it many times, decorating almost any publication related to atoms: a dot surrounded by several circles, usually foreshortened into intersecting ellipses. That model has now been out of date for half a century. But symbols have long lives: Father Time is still depicted with a sand-glass, not a wristwatch.

Arthur Holly Compton: In 1911, Ernest Rutherford, later Lord Rutherford, discovered the nucleus of the atom.

Mark Oliphant: In 1912 Niels Bohr spent nearly six months with Rutherford, during which he became fascinated with the structure of the atom as revealed by Rutherford's work. Chadwick was much impressed by Bohr, by his intuitive grasp of and interest in all science, and by his kind and generous nature. They became lifelong friends.

Niels Bohr, *writing on June 19, 1912*: It could be that I've perhaps found out a little bit about the structure of the atoms. If I'm right, it would not be an indication of the nature of a possibility, but perhaps a little piece of reality. I may yet be wrong, for it hasn't been worked out fully yet. You can imagine how anxious I am to finish quickly.

Otto R. Frisch: No other physicist of our time, except perhaps Einstein, has so strongly influenced our thinking in general, not just in physics. His model of the atom brought him immediate fame in 1913—with the electrons circling around the nucleus like miniature planets, confined to certain allowed orbits except when they jumped from one orbit to another in the process of absorbing or emitting radiation. That picture was so astonishing and unorthodox. Bohr himself was very much aware of the crudeness of that model; it resembled the atom no more than a quick pencil sketch resembles a living human face. But he also knew how profoundly difficult it would be to get a better picture.

Niels Bohr: Abstract thinking, which throughout the ages has been one of the most powerful of man's aids in lifting the veil that shrouds the laws of Nature from the eyes of the uninitiated observer, has proved of the utmost importance for enabling the insight into the structure of atoms.

Werner Heisenberg: To those of us who participated in the development of atomic theory, the five years following the Solvay Congress in Brussels [in 1911] looked so wonderful that we often spoke of them as the golden age of atomic physics. The great obstacles that had occupied all our efforts in the preceding years had been cleared out of the way; the gate to that entirely new field—the quantum mechanics of the atomic shell—stood wide-open, and fresh fruits seemed ready for the plucking.

Arthur Holly Compton: In 1919 Rutherford made the further startling discovery that when an alpha particle (i.e., a helium nucleus) strikes the nucleus of a nitrogen atom, a proton (i.e., a hydrogen nucleus) is sometimes emitted. Here was artificial transmutation, the changing of one chemical element into another. Helium acts on nitrogen to produce hydrogen. What is more, nuclear energy is released. This was shown by the fact that the proton escaped with an energy greater than that of the incident alpha particle. Here at last was a lead toward the release of atomic power.

C. P. Snow: As soon as Rutherford got onto radioactivity, he was set on his life's work.

Arthur Holly Compton: On writing about it to an American friend, Rutherford commented that the influence of this discovery on the course of history might eventually be greater than that of the world war that had just been fought.

Henning Pleijel: Lord Rutherford suggested that, apart from protons and electrons, there also existed particles of the same weight as a proton but without any electric charge. To this particle was given in advance the name of "neutron." This neutron had long been searched for but without any result.

* * *

The world of physics through the first half of the twentieth century was a very tiny community, a fact represented in part by the groundbreaking science of Marie Curie's daughter Irène, who went on to marry physicist Frédéric Joliot, and make key discoveries building on her mother's work. Discoveries were traded between and built upon one after another across this small field as the 1920s and 1930s progressed. Few of those discoveries would prove as transformative as the quest for Rutherford's elusive "neutron."

Enrico Fermi: Joliot and Irène Curie at the end of the year 1933 obtained the first cases of artificial radioactivity by bombarding boron, magnesium, and aluminium with α-particles from a polonium source. They produced thus three radioactive isotopes of nitrogen, silicon and phosphorus, and succeeded also in separating chemically the activity from the bulk of the unmodified atoms of the bombarded substance.

Leo Szilard: In 1932, while I was still in Berlin, I read a book by H.G. Wells called *The World Set Free*. This book was written in 1913, one year before the World War, and in it H.G. Wells describes the discovery of artificial radioactivity and puts it in the year of 1933, the year in which it actually occurred. He then proceeds to describe the liberation of atomic energy on a large scale for industrial purposes, the development of atomic bombs, and a world war which was apparently fought by an alliance of England, France, and perhaps including America, against Germany and Austria, the powers located in the central part of Europe. This book made a very great impression on me.

Herbert L. Anderson: The solid scientific fact that H.G. Wells had at his disposal when he wrote this book was what was known then about natural radioactivity: that uranium disintegrated by emitting alpha particles. This was a process yielding a million times more energy per atom than in ordinary combustion. The trouble was that it took place very slowly. What was needed, H.G. Wells realized, was a way to speed it up. Then, from a pound or two of uranium, enough energy could be obtained to light a great city, power the wheels of industry, drive airplanes and, inevitably, fashion devastating weapons of war. Those who knew Szilard would understand instantly why this idea would excite him and why he would keep turning it over and over in his mind until he could figure out what he could do with it.

Leo Szilard: In London in September 1933, I read in the newspapers a speech by Lord Rutherford. He was quoted as saying that he who talks about the liberation of atomic energy on an industrial scale is talking moonshine. This set me pondering as I was walking the streets of London, and I remember that I stopped for a red light at the intersection of Southampton Row. It suddenly occurred to me that if we could find an element which is split by neutrons and which would emit two neutrons when it absorbed one neutron, such an element, if assembled in sufficiently large mass, could sustain a nuclear chain reaction. I didn't see at the moment just how one would go about finding such an element, or what experiments would be needed, but the idea never left me. In certain circumstances it might become possible to set up a nuclear chain reaction, liberate energy on an industrial scale, and construct atomic bombs. The thought that this might be in fact possible became a sort of obsession with me.

Laura Fermi: In January 1934, the French physicists Frédéric Joliot and his wife Irène Curie announced that they had discovered artificial radioactivity.

Mark Oliphant: One morning Chadwick read the communication of the Curie-Joliots in the [French physics journal] *Comptes Rendus*.

James Chadwick: As I told Rutherford about the Curie-Joliot observation and their views on it, I saw his growing amazement; and finally he burst out "I don't believe it." Such an impatient remark was utterly out of character, and in all my long association with him I recall no similar occasion. I was convinced that there was something quite new as well as strange. A few days of strenuous work were sufficient to show that these strange effects were due to a neutral particle and to enable me to measure its mass: the neutron postulated by Rutherford in 1920 had at last revealed itself.

Niels Bohr: We not only believe the existence of atoms to be proved beyond a doubt, but also we even believe that we have an intimate knowledge of the constituents of the individual atoms. According to our present conceptions, an atom of an element is built up of a nucleus that has a positive electrical charge and is the seat of by far the greatest part of the atomic mass, together with a number of electrons, all having the same negative charge and mass, which move at distances from the nucleus that are very great compared to the dimensions of the nucleus or of the electrons themselves. In this picture we at once see a striking resemblance to a planetary system, such as we have in our own solar system.

Richard Feynman, *physicist*: If, in some cataclysm, all of scientific knowledge were to be destroyed, and only one sentence passed on to the next generations of creatures, what statement would contain the most information in the fewest words? I believe it is the *atomic hypothesis*—or the atomic *fact*, or whatever you wish to call it—that *all things are made of atoms—little particles that move around in perpetual motion, attracting each other when they are a little distance apart, but repelling upon being squeezed into one another.*

Otto R. Frisch: Atoms are not *that* small, about a thousand times smaller than microbes which you can see under an optical microscope. An ion microscope shows quite clearly the beautiful regular pattern of atoms on the point of a sharp needle. But atomic nuclei are *really* small. Try to think of something a thousand times smaller than an atom and you are still not down to the size of atomic nuclei; you need another factor of twenty or so. If an atom were enlarged to the size of a bus, the nucleus would be like the dot on this i.

Maurice Goldwater, *physics student*: What one might call the "neutronic age" started there in 1932 with Chadwick's discovery of the neutron.

Arthur Holly Compton: It is this particle whose use ten years later made possible the nuclear chain reaction.

I. I. Rabi: The neutron is really what makes the atomic bomb tick.

* * *

Otto Hahn: It was especially the Italian scientist [Enrico] Fermi who first realized the great importance of neutrons for the production of nuclear reactions.

Laura Fermi: After Enrico learned of Joliot and Curie's discovery, he decided he would try to produce artificial radioactivity with neutrons. Being a man of method, he did not start by bombarding substances at random, but proceeded in order, starting from the lightest element, hydrogen, and following the periodic table of elements. Hydrogen gave no results: when he bombarded water with neutrons, nothing happened. He tried lithium next, but again without luck. He went on to beryllium, then to boron, to carbon, to nitrogen. None were activated. Enrico wavered, discouraged, and was on the point of giving up his researches, but his stubbornness made him refuse to yield. He would try one more element. That oxygen would not become radioactive he knew already, for his first bombardment had been on water. So he irradiated fluorine. Hurrah! He was rewarded. Fluorine was strongly activated, and so were other elements that came after fluorine in the periodic table.

Enrico Fermi: A systematic investigation of the behavior of the elements throughout the Periodic Table was carried out by myself, with the help of several collaborators, namely Amaldi, d'Agostino, Pontecorvo, Rasetti, and Segrè.

Edoardo Amaldi: We worked with incredible stubbornness. We would begin at eight in the morning and take measurements, almost without a break, until six or seven in the evening, and often later.

Otto Hahn: Fermi and his co-workers irradiated practically all of the elements of the Periodic System with neutrons, and made numerous artificial radioactive elements.

Laura Fermi: When, in the course of their researches, they came to bombard with neutrons the last element of the periodic table, uranium, whose atomic number is 92, they found that it became active, that more than one element was produced, and that at least one of the radioactive products was none of the existing elements close to uranium. Theoretical considerations and chemical analysis seemed to indicate that a new element of atomic number 93, an element which does not exist on the earth because it is not stable, was among the disintegration products of uranium.

I. I. Rabi: Fermi and his school of physicists in Italy were among the first to realize the power of the neutron. Since the neutron carries no charge, there is no strong electrical repulsion to prevent its entry into nuclei. In fact, the forces of attraction which hold nuclei together may pull the neutron into the nucleus. When a neutron enters the nucleus, the effects are about as catastrophic as if the moon struck the earth. The nucleus is violently shaken up by the blow, especially if the collision results in the capture of the neutron. A large increase in energy occurs and must be dissipated, and this may happen in a variety of ways, all of them interesting.

Laura Fermi: They sent their first report to *Ricerca Scientifica* in May 1934, not to claim the discovery of a new element but rather to relate what indications they had found that such an element might have been produced. *The New York Times* published a two-column article under a two-line headline: "Italian Produces 93rd Element by Bombarding Uranium."

Lise Meitner: From 1934 to 1938, Otto Hahn and I were able to resume our joint work, the impetus for which had come from Fermi's results in bombarding heavy elements with neutrons.

Otto Hahn: I remember our co-worker Max Delbrück, who was Lise Meitner's assistant, expressing his amazement that after having received this exciting news about Fermi's work in Italy we could sleep a wink before repeating the experiments. That decision led to the work on which Lise Meitner and I thereupon started, work that lasted more than four years. We were soon joined by Fritz Strassmann, who had been working at our institute since 1929. We soon ascertained that Fermi was right, but we also found that what happened when uranium was bombarded with neutrons was very complicated indeed.

Luis Alvarez: Soon afterward a German chemist, Ida Noddack, published a critical demurrer: Fermi could not claim the discovery of new transuranium elements, she argued, until his unidentified radioisotopes had been compared with every element in the periodic table. No one took Noddack seriously. The notion that uranium could turn into a lighter element in the middle of the periodic table under bombardment by nothing more energetic than thermal neutrons was self-evidently ridiculous; to do so, it would have to split.

Laura Fermi: A controversy over element 93 had started and dragged on inconclusively.

Luis Alvarez: I was bothered at the time that the Fermi transuranics didn't fit the pattern of other radioactive elements. Instead of decaying, as we said, "downhill to the floor of the valley of stability," they decayed uphill, into a region that ought to be progressively more unstable. I knew something was off-key, as did everyone familiar with nuclear theory, but the correct explanation entailed such a radical departure from contemporary understanding that no one pursued the matter.

"My days were numbered"

DARKNESS FALLS ON EUROPE

The rise of Adolf Hitler's Third Reich disrupted the continent's golden age of atomic discovery.

The advances of physics through the 1930s were inseparable from the darkening clouds of far-right fascism on the European continent. The rise of Adolf Hitler and his National Socialist Party in Germany and Benito Mussolini in Italy destabilized much of Europe's scientific progress, particularly as anti-Semitic politics and pogroms targeted many of the biggest names in physics. Those fascist governments came to power alongside ruinous inflation caused by the fallout of World War I; over the course of 1923, the German mark fell from 400 to the dollar to 7,000 to finally 4.2 trillion to the dollar by November. Foreigners found themselves living like royalty as pensioners starved.

Even beyond Germany and Italy, scientists across Europe watched the enveloping cloak of fascism warily—nowhere more so than in Hungary. While there were just 350 Jewish families in Hungary on the eve of World War II, that small group possessed one of the greatest generations of scientific talent in world history, including physicists Eugene Wigner and Edward Teller, computer pioneer John von Neumann, and the space-defining aerospace engineer Theodore von Kármán. "Out of the prospering but vulnerable Hungarian Jewish middle class came no fewer than seven of the twentieth century's most exceptional scientists," historian Richard Rhodes wrote. "The mystery of such a concentration of ability from so remote and provincial a place has fascinated the community of science."

None of them—nor their colleagues elsewhere in the continent—would find themselves immune to the hate and war of the 1930s.

Albert Einstein, *writing in December 1919*: Antisemitism is strong here and political reaction is violent.

Werner Heisenberg: The end of the First World War had thrown Germany's youth into a great turmoil. The reins of power had fallen from the hands of a deeply disillusioned older generation, and the younger one drew together in an attempt to blaze new paths, or at least to discover a new star by which they could guide their steps in the prevailing darkness.

The summer of 1922 ended on what, for me, was a rather saddening note. My teacher had suggested that I attend the Congress of German Scientists and Physicians in Leipzig, where Einstein, one of the chief speakers, would lecture on the general theory of relativity. The lecture theater was a large hall with doors on all sides. As I was about to enter, a young man pressed a red handbill into my hand, warning me against Einstein and relativity. The whole theory was said to be nothing but wild speculation, blown up by the Jewish press and entirely alien to the German spirit.

At first I thought the whole thing was the work of some lunatic, for madmen are wont to turn up at all big meetings. However, when I was told that the author was a man renowned for his experimental work I felt as if part of my world were collapsing. All along, I had been firmly convinced that science at least was above the kind of political strife that had led to the civil war in Munich, and of which I wished to have no further part. Now I made the sad discovery that men of weak or pathological character can inject their twisted political passions even into scientific life.

Rudolf Peierls: The economic situation in Germany was getting worse, unemployment was high, and political life was becoming more violent. Assassinations had been common during the whole period of the Weimar Republic, and now the brown shirts of the National Socialists were increasing in number and in aggressiveness. Yet few people had any inkling of the disaster that was imminent.

Sigmund Freud, *December 7, 1930*: We are moving toward bad times. I ought to ignore it with the apathy of old age, but I can't help feeling sorry for my seven grandchildren.

Leo Szilard: I reached the conclusion something would go wrong in Germany very early. I reached in 1931 the conclusion that Hitler would get into power, not because the forces of the Nazi revolution were so strong, but rather because I thought that there would be no resistance whatsoever.

Albert Einstein, *writing in his diary, December 1931*: I decided today that I shall essentially give up my Berlin position and shall be a bird of passage for the rest of my life.

Otto R. Frisch: I have never been politically conscious. In the early thirties in Hamburg I didn't pay any attention to the general crisis atmosphere; with a sarcastic smile I observed the repeated changes of government and the much joked-about ineptness of Hindenburg, the famous general who had been made President of the Republic of Germany. When a fellow by name of Adolf Hitler was making speeches and starting a Party I paid no attention. Even when he became elected Chancellor I merely I shrugged my shoulders and thought, nothing gets eaten as hot as it is cooked, and he won't be any worse than his predecessors.

Louis Fischer, *correspondent,* The Nation: How did Hitler come to power in Germany? Hitler's policy, at home and abroad, has always been to reveal his plans. Hyper-suspicion of propaganda, however, led many people to doubt what he said. The Nazis boasted that they would rule Germany, and Hitler painted a picture of his future game. "Heads will roll," he said. He would destroy democracy. Yet democracy tolerated him and helped him take office in order to destroy democracy. This peaceful death of German democracy is one of the strangest chapters in history. German democracy marched to its grave with eyes wide open, and singing, "Beware of Adolf Hitler." Democracy is temperate. Its foe is extremism. In Germany, extremism was the thermometer of a sick social system and an ailing economy.

Eugene Wigner: Most Germans seemed strangely unconcerned with Hitler. They had not sought him, but when he came they said, "Well, the man is impressive. Let us see what he does." Few of them expected him to lead Germany into a disastrous war. They watched with interest as he blamed their hardships on Jews and on other nations. But most of them thought he would stop short of a war. After all, Hitler had managed to take power in Germany without a war.

***Bulletin, International News Service, January 30, 1933*:** Adolf Hitler, Nazi chieftain who began life as a house painter and street sweeper, achieved his life's ambition today when he was appointed Chancellor of the Reich.

John Gunther, *Europe correspondent*, Chicago Daily News: The night of February 27, 1933, a few days before the March 5 elections which were to confirm Hitler's chancellorship, the building of the German Reichstag in Berlin was gutted by fire. This fire destroyed what remained of the German republic. It not only burned a public building; it incinerated the communist, social democratic, Catholic, and nationalist parties of Germany. It was discovered at about nine-fifteen on a winter evening back in 1933, but its embers are burning yet.

In the flames of the Reichstag fire disappeared the old Germany of Bismarck, William II, and the Weimar constitution. In its smoke arose Hitler's Third Reich.

Leo Szilard: Hitler came into office in January '33, and I had no doubt what would happen. I lived in the faculty club of the Kaiser Wilhelm Institute in Berlin-Dahlem and I had my suitcases packed. By this I mean that I had literally two suitcases standing in my room which were packed; the key was in it, and all I had to do was turn the key and leave when things got too bad. I was there when the *Reichstagsbrand* occurred, and I remember how difficult it was for people there to understand what was going on. A friend of mine, Michael Polanyi, who was director of a division of the Kaiser Wilhelm Institute for Physical Chemistry, like many other people took a very optimistic view of the situation. They all thought that civilized Germans would not stand for anything really rough happening.

Otto R. Frisch: I didn't take Hitler at all seriously at first. I had the feeling: "Well, chancellors come and chancellors go, and he will be no worse than the rest of them." Things began to change, and of course when the racial laws were published, by which people of partly or wholly Jewish origin had to be dismissed from the universities, I realized that my days were numbered.

Edgar Ansel Mowrer, *Berlin correspondent,* Chicago Daily News: The elimination of Jews from German public life—if not from Germany altogether—was one of the chief promises of National-Socialist propagandists and apparently rarely failed to elicit approval.

Ralph W. Barnes, *datelined Nuremberg, Germany, September 15, 1935*: Stringent new laws depriving German Jews of all the rights of German citizens and prohibiting marriages between Jews and "Aryans" (Gentiles) were decreed by a subservient, cheering Reichstag here tonight, after an address by Chancellor Adolf Hitler.

Hermann Göring, *air minister and Prussian premier, German Reich*: We must preserve the Germanic and Nordic purity of the race, and must protect our women and girls with every means at our disposal. In this pure blood stream will blossom forth a new era of Germanic happiness. Never again will we let our Germanism be infected and ruined by Jewish infiltration. Our newly won freedom requires a new symbol. The swastika has become for us a holy symbol. It is the anti-Jewish symbol of the world.

Eugene Wigner: The situation for Jews in Germany rapidly became intolerable. I would now need a permanent home outside Europe. I hoped against hope that fascism would subside and Hitler be replaced or subdued. But I did not expect it to happen. By 1933, I saw Europe as a sinking ship.

Leo Szilard: How quickly things move you can see from this: I took a train from Berlin to Vienna on a certain date, close to the first of April, 1933. The train was empty. The same train on the next day was over-crowded, was stopped at the frontier, the people had to get out, and everybody was interrogated by the Nazis. This just goes to show that if you want to succeed in this world you don't have to be much cleverer than other people, you just have to be one day earlier than most people. This is all that it takes.

Werner Heisenberg: The golden age of atomic physics was now fast drawing to an end. In Germany political unrest was increasing. For a time I tried to close my eyes to the danger, to ignore the ugly scenes in the street. But, when all is said and done, reality is stronger than all our wishes.

Otto R. Frisch: Disturbing rumors were rife. Some of my Jewish friends had warned me not to be out at night because Jews had been beaten up in the dark. I remember walking home late one night when I heard fast footsteps ring out in the empty street; I wondered if it was one of those anti-semitic brutes on the rampage. Of course to break into a run would have given me away at once; I kept my speed though the footsteps rapidly came nearer and finally pulled up beside me. A burly fellow in S.A. uniform pulled off his cap and greeted me with great politeness; it was the son of my landlady. He explained to me that he had to join this para-military force because otherwise he would not have been allowed to complete his law studies; there were many like him who disliked the Nazis but couldn't afford not to join.

The persistent stories of concentration camps, of synagogues burnt, of beatings and torture, all were stoutly denied by the German newspapers as mere "horror propaganda" put out by the enemies of Germany. Some of my friends told me the stories were true, indeed that the truth was worse. But I wouldn't believe that Germany had changed so suddenly and so horribly, and that all the newspapers could so consistently be telling lies.

Kurt Mendelssohn, *chemist*: Breslau, where I had a post at the university in 1933, was ahead of most German cities in establishing Nazi terror. We decided to leave forthwith, ostensibly to spend Easter in Berlin. In Berlin, I bought a ticket to London. When I woke up in [London] the sun was shining in my face. I had slept deeply, soundly, and long—for the first time in many weeks. The night before I had arrived in London and gone to bed without fear that at 3 a.m. a car with a couple of S.A. men would draw up and take me away.

P. B. Moon, *physicist, Cambridge*: [Rutherford] did a very great deal for the refugees from Hitler's Germany, finding places for some of them in his laboratory and scraping together what money he could to keep them and their families going until they could find established posts.

Otto R. Frisch: In Copenhagen I heard for the first time the suggestion that the fire that had devastated the German Parliament had not been started by the accused Communist, van der Lubbe, but had been deliberately laid by the Nazis in order to work up public opinion against the Communists; it was an idea that startled me at first but then seemed plausible. After my return to Hamburg my one remaining colleague in the department, Knauer, gave me dinner at his lodgings and wanted to hear what people abroad said about the fire. Although he had become a Nazi Knauer had never let the anti-semitic party line interfere with our friendship. Quizzed about the fire I tried to hold my peace and talk of other things. But when he insisted I did tell him that people were convinced that the fire had been laid by the Nazis for political reasons. He was horrified. "But how can anybody think such a thing of people like Hitler or Göring; just look at their faces!"

Knauer kept his friendly and helpful attitude to the last and made my departure easy by finding a small freighter that was going to London and had one cabin for a passenger. On that cockleshell, on a windy day in October 1933, I left Germany with all my belongings in several trunks which kept sliding forth and back in my cabin as the ship rolled and pitched across the North Sea while I braced myself in my berth, unable to sleep.

Werner Heisenberg: When I returned to my Leipzig Institute at the beginning of the summer term of 1933, the rot had begun to spread. Several of my most capable colleagues had left Germany, others were preparing to flee. Even my brilliant assistant, Felix Bloch, had decided to emigrate, and I myself began to wonder whether there was any sense in staying on.

Bulletin, Associated Press, August 2, 1934: Adolf Hitler made himself absolute dictator of Germany today. He concentrated in his own hands the functions of President and of Chancellor as soon as the aged President Paul von Hindenburg had died at Neudeck.

Laura Fermi: It was almost unbelievable. Germans were the traditional foes of Italians, since the first World War, a fallen foe. The newly risen Fuhrer of Germany was held to be a none-too-intelligent imitator of the Duce, a puppet obediently waiting for directives from the Fascist Master. The puppet had taken some initiative of his own. In March, 1935, he had denounced the Versailles Treaty and declared that Germany would rearm. The Fuhrer had in store another of his spring surprise moves: in March, 1936, his troops occupied the demilitarized Rhineland. By then Mussolini was on bad terms with France and England, but dreaded and opposed a strong Germany.

Leo Szilard: When the German troops moved into the Rhineland and England advised France against invoking the Locarno pact [in March 1936], I knew that there would be war in Europe.

Edoardo Amaldi: "*Physics as soma*" [roughly, "physics is the cure," a reference to Aldous Huxley's *Brave New World*] was our description of the work we performed while the general situation in Italy grew more and more bleak, first as a result of the Ethiopian campaign and then as Italy took part in the Spanish Civil War.

Eugene Wigner: Hitler's campaign against the Jews cost him most of the greatest people I had studied with. If Hitler did not personally fire us all from our jobs, he made life unsafe for us in Nazi countries. And he forced us to follow politics. Many other important physicists fled as well, Enrico Fermi, Edward Teller, and Hans Bethe among them. Most of us resettled in the United States. Perhaps the United States should erect a great stone monument to Adolf Hitler for his dedication to advancing the American natural sciences. Not even Joseph Stalin scattered scientists like Hitler.

"I stopped the barber in mid-snip"

FLEEING FASCISM

The Fermi family upon arrival in America.

By 1938, war was enveloping Europe and those scientists who could plan their escapes came mostly to US and British institutions, labs, and universities. But the physicists of Europe had one last important discovery to contribute: The process that would come to be known as "fission," the chain reaction that unlocked the near-inexhaustible energy of the atom and illuminated the path toward both atomic weapons and nuclear power.

Laura Fermi: The Italian government seemed to have gone crazy. The first anti-Semitic laws were passed early in September. We at once decided to leave Italy as soon as possible. Enrico wrote four letters to four American universities, in which he stated that his reasons for not accepting their previous offers had ceased to be. He dared write nothing more specific. We were still in the Alps and four letters, all in the same handwriting, all going to America, if mailed at the same village could not fail to arouse suspicion. We took advantage of a car trip and mailed Enrico's letters at four towns miles apart. Enrico received five offers of positions in America. He accepted that of Columbia University. To Italian officials he declared that he was embarking on a six-month visit to New York.

Emilio Segrè: In the fall of 1938, at a physics meeting in Copenhagen, Fermi was confidentially informed by Bohr that his name was high on the list of candidates for a Nobel prize. Such a disclosure was most unusual but was prompted by an effort to ascertain that the award would not embarrass him. There had been cases in which dictatorships had forced a recipient to renounce the award or had otherwise harassed him. The Swedish Academy was thus taking precautions. The nomination to the award was hardly surprising, but it called for some adjustments in Fermi's emigration plans.

Laura Fermi: To prospective emigrants, who would be allowed to take along fifty dollars apiece when leaving Italy for good, the Nobel Prize would be a godsend. However, the existing monetary laws required Italian citizens to convert any foreign holdings into lire and bring them into Italy. Hence our decision to go to Stockholm and from there directly to the United States, if Enrico were to be awarded the Nobel Prize.

Emilio Segrè: Once Fermi made a decision, he never looked back.

Laura Fermi: Early on the morning of November 10, 1938, I found myself answering the telephone in the hall of our home. "Is this Professor Fermi's residence?" asked the operator's voice. "I wish to inform you that this evening at six Professor Fermi will be called on the telephone from Stockholm." My drowsiness vanished at once. *A call from Stockholm!* I ran back into our bedroom. Enrico's head was still sunk in the hollow of his soft pillow. "Wake up, Enrico! This evening you'll be called on the telephone from Stockholm!" Calm, but immediately alert, Enrico propped himself up on his elbow and replied: "It must mean the Nobel Prize."

Emilio Segrè: On December 6, 1938, the Fermi family—Enrico, Laura, the two children, Nella and Giulio—and a maid boarded the train at Rome. Amaldi and Rasetti went to the station to say goodbye. Everyone understood that the departure signified the end of a memorable period in their lives.

Laura Fermi: There was the prize award on December 10, the anniversary of Nobel's death. Only the prizes for literature and for physics were awarded in 1938. Pearl Buck, the American writer of novels with Chinese background, and Enrico sat in the center of the stage in the Concert Hall. Enrico sat stiff because he could not do otherwise. Stiff with the expectation of a dreaded but likely mishap: that the heavily starched front of his evening shirt might suddenly snap and thrust out in a protruding arc between the silk lapels of his full dress suit, with an explosive sound, at his first incautious move, as it had done many times before. Although dedicated to measurement, Enrico had not yet recognized that fronts of ready-made shirts were too long for him.

Edward Teller: The Fermis used the prize money to travel on to New York, where Enrico settled in as a professor at Columbia.

Emilio Segrè: The Fermis landed in New York on January 2, 1939, and Fermi turned to his wife and said: "We have founded the American branch of the Fermi family." I can imagine his smile.

* * *

The Fermis were hardly the only ones to find their quiet lives of science interrupted as the war years began. Even as some others fled, the work continued, and uncovering the next step in the quest to understand and harness the atom fell to the newly displaced Lise Meitner and her colleague chemists Otto Hahn and Fritz Strassmann, along with her nephew Otto Frisch.

Edward Teller: The chairman of the physics department at The George Washington University asked me to give a talk about atomic theory to the faculty of the university. During the question period following my lecture, someone asked, "How long before a practical use of nuclear energy might be worked out?" I predicted, "It may take a year, a hundred years, or it may never happen." I was wrong. As I was speaking, two chemists at the Kaiser Wilhelm Institute in Berlin were beginning to examine the first key to unlocking nuclear energy. That key had been lying around unused for half a dozen years.

Otto R. Frisch: Lise Meitner had been working in Berlin with the chemist Otto Hahn for about thirty years, and during the last three years they had been bombarding uranium with neutrons and studying the radioactive substances that were formed.

Otto Hahn: In spite of more or less trivial interference on the part of the regime, work had been going ahead smoothly so far. Professor Lise Meitner had not been troubled by anybody in those first years, for, being an Austrian, she was protected by her foreign nationality. Professor Thiessen, Director of the Kaiser Wilhelm Institute of Physical Chemistry, which had meanwhile been transformed into a model institution of National Socialist science, treated Lise Meitner with all due courtesy for as long as she stayed in Berlin. But now came the year 1938.

Otto R. Frisch: The occupation of Austria in March 1938 changed my aunt, the physicist Lise Meitner—technically—from an Austrian into a German. She had acquired fame by many years' work in Germany, but now had to fear dismissal as a descendant of a Jewish family. Moreover, there was a rumor that scientists might not be allowed to leave Germany; so she was persuaded—or perhaps stampeded—into leaving at very short notice, assisted by friends in Holland.

Otto Hahn: Now for Lise Meitner too the situation became critical.

Lise Meitner: I decided that it was high time to get out with my secrets.

Otto Hahn: We decided to get her across the frontier illegally, and as quickly as possible. On the evening of 16 July Professor Coster arrived from Holland and came straight to the institute. He brought with him an assurance that the Dutch would permit Lise Meitner to enter Holland without a visa. Aided by our old friend Paul Rosbaud, we spent the night packing the clothes she most needed and some of her valuables. I gave her a beautiful diamond ring that I had inherited from my mother and which I had never worn myself but always treasured; I wanted her to be provided for in an emergency. On the morning of 17 July, accompanied by Professor Coster, Lise Meitner left in all secrecy, not knowing what that day might hold in store for her. We agreed on a code-telegram in which we would be let known whether the journey ended in success or failure.

Lise Meitner: I took a train for Holland on the pretext that I wanted to spend a week's vacation.

Otto Hahn: The danger consisted in the SS's repeated passport-control of trains crossing the frontier. People trying to leave Germany were always being arrested on the train and brought back. Lise Meitner was lucky; she succeeded in crossing the frontier to safety.

Lise Meitner: At the Dutch border, I got the scare of my life when a Nazi military patrol picked up my Austrian passport, which had expired long ago. I got so frightened, my heart almost stopped beating. I knew that the Nazis had just declared open season on Jews. For ten minutes I sat there and waited, ten minutes that seemed like so many hours. Then one of the Nazi officials returned and handed me back the passport without a word. Two minutes later I descended on Dutch territory, where I was met by some of my Holland colleagues. There I obtained my Swedish visa.

Otto R. Frisch: In the autumn she accepted an invitation to work in Stockholm, at the Nobel Institute led by Manne Siegbahn. I had always kept the habit of celebrating Christmas with her in Berlin; this time she was invited to spend Christmas with Swedish friends in the small town of Kungälv (near Gothenburg), and she asked me to join her there. That was the most momentous visit of my whole life.

Otto Hahn: When we had carried out the indicator experiments that proved barium was present, I wrote some personal letters to Lise Meitner, telling her of our results. In my letter of 19 December, I wrote, "The thing is: there's something so odd about the 'radium isotopes' that for the moment we don't want to tell anyone but you. The half-lives of the three isotopes are pretty accurately determined; they can be separated from all the elements except barium; all reactions are correct. Except for one—unless there are some very weird accidental circumstances involved: the fractionation doesn't work. We are more and more coming to the awful conclusion that our Ra isotopes behave not like Ra, but like Ba. Strassmann and I agree that for the time being nobody should know but you. Perhaps you can put forward some fantastic explanation. We ourselves realize it can't really burst into Ba."

Fritz Strassmann: Lise Meitner was the intellectual leader of our team, and therefore she belonged to us—even if she was not present for the "discovery of fission."

Otto R. Frisch: When I came out of my hotel room after my first night in Kungälv I found Lise Meitner studying a letter from Hahn and obviously worried by it. I wanted to tell her of a new experiment I was planning, but she wouldn't listen; I had to read that letter. Its content was indeed so startling that I was at first inclined to be skeptical.

Laura Fermi: Lise Meitner became the first scientist outside Germany to learn of Hahn's and Strassmann's discovery. She realized what had happened—some uranium atoms had split into two almost equal parts. In order to talk the matter over at leisure, the aunt and nephew took a long walk in the snow. Physical exercise, they thought, might clear their minds. Lise Meitner did most of the talking, urgently, convincingly.

Otto R. Frisch: We both sat down on a tree trunk—all that discussion had taken place while we walked through the wood in the snow, I with my skis on, Lise Meitner making good her claim that she could walk just as fast without—and started to calculate on scraps of paper. Lise Meitner remembered the empirical formula for computing the masses of nuclei and worked out that the two nuclei formed by the division of a uranium nucleus together would be lighter than the original uranium nucleus by about one-fifth the mass of a proton. Now whenever mass disappears energy is created, according to Einstein's formula $E = MC^2$, and one-fifth of a proton mass was just equivalent to 200 MeV. It all fit!

Arthur Holly Compton: Here would be a source of energy enormously greater than any that science had heretofore known.

Laura Fermi: Once he became convinced, Frisch felt, like his aunt, that they should not keep the news to themselves. They decided to inform Niels Bohr at once. Bohr lived in Copenhagen, Denmark, and so aunt and nephew hastened from Sweden to that city.

Otto R. Frisch: I traveled to Copenhagen in considerable excitement. I was keen to submit our speculations—it wasn't really more at the time—to Bohr, who was just about to leave for the U.S.A. He had only a few minutes for me; but I had hardly begun to tell him when he smote his forehead with his hand and exclaimed: "Oh what idiots we all have been! Oh but this is wonderful! This is just as it must be! Have you and Lise Meitner written a paper about it?" Not yet, I said, but we would at once; and Bohr promised not to talk about it before the paper was out.

Arthur Holly Compton: The conversation became so intense that only with difficulty could Bohr tear himself away to catch the train.

Otto R. Frisch: The paper was composed by several long-distance telephone calls, Lise Meitner having returned to Stockholm in the meantime. I asked an American biologist who was working with Hevesy what they call the process by which single cells divide in two.

William A. Arnold, *Frisch lab partner*: Frisch looked up at me and said, "You work in a microbiology lab—what do you call the process in which one bacterium divides into two?" I answered "Binary fission." He wanted to know if you could call it "fission" alone, and I said you could.

Otto R. Frisch: "Fission," he said, so I used the "nuclear fission" in that paper. It was sent off to *Nature*. About five weeks passed before *Nature* printed those notes.

John A. Wheeler, *nuclear physicist, Met Lab*: On Monday, January 16, 1939, I taught my morning class at Princeton University, then took a train to New

York and walked to the dock where the Danish physicist Niels Bohr was scheduled to arrive on the MS *Drottningholm*. I was not the only one who decided to welcome Bohr personally. While I was waiting on the dock, who should turn up but the Italian physicist Enrico Fermi and his wife, Laura, who, with their two children, had arrived in the United States only two weeks earlier.

Herbert L. Anderson: Bohr came through New York on his way to Washington. He was anxious to see Fermi's reaction to his great news. Bohr came right over and grabbed me by the shoulder. "Young man," he said, "let me explain to you about something new and exciting in physics." Then he told me about the splitting of the uranium nucleus. Suddenly everything I had done in the last five years began to make sense. Neutrons brought about the fission of uranium, and neutrons had become my field.

I. I. Rabi: By nightfall Fermi was already speculating on the size of the crater which would be produced if one kilogram of uranium were to disintegrate by fission. Similar scenes were occurring all over the world. The race for the atomic bomb was on.

Luis Alvarez: I learned about the discovery of nuclear fission in the Berkeley campus barbershop while my hair was being cut. Buried on an inside page of the *San Francisco Chronicle* was a story from Washington reporting Niels Bohr's announcement that German chemists had split the uranium atom by bombarding it with neutrons.

***Associated Press, "200 Million Volts of Energy Created by Atom Explosions,"* San Francisco Chronicle, *Monday, January 30, 1939, page 2*:** American scientists heard today of a new phenomenon in physics—explosion of atoms with a discharge of 200,000,000 volts of energy.

Luis Alvarez: I stopped the barber in mid-snip and ran all the way to the Radiation Laboratory to spread the word.

Philip H. Abelson: My memories of the day that news of uranium fission came to the Berkeley Radiation Laboratory are vivid. That morning, as a member of the cyclotron crew, I was at the control console operating the machine. About 9:30 a.m., I heard the sound of running footsteps outside, and immediately afterward Alvarez burst into the laboratory. When Alvarez told me the news, I almost went numb.

Luis Alvarez: As people arrived at the laboratory that morning, we told them the news. Everyone found it hard to believe. I tracked down Robert Oppenheimer. He instantly pronounced the reaction impossible and proceeded to prove mathematically that someone must have made a mistake. The next day Ken Green and I demonstrated the reaction. I invited Robert over to see the very small natural alpha-particle pulses on our oscilloscope and the tall, spiking fission pulses, twenty-five times larger. In less than fifteen minutes he not only agreed that the reaction was authentic, but also speculated that in the process extra neutrons would boil off that could be used to split more uranium atoms and thereby generate power or make bombs. It was amazing to see how rapidly his mind worked.

Glenn Seaborg: I do not recall ever seeing Oppie so stimulated and so full of ideas. As it turned out, I was privileged to witness his first encounter with the phenomenon that was to play such an important role in shaping the future course of events in his life.

J. Robert Oppenheimer, *letter to William Fowler, January 1939*: The U business is unbelievable. We first saw it in the papers, wired for more dope, and have had a lot of reports since. In how many ways does the U come apart? At random, as one might guess, or only in certain ways? It is I think exciting, not in the rare way of positrons and mesotrons, but in a good honest practical way.*

Philip Morrison: When fission was discovered, within perhaps a week there was on the blackboard in Robert Oppenheimer's office a drawing—a very bad, an execrable drawing—of a bomb.

* In Oppenheimer's letters, this letter is dated "January 28?, 1939," but there's reason to believe it was written at least a bit later, since it seems like word of the events didn't get to Berkeley until two days later.

"We were all green"

ADJUSTING TO THE NEW WORLD

Albert Einstein and Leo Szilard worried together about the possibility of a bomb.

For the still-tiny circle of scientists who understood the potential of fission, the leap from the theoretical to the potential of an atomic bomb came quickly and with fierce urgency given how many had fled Nazism and the creep of authoritarian regimes of Europe. They resolved to force their newly adopted home country of the US to pay attention.

Eugene Wigner: Eagerly, Leo Szilard and I discussed the atomic bomb with our university colleagues. Szilard knew the crucial questions: *How could we reach the men who controlled American warfare? And how could we persuade them of the military value of an atomic bomb project?* Our academic colleagues, for all of their eminence, had little authority in warfare and few resources. Szilard knew that we could hardly make an atomic bomb without federal support.

But he disliked this idea; and like most men he was reluctant to face that which he disliked. He was afraid that the government would saddle uranium research with an awful load of bureaucracy.

Arthur Holly Compton: In the United States the first steps toward putting atomic energy to military use were taken almost immediately after uranium fission was discovered. At the urging of Szilard and Fermi, Professor George B. Pegram of Columbia University wrote to Admiral S. C. Hooper, then director of the technical division of naval operations.

Eugene Wigner: Enrico Fermi was invited to meet some Navy men, including a man named Ross Gunn. The talk was a distinct failure. Fermi got nothing more from it but $2,000 for isotope research. The Army and the Navy had their own thinking, and they found atomic bombs alien. They said, "It's just some crazy worrying by a few foreigners." And, in a way, they were right. There was something crazy about touting an atomic bomb, when so little of the crucial work had been done.

Laura Fermi: On that same March 16 when Professor Pegram had written his letter, Hitler had annexed what was left of Czechoslovakia after the Munich dismemberment. War was approaching. There could be little doubt of it.

Edward W. Beattie, Jr., *correspondent, United Press*: The murder of Czechoslovakia is just a little red-inked stamp on page 19 of my passport, with the date of March 14, 1939, and the word "Prejezd," which I guess must mean entry. There is no exit stamp because the German army marched in next day, and it took a military pass to leave Prague. The one scene that was most poignant was the entry of the first heavy German column into Wenceslas Square in midmorning of March 15. Dense snow slanted down. The crowd jammed so close it was almost impossible to move. A rumble grew down the side street, and the first German tanks and armored cars, their crews sitting tight-lipped with sub-machine guns at the ready turned into the square. As they clattered across the pavement, a wave of sound swept with them and grew into a chorus of thousands of voices, as the Czechs sang their national anthem into the mouths of German guns.

Edward Teller: The four of us who had worked in Germany knew well the excellence of the physicists who were likely to be considering similar questions about fission. We argued that, from now on, we should not publish the results of fission research lest the Nazis learn from them and apply them to making a nuclear explosive. Bohr, however, took the opposite view with deep conviction.

Niels Bohr: Openness is the basic condition necessary for science. It should not be tampered with.

Edward Teller: He thought we were unduly alarmed: Separating the two forms of uranium and accumulating a sufficient quantity of U-235 would require efforts so huge as to be impractical. "You would need to turn the entire country into a factory," he declared.

Arthur Holly Compton: Now that a chain reaction appeared likely, uranium fission became a matter involving the nation's safety. At Leo Szilard's urgent plea, the new discovery was withheld from publication.

* * *

Leo Szilard: At this point both Wigner and I began to worry about what would happen if the Germans got hold of large quantities of the uranium which the Belgians were mining in the Congo. We began to think: Through what channels could we approach the Belgian government and warn them against selling any uranium to Germany? It occurred to me that Einstein knew quite well the Queen of the Belgians, and so I suggested [to Wigner] that we visit Einstein, tell him about the situation, and ask him whether he might not write to the Queen.

Eugene Wigner: Einstein somehow knew the Belgian Royal Family, so we felt he ought to write this letter. It was not customary for physicists to be on familiar terms with European royalty, but then Einstein was not an ordinary physicist.

Leo Szilard: We knew that Einstein was somewhere on Long Island but we didn't know precisely where, so I phoned his Princeton office and I was told he was staying at [a] Dr. Moore's cabin at Peconic, Long Island. Wigner had a car and we drove out there and tried to find Dr. Moore's cabin.

Eugene Wigner: July 16, 1939, was a Sunday. Szilard and I got terribly lost trying to find the house.

Leo Szilard: We drove around for a half an hour, asking everybody we met—no one knew Dr. Moore's cabin.

Eugene Wigner: We knew the street name, and along the way asked a good many people where the street was. No one could tell us.

Leo Szilard: We were on the point of giving up and going back to New York when I saw a boy aged maybe seven or eight standing on the curb. I leaned out of the window and I said, "Say, do you by any chance know where Professor Einstein lives?" The boy knew that and he offered to take us there, though he had never heard of Dr. Moore's cabin.

Eugene Wigner: There we found Einstein dressed in an old shirt and unpressed pants, apparently perfectly content to be thinking only of physics.

Leo Szilard: We discussed the situation with Einstein. This was the first Einstein had heard about the possibility of a chain reaction. He was very quick to see the implications and perfectly willing to do anything that needed to be done.

Eugene Wigner: Einstein was not interested in nuclear physics. Indeed, he thought that all of quantum theory was largely an error. And who knows, perhaps someday Einstein will be proved right on that; though, if so, it has certainly been quite a useful error. On this July day, we spoke deeply. As usual, we spoke German. Einstein was quite receptive. Though he had rarely thought about nuclear chain reactions before, within ten minutes he grasped the situation. He understood the meaning of a chain reaction scientifically, remarking that for the first time in history, men would tap energy from a source other than the sun.

Leo Szilard: Einstein was willing to assume responsibility for sounding the alarm even though it was quite possible that the alarm might prove to be a false alarm. The one thing that most scientists are really afraid of is to make a fool of themselves. Einstein was free from such a fear and this above all is what made his position unique on this occasion.

Eugene Wigner: Einstein realized the political and military meaning of nuclear fission: that it could yield explosives strong enough to make the Nazis invincible. And Einstein was just as horrified as I was by that prospect. He volunteered to do whatever he could to prevent it.

Leo Szilard: This story shows that we were all green. We did not know our way around in America, we did not know how to do business, and we certainly did not know how to deal with the government.

Herbert L. Anderson: Szilard acted on a suggestion from Gustav Stolper, a Viennese economist and friend of long standing. He went to see Alexander Sachs, a Lehman Corporation economist, reputed to have ready access to the White House.

Leo Szilard: Stolper telephoned Dr. Sachs and I went to see him and I told him my story. Sachs said that if Einstein were to write a letter he would personally deliver it to President Roosevelt, and that he thought that it was no use going to any of the agencies, the War Department, or any of the government departments, because they would not know how to handle this. This should go to the White House.

Alexander Sachs: I felt it was essential that an opinion should be written by the one man whom the world recognized as the preeminent scientist of our day—not only the preeminent scientist but one of the greatest humanitarians because he had left Nazism. He had anticipated the trend of events.

Herbert L. Anderson: The best approach was to go directly to the top.

Leo Szilard: This sounded like good advice, and I intended to follow it. In the meantime Teller had arrived in New York and I asked Teller to drive me out to Long Island—he had a car.

Edward Teller: In early August, he asked, "Could you drive me to the end of Long Island to see Einstein tomorrow?" Szilard accomplished the extraordinary, but he had not learned to drive. Unfortunately, Szilard knew only Einstein's general whereabouts, not his address. Once we were in the right neighborhood, we began inquiring about the famous professor, with no result. Finally, we asked a little girl with long braids, about eight years old. She had never heard of Professor Einstein, but she knew a nice old man with long white hair. We were, she told us, almost in front of his house.

Leo Szilard: Teller and I discussed with Einstein this new approach of writing to the President. Einstein was perfectly willing to do this. We discussed a little bit what should be in this letter. I said I would draft it and send Einstein perhaps one or two drafts for him to choose. I prepared a long draft and a short draft.

Janet Coatesworth, *secretary to Leo Szilard*: I was quite young when I worked as his secretary, but he was always very patient with me. He was dictating one day in 1939 and he mentioned a "dreadful weapon" and he also said something about writing to the President of the United States. That convinced me! I was sure I was working for a "nut"! A nice nut, but a nut. I am quite certain he was aware of this most unflattering judgment of mine, for he began to look very amused and his face took on a look of absolute mischief and merriment.

Leo Szilard: We did not know just how many words one could put in a letter which a President is supposed to read. How many pages does the fission of uranium rate? So I sent Einstein a short version and a longer version; Einstein thought the longer one was better.

Edward Teller: Einstein read the letter with great care. Einstein signed the letter, and we left.

Albert Einstein, *letter to President Franklin D. Roosevelt*: Some recent work by E. Fermi and L. Szilard, which has been communicated to me in manuscript, leads me to expect that the element uranium may be turned into a new and important source of energy in the immediate future. Certain aspects of the situation which has arisen seem to call for watchfulness and, if necessary, quick action on the part of the Administration.

In the course of the last four months it has been made probable—through the work of Joliot in France as well as Fermi and Szilard in America—that it may become possible to set up a nuclear chain reaction in a large mass of uranium by which vast amounts of power and large quantities of new radium-like elements would be generated. Now it appears almost certain that this could be achieved in the immediate future.

This new phenomenon would also lead to the construction of bombs, and it is conceivable—though much less certain—that extremely powerful bombs of a new type may thus be constructed. A single bomb of this type, carried by boat and exploded in a port, might very well destroy the whole port together with some of the surrounding territory. However, such bombs might very well prove to be too heavy for transportation by air. In view of the situation you may think it desirable to have more permanent contact maintained between the Administration and the group of physicists working on chain reactions in America.

I understand that Germany has actually stopped the sale of uranium from the Czechoslovakian mines which she has taken over. That she should have taken such early action might perhaps be understood on the ground that the son of the German Under-Secretary of State, von Weizsäcker, is attached to the Kaiser-Wilhelm-Institut in Berlin where some of the American work on uranium is now being repeated.

Leo Szilard: The letter was dated August 2, 1939. I handed it to Dr. Sachs for delivery to the White House.

Alexander Sachs: I sought and waited for a proper opportunity to see the President. I felt the mere delivery of memoranda was insufficient. Our system is such that national public figures are punch-drunk with printer's ink. This was a matter that the Commander in Chief and the head of the Nation must know. I could only do it if I could see him for a long stretch and read the material so it came in by way of the ear and not as a soft mascara on the eye.

Eugene Wigner: Within two months, England and Germany were at war.

Gen. Douglas MacArthur: On September 1, 1939, Hitler attacked and successfully overran Poland.

Stanislaw Ulam: It was a very hot, humid, New York night. I could not sleep very well. It must have been around one or two in the morning when the telephone rang. Dazed and perspiring, very uncomfortable, I picked up the receiver and the somber, throaty voice of my friend the topologist Witold Hurewicz began to recite the horrible tale of the start of war: "Warsaw has been bombed, the war has begun," he said. At that moment, I suddenly felt as if a curtain had fallen on my past life, cutting it off from my future. There has been a different color and meaning to everything ever since.

Otto R. Frisch: Hitler had been presented with an ultimatum, asking him either to withdraw his troops from Poland or to consider himself at war with Britain; we all sat round the radio and there was a great feeling of tense sobriety when we were told that the deadline had passed and that the war was on.

Luis Alvarez: War came to Europe and changed all our lives.

* * *

Alexander Sachs: I brought the material over to President Roosevelt and met with him on October 11, 1939. The President remarked, "Alex, what you are after is to see that the Nazis don't blow us up." I said, "Precisely." He then called in [military aide] General [Edwin] Watson, lovable "Pa" Watson, and said, "This requires action." General Watson went out with me and the informal group was established.

Edward Teller: Roosevelt acted at once. The president set up an Advisory Committee on Uranium, and appointed D. Lyman Briggs, the head of the Bureau of Standards, its chairman. Briggs called a meeting for October 21.

Eugene Wigner: The first meeting I attended at the National Bureau of Standards was in Washington, D.C., on October 21, 1939. Early in the meeting, Szilard pointed out that making a chain reaction would require money to perform experiments and to acquire uranium supplies and graphite. Szilard also suggested creating a permanent committee between the physicists and the government. Teller and I supported Szilard. The colonels kept rather aloof. I had the feeling that these soldiers and government men were just like the others I had approached: they were friendly, they smiled, but they never expected to see a working atomic bomb in this world.

Leo Szilard: The Washington meeting was followed by the most curious period in my life. We heard nothing from Washington at all. I had assumed that once we had demonstrated that in the fission of uranium neutrons are emitted, there would be no difficulty in getting people interested; but I was wrong. It is an incredible fact, in retrospect, that between the end of June 1939 and the spring of 1940, not a single experiment was under way in the United States which was aimed at exploring the possibilities of a chain reaction in natural uranium.

Arthur Holly Compton: The failure of the appeal of Einstein and his associates hinged on the fact that research in new fields of science had not been recognized by the United States government as a significant source of national strength. There was at Washington no individual or office having power to deal adequately with a new scientific development whose importance, though urgent and vital, was ill defined. It was simply not in our tradition. The truth is that our government, like its citizens, even in late 1939, had hardly begun to ready itself for war.

Edward Teller: During that academic year, the fission research at Columbia developed slowly. I was uncertain whether I wanted to remain a bystander or become a participant. I was content and pleased with the way my small world was running. Although I was happy in academia, the possibility of the new weapon made me worry.

In early May 1940, together with a few thousand other scientists, I was invited to attend a Pan American Congress at which President Roosevelt was to speak. Two days before the meeting, the phony war turned into a fast-moving conquest. Using modern tanks and dive bombers to prepare the way, the Nazi armies swept triumphantly through Holland, Belgium, and Luxembourg. The Nazi *Blitzkreig*, the lightning-strike war, was terrifyingly effective. I decided to accept the invitation and hear the president. President

Roosevelt talked that day about inherent human rights and the blessings of democracy, and about the progress made through science and technology in conquering disease and poverty. Then he became more specific about the war.

Franklin D. Roosevelt, ***President of the United States, address before the Eighth Pan American Scientific Congress, Washington, DC, May 10, 1940*****:** You who are scientists may have been told that you are in part responsible for the debacle of today because of the processes of invention for the annihilation of time and space, but I assure you it is not the scientists of the world who are responsible, because the objectives which you held have looked toward closer and more peaceful relations between all nations through the spirit of cooperation and the interchange of knowledge.

The great achievements of science and even of art can be used in one way or another, to destroy as well as create. They are only instruments by which men try to do the things they most want to do.

Can we continue our peaceful construction if all other continents embrace by preference or by compulsion a wholly different principle of life? No, I think not.

Surely it is time to use every knowledge, every science we possess, to apply common sense and above all to act with unanimity and singleness of purpose.

I am a pacifist. You, my fellow citizens of twenty-one American republics, are pacifists too. But I believe that you and I, if in the long run it be necessary, will act together to protect and defend by every means at our command, our science, our culture, our American freedom and our civilization.

Edward Teller: Seated in the crowd of thousands that day, I had the peculiar feeling that the president was speaking directly to me. Perhaps that is what is meant by charisma. But I also suspected that, out of all those present, the president and I were probably the only people who associated "using every knowledge, every science we possess" with the race for the atomic bomb. Roosevelt's speech resolved my dilemma. I was one of the fortunate helped to escape from the Nazi threat. I was now enjoying the comforts and many benefits of living in a democracy. I had the obligation to do whatever I could to protect freedom.

Not long after Roosevelt's address, I went off to give a Sigma Pi Sigma lecture series. While I was traveling from campus to campus, the Nazi armies were sweeping through France. Every day, the situation looked more terrible. The brave resistance at Dunkirk provided the only little spark of hope, but in the midst of the Nazi victory, I hardly noticed it.

Vannevar Bush: Germany swept across France, conquered it with ease, and nearly trapped the whole British army. Russia stood aside, to wait for the rest of Europe to exhaust itself and then to pounce. Nazi submarines threatened to cut off Britain's food supplies and starve her out. Hitler's might had been vastly underestimated. It looked as though later we might face, alone, a Nazi enemy master of all the production facilities of Europe, allied with Japan to conquer the world, and in a fair way to do it.

Sen. James F. Byrnes, *Democratic US senator from South Carolina*:* It was the disaster at Dunkirk that at last aroused our people. Our hatred of war was at odds with our growing recognition that the conflagration was creeping ever closer to our shores.

Vannevar Bush: We were all drawn together early by one thing we deeply shared—worry. We were agreed that the war was bound to break out into an intense struggle, that America was sure to get into it in one way or another sooner or later, that it would be a highly technical struggle, that we were by no means prepared in this regard.

Arthur Holly Compton: The government's unpreparedness for handling uranium research was one of several examples that shocked certain members of the National Academy of Sciences into action. At their suggestion President Roosevelt created the National Defense Research Committee.

Vannevar Bush: The National Defense Research Committee was launched [on June 27, 1940] over a year before we entered World War II, as a civilian

* Byrnes held a variety of key top positions through the Roosevelt and Truman years; at the start of the war in Europe, he was in the Senate, but he was nominated to the Supreme Court in 1941, then left in 1942 to aid the war effort—spending the duration as first the director of the Office of Economic Stabilization and, later, the director of the Office of War Mobilization from 1943 to 1945. In 1945, in the final month of the war, Harry Truman nominated him to be secretary of state.

organization of scientists and engineers for the purpose of developing new weapons for military use.

Laura Fermi: Why were the persons acting this drama all foreign-born? In Italy, I reflected, universities are government-controlled; a channel between universities and government is always in existence and does not need to be opened. These people—these Hungarian-, German-, and Italian-born—knew the organization in dictatorial countries; it occurred to them that there might be ties between research and military applications, that in Germany all scientific work might have been enrolled in the war effort.

In the face of a national emergency, totalitarian regimes are more efficient than democracies, at least during the first stages of the game. They are better equipped. A dictator holds in his hands all the strings and can pull them and mobilize the country at a moment's notice. A democracy has either no strings at all or long pieces of red tape.

Emilio Segrè: Fermi used to say, whenever somebody bragged about his Pilgrim ancestry, or when he heard about the Daughters of the American Revolution, that he and other newly arrived refugees were the true, new pilgrims, who understood and appreciated some American ideals better than the American-born.

Alexander Sachs: One great advantage that we had was these refugees, these scientists themselves, responded to that very sprit of freedom that brought the Pilgrim Fathers over here. They were saturated by ideas and motives which the regimented scientists could not have, and so the transplanted and the American scientists, if given the means, would make advances much faster.

Eugene Wigner: It was refugees from other parts of Europe who saw most clearly that a war was coming. We reported the menace to our adopted countries. Both in England and in the United States, we did all we could to herald the danger and to alert those in power.

"A special medal to be given to meddling foreigners"

THE M.A.U.D. COMMITTEE

England, under air assault during the Blitz, first pushed the idea of building a bomb.

While nuclear fission research stalled in the US and war began in Europe, other scientists in the United Kingdom continued to calculate the possibility of a bomb and worriedly advocated for action, even as they similarly struggled to navigate unfamiliar government bureaucracies.

Otto R. Frisch: Back in Copenhagen I did some experiments which gave the first physical, not chemical, evidence of fission; but on the whole I felt, as I wrote to my mother, like a man in the jungle who finds he has caught an elephant by the tail and does not know what to do next. The idea clearly opened fascinating vistas, but I did nothing about it. Threat of war had become palpable in the spring of 1939; and I did not feel like starting any new work that might soon be stopped. Having left Germany because of Hitler's race laws and believing that Denmark was now in danger of invasion, I felt that I had better go elsewhere. I gratefully accepted an invitation from Mark Oliphant, head of the physics department of the University of Birmingham, to visit him during the summer of 1939 to discuss what had best be done. We were still discussing when war was declared, and I stayed.

Rudolf Peierls: Quite soon tribunals were set up to classify all enemy aliens into three categories: those in the first category were trusted, and freed from practically all restrictions; the second category were those about whom too little was known, and for whom the restrictions continued; and the third category were suspected of being enemy agents and were interned. We were placed in the first category.

Otto R. Frisch: After studying the theory of thermal diffusion, I decided to build a Clusius separation tube to produce a small sample of enriched uranium. This experiment was begun in an unused lecture room, because by that time all the laboratories in the physics department were being used for development work on radar. That was, of course, highly secret work to which I was not admitted, being technically an enemy alien. For my work not much help could be offered, so my Clusius tube made slow headway and was finally abandoned.

My friend and colleague Rudolf Peierls had improved a formula—first proposed by Francis Perrin—for estimating the critical size of a chain reacting assembly. That formula contained parameters, such as the fission cross-section and the number of neutrons emitted per fission, which were hardly known at the time. I had to make guesses, which were overoptimistic as I later realized, and was staggered to get the result that a couple of pounds of Uranium-235 would be sufficient to make an atomic bomb.

Rudolf Peierls: One day, in February or March 1940, Frisch said, "Suppose someone gave you a quantity of pure 235 isotope of uranium—what would happen?" We started working out the consequences. We had all the data to insert in my formula, and we were amazed how small this turned out to be. We estimated the critical size to be about a pound, whereas speculations concerned with natural uranium had tended to come out with tons. Our estimate turned out to be rather too low, but the order of magnitude was right.

Otto R. Frisch: We came to the conclusion that with something like a hundred thousand similar separation tubes, one might produce a pound of reasonably pure Uranium-235 in a modest time, measured in weeks. At that point we stared at each other and realized that an atomic bomb might after all be possible.

Rudolf Peierls: We were quite staggered by these results. In a classical understatement, we said to ourselves, "Even if this plant costs as much as a battleship, it would be worth having."

Otto R. Frisch: I have often been asked why I didn't abandon the project there and then, saying nothing to anybody. Why start on a project which, if it was successful, would end with the production of a weapon of unparalleled violence, a weapon of mass destruction such as the world had never seen? The answer is very simple. We were at war, and the idea was reasonably obvious; very probably some German scientists had had the same idea and were working on it. A German scientist, Gustav Hertz, had been one of the first to separate isotopes—of neon, not uranium—in significant quantities, and the possibility was well known to the physics community.

Rudolf Peierls: For all we knew, the Germans could already be working on such a weapon, and the idea of Hitler getting it first was most frightening. It was our duty to inform the British government of this possibility. At the same time our conclusion had to be kept secret; if the German physicists had not yet seen the point, we did not want to draw their attention to it.

Frisch and I sat down to write a memorandum stating our analysis and conclusions. It was written in two parts: one was technical and gave the arguments, and the other was nontechnical and summarized the conclusions. We discussed radioactivity and the spread of radioactive fallout. We pointed out that use of this weapon would probably kill large numbers of civilians "and this may make it unsuitable as a weapon for use by this country." But as there was no effective defense, other than the threat of retaliation with the same weapon, it would be worth developing as a deterrent, even if one did not intend to use it as a means of attack. We did not entrust this document to a secretary. We typed it up ourselves—or rather, I did, because I had a typewriter and was familiar with it.

Otto R. Frisch: Peierls and I went to talk it over with Oliphant.

Rudolf Peierls: We did not know how to send a secret communication, or, for that matter, where to send it.

Mark Oliphant: Peierls and Frisch came to me in 1940. They convinced me that if the less prevalent isotope of uranium could be separated in a pure form, it might be possible to make a weapon.

Otto R. Frisch: He told us to send our report to Henry Tizard, who was advising the government on scientific problems concerned with warfare. That report was sent off within a couple of weeks and was decisive in getting the British Government to take the atomic bomb seriously.

Rudolf Peierls: Tizard passed the paper on to G. P.—later Sir George—Thomson, who was the chairman of a committee concerned with the possibility of a nuclear chain reaction. The committee was about to disband itself. They saw no immediate prospect of success.

Mark Oliphant: The committee generally was electrified by the possibility [of the Peierls-Frisch memo].

James Chadwick: I was asked if I would take charge of the experimental work required to look into this matter. Of course, I said, "Yes."

Rudolf Peierls: The name of the [new] committee was the M.A.U.D. Committee, and that name has an amusing origin.

Otto R. Frisch: A telegram had been received from Niels Bohr which ended with greetings to "Maud Ray, Kent." Nobody had heard of such a person, and we all tried to read some subtle meaning into that name. We were all convinced that Bohr wanted to convey some secret message.

Rudolf Peierls: This puzzle led to the suggestion of the name "Maud Committee," or M.A.U.D. to look more official. It was unfortunate that many people associated with it were convinced the letters stood for "Military Applications of the Uranium Disintegration"!

Otto R. Frisch: Much later we learned that Maud Ray was an old friend of the Bohr family.

Rudolf Peierls: I needed some regular help—someone with whom I would be able to discuss the theoretical technicalities. I looked around for a suitable person, and thought of Klaus Fuchs. He was a German, who as a student had been politically active as a member of a socialist student group (which was essentially communist) and had to flee for his life from the Nazis. In due course he got a full clearance, and he started work in May 1941. Fuchs became a lodger in our house, and he was a pleasant person to have around. His appointment did indeed provide me with support in the research work that was as efficient as I had hoped.

James Chadwick: I remember the spring of 1941 to this day. I realized then that a nuclear bomb was not only possible—it was inevitable. Sooner or later these ideas could not be peculiar to us. Everybody would think about them before long, and some country would put them into action. I had nobody to talk to—the chief people in the laboratory were Frisch and Rotblat. However high my opinion of them was, they were not citizens of this country, and the others were quite young boys. There was nobody to talk to about it. I had many sleepless nights. I did realize how very, very serious it could be, and I had then to start taking sleeping pills. It was the only remedy. I've never stopped since then. I don't think I've missed a single night in all those years.

Rudolf Peierls: It was decided to increase the resources necessary for this work and to set up an organization that could handle a larger project. The project received a new code name, "Tube Alloys." It meant nothing but sounded like a very dull but practical organization.

Robert Serber: The MAUD committee reported that a bomb could be built in two years at a cost of 50 million pounds.

Mark Oliphant: The minutes and reports of the Maud Committee had been sent to Lyman Briggs, chairman of a similar committee in the United States, and we were puzzled to receive virtually no comment. In 1941 I went to the United States on radar business and was asked to make discreet enquiries about this situation. I called on Briggs in Washington, only to find that this inarticulate and unimpressive man had put the reports in his safe and had not shown them to members of his Committee.

Leo Szilard: Oliphant realized that something was very wrong and that the work on uranium was not being pushed in an effective way. He travelled across this continent from the Atlantic to the Pacific and disregarding international etiquette told all those who were willing to listen what he thought of us. Considerations other than those of military security prevent me from revealing the exact expressions which he used.

One of the key stops Oliphant made during his cross-country Paul Revere–style warning trip was Berkeley, California, where professor Ernest O. Lawrence had founded the Radiation Laboratory. Much of the "Rad Lab," as it is known for short, centered around Lawrence's ever-expanding ambitions for a "cyclotron," a massive magnet array that helped in atomic experiments. The University of California–Berkeley, which also hosted a theoretical physics division led by J. Robert Oppenheimer, had, by the start of the 1940s, become a central focal point for anyone interested in the atom.

Mark Oliphant: Amazed and distressed, I reported the situation to Vannevar Bush and James B. Conant, who were responsible for the application of science to a war in which America was rapidly becoming involved, although officially still neutral. Not satisfied with their response, I raised the question with Ernest Lawrence, inventor of the cyclotron and the most dynamic member of the Briggs Committee. He was deeply interested, and I am sure that it was his influence which led to a very rapid escalation of effort in America.

Arthur Holly Compton: Lawrence had come as a graduate student to the University of Chicago in the fall of 1923 when I began my work there as a young professor of physics. After he had gone to the University of California as professor of physics, Lawrence stopped one day in Chicago to show me his plans for a device that he called a "cyclotron." This can be described most simply as an electric motor whose rotating armature is replaced by a revolving stream of atomic particles. When these particles gain enough speed, they fly out at a selected point in the periphery of the field magnets, forming a high energy "beam" that is useful for many experimental purposes. I encouraged him to go ahead with its construction. Its success was remarkable, and the use of the cyclotron was of epochal importance in nuclear physics. His "Radiation Laboratory" at Berkeley early became a mecca for nuclear physicists and chemists from all over the world.

Emilio Segrè: Few machines were to be as productive of important discoveries in nuclear physics as the 60-inch cyclotron, which started working at the beginning of 1940.

Luis Alvarez: Ernest Lawrence's greatest invention was doing physics in cooperative teams. I was enormously stimulated by it.

Glenn Seaborg: Ernest Lawrence had been awarded the 1939 Nobel Prize for his invention of the cyclotron. Lawrence was off playing tennis; his secretary had difficulty convincing the people at the Berkeley Tennis Club that the message was worth calling him off the court to receive. Lawrence was not only the first Nobel winner at the University of California but also the first from any state university in the United States. Major breakthroughs in science had traditionally come in Europe, especially Germany and England. When American scientists emerged, Harvard practically held a monopoly. It was one of the first steps in proving that we were building a public university that could compete with the best of the private institutions.

Arthur Holly Compton: Ernest Lawrence was also one of those who early showed his alertness to the need for American science to get ready for the military showdown between the Axis powers and the free world.

Ernest O. Lawrence: [The Nazis] have taken every advantage of modern technical developments, while the Allies have gone along traditional lines. I hope we will look at the problem of warfare scientifically. We need research and more research.

Leo Szilard: If Congress knew the true history of the atomic energy project, I have no doubt but that it would create a special medal to be given to meddling foreigners for distinguished services, and Dr. Oliphant would be the first to receive one. He discussed his concern with E. O. Lawrence, who in turn approached Compton, and as a result of this agitation it was decided to reorganize the project.

Arthur Holly Compton: In early September of 1941, Ernest Lawrence called me by phone from Berkeley. Certain new developments made him believe it would be possible to make an atomic bomb. I made a date for Lawrence to see me in Chicago the following week when James B. Conant, President of Harvard University, was also to be there. It was a cool September evening. My wife greeted Conant and Lawrence as they came into our home and gave us each a cup of coffee as we gathered around the fireplace. Lawrence began by telling briefly of new results from England and how this work was confirmed by experiments in the United States. This work had convinced him of the feasibility of making an atomic bomb using only a few kilograms of fissionable material. He described recent Berkeley experiments, indicating that the bomb could be made equally well either with Uranium-235 or with a new chemical element discovered in his laboratory which was soon afterwards named "plutonium."

Glenn Seaborg: Under normal circumstances, we would have rushed to publication to establish our claim to the discovery of a new element. But the war had changed everything. The world would not learn of the discovery for more than four years. At first, we gave the new element no name, simply referring to it as 94. But even that revealed too much for casual conversations around the Faculty Club or the lab, so we adopted the code name of "copper" for element 94 and "silver" for element 93. This code worked well enough through 1941, until some experiments required the use of some real copper, which we then referred to as "honest-to-God copper." A year after its discovery we finally named our new element. It was so difficult to make, from such rare materials, that we thought it would certainly be the heaviest element ever formed. So we considered names like *extremium* and *ultimium*. Fortunately, we were spared the inevitable embarrassment that one courts when proclaiming a discovery to be the ultimate in any field by deciding to follow the nomenclatural precedents of the two prior elements: uranium and neptunium. We briefly considered the form plutium, but plutonium seemed more euphonious. Each element has a one- or two-letter abbreviation. Following the standard rules, this symbol should be Pl, but we chose Pu instead. We simply followed the planetary precedent.

James B. Conant: Discoveries of fundamental significance had been made by American physicists largely working outside the official framework of the advisory committee. Using the atom smasher Lawrence had invented—the cyclotron—his associates in Berkeley had produced the hitherto-unknown element No. 94; it was christened plutonium. Before long, experiments with tiny amounts of material had confirmed what the theoreticians had surmised, namely, that the new element, like one of the uranium isotopes, underwent spontaneous fission. Already, though hardly enough of the element had been manufactured to be seen, more than one physicist in the United States and England had begun to whisper that the large-scale production of plutonium might prove to be the essential step in a scheme for releasing atomic energy.

Arthur Holly Compton: The most critical problem in making a plutonium bomb was to establish a nuclear chain reaction that would supply the neutrons needed to make Pu-239 from U-238. It was thus the idea of the plutonium bomb that gave military significance to the chain-reacting pile.

James B. Conant: Bush enlarged the National Academy Committee and asked for another review of the situation. The two new members of Compton's committee were the chemical engineer, W. K. Lewis, and a physical chemist who had transformed himself during the past year into the NDRC expert on explosives—Professor George B. Kistiakowsky of Harvard. Kistiakowsky was well aware of the research work on separating Uranium-235, but had been thinking in terms of power. When I retailed to him the idea that a bomb could be made by the rapid assembly of two masses of fissionable material, his first remark was that of a doubting Thomas. "It would seem to be a difficult undertaking on a battlefield," he remarked.

George B. Kistiakowsky: I was brought in with a specific assignment of describing what would be the effect of an atomic explosion of several kiloton TNT-equivalent force, which was, at that time of course, an unknown quantity. I brought one of my young associates to do a careful survey calling together all of the information on accidental large—mostly industrial—explosions. Out of that, we plotted a scaling wall with the size of the damaged area as a function—an estimated size. I also described how explosives could be used to initiate the nuclear explosion. I described it as a case when you have the fissionable material in the middle and the explosives around it, and I said you just explode it so that it explodes symmetrically on all sides.

James B. Conant: A few weeks later when we met, George's doubts were gone. "It can be made to work," he said. "I am one hundred percent sold." My doubts about Briggs' project evaporated as soon as I heard George Kistiakowsky's considered verdict. I had known George for many years. I had complete faith in his judgment. If he was sold on Arthur Compton's program, who was I to have reservations?

Abraham Pais: Much has been written about Einstein's letters to President Roosevelt on the importance of the development of atomic weapons. Opinions on the influence of these letters are divided. It is my own impression that this influence was marginal. He only decided to go ahead with full-scale atomic weapons development in October 1941. At that time he was mainly influenced, I believe, by the British efforts. In his later years, Einstein himself said more than once that he regretted having signed these letters: "Had I known that the Germans would not succeed in producing an atomic bomb, I would not have lifted a finger."

2nd Lt. R. Gordon Arneson, ***staff assistant for atomic energy, War Department*****:** It was only when the British came up with their MAUD committee report which said a bomb was feasible that we got energized.

Arthur Holly Compton: I called our National Academy Committee together once more in Cambridge, Massachusetts, in mid-October. Two major questions remained to be answered. First, how destructive would an atomic bomb be? Second, what would it require in time and cost to produce the bomb? I asked the theoretical physicists on our committee to solve the first problem. The second I put up to the engineers. To neither of the questions were the experts willing to attempt an answer.

After some discussion, I suggested a total time of between three and five years, and a total cost—assuming that only one method of producing U-235 or plutonium would be followed—of some hundreds of millions of dollars. None of the committee members objected. The time estimate was used in our submitted report. At the suggestion of Bush the cost estimate was played down, lest the government should be frightened off.

I have always been rather proud of these forecasts, considering the limited data. The actual time required was three years and eight months. The cost of producing the plutonium used during the war was about 400 million dollars. The total atomic bomb program used about 1,500 million dollars by the end of the war, but this involved carrying through to production not one but four methods for making fissionable material. I presented the report personally to Vannevar Bush on November 6, 1941. We spent an hour discussing its contents and what the next action should be. Bush took the report at once to President Roosevelt. In Bush's hands was also a report from the British that covered the same general ground. The British and American reports agreed that the bombs could probably be made, that they would be so destructive that they might well turn the tide of the war, and that this possibility was one of which the Germans were well aware.

James B. Conant: In the last days of November, Bush sent the report of Arthur Compton's committee to the President. This report was explicit about an atomic explosive: "A fission bomb of superlatively destructive power will result from bringing quickly together a sufficient mass of element U-235."

Arthur Holly Compton: The first steps toward getting the atomic program under way had already been worked out between Vannevar Bush and James Conant in agreement with the President's committee on top policy. Conant was to head a small group, given the name of the S-1 Committee, which was to see that the investigations went ahead with all possible speed.

James B. Conant: The responsibility for the atomic business was taken out from the National Defense Research Committee and given to this special group, of which I was Chairman, reporting to Bush.

Arthur Holly Compton: The members of the S-1 Committee were: Chairman, Dr. Conant; Vice Chairman, Dr. Lyman J. Briggs, Director of the National Bureau of Standards, to whom the President had originally delegated the government's responsibility for study of the field of atomic energy; Dr. Eger V. Murphree, Director of Research for the Standard Oil Development Company of New Jersey; Ernest Lawrence; Harold Urey; and myself.

After the meeting of the committee, I went with Bush and Conant to lunch at the old Cosmos Club.

James B. Conant: Compton was talking about producing a new element, plutonium, which had not yet been seen except in microscopic amounts. Yet it was proposed to produce large amounts of plutonium by the operation of a pile. The contents of the pile would then be put through a series of chemical reactions in order to separate the plutonium from the uranium. To my objection that the chemistry of the element was largely unknown, Compton replied that intensive research would produce the necessary knowledge.

Arthur Holly Compton: This was Saturday. I went from the luncheon table to my room and wrote out a preliminary plan of attack and an initial operating budget. Though devising the method for building the bomb was my most important assignment, it did not seem to call for first attention. If plutonium was to be made, we needed to get into action at once.

Laura Fermi: It was only on December 6, 1941, the day before Pearl Harbor, three years after the discovery of uranium fission in Germany, that the decision to make an all-out effort in atomic energy research was announced by Vannevar Bush, director of the Office of Scientific Research and Development.

Arthur Holly Compton: This was December 6th, 1941. The nation had yet one day of peace.

"The 'take-it-or-leave-it note' "

DECEMBER 7, 1941

Japan's attack on Pearl Harbor ended the US's hopes of staying out of the war.

Just as Germany's war in Europe began with Hitler's advances across Europe in the 1930s, Japan had been steadily advancing through Asia that decade as well—starting even earlier with the conquering of Manchuria in 1931. In 1937, Japan launched a full-scale war with China by invading the mainland; its capture of the then capital, Nanking, in December 1937 was followed by the mass murder and rape of civilians—perhaps upwards of 200,000 were killed in the "Rape of Nanking," which presaged other brutal atrocities and war crimes as imperial Japanese forces began a wider conquest across the Pacific. Through the summer of 1941, the still-isolationist-minded US had tried to navigate around becoming involved in the conflicts in either Europe or the Pacific.

After years of heeding the isolationist political currents at home, Franklin Roosevelt found his hand forced by the surprise Japanese attack on Pearl Harbor, which killed some 2,400 US personnel, destroyed much of the US Pacific Fleet, and cleared the way for the Empire of Japan to sweep down across the Pacific to the very edge of Australia in the months ahead. The attack spurred the US into war in a matter of days and gave even more urgency to the efforts to research an atomic bomb.

Joseph C. Grew, *US ambassador to Japan*: In 1931 came their invasion of Manchuria. In 1937 came their invasion of China south of the wall, and while their Army eventually floundered in China, due to the magnificent fighting spirit of Chiang Kai-shek, his courageous armies, and his determined people, nevertheless the warfare which then ensued proved a practical training for the Japanese soldiers and sailors, who tirelessly developed and perfected the tactics they subsequently used in their landings and conquests to the south.

Robert Guillain, *Tokyo correspondent, Havas News Agency:** Ten years of imperialistic expansion, marked by the conquest of Manchuria in 1931, the step-by-step invasion of northern, central and southern China from 1937 to 1939, the first move against Singapore with the Tonkin invasion in 1940, and the occupation of Cochin China in 1941, led the Japanese war toward fusion with Hitler's war; it was entirely natural that the two should blend into a single world conflict.

Masuo Kato, *US correspondent, Domei News Agency*: In July, the Japanese Army marched into Indo-China. Convinced that the move into Indo-China was to establish a springboard for a southern invasion, the United States on July 26, 1941, froze all Japanese assets in America, an action that had previously been taken against Axis Germany, and peace conversations were, for the moment, meaningless.

Henry C. Wolfe, *war correspondent*: A general war in the Pacific appeared imminent. But the United States matched Nippon's moves with several blitz

* Havas, originally founded in 1835 and the world's oldest news service, was relaunched and renamed after the French occupation by the Nazis as Agence France-Presse.

moves of her own. We clapped an oil embargo on Japan and froze her credits in America. We incorporated the armed forces of the Philippines into the Army of the United States. And we made Lieutenant General Douglas MacArthur commander of the combined Filipino-American defense establishment.

Gen. Douglas MacArthur: We began an eleventh-hour struggle to build up enough force to repel an enemy. Too late, Washington had come to realize the danger. My orders from Washington were not to initiate hostilities against the Japanese under any circumstances. The first overt move in the Philippine area must come from the enemy.

Robert Guillain: For six months, nationalist propaganda, whipped up by the German colony, exploited by the military clique, had violently assailed America and exalted Hitler's victories. The United States, said the newspapers, by imposing economic sanctions on Japan, depriving it of oil, scrap iron, loans, trade, was strangling Japan. America must "reconsider its attitude" or Tokyo's patience would run out. Threats by General Hideki Tojo, successive waves of troop mobilization, civil-defense drills all clearly pointed to war.

Joseph C. Grew: When the Japanese militarists, committed absolutely to the course of conquest, took measure of their military resources and perceived the extent of democratic rearmament, they had to gamble. The gamble was heroic, but not that of a mere game of chance. Their well-planned campaigns southward were brilliant accomplishments.

Masuo Kato: The shadow of Hitler's Germany hung heavily over Japanese official thinking. The military education of many officers of the Army had been largely German-influenced, and pro-German sentiment was predominant in Army circles as a result. The fact that Nazism was an ideal doctrine for a militaristic state made many of these same officers pro-Nazi also, and the pressure of the China War had made Japan a virtual military dictatorship long before she attacked the United States and Great Britain. Admiration for German military methods and emulation of them led Japan's military leaders into the error of believing that Germany would certainly be victorious in the European war and that any course except to support her would be folly.

Nogi Harumichi, ***university student, Patriotic Students' Alliance*****:** Beginning in 1939, Hitler's newsreels were shown every day. When I played hooky, I always went to see them. I'd watch those stirring movies about Hitler and wonder, "What's the matter with the Japanese army in Manchuria? Why can't they just annihilate the British or the Americans? Hitler took all of Poland and united it with Germany!" Japanese youth at that time adored Hitler and Mussolini and yearned for the emergence of a Japanese politician with the same qualities. We wanted decisive action.

Robert Guillain: It had mainly been Hitler's insistence and example that had pushed Tokyo into the war. The Japanese were dazzled by the early German victories, fascinated by Hitler, bewitched by the promise of the coming partition of the world. This ineluctable train of events coincided with a calculated, premeditated design: Japan was bursting with a desire to prove itself as much a world power as the Western countries of which it had so long been the docile, patient pupil. This Asian people was determined to force its way on to the stage of history by chasing the white race out of Asia. This was an old ambition, nursed since Japan's first contact with the Western world.

Masuo Kato: After Japan's surrender Lieutenant General Ryukichi Tanaka, former chief of the Military Administration Bureau, summarized in a newspaper article the Army's estimate of the military situation before Pearl Harbor. Germany was expected to smash Russia by the end of 1942. If Great Britain then capitulated to Germany, as seemed likely, the American people would lose their stomach for war. Therefore Japan could anticipate victory by the end of 1942. Fantastic now, that hypothesis gave the Army the foundation of its political power. On the diplomatic side, Germany had convinced Matsuoka that the Tripartite Alliance could provide Japan with a means of neutralizing the United States in the Pacific.

Robert Guillain: The war against America was the coronation of three generations of effort that had already crystallized in war three times: in China in 1895, against Tsarist Russia in 1904, and World War I, which Japan entered in 1915. All this indicates that we must look beyond the logical causes of the Pacific war. Its true causes were basically emotional.

Masaichi Kikuchi, ***officer candidate, Imperial Japanese Army*****:** We grew up in a world where everyone who was not Japanese was perceived as an enemy. Chinese, British, American. We were schooled to regard them all as evil, devilish, animalistic. Conflict was commonplace for our generation, from Manchuria onwards.

2nd Lt. Tominaga Shozo, ***232nd Regiment, Thirty-Ninth Division, Imperial Japanese Army, based in central China*****:** A new conscript became a full-fledged soldier in three months in the battle area. As the last stage of their training, we made them bayonet a living human. When I was a company commander, this was used as a finishing touch to training for the men and a trial of courage for the officers. Prisoners were blindfolded and tied to poles. The soldiers dashed forward to bayonet their target at the shout of "Charge!" Some stopped on their way. We kicked them and made them do it. After that, a man could do anything easily. Everyone became a demon within three months.

Masuo Kato: Although as early as September 1941 some members of the Japanese Embassy staff were darkly predicting "war or at least a showdown," I was convinced throughout that war could be avoided. Renewed talks with President Roosevelt and Secretary Hull began at the White House on November 17, and by November 20 there was considerable hope that a solution might be reached. Secretary Hull's note of November 26, which stated the United States position toward Japan, was called by the press the "take-it-or-leave-it note." The November 26 note to the Japanese Government should have made it obvious that there was no longer hope for the negotiations, but there still seemed not the slightest inkling in the Embassy that war was to strike within a few days.

Robert Guillain: It is easy to see today what madness it was for Japan to attack the United States in December 1941, but I can attest that even at the time, there was not a single foreigner living in Tokyo to whom that folly was not glaringly evident. Not one of the foreign observers whose painful privilege it was to watch the march of events closely failed to foresee from the very first day that the disproportion between the United States and Japan must sooner or later lead to an American victory.

Edwin Nakasone, ***age 14, Oahu, Hawaii*****:** December 7, 1941—Mama and papa asleep, the rest of the family asleep. I'm having breakfast—our kitchen door faced the west. There's a mountain range, the Wai'anae Range, and then there's a cut—the Kolekole Pass. I was watching it, eating my breakfast—I recall vividly my breakfast was Kellogg's Corn Flakes. We didn't have enough milk, and we didn't have too much in the way of ice box room, so a lot of time we were eating it with Carnation Milk.

I see this beautiful formation of about fifteen planes coming through Kolekole Pass, and they swooped down on Schofield Barracks and began strafing. They swooped up into the air and went after Wheeler airfield. There, again, in beautiful formation, they dove down—one after another—and I see little pellet-like things dropping down from the planes. And I said, "Oh my God—they're making a horrible mistake!" I was of the opinion that this is the Navy playing war games against the Army and bombing Wheeler airfield. I hear this "boom, boom, boom" and see all this debris going up. We're no more than three miles away, up on the heights looking down. I could see quite clear what was going on.

I dashed outside, looked up, and there was a Zero fighter coming, no more than 2,000 feet at the most above in the air, and I see the great big red balls of Japan on both wings and the fuselage. I was most surprised. To this day, I still recall the Japanese pilot—the cockpit was open, he had his neckerchief around him, flowing out, he had the goggles on, and I still remember his face as he came roaring over our homes.

Pvt. Russell McCurdy, ***gun director, USS*** **Arizona,** ***US Marine Corps*****:** That morning at 0755 I was getting ready for liberty, getting cleaned up in the forward head. I felt a small thud like a water barge striking us. Then I felt another thud like that—I discovered later it was bombs exploding. I went up on deck and there were guys pointing up in the air at planes going overhead, and there were explosions over on Ford Island. General Quarters sounded, and then machine-gun fire and our antiaircraft guns came into action. The Japanese planes were swooping all around us, and I watched torpedo planes coming in low from across the harbor, heading toward Battleship Row. Then there was a really violent explosion in the front part of the ship, which caused the old *Arizona* to toss and shake. First the ship rose, shuddered, and settled down by the bow. We got to the deck and it was chaos. There were charred bodies everywhere. The passageways were like white-hot furnaces.

Leonore Rickert, ***nurse, US Navy, Pearl Harbor Naval Hospital*****:** I was on duty on Sunday morning, December 7. I looked over toward Ford Island and could see things blowing up, and knew we had a problem. When the captain came to the ward he said the Japanese were attacking. New patients were starting to come in, and they were burned from being thrown off the ships and into the water where there was burning oil. They were terribly burned.

Capt. Paul W. Tibbets, ***engineering officer, 90th Squadron, Third Attack Group*****:** On a Saturday in the first week of December 1941, at Fort Bragg, North Carolina, we went up to fly attack missions over some ground troops as part of an army maneuver. The next day we flew back to Savannah. It was a reasonably sunny day, and I had tuned my radio to a station in Savannah. Suddenly the music in my earphones ceased and a voice broke in. A mile over the red clay earth of Georgia, I learned that the Japanese had bombed Pearl Harbor.

Edward Teller: Our closest friends that year, the Fermis, the Mayers, and the Ureys, all lived outside New York City, in Leonia; therefore, although we lived near the university, Mici and I did a considerable amount of commuting. One Sunday in December, Mici and I stopped to buy gas on our way to the Fermis. The gas station attendant was listening to a radio inside, and when he finally came out to the car, he told us that Pearl Harbor had been bombed. "Where is Pearl Harbor?" I asked. So it was that we learned that the United States was at war.

Frances Perkins, ***US Secretary of Labor*****:** It was shocking. There was terrific excitement. We sat down near the desk of the president. The president's pride in the Navy was so terrific that he was having actual physical difficulty in getting out the words that the Navy was caught unawares, that bombs dropped on ships that were not in fighting shape and not prepared to move, but were just tied up. I remember that he said twice to Knox, "Find out, for God's sakes, why the ships were tied up in rows."

Henry Stimson, ***US Secretary of War, diary, December 7, 1941*****:** When the news first came that Japan had attacked us, my first feeling was of relief that the indecision was over and that a crisis had come in a way which would unite all our people. This continued to be my dominant feeling in spite of the news of catastrophes which quickly developed. For I feel that this country united has practically nothing to fear, while the apathy and divisions stirred up by unpatriotic men have been hitherto very discouraging.

Gen. George C. Marshall, ***chief of staff, US Army*****:** A democracy has a very hard time in a war particularly at the start of a war. They can never get ready in advance. The conditions are such that they are very susceptible to surprise action and the arbitrary government like the Hitler government has every advantage in those respects. They are just bound to win at the start unless they are very, very stupid. Of course, in the end, if the democracy is a firm democracy, it builds up a power which outlasts the other and the dictatorship bogs down. But it hadn't bogged down yet.

Cmdr. Edwin Layton, ***intelligence officer, US Pacific Fleet, Pearl Harbor*****:** One final shock was in store for the president before the day came to a close. News arrived at the White House just before midnight that an air raid had wiped out most of the Philippines air force. It was a reprise of Pearl Harbor. The Japanese planes from Taiwan swept in in well-coordinated waves to strafe and bomb Clark Field and the other airstrips north of Manila at lunchtime. General [Lewis] Brereton's planes were swallowed like sitting ducks in a holocaust of exploding bombs and blazing gasoline. In less than half an hour, three quarters of the fighters in MacArthur's command had been reduced to charred skeletons. At a single blow it had removed our ability to strike back and guaranteed the success of the impending Japanese invasion of the islands.

Sgt. Paul Metro, ***radar, 393rd Bombardment Squadron*****:** The next day President Roosevelt came on the radio to announce the declaration of war on Japan. Two days later, Germany and Italy declared war on the US.

Tojo Hideki, ***prime minister of Japan, radio address, December 8, 1941*****:** I am resolved to dedicate myself, body and soul, to the country, and to set at ease the august mind of our Sovereign. And I believe that every one of you, my fellow countrymen, will not care for your life but gladly share in the honor to make of yourself His Majesty's humble shield. The key to victory lies in a "faith in victory." For 2,600 years, since it was founded, our Empire has never known a defeat. This record alone is enough to produce a conviction in our ability to crush any enemy no matter how strong. Let us pledge ourselves that we will never stain our glorious history, but will go forward. The rise or fall of our Empire and the prosperity or ruin of East Asia literally depend upon the outcome of this war. Truly it is time for the one hundred million of us Japanese to dedicate all we have and sacrifice everything for our country's cause.

Scribe First Class Noda Mitsuharu, ***clerk, Headquarters Combined Fleet, Imperial Navy*****:** After the successful attack on Pearl Harbor, we sailors talked about the opportunities we might get. My dream was to go to San Francisco, and therc head up the accounting department in the garrison unit after the occupation. All of us in the navy dreamed of going to America.

PART II

IMAGINING *a* BOMB

1941–1942

"The war must be won"

SETTING UP THE MET LAB

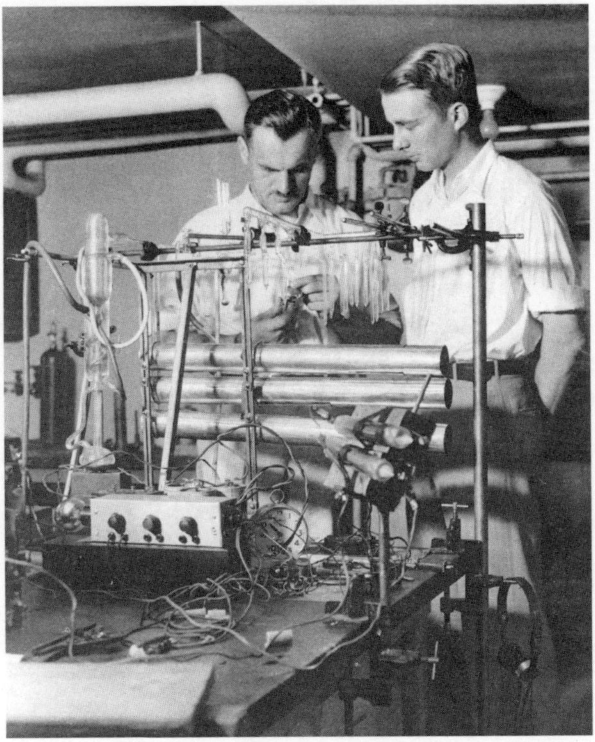

Arthur Holly Compton, with his student Luis Alvarez, recruited far and wide for the Met Lab.

While the United Kingdom rejoiced that the US had finally joined the war, the early months of World War II for the US were dark. The Japanese Navy and Army marched down through the Pacific, defeating US garrisons in the Philippines, taking Hong Kong, Singapore, and Burma, among many others, seizing island after island, virtually all the way to the edge of Australia. Spurred on by America's official entry into the war, the nation's nuclear physicists descended on Chicago to dive into the practical questions of a now suddenly all-too-serious effort to make atomic weapons a reality and how to build and harness chain reactions. The new team in Chicago, headed by Arthur Holly Compton, grew almost as exponentially as a chain reaction itself: Just forty-five strong in March, by June the Met Lab boasted a staff of more than 1,200.

Arthur Holly Compton: The attack on Pearl Harbor was from an immediate technical point of view very well done. It was skillfully planned, executed with precision, and gave a crippling blow to our Navy. But from a broader military perspective, what a mistake! Its immediate effect was to unite all Americans toward the nation's defense. If we invited a scientist to take part in our project, his only question was whether it was this or some other branch of the war effort in which he could be more useful. Universities and business organizations gave us every possible cooperation. The war must be won.

Glenn Seaborg: It felt as if there was not a moment to waste. It's hard for anyone who didn't live through World War II to imagine the desperation and sense of impending doom that we felt, hard to imagine that we believed that Germany and Japan could conquer the world.

Adm. Chester W. Nimitz, *commander-in-chief, US Pacific Fleet*: We have taken a tremendous wallop, but I have no doubt of the ultimate outcome.

Vice Adm. William "Bull" Halsey, Jr., *commander, Carrier Division 2, US Pacific Fleet*: Before we're through with 'em, the Japanese language will be spoken only in Hell.

Eugene Wigner: On December 8, 1941, the very day after the Japanese bombed Pearl Harbor and brought America directly into the war, I heard from Arthur Compton again. He told me that the Uranium Project was being reorganized.

Norman Hilberry, *associate director, Chicago Met Lab*: I was teaching at NYU and Ann and I had gone into our first faculty party just before Christmas '41. Our babysitter called and told us a telegram had come. It was from Compton. "Have important war job for you. Please report earliest possible moment." I got on the train and went to Chicago, PDQ. He told me what he could. I went to the Physical Society meeting to recruit and reported back to Chicago in January of '42.

Arthur Holly Compton: To make atomic bombs, fissionable material was needed, and this could be either of two kinds. One of these was Uranium-235 that must be separated from its much more abundant isotope, Uranium-238, by a very difficult mechanical process. The other fissionable material was plutonium. This would be produced by a steady nuclear chain reaction with ordinary uranium, as a result of which a small fraction of the Uranium-238 would be transmuted into Plutonium-239. This plutonium would then be extracted chemically from the uranium. The prime problem was to find a way of producing some hundreds of pounds of Uranium-235 or of plutonium.

Norman Hilberry: At that meeting every reactor type was discussed.

Arthur Holly Compton: We reached the decision to pursue four parallel methods, four horses in a race: Ernest Lawrence used his Radiation Laboratory at the University of California as the center for development of magnetic separation of U-235; Harold Urey coordinated the gaseous diffusion studies at Columbia University; E. V. Murphree was put in charge of the development of the centrifuge method, using the facilities of the Standard Oil Development Company's laboratory at Bayway, New Jersey, and cooperating with J. W. Beams at the University of Virginia; I had the task of developing a method for producing plutonium. The method of thermal diffusion was being developed by the Naval Research Laboratory independently of the S-1 Committee. Though in one sense competing, these various groups were also cooperating closely.

Leona H. Woods, *physics graduate student, University of Chicago*: The next problem was to create the central laboratory. Columbia was a possible site, but Harold Urey's diffusion project was there and was expanding fast into the available university space. Instead, Compton decided on Chicago because he had access to laboratory facilities and office space at the University of Chicago, because housing was more available, and because Chicago was safer against military attack than were coastal cities. At that time, the Japanese Navy was unopposed in the Pacific; there was great fear of attacks on the West Coast; and there had been a German submarine landing on the East Coast of the United States.

John H. Manley, *physicist*: The work toward a chain-reacting pile, which had been going on at Columbia and at Princeton primarily, but at Chicago also, was being consolidated by Arthur Compton at Chicago in this newly named—deliberately to be misleading—"Metallurgical Laboratory."

Eugene Wigner: Just as the "sanitarium" where I stayed as a child was not chiefly concerned with the sanity of its patients, so this Metallurgical Laboratory was not designed for metallurgy. The name disguised a laboratory that was trying to create a nuclear chain reaction. And not any nuclear chain reaction, but one of enormous power, which is quite a different thing.

Luis Alvarez: Arthur phoned me in Cambridge and asked me if I would come to Chicago to talk with him about a matter of great urgency. As soon as I could arrange air travel priority, I was there. In the course of my visit Ernest Lawrence came to Chicago to try to persuade Arthur to move the pile program to Berkeley. His argument was convincing: his Radiation Laboratory had support facilities for such a project and experience in the administration of large projects. Ernest and Arthur were scientific peers. I fitted in several rungs below them and felt a strong emotional attachment to each. I remember in particular my surprise at their behavior during a very long and decisive meeting in Arthur's bedroom—he had the flu and felt miserable. Ernest argued in favor of moving everyone to Berkeley. Arthur resisted, sensing that in Berkeley he would be reduced to a cog in Ernest's large machine. In all the years I had been Arthur's student, I had never seen him fight so hard for anything. The discussion between the two men became increasingly acrimonious.

Arthur Holly Compton: Lawrence objected: "You'll never get the chain reaction going here. The whole tempo of the University of Chicago is too slow."

"We'll have the chain reaction going here by the end of the year," I predicted.

"I'll bet you a thousand dollars you won't," he challenged.

"I'll take you on on that," I answered, "and these men are the witnesses."

"I'll cut the stakes to a five-cent cigar," countered Lawrence.

"Agreed."

Luis Alvarez: I was shocked; I'd never heard either Ernest or Arthur bet so much as a nickel on anything. Then they both looked at me, obviously embarrassed that I had heard these intemperate remarks and witnessed such uncharacteristic behavior. When they cooled down, they canceled the bet. That was unfortunate for Arthur. He would have won the bet with three weeks to spare.

Leona H. Woods: The Metallurgical Laboratory moved from Columbia University where it had been initiated to the University of Chicago in the early spring of 1942, bringing with it Nobel laureate Enrico Fermi and his colleagues Leo Szilard, Walter Zinn, Herbert Anderson, John Marshall, Albert Wattenberg, and several other experimental physicists who participated in the establishment of the first chain reaction, as well as future Nobel laureate Eugene Wigner and other theoreticians such as Edward Teller and John Wheeler.

Herbert L. Anderson: The Metallurgical Laboratory acquired a great sense of urgency. It grew rapidly in size and number of personnel, and its work was classified. Fermi's little group of physicists was quickly outnumbered by the influx of many other groups: chemists to work out the chemistry of the fission products and the separation of plutonium; engineers to design the plants; metallurgists to fabricate uranium metal; and even doctors and biologists to study the effects of radiation and to recommend safeguards against such hazards.

Albert Wattenberg: When we went to Chicago, the original New York group was split into two main groups—one under Zinn and another under Anderson—and an appreciable number of additional people were brought in to work with us. Another group under Volney Wilson was in charge of the controls and instrumentation development. Before the war, Wilson understood what nuclear bombs would do, and he had been unwilling to work on the project. However, in the fervor created by the war, he decided he should work on the project.

Alvin M. Weinberg: Fermi's and Wigner's groups got along well. Fermi's aim was to show that a chain reaction was achievable; Wigner's aim was to design a large, high-power reactor to produce plutonium. Fermi's experiments provided the basic data on which Wigner's group based its designs for the big reactors.

Arthur Holly Compton: Typical of the necessary adjustments was that of finding living quarters for the people coming to Chicago. Until a housing office could be put into effective operation, my wife gave what help she could. She found rooms in a friend's home for Laura and Enrico Fermi and their two children until more permanent accommodations could be secured. Fermi's two assistants, Herbert Anderson and John Marshall, were installed in our older son's room in our home. My wife rallied the help of other ladies who knew Chicago to see that the newcomers would find schools for their children, locate convenient shops, and pick a suitable doctor or dentist. Working with [project administrator] Joyce Stearns, she arranged some simple parties where the incoming men and women could get acquainted. Rapidly there developed a spirit of high group morale.

Eugene Wigner: Two methods of fission were then known. The first was based on Uranium-235, the rare isotope of uranium. The second was based on Plutonium-239, a new element that could be produced in a nuclear reactor. The chief task of my group was to design a nuclear reactor. We felt sure that a nuclear chain reaction could be made and controlled. We even knew crudely what had to be done: to make a chain reaction producing plutonium, and to understand the separation of the plutonium and the dissipation of heat that the fission process produces.

Arthur Holly Compton: The way was now clear for our main task: to develop a method of producing some hundreds of pounds of plutonium.

Albert Wattenberg: One of the first things that had been established about fission was that several neutrons were emitted during the fundamental fission process. The concept for a self-sustaining chain reaction required that these neutrons be slowed down and made to collide with uranium so that more fission would result with the emission of more neutrons to sustain the reaction. The feasibility hinged on not losing too many of the neutrons and quantitatively understanding the various neutron loss processes.

John H. Manley: The months spent at the Met Lab were thrilling, hectic and varied. One problem was to find materials to slow down neutrons. The main scheme was to use graphite.

Albert Wattenberg: The exponential piles that we had built at Columbia had given results indicating that even an infinite amount of material would not lead to a self-sustaining structure. This was mainly because of the impurities in the graphite. During the spring, some new graphite arrived, and the exponential piles we built and measured in Chicago indicated that it would be feasible, with a very great deal of material, to build a chain-reacting structure; thus, it was very worthwhile to continue to get the better quality graphite and also to improve the quality of the uranium oxide that we were obtaining.

Leona H. Woods: If the uranium were in the form of metal, then less total material would be needed and the reactor could be smaller. By the time John Marshall arrived at Chicago, Szilard had obtained some small pieces of solid uranium metal somewhere, and, with these pieces, John began to find out how to melt and cast uranium, using furnaces he built in 50-gallon oil drums lined with asbestos insulation. The metal-casting work was transferred to John Chapman's laboratory at M.I.T. John and some other scientists from Chicago went to M.I.T. and, in about three months, had cast six tons of uranium metal in long rods of a few inches diameter which they then sawed into lumps of a few inches long each, using a machine-driven hacksaw. The sparks that flew from the saw were dramatic.

Herbert L. Anderson: Planning for Chicago Pile #1 began early in July as soon as it became evident that sufficient purified uranium and graphite would be delivered by November; Norman Hilberry had carried through a remarkably successful procurement effort.

Eugene Wigner: By July 1942, [Met Lab engineer] Gale Young and I had rough plans for a great 100,000-kilowatt pile to be made of uranium lumps in a graphite cylinder 12 feet high and 25 feet around. It would be cooled by water. This design was further improved throughout the year, and eventually became the basis of the nuclear reactor built in Hanford, Washington. The design that my Met Lab group finally adopted for the nuclear reactor was a roughly cubic form, about 6 yards in each direction. We figured how to insert the uranium, how to remove it, and many other such things. It seemed as complex as designing a factory.

Alvin M. Weinberg: We were writing on a tabula rasa. Everything was new and untried. Discoveries came easily.

"You can't spend that much money any faster"

FDR'S OK

Vannevar Bush, James B. Conant, and Leslie Groves (*left to right*) became the key drivers of the Manhattan Project.

Over the spring and summer of 1942, the first concrete plans required to create an atomic bomb began to come together—or, more accurately, the first plans for future research that would lead to future specific plans that could lead to the necessary production of plutonium and uranium. Work proceeded on an ever-increasing number of parallel tracks as the still-developing team settled on the organizational structure for the work ahead, as well as the physical locations where production facilities would be built, and began to think in earnest about just how to build the bomb itself.

Norman Hilberry: We were told to prove that you could *not* make a bomb, that you could *not* get a chain reaction. The first deadline we faced was the May 15 meeting of the S-1 Committee in Washington, when the budgets for the next year had to be put in. The intent had been, at that time, that the whole effort would be concentrated on the most promising project. We got the chemists working like mad on what the impurities were in these materials that Fermi was using, both in the graphite and in the oxide, and then try to estimate what could be done if these [impurities] could be eliminated. Compton went into that meeting and announced point blank that it would work. He put the numbers down, "Here is what we have. This is what we know the impurities are. We know we can remove these thus and so, and we know we can remove these thus and so." There was no question about "Will it work?"

James B. Conant: As news arrived during the early spring of 1942, Bush realized that sometime in May decisions involving very large expenditures of money would have to be made. The uncertainties had been growing less as the results from various research projects kept coming in. New measurements enabled the theoreticians to estimate that the minimum amount of Uranium-235 that would explode—the critical mass—if assembled rapidly would be between 2.5 and 5.0 kilograms. Such quantities were quite different from 100 kilograms which was the upper limit of the range of values estimated by the committee of the National Academy of Sciences.

The three program chiefs and I met with Murphree and [Army Corps of Engineers construction commander] General [Wilhelm] Styer on May 23, 1942. After considering all the pros and cons, the group recommended to Bush that he ask the President to authorize a construction program based on the assumption that a start should be made in each of four ways to manufacture a bomb—these were three separation schemes (the electromagnetic, the gaseous diffusion and the centrifugal) and the production of plutonium in a pile. We had, in effect, told Bush that since we could not decide on which of four horses to place our bet, all four should be kept in the race, though we thought they might be running neck and neck until the final lap.

Vannevar Bush: When I told Mr. Stimson that progress on the bomb had reached the point where a very large amount of money had to be spent for manufacturing facilities and so forth, I suggested to him that the Army take over at that point.

James B. Conant: The total construction cost we estimated as $80 million and an annual operating cost as $34 million. The project, we believed, would yield a few atomic bombs by July 1, 1944. I recall vividly the argument about the time schedule. "Why nearly two years' delay?" I asked. "Why is it not possible to speed up the construction?" To which Murphree, speaking as an experienced chemical engineer, replied—I remember clearly the words he used—"Doctor, you can't spend that much money any faster."

Col. Leslie Groves: Bush's recommendation was very clear that it was now time to put the work of constructing and of building the plants in the hands of the Army engineers.

Gen. George C. Marshall: It fell to me to make the preparations and still do it with secrecy.

Arthur Holly Compton: Bush laid the evidence before the top policy committee of Vice President Wallace, Secretary of War Stimson, and Chief of Staff General Marshall. With their approval, the recommendation of Bush and Conant was brought to President Roosevelt on 17 June. The response was immediate.

Franklin Delano Roosevelt, *note to Vannevar Bush*: V.B. OK. FDR.

Vannevar Bush: One of the most extraordinary things of the war, of course, was that Stimson and Roosevelt backed atomic energy development without any hesitation, completely and fully. This was a courageous thing to do because this development was unlike anything ever seen before. Usually when you are undertaking a development, you can make one part of it, and demonstrate that, or you can make a small-scale model and prove that the theory behind it is right. In the case of the atomic bomb this was impossible. It could be tested only at full-scale. Stimson and Roosevelt were backing something which was to them only some figures on a piece of paper calculated by physicists.

Gen. George C. Marshall: I was rather amused at myself because as time wore on, these long statements that would come, that were filled with complicated procedures necessary in these matters and the technical terms involved—I spent so much time with the *Encyclopedia Britannica* or the dictionary trying to interpret what they said that I finally just gave it up, deciding that I never would quite understand it all. What I must understand was all the procedure concerned with getting this thing done.

James B. Conant: The first Army officer to be brought into the project on a full-time basis was Colonel James C. Marshall.

Col. James C. Marshall, *Army Corps of Engineers*: On June 17, 1942—a Wednesday—I received a teletype from the Office of the Chief of Engineers directing me to report to the Chief of Engineers the next morning. On arrival in Washington, I went to General Styer's office. He came out and said, "Okay Mrs. Matheson, let me have the S-1 file." He handed me, as I recall, about five sheets of paper, maybe six, and I said, "Is this all there is?"

He said, "Yes, read this first letter." There was a letter from Vannevar Bush to President Roosevelt dated a few days before. The letter contained three or four pages and stated that the status of the art or science, whichever they wanted to call it, concerning atomic fission—a word which struck me just out of the blue. I had never heard of it before. The letter said that atomic fission was about ready to happen. Styer says, "The White House has a fund of $200,000,000 to be spent at the discretion of the president." He said, "Tomorrow you go over and tell [Eugene] Reybold, the Chief of Engineers, that you've got a new job and that you need some money. Vannevar Bush's outfit over there at OSRD [Office of Scientific Research and Development] is running both. All of their contracts with the universities, laboratories and others around the country are about to run out. They will run out June 30th. They must have money."

Anyhow, after an hour or two of this and being told what my mission was for the next day, he handed me the papers. They were marked "Secret." He said, "Keep them in your possession." I said, "Is this all I get?" He said, "Yes, I will tell Reybold to issue orders forming a new district, making you District Engineer. You report direct to this office."

Col. Leslie Groves: Somervell and Styer—without any discussion with General [T. M.] Robins or myself—set up this special engineer district and selected for it Colonel Marshall. If they had talked to me about it, I would never have recommended Marshall for the job, because he just was not fitted for it. He was too nice a fellow, he was too amenable to scientific advice, and he also was very set on building up a neat organization where everything fell into line—all the paperwork was competently handled and all the rest of it. He did not have the physical strength to carry on such a thing.

Col. James C. Marshall: I started out on finding the money the next day. Styer says, "Go to Reybold and tell him you need $15,000,000, and he is not to ask you any questions." So I go into General Reybold—a three-star general at the moment—and said, "General, I am over here with orders from General Styer to get a sum of money, and you are not to ask any questions." He said, "How much do you want?" I said, "I want $15,000,000." He immediately reached for the telephone, said, "Get me Styer on the phone—no, get me Somervell."

"Bill, this is Reybold." He said, "I've got a crazy man here sitting at my desk who says he wants me to give him a check for $15,000,000, and he won't tell me what it's for. What should I do?" I heard Somervell say, "Give him the money and quit asking questions." No one in the Chief of Engineer's office, regardless of his rank—civilian or military man—could sign a check in excess of $5,000,000. So we had to get a first lieutenant from the Finance Department to come over and sign a Treasury check for $15,000,000. I then walked over to 15th Street NW, somewhere up there where OSRD was at the time. Dr. [Irvin] Stewart, who was Bush's right-hand man, said, "I hope you have some money. You are supposed to be the man. We need $15,000,000 in order to preserve the continuity of our contracts with University of Chicago, University of California, Berkeley, and so forth and so on." I handed him the check.

Col. Leslie Groves: On June 18, immediately after receiving orders to set up his special district, Colonel Marshall had informed General Eugene Reybold, the Chief of Engineers; General Robins, the Deputy Chief of Engineers and Chief of Construction; and me, the Deputy Chief of Construction, of his new assignment. He did not reveal many of the details of his work, but he did ask that we give him every possible assistance. When he first told us of his *carte blanche* instructions, Robins and I were rather skeptical about how long it would be before his priority would be overridden by some other super-important project. We had seen this happen before.

Lt. Col. Kenneth D. Nichols: On Friday, June 19, 1942, Colonel Marshall unexpectedly called from Washington. "Come to see me Sunday morning in Syracuse about a very technical project," he said. "I can't tell you any more over the phone." Sunday morning, as I came into his office he greeted me, "Nick, I am giving you fifteen seconds to volunteer for a very important technical project, or be drafted." After he had given me a very short description of the nature of the project, I didn't need the fifteen seconds. With volunteering settled, Marshall handed me a large envelope that contained most of the top secret information he knew about the new project. I was to read them in his presence.

Col. James C. Marshall: I got Nichols transferred to me. He was a Ph.D.—even though it was in hydraulics, I thought I needed somebody who at least had a degree beyond a B.S.

* * *

With the work officially in the hands of the military, the scientists and personnel in the new project needed to begin building the infrastructure to support and develop their studies further, as well as what would surely be large production facilities to actually ready the uranium and plutonium for development of a possible bomb.

Arthur Holly Compton: One important question was where the various operations might be carried on. A place was needed first of all for setting up the experimental reactor. As my wife and I were horseback riding one Saturday afternoon with our friend, George McKibben, a Chicago lawyer, we located a sequestered part of the Cook County recreational area that seemed suitable for the purpose. McKibben, of course, had no idea as to our objective; but when he saw our interest in this well-hidden region only twenty miles from the city of Chicago he immediately put us in contact with the officials of the Cook County Forest Preserve. On the maps of the area this site was called "Argonne Forest."

Col. Leslie Groves: The plan then was to concentrate all facilities required for the production of fissionable materials at a single site.

Arthur Holly Compton: Throughout the spring we had been on the lookout for a site suitable for our plutonium production plant.

Gen. George C. Marshall: We had to construct these huge plants which were going to be required and still try to do it in secrecy.

Arthur Holly Compton: Essential requirements were ample electric power, a good supply of water for cooling, a rugged terrain that would prevent an explosion in one portion of the plant from causing widespread disaster, adequate transportation, available labor supply, a climate that would permit winter construction, and preferably remoteness from the seacoast to make enemy attack more difficult. The Tennessee Valley fitted all these conditions except, surprisingly enough, that just at this time, because of the heavy demands of the new electrical industries that had moved into the area, there was little more power available than that needed to meet existing requirements. Thomas Moore, our chief engineer, Richard Doan, Director of the Metallurgical Laboratory, and Norman Hilberry, associate project director, had gone to Knoxville early in May 1942. A day or two later my wife and I appeared in Knoxville as if for a holiday at the Great Smoky Mountains. The others had already inspected several sites under guidance of officials of the Tennessee Valley Authority. I spent half a day with them going over the Clinch River territory. We reported to Washington that the Tennessee area was our choice.

Col. Leslie Groves: That area seemed to meet all the requirements, and beyond that, it gave promise of being a pleasant place for the permanent operating force to live. This was most fortunate because we anticipated that many of the operating personnel would have to be imported, since the specialized skills we would need would be difficult to recruit locally.

Arthur Holly Compton: A month later, when the Army was assigned its responsibility, Colonels K. D. Nichols and J. C. Marshall inspected the sites again and confirmed our recommendation.

Col. Kenneth D. Nichols: Marshall and I left for Knoxville the evening of June 30 to look at sites. During the three days we spent in Tennessee, we looked at four locations that met our primary requirements. Apart from having the TVA power and water, the location had the necessary isolation because the Clinch River provided a boundary on three sides, and a mountain ridge protected the north side. The area also had the necessary number of valleys and ridges to help isolate the separate plants from each other.

Col. James C. Marshall: I figured if you're going to have a high explosive plant in these valleys, they would be separated from each other and in the case of an explosion they would naturally go up rather than spreading out.

Gen. George C. Marshall: In all these things, it was exceedingly difficult to keep them secret when you had to get at big money and build these great plants without explanation. I think only the fact that we were building so many of them diverted the public attention from these particular ones.

* * *

One of the biggest challenges of the summer of 1942 was imagining how a future atomic bomb—which had been proven on paper only—would actually function as an explosive device. To solve that particular piece of the ever-evolving puzzle, Compton enlisted the help of UC-Berkeley's star theoretical physicist, the close colleague of Ernest Lawrence, and the professor who more than anyone in the 1930s had helped to establish the US as a focal point of theoretical physics.

Leona H. Woods: Compton appointed J. Robert Oppenheimer to head a small theoretical group studying the physics of the bomb.

Arthur Holly Compton: I had met Robert Oppenheimer in 1927 when he was a member of the colony of American students of James Franck and Max Born at Göttingen. A specialist in the problems of nuclear physics, he was one of the very best interpreters of the mathematical theories to those of us who were working more directly with the experiments. I had also dealt with "Oppie" in some rather delicate negotiations involving a professional organization that in some of its branches had been infiltrated by Communists.

I. I. Rabi: Oppenheimer understood the whole structure of physics with extraordinary clarity, and not only the structure, but the interactions between the different elements. Hardly any branch of physics was foreign to him. As well as theoretical physics, he also had a vast knowledge of experimental results and methods at his fingertips and would continually amaze experimenters by his great knowledge of their own subject—in some respects exceeding their own, especially in fields of great current interest. It is therefore not surprising that he became an almost mythical figure, especially to experimenters.

Robert Serber: Oppenheimer's fascinating personality played a major part in his unique powers as a teacher. Oppenheimer's course in quantum mechanics was well established. "Oppie"—as he was known to his Berkeley students—was quick, impatient, and had a sharp tongue. Now, after five years of experience, he had mellowed—if his earlier students were to be believed. His course was an inspirational, as well as educational achievement. He transmitted to his students a feeling of the beauty of the logical structure of physics and an excitement in the development of the science. Almost everyone listened to the course more than once, and Oppie occasionally had difficulty in dissuading students from coming a third or fourth time.

James B. Conant: As an outstanding theoretical physicist, he had already helped Lawrence in designing the electromagnetic method of separating U-235. Now it was suggested that Oppenheimer turn his attention to the design of a bomb.

John H. Manley: Oppenheimer wanted help from someone with more experimental experience than he had and he accepted the position on the condition that an assistant be chosen who would fill in this gap. I may note parenthetically that almost anybody would have had more experimental experience than Oppenheimer. He had essentially zero laboratory experience. He was an outstanding theorist and did understand the laboratory techniques, but not as an operator. Anyway, I was Compton's choice.

Arthur Holly Compton: After a few weeks spent at Chicago in laying his plans and recruiting his key men, Oppenheimer called together in June 1942 at Berkeley, California, a group of the nation's most competent theoretical physicists. Their task was to figure out how the bomb might be made to explode and what its effect would be.

Hans Bethe: We met in Berkeley for the summer of 1942. We first thought it would be a very simple thing to figure out this problem and we soon saw how wrong we were.

Emilio Segrè: Hans Bethe, Robert Serber, Edward Teller, E. J. Konopinski, and two younger physicists, Stanley Frankel and Eldred Nelson, worked on this project. As they proceeded in their calculations, they needed more and more experimental data that had not been measured, and we tried to help them out as much as possible. At the time such data were few and unreliable.

J. Robert Oppenheimer: We had an adventurous time. We spent much of the summer of 1942 in Berkeley in a joint study that for the first time really came to grips with the physical problems of atomic bombs, atomic explosions, and the possibility of using fission explosions to initiate thermo-nuclear reactions. After these studies there was little doubt that a potentially world-shattering undertaking lay ahead. We also began to see how rough, difficult, challenging and unpredictable this job might turn out to be.

Luis Alvarez: I remember a most interesting afternoon we spent together, during which time Oppenheimer told me for the first time the possibility of building a thermonuclear weapon. He told me in some detail of the scientific design, as he then envisaged it, and pointed out how it would be triggered. As Dr. Oppenheimer pointed out to me, there was no apparent limit to the magnitude of the explosion.

J. Robert Oppenheimer: After our conferences were over, I went and reported to Compton who was off on a summer holiday about this aspect of it, as well as others.

Arthur Holly Compton: I'll never forget that morning. I drove Oppenheimer from the railroad station down to the beach looking out over the peaceful lake. There I listened to his story. What his team had found was the possibility of nuclear fusion—the principle of the hydrogen bomb. This held what was at the time a tremendous unknown danger. Hydrogen nuclei, protons, are unstable, for they could combine into helium nuclei with a large release of energy. To set off such a reaction would require a very high temperature. But might not the enormously high temperature of an atomic bomb be just what was needed to explode hydrogen? And if hydrogen, what about the hydrogen of sea water? Might the explosion of an atomic bomb set off an explosion of the ocean itself? Nor was this all. The nitrogen in the air is also unstable, though in less degree. Might it not be set off by an atomic explosion in the atmosphere? These questions could not be passed over lightly. We agreed there could be only one answer. Oppenheimer's team must go ahead with their calculations. Unless they came up with a firm and reliable conclusion that our atomic bombs could not explode the air or the sea, these bombs must never be made.

"We might have called it Hoboken"

CREATING THE MANHATTAN ENGINEER DISTRICT

At the Met Lab, Enrico Fermi (*left*) worked to perfect a chain reaction.

The creation in the summer of 1942 of what was ultimately dubbed the Manhattan Engineer District gave new energy and structure to the sprawling exploration of atomic energy in numerous labs, most of which remained a theoretical exercise more than reality, as well as the official shorthand that history would remember the effort as: The Manhattan Project.

Col. Leslie Groves: The question of a name for the project came up. Toward the end of June, Reybold told us that the new establishment was to be called the "Laboratory for the Development of Substitute Materials" or "DSM." I demurred on the grounds of security, feeling that the name was bound to arouse curiosity. Reybold decided no change would be made. Before we parted, it was decided definitely to hire [the Boston-based construction firm] Stone and Webster as the over-all architect-engineer-managers.*

Col. James C. Marshall: Reybold insisted I open up a District Headquarters right upstairs over him in the Chief's Office. I objected and I said, "I'll have Nichols down here in Washington. I want to go to New York where I can get office space. You can't get office space here. If you're trying to hide something, you can hide it in New York City a lot easier than you can hide it in Washington." I leased floor-by-floor eight or nine floors in 261 5th Avenue down here at 29th Street.

Col. Leslie Groves: On August 11, Marshall handed me the draft of a general order to be published that day announcing the formation of the new district. In it he used the designation "DSM." I again objected to this term because I felt that it would arouse the curiosity of all who heard it.

Col. James C. Marshall: I said, "Why not call it the Manhattan District? I'm in Manhattan." So that was the Manhattan District.

Col. Kenneth D. Nichols: Giving the project that name would focus attention away from the actual site of the plants. The chief of engineers issued Order No. 33 on August 13, 1942, setting up an engineer district without territorial limits, to be known as the Manhattan Engineer District.

Gen. George C. Marshall: The Manhattan Project was the name least liable to arouse some feeling of a mystery. We might have called it Hoboken, but we called it Manhattan.†

* The original contract for Stone and Webster imagined the firm would lead the $80 million construction efforts across the atomic project, but as the scope (and complexity) of the task ahead became clear, it instead became one partner among many.

† In project parlance, the "Manhattan Engineer District" would refer specifically to the army's atomic effort, while the "Manhattan Project" referred to the wider umbrella of labs, scientists, factories, and facilities across the nation that supported the effort.

Mere weeks after the project was officially named, Colonel Groves found himself—most unwillingly—put in charge of it.

Vannevar Bush: When Styer first recommended Groves' appointment, I said to Styer that it wouldn't do at all; I was sure that Groves would get into trouble with the scientists. After some time, Styer sat down with me again and he said, "Look, there isn't another man in the U.S. Army that can do this job with the skill that Groves would use. We'll have to appoint him, and then you and I'll have to sit on the lid to be sure that he doesn't get into trouble with the scientists."

Col. Leslie Groves: One day in mid-September, a few minutes after I had finished testifying before a Congressional committee on a military housing bill, I met Somervell outside in the hallway. He went on to say: "The Secretary of War has selected you for a very important assignment, and the President has approved the selection." My spirits fell as I realized what he had in mind. I did not know the details of America's atomic development program at that time, but because of the nature of my responsibilities I knew of its existence and its general purpose. Though a big project, it was not expected to involve as much as $100 million altogether—much less than our total overall spending in a normal week. Magnitude aside, what little I knew of the project had not particularly impressed me.

Later that morning, I saw Styer at his office in the Pentagon. He confirmed my worst premonitions by telling me that I was to be placed in charge of the Army's part of the atomic effort. When I returned home that evening I told my wife and daughter and wrote to my son, a cadet at West Point, that I had a new job, that it involved secret matters and for that reason was never to be mentioned.

Vannevar Bush: Styer was right when he insisted that Groves was the man for the job.

Col. Leslie Groves: Before I left, Styer told me that General Marshall had directed that I be made a brigadier general, and that the list of new promotions would be out in a few days. I decided at once, and Styer agreed, that I should not take over the project officially until I could do so as a brigadier.

I thought that there might be some problems in dealing with the many academic scientists involved in the project, and I felt that my position would be stronger if they thought of me from the first as a general instead of as a promoted colonel. My later experiences convinced me that this was a wise move; strangely enough, it often seemed to me that the prerogatives of rank were more important in the academic world than they are among soldiers.

Col. Kenneth D. Nichols: Groves decided to establish his headquarters in Washington, at least initially. He soon found that the capital was the ideal place from which to work. He was able to stay in touch with the War Department and other government agencies while also readily reaching out into the field.

Col. Leslie Groves: The office out of which I was to control the Manhattan Project consisted of two rooms. As I consider Washington today, it seems incredible that these accommodations were as limited as they were. My secretary, Mrs. O'Leary, who was soon to become my chief administrative assistant, and I occupied one room. The only furniture added was one, and later another, heavy safe.

* * *

The most significant—and first—move Groves made as the new head of the Manhattan Project was to establish it as the nation's top priority endeavor, upgrading the mid-level war priority status the S-1 Committee's work had been operating under through the spring and summer.

Col. Leslie Groves: The situation during the summer of 1942 was not promising for any operation that did not hold the very highest priority. Stone and Webster estimated at the time that the construction of a pilot plant for the electromagnetic separation process would take eleven months under an AA-3 priority, the highest then available to the MED; yet the same job could be completed in eight months if an AA-1 rating were obtained.

I did not see how we could possibly get the job done with nothing better than an AA-3 priority, and I did not feel inclined to fail by default. It seemed quite simple to me—if ours was really the most urgent project, it should have the top priority. On September 19, I called upon Donald Nelson, the head of the War Production Board, and stated my views very simply but most definitely. His reaction was completely negative; however, he quickly reversed himself when I said that I would have to recommend to the President that the project should be abandoned because the War Production Board was unwilling to co-operate with his wishes.

James B. Conant: The thing could've never have been built unless Groves had been able to get such top priority.

Col. Leslie Groves: Up to this time, I had asked no questions about the scientific difficulties and the probability of success in overcoming them, because it was not necessary for me to know them in order to carry out my responsibilities, which had involved chiefly assistance, where wanted, to Marshall in the site location and the procurement of land, equipment and materials. Now, I was particularly concerned with determining to what extent our work would be based on real knowledge, on plausible theory or on the unproven dreams of research scientists. Next, I wanted to know about the available supplies of raw materials.

Col. Kenneth D. Nichols: Groves was horrified at the information I gave him.

Col. Leslie Groves: In fact, I *was* horrified. It seemed as if the whole endeavor was founded on possibilities rather than probabilities. Of theory there was a great deal, of proven knowledge not much. Even if the theories were correct, the engineering difficulties would be unprecedented.

Arthur Holly Compton: In his first review of the situation, Groves realized that the project needed immediate strengthening in its industrial phases. The first task was to get production in hand. Within twenty-four hours Groves had made his own personal inspection of the Tennessee Valley area and had approved the selection of a site along the Clinch River. Steps were immediately initiated to take over the area of almost eighty square miles that became Oak Ridge. Here was established the headquarters of the Clinton Engineer Works, named for the neighboring old village of Clinton.

Col. Kenneth D. Nichols: Receiving his star on the twenty-third, Groves officially took charge of the project. That afternoon, he attended a meeting in the secretary of war's office to decide on the form and makeup of the policy supervision of America's atomic bomb effort.

Vannevar Bush: Part of the plan for the Manhattan District, as I worked it out with Mr. Stimson, was the creation of a Military Policy Committee. This consisted of myself as chairman, with Conant as my deputy, General Styer, and [Deputy Chief of Naval Operations for Materiel] Admiral [William R.] Purnell. It served as a sort of board of directors for General Groves. It met frequently, had no staff or secretary present, kept no formal records, but provided a point at which every important move could be discussed and closely examined. I know its existence helped Groves. No one who has not been placed in a post of heavy responsibility can realize what a lonesome feeling it is when there is no equivalent of a board present, and one reports to a chief who is rarely accessible.

Arthur Holly Compton: More clearly than the others of us on the S-1 Committee, Conant saw the magnitude of the operations that must be undertaken if atomic bombs were in fact to be of use in the present war. On a recent visit, he had expressed himself with vigor: "You are after elephants with a peashooter." We must work on a larger scale if significant production was to come.

Col. Kenneth D. Nichols: Despite his initial unhappiness with the assignment, once Groves fully took over the reins of the project, I never again heard him voice a single word of regret. Once in charge, he quickly moved to assume de facto control not only of construction but also control of all research and development, operation of the plants, development of the bomb, and the military aspects of the project.

Eugene Wigner: What an interesting man Groves was! I must admit that many of my physicist colleagues quite disliked him. But I liked Groves. He was a boss in every sense of the word. General Groves had the body of a boss, too, really a quite striking physique. He was more than a little fat; and he must have known that he was. Groves was a dynamic leader who used his great brawn to effect.

Col. Kenneth D. Nichols: General Groves is the biggest S.O.B. I have ever worked for. He is most demanding. He is most critical. He is always a driver, never a praiser. He is abrasive and sarcastic. He disregards all normal organizational channels. He abounds with energy and expects everyone to work as hard or even harder than he does. Although he gave me great responsibility and adequate authority to carry out his mission-type orders, he constantly meddled with my subordinates. And if I had to do my part of the atomic bomb project over again and had the privilege of picking my boss I would pick General Groves.

Capt. Joseph Volpe, *legal adviser, Manhattan Project*: He was decisive. As a matter of fact, I learned one thing in my work with the General that I think is, stood me in good stead over the years and that was once you decide, move on to something else. Don't worry about it, don't lose any sleep over it. Get on with the next task. And he had a great knack for that. As you know he made some extraordinary decisions to build things that were not proven scientifically or technically.

Brig. Gen. Leslie Groves: I think it is important to realize that when I made scientific decisions—in case there are any questions that come in of not knowing all the theories of nuclear physics, which I did not—nobody else knew anything either. We were groping entirely in the dark.

Edward Teller: I heard about a pep talk our general had given when he visited Ernest Lawrence's laboratory in Berkeley. At its conclusion, he turned to Lawrence and said, "Professor, I expect success. Remember your reputation depends on it." Nobel Laureate Lawrence never blinked an eye. But after the meeting, he took the general to his favorite watering spot, Trader Vic's, for dinner. There, after they had enjoyed a few Maitais, Lawrence turned to Groves and said, "You know, General, my reputation is made. It is *yours* that depends on the outcome of the Manhattan Project."

Brig. Gen. Leslie Groves: On October 5, 1942, I paid my first visit to the Metallurgical Laboratory at the University of Chicago, where Arthur Compton and I spent the morning inspecting the laboratory facilities and discussing with a number of scientists the work on which they were engaged.

Alvin M. Weinberg: General Groves was introduced to the staff at a large meeting in the Eckhart Hall lecture room. After being introduced by Arthur

Compton, the general spoke for a few minutes. I cannot remember now what he said, but he made a bad impression on us—too military in manner, somehow too overbearing. I never quite overcame the first impression, though in retrospect I must concede he did a remarkable job.

Brig. Gen. Leslie Groves: As the meeting was drawing to a close, I asked the question that is always uppermost in the mind of an engineer: With respect to the amount of fissionable material needed for each bomb, how accurate did they think their estimate was? I was horrified when they quite blandly replied that they thought it was correct within a factor of ten. My position could well be compared with that of a caterer who is told he must be prepared to serve anywhere between ten and a thousand guests. But after extensive discussion of this point, I concluded that it simply was not possible then to arrive at a more precise answer.

Col. Kenneth D. Nichols: As a result of his visiting Chicago, Groves was aware for the first time of the size and difficulty of the project.

Brig. Gen. Leslie Groves: Up until this time, only infinitesimal quantities of plutonium had been produced, and these by means of the cyclotron, a laboratory method not suitable for production in quantity. And by quantity production of plutonium, I do not mean tons per hour, but rather a few thimblefuls per day. Even by December, 1943, only two milligrams had been produced.

"A bomb laboratory was a good idea"

THREE BIG DECISIONS

Leslie Groves and J. Robert Oppenheimer were an unlikely but highly successful pair.

Over the course of the fall of 1942, General Groves and the leaders of the now officially named Manhattan Engineer District made three foundational decisions that would shape the future arc and success of their project: Choosing the director of the effort to build the bomb—what would be known as "Project Y"—as well as the site of its main laboratory and its main contractor, a company best known at the time for its recent invention of nylon, the first synthetic polymer, which had remade American fashion in the 1930s.

Col. Kenneth D. Nichols: Some of the key scientists greatly underestimated the time and effort that would be required to develop the weapon. They saw no urgency in starting it because they thought it could be done in a few months with less than a hundred men.

John H. Manley: The physics of an explosive chain reaction is really very different from the physics of the chain-reacting pile. In the latter, the pile has to operate on slowed down or moderated neutrons, but not so in the chain reaction for a bomb. It must go fast and be propagated by fast neutrons, otherwise the reaction time would be so long that the material would simply expand and you'd get a fizzle with no real explosive result.

Joseph O. Hirschfelder, *physicist, University of Wisconsin*: Their idea was to make the atom bomb in the form of two hemispheres of enriched uranium, using a miniature gun to shoot one of these hemispheres, as a projectile, into the other hemisphere, which served as a target. As long as these hemispheres were apart, the bomb was inert; when they came together the enriched uranium sphere would exceed the critical mass and the bomb would explode. All of this seemed to them exceedingly simple and would require a staff of the order of fifty scientists and maybe up to fifty additional assistants.

Brig. Gen. Leslie Groves: Discussions with Arthur Compton, Conant, and Bush made it clear to me that these estimates were dangerously overoptimistic and that the work should be started at once. A difficult question arose: Who should be the head of it? I had not before been confronted with this special problem, for the directors of the other laboratories connected with the project had been appointed before my arrival upon the scene.

Arthur Holly Compton: A person suited to head the unique task of devising and building atomic bombs needed unusual qualifications. A critical part of the job would be working out an adequate theory of the fission explosion. But experiments also would have to be done, and some of these would be extraordinarily difficult. What is more, this work would necessarily be carried out under conditions of almost unprecedented seclusion. The leader of this enterprise must be a person of such human understanding that he could keep a group of high-strung specialists working smoothly together while largely separated from outside contacts.

Brig. Gen. Leslie Groves: Although Oppenheimer headed the study group at Berkeley, neither Bush, Conant nor I felt that we were in any way committed to his appointment as director of Project Y. I did not know Oppenheimer more than casually at that time. Our first meeting had been on October 8 at the University of California, when we had discussed at some length the results of his study and the methods by which he had reached his conclusions. Shortly afterward, I asked him to come to Washington and together we had explored the problem of exactly what would be needed to develop the actual bomb.

Victor Weisskopf, *physics professor, University of Rochester*: It was an inspired but by no means obvious choice. Certainly he was the central figure in nuclear physics. No other man commanded so much respect of his colleagues; but he never was director of a large research operation, he did not have what one calls "administrative experience."

Brig. Gen. Leslie Groves: Oppenheimer had two major disadvantages—he had had almost no administrative experience of any kind, and he was not a Nobel Prize winner. Because of the latter lack, he did not then have the prestige among his fellow scientists that I would have liked the project leader to possess. The heads of our three major laboratories—Lawrence at Berkeley, Urey at Columbia, and Compton at Chicago—were all Nobel Prize winners, and Compton had several Nobel Prize winners working under him. There was a strong feeling among most of the scientific people with whom I discussed this matter that the head of Project Y should also be one. However, because of the prevailing sentiment at that time, coupled with the feeling of a number of people that Oppenheimer would not succeed, there was considerable opposition to my naming him.

Col. Kenneth D. Nichols: On October 15, Groves asked Oppenheimer to join us [in Chicago] to continue the discussion about the location and organization of the bomb lab. With many issues still remaining as the departure time for the 20th-Century Limited approached, Groves invited Oppenheimer to join us on our way back to New York. After dinner on the train, the conversation continued in my small roomette, with Groves, Marshall, Oppenheimer, and myself crowded into the small space with no elbow room. Despite the close quarters and the late hour, the discussion proved most fascinating. It covered all aspects of setting up an organization, building the needed facilities for laboratories and housing, procuring scientific equipment, and dealing with such expected issues as recruiting scientists and confining them in a laboratory in a remote area, and whether the scientists should be commissioned as officers in the Corps of Engineers. When Oppenheimer left the train in Buffalo, there remained no doubts in my mind that he should direct the new lab despite the difficulties we would have in clearing him.

Brig. Gen. Leslie Groves: In a few weeks it became apparent that we were not going to find a better man; so Oppenheimer was asked to undertake the task. But there was still a snag. His background included much that was not to our liking by any means. The security organization, which was not yet under my complete control, was unwilling to clear him because of certain of his associations, particularly in the past.

Col. Kenneth D. Nichols: Before the war, Oppenheimer had become involved with left-wing or Communist-leaning groups and had enjoyed friendships with known or suspected Communists, including his brother, Frank; his girlfriend; and his wife. While he had broken contacts with the questionable organizations once he began work on the bomb project, he retained many of his friendships. Even though the USSR was on our side, these contacts were considered to be security risks.

J. Robert Oppenheimer: I might well have appeared at the time as quite close to the Communist Party, perhaps even to some people as belonging to it. As I have said, some of its declared objectives seemed to me desirable. But I never was a member of the Communist Party, I never accepted communist dogma or theory; in fact, it never made sense to me. I had clearly formulated political views. I hated tyranny and repression and every form of dictatorial control of thought. In most cases I did not in those days know who was and who was not a member of the Communist Party. No one ever asked me to join the Communist Party.

Vannevar Bush: Groves took the matter up with Conant and me. We both knew Oppenheimer's history. Groves had looked it up very thoroughly and we had quite a conference on it. We had the evidence of Oppenheimer's leftist tendencies, the question of whether his wife was inclined to be a Commie, and the question of his younger brother, who is still more inclined to be. We also knew that Oppenheimer was highly respected by the scientists. Both Conant and I felt perfectly sure that the man was loyal. We went over all the angles of the thing and then Groves made the appointment.

Brig. Gen. Leslie Groves: I have never felt that it was a mistake to have selected and cleared Oppenheimer for his wartime post. He accomplished his assigned mission and he did it well. We will never know whether anyone else could have done it better or even as well. I do not think so.

* * *

The choice of Oppenheimer to head Project Y would come to define the Manhattan Project in myriad ways, not least of which was Oppenheimer's subsequent influence on both the decision to build a centralized laboratory and, specifically, its location in the Southwest. Oppenheimer and Groves made a seemingly unlikely pair—a wisp-thin thirty-eight-year-old scientist schooled in the Old World's and New World's most elite institutions, from Göttingen to Harvard, deeply rooted in the theoretical and academia; the other a stout and exacting forty-two-year-old West Point grad who had helped lead the construction of the Pentagon, the world's largest office building, and equally deeply rooted in the practicalities and proclivities of bureaucracies—but it would prove to be one of the most fruitful working relationships in the history of the US government.

J. Robert Oppenheimer: We began to notice how very much needed doing and how much the little laboratories were suffering from their isolation. There was supposed to be security and the result was that people would not know what was going on anywhere else. Work was duplicated, and there was almost no sense of hope or direction in it. By the fall of 1942, not only the theoretical people but anyone who knew the experimental situation realized that this had to be pulled together. These were the considerations that led me to say to General Groves, who had by then been brought into the project as its head, that I thought a bomb laboratory was a good idea.

John H. Manley: The problem of liaison among all the groups was a fantastically difficult one. We couldn't, of course, use long distance telephone; our work was classified. Teletype connections that could carry classified messages were limited and next to hopeless for trying to unsnarl experimental difficulties among these various groups. It didn't take very long for Compton and Oppenheimer and me to realize that we just couldn't run a railroad in this fashion and get anywhere in finding out the necessary properties of the materials from which to build a bomb.

Lt. Col. John Lansdale, ***counterintelligence chief, Manhattan Project*****:** We had originally planned to put this laboratory at Oak Ridge—that was the original purpose of the acquisition of so much of the land down there before we understood how big the project was going to be. Dr. Oppenheimer and various of his associates were quite strong in their feeling that the fastest and best progress could be made if we could find a place where the principle of compartmentalization which we had adopted generally for the whole project could be laid to one side—an isolated place where means of egress and ingress could be easily controlled and means of communication monitored.

Lt. Col. John H. Dudley, ***Manhattan Engineer District, Army Corps of Engineers*****:** My first connection with this work was in the very pleasant fall weather of October, 1942. I was borrowed from my district to travel around the West to locate a site for a mysterious installation. At that time, in fact all the way through, I was not supposed to know its purpose. I was simply given a set of criteria to follow.

Col. Kenneth D. Nichols: The initial criteria included a location more than two hundred miles from any border or ocean, in a sparsely settled area with a rather mild climate, in a natural bowl surrounded by hills.

Edwin McMillan, ***physicist, UC-Berkeley*****:** Colonel Dudley said that he visited most of the small towns in the Southwest. He said he traveled thousands of miles on two-lane roads.

Lt. Col. John H. Dudley: Two-lane roads—one lane for the left wheels and one lane for the right wheels. When the going got tough, I switched to a jeep, and when it got even tougher, I rode a horse.

Brig. Gen. Leslie Groves: Dudley confirmed our preliminary views that there were only two general areas that might be satisfactory. One would lie somewhere along the Santa Fe Railroad, in New Mexico or Arizona, while the other would be in California. While shielded by surrounding mountains against the chance of an accidental explosion, the teeming millions of Los Angeles County were too near for us to maintain the security we deemed necessary.

Lt. Col. John H. Dudley: The best place I found that fitted the criteria was Oak City, Utah. It is a delightful little oasis in south central Utah. The railroad was only 16 miles away, over a nice easy road. The airport was not too distant. The water supply was good. It was surrounded by hills, and beyond there was mostly desert. However, I noticed one thing: If we took over this area we would evict several dozen families and we would also take a large amount of farm acreage out of production. I recommended to Colonel Marshall that we skip over Oak City to avoid these adverse effects. Instead, I suggested the second choice, Jemez Springs, New Mexico.

Col. Kenneth D. Nichols: To confirm the choice, Dudley arranged for Oppenheimer and Edwin McMillan to meet him and Groves in New Mexico on November 16.

Edwin McMillan: We were supposed to get horses and Colonel Dudley was to meet us and ride the boundaries. We went up to Jemez Springs and we met Dudley there.

Lt. Col. John H. Dudley: Oppenheimer took one look at Jemez Springs and proceeded to change the criteria.

Col. Kenneth D. Nichols: Despite his earlier enthusiasm, Oppenheimer, seeing the site for himself, found it unacceptable because "the surrounding cliffs would give his people claustrophobia and he refused to ask them to live in a house that had been previously occupied by a Mexican or an Indian."

Edwin McMillan: We were arguing about this when General Groves showed up.

Lt. Col. John H. Dudley: On meeting us at Jemez Springs, Groves was unhappy that we did not have a site picked. So he asked Oppenheimer if there was something else around that had prospects. Oppy proposed Los Alamos as though it was a brand new idea.

Col. Kenneth D. Nichols: In fact, as early as August 29, the district engineer's office in Albuquerque had made inquiries about Los Alamos, and Dudley had visited it during his own search. Using the initial set of criteria, however, he had rated it a poor second to Jemez Springs.

Edwin McMillan: Oppenheimer said, "Well, if you go on up the canyon, it comes out on top of the mesa and there's a boys' school there, which might be a useful site." We all got in cars. We went up to Los Alamos Ranch School.

Brig. Gen. Leslie Groves: In the hope of finding something more suitable, we drove over the mountains toward Santa Fe, to look at a possibility suggested by Oppenheimer. As we approached Los Alamos, we came upon a boys' boarding school that occupied part of the area.

Edwin McMillan: I remember arriving there, and it was late in the afternoon. There was a slight snow falling, just a tiny drizzly type of snow. It was cold, and there were the boys and their masters out on the playing fields in shorts. This is really a place for hardening up the youth.

Stirling A. Colgate, *student, Los Alamos Ranch School*: The Ranch School was established for boys to learn to ride and be, if not cowboys, at least highly educated cowboys, and have a feeling for the outdoors, and pack trips, and riding a lot. And many sports, but not any team sports. The education here was extraordinarily intense. Quite frankly, because of the money that went into this Ranch School, it was a rather expensive place, and you had to have reasonably wealthy parents, though there were a few scholarships. The quality of the teachers, the number in classes, and the intensity of the education was just beyond comparison.

Col. James C. Marshall: It was on a mesa quite high, about 8,000 feet high, several thousand feet higher than Santa Fe.

Edwin McMillan: Soon as Groves saw it, Groves said, "This is it."

Brig. Gen. Leslie Groves: It was quite evident that this would be an isolated site, with plenty of room for expansion. The fact that there were already a number of buildings at Los Alamos, though nowhere nearly as many as we would ultimately require, meant that we could move in our first people at once and expand on that base. This would save us months in getting started. From the standpoint of security, Los Alamos was quite satisfactory. It was far removed from any large center of population, and was reasonably inaccessible from the outside.

Col. Kenneth D. Nichols: Groves immediately set into motion the process to acquire the school buildings and property.

Col. James C. Marshall: We bought the whole school—the horses, the canoes, the skis, the tennis ranges, everything.

Stirling A. Colgate: About December that year, two men showed up at school, and we were required to say our yes sirs to a Mr. Jones, who was wearing a fedora, and to a Mr. Smith, who was wearing a porkpie hat. The names were obviously pseudonyms. Not only was everybody showing them great deference, but Mr. Jones seemed most uncomfortable every time someone referred to him by that name.

The four of us who were seniors had studied physics. The pictures in our physics textbook made it easy for us to recognize Mr. Jones as Ernest Lawrence and Mr. Smith as Robert Oppenheimer. Furthermore, the discovery of fission had been big news. In fact, we were even aware of the idea of a chain reaction.

Clearly, the school was about to be converted to a laboratory to work on a very secret physics project. Why else would top physicists be visiting a place out at the end of nowhere with no water, no roads, no facilities? What was really going on was obvious! We were secretly amused by the pretense.

Henry Stimson, *letter to A. J. Connell, head of the Los Alamos Ranch School, December 1, 1942*: You are advised that it has been determined necessary to the interests of the United States in the prosecution of the War that the property of the Los Alamos Ranch School be acquired for military purposes.

It is requested that you refrain from making the reasons for the closing of the school known to the public at large.

A. J. Connell: They did permit us, however, to finish the first half-year by cancelling the Christmas holidays and working right through until January 21st. Stirling, Bee, Ted, and Collier all graduated on January 22nd, having qualified for our diplomas and passed special college boards, given in Santa Fe a few days before.

Stirling A. Colgate: Oppenheimer gave a superb talk at our commencement. He stood in front of the fireplace in the lodge, and graced this project with a set of words that I wish were recorded. I have never seen them, but it was an extraordinary talk that he gave about closing the Ranch School. He made us all realize the tremendous importance of what he felt was going to happen here. It was tried to impress on us that we shouldn't talk about what happened here, and, certainly, I never did.

John H. Manley: It wasn't very long after the Los Alamos site selection that Groves succeeded in getting the University of California to be the contractor to operate the new laboratory. [Until 2006] this was the eastern-most campus of the University of California, the Los Alamos campus in New Mexico.

* * *

Col. James C. Marshall: Gradually, Nichols and I together got the word across to Vannevar Bush and Conant and all of the Nobel Prize people over there on these committees that this was a big engineering job and that you could not take test tube experiments and these milli/microsecond things in minute quantities that [Harold] Urey and John Dunning and these people had been playing with. Nobody had any U-235.

Brig. Gen. Leslie Groves: I had begun to realize that we were involved in an enormously bigger undertaking than I had previously understood and that it was unreasonable to expect Stone and Webster to carry the full burden of all the engineering.

Eugene Wigner: General Groves looked for a large industrial firm to perform much of this work.

Arthur Holly Compton: These tasks fit most closely with those of a diversified chemical industry concerned with large-scale production. The prime American industrial organization operating in this field was the E. I. DuPont de Nemours Company of Wilmington, Delaware.

Col. Kenneth D. Nichols: At a meeting with Vice President Willis Harrington and Dr. Charles Stine, also a company vice president and distinguished chemist, Groves proposed that DuPont take over the entire plutonium project, not just working on the chemical process for separating out the plutonium.

Brig. Gen. Leslie Groves: During the following week the top officials of DuPont discussed our proposal, and at their request eight of their key employees were permitted to visit the Chicago laboratory, where they went over the status and plans of the project with Compton and his associates, and received all available theoretical and experimental data.

Col. Kenneth D. Nichols: Representing some of the best engineering and scientific talent in the company, the DuPont investigators—including Stine, Roger Williams, Thomas Gary, and Thomas Chilton—arrived in Chicago on November 4 and spent several days observing every aspect of the activities at the lab. After the group returned to the company's headquarters in Wilmington, DuPont scheduled a meeting to discuss their findings, and on the tenth I accompanied Groves to the conference in Wilmington.

Brig. Gen. Leslie Groves: On November 10, I went to Wilmington to see [DuPont president Walter S.] Carpenter. My purpose was to convince him that DuPont must take over the entire plutonium project. When I entered his office I knew that I had a staggering proposal to put up to him.

Walter S. Carpenter: Our reaction at that time was that we were asked to take on a job about equivalent to perpetual motion. Recovering the power of the atom just seemed to be one of those things at that time, which was just beyond all conceivable reach.

Crawford Greenewalt, *assistant director, chemical department, DuPont Corporation*: There was no assurance that any of these elements would operate. There was no assurance that you could make a reactor run at the high power levels that were required to produce plutonium. There was no assurance that the plutonium, if produced, could be separated. There certainly was no assurance at that time that an atomic bomb could be made, even given the plutonium.

Walter S. Carpenter: Groves told us that President Roosevelt, Secretary of War Stimson, and General Marshall, Chief of Staff, all felt that this was a matter of the utmost urgency. He pointed out that victory in the war would go to the nation that solved thc problem first.

Crawford Greenewalt: I had my doubts—like all these people were eminent scientists but none of them were engineers and the DuPont company is being asked to undertake this major undertaking.

Brig. Gen. Leslie Groves: They pointed out that even in one of their own fields of specialization they would not attempt to design a large-scale plant without the necessary data that could be accumulated only by a long period of laboratory research, followed by semi-works operation: for example, it had taken them many years to get nylon into mass production; yet the nylon process was simple compared to what we were asking of them.

Eugene Wigner: Resisting General Groves was never easy when he wanted something, and during the war it was nearly impossible.

Walter S. Carpenter: We had really no alternative, but to go ahead.

Norman Hilberry: Boy—that bunch—you understood why DuPont was the company it was. They were the hardest-nosed, sharpest bunch of characters you ever ran into. DuPont took absolutely no responsibility for the basic science. "That's yours," they said. "We will take full responsibility for the engineering development, for the construction and for the operation." The cut was clean. A straight, clean operation.

Dale Babcock, *chemist, DuPont Corporation*: In November of '42, Crawford called a few of us together and said, "I am going to describe to you people something that is heresy to chemists. We are going to make a new atom, on a scale of pounds per year. That new element is plutonium." To persons who were chemists all their lives, that was heresy, absolute heresy. In December, I was taken out of nylon and put on this development full time.

"Let's make a deal, Colonel"

MAKING THE PILE

The experimental piles in Chicago covered everything in graphite dust.

While the Manhattan Engineer District started up, the scientists at the Met Lab in Chicago, under Arthur Holly Compton, worked to ready the first chain-reacting pile of uranium, the landmark step in all the bomb development work to come. The site of their groundbreaking experiments to create "exponential piles" was about as unlikely a venue for scientific breakthroughs imaginable: Underneath the west stands of the old football stadium at the University of Chicago's Stagg Field in a disused squash court.

Leona H. Woods: Between April and October, in the west stands, eighteen stacks of graphite and uranium were built in various arrangements of lump size and distance apart, some including powdered metal and some including cast metal.

Albert Wattenberg: Slowly, our work progressed. The exponential piles built in August were a real turning point. They were the first exponential piles to indicate that one could build a self-sustaining nuclear chain reaction if one had an adequate amount of material.

Leona H. Woods: In late August, the pile experiments in the grimy halls under the west stands showed that, without a doubt, a lattice of graphite and uranium oxide lumps could be put together which would chain-react at a size realizable with the materials on hand. Furthermore, metal was beginning to be delivered from M.I.T., the inclusion of which would make the critical size of the chain-reacting pile somewhat smaller than if it were built only with oxide lumps in the lattice.

Albert Wattenberg: As experiments gave us information as to which were the best materials and the best geometry and as the theoretical estimates became more reliable, more definite commitments were made to build an experimental pile which it was hoped would be self-sustaining.

Herbert L. Anderson: To make the best use of the material that would be available, it was decided to build the pile in a spherical shape and to make provision for substituting carbon dioxide for air within the structure. We decided to mount the pile on a cradle of wood timbers and to enclose the whole structure within a halon cloth tent.

Leona H. Woods: Sometimes Herb took me with him on his tour of the lumberyards on Chicago's South Side to buy large numbers of 4-by-6-inch timbers.

Herbert L. Anderson: I spent the summer contracting for an awesome number of 4-by-6-inch timbers. I remember the astonishment with which my inquiry was received at the Sterling Lumber Company which became a main supplier.

Leona H. Woods: He also ordered a huge square rubber and canvas balloon to enclose the graphite and wood assemblage. The reason for this was that it might have become necessary to replace the air in the cracks between the graphite bricks with some other gas, say helium, in order to allow the chain reaction to occur because air might absorb too many neutrons.

Herbert L. Anderson: For the balloon cloth enclosure I went to the Goodyear Rubber Company in Akron, Ohio. The company had a good deal of experience building blimps and rubber rafts but a square balloon 25' on a side seemed a bit odd to them. In wartime a lot is done with no questions asked. I had good credentials and a high priority rating, and that was good enough for them. They built the balloon in short order to my specifications, suppressing a justifiable curiosity.

Leona H. Woods: There was no heat in the building because it was used for strenuous exercise, and heat was not needed. While the pile experiments of the type begun at Columbia were going on, the lack of heat didn't matter. But, after September, when Chicago begins to feel winter set in, there is a penetrating cold under the stands. The boys and staff kept warm by hard work, but the guards had to stand around freezing.

Walter Zinn: To help, we tried charcoal fires in empty oil drums—too much smoke. Then we secured a number of ornamental, imitation log, gas-fired fireplaces. These were hooked up to the gas mains, but they gobbled up the oxygen and replaced it with fumes which burned the eyes. The scientists and technicians could use physical activity to keep warm, but the security guards had to stand in one place at the entrance. The University of Chicago came to the rescue. Years before, big league football had been banned from the campus: we found in an old locker a supply of raccoon fur coats. Thus, for a time we had the best dressed collegiate-style guards in the business.

Herbert L. Anderson: For the construction of the pile Fermi assigned the responsibility jointly to Zinn and me. Our two groups combined for a concerted effort. Two special crews were organized: one machined the graphite, the other pressed the uranium oxide powder using specially made dies in a large hydraulic press. Both crews managed to keep their output up to the rate of the deliveries. A separate group under Volney C. Wilson was in charge of control and measuring devices.

Albert Wattenberg: As well as building piles and making neutron measurements, younger physicists such as myself would work with a crew of high school age kids pressing the uranium oxide pseudospheres and would supervise the drilling of the holes in the graphite bricks. We must have had to drill over 40,000 holes about 3-¼" diameter and with shaped bottoms in order to fit the pseudospheres of uranium oxide. The tough high school kids used for the production work had quit school to earn a little money while waiting to be drafted.

Herbert L. Anderson: In our report for the month ending October 15, Zinn and I could state that 210 tons of graphite had been machined.

Albert Wattenberg: As well as measuring exponential piles, Zinn took charge of the machining of the graphite and the pressing of the uranium oxide. I feel that Wally Zinn's enormous contribution and cleverness in this project have not been adequately appreciated. Zinn really had a full grasp of the steps and processes needed to build a pile. He was exceptional at devising straightforward, reliable, and efficient solutions to an enormous variety of physics and engineering problems. With about half a dozen young physicists, one millwright, and about thirty kids who had dropped out of high school, he carried a major share of the physics measurements of the exponential pile program, and he machined all the graphite blocks and pressed the uranium oxide briquettes for those exponential piles and for the first self-sustaining pile. Zinn drove people hard; he obtained very high quality work from them and also gave them a great deal of satisfaction in accomplishment.

* * *

Leona H. Woods: Where did the Manhattan District get the uranium that went into CP-1 (chain-reacting Pile-1)? A strange but true tale is that it was thanks to the foresightedness of Edgar Sengier, head of Union Minière, Katanga—a Brussels-based firm.

John Gunther: Probably not one American in a hundred thousand has ever heard the name Edgar Edouard Sengier, nor is he well known in Europe outside of a limited circle. So far as I know, no photograph of him has ever appeared in an American newspaper or magazine of wide circulation. Edgar Sengier is, in his field, one of the great unknowns of our time. This is all the more remarkable because it was Mr. Sengier who made it possible for the United States to make the atomic bomb.

Col. Kenneth D. Nichols: Initially, the scientists did not even have enough of the element for experimental purposes and had no real idea of how much we would need once the separation plants went into operation.

Brig. Gen. Leslie Groves: It is sobering to realize that but for a chance meeting between a Belgian and an Englishman a few months before the outbreak of the war, the Allies might not have been first with the atomic bomb. For the most important source of uranium ore during the war years was the Shinkolobwe Mine in the Belgian Congo and the most important man concerned with its operation was M. Edgar Sengier.

Col. Kenneth D. Nichols: The Shinkolobwe mine represented a freak occurrence in nature. It contained a tremendously rich lode of uranium pitchblende. Nothing like it has ever again been found. The ore already in the United States contained 65 percent U-308, while the pitchblende aboveground in the Congo amounted to a thousand tons of 65 percent ore, and the waste piles of ore contained two thousand tons of 20 percent U-308. To illustrate the uniqueness of Sengier's stockpile, after the war the MED and the AEC considered ore containing three-tenths of 1 percent as a good find.

Brig. Gen. Leslie Groves: In May of 1939, Sengier happened to be in England, in the office of Lord Stonehaven, a fellow director on the Union Minière Board, when Stonehaven asked him to receive an important scientist. This turned out to be Sir Henry Tizard, the director of the Imperial College of Science and Technology. He asked Sengier to grant the British Government an option on every bit of radium-uranium ore that would be extracted from the Shinkolobwe Mine. Naturally, Sengier refused. As he was leaving, Sir Henry took him by the arm and said most impressively: "Be careful, and never forget that you have in your hands something which may mean a catastrophe to your country and mine if this material were to fall in the hands of a possible enemy." This remark, coming as it did from a renowned scientist, made a lasting impression on Sengier.

Arthur Holly Compton: Sengier sensed that this uranium ore might be of military value.

Brig. Gen. Leslie Groves: Sengier left Brussels in October of 1939 for New York, where he remained for the rest of the war. From there, he managed the operations of his company, both inside and outside the Belgian Congo. Toward the end of 1940, fearing a possible German invasion of the Belgian Congo, Sengier directed his representatives in Africa to ship discreetly to New York, under whatever ruse was practicable, the very large supply of previously mined uranium ore, then in storage at the Shinkolobwe Mine. In accordance with Sengier's instructions, over 1,250 tons of uranium ore were shipped by way of the nearest port, Lobito, in Portuguese Angola, during September and October of 1940.

Arthur Holly Compton: He ordered the ship laden with this ore to proceed to New York. There the ore was stored in a warehouse.

Capt. Lewis L. Strauss, *US Naval Reserve, Office of Naval Research*: He had managed to divert to the United States some two thousand steel drums containing about twelve hundred tons of ore. These were stacked in the open at Port Richmond, Staten Island, New York, and plainly marked "Uranium Ore, product of the Belgian Congo." They apparently excited no interest.

Col. Kenneth D. Nichols: Early in 1942, while in Washington on other matters, he mentioned this stockpile to State Department officials concerned with international economic affairs.

Brig. Gen. Leslie Groves: As is now well known, the State Department was not informed of the atomic project until shortly before the Yalta Conference in February of 1945. Nevertheless, it is hard to understand why, with Sengier so insistent on the value of the uranium ore, and knowing that the ore contained radium, the State Department officials did not make a serious effort to determine the real value of the ores.

Col. Kenneth D. Nichols: I first learned of Sengier's supply of ore on September 7 [1942]. Taken by surprise, I immediately began to ask about the stockpile. I visited Sengier in his New York office on September 18 to discuss purchasing his stockpile. I found the Belgian a courteous gentleman in his sixties. He had a somewhat pallid face, and his light hair was thinning. He was immaculately dressed, and he spoke excellent English in rather curt sentences.

Brig. Gen. Leslie Groves: When Nichols opened the conversation, Sengier was somewhat guarded in his reply, recalling how the State Department had consistently ignored his repeated proddings.

Edgar Sengier: The colonel confirmed his credentials. I asked him when he would like to have the shipment and he told me, "Right now." So I told him, "I just happen to have a thousand tons of ore stored right here in New York City."

Brig. Gen. Leslie Groves: He said: "Colonel, will you tell me first if you have come here merely to talk, or to do business?" Nichols answered diplomatically, as always, that he was there to do business, not to talk.

Col. Kenneth D. Nichols: Perhaps too flippantly, I answered, "Yes. I have more authority, I'm sure, than you have uranium to sell." After thinking about it for a moment, he demanded to know, "Will the uranium ore be used for military purposes?" I hesitated. I didn't know what I should say to a foreigner about the country's most secret war project. Sengier rescued me: "You don't need to tell me how you'll use it. I think I know. All I want is your assurance as an Army officer that this uranium ore is definitely going to be used for war purposes." I could, of course, give him that assurance. He replied, "Good. Then let's make a deal, Colonel."

Arthur Holly Compton: When Sengier was assured on these two points, he immediately noted on a sheet of yellow paper the conditions of sale of the ore to the United States government.

Col. Kenneth D. Nichols: The draft agreement contained only eight sentences.

Brig. Gen. Leslie Groves: This was typical of the way in which a great many of our most important transactions were carried out. Once the seller understood the importance of our work (and there was no need to explain it in this case), he was invariably perfectly willing to deliver his goods or his services on our oral assurance that fair terms and conditions would be settled at a later date. We always promised that he would not be out-of-pocket for any expenses incurred if for some reason final agreement was not reached. And we always kept that promise.

Leona H. Woods: This ore went to the metals production plants and was converted into fuel elements in CP-1. The six tons of metal arrived in time to be placed at the center of the pile. This more dense material allowed the pile to become chain-reacting at a smaller size than had been previously planned for.

* * *

Albert Wattenberg: After exponential pile No. 18 was built there no longer was any doubt for quite a few of us that we were building a chain-reacting pile. However, before we finished building the first self-sustaining pile, several incidents occurred which could have led to serious delays in our getting the job done.

Herbert L. Anderson: Around October 20 labor difficulties arose.

Albert Wattenberg: We had planned to move the material to a new laboratory at the Argonne Forest near Chicago. But construction of the building was halted due to labor problems.

Herbert L. Anderson: It was clear that we would be ready to assemble the pile before the building was completed. Fermi became concerned about a serious delay.

Albert Wattenberg: The squash court under the West Stands at Chicago where we had been building all of our exponential piles was just barely large enough to contain the chain-reacting pile.

Arthur Holly Compton: Early in November Fermi came into my office. "I believe we can make the chain reaction work safely right here in Chicago." We discussed the matter back and forth until we were both satisfied. According to Fermi's calculations, which I carefully checked, we would be working under conditions that it should take some minutes for the reaction to double its power. If this proved correct, there would be ample time for adjustments, and the reaction would be under full control.

Brig. Gen. Leslie Groves: Several experiments carried out while the pile was under construction indicated that the chances of any untoward happening were very slight.

Arthur Holly Compton: The only reason for doubt was that some new, unforeseen phenomenon might develop under the conditions of release of nuclear energy of such vastly greater power than anyone had previously handled. We would also take whatever other precautions we could think of, even though these might appear superfluous. After all, the experiment would be performed in the midst of a great city. We did not see how a true nuclear explosion, such as that of an atomic bomb, could possibly occur. But the amount of potentially radioactive material present in the pile would be enormous and anything that would cause excessive ionizing radiation in such a location would be intolerable.

Brig. Gen. Leslie Groves: If the pile should explode, no one knew just how far the danger would extend. Stagg Field lies in the heart of a populous area.

Arthur Holly Compton: As a responsible officer of the University of Chicago, according to every rule of organizational protocol, I should have taken the matter to my superior. But this would have been unfair. [University of Chicago] President [Robert] Hutchins was in no position to make an independent judgment of the hazards involved. Based on considerations of the University's welfare the only answer he could have given would have been no. And this answer would have been wrong. So I assumed the responsibility myself. I told Fermi to go ahead with the critical experiment.

Brig. Gen. Leslie Groves: I learned then that nothing is harder for the man carrying the ultimate responsibility, in this case myself, than to sit back and appear calm and confident while all his hopes can easily be destroyed in a moment by some unexpected event over which he has no direct control.

* * *

Herbert L. Anderson: On Monday, November 16, we opened the rubberized balloon cloth envelope and started erection of the pile inside it. We organized into two shifts: Wally Zinn took the day shift, mine was the night shift.

Leona H. Woods: At the doubles squash court under the west stands at Chicago, on November 14, the balloon cloth was laid out on the floor and the first layer of the graphite matrix supported on the 4-by-6-inch timbers began to be laid down.

Albert Wattenberg: A circle was drawn to indicate where the first graphite bricks should be placed, and the construction of the first chain-reacting pile began.

Leona H. Woods: We proceeded at a rate of somewhat more than two layers per day, and by November 20, the fifteenth layer of the graphite-uranium matrix was being laid.

Arthur Holly Compton: Not nearly enough uranium metal was going to be ready in time. The few tons that would be delivered were reserved for use near the middle of the pile, where their effect would be greatest. For the outer portions of the pile, uranium oxide purified by Mallinckrodt [Chemical Works] and now coming in sufficient quantity would have to be used. This oxide we had to form, using a hand press, into compact lumps that could be built into the structure. The pile went up as rapidly as the materials arrived.

Herbert L. Anderson: There were no detailed plans or blueprints for the frame or the pile. Each day we would report on the progress of the construction to Fermi, usually in his office in Eckhart Hall. There we would present our sketch of the layers we had assembled and indicate what we thought could be added on the following shifts. Since some of the graphite was of better quality than the rest it was important to arrange its disposition carefully. Fermi spent a good deal of time calculating the most effective location for the various grades of graphite on hand.

Albert Wattenberg: From the middle of October until December 2, we were on a regime of about 90 hours of work a week. All we did was to work and sleep, and sometimes we didn't even get to eat meals. Sometimes we thought of why we were doing it; several times we discussed what we would do if the Nazis won—where we would try to hide in the United States? We were fairly certain we would be killed if we were caught. One morning very early Dr. Alvin Graves came in (he was slightly older than the rest of us) and wanted to take over what I was doing, although he wasn't due in until late that afternoon. He said he just couldn't sleep. He felt the Nazis were working, that they were pushing ahead to get there before us. We were in a real race, and he felt he shouldn't be taking a day off.

Herbert L. Anderson: One important detail was the location of the cadmium control strips. These were needed to keep the pile from becoming too reactive once it began to approach the critical size. We wanted a number of control rods distributed widely in the structure. This meant that some had to be installed at a rather early stage. A simple design for a control rod was developed which could be made on the spot: cadmium sheet nailed to a flat wood strip was inserted in a slot machined in the graphite for this purpose. The strip had to be inserted and removed by hand. Except when the reactivity of the pile was being measured, they were kept inside the pile and locked using a simple hasp and padlock, the only keys to which were kept by Zinn and myself. One special, particularly simple, control rod was built by Zinn; it operated by gravity through weights and a pulley and was called "Zip." It was to be pulled out before the pile went into operation and held by hand (Zinn's) with a rope. In case of an emergency or if Zinn collapsed, the rope would be released and Zip would be drawn into the pile by gravity.

Leona H. Woods: Everything and everybody soon became black with graphite dust; there was a black haze in the air that scattered the beams from the floodlights. Walter Zinn forbade me to help with construction because he said he didn't want to discover he had been cussing out a girl when I took off my dust mask and cap—he was ready and versatile at cussing. It was just as well because there was plenty for me to do.

Meta Newson, ***project spouse of physicist Henry W. Newson*****:** The first two years after we were married, from 1934 until 1936, we were in California with Ernest Lawrence, at the cyclotron at Berkeley. When the Manhattan Project started, my husband was at Stagg Field. When I went to Stagg Field to pick him up in the evenings—I couldn't go in, he would have to come out—he came out one day with little blocks of graphite. I thought, "That idiot, he is starting to play with blocks."

Arthur Holly Compton: The graphite dust made the floor more slippery than a dance floor.

Herbert L. Anderson: Once the 15th layer had been reached, we introduced the practice of measuring the neutron activity at a fixed point in the structure. Each day the measurements of the activity were reported to Fermi who used it to improve his estimate of how much bigger the pile would have to be.

Alvin M. Weinberg: Fermi was able to accurately predict how many layers were needed for criticality.

Herbert L. Anderson: As the pile grew the estimate of its critical size became increasingly accurate. Thus, we could tell that on the night between December 1st and 2nd, during my shift, the 57th layer would be completed and the pile could be made critical.

Albert Wattenberg: About eight weeks prior, Fermi had started a series of weekly lectures which continued until November 20.

Luis Alvarez: His brilliance as a lecturer was astonishing. I had never heard such lucid lectures, delivered without notes but as polished as if Fermi had been reading them from a book. My friends and I attributed his flawless performances to careful rehearsal. Later, when I worked with him, I understood that he simply knew his subject so well that he could improvise a finished presentation only minutes before he walked into the room.

Herbert L. Anderson: That night the construction proceeded as usual with all cadmium rods in place. When the 57th layer was completed, I called a halt to the work in accordance with the agreement we had reached in the meeting with Fermi that afternoon. All the cadmium rods but one were then removed and the neutron count taken, following the standard procedure which had been followed on the previous days. It was clear from the count that once the only remaining cadmium rod was removed, the pile would go critical. It was a great temptation for me to pull the final cadmium strip and be the first to make a pile chain react. But Fermi had anticipated this possibility. He had made me promise that I would make the measurement, record the result, insert all cadmium rods, lock them all in place, go to bed and nothing more.

"The clicks merged into a roar"

CHAIN REACTION

The final appearance of the chain-reacting pile.

In early December 1942, the world war still appeared that it could go either way. Far from Chicago, some of the war's fiercest moments flashed—including battles in North Africa and Guadalcanal—and warnings were just beginning to come about how brutal the conflict's cost was turning out to be. The State Department had recently warned that approximately half the estimated four million Jews in Nazi-occupied Europe had been slain in an "extermination campaign," leading Jewish communities across the Allied nations to hold vigils and declare Wednesday, December 2, 1942, an international day of mourning. Underneath the old stadium at the University of Chicago, the day would be remembered for other historic reasons. There, the Chicago Met Lab believed it was ready to start up the world's first artificial nuclear reactor. The final "pile" was a massive undertaking, costing about a million dollars and involving some 45,000 graphite blocks—totaling more than 300 tons—alongside more than 5 tons of uranium metal and 40 tons of uranium oxide.

Arthur Holly Compton: Wednesday, 2 December, was a cold day in Chicago, about 10 degrees, with a raw wind. The "L" and the street cars were jammed, for it was the second day of gas rationing. Motor traffic was down 40 percent.

Walter Zinn: It was a very cold day. To those of us who worked in the West Stands cold was not a new experience. That gloomy structure with its high stacks of graphite bar filling all corridors, stairwells, and wherever 500 tons of the black stuff would be stored was completely unheated. Perhaps the importance of our jobs had something to do with it, but we really worked fast to keep warm.

Arthur Holly Compton: That morning, on schedule, W. K. Lewis brought his reviewing committee back to Chicago, returning from Lawrence's laboratory in California. They were stopping over between trains. We met the committee in a comfortable conference room of Eckhart Hall. "Where is Fermi?" Lewis inquired. We would like to talk over these questions with him." "I'm sorry," I replied, "but Fermi has an important experiment in hand in the laboratory and has asked to be excused. Here are others of us who will be glad to discuss your questions." The members of the committee surely guessed what Fermi was doing, but in not telling them the code of secrecy was being observed.

Albert Wattenberg: On December 2, we began by checking that the neutron intensity was the same as Herb Anderson had measured the previous night, when all except one of the cadmium rods in that pile had been removed. The rates on some of the other instruments were checked and some adjustments were made in anticipation of the neutron intensity's increasing as we proceeded in the morning.

Arthur Holly Compton: Tests showed that the pile, only about three-fourths of the size that had been thought necessary, was ready to give a chain reaction. This reaction was held down by control rods coated with cadmium that swallowed up all neutrons within reach. To make the reaction work it should now only be necessary to pull these control rods out of the pile.

Herbert L. Anderson: Fermi had prepared a routine for the approach to criticality. The last cadmium rod, attended by George Weil, was pulled out step by step. At each step a measurement was made of the increase in the neutron activity, and Fermi checked the result with his prediction, based on the previous step.

Albert Wattenberg: The rest of us gathered on the narrow balcony at the other end of the squash court. At one end of the balcony were the electronics, scalers, and a pen recorder attached to detectors on the pile. Some of the younger physicists would read and plot the readings from the scalers; Fermi could look at their data or at the pen recorder; they were independent measurements of the neutron intensity.

Leona H. Woods: Fermi and I repeated Herb's flux measurement with the standard boron trifluoride counter.

Albert Wattenberg: The most important thing was to establish the position of the control rod at which the pile would become self-sustaining, that is, the critical point. The next thing was to establish how fast the intensity would rise if he moved the rod beyond that point. From the first couple of measurements, he obtained the value of the constant, which was what he had hoped it would be.

Leona H. Woods: The new point fell exactly on Fermi's extrapolated line; it intercepted zero at half a layer less than number 57.

Albert Wattenberg: Fermi periodically read some numbers and did a quick calculation on his little slide rule of the exponential rate of rise of the neutron intensity in the pile. After the intensity had leveled off, he then told Weil to move the cadmium rod another six inches. The neutron intensity in the pile rose further and then again leveled off. The pile was still subcritical. Fermi had been busy noting the values on the back of his slide rule and calculating the rate of rise. After it had stabilized, Fermi told Weil to move the rod out another six inches. Again the neutron intensity increased and leveled off. The pile was still subcritical.

Norman Hilberry: Clearly if there were any new law of physics, it would begin to show up in an actual deviation of the observed graphs from those Fermi had computed. And each time, it hit absolutely right on the nose. I am sure that long before Fermi finally said, "George, pull it out another ten inches," the question had long since been settled in his mind. It was long since settled in mine too.

Albert Wattenberg: It was 11:30 a.m., and Fermi said, "I'm hungry. Let's go to lunch."

Leona H. Woods: We agreed to meet again at two o'clock. Herb, Fermi, and I went over to the apartment I shared with my sister—it was close to the stands—for something to eat. I made pancakes, mixing the batter so fast that there were bubbles of dry flour in it. When fried, these were somewhat crunchy between the teeth, and Herb thought I had put nuts in the batter.

Arthur Holly Compton: About the middle of the morning the telephone rang. It was Volney Wilson's voice: "I thought you would want to know that Fermi is ready to start the critical experiment." Wilson explained that space in the laboratory was at a premium but told me that if I wanted to bring with me one other person it should not too greatly disturb the experiment. I picked rather the youngest member of the group, Crawford H. Greenewalt, then at the age of forty the director of research of one of the important divisions of the DuPont Company.

Crawford H. Greenewalt, *chief liaison to the Manhattan Project, DuPont Corporation*: Why he picked me out of the three I do not know but he did.

Arthur Holly Compton: I reasoned that he would probably remember longer than the others what he would see, and it should be something worth remembering.

Crawford H. Greenewalt: Of course it was an exciting thing because actually I never regard this particular experiment as really critical. That is, there are many first experiments that do not work and this does not mean that it cannot be made to work. This is just the first try and it was interesting, but I did not consider it as critical in determining whether or not the project fell flat or whether it went on. I am quite sure that if it had not worked, if the experiment had failed for some reason or other, they would have found some way of trying again.

Leona H. Woods: We put on the usual gray—now black with graphite—laboratory coats and entered the doubles squash court containing the looming pile enclosed in the dirty, grayish-black balloon cloth and then went up on the spectators' balcony. The balcony was originally meant for people to watch squash players, but now it was filled with control equipment and read-out circuits glowing and winking and radiating some gratefully received heat.

Arthur Holly Compton: We entered onto a balcony at one end of the squash court laboratory. At the opposite end of the room was the massive pile of graphite blocks, within which the uranium was embedded. On the balcony with us were twenty others, including Fermi.

Eugene Wigner: Leo Szilard was able to bring himself to attend the event. His sense of history was apparently greater than his jealousy of Fermi.

Albert Wattenberg: Herb Anderson, Bill Sturm, and Leona Woods were recording the readings from instruments. Somehow we got a public address system and Bill Overbeck was set up to call out the neutron counts. Fermi was set up to watch the pen on the recording chart which was attached to a neutron detector.

Herbert L. Anderson: Then back from lunch, Fermi called for another increase in activity. Again predicted it on the nose, you see. And then finally he says, "Now we will make a chain reaction for the first time in the history of man. We will pull the rod out."

Crawford H. Greenewalt: They had on the platform buckets of strong cadmium nitrate solution. The idea was that if the reaction could not be controlled by the control rods and seemed to be getting away they were to run out on top of the structure and pour the buckets of cadmium nitrate physically, by hand. This was supposed to stop the reaction, but this was simply the remote precaution.

Albert Wattenberg: We had several different types of safety rods. One of them, called "Zip," which was designed by Zinn, operated by gravity. Wilson's group had built a series of safety rods which could be activated remotely by pushing a button. An additional gravitational safety rod was tied out with just a rope on the railing of the balcony where we stood. Norman Hilberry had an axe to cut that rope if human intervention were required to shut the pile down in a hurry.

Leona H. Woods: Each person had a job. I read the counts of the standard boron trifluoride counter in a loud voice: "Two, two, three, one . . ."—these being the counts in 10-second intervals with the control rod still inside the pile.

Albert Wattenberg: The trace on the paper on which the neutron intensity was being recorded showed the intensity rising slowly, at the rate that Fermi expected.

Arthur Holly Compton: The data fitted his calculated line with remarkable precision.

Herbert L. Anderson: At first you could hear the sound of the neutron counter, *clickety-clack, clickety-clack.*

Leona H. Woods: The last control rod, manned by George Weil, was pulled out foot by foot, at the voiced instruction of Fermi on the balcony above him. After each foot, there was a halt to measure the increased neutron flux shown by the pen recorder, which Fermi checked with his slide rule against his predicted flux increase. When the cadmium control rod was pulled out to each new position he asked for, you could hear the sound of the clicking boron trifluoride counter increase. I called, "Eight, sixteen, twenty-eight, sixty-four . . ."; then the clicks merged into a roar too fast to read.

Herbert L. Anderson: The clicks began to merge into a roar; the counter couldn't follow anymore.

Leona H. Woods: Fermi switched on the chart recorder attached to the ion chamber, and everyone watched the pen rise rapidly and level off. "Another foot George." The pen rose rapidly and leveled off. "Another foot George . . ."

Crawford H. Greenewalt: The thing that I remember best is Enrico Fermi's complete calmness. He was walking around as if he was simply waiting for the barber to say, "Mr. Fermi, come have your hair cut." It was just as casual and calm as that. Every so often he would pull a little three-inch slide rule out of his pocket, and make a few stabs with it.

Herbert L. Anderson: "The pile has gone critical," he announced. No one present had any doubt about it.

Leona H. Woods: Everyone could see that the pen line was rising without leveling off—up and up.

Herbert L. Anderson: Then everyone began to wonder why he didn't shut the pile off. But Fermi was completely calm. He waited another minute, then another.

Leona H. Woods: What happened was that Fermi waited—and waited—to test Volney Wilson's control circuits. Suddenly bells rang, startling everybody; the ion chamber flux had passed the level preset for safety. Wilson reached over and tore the connecting wires out of the wall to stop the bells.

Electric motors drove in the safety rods; like the control rods and the zip, the safety rods were coated with cadmium foil, and this metal absorbed so many neutrons that the chain reaction was stopped. Volney Wilson called these "scram" rods. He said that the pile had "scrammed," the rods had "scrammed" into the pile. This word has entered the vocabulary of power-plant operation, and also of nuclear submarines, so that any shutdown of the reactors is called a scram.

Albert Wattenberg: The radiation and the neutron intensity and the counting rates all decreased almost instantaneously. We had built the pile, and Fermi had established that we could get a self-sustaining nuclear reaction that we could control in a very predictable manner.

Crawford H. Greenewalt: It worked. We all heaved a sigh of relief.

Leona H. Woods: At the instant that the safeties went in, the pile had achieved a power of only about 1/2 watt, barely enough to light a flashlight; but the chain reaction had been demonstrated.

Herbert L. Anderson: No cheer went up, but everyone had a sense of excitement. They had been witness to a great moment in history. Only forty-three persons were present at the experiment, mostly the scientists who had done the work.

Leona H. Woods: We began to lock in all the control and safety rods and to turn off the power supplies. We were nearly ready to leave, taking off our dirty gray laboratory coats and putting on our outdoor coats when in came Eugene Wigner, alone, with one small bottle of Chianti. We were only about twenty people, the visitors and the high brass all having long since left. Eugene had, miraculously, not only the tiny bottle of Chianti but also some paper cups. These he filled with a few drips each and passed them around in the midst of that dingy, gray-black surrounding without any word whatsoever. No toast, nothing, and everyone had a few memorable sips. No toast? Why not? There was a greater drama in the silence than if words had been spoken. Everyone was thinking: *If we did it, haven't the Germans already achieved the chain reaction?*

Albert Wattenberg: After all the others had left, I stood there just looking at the pile. I had a tremendous feeling of accomplishment. Then my mind wandered in the wrong direction—I started thinking about the work that lay ahead. So I went around and checked that all of the rods were locked in place, that all the power supplies were turned off. I hung up the Chianti bottle on the wall. I then went home to my room to sleep for twelve hours.

* * *

Arthur Holly Compton: When the committee had left, I picked up the phone and called Conant.

James B. Conant: The way the story is usually told, I was in my office in Cambridge. Actually, I was in Washington in my quarters in the dormitory attached to the Dumbarton Oaks Library and Collection of Harvard University, where I had been staying several days each week since Pearl Harbor. I was waiting for news. Therefore I was not surprised when I heard Arthur say: "Our Italian navigator has just landed in the new world."

Arthur Holly Compton: Then, half apologetically, because I had led the S-1 Committee to believe that it would be another week or more before the pile could be completed, I added, "the earth was not as large as he had estimated, and he arrived at the new world sooner than he had expected."

James B. Conant: My apprehension influenced my immediate question: "Were the natives friendly?" There was no prearranged code, but Arthur knew that I was asking whether everything had proceeded according to prediction. "Everyone landed safe and happy," he replied.

Leona H. Woods: Enrico and I trudged back toward home through the blue-shadowed snow, the temperature well below zero. Herb had already disappeared, doubtlessly to clean up for a party that Laura was giving that night. Enrico and I didn't say a word; I don't know what he was thinking, but I was thinking, "Of course, the Germans have already made a chain reaction because we have, and they have been ahead until now. When do we get as scared as we ought to and work harder?"

Seeking to probe his thoughts, I asked Fermi, when do we get scared? Could our work go faster?

Laura Fermi: In December, 1942, I gave a large party for the metallurgists who worked with Enrico and for their wives.

Leona H. Woods: Laura's party had been scheduled weeks before. That it happened to fall on the same day as the chain reaction demonstration was pure coincidence. Laura was so little aware of the major events of the day that after the tired and exultant Enrico got home, she asked him to go out and buy cigarettes for the party! And it was snowing.

Laura Fermi: As the first bell rang shortly after eight in the evening, Enrico went to open the door, and I kept a few steps behind him in the hall. Walter

Zinn and his wife Jean walked in, bringing along the icy-cold air that clung to their clothes. Walter extended his hand to Enrico and said: "Congratulations." "Congratulations?" I asked, puzzled, "What for?" Nobody took any notice of me.

Leona H. Woods: I got there on time, about eight o'clock, and almost instantly people began to arrive in large numbers. As each couple came through the door, stamping off snow and pulling off overshoes, they had congratulations for Enrico.

Laura Fermi: Every single man congratulated Enrico. He accepted the congratulations readily, with no embarrassment or show of modesty, with no words, but with a steady grin on his face.

Leona H. Woods: Laura was mystified—*what was going on?*

Laura Fermi: My inquiries received either no answer at all or such evasive replies as: "Ask your husband," or: "Nothing special. He is a smart guy. That's all," or: "Don't get excited. You'll find out sometime." I had nothing to help me guess. Enrico had mentioned nothing worthy of notice, and nothing unusual had happened, except, of course, the preparations for the party. And those did not involve Enrico and provided no ground for congratulating.

Leona H. Woods: She came to me and begged me to tell her what Enrico had done. I was struck dumb by her question and became a silent statue. *How could I, the youngest member of a totally secret project, say one word that would inform her, this beautiful lady whom I admired so intensely and would not disappoint for anything?* My mind gradually unthawing, I decided to use an analogy. I said that Enrico had done something equivalent to sinking a Japanese admiral's ship—this at a time when the American fleet in the Pacific had been totally wiped out, and we were at the mercy of the Japanese. Even the capture of Hawaii and invasion of the West Coast of the United States were possible. So I replied, "He sank a Japanese admiral." This was perhaps the most embarrassing moment of my life, quite unknown to anyone else.

Laura Fermi: Two years and a half elapsed. One evening, shortly after the end of the war in Japan, Enrico brought home a mimeographed, paper-bound volume. "It may interest you to see the Smyth Report," he said. "It contains all declassified information on atomic energy. It was just released for publication, and this is an advance copy." It was not easy reading. I struggled with its technical language and its difficult content until slowly, painfully, I worked my way through it. When I reached the middle of the book, I found the reason for the congratulations Enrico had received at our party.

Herbert L. Anderson: The original pile in the West Stands, dubbed CP-1, had a short life. It lived for three months, but those were three very active months for the first chain reactor. It turned out to be a marvelous experimental tool. Its sensitivity for neutron absorption and production was beyond the wildest dreams of those of us who had struggled so hard to make such measurements before. The pile became an indispensable device for the design of its successors. The building at the Argonne site was now complete, and we had a whole group of young and eager engineers from DuPont to help us. We did not hesitate to disassemble and rebuild the pile at the Argonne site.

Albert Wattenberg: I had sentimental feelings about CP-1. I remembered the circle which had been drawn on the floor of the balloon cloth to indicate where we should lay the first bricks. As we got close to the bottom layers, I dug down and made sure to get out what I thought was the first graphite brick that had been laid, namely, the cornerstone of CP-1. I moved these out to our laboratory at Site A and the Chianti bottle hung on the wall of that laboratory until the straw string began to look rather weak.

* * *

Arthur Holly Compton: The atmosphere was now one of confidence. The nuclear reaction was an accomplished fact.

Col. Kenneth D. Nichols: Franklin Matthias and I went to Wilmington on December 14 to discuss with DuPont officials the site requirements for the relocated plutonium process. Given the needs for a much larger area than the Tennessee site and a great deal of electric power and water, relatively few suitable locations existed. The area in central Washington State near the Grand Coulee Dam seemed to offer the most promising site, and on the fifteenth,

Matthias and A.E.S. Hall and G. P. Church of DuPont left to survey that area, and other locations in California and Nevada.

Col. Franklin T. Matthias, *officer-in-charge, Hanford Engineer Works*: I thought the Hanford site was perfect the first time I saw it. We flew over the Rattlesnake Hills up to the river, so I saw the whole site on that flight. We were sure we had it. I called General Groves from Portland, and told him I thought we had found the only place in the country that could match the requirements for a desirable site. It had so much in favor of it—an area with almost no people, very undeveloped, it was obvious it had been built by the Columbia River in early times working across the valley leaving gravel behind it, and there's nothing better than gravel, deep gravel, for foundations, for earthquake protection, anything you want. It had all the advantages.

Brig. Gen. Leslie Groves: The Hanford site was one of the largest procurements of land handled during the war, or at any other time. The total acreage taken was something less than a half-million acres.

Arthur Holly Compton: This decision to develop another vast area for carrying on the atomic project added very substantially to its total cost. It was about a similar occasion that General George C. Marshall was speaking when, years later, he told me the following story. General Groves came to see him at his office in Washington. Marshall kept him waiting for some minutes while he finished an item on his desk. Then he turned to examine Groves's memorandum. It was a statement that added facilities would require an additional hundred million dollars. He read the memo and, as was his custom, handed it back with only a kind comment to indicate his approval. As Groves was about to leave, Marshall called him back. "General," he said, "you may be interested to know why I kept you waiting when you came in. I was writing this check for three dollars and fifty-two cents for grass seed for my lawn."

Eugene Wigner: Just two weeks later, the plans for the reactor plant in Hanford, Washington were passed out. They reflected the will of the Army to build production-scale nuclear reactors. What confidence all of us had in Enrico Fermi's team. He inspired it. He deserved every bit of it.

Alvin M. Weinberg: By the end of 1942 Wigner had completed the design of a 500 megawatt water-cooled reactor that would produce 500 grams of plutonium per day. The report CE-407, "Preliminary Process Design of Liquid-Cooled Power Plant Producing 5x105 kw," was dated January 9, 1943. As I think back on Wigner's design of the Hanford plutonium producing reactors, I can think of only one analogy: Mozart, who would compose a piano concerto in a few days. The whole thing was accomplished in about four months.

Col. Kenneth D. Nichols: With the selection of Los Alamos for the bomb development laboratory and the Hanford site for the plutonium production plants and with the acquisition of the CEW site, the Manhattan Project had the locations for its major facilities. Thus, by the end of the year, work was under way on three methods of producing fissionable material, with the goal of producing at the earliest possible date an atomic bomb that could fit into the bomb bay of a B-29.

Arthur Holly Compton: After December 1942 what determined when the bombs were ready was simply the time required to design and build the plants, to produce the materials, and to fabricate the materials into bombs.

Col. Kenneth D. Nichols: The December 1942 progress report for President Roosevelt provided estimates for beginning bomb production as possibly June 1, 1944, a better chance before January 1, 1945, and a good chance during the first half of 1945. The total cost was estimated as about $400 million.

Gen. George C. Marshall: I obtained the first money [for the Manhattan Project] by taking 20 percent of the appropriations concerning such matters in the development of bombs, artillery, and kindred matters, which was legal. You could divert 20 percent away from an appropriation to a somewhat similar matter—one connected with defense, for example—and this bomb was certainly connected with defense.

Vannevar Bush: The way in which the money was raised was interesting. Each year, after the Manhattan District had been established, Secretary Stimson and I went up on Capitol Hill and met first with the leaders of the House and then with their counterparts in the Senate. This included, of course, the Chairman of the Appropriations Committee of the House, the Senior Minority Member, and the Majority Leader of the House—about five or six men. I told them of the difficulties of development, the enormous cost, the probable timetable, the size of the bomb when it was developed. We included, also, estimates of where we thought the Germans stood. Now this was an excellent way to do it because then the item for the money on the Manhattan District was buried in Army Appropriations; when it came up, for example, in the House Appropriations Committee, the Chairman would say, "Well now, don't inquire into that item, gentlemen; I've inquired into it very thoroughly and I can assure you that it's all right." There never was the slightest leak from that source.

PART III

MAKING *the* BOMB

1942–1944

From late 1942 through the winter of 1945, the work of the Manhattan Project unfolded at numerous sites around the country simultaneously, from the Rad Lab in Berkeley to the Met Lab and Argonne Lab around Chicago to Columbia University in New York.

The project's three major facilities at Oak Ridge, Tennessee, Los Alamos, New Mexico, and Hanford, Washington, each had to be built from scratch—creating some of the most advanced scientific facilities in the world in remote, isolated locales, amid wartime labor and materials shortages, to focus on industrial processes based on novel and largely untested methods, all under a heavy cloak of secrecy and misdirection. At nearly every turn, project planners, engineers, and scientists realized they had underestimated the complexity and scale of the work ahead.

The division of labor, for the most part, fell into three distinct lanes of effort: Oak Ridge was the center of the Manhattan Project's uranium refinement; Hanford focused on plutonium; and Los Alamos brought together the world's top scientists on a remote mesa to design and build the working bombs themselves.

For organizational and comprehensibility purposes, I have mostly organized the narrative in this part by geographic location rather than strictly chronologically—telling the stories of Oak Ridge, Los Alamos, and Hanford distinctly, even though time-wise they all overlapped from 1942 through 1945. The order ahead follows roughly when each location's primary work unfolded: In the roughest chronological terms, the Oak Ridge "Y-12" calutrons begin uranium production first, in November 1943; while the bomb design work peaks in 1944 at Los Alamos; and the Hanford plutonium facilities begin production last in September 1944, when their "B Reactor" comes online.

"Stay right here and go to work"

OAK RIDGE: CREATING THE CLINTON ENGINEER WORKS

The seizure of the land for Oak Ridge disrupted residents like J. Nash Copeland and his store.

When Leslie Groves and the US government requisitioned a vast expanse of land in Tennessee, the Manhattan Project still had little idea what precisely would be built there. The site—known first as the Clinton Engineer Works and later Oak Ridge—would ultimately host the first of the mega-facilities built to ready uranium for the bomb. The region around the Clinch River was mountainous and still quite rural; the dams of the Tennessee Valley Authority were just beginning to bring electrification to many of the small communities around Black Oak Ridge. As families—many of whom had lived in the Tennessee hills for generations and even centuries—were moved out, engineers and scientists drew on the work of Ernest Lawrence's Berkeley calutrons and other Manhattan Project labs to build some of the largest industrial facilities in the US.

Alvin M. Weinberg: Almost immediately after the Army took over the project in September 1942, Tennessee was chosen as site "X" for all the production plants—the three isotope-separation plants (K-25 gaseous diffusion, Y-12 electromagnetic separation, and, later, S-50 liquid thermal diffusion) and the plutonium-producing piles.

Brig. Gen. Leslie Groves: Here would be located all our uranium separation plants—the plants designed to separate the easily fissionable Uranium-235 from the more abundant but much less fissionable isotope, Uranium-238.

Paul Elza, *engineer, Tennessee Valley Authority*: In very late '42, there were rumblings throughout the countryside about something big going on out near Clinton. Most people were quite busily engaged in many other things, and paid relatively little attention to it. Word and rumor began to spread that it was going to be a great artillery range or a bombing practice location—that caused some concern in the population. It was natural for one of those things about which we all speculated was that it would be some great new secret weapon, and of course that wasn't too far from the mark.

Horace V. Wells, Jr., *publisher,* The Clinton Courier-News: The take over—this was a rather difficult period for the county. The U.S. Army sent in people to handle the acquisition of the property for the then-called Clinton Engineer Works.

J. Nash Copeland, *owner, general store, Robertsville*: They just came down, looked around, issued an "Order of Taking," and told us to get out of the property. November the 15th they told us to move. We moved out December the first of 1942. I'd built a four-room house with running water in it and I had improved our house by adding a bathroom and put in running water and electricity. I'd improved the store building and I had a warehouse building and I still only was offered the same price when the government came in to take it over that I had paid for in 1935. We had one little lady lived on the hill, Ms. Dicey—she had an acre and a little house and a little barn thing. They only gave her $75 for her total property there—believe it or not. Wasn't even enough to move the woman.

Horace V. Wells, Jr.: Here were people who had land that had been in their family from the original grant, from the state of North Carolina, for service in the Revolutionary War. The land had never been sold and it was the only home they had. They had been making a living there, they were satisfied. The government came in and offered prices that felt too low—and in fact were too low to go and buy comparable land anywhere else.

J. Nash Copeland: We had a mass meeting at the Scarboro School at that time and the building was just about full. I don't believe there was hardly a family here that wasn't represented, and they were unanimous in telling the government that they weren't treated right in purchasing the property. The only reason people here gave up their homes as easy as they did is because they thought it was wartime and they thought they were doing their part in helping the war effort.

Paul Elza: We were at war—we were in rather desperate circumstances up until that time. Remember things hadn't gone entirely well for us and people were in the mood of sacrifice. They were in the mood of being cooperative. You could stop a man on the street and tell him, persuasively, that you needed the coat off his back for the war effort and chances are at that moment he'd shuck his coat off and hand it to you and never look back.

Arthur Holly Compton: The speed with which the construction went ahead at Oak Ridge was phenomenal. In December 1942 ground was broken for the administration building. During the following winter work started on the electromagnetic separation plant, the plutonium semiworks, and the residential areas. In June 1943 a steam power plant of a quarter-million kilowatts was begun to supply the electricity for the plants that were being erected.

Col. James C. Marshall: We had a contest in the District there and offered a $25 bond to anybody that would name the place down there. We got 94 percent, I think, of the several hundred replies to the contest were all Shangri-La, so I vetoed that.

Charles E. Normand, ***project staff, Y-12 Plant, Tennessee Eastman Corp.*****:** We were told that we were going out to "the site," which was now referred to a little more specifically as Clinton Engineer Works, though we still didn't know where it was. As a matter of fact, when we got on the train to come out, the senior member of our party had all of our tickets in a sealed envelope and we weren't allowed to open it until we were out of town on the way.

Col. James C. Marshall: One day O'Meara came in and he said, "If we're going to open up a town down there, I've got to have a name for it." We called it the Clinton Engineer Works to disguise it like the "Such and Such Ordnance Works"—Badger Ordnance Works and Twin Cities Ordnance Works and things like that. O'Meara said, "The Post Office won't stand for that many words in the name."

I said, "Well, we can't call it Clinton, because there is a town Clinton." We thought of several names, and I remember sitting in the office down here with Virginia Olsson. She sat in the same office I did, Nichols was here and Blair was here in separate rooms. I asked Ms. Olsson to bring me a map. I saw the principal ridge there was marked Black Oak Ridge. I said, "Okay, call it Black Oak Ridge." And he rubbed his hands, and he said, "I told you, we could not have three names in the town like that. The Post Office Department doesn't like it." I said, "Well, call it Oak Ridge and get the hell out of here!" And so it was named.

* * *

With the land cleared and in government hands, work began on the uranium plants. Just as Groves had enlisted DuPont as the main contractor for the plutonium project, he turned to a local powerhouse industrial firm to handle the construction and management of the new uranium plants. The construction project alone would employ about 15,000 people, and training was soon underway for 5,000 more personnel to operate and maintain the plants. The original plans for the Clinton Engineer Works envisioned housing and facilities to support about 13,000 people, but population estimates quickly leapt to 30,000, then 45,000, and ultimately there were 75,000 people working in and around Oak Ridge by the end of World War II, making the secret community the fifth-largest city in Tennessee.

Brig. Gen. Leslie Groves: Long before the essential research was well started and before the equipment could be designed, we had to start designing and constructing the building to house it. Stone and Webster was in charge of this operation. The research on which all design was based was carried out in the Radiation Laboratory of the University of California, under the direction of Dr. Lawrence; and to operate the plant we selected Eastman Kodak, whose subsidiary, Tennessee Eastman, was an extremely competent organization with much experience in chemical processes.

Col. Kenneth D. Nichols: Tennessee Eastman already was involved in war work and was responsible for the Holston Ordnance Works, an explosives plant near Kingston, Tennessee. They knew industrial chemical operations, the labor situation in Tennessee, and had the full technical, managerial, and financial backing of Eastman Kodak. Tennessee Eastman worked closely with Stone and Webster and took full responsibility for developing the chemical process based on work done at Berkeley.

Horace V. Wells, Jr.: We had a tremendous influx of people during the early days—people were living in barns and chicken houses. Automobile firms went out of business [during the war], so some of the garages were converted into dormitory arrangements. People just placed anywhere.

Edward S. Bettis, *nuclear engineer, Y-12 Plant, Tennessee Eastman Corp.*: I was told absolutely nothing, absolutely nothing. As a matter of fact, my interview for the job took place on the fire escape on the old Empire Building in Knoxville. I remember asking the man who interviewed me, "What are we going to do?" He said, "I can't tell you." I said, "When will you be able to tell me?" He said, "We won't tell you. Ever."

John Shacter, *chemical engineer, K-25 Plant, Union Carbide:** They had a big hall with the interviewers—mine was named Kleintop—he said, "I can't tell you anything about the work. It's wartime stuff. But it's got a lot of math and engineering, and it's interesting, and it's fast moving, and if you want the job, you're going to have to stay right here and go to work."

* Through World War II, the company that helped run the Oak Ridge facility was known as the Carbide and Carbon Chemicals Company, which later evolved into the modern-day Union Carbide. Since the company is referred to in oral histories and memories as both, I've changed all references to Union Carbide for simplicity.

Paul Elza: I looked up from my desk [at the Tennessee Valley Authority] and there appeared in the door Lee Warren. He was a brusque sort of rough-talking character and I heard him call out, "Where in the hell's Elza?" I stood up at my desk and held up my hand to wave to him and he came back. He loomed over my desk and says, "I want you to go with me." I says, "Alright when?" And he says, "Now." He says, "I can't tell you anything about it. I can't tell you what you'll be doing," and he says, "I can't tell you anything except you won't be paid any less money than you are here." It turned out that that man had gone throughout TVA and had picked and selected people that he wanted to come to Oak Ridge. I came with him, he stopped by an employment office and there were signs around saying Tennessee Eastman Corporation, and he said these are the people who are going to put you on the payroll. We then came through Clinton—and through what was even then known as Elza Gate—and we were taken up to a building that looked like a huge Army barracks.

Waldo E. Cohn, *biochemist, Metallurgical Laboratory*: A lot of my recruiting took place by phone calls from my old colleagues at Berkeley and whatnot. They hedged around—it would be something in line with my expertise and that I would find it very exciting, so forth and so on. Anyway, there were enough hints dropped to make me interested.

Brig. Gen. Leslie Groves: There were only three electrical suppliers in the country whom we considered suitable for the manufacture of the type of equipment in the quantities needed for the electromagnetic project. To avoid overloading them, we divided our requirements among them: General Electric produced power supply equipment, Allis-Chalmers the magnets, and Westinghouse the process bins and allied parts. Building and operating such a plant as this presented many new industrial problems as laboratory experiments using raw materials measured in grams were expanded to handle tons. More than fifty key specialists were transferred from Berkeley to Tennessee Eastman.

Edward S. Bettis: Eastman had only a very few of their employees that they put here. They had to recruit all the others—some of us they called "key personnel" were given training in the policies of the company and how the company was run, and we in turn had to indoctrinate others. Although my job was a day job, I've gone out many times at two o'clock in the morning to conduct these training classes in Eastman policy—I was just one of many.

Brig. Gen. Leslie Groves: To wring out the utmost in the way of support for the electromagnetic project, we invited the presidents of Westinghouse, General Electric and Allis-Chalmers to visit Oak Ridge. The speed with which the plant could be completed depended largely on how quickly their companies could deliver the key parts, and we wanted these men to see for themselves just how their equipment was to be used and to gain a firsthand realization of the complexity and magnitude of the project. The results of the visits were quite noticeable.

Meyer Silverman, *chemical engineer*: The job offer in Oak Ridge looked attractive. Just as the interview was ending, [they] asked me, "By the way, what does Mrs. Silverman do?" I said, "Well, recently she has been working as secretary to a couple of patent attorneys at RCA." [My interviewer] said, "You hear that! Grab them immediately!" They were short of competent professional secretarial help.

Obie Amacker, *labor relations, X-10 Plant*: I was not able to learn anything about the project until I reported to Oak Ridge. There, I became reacquainted with some chemists whom I had worked with in Alabama. These chemists had disappeared to Oak Ridge and the University of Chicago, and I did not know what they were doing after they disappeared.

Marjorie Ketelle, *project spouse*: I was very anxious to get down here. I remember the day that the great, big burly man came to move our small amount of furniture—we didn't have very much. He was putting ours in the same van as several other people's that were coming here. He came in and said, "Well, so you are going down to Hell, Tennessee." It was a terribly bad thing to have someone tell you.

"The gigantic scale of everything"

OAK RIDGE: Y-12

Tennessee Eastman delighted in how its female calutron operators outperformed the physicists themselves.

The centerpiece of the Oak Ridge complex was known as the Y-12 plant, which used giant magnets to separate uranium isotopes. The scale boggled the imagination given how tiny the finished output was. By the time they were at full operation, the ten buildings that ultimately made up the Y-12 electromagnetic separation facility housed some 2,000 cyclotrons, modeled on Ernest Lawrence's work in Berkeley. Together they separated about 100 grams—equal to about a half-cup—of Uranium-235 each day. Construction work on Y-12 began long before the Radiation Laboratory had finished designing the machines that would go inside it—or, for that matter, before they'd even proved the design would work at all. Groundbreaking for the Y-12 plant occurred on February 18, 1943.

Luis Alvarez: It was Ernest's idea to build a thousand enormous mass spectrometers, dubbed calutrons, to separate U-235 from U-238. The scale of his proposal led everyone to question his sanity at first, but with a series of increasingly large test devices he demonstrated that he was on the right track. Understanding that the 184-inch cyclotron could be converted to a large-scale calutron, everyone pitched in to complete construction ahead of schedule. The big magnet went up first and its building around it. When I visited the new laboratory on the hill in March 1943, I found all this activity amazing. My old love for magnets, vacuum plumbing, and cyclotron electronics was rekindled.

Christopher Keim, *project staff, Y-12 Plant*: The name calutron is a condensation of "cyclotron" and California, where the cyclotron was developed.

Brig. Gen. Leslie Groves: We would never have attempted it if it had not been for the great confidence that we, particularly Bush, Conant and I, had in the ability and drive of Dr. Ernest O. Lawrence of the University of California. Rather early in the American effort, Lawrence had proved to his own satisfaction that electromagnetic separation was feasible, but he stood almost alone in this optimism.

Col. Kenneth D. Nichols: Ernest Lawrence provided outstanding scientific leadership for the design, construction, and operation of the electromagnetics plant (Y-12). In my opinion, Lawrence probably was the most dynamic of all the physicists involved in producing the atomic bomb.

Brig. Gen. Leslie Groves: The method called for a large number of extremely complicated, and as yet undesigned and undeveloped, devices involving high vacuums, high voltages, and intense magnetic fields. As a large-scale method of separating Uranium-235, it seemed almost impossible. Dr. George T. Felbeck, who was in charge of the gaseous diffusion process for Union Carbide, once said it was like trying to find needles in a haystack while wearing boxing gloves.

Paul Elza: When these calutrons are set up, they're set up inside a huge magnet. These magnets are laid out in the shape of a racetrack—an elliptical shape. They are quite large. All of us who worked on it referred to them as racetracks. All of the units are operating to separate the Uranium-235—the fissionable isotope of Uranium that you want in order to get fission and get the weapon.

Brig. Gen. Leslie Groves: In every way, this process was one of the major efforts of the MED [Manhattan Engineer District]. Its purpose was to separate Uranium-235 from uranium as it occurs in nature and to do so in sufficient quantity, and of the concentration necessary, for use in atomic weapons. Basically, electromagnetic separation of isotopes is based on the principle that an ion describes a curved path as it passes through a magnetic field. If the magnetic field is of constant strength, the heavier ions will describe curves of longer radii. The various isotopes of an element, since they differ in mass, can be isolated and collected by such an arrangement.

Col. Kenneth D. Nichols: By the middle of March 1943, the scope of the Y-12 plant was determined. There would be five racetracks of ninety-six tanks each for the Alpha stage. Lawrence finally had acknowledged that a second—or Beta—stage would be needed. The Beta tanks were smaller, arranged in the form of a rectangle, with the plant consisting of two units of thirty-six tanks, two sources each. For the Beta plant, everything had to be more precise because this plant would be handling 10 to 36 percent U-235 enriched material as compared to only 0.7 percent U-235 material in the Alpha stage, and losses could not be tolerated.

Brig. Gen. Leslie Groves: The electromagnetic plant was built in a restricted area of about 825 acres in the central-south-eastern part of the reservation, approximately five miles from the commercial district of Oak Ridge, which was the town site of the overall development. From the standpoint of employment, this plant was the largest in the Clinton works.

Col. Kenneth D. Nichols: Lawrence toured the entire electromagnetics project in May 1943 and was amazed at the scope and magnitude of the effort. As a result of designing and building cyclotrons, Lawrence had far more experience with large equipment than most scientists. But even so, he had difficulty comprehending what was involved in building 552 calutrons and accompanying magnets and controls. However, his amazement at the progress increased his enthusiasm and his dedication to final success. Moreover, his enthusiasm permeated the entire project.

* * *

The enormous scale and material needs of the Y-12 plant proved especially challenging amid wartime shortages and the competing priorities for industrial manufacturing across the country and the war effort. One of the major early hurdles proved to be a shortage of copper for the wiring of the magnets, causing the Manhattan Engineer District to locate and source a creative alternative.

John Shacter: The gigantic scale of everything—you know, we had bicycles riding up and down the plant. [I was] impressed as heck.

Brig. Gen. Leslie Groves: Substances that had previously had very limited application were needed in staggering quantities. For example, each alpha track used four thousand gallons of liquid nitrogen every week.

Col. Kenneth D. Nichols: Copper was required for electric windings to form the large electromagnets. The pilot unit, originally planned for the Berkeley campus, would need 120 tons of copper, while the full-scale plant to be built in Tennessee would need five thousand tons or more of the metal. Copper was in desperately short supply because of the demands of the war industries.

Col. James C. Marshall: They said we can't have copper to build the magnets in the Y-12 Plant. I heard from somebody that you could use silver. I remember calling up on the phone to Gus Klein at Stone and Webster. I said, "Will you compare, over the phone, the conductive qualities of pure silver and pure copper and disregard the cost? What is the resistance, the electrical properties, and the thermal properties?" Then I could figure out with all the stages and all the magnets needed in that Y-12 Plant.

Col. Kenneth D. Nichols: For the electromagnetic process, silver could substitute at the ratio of eleven to ten.

Col. James C. Marshall: I then said to somebody, "Where can we get silver?" Somebody said, "Well how about getting all this stuff from [Treasury Secretary] Mr. [Henry] Morgenthau? He's got I don't know how many hundreds of millions of dollars' worth of silver up there at West Point."

Col. Kenneth D. Nichols: Since the government would own the plants and the silver could be returned after the war, we decided we should approach the U.S. Treasury to borrow the needed metal from the silver repository. As a result, I visited Assistant Secretary of the Treasury Daniel Bell. He explained the procedure for transferring the silver and asked, "How much do you need?" I replied, "Six thousand tons." "How many troy ounces is that?" he asked. In fact, I did not know how to convert tons to troy ounces, and neither did he. A little impatient, I responded, "I don't know how many troy ounces we need, but I know I need six thousand tons—that is a definite quantity. What difference does it make how we express the quantity?" He replied rather indignantly, "Young man, you may think of silver in tons, but the Treasury will always think of silver in troy ounces."

With our contrasting perspectives expressed, we then settled on a form of agreement that was ultimately used to transfer some 14,700 tons of silver from its storage place at West Point to New Jersey, where it was melted down and cast into large ingots for shipment to Allis-Chalmers in Milwaukee for further processing.

Brig. Gen. Leslie Groves: Under the terms of the final agreement, six months after the end of the war an equal amount of silver would be returned to the Treasury. It was further agreed that no information would be given to the press on the removal of the silver, and that the Treasury would continue to carry it on their daily balance sheets.

Col. Kenneth D. Nichols: Each month during the war, I signed an inventory for the Treasury stating that we had in our possession over four hundred million troy ounces of silver—expressed to hundredths of an ounce.

Col. James C. Marshall: Allis-Chalmers wound it on the magnets, and those magnets were big enough to require two long freight cars, and they were shipped to Oak Ridge. That was a major operation in itself.

Col. Kenneth D. Nichols: We established very strict procedures to avoid loss, and when the silver was returned to the Treasury after the war "less than one thirty-six-thousandth of 1 percent of the more than 14,700 tons of silver—was missing."

"Oh, the mud!"

OAK RIDGE: LIVING INSIDE THE GATES

Trailer parks and housing developments sprouted all over the hills around Oak Ridge.

The tens of thousands of newly arrived transplants found almost everything lacking in Oak Ridge—from entertainment to roads. Few of them—and even fewer of the local residents—understood exactly what was taking place inside the gates of the Clinton Engineer Works and even many plant workers wondered at the goal of the vast industrial processes around them. The only Manhattan Project facility located in the Jim Crow South, Oak Ridge was also the only site to encounter legal segregation against Black workers.

Col. Kenneth D. Nichols: From the spring of 1943 to the end of 1944, a tremendous construction effort ensued at all the Manhattan Project sites. At the CEW, the construction of the central facilities, family housing, schools, commercial facilities, dormitories, and barracks or hutments for construction workers became an ever-expanding program. For temporary housing, we rounded up every trailer we could locate from every part of the United States. A separate construction camp, which we hoped would live up to its name, Happy Valley, was located near the gaseous diffusion plant to lessen travel time for the seventeen thousand construction men working there.

James Reagan Justice, ***cafeteria manager, Clinton Engineer Works*****:** [The locals] hadn't the slightest idea [what was going on]. They'd see these trains loaded with something going in to Oak Ridge and nothing coming out. They couldn't figure it. They didn't have any manufacturing or anything over there. There wouldn't be anything coming out. That's the thing I heard, more than anything else: "What in the world could they be making when they weren't shipping anything out of there?"

Colleen Black, ***leak detector, K-25 Plant*****:** Everything came in and nothing came out.

Col. Kenneth D. Nichols: During the month of May we finished 1,288 family units, which brought the total to 7,041 residences, exclusive of 113 efficiency apartments. Eighteen dormitories were finished during the month. Every time we expanded the plants, we had to authorize more houses and town facilities of all kinds to provide for the welfare of the new influx of workers. We even built a jail, but then had to face the jurisdictional question of whether we had the authority to lock the door.

Charles E. Normand: One of the things that impressed me [upon arriving] was the size of the operation—a little bare, rocky hill had stacked crated bathtubs covering that whole hilltop, waiting to be put into houses, none of which were built yet. A whole hilltop covered with bathtubs stacked three layers deep was an impressive introduction to the place.

Col. Kenneth D. Nichols: Marshall argued for exception to the cost limits placed on expenditures for housing. Groves, however, expressed the belief that houses should be quite small and extremely simple in the interests of economy. In turn, Marshall argued that primitive housing could not be expected to meet family requirements of the class of personnel contemplated for the project and that comfortable and modern quarters would have to be provided, at least to the maximum extent that could be reached under the money limitations expected.

Col. James C. Marshall: For instance, I wanted to put a fireplace in every house we built in Oak Ridge. We started out I built 1,000. He said, "You're crazy, you don't need that many." Well then we had 3,000 going in a matter of two or three months, all on my say-so. All of the first 3,000 had fireplaces. Groves said, "That's silly, people like the pioneer experience." I said, "You can build Army barracks if you want to out in Los Alamos. I don't care what you build out in Richland. You can't have fireplaces there because there's no wood to burn in them." But I said, "At Oak Ridge, there is going to be a screened-in porch and there's going to be a fireplace in each house." I had the say-so for Oak Ridge.

Arthur Holly Compton: Our house at Oak Ridge was like three thousand others. It was across the road from a similar house occupied by Colonel Nichols, the commanding officer of the area. This little knoll where we lived accordingly became known as "Snob Knob." The widespread community spirit made the best of the difficulty of living in this construction area. When my wife and I arrived to occupy our just completed house, our car was filled with odds and ends. As we were sweeping the floors and clearing away the rubbish, across the road came a neighbor bearing a bucket and a broom. She introduced herself as Jackie Nichols. She was the wife of the commanding officer. What could she do to help put our house in order? A few weeks later President Conant came to Oak Ridge. As he stepped in the door of our house he exclaimed, "Why, Betty, you have made a home of this." "That's the idea, Jim," was her reply.

Karl Z. Morgan, *health physicist, University of Chicago*: I came to Oak Ridge in September of 1943, and my family joined me here a few months after that. I stayed at what was called the Guest House. It was just a big barn in those days and we slept in one big room that had about thirty cots.

John Michel, ***project staff, K-25 Plant*****:** When I first came down here, I went on shift work—rotating shift. So two thirds of the time I was trying to sleep when other people weren't there, but still a lot of noise around the dorm—thin walls and minimal structures.

Bonnie Hicks, ***chef*****:** There were these huge trailer parks here. This is something that the people in Knoxville didn't seem to realize at that time—some of the highest educated people in the world were living in trailers. That's all they had to live in. As far as my friends and relatives in Knoxville, they just didn't live in trailers. If you did, you were a very lower-class person as a rule.

Hetty Horton, ***teacher*****:** This was a segregated town when we came and they went by the Southern rules. [Black employees] had their own school. They didn't have a high school for a while. They use to have to take the bus and go to Knoxville.

Hal Williams, ***construction worker, K-25 Plant*****:** I would be working with a white fella all day beside him—well when quittin' time come, they went to their shack and I went to mine. That's a different world. We didn't even clock out on the same clock.

R. L. Ayers, ***cafeteria worker, K-25 Plant*****:** White people had barracks and dormitories, but Black people had huts to live in and that was it for the Black people. The huts were something like a box, made like a box. It had four beds in it. And if they needed more space they would put 8 beds in it, double beds. It had a big pot belly stove in the center of the floor and that was the heat. So we had no running water, no place to cook and no bathrooms in this place. They had a big long place, they called it the latrine. That's where you had to go to do your washing, do your cooking if you wanted to cook anything, take a bath and use the bathroom. If you were Black, even if you had a master's degree it made no difference. All you could do was sweep up, clean up. In '43, that's all that you could do. So, I wasn't making but $1.47 an hour, but it was better than where I came from. This place was owned and operated by the federal government and it was sad the way that the Black people were treated.

Hal Williams: They had a Skyway Theater for folks to drive in in their cars. It was a long time before a Black could drive his car there to it. He could come out there and sit up in the ground and listen to the movies—sure look at it—but he couldn't drive up there like the white did.

* * *

Col. Kenneth D. Nichols: We ultimately completed more than three hundred miles of paved roads throughout the reservation, including a four-lane highway down the center of the main valley connecting the town of Oak Ridge with the gaseous diffusion plant (K-25), within the town site, and branch roads to the electromagnetic plant (Y-12), the plutonium semiworks (X-10), and to each of the five security entrance gates. We also had to build a complete water purification plant and two sewage treatment plants. The electric distribution system, telephone, water, and sewage systems had to be expanded continually to meet the exploding population of Oak Ridge. The railroad connections to the L & N and the Southern Railroad were faced with hauling the millions of tons of supplies needed for the three plants, the central facilities, and the town.

Charles E. Normand: Things were moving very fast. No sidewalks, no pavement. The streets had had rock put on them. In fact they followed a general pattern. They would bulldoze the streets out, place crushed stone on them and then come along with a big de-ditching machine and dig a trench right down the middle to lay the water main and then it would all have to be done over again.

Karl Z. Morgan: One day I heard a plaintive call from a young lady who was ahead of us crossing the road, looked up, and she was stuck in the mud. At that time, they issued boots to everybody that worked at the Laboratory—women and men—and it was up to the top of her boots and she wasn't able to move. Some us got out to her and pulled her out, but her boots are still there. They're buried under the highway, I guess, today.

James Reagan Justice: Oh, the mud! I never saw so much mud as that in my life. That was the worst mud ever. And they had thousands and thousands of loads of gravel in there and it'd just sink out of sight.

Hetty Horton: Your shoes just got wrecked.

Karl Z. Morgan: Each of us had three or four pairs of shoes we would have to clean in the evening because of the mud and pick up the pair of shoes that had been worn the farthest back and then get on the bus and go to work.

Paul Elza: All back in the woods behind the houses there had been boardwalks built throughout the townsite, so that very few people used the roads when they were walking. They went everywhere they needed to go on the boardwalks.

James Reagan Justice: In Knoxville, they could tell an Oak Ridger by his shoes: he'd have mud all over them.

Ernest M. Lees, *maintenance worker*: I always felt that Knoxvillians resented all of us foreigners.

Karl Z. Morgan: Although many of us came from the South—I'm a Southerner—they thought all of us were Yankees.

Paul Elza: With this enormous influx of population, there were shortages of anything and everything—not only was it wartime, but here was a concentration of one of the biggest activities going on, and in a small area, and in an area that was not heavily populated there to fore. Accordingly, everything was short. You never could find enough of anything. The people outside tended to blame that on Oak Ridge. The schools were all over crowded. The movie theatres were over crowded. The places to eat were over crowded and it was always them damned Oak Ridgers that were creating the clutter and the bother.

Col. Kenneth D. Nichols: We decided that the district should not try to staff and manage all the required facilities in the town. Consequently, we contracted with Turner Construction Company to take on town management and operations. George Horr, a vice president of Turner, had been the project manager for construction of the Rome Air Depot, so Marshall and I were well acquainted with both him and the company.

Turner organized a special company called Roane-Anderson—named for the two counties involved in the CEW site. They organized and operated the bus lines, garbage collection, the school system, the hospital, management of all the housing, the hotel, the fire department, central eating facilities, and practically everything else pertaining to town operation, including delivering coal to individual houses.

James Reagan Justice: We brought meat by the car load, we brought produce by the truck load and we brought potatoes by the car load. At that time there was 700 employees in the cafeteria alone.

Charles E. Normand: One wing of the cafeteria was a recreation room where we would meet and play ping pong. One of the big events for about once a week, they would get in a shipment of beer. It would come to the cafeteria, and after dinner, the group from the recreation room would be served beer.

Col. Kenneth D. Nichols: The school system posed a special problem. The school population increased every day. Additional teachers and school buildings had to be made available as needed for children arriving at Oak Ridge from all parts of the United States and all having different backgrounds and educational needs.

Hetty Horton: The first newspaper that the school put out only put the first names of the children. They couldn't use any last names because some were famous scientists' children.

Paul Elza: I suppose most people here had 98 percent of their existence inside the gates.

Leta Orrison, *project spouse*: People were so hungry for friendship. Everybody was a stranger. So you may have met your best friend sitting at the bus stop.

Mary Michel, *teletypist, K-25 Plant*: Security was pretty strict. I know that I belonged to a group for a while, that called themselves the St. Stephens Episcopal Choir, but we always had great parties afterward and one of the guys started talking too much. The people kept saying, "Oh, this guy is going to say the wrong things sometime to the wrong person," and sure enough one day he vanished. I never knew what happened to him. He was definitely removed. I often wondered what happened to him.

Ernest M. Lees: I was amused on some occasions how well some of us were oriented on security. We'd get to talking with someone, "Well, where do you work?" "Clinton Engineer Works." "Yeah, I know Oak Ridge, but where? Who do you work for out there?" "Clinton Engineer Works." They couldn't even tell us Stone and Webster, or whoever the other companies—they wouldn't say, just "Clinton Engineer Works."

Paul Elza: It was always taken for granted that no one was from here. One evening at a gathering, one of these dowager types from Cambridge, Massachusetts came up to me and said, "Mr. Elza, where are you from?" I said, "Well ma'am I'm from right here." She said, "You mean you were born here?" I said, "Yes ma'am." And she said, "and you grew up here?" And I said, "yes ma'am, right here." And she turned to her husband across the room and she says, "oh dear come here—they're training some of the natives to work on the project!" It was a thing of surprise if you found someone that happened to be born and grew up right here.

Col. Kenneth D. Nichols: For all town problems, the residents were advised to call Roane-Anderson. I really caught hell one day when Jackie phoned my office. Miss Olsson told me that Mrs. Nichols was stuck in the mud and wanted to know what to do about it. Busy with a problem, I adhered to my own orders and simply said, "Tell her to call Roane-Anderson, like everyone else has to do." That was the last I heard about it until I returned home for dinner. Then I heard plenty.

"The drive to get this work done"

OAK RIDGE: MAKING U-235

The "racetrack" calutrons were the centerpiece of Oak Ridge's uranium efforts.

By November 1943, the Y-12 plant was starting to show real progress, but gremlins in the production process bedeviled engineers for months. Although by February 1944 the plant had refined enough uranium to deliver some samples to Los Alamos, ultimately, in July 1944, Lawrence and Groves decided to completely redesign the complex "racetracks" that refined the uranium to fix numerous problems and speed production.

Col. Kenneth D. Nichols: Work on the plants themselves provided an ongoing challenge. Construction of the electromagnetic plant generated unexpected and difficult problems. The first alpha building with the equipment for the first racetrack was completed and placed in operation on November 13, 1943, my thirty-sixth birthday. However, as a birthday present it proved to be a real dud, as its operation ran into difficulties immediately. Operators could not sustain a beam in the calutrons. Vacuum could not be maintained because of leaks. However, the worst problem was that the magnets shorted out, causing us to stop operations completely to locate the cause. Groves was at his best or worst, depending on one's point of view, in pinning down the cause of the trouble. He was extremely disturbed about the situation, and his caustic comments and persistent inquiries irritated practically everyone. Even Ernest Lawrence received some sarcastic comments when he recalled that he had experienced a similar problem with his cyclotron. The stress, long hours of work, frequent meetings, major but honest differences of opinion, and flaring tempers generated hard feelings.

Graydon Whitman, ***mechanical engineer, Y-12 Plant, Special Engineer Detachment*****:** They had had a lot of trouble with their start-up. I was assigned to 9201-2, an Alpha Building, in Major Repair. There was a shortage of people who knew a screwdriver from a pair of pliers. There were a lot of tough problems they were having.

Brig. Gen. Leslie Groves: One difficulty, which was unforeseen, because we lacked experience with magnets of such enormous power, was that the magnetic forces moved the intervening tanks, which weighed some fourteen tons each, out of position by as much as three inches. This put a great strain on all the piping connected to them. The problem was solved by securely welding the tanks into place using heavy steel tie straps. Once that was done, the tanks stayed where they belonged.

Arthur Holly Compton: Runs were made testing the chemical extraction process. Each test worked more successfully than the one before.

Graydon Whitman: At the end of thirty days of normal operation, a calutron was taken down and the U-235 recovered from the pockets. The thing was sent to a wash area where it was washed in dilute nitric acid, everything cleaned up, and all the parts brought back, and then reassembled. It's complicated. There was just a continuous line of calutrons to reassemble; it was like a production line. The drive to get this work done—I've never seen anything like it.

Col. Kenneth D. Nichols: There was considerable question concerning operators. Would it take hundreds or even thousands of Ph.D.s to operate the plant?

Connie Bolling, ***staff supervisor, Y-12 Plant*:** They sent some of us to Livermore, California, to learn from E. O. Lawrence, who built the first calutron. They didn't tell us where we were going, and Oak Ridge wasn't named. We didn't know any of the scientists that were training us—they didn't even have name cards, and there wasn't any writing down of anything. They trained us, and then we came back to the Y-12 plant. We had to teach for a whole year the operators how to work those calutron machines, and for one whole year that is all I did.

Col. Kenneth D. Nichols: Tennessee Eastman started plans for training personnel and decided not to use Ph.D.s to operate the control units. Instead, they planned to use girls from Tennessee having only a high-school education or less. In Berkeley, many of the scientists were skeptical about this decision.

Louise Keaton, ***control panel operator, Y-12 Plant*:** I graduated high school and then went to Oak Ridge to work. I just went directly to work. We called calutrons "cubicles." I was a cubicle operator. They were big on each side of a long aisle.

Marjorie Walls, ***control panel operator, Y-12 Plant*:** They had a row of calutrons that way and a row back this way. We were busy watching numbers on those things. We had to keep a certain ratio in order to get a better grade of separation of uranium. At first I looked at those and I thought, "I'll never be able to keep up with this." But you do.

Louise Keaton: I operated four—two on each aisle. I remember my badge number: 18157. When we went to work, we changed clothes into a blue uniform. Then, when we came out, we left that uniform and it was laundered and ready for us for the next shift. It was fun. The cubicles sometimes would have flurries—what we called flurries—and you had to keep operating and adjusting knobs so that you could make good readings. If they got out of control, when they could get into flurries, we operated a knob between them and got them back and they would make terrible noises. In the back of each one of the cubicles or calutrons, there was a small window and we were told never to look in that window.

Col. Kenneth D. Nichols: Tennessee Eastman's proposal to train operators with only a high-school education was working remarkably well. As each new unit was turned over to Tennessee Eastman by Stone and Webster, Ernest Lawrence, with a team of scientists from Berkeley, took over operations to eliminate the bugs in the unit. When they achieved a reasonable operating rate, they transferred the unit to Tennessee Eastman. As a result of my comparing production data for the various units, I pointed out to Lawrence that the young "hillbilly" girl operators were outproducing his scientists. He claimed that this was because his men were experimenting on ways to improve operations. Thereupon I challenged him to make a production race between his Ph.Ds and the young local girls. He agreed and he lost. The girls won because they were trained like soldiers "to do or not to do—not to reason why." In contrast, the scientists could not refrain from time-consuming investigation of the cause of even minor fluctuations of the dials. This little contest provided a big boost in morale for the Tennessee Eastman workers and supervisors.

Marjorie Walls: Most of the operators were women—the young men were gone.

Col. Kenneth D. Nichols: We had difficulty finding sufficient technical talent. Fortunately, we seized the opportunity to select qualified men to form a Special Engineer Detachment (SED). The largest SED units were at the CEW and Los Alamos. At a Military Policy Committee meeting with James C. White, president of Tennessee Eastman, about the difficulties of finding sufficient operators, White commented on how helpful the Army had been. He turned to Admiral Purnell and asked, "What can the Navy do to help us?" In response, Purnell arranged for about sixty young commissioned officers with technical education to be assigned to the MED. They would be assigned to a separate dormitory they called "Good Ship Never Sink."

* * *

The other major effort at Oak Ridge to refine uranium was known as the "K-25" plant, a name derived from the plant's contractor, the Kellex Corporation, and

Uranium-235, which is often shortened in scientific speak to just "25." It relied on what was known as the "gaseous diffusion method" to separate U-235 from U-238, a process that had been the primary recommendation of the British scientists working alongside the M.A.U.D. Committee and the Tube Alloys project as early as 1941. That work had been expanded upon by Columbia University's John R. Dunning and others who designed a process to turn uranium metal into uranium hexafluoride gas that would be pumped through a barrier filled with tiny, microscopic holes. Like Y-12, work began on K-25 long before scientists at Union Carbide, Kellex, and other labs had even figured out how to make such a porous barrier. The finished plant was housed in a mile-long, U-shaped building—the largest roofed building in the world at that time.

Hubert Barnett, *maintenance supervisor, K-25 Plant*: Columbia University did the theoretical design of the plant—there had never been a diffusion plant before. I spent all my time working with Kellex on getting information, getting the proper drawings that we needed to train our people, because not only did we have to get qualified people but we had to train them in maintenance activities that they've never been exposed to before. It was all special.

Mike Linden: I was actually working in Philadelphia for the General Electric Company when the war manpower commission said, "Get your tail to New York on Monday morning." Arrived in New York and went to work for the Kellex Company at Columbia University at the Nash Building doing vacuum testing. From there, the entire group eventually, except for a few of us, moved to Oak Ridge with Union Carbide.

Brig. Gen. Leslie Groves: The gaseous diffusion method was completely novel. It was based on the theory that if uranium gas was pumped against a porous barrier, the lighter molecules of the gas, containing U-235, would pass through more rapidly than the heavier U-238 molecules. The heart of the process was the barrier—a porous thin metal sheet or membrane with millions of sub-microscopic openings per square inch. These sheets were formed into tubes which were enclosed in an airtight vessel, the diffuser. As the gas, uranium hexafluoride, was pumped through a long series, or cascade, of these tubes it tended to separate, the enriched gas moving up the cascade while the depleted gas moved down. However, there is so little difference in mass between the hexafluorides of U-238 and U-235 that it was impossible to gain much separation in a single diffusion step.

Donald Trauger, *Columbia University physicist, K-25 Plant*: To make weapons grade material we required many stages, many repetitions of the gas passing through barriers and a little bit of separation with each pass.

Brig. Gen. Leslie Groves: This was why there had to be several thousand successive stages.

Donald Trauger: The barrier was tiny pieces that were an inch—an inch square was a fairly large piece at that time, but they envisioned that for a plant of K-25's size would require a large area of barrier, in many little pieces that somehow fit together, that you could measure it in acres. To go from these little pieces that were an inch square, about as large as they would make at the time, was a daunting undertaking.

Brig. Gen. Leslie Groves: The basic piece of equipment was the isotope separation column, 102 of which were arranged to form an operating unit which we termed a "rack." The column was a vertical pipe, forty-eight feet long, of nickel pipe surrounded by a copper pipe. The copper pipe was encased in a water jacket contained in a four-inch galvanized-iron pipe. The copper pipe was cooled with water at a moderate temperature. The columns were arranged in three groups, each of seven racks, making a total of 2,142 columns.

Mike Linden: The entire system at K-25's success depended on being leak-tight so far as possible. The helium mass spectrometer was the tool at the University of Minnesota that we used in doing our vacuum testing.

Brig. Gen. Leslie Groves: At first the operation was not too satisfactory. We were badly handicapped by the complete lack of pilot plant experience, the lack of trained people and, as it turned out, by an insufficient supply of steam. We were also plagued by leaks of the process material and by high-pressure steam leaks.

Colleen Black: My father worked for Midwest Pipe and we were in the same building. It was huge, and the pipes would come down and would go on the

1

Lise Meitner and Otto Hahn were key to unlocking nuclear fission.

2

Werner Heisenberg and Niels Bohr.

3

Robert Oppenheimer, Glenn Seaborg, and Ernest Lawrence.

4

Lawrence's team pose beneath the magnet for their giant cyclotron; Oppenheimer is standing in the middle of the back row.

5

The Berkeley Rad Lab cyclotron became the model for Oak Ridge.

6

Students at the Los Alamos Ranch School pose outside the house that during the war would become the Oppenheimers' home.

7

The Chicago Met Lab who built CP-1. *Back row, from left*: Norman Hilberry, Samuel Allison, Thomas Brill, Robert Nobles, Warren Nyer, and Marvin Wilkening; *middle row, from left*: Harold Agnew, William Sturm, Harold Lichtenberger, Leona Woods, and Leo Szilard; *front row, from left*: Enrico Fermi, Walter Zinn, Albert Wattenberg, and Herbert L. Anderson.

8

Sending money home on payday in Hanford.

9

Swing dancing at Oak Ridge.

10

A Women's Army Corps (WAC) unit marches at Oak Ridge.

11

Arthur Holly Compton's badge at Hanford used a pseudonym for security.

Meals at Los Alamos Fuller Lodge were always lively.

12

13

Reminders to keep the project work secret were everywhere.

A selection of security badge photos from Los Alamos. **(14–31)**

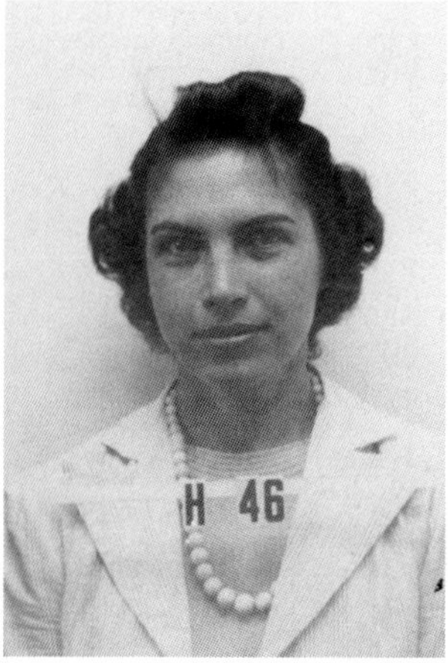

Mary Argo

Kenneth T. Bainbridge

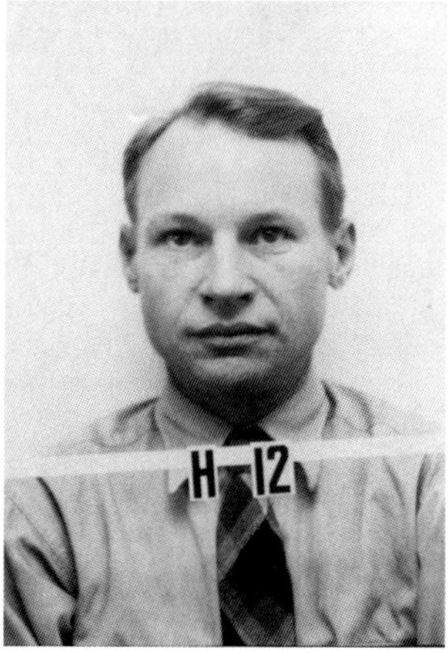

Berlyn Brixner

Richard P. Feynman

Klaus Fuchs

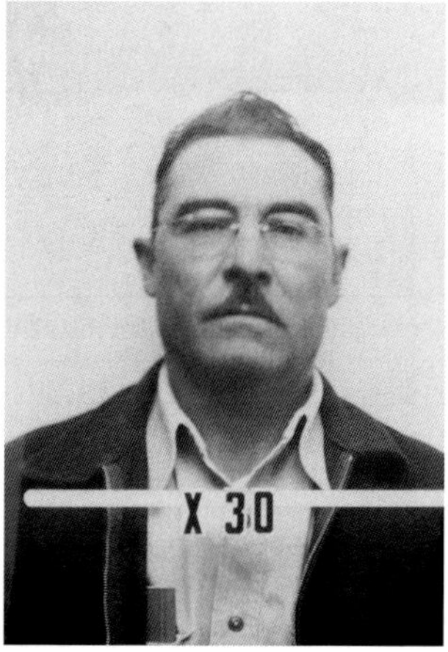

J. J. Gutierrez

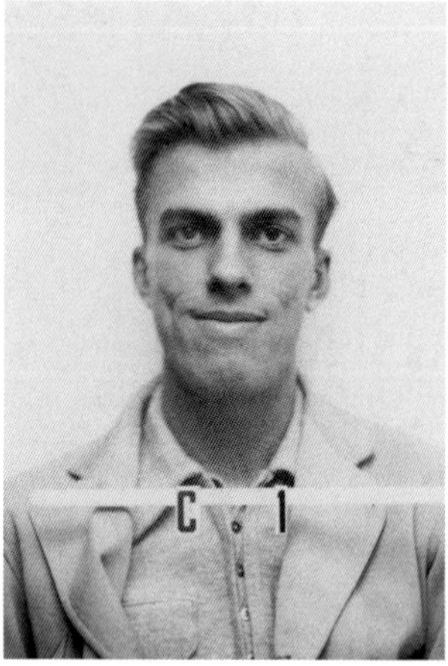

Louis Hempelmann

George B. Kistiakowsky

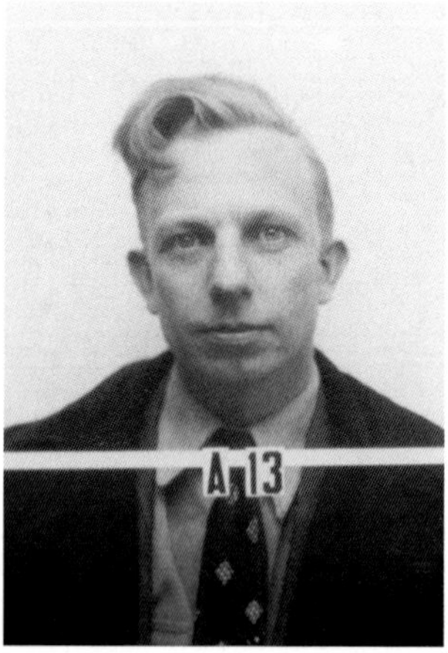

John H. Manley

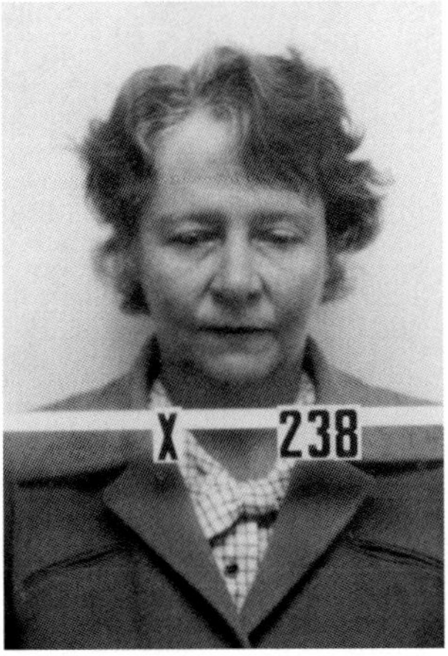

Dorothy McKibbin

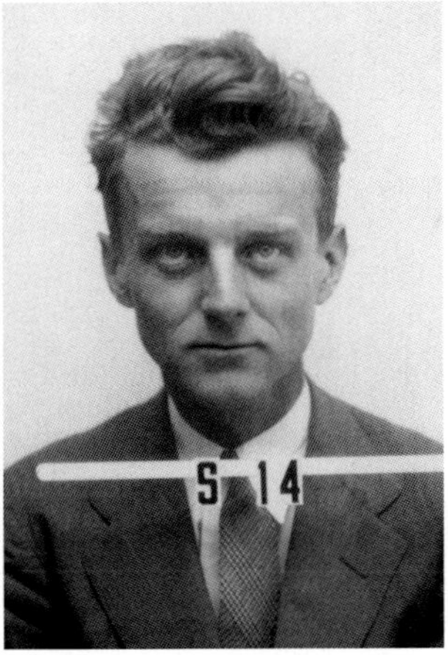

S. H. Neddermeyer

Paul Numerof

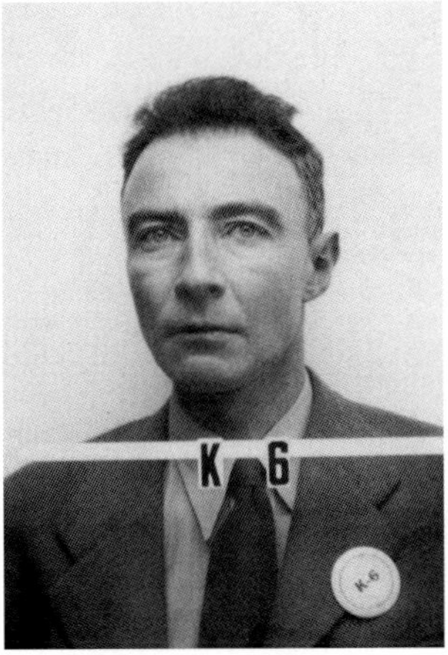

J. Robert Oppenheimer

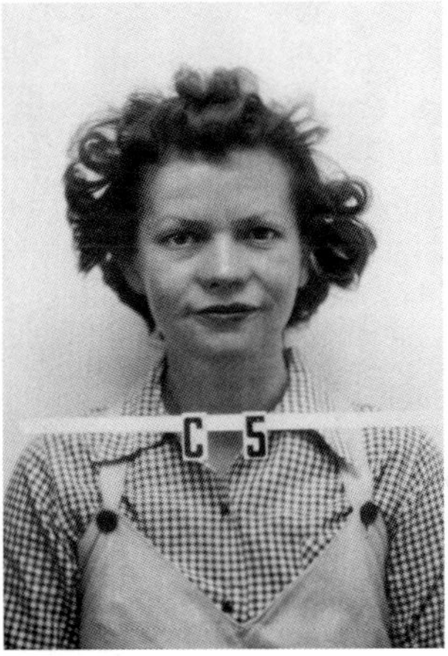

Katherine Oppenheimer

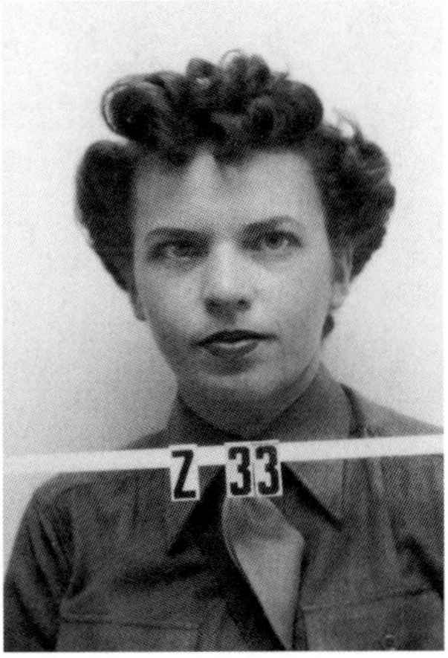

Eleanor Stone Roensch

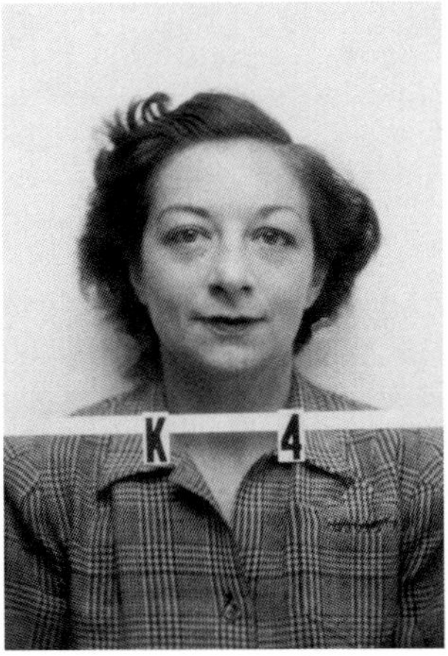

Charlotte Serber

Stanislaw Ulam

John von Neumann

32

Curtis LeMay, *center*, adopted new firebombing tactics when he arrived to lead the B-29 air war against Japan in the spring of 1945.

33

A single March raid killed 100,000 residents of Tokyo.

machines and our [mass spectrometer] machine would take all this air out of them and then we would try to find where the leak was. We'd mark the pipe with glyptal [paint] and they would take it back and fix the leak.

Brig. Gen. Leslie Groves: By October it was evident that too much steam was leaking out at the screwed unions at the bottom and top of the columns. We decided, therefore, to replace all of them with new welded connections. By January, all the twenty-one racks were again ready except for a few small piping changes found to be necessary on the basis of our operating experience.

Colleen Black: I had no idea what was going in the pipes. They were great big pipes, little bitty pipes.

Hubert Barnett: I would say that we had 7,000 employees in the plant when the war ended. I'd say not over fifty people knew what the hell was going on.

Brig. Gen. Leslie Groves: It was not until January, 1945, that these difficulties were entirely ironed out. Peak production was reached the following June.

William Wilcox, *chemist, Y-12 Plant*: K-25 was so much more efficient—less than 10 percent of the cost of what it was costing at Y-12.

* * *

Late in 1944, engineers rushed to build a third plant—S-50—that focused on another uranium refinement process known as thermal diffusion, developed by Philip Abelson. It became fully operational in March 1945, helping to feed slightly more refined uranium into the Y-12 calutrons and speed up the refinement process there. Ultimately, it sped up uranium production by about a week.

Brig. Gen. Leslie Groves: If I had appreciated the possibilities of thermal diffusion, we would have gone ahead with it much sooner, taken a bit more time on the design of the plant and made it much bigger and better. Its effect on our production of U-235 in June and July, 1945, would have been appreciable. Whether it would have ended the war sooner, I do not know.

"His eyes had that special intensity"

LOS ALAMOS: PROJECT Y

Many of the nation's top scientists disappeared into the hidden mesa of Los Alamos.

Even with the construction of vast production facilities and factories underway, scientists were only beginning in 1943 to design the bomb itself. That would be the task of the team Oppenheimer assembled on a remote mesa in New Mexico, part of the ultimately 54,000-acre site, purchased by the government for about $440,000, known colloquially as Los Alamos. It would be a task, like many on the Manhattan Project, far larger and more complex than first imagined.

J. Robert Oppenheimer: The last months of 1942 and early 1943 had hardly hours enough to get Los Alamos established.

Brig. Gen. Leslie Groves: The task for which Project Y, as the bomb development was called, was brought into being was without precedent. It would require the utmost in collaboration among civilian engineers, metallurgists, chemists and physicists, as well as military officers, some of whom would have to use the final weapons in combat. Many of the most difficult problems encountered at Los Alamos could not even be anticipated until work was well under way throughout the entire project. For this reason, scheduling at the Y site was both definite and indefinite. The bomb had to be ready as soon as sufficient quantities of atomic explosives were available, yet no one could say when this would be.

J. Robert Oppenheimer: Even though we then underestimated the ultimate size of the laboratory, which was to have almost 4,000 members by the spring of 1945, and even though we did not at that time see clearly some of the difficulties which were to bedevil and threaten the enterprise, we knew that it was a big, complex and diverse job. Even the initial plan of the laboratory called for a start with more than 100 highly qualified and trained scientists, to say nothing of the technicians, staff, and mechanics who would be required for their support, and of the equipment that we would have to beg and borrow since there would be no time to build it from scratch.

Brig. Gen. Leslie Groves: The big problem in getting good people arose from the fact that the scientific resources of the country, particularly in this general area, were already fully engaged on important war work.

J. Robert Oppenheimer: The primary burden of this fell on me. To recruit staff I traveled all over the country talking with people who had been working on one or another aspect of the atomic-energy enterprise, and people in radar work, for example, and underwater sound, telling them about the job, the place that we were going to, and enlisting their enthusiasm.

Arthur Holly Compton: Oppie drew to Los Alamos a group of exceedingly able and resourceful men. From Princeton, the University of California, the University of Chicago, the University of Minnesota, the University of Wisconsin, and many other institutions they rallied to join him.

Robert R. Wilson, ***physicist, Princeton University*****:** "My God," I exclaimed to my wife as I hung up the phone, "Robert Oppenheimer is coming to visit." We were then in Princeton where I had been working at the university on a project to separate the rare bomb-making isotope of uranium. Oppy explained that he had been chosen to head up a new laboratory in the west, the purpose of which was to work out just how to assemble a nuclear bomb out of the fissionable material that would, as we then believed, be available in another year. Oppy asked me to join his new laboratory. I agreed on the spot. Then he suggested that we go on to convince my colleagues to come as well. To a man, almost, they did.

Bernice Brode, ***project spouse of physicist Robert Brode*****:** It was wartime Washington early in March of 1943 when our friend J. Robert Oppenheimer came to see us in our chilly living room. Heat was rationed, and our rented house in Chevy Chase was cheerless and damp. But Oppie did not notice. I could see he was burning with an inner fire as he told us about his new war project, to be situated in the desert of New Mexico. I remembered how he once had said that his two loves—physics and desert country—never existed together. Had he joined them at last? He was vague about everything, but his eyes had that special intensity, peculiar to him, when he said to me, "I think you will like that life up there, Bernice. It will be quite nice, even in wartime." He made it seem like high adventure rather than patriotic duty, and I felt it was not to be missed.

Edward Teller: During the winter, Oppie had asked me to help him with recruitment. As part of that task, I wrote a description for a prospectus without having seen the laboratory grounds; I mentioned among other things that the school was built around "a small lake." When I arrived, I came face to face with that body of water: It was and is, in the best of times, a pond. Fortunately, those whom I unintentionally led astray preferred teasing me to being angry.

Brig. Gen. Leslie Groves: One other major handicap was that we could not hold out any financial inducement to the people we wanted. It had been decided, after consultation with the Military Policy Committee, that, in keeping with the general policies of the OSRD [Office of Scientific Research and Development], we should not offer any increase in pay to people recruited for the Manhattan Project. However, academic personnel who had formerly been paid on the basis of a nine-months work year were given increases whereby they were paid for the full twelve months of work, at the original monthly rate.

Col. Kenneth D. Nichols: Dr. Conant had suggested that in view of the secrecy and the military nature of the work, we commission the scientists as officers in the Corps of Engineers and operate Los Alamos as a military laboratory. Oppenheimer was amenable to this type of organization, and he actually took initial steps toward becoming a commissioned officer.

J. Robert Oppenheimer: For a time there was support for making it a military establishment, in which key personnel would be commissioned as officers; and in preparation for this course I once went to the Presidio to take the initial steps toward obtaining a commission.

Col. Kenneth D. Nichols: Oppenheimer ran into difficulties with the military concept when he tried to recruit Robert F. Bacher and Isidor I. Rabi. They both refused to accept commissions.

Robert R. Wilson: Rabi and Bacher—and perhaps others—managed to talk Oppy out of his determination to have everyone in the new lab inducted into the army. Before that, as Oppy and I had traveled about the country on various missions connected with the Los Alamos project, we had argued fiercely about his suggestion of our becoming soldiers in uniform. I argued the impracticality of scientists taking arbitrary orders from above—all the orders from above that I had seen for the past year had seemed a bit nonsensical. Nor are scientists at their best in unquestioningly following orders. I wondered if we could function at all in those circumstances.

Luis Alvarez: It wouldn't have worked. Bob Wilson and Joe Kennedy, for example, who were under thirty but led the experimental nuclear-physics and chemistry divisions, would have been unable to argue with more senior but less knowledgeable officers. I don't think science can be done under authoritarian arrangements. Young people very often know better than their elders.

J. Robert Oppenheimer: We had a long hassle about that. In a letter which reached me early in 1943, signed by Groves and Conant, it was agreed that initially the workers in the laboratory would be civilians. It was contemplated that later at the more critical phases the key people would be commissioned. That plan was dropped, essentially because the numbers got so big and there was no need for it, and it became impractical.

* * *

Lt. Col. John H. Dudley: We set up an office in Santa Fe on the fourth of January, 1943. A few days later we set up an office for Oppenheimer in another building. The initial construction contract looked like $300,000. Within a year that first contract had gone to $7.5 million, a 25-fold increase. And it was only the first contract; there were many others because there were major difficulties in the construction and major expansions.

Brig. Gen. Leslie Groves: From the beginning, the procurement of equipment and materials was difficult, not only because our needs were unusual but because some all-important equipment could be obtained only by negotiation or borrowing from universities.

Hugh T. Richards, *physicist, Rice University*: The Manhattan Project requisitioned most of our lab equipment and tools. An army inspector came to sign for and supervise the packing. He was of course completely baffled by most of the items and could only write down what we told him, but when it came to small hand tools, he beamed and insisted on more details, e.g. pliers had to be identified as slip-joint gas pliers!

J. Robert Oppenheimer: It took from perhaps October or November 1942 until March of 1943 to get the rudiments of a laboratory. We stole a cyclotron from Harvard, some [Van de Graaff] accelerators from Wisconsin.

Edwin McMillan: Los Alamos had to get equipment, nuclear equipment, and I went to several laboratories that had cyclotrons of the right size, and the one that was best suited, in the best condition, portable, or as close to portable as a cyclotron gets, was the Harvard cyclotron. On my recommendation it was taken, and for many years after that some people at Harvard were very angry with me. Of course, in the meantime, construction was going on, housing, laboratories and so on. Oppenheimer and his immediate staff arrived on March 15, 1943, so from the middle of March perhaps 20 research people were there. I followed very shortly after that, Mrs. McMillan came on April 1, and from then on the laboratory grew rapidly.*

Leona H. Woods: All the equipment—the cyclotrons, the Van de Graaff, the betatron, the machine-shop equipment, and construction material—had to travel up the original amusement park ascent to the mesa. Surprisingly, little of it fell over the edge. A dramatic story was that Sam Allison, who had driven to Santa Fe with everyone's ration coupons to buy liquor, was washed into the drain that comes through Espanola by a flash flood on his way back. Sam and the liquor were rescued safely, but the car suffered a few dents.

Stanislaw Ulam: I received an official invitation to join an unidentified project that was doing important work, the physics having something to do with the interior of stars. The letter inviting me was signed by the famous physicist Hans Bethe. A student of mine, Joan Hinton, had left for an unknown destination a few weeks before. Soon after, other people I knew well began to vanish one after the other, without saying where—cafeteria acquaintances, young physics professors and graduate students like David Frisch, and his wife Rose, who was a graduate student in my calculus class, Joseph McKibben, Dick Taschek, and others.

Finally I learned that we were going to New Mexico, to a place not far from Santa Fe. Never having heard about New Mexico, I went to the library and borrowed the Federal Writers' Project Guide to New Mexico. At the back of the book, on the slip of paper on which borrowers signed their names, I read the names of Joan Hinton, David Frisch, Joseph McKibben, and all the other people who had been mysteriously disappearing to hushhush war jobs without saying where.

* McMillan was an early pioneer of the Berkeley Rad Lab with Lawrence, where he is credited with discovering Beryllium-10. Even before the US entered World War II, he'd decamped to MIT to work on the secret effort to develop radar before ultimately joining the Manhattan Project. He and Glenn Seaborg shared the 1951 Nobel Prize in Chemistry for their discoveries of Beryllium-10 and plutonium.

Ens. Donald F. Mastick, *US Naval Reserve*: I traveled to Los Alamos in early 1943 under rigorous security, being the second technical person in residence there. Those were very active times; the pressure to move ahead was intense and exhilarating.

Robert Bacher: Nobody was supposed to know where we were going. I just disappeared into thin air.

* * *

Dorothy McKibbin, *director, Los Alamos Lab project office, Santa Fe*: 109 East Palace was the Los Alamos Santa Fe office which served as a reception desk, information center, and travel bureau. Scientists arrived there breathless, sleepless, and haggard, tired from riding on trains that were slow and crowded. Often the traveler arrived days after he had been expected and settled down with a sigh into a chair at 109 East Palace as if he could never move again.

Most of the new arrivals were tense with expectancy and curiosity. They had left physics, chemistry, and metallurgical laboratories, had sold their homes or rented them, had deceived their friends, and then had launched forth into an unpredictable world. They walked into the thick-walled quietness of the old Spanish dwelling at 109 East Palace expecting anything and everything, the best and the worst. The scientists often arrived in a frantic hurry. One dashed in hatless and breathless after a hectic rush from Johns Hopkins University and panted in dismay, "What, no ride up for an hour and a half? Why, I cut short a seminar in order to get here now!"

John H. Manley: In April of 1943, people started coming into Santa Fe, reporting to Dotty McKibbin at 109 East Palace, asking for further instructions: where do they go from there? She'd tell them how to cover the last leg, which was that 35-mile trip. I had to stay a few days when I arrived in Santa Fe just about April Fool's Day in order to get the accelerator from Illinois unpacked. It was in the freight yard, in a boxcar and I had to make arrangements to get it on a truck and up to Los Alamos. I remember it was April fourth when I drove off with a man and his truck, and the accelerator in the back end of the truck, to my unseen destination of Los Alamos. I was quite concerned most of that 35-mile drive for the cargo in the back of the truck. It was a steep old country gravel road full of turns and sharp bends as it climbed the last 12 miles from the Rio Grande crossing at 5,500 feet above sea level to the 7,200-foot altitude of Los Alamos. We managed to make it and pulled up in the laboratory area.

L. D. P. King, *physicist, Water Boiler Reactor Team*: The first ride to the hill was memorable. Wandering through the several little Spanish villages past San Ildefonso Pueblo and then climbing an incredible series of switchbacks to get to the top of Los Alamos Mesa, all on a rough gravel road, is not easily forgotten.

Charlotte Serber, *project spouse*: When the first hundred or so scientists and their wives arrived, they met endless unexpected situations and hardships. Everything was makeshift. Los Alamos was in no way ready to receive them. The housing had not been completed. The fence around the Post was half-finished. The Tech Area was an empty shell without power, gas, telephone, furniture, or equipment, and it was separated from the Post proper only by fence posts.

J. Robert Oppenheimer: We started out the job with a large meeting—this would have been April 1943—that I called, all the people there and a number of others whom I hoped to lure there, and many of whom were in fact later to come, to discuss the technical.

L. D. P. King: Oppenheimer's first step following the creation of Project Y was to hold a series of conferences at Los Alamos on April 15–24, 1943. These meetings were to brief the initial staff on the present state of knowledge and chart a course for theoretical and experimental work at Los Alamos.

John H. Manley: If there were any ground-breaking ceremonies at Los Alamos like champagne or cutting ribbons, I was unaware of them. Most of us who were there felt that the conference in April, 1943, was really the ground-breaking ceremony.

Emilio Segrè: Oppenheimer had invited some thirty scientists to the gathering, including the future leaders of the project and consultants like Fermi and Rabi.

In the conference's five sessions, Robert Serber systematically described all that was known concerning a possible bomb. Serber's lectures were followed by discussion of what to do, as well as by animated debates on the laboratory's organization.

John H. Manley: There were long discussions of all problems which could be foreseen and decisions on assignment of responsibilities.

Robert Bacher: It was mostly devoted to elaborating the unknown physics information that was needed for knowing whether an atomic bomb would work or not. There were fundamental things where the information just wasn't known. For example, nobody knew how fast the neutrons came out; some of them were known to be delayed. But even the ones that came quite promptly—you could say, "Well, they probably come right away." But they had to get out of there in a time like 10^8 seconds—that's a hundredth of a millionth of a second—and nobody had any idea of whether that was it at all. Any measurements made up to that time only went down to about a hundredth of a second.

Edward U. Condon, ***notes on opening lecture by Robert Serber, Los Alamos, April 1943*****:** The object of the project is to produce a practical military weapon in the form of a bomb in which the energy is released by a fast neutron chain reaction in one or more materials known to show nuclear fission.

Victor Weisskopf: Not much more was known than the fundamental ideas of a chain reaction.

J. Robert Oppenheimer: My directive was to lose no day in preparing an atomic bomb. The definition of an atomic bomb was that it should be at least equal to 1,000 tons of TNT in explosive force. This sense of pressure started at the beginning and never let up.

Charlotte Serber: Everyone was put to work, usually at unfamiliar jobs such as rigging, teamstering, chauffeuring, and clerking. I had been hired on the Project as the Scientific Librarian, but since no books or reports had arrived yet, I also did another job. For the first month or two, I worked in the Director's Office, helping Priscilla Greene, the Executive Secretary.

John H. Manley: It is hard to re-create the atmosphere of those days. Let me try with an illustration. Just before Los Alamos really got going, the last measurements on how much Uranium-235 might be needed for a weapon had increased over the previous low estimate by almost a factor of two; it was about five kilograms in absolute amounts. These five kilograms meant nearly two months extra production for each weapon. Maybe, if we were really clever and got an extremely good material that could reflect back neutrons and behave properly, we could get back most of that factor of two that we had just lost. We were playing that kind of a game almost continually. You get experimental results which say things are worse than expected. Then you try to be smart and get some better material or a new device or do things another way.

J. Robert Oppenheimer: We were building a town at the same time that we were building the laboratory.

Robert R. Wilson: We were small enough in numbers to be put up at Fuller Lodge, the elegant central log-building of the Los Alamos school. There the grocer, the plumber, the school master were also housed. There we all took our meals under the baleful eye of the spinster dietician of the school, who was now watching in stern disapproval our food habits, our conversation, our moral convictions, our politics—we failed on all counts. Since then, I have also had occasions to try to set up an eating facility and am more sympathetic. At the time, the possibility that she was a Nazi agent trying to starve us to death did not seem all that far-fetched.

Emilio Segrè: Fermi, Rossi, I, and perhaps some other Italian-speaking physicist, were lunching one day during this period at Fuller Lodge, and as usual, we slipped into Dante's language; as usual, talking loudly. General Groves was nearby, and he let us know that he did not like us speaking Hungarian in public; he delicately hinted that if we wanted to speak foreign languages, we had better go into the woods.

Robert R. Wilson: For a time—was it weeks or was it only a few days—we happy few ran the project; we were the project. Then, other people, rank outsiders, began to arrive.

John H. Manley: I think we really must have made some sort of a record and I'm still moderately proud of the little part I had in it: all four of these accelerators, the cyclotron, two Van de Graafs and a Cockcroft-Walton were operating and giving data on experiments within two or three months after they were trucked up to Los Alamos. This would have been a feat on any university campus, but at Los Alamos the buildings weren't even finished, the workmen were still in there, special wiring and plumbing had to be installed for all of these machines, and shops and stocks and everything else were just getting organized. I can add to the picture of our early complications by reminding you that the only telephone line to Los Alamos from the outside world was a Forest Service line. If you manipulated the crank on the side of the box with enough vigor sometimes you got a response from the outside world.

Franklin D. Roosevelt, *letter to J. Robert Oppenheimer, June 29, 1943*: The successful solution of the problem is of the utmost importance to the national safety, and I am confident that the work will be completed in as short a time as possible as the result of the wholehearted cooperation of all concerned. I know that you and your colleagues are working on a hazardous matter under unusual circumstances.

Arthur Holly Compton: By early July experiments with the cyclotron were under way.

Hugh T. Richards: For a couple of weeks in July our group had the world's supply of plutonium, a barely visible speck (a few hundred micrograms) prepared by cyclotron bombardment at Washington U. (St. Louis). We compared the neutrons emitted from our small Pu sample to a known U-235 sample. This was in fact the first experiment completed at Los Alamos and everyone in the group had devoted all free hours to the project.

J. Robert Oppenheimer: We were finding out things that nobody knew before.

"Exciting, stimulating and even awe-inspiring"

LOS ALAMOS: WORKING ON THE MESA

Much of life at Los Alamos was basic, but most residents remember it as a grand adventure.

The earliest estimates for the Los Alamos laboratory imagined just a few hundred personnel, but the population jumped by more than that effectively every month through the end of the war. Los Alamos's population stood at 3,500 by the end of 1943, about 5,700 by the end of 1944, and more than 8,000 by the end of 1945. All of their supplies to support the new community and laboratory complex—and all of the new personnel—would have to be trekked over a small, treacherous twenty-five-mile road.

Brig. Gen. Leslie Groves: As the work got under way some amazing rumors began to circulate through Santa Fe, some thirty miles away. Typical of these was that old stand-by that we were building a home for pregnant WACs [soldiers from the Women's Army Corps]. The near-by local population followed the construction of the enclosure's fence with great interest to see whether it was designed to keep people in or to keep them out.

Dorothy McKibbin: Santa Feans soon became accustomed to the queer ways of the scientists. They claimed they could spot these people from a great distance. Frequently, a clerk in a shop, prompted more by western hospitality than by curiosity, automatically inquired, "Where are you from?" The answer was always a stammered "Box 1663," as the speaker faded into the background. Security allowed them to say no more. Santa Feans knew what Box 1663 meant and felt smug about it.*

Brig. Gen. Leslie Groves: After a number of Navy officers had been assigned to the project, and were seen on the streets of Santa Fe, rumors burgeoned about the new type of submarine that was being perfected on the Hill, as Los Alamos came to be known locally. Although the nearest navigable body of water was many hundreds of miles away, this rumor sounded entirely plausible to a number of people.

Edward Teller: The newly established laboratory procedures were as strange as our setting. Almost all of us were accustomed to an academic atmosphere, to having time to sit and think quietly by ourselves, to nurturing a novel idea slowly, and to casual chats with colleagues. But at Los Alamos, almost constant collaboration was necessary, all the work was done at a feverish pace, and one's new good idea, once hatched, could be taken away and given to others to develop—which, for many scientists, felt a little like giving one's child to someone else to raise.

Stanislaw Ulam: It is difficult to describe for the general reader the intellectual flavor, the feeling, of a scientific "atmosphere." There is no specific English

* While PO Box 1663, the mail drop for the scientists atop the mesa, is the most famous mailing address of the Los Alamos Lab and Project Y site, the military utilized more than a half-dozen specific PO Boxes for the site, including #180 for military and technical staff and #1539 for medical staff.

word for this impression. It was on the first or second day in Los Alamos that I met [Richard] Feynman, and remarked to him about my surprise that $E = MC^2$—which I of course believed in theoretically but somehow did not really "feel"—was, in fact, the basis of the whole thing and would bring about a bomb. What the whole project was working on depended on those few little signs on paper. Einstein himself, when he was first told before the war about radioactive phenomena showing the equivalence of mass and energy, allegedly replied, "Ist das wirklich so?" *Is that really so?*

Paul Numerof, *chemist, Special Engineer Detachment, Los Alamos*: The laboratory was quite a surprise. To find such a superb facility on the plateau of a mountain in the wilds of New Mexico had to be the last thing anyone would expect. Nothing was lacking. It had everything that any chemist could want. There were five civilians and another soldier working there already. I was the sixth chemist. These men, and another who joined us later, were to be my scientific colleagues for twenty-two months.

Frederic de Hoffmann, *physicist*: Meetings on subjects under consideration occurred spontaneously. It took me many years to realize that all the instant problem-solving I had seen was not the rule of how physics got done, but the rare exception. At Los Alamos one really expected it to be the rule.

Rudolf Peierls: In return for the isolation of the place, Oppenheimer had wrung from Groves the concession that there was to be no compartmentalization within the laboratory. Every scientific member was allowed to know everything that went on in the laboratory, except for a few strictly military matters. This helped greatly to make the work efficient.

Brig. Gen. Leslie Groves: Compartmentalization of knowledge, to me, was the very heart of security. My rule was simple and not capable of misinterpretation—each man should know everything he needed to know to do his job and nothing else.

Col. Kenneth D. Nichols: Groves ardently supported compartmentalization of the atomic bomb project. The scientists did not favor the idea, as it directly contradicted the belief that science thrives on the free exchange of all information. At Los Alamos, they insisted on complete open discussion of all aspects of bomb design and won the support of Oppenheimer. Groves reluctantly approved it.

Leona H. Woods: The internal policy at Los Alamos was that everyone there with sufficient technical background had complete access to all information.

J. Robert Oppenheimer: It turned out over and over again this was a wise policy. Good ideas came from places that you would not have expected. Enthusiasm and understanding could be generated because people knew what it was all about.

Paul Numerof: Every Monday night in the smaller of the two theaters at Los Alamos, there were reviews of the status of the project: what was going well, what was not going well, what was being done to solve problems. Often there were guest speakers from other laboratories around the country. It was exciting, stimulating and even awe-inspiring to be in the presence of these luminaries, men of whom I had heard and whose publications I had read.

Luis Alvarez: Any properly cleared technical person could attend and anything and everything about the secret work of Los Alamos could be discussed.

Rudolf Peierls: One of the groups would present a report on its work. He would also announce any interesting news, such as the results of some crucial tests or the arrival of some samples of Uranium-235 or plutonium. The meetings were held in the closely guarded cinema.

Lt. Dr. Henry L. Barnett, ***pediatrician, Army Medical Section, Los Alamos*****:** I went to the colloquia and I didn't understand very much. Louie Hempelmann, at one point, left a lecture and said there was only one word he understood and that was, "Fermi."

Joseph O. Hirschfelder: As each new problem developed, experts were recruited to solve that problem. For example, I was brought in to prescribe the characteristics of the gun and gunpowder to be used in the enriched uranium atom bomb. In three weeks I completed the final specifications for the internal ballistics of the gun and the charge of gun powder. My situation at the end of the first three weeks represented a typical personnel problem at Los Alamos: After the expert had solved his problem, what did you do with him? Generally the expert was transferred to some other problem area where he might, or might not, be knowledgeable. By the time that the atom bomb was tested, Los Alamos was three deep in experts.

Edward Teller: Project Y, as Los Alamos was code-named, was perennially shorthanded. By the time Los Alamos was organized, most American scientists were already involved in war work. The several talented British physicists, among them James Tuck and Rudolf Peierls, were particularly appreciated because no one needed to orient these newcomers to the work. The British were firmly convinced, then and afterwards, that they had started the atomic bomb project with their Tube Alloy program. The following summer, another member of the British contingent, Klaus Fuchs, arrived after having spent some months working at Columbia.

Paul Numerof: Fuller Lodge's upper floor was used for visitors and the ground floor was a large open auditorium. A piano stood at one end. On the evening of my memory, on my way back to the lab, I heard someone at the instrument. I stopped in to listen. I recognized the pianist as Otto Frisch, who with his aunt, Lise Meitner, first estimated the energy release in nuclear fission. I waited until he had finished the magnificent Mozart Sonata he was playing and then applauded. He stood up, smiled, and waved. I waved in return and continued on my way. The experience was surreal.

Victor Weisskopf: The great world of international physics was assembled inside the fence.

Eugene Wigner: The Hungarian scientists working on the Manhattan Project—principally Szilard, Teller, von Neumann, and Wigner—were thought to be queer by the Americans. They often called us the "Martians." The label was unreasonable. We Hungarians had no more contact with Mars than they did. But we had imagination and some far-reaching desires. A spur to our success was probably the fact of our forced emigration. Emigration can certainly be painful, but a young man with talent finds it stimulating. Outside your own nation, you lack a ready place. You need great ingenuity and effort just to find a niche. Hard work and ingenuity become a habit.

Otto R. Frisch: Niels Bohr also came to Los Alamos. He arrived with his son, Aage. In the autumn of 1943 Niels Bohr had escaped from Denmark when he and his family crossed the sound to Sweden in small boats on a dark night; word had gone round that the Germans were about to pick up and imprison all the Jews in Denmark, and Bohr had a Jewish mother.

Margrethe Bohr, *spouse*: We had to get away the same day.

Aage Bohr: The stay in Stockholm lasted only a short time. A telegram was received from Lord Cherwell with an invitation to come to England. My father immediately accepted and requested that I should be permitted to accompany him.

Otto R. Frisch: He was taken in a Mosquito bomber, seated in the bomb bay, where he became unconscious because the headphones didn't fit his very large head and so he didn't hear when the pilot told him to turn on the oxygen.

J. Robert Oppenheimer: The Royal Air Force was not used to such great heads as Bohr's.

Aage Bohr: The pilot realized that something was wrong when he received no answer to his inquiries, and as soon as they had passed over Norway he came down and flew low over the North Sea. When the plane landed in Scotland, my father was conscious again.

J. Robert Oppenheimer: Once in England and recovered, he learned from Chadwick what had been going on [with the atomic bomb]. To Bohr the enterprises in the United States seemed completely fantastic.

Edward Teller: When I heard that Bohr was coming, I began looking forward to reminding him that he had said it was impossible to build a fission weapon. But Bohr spotted me at the end of a long corridor, came running, and immediately squelched my chance of having been right. "Teller," he said, "didn't

I tell you that you could not make a nuclear explosive without turning the whole country into a huge factory? Now you have gone ahead and done it!"

J. Robert Oppenheimer, ***letter to Brig. Gen. Leslie Groves, November 2, 1943*****:** After you gave me the list during your last visit of the men whom we may expect from the United Kingdom, it occurred to me that it might be wise before they arrive here to give them new names. This refers especially to Niels Bohr. I am thinking of the fact that mail will be addressed to them, that they may on occasion originate or receive long-distance calls, that they will be making some local purchases, and that for all these routine matters it would be preferable if such well known names were not put in circulation.

It has, in fact, troubled us some that we are forced to place calls for Dr. Conant, Fermi, Lawrence, etc. This does not happen very often, but in view of the fact that we try not to use these names over the telephone, the placing of the calls themselves seems to us rather unwise. I doubt whether at this late date it would be practicable to assign new names to those who have been associated with the project in the past. In the case of Bohr and Chadwick I think it would be advisable to do so before they get here. Sincerely yours, J. R. Oppenheimer

Edward Teller: One of the more futile security measures was to change distinctive famous names into common ones. Those of us who were not so famous suffered only a minor deprivation of identity. Our driver's licenses were made out with a number instead of a name, and "Post Office Box 1663, Santa Fe, New Mexico" instead of an address. But Niels Bohr was famous, so he was transformed into Nicholas Baker. The group of us who had known him at his Institute in Copenhagen soon modified that alias to Uncle Nick.

Stanislaw Ulam: It was well known throughout Los Alamos that Nicholas Baker was Niels Bohr nevertheless, his true name was never supposed to be mentioned in public. At one colloquium, Weisskopf referred to "the well-known Bohr principle." "Oh excuse me," he fumbled, "the Nicholas Baker principle!" General laughter greeted this security breach.

Arthur Holly Compton: At the order of General Groves, some of us who were known to be associated with work in atomic physics were given fictitious names to be used when away from our home bases. This precaution led into a variety of amusing and sometimes embarrassing incidents. I well recall an experience at Cheyenne, Wyoming. Trouble had developed at the Hanford plant. General Groves requested me to fly out at once. For the first time in nearly three years I was permitted to travel by air. I was handed tickets in the name of Black. It was late at night and I had been sleeping on the plane. After a pause at the Cheyenne airport, the stewardess was checking over the names as we returned on board. "Name, please?" I was puzzled. I remembered that I had been given the name of some dark color. *Was it Black or Brown?* Fortunately, I guessed right and the stewardess let me pass.

Bernice Brode: The strangest feature of all to us was the security. We were quite literally fenced in by a tall barbed wire barricade surrounding the entire site and patrolled along the outside by armed MPs. We felt cozy and safe, free from robbers and mountain bears. We never locked our doors. In our second year, extra MPs were sent to guard the homes of the Oppenheimers and [Capt. William "Deak"] Parsons, making round-the-clock patrols. Some of the practical housewives cooked up a scheme to use these MPs as babysitters in the immediate neighborhood. What could be safer than a man with a gun guarding the precious small-fry? The children were sure to be impressed and behave accordingly. Martha Parsons never hired a babysitter as long as the MPs remained around her house, and Kitty Oppenheimer once got real service when the guard came to the front door of the house she was visiting to tell her that little Peter was crying. Soon after, the sergeant in charge put his foot down, no more babysitting for his crack MPs!

Ralph C. Sparks, *Special Engineer Detachment*: At one of our regular Wednesday evening security lectures—this one on loose talk in the barracks—Major de Silva announced that "last Monday night about 10:30 there were five soldiers holding a discussion about their work in the Tech Area. It occurred in Barracks C at the west end." Then came the usual stern warning: "If this ever happens again there will be a court-martial and a firing squad will be summoned to carry out the punishment." The five who were discussing our problems in the Tech Area were Sandy Simons, Bob Alldredge, Louis Jacot, Jim Maxim and me. All five of us knew there was a G-2—intelligence—agent in that group, but we didn't know who he was. As a result, none of us would speak to each other for several months. After the war was over, I visited Jim Maxim at his home in Maine and he finally admitted he was a G-2 agent and had turned us in to Major de Silva. He was very apologetic and sad as he related what his duties were while he was in the Army.

Brig. Gen. Leslie Groves: By the end of the war the MED's force of "creeps," as they became known, numbered 485.

Jane S. Wilson, *project spouse*: Because any representative listing of Project personnel would have revealed a suspicious concentration of nuclear physicists, such lists were forbidden. For this reason, we were prohibited from depositing money in Santa Fe, and all our banking was done by mail. Automobile licenses and New Mexico state income taxes were made out to numbers rather than to names. Drivers' licenses were also anonymous. As far as the New Mexico records were concerned, one was driver 66 or driver 23.

Lt. Col. John Lansdale: We established a system of monitoring telephone calls and mail. We established a post office, you might say, down in Santa Fe in an office. We censored all mail on a spot check basis, and the mail of the more important scientists and those upon whom we had derogatory information 100 percent.

Jane S. Wilson: Our mail was censored. Furthermore, our correspondents were not supposed to know that it was censored. The method was simple. Mail went into the box unsealed, the censor read it, sealed it, and sent it on its way. Or, if he didn't approve of the letter, he sent it back. Sometimes this system proved useful. If one of us intended to send a letter with an enclosure, such as a check, and then forgot to enclose it, the letter would come back with a note from the censor politely chiding the sender for his absent-mindedness.

* * *

Emilio Segrè: [The] British Mission, headed by Sir James Chadwick, included among others my old friends Rudolf Peierls, Otto Frisch, and P. B. Moon. The British Mission unfortunately also included Klaus Fuchs, a German refugee who became a Russian spy. I had exchanged only a few words of introduction with him, but he passed under our window every day at noon, presumably going to lunch. Elfriede noted his sad aspect and, not knowing who he was, nicknamed him "il Poverino" (the poor soul). She was dismayed later in hearing that the "Poverino" was a spy.

Brig. Gen. Leslie Groves: The most disastrous break in security was that resulting from the treasonable actions of the English scientist, Klaus Fuchs. Our acceptance of Fuchs into the project was a mistake. But I am at a loss when I try to determine just how we could have avoided that mistake without insulting our principal war ally, Great Britain, by insisting on controlling their security measures.

Ralph C. Sparks: It was ironic that there were only about 100 scientists who had white badges that entitled them to know everything that went on in the Tech Area. One such white-badge man was Klaus Fuchs, one of the physicists who came to Los Alamos with the British Mission.

Edward Teller: Fuchs, a polite and gracious bachelor, was generous with his time. He was willing to help with any project, whether it was to discuss a colleague's problem and suggest possible new approaches or to act as a chauffeur for wives whose husbands had no time for that. His services earned him a fond spot in many hearts.

Luis Alvarez: When there were parties at Los Alamos, he would take care of the children of the people who went to the parties so he had an excuse not to go. He was not a particularly social person. I recognized him and nodded to him in the halls.

Robert Bacher: He was a very quiet, very retiring person.

Luis Alvarez: A very retiring person.

Cmdr. Norris Bradbury, ***US Navy, head of E-5, the Implosion Experimentation Group, Los Alamos Lab*****:** I think it must be said in fairness to Fuchs that he worked extremely hard and effectively for Los Alamos and this country. He appears to have a divided or double loyalty. I think his accomplishments at Los Alamos it must be said were very effective.

* * *

Much of the unique flavor of Los Alamos flowed from the personality and intensity of the lab director, J. Robert Oppenheimer, whose role ranged from chief administrator to recruiter to something of a scientific mascot.

Joseph O. Hirschfelder: Oppy was a frail, sensitive, lonely man whose life was tragic. When he was thirteen years old, he had tuberculosis and his parents took him to New Mexico where they bought a ranch in a mountain valley far from any habitation. There, Oppy whiled away the time while recuperating by studying Sanskrit. He was absolutely brilliant. However, in spite of Oppy's eminence as a physicist he published very few articles; indeed, he set such high standards for his own research that he could seldom satisfy his own standards. This made him unhappy. Oppy had a wonderfully clear understanding of the basic principles of physics and had a genius for finding other people's mistakes. Thus, physicists from all over the world came to him for advice and help.

Otto R. Frisch: Oppenheimer used to greet newcomers with the words "Welcome to Los Alamos, and who the devil are you?" His slight figure with the broad-brimmed porkpie hat was unmistakable.

Rudolf Peierls: On our first evening there, the Oppenheimers asked Genia and me for dinner. This started with dry martinis, and we each had two. We did not then realize that the altitude substantially reduces one's tolerance for alcohol, until one gets acclimatized in a week or so. After dinner we found we had great trouble getting up from the table and walking home. This was only slightly aggravated by the fierceness of Robert's martinis. He had strong views on questions of style in food and drink. Martinis had to be strong. Coffee had to be black. When coffee was served in their house, there was never any cream or sugar on the table. They would be provided on request, but the hosts started from the assumption that the guests would want to have their coffee the proper way. Steak had to be rare.

Luis Alvarez: Remembering the unworldly and longhaired prewar Robert, I was surprised to see the extent to which he had developed into an excellent laboratory director and a marvelous leader of men.

Brig. Gen. Leslie Groves: Naturally I am prejudiced, because I selected him for the job, but I think he did a magnificent job as far as the war effort was concerned. In other words, while he was under my control and you must remember that he left my control shortly after the war was over.

Hans Bethe: He knew and understood everything that went on in the laboratory, whether it was chemistry or theoretical physics or machine shop. He could keep it all in his head and coordinate it. He understood immediately when he heard anything, and fitted it into the general scheme of things and drew the right conclusions. There was just nobody else in that laboratory who came even close to him in his knowledge. There was human warmth as well. Everybody certainly had the impression that Oppenheimer cared what each particular person was doing. In talking to someone he made it clear that that person's work was important for the success of the whole project.

Joseph O. Hirschfelder: Every Sunday Oppenheimer would ride his beautiful chestnut horse from the cavalry stable at the east side of town to the mountain trails on the west side of town greeting each of the people he passed with a wave of his pork-pie hat and a friendly remark. He knew everyone who lived in Los Alamos, from the top scientists to the children of the Spanish-American janitors—they were all Oppenheimer's family. His office door was always open and each of us could walk in, sit on his desk, and tell him how we thought that something could be improved. Oppy would listen attentively, argue with us, and sometimes dress us down with clever cutting sarcasm. At all times he knew exactly what each one of us was working on, sometimes having a better grasp of what we were doing than we did ourselves.

Edward Teller: I consider Dr. Oppenheimer's direction of the Los Alamos Laboratory a very outstanding achievement due mainly to the fact that with his very quick mind he found out very promptly what was going on in every part of the laboratory, made right judgments about things, supported work when work had to be supported, and also I think with his very remarkable insight in psychological matters, made just a most wonderful and excellent director.

J. Robert Oppenheimer: I have never known a group more understanding and more devoted to a common purpose, more willing to lay aside personal convenience and prestige, more understanding of the role that they were playing in their country's history. Time and again we had in the technical work almost paralyzing crises. Time and again the laboratory drew itself together and faced the new problems and got on with the work. We worked by night and by day; and in the end the many jobs were done.

Col. Kenneth D. Nichols: Success remained about a fifty-fifty proposition. Faint hearts and pessimists had no place in the Manhattan Project. I always had the gut feeling that we would succeed.

Victor Weisskopf: One of the most important factors that kept us at work was the common awareness of the great danger of the bomb in the hands of an irresponsible dictator.

Edward Teller: It was hard not to feel that we were far from our goal. Earlier, Bohr had told us that Heisenberg was working on the German atomic bomb. For those of us who knew Heisenberg and the many other talented German physicists, the idea of their work was deeply disturbing. The thought of how far the Germans might have come in the years since the discovery of fission was enough to give us all nightmares.

George B. Kistiakowsky: That was the driving force of Los Alamos.

J. Robert Oppenheimer: The deadline never changed. It was as soon as possible.

"Mushroom-like growth was a constant"

LIFE ON BATHTUB ROW

The "Big House" at Los Alamos, one of the old Ranch School buildings, became a focal point of lab life.

Los Alamos—known as Site Y to the government and "The Hill" to most of its residents—provided odd living arrangements: A romantic desert mountain community, richly infused with Native American culture and history, hurriedly thrown together with government-issue furniture and bureaucracy mixed with some of the most advanced technology in the world.

Otto R. Frisch: I was given a room in one of the original school buildings, a magnificent blockhouse which was traditionally built from big tree trunks and generally known as the Big House. Here, on the whole, were the quarters for bachelor scientists. Married ones were given individual houses, which were going up at a great rate.

Ruth Marshak, *teacher*: The Housing Office was in one of the Ranch School buildings, and it was the Housing Office which we new, confused arrivals sought on our first morning. Locating any place on the mesa was difficult; the sprawling town had grown rapidly and haphazardly, without order or plan. Roughly in the center of town was Ashley Pond, a shallow little pool, with the laboratories on the one side and the hospital on the other. To the west stretched a section of four and eight-family dwellings, identical in appearance, hunter green in hue. This section terminated in tight rows of barracks, housing for the enlisted military personnel, which overlooked the horse pasture. East of the pond was the oldest housing, consisting of green duplexes for childless couples, four-family houses for larger families, and Bathtub Row.

Rudolf Peierls: The old log houses had the distinction of containing bathtubs, as opposed to mere showers, and the street on which they stood was known as "Bathtub Row."

Luis Alvarez: The Army built apartments in barracks style with tin showers. The apartments came in various sizes, the commonest being four-family units, with two families above and two below.

Rudolf Peierls: We were told, apologetically, that no room was left for us in Bathtub Row or in any of the houses nearby in the more desirable part of town. There was only a flat on the "other" side of town. We said, "Never mind; when we live there it will become respectable." Sure enough, when the Fermis arrived a little after us, they moved into the flat above us.

Jane S. Wilson: The military administration, with what struck me as typical perversity, had given each apartment a splendid modern electric refrigerator with one hand and a hideous, curvaceous, very bleak wood and coal-burning range with the other. One frightened look at this item, familiarly known as the Black Beauty, and I was in tears.

Robert R. Wilson: Worst of all was the cook stove, an old-fashioned wood range. My wife had never seen such an object. Then too, at an altitude of 7,200 feet, it did take an unconscionably long time to hard boil an egg. When Oppy brought General Groves on an inspection tour, my wife felt that the time had come to make a strike, not only for herself but for every housewife on the Hill. "Yes, General," she simpered, "everything is fine, just fine. One little thing—the stove. I can't get it to work, and we are growing tired of cold meals."

"Nonsense," said the General briskly. "These stoves are wonderful devices. I was raised on them. I'm an old farm boy. Let me show you how it's done." The General marched into the kitchen and fiddled with the obdurate "Black Beauty." The General's hands grew smudgy. Black spots dappled his tan uniform. Time passed. He was not able to light a fire. "There!" said the General, wiping his hands against his pants. "You see how it's done!" He marched out of the kitchen, head very high. The next day, G.I. electric hot plates were distributed to every household on the site.

Jane S. Wilson: I did all my cooking on two hot plates plus my own electric broiler and electric roaster. With such implements, I would nonchalantly whip up dinner, occasionally for as many as thirty-five. This was difficult but not impossible, except when the power was shut off. There were periods when this happened frequently, sometimes for hours at a time. If dinner happened to be ready, we ate by candlelight. If our meal was not yet cooked, occasionally we did not eat at all.

Bernice Brode: All the kitchens faced on the road, so that the fronts of the houses were really the backs. Callers came in via the back, or kitchen, doors from the steps that were just off the road.

Rudolf Peierls: The houses were heated by hot air from a coal-burning furnace, and one thermostat served the upstairs and downstairs flats. Our living room contained the thermostat that controlled both our flat and that of the Fermis. We had to remember to set the thermostat to a higher temperature when we had a party, and perhaps a log fire, to prevent the Fermis from getting too cold; and to set it down when we opened our windows, or the Fermis would get roasted. Not all ground-floor tenants remembered these finer points, and there was a good deal of friction.

Kathleen Mark, *project spouse*: Perhaps the most surprising thing about living in a Los Alamos house was the service we received. When the coal bin was empty, or often before, men appeared in a large truck to fill it up again. When the wood box was empty, it was promptly refilled.

Alice Kimball Smith, *project spouse*: The mushroom-like growth was a constant source of jokes. One might be picking tall white yuccas and fiery paintbrush in a quiet mountain meadow one Sunday and come back two weeks later to find it covered with government trailers or Nissen huts.

Phyllis K. Fisher, *project spouse*: Nameless dirt streets and roads were located in reference to the water tower. One lived "north of the tower" or "east of the tower." The growing town quickly outstripped its limited water supply and also put a strain on an inadequate power supply. Housing continually lagged behind the population increase. There were, clearly, too many of us for our meager resources. And so the weathered and worn water tower represented our point of reference as well as our forlorn hopes for survival on our bleak mesa.

Ralph C. Sparks: The mess hall was still "Army" and we had all come to call the West Mess Hall by a more appropriate name, "Worst Mess Hall." One day at the noonday meal, the coffee—a huge stainless steel monster—failed to give coffee. The mess sergeant removed the lid and peered into the pot. He reached in and pulled out a large mop. The mop looked as though it had seen duty in World War I and had been in the pot since then. Somehow we all lost our desire for coffee for some time.

* * *

T/3 Eleanor "Jerry" Stone: Los Alamos was small and compact. A main road connected East Gate at one end with West Gate at the other.

Bernice Brode: The Technical Area—called Tech Area, T Area or simply T—where the main work of the project was done, resembled a small factory, a two-story clapboard building painted, of course, green. The windows were large and pleasant, like those in our houses, although innocent of any washing since the original putty was smeared on. Originally the one building, designed as a laboratory only, was built along West Road. But we soon grew in all directions, adding wings wherever possible. The Tech Area had its own fence around it, and a special badge was required to enter the gate guarded by MPs. The badges came in assorted colors indicating the areas to which the bearer had access. White was the highest form, also admitting the wearer to the testing area in the canyons. Mine was orange; though one of the lower forms, it allowed me to roam at will inside T.

Charlotte Serber: The Tech Area originally contained a group of buildings named T to Z, respectively, which housed the administrative offices, laboratories, library, warehouse, and shop. From this modest beginning, the place mushroomed into so many buildings that to name them we quickly ran through the English alphabet, moved into Greek and Hebrew, and finally into mathematical symbols. The first buildings were drab and badly planned with soft, unvarnished floors, small windows, and poor incandescent lighting. Later, buildings varied from the elegant structure built for the chemists, which sported glass partitions, battleship linoleum, and an overabundance of fluorescent lighting, to the beaverboard chicken-coop built for the theoretical physicists.

T/3 Eleanor "Jerry" Stone: All activity in those days centered around the Tech Area and overflowed twice a day to the Tech PX for coffee breaks. On my second day in Los Alamos, I was assigned to work in the Tech PX. Although my Army job was classified "Communications," my Tech Area clearance had not been completed, and Army personnel do not remain idle. I reported for duty to Sergeant White, a dour-faced Arkansas boy, and was introduced to my first Spanish-speaking people, Ramon and Linda, both teen-agers. They taught me the intricacies of putting together milk shakes. Soon it was coffee time, and the mob was upon us. Hardly could we recover from one rush, when another came. I never had a chance to look at the clock until I was excused at 6 p.m. Then I headed dog-tired down the side of the road straight for my bunk.

Charlotte Serber: When the public-address system was installed, our favorite PBX operator happened to be on, and she christened the machine in dulcet tones, "At the sound of the gong, it will be 5:30. Everyone please go home."

In about its second week of infancy, we still treated the PA as a fancy toy, serenading one of the senior scientists with "Happy Birthday." Such frivolous behavior was officially discouraged, but nevertheless practical jokes on the PA continued to crop up at times. An operator, by request, insistently paged Werner Heisenberg at intervals for two days. Finally, a sympathetic soul took pity on her and explained that if she really wanted him she had better cable Berlin.

Bernice Brode: Every room in T had a loudspeaker over which came diverting messages. "Attention please. Will the person who took the Sears Roebuck catalog from Harold Agnew's room please return it immediately. Repeat—immediately." "Attention please. Will the owner of the lady's blue bicycle with the outsized basket please remove it. The bulldozer is coming and the bicycle is in danger." I dashed out, for it sounded like mine—it was.

T/3 Eleanor "Jerry" Stone: The paging system, however, was in almost constant use, chanting for Kistiakowsky, Bethe, Fermi, Teller, Mitchell, Serduk, Segrè, Perlman, Linschitz, as well as for hastily needed, little-known technicians and two popular characters, J. J. Gutierrez and John Marsh, maintenance men. These last two must have been the busiest men in town; we paged them consistently twenty times a day.

Hugh T. Richards: The name most commonly heard over the loud speaker paging system in the tech area was J. J. Gutierrez, a Hispanic in charge of the janitorial staff.

Otto R. Frisch: Most scientists worked in groups of about a dozen people, headed by a group leader, but there were some exceptions. For instance, I was not put into any group, but worked for a while as a sort of visiting plumber, going round to see what various groups were doing, and offering advice when required, particularly on questions of instrumentation.

Laura Fermi: Enrico was the leader of the "F Division," in which F stood for Fermi. When he arrived at Los Alamos, he managed to gather a group of very brilliant men. One of them was his imaginative friend Edward Teller; another was Herbert Anderson, Enrico's inseparable collaborator.

Herbert L. Anderson: Four groups were placed in the F Division. One, under Edward Teller, pursued the theoretical study of the "Super"—the hydrogen bomb—in which Teller had been engaged for some time. Egon Bretscher headed another group on the "Super," which was the experimental counterpart of Teller's. Fermi's greatest personal participation was in the other two groups: the Water Boiler group under L. D. P. King, and the group under me called F-4. The water boiler Pere King was building was an extremely simple nuclear reactor, and though small in size (only one foot in diameter) it could serve as a strong source of neutrons. It used enriched uranium in water solution, a novel product of the new "atomic" technology, undreamed of only six years earlier. My group—Darragh Nagle, Julius Tabin, and I—was available for other problems that might come up.

Eugene Wigner: When people discuss the Manhattan Project, they often linger too long on the physicists. We had some wonderful chemists too, whose work was essential to our success. Glenn Seaborg was my favorite: a tall, friendly, brown-haired real American. The nuclear chain reaction made plutonium, which had to be separated from the uranium in the reactor. With talented men assisting him, Seaborg did much of this separation work. After the war, Seaborg shared the 1951 chemistry Nobel with Edwin McMillan for related work with transuranic elements.

Ralph C. Sparks: Some of the scientists who came to my shop with their sketches of equipment to be made, drew them on scraps of paper or an old brown paper bag. The scientist would proceed to enhance the sketch with a verbal description of what was wanted, which seldom concurred with the sketch. I would jot down the verbal description below the sketch, then sit at my desk and draw a conventional three-dimensional machine-shop drawing.

Bernice Brode: These SED boys were quite different from the regular Post soldiers. They looked, in spite of the uniforms, like budding professors instead of combat troops. Shortly after they came up to the Hill, some high brass from Washington came for a formal military review in the baseball field in front of the Big House. All of us came with our children to see the show. The MPs, the Post soldiers, the WACs, and even the doctors made a fine showing as they marched across the field, but the newly arrived SED boys were terrible. They couldn't keep in step.

Ralph C. Sparks: The 9812th Special Engineer Detachment in the Manhattan Corps of Engineers, otherwise known as SED, was indeed a very well-educated and skilled group of men. The information about our detachment published in 1946 said more than 35 percent of the men had college degrees, some with master and doctoral degrees. Most of the others had skilled training and many had ten years experience. Many developments and patents were the work of this group of SED soldiers in the technical area. When I arrived on the Hill [in 1943], there were about 188 men who had arrived.

George B. Kistiakowsky: The Special Engineer Detachment was very important. General Groves insisted that, in distinction to technical staff civilians, most of whom lived quite comfortably in a highly hierarchically organized society, the enlisted personnel be given only what the Army regulations stipulated as the minimum comforts: minimum housing, minimum recreation, minimum food facilities. And this meant 40 square feet per man in the barracks, including part of the recreation area. Try to recreate yourself in that area. The poor SEDs, of whom we had more than a thousand at the end of the war, really felt themselves the pariahs of Los Alamos.

Val L. Fitch: At Los Alamos I was assigned to an upper bunk in a recently completed barracks, a spot that was to be home for another year and nine months. I quickly learned the army situation from the SEDs already there. We lived in single floor barracks, roughly sixty men to a unit. As the summer and fall of 1944 progressed the size of the SED contingent continued to increase as fast as new barracks were built. The fundamental dichotomy in the army existence and the work alongside civilians troubled some of the SEDs. They considered themselves miserably exploited by the system. On the other hand, many of us found our work in the laboratory intellectually stimulating, and we spent long hours there working on and learning new things. We considered this army assignment extraordinarily fortuitous.

* * *

Emilio Segrè: On average, the members of this group were young, about thirty-two years old; some who were a little older had barely passed forty and were already quite famous. Several who would become famous later were about twenty years old at the time. There were eight future Nobel prize winners—Alvarez, Bethe, Bloch, Chamberlain, Feynman, McMillan, Rabi, Segrè. Oppenheimer was thirty-nine.

Bernice Brode: There were almost no old people, so those of us in our early forties were the senior citizens. We had no invalids, no in-laws, no unemployed, no idle rich and no poor.

Elsie McMillan, *project spouse*: Los Alamos had a small hospital with only two bedrooms, a waiting room, a pharmacy, and an operating room which at first could not be used because we did not have the proper anesthetic for the altitude. We had only two doctors, James Nolan, who had been a cancer specialist, and was the physician for the people who were there, and Louis Hempelmann, who was the radiologist for the technical area. We had three nurses, Pete and Sarah and Peggy. Food had to be brought over from the lodge, and it got cold.

Dr. Louis Hempelmann: I was supposed to be the medical director for the laboratory, with specific emphasis on radiation. I didn't even know that there was such a thing as occupational medicine. We operated in the most primitive way, really. Then Oppie called me and asked me if I could get someone to take care of the health of the town, of the total population. I got a classmate of mine named Jim Nolan, who had gone into gynecology. He was trained as a surgeon, and then went into obstetrics and gynecology. He was a very good obstetrician, fortunately, which was the main thing we had to deal with. Also, he was a good surgeon, so he could set bones and things like that.

Lt. Dr. Henry L. Barnett: Louie Hempelmann, who had been in medical school with me, was a radiologist in Rochester. He always ranked first in the class, and I ran second. Louie asked me whether I'd be interested in a job where I would be doing pediatrics. I got an order I should report to 109 Palace Street in Santa Fe, New Mexico. There was a surgeon there that Louie had gotten, Jim Nolan, who was also in our class. The next one they wanted was a pediatrician, so they got me.

Shirley B. Barnett, *project spouse*: Since the hospital was centrally located, no operation or emergency went unnoticed by the local gentry. I remember waiting one night outside the hospital with Anne, Jim [Nolan's] wife, while Jim and Henry were in the operating room taking care of an emergency. Anne was expecting a baby within a week or two. When a car drove up and the occupants spotted us standing in the shadows, they asked why the operating room lights were on. They wondered audibly if Anne's baby was being born. Anne stepped out from the shadows and reassured them. As the car drove off, Anne made a fervent wish that her baby be born during the day, so as to assure her some chance of a head start on knowing whether her baby was a boy or a girl. Her wish was not granted, but her child was born during a night of comparative quiet on the mesa. The announcement was made next morning to a proud community, who felt that the birth of its first child was something in the way of a major event and a matter for loud huzzahs. Our birth rate after this—Anne's baby was born in August 1943—was fairly high.

Ruth Marshak: The General was reputed to have complained to Dr. Oppenheimer about the number of children being born on the Hill. Couldn't something be done about it, the General wanted to know. A jingle celebrating this remark went in part: *The General's in a stew / He trusted you and you / He thought you'd be scientific / Instead you're just prolific / And what is he to do?*

Shirley B. Barnett: Eighty babies were born during the first year, and about ten a month thereafter. "Rural Free Delivery," people said, jokingly. Henry's pediatric practice increased steadily.

Elsie McMillan: The birth certificates of all babies born there said: place of birth, Box 1663, Sandoval County Rural. My God, was that box ever full of babies!

Bernice Brode: Our school at Los Alamos was the most exclusive in the country—and our worst problem. In the beginning, everyone was completely unrealistic about the school, and we all had to learn the hard way. The earliest organizers seemed to proceed on the assumption that the school would be the least of their troubles. With all those thoroughly educated people to be hired, why wouldn't it be a cinch to set up and run a fine school for their kids?

Rudolf Peierls: The science teaching was weak. This paradox was explained by the fact that most of the teachers were wives of scientists and included some first-rate scholars. However, those with scientific qualifications preferred work in the laboratory, so teachers with poor science backgrounds had to teach science also.

Ruth Marshak: We teachers worked under difficulties. When an experimental blast in a nearby canyon would rock the school to its expensive foundation, there would be a frightened silence in the classroom, and then we would begin again on Henry Wadsworth Longfellow.

Phyllis K. Fisher: Our "quiet" was punctuated from time to time by explosions down in the canyons. These explosions were often enough to shake our flimsy houses and set all the pictures on the walls askew.

T/3 Eleanor "Jerry" Stone: There were many loud blasts. When the ground shook and the air smelled of firecrackers, we knew the scientists were testing explosives. When I washed my hair, I could smell that firecracker smell, but it was combined with the smell of the pines.

* * *

Charlotte Serber: Until we had a formal Personnel Office in full swing, most housewives were transformed into working wives by the grapevine. Working conditions included forty-eight hours to the work week, two weeks of vacation with pay, sick leave, one day off a month for a shopping trip to Santa Fe, maids available through the Housing Office, and a nursery school for her children. The working wife's salary, which was set very arbitrarily, was influenced less by her previous work history than by the fact that she really had no bargaining power.

Bernice Brode: I worked for some months as a computer—as we computing-machine operators were called then—in the theoretical wing at T. After three months of computer training, we were moved to the theoretical wing of T to work under mathematician Moll Flanders. After hours, Professor Flanders and his family contributed greatly to our musical life. All the family sang and played instruments, and Moll himself conducted our chorus and orchestra. He wore an unusual but becoming full beard, and when we asked why, he replied in his New England accent, "If you had three women in the family and only one bathroom, would you not do likewise?"

Edward Teller: A further source of unhappiness was the limited availability of domestic help. Mici, like most of the wives, eventually went to work at the laboratory in the computations division because of the terrible shortage of personnel. With Paul a baby, she had to have help to do so. At that time, household helpers were in such short supply that they were rationed.

Charlotte Serber: Within about fifteen miles of Los Alamos there are three Indian pueblos, two towns, and a number of small farms, the closest being San Ildefonso Pueblo. In May 1943, the Security Office granted us permission to bring San Ildefonso women up to do housework for the working women. An Army carryall was to transport the original eight or ten Indians up to the Hill at 8:30 and down again at 5:30 each day. Most of us got from three to six half-days of work a week and were delighted at this unexpected relief from housework. As more and more people arrived on the Hill and because the press of work in the Tech Area never eased up, the demand for Indian maids grew tremendously.

Phyllis K. Fisher: It was always a thrill to visit the different Indian pueblos scattered throughout the valley, to get to know some of the local people, to begin to appreciate their art and philosophy, as well as their festivals. We came to realize that we were surrounded by a rich, intriguing, and very special world. Around us was a lovely area that invited exploration.

Bernice Brode: The Indian dances, whatever else they meant to the Indians, provided good fun and a show for everyone. Los Alamos people provided an enthusiastic audience, and the Indians liked it. Some of the dances were held on weekdays, but when it was understood that our men could come only on Sunday, their one day off, some of the dances were switched. The dances also increased in variety, we noticed, and we suspected the Indians were making up new non-traditional ones, since we were enthusiastic but uncritical and would not know the difference.

Paul Numerof: One of the civilian men in the lab had his own car, and he would often arrange trips to several of the Indian pueblos in the area. One of them, San Ildefonso, was the home of a woman named Maria Martinez, who became famous for her black-on-black pottery. We would drive up to the central square of the pueblo and wait. Eventually doors to the homes that faced the square would open and Indian women would appear with their pottery carried in their large billowing skirts. They would form a semicircle, place blankets on the ground, and put their pottery on them. Not a word was said. Buyers would walk up and down, pick up the pieces, and ask questions. It wasn't until much later in life that I appreciated fully what an opportunity I had missed. A 12-inch Maria Martinez plate, black-on-black, that I could have bought for $12 in 1944, now could be worth about $12,000 (if it were even available from a collection). My problem was that $12 was almost half of my monthly paycheck.

Charlie Masters, *teacher, Los Alamos school*: A phenomenal amount of black ware was produced, for the Los Alamos folk had an insatiable appetite for these plain, rich bowls, plates, vases, plaques, and candlesticks. It became almost impossible to buy a new piece not sanctioned by the taste of the Hill or to find a potter with the time to make one. It cost me four Sunday visits to San Ildefonso, I recall, to buy a bowl of two-toned brown (or red, as the Indians prefer to call it) which I had rashly promised as a birthday gift.

* * *

Emilio Segrè: The mess hall in Fuller Lodge had a porch opening onto a lawn, and from it we had a spectacular view on the Sangre de Cristo Mountains, dominated by the Truchas Peak, across the Rio Grande valley. The view from Fuller Lodge could not fail to impress whoever saw it for the first time. The view from Fuller Lodge became even more dramatic in late spring and summer at 4 p.m., when every day a big thunderstorm started illuminating the horizon toward the Sangre de Cristo Mountains, with brilliant lightning criss-crossing the sky. The storm lasted a few hours and by eight o'clock it was over, giving way to a serene night. The phenomenon was perfectly regular: at noon big cumulus clouds started forming in a sky that early in the morning had been perfectly clear; the clouds grew and rose in the sky, until they climaxed in the afternoon's thunderstorm. These summer storms cooled the days, which otherwise would have been hot, in spite of the altitude. Thus the climate was most pleasant, with moderately cold winters that permitted skiing.

The Fuller Lodge at the Los Alamos Ranch School.

Edward Teller: In retrospect, it is hard to imagine where we found the energy to go hiking and horseback riding, visit the nearby Indian pueblos for festivals, explore the ancient Indian ruins a few miles away at Bandelier, give and attend parties, and manage routine chores while working long hours on the atomic bomb as well. But we did.

Rudolf Peierls: The scope for leisure activities was limited. There was a cinema, but not much else. People with musical talents arranged music groups. Barn dancing was popular, and there was a "horsy set." There were also many parties, large and small. Being an army base, Los Alamos did not have a wine store, and drink had to be bought in Sante Fe. Whisky and gin were in short supply, but there was plenty of Mexican vodka. As most Americans like martinis, a mixture was made with vodka in place of gin, and nicknamed Martinovich. John von Neumann consumed fifteen of these one evening in our house. Next day he said, "I know my stomach has a cast-iron lining, but it must have developed a crack!"

Edward Teller: Many activities took place on the mesa itself. I helped at the radio station, played chamber music, and had my only experience as a thespian when I played the part of a corpse in a production of *Arsenic and Old Lace*.

Bernice Brode: Little publicity was needed for a forthcoming play. Nearly everyone on the Mesa had been part of the rehearsal, been approached for props, or been asked to help out in some way, so every performance was assured of an appreciative and capacity audience. After the play it was the custom for the players to come out in grease paint and be congratulated by their public. Then we pushed back the chairs and benches and danced until midnight to music often provided by Mr. Olmstead's jazz band. One of our biggest hits was *Arsenic and Old Lace* with Betty Brixner as the old lady. Betty was a pretty blonde of twenty-five, so she had a good deal of acting to do but carried it off very well. The high spot of the show was the end of the last act when the dead bodies were brought up from the cellar. It was kept top-secret so well that the audience was unprepared to see Oppenheimer brought up stiff as a corpse and laid on the floor, then Deak Parsons, then Bob Bacher, Cyril Smith, Harold Agnew and others. Cyril Smith remarked on the way home that it was the most restful occupation he had on the Mesa.

Val L. Fitch: Those of us who immediately got involved in the hiking, skiing, skating, and folk dancing activities came to love dearly that part of the country. Most of the noted physicists at Los Alamos hiked and skied, and I came to know more of them on the ski slopes than I did at work. Niels Bohr skiing, albeit modestly, was a memorable sight. Being gently chastised by Enrico Fermi for inadequately—in his opinion—filling in the sitzmark from a skiing spill was more an honor for me than a rebuke. Mrs. Rudolf Peierls, directing traffic over all the ski slopes from the stoop of the warming hut at the bottom, is not to be forgotten. Where else in the army could one, on a moonlit night, go skiing a few hundred yards from his barracks as I did?

Shirley B. Barnett: The natural hazards of transplanting a large group of urban dwellers into a country where vigorous outdoor exercise is very much the thing took its toll. There were horseback-riding accidents, skiing accidents, and even one Ping-Pong accident. Touch football provided its share of dislocations and sprains, with tennis trailing along behind. By the time the community had reached its top population, around 7,000, our vital statistics in relation to accidents were on a par with any.

Otto R. Frisch: Teller had lost a leg in a traffic accident while young, but he never let on. His artificial leg merely gave him a slight limp, and he didn't mind going for long walks; he even often joined us when we went skiing, but then wore snow shoes rather than skis.

Stanislaw Ulam: Enrico was fond of walking, several times we walked all the way from Los Alamos down the walls of a canyon and along a stream to the Bandelier National Monument. It was a walk of seven or eight miles during which we had to cross the stream more than thirty times. The walk lasted several hours, and we discussed many subjects.

Leona H. Woods: Enrico took me on the usual hikes around Los Alamos, such as climbing Lake Peak across the valley of the Rio Grande, one of the high peaks in the Sangre de Cristo range. We found arrowheads and marveled at the patience it took to chip out these weapons so carefully. Obviously the Department of Defense was a cottage industry in those days, circa A.D. 1300. Pot shards are everywhere. It is puzzling how so many pots could have been broken along every trail.

Otto R. Frisch: On the long walks which were his recreation he liked to talk physics to his guard. One day he said pensively—he had acquired a good command of English but had never lost his Italian accent—"my bodyguarde, now he know so much physics, he will soon neede bodyguarde himself."

"It really worked!"

OAK RIDGE: GLIMPSING PLUTONIUM

The X-10 "semi-works" plant at Oak Ridge started creating plutonium.

The work to refine plutonium at the Hanford Engineer Works in the dry desert of eastern Washington State really began across the country at Oak Ridge's Clinton Engineer Works, where the Manhattan Project first designed and built a pilot "semi-works" graphite reactor known as X-10 under the leadership of the University of Chicago's Met Lab and DuPont. That reactor, the first built after the Met Lab's December 1942 success with CP-1, produced the first meaningful amounts of plutonium the world had ever seen. Constructed on a crash schedule beginning in February 1943, the reactor was online by November and the first plutonium emerged later that month.

Arthur Holly Compton: By mid-October the pattern for the first experimental reactor at Chicago had been agreed upon. It was of prime importance that the pilot plant at Oak Ridge be of the greatest possible value to DuPont in building and operating the Hanford plant. Accordingly, Whitaker spent a considerable part of several months at Wilmington working with the DuPont men on the plans for the plant's construction and operation. A design was agreed upon that had considerable similarity to the Wigner plans for the Hanford production plant.

Alvin M. Weinberg: Wigner likes to say I designed by myself the X-10 reactor at Oak Ridge in early 1943, but it really wasn't much of a thing. There really wasn't much design that had to be done there. I was responsible for deciding what the lattice spacing was—the geometry of the nuclear pile. The X-10 reactor was built in nine months. Perhaps the most serious problem was the canning of the metallic uranium slugs. Each slug was four inches long and about one inch in diameter. It was placed in a thin aluminum can that was then welded shut. Unfortunately, the welded end caps sometimes leaked, and many slugs had to be rejected. But eventually enough nonleakers were accumulated to load the pile. On November 4, 1943, the X-10 reactor went critical for the first time. Fermi had come from Chicago to supervise, and though I was not there, I was told that all went pretty much as planned.

Charlie W. M. Mathis, *project staff, X-10 Reactor*: In this reactor we transmuted uranium into small quantities of plutonium that were used for extraction process development and testing to evaluate its properties. We discharged the irradiated uranium fuel down the back of the reactor into a pit. On the other side of the wall were the handlers, dissolvers, dipping down to pick up the fuel elements.

Alvin M. Weinberg: The significance of the X-10 to Hanford was that nobody had ever extracted plutonium on a large scale, separation had always been done on a micro-scale. This was the first time in human history that mankind was handling radioactivity on this enormous scale. X-10 was the first reactor that produced significant amounts of heat, a thousand kilowatts. Secondly, it was the first reactor in which sizeable amounts, meaning gram quantities, of plutonium were produced, about one gram a day. The Hanford reactors each one initially produced about 250 grams a day.

Col. Kenneth D. Nichols: The pile operated beautifully and eventually reached a power level equivalent to 1,800 kilowatts, about twice the design capacity. We were jubilant. In December, 1.54 milligrams of plutonium were separated and shipped to the met lab for experimentation. In March there was great excitement when the first gram of plutonium was produced. I felt elated. We were now on the road to success. Compton and Whitaker invited Groves and me down to the semiworks to see it. Compton opened the glass door and reached in under the ventilation hood to pick up a small glass vial containing a single gram of green liquid. He handed it to me. Whitaker hurriedly picked up a stainless-steel pan and held it under my hand, saying, "For God's sake, don't drop it on the floor." As Groves reached for it, Whitaker grabbed it and replaced it safely under the hood.

Alvin M. Weinberg: I was awestruck when Sam Allison, who was then director of the Metallurgical Laboratory, showed a few of us a small vial filled with a green solution of a dissolved salt of plutonium, probably plutonium nitrate. So the crazy idea of manufacturing a new element on a large scale was not so crazy after all: It really worked!

"The predicament was grave"

LOS ALAMOS: DESIGNING THE BOMB

The "Tech Area" of Los Alamos.

The main, day-in, day-out work of the Manhattan Project scientists at Los Alamos was designing not one but two different nuclear devices, using plutonium and uranium. There are competing—but not necessarily mutually exclusive—stories about the origins of the "Thin Man" and "Fat Man" names for the project's bomb designs. One story holds that the names were deliberately chosen to honor Franklin Roosevelt and Winston Churchill—or perhaps used by the military to confuse enemy surveillance, who would imagine the B-29s being modified to carry "Thin Man" and "Fat Man" were meant for VIP transport. By contrast, Robert Serber says the names, instead, were an homage to detective novelist Dashiell Hammett—with

"Thin Man," which featured a long, thin bomb design, honoring Hammett's 1934 novel of that title and "Fat Man," a legitimately fat and round bomb, named after the character Kasper Gutman in The Maltese Falcon, *which had just come out as a Humphrey Bogart movie in 1941.*

As they got into the work, though, the design for "Thin Man," the proposed plutonium-fueled gun-type atomic bomb, had to be abandoned, delivering perhaps the most severe crisis to Los Alamos of its short existence. Instead, thoughtful work and a quick pivot by Oppenheimer would lead to the bomb known as "Little Boy."

Stanislaw Ulam: Most of the physics at Los Alamos could be reduced to the study of assemblies of particles interacting with each other, hitting each other, scattering, sometimes giving rise to new particles.

Luis Alvarez: The easiest way to start a nuclear explosion is to bring two subcritical pieces of fissionable material quickly together in a gun to make a critical mass. A critical mass is not some absolute number of kilograms of fissionable material. The amount of fissionable material to be used depends on the density of the material chosen and its shape.

Edward Teller: Szilard's original idea for a fission weapon was simple enough: Start from one neutron and let it multiply. After sufficient neutron multiplication occurs, a few pounds of fissionable material will liberate energy equivalent to thousands of tons of high explosives. There is just one small hitch: that multiplication must occur in less than one one-millionth of a second. Otherwise, the material will predetonate—fly apart with moderate energy before a full chain reaction can occur.

Robert Bacher: You've got to get it together pretty fast, because if you don't, it will just go poof as you put it together.

Edward Teller: The most obvious way to assemble the critical mass was to use a high-velocity gun to propel one-half of the nuclear material into the properly positioned second half. But this solution created new problems. First, building a device that could be transported by plane was a challenge, and separating the fissionable material into two portions meant that the device had to be large. Second, shooting half of the material with sufficient accuracy, velocity, and reliability was difficult, and there was also a danger that the rebound from the impact of the projected material would break the system apart before the initiating neutrons could be injected and could multiply.

Edwin McMillan: The gun method—firing two chunks of fissionable material together at high speed and then releasing some neutrons to start the chain reaction. The gun method was *the* method.

Robert Christy, *physicist, Los Alamos Lab*: It was such a straightforward assembly that no one was worried about it. At that time, everyone felt that they could predict exactly what would happen.

Robert Bacher: This was indeed the method subsequently used to make the Hiroshima bomb. It had a number of difficulties, but it looked straightforward, and with the known nuclear constants of Uranium-235 it should be something that could be done without a wholly new art being developed.

Edward Teller: Those problems proved only moderately difficult. Solutions to the mechanics of size and of combining the material were worked out, and the problem of rebound was overcome by activating a neutron source just as the halves were in proper position.

Robert Bacher: There seemed to be no reason why plutonium shouldn't work this same way, too, though there was very much less known about its nuclear properties.

* * *

Edward Teller: After we had been working for a few months, a real difficulty showed up. We had assumed that a uranium or plutonium nucleus would not split unless it was struck by a neutron. In the summer of 1943, Emilio Segrè discovered that Uranium-238, Plutonium-239, and Plutonium-240 all undergo fission spontaneously.

Robert Bacher: When a pilot plant at Oak Ridge came into operation, we got some of the first samples out of that. We had decided we had to make measurements on this to find the nature of the work and to check for neutron emission. This was done—very fine physics—under the direction of Emilio Segrè from Berkeley.

Emilio Segrè: The difficult, but important, part of the work came with the study of Pu-239. Once we had milligram samples, we soon recognized that Pu-239 had a rate of spontaneous fission high enough to interfere seriously with the proposed methods of bomb assembly through pre-detonation. These findings, starting in April 1943 with a few counts, became firmer with better samples and longer observation times. We also checked the number of neutrons emitted per spontaneous fission.

Robert Bacher: What was found by Segrè and his group at Los Alamos was that the material produced in this pilot plant at Oak Ridge had different properties from the material we'd had before. It emitted neutrons, indicating spontaneous fission. This created a major problem. The more we found out about how sensitive this was to the amount of irradiation in the nuclear pile where it was made, the more we became convinced that it just wasn't possible to make a bomb out of it. We were then struck with the difficult problem that with the way we were making a bomb—using the gun assembly—you couldn't use plutonium. Plutonium was valueless to us. We were all glum. That caused a great crisis for the whole project.

Emilio Segrè: By July 1944, our results brought the Los Alamos lab to a real crisis, although the relevant information was based on a few counts only. Spontaneous fission in plutonium was so frequent that the plutonium alternative for making a bomb was excluded unless one could invent and develop a totally different assembly method.

James B. Conant: For the first time it was discovered that the plutonium as manufactured contained an isotope with undesirable nuclear properties. As a consequence, neutrons were being constantly emitted from the material. It could not be certain that two portions of the fissionable material could be brought together without a chain reaction starting before the total was well above the critical mass. In all the arguments in favor of the plutonium route to an explosive, it had been assumed that the design of a bomb could be made irrespective of whether U-235 or plutonium made in a pile was the fissionable material. The assumption was now shown to be wrong.

Emilio Segrè: The predicament was grave indeed, it meant that about half of the total work of the project might be useless for war purposes.

John H. Manley: This terrible shock, and an inescapable one, was that the gun assembly method could not be used for plutonium.

Col. Kenneth D. Nichols: There was no question that the gun method could not be used for plutonium. Evidence was overwhelming.

John H. Manley: The choice was to junk the whole discovery of the chain reaction that produced plutonium, and all of the investment in time and effort of the Hanford plant, unless somebody could come up with a way of assembling the plutonium material into a weapon that would explode. It was again a Los Alamos challenge to do just that. It was the only possible way out at that stage of the game.

Col. Kenneth D. Nichols: Development of implosion on a crash basis was the only possibility worth considering. My concern was Hanford. What to do about it? We did not know how long it would take to develop an implosion weapon. I thought that we should proceed at Hanford until scientists at Los Alamos determined it was absolutely impossible to develop an implosion bomb in time to be useful in this war. Not to continue building Hanford ran the obvious risk of determining that an implosion bomb was feasible, but then not having plutonium to fuel it. On the other hand, continuing to build would make our loss that much greater if implosion proved impossible. Groves again demonstrated guts by approving continued construction at the Hanford Engineer Works at the same urgent pace.

James B. Conant: An alternative weapon had to be found at once. Fortunately, a design was already at hand, but far from complete. It had been suggested some months earlier by a member of the Los Alamos staff, S. H. Neddermeyer. It was known as the implosion weapon. The principle was simple. A mass of fissionable material not quite critical would become critical if powerfully compressed. The compression was to be brought about by means of specially designed conventional explosives. To reduce this idea to practice, a whole new branch of the science of explosives had to be developed.

Emilio Segrè: Fortunately, the implosion method invented and suggested by Seth Neddermeyer avoided the pre-detonation problems connected with the slowness of the gun assembly of the bomb.

Robert Bacher: Work on implosion that Neddermeyer had started had gone ahead slowly, but it was far from indicating that it was a usable method.

Luis Alvarez: Implosion involved compressing a subcritical mass of fissionable material to higher density with shock waves from a surrounding high-explosive shell, squeezing it to supercriticality. The immediate and obvious advantage of implosion is that the material "assembles" so quickly under the pressure of the high-speed shock wave that it doesn't have time to predetonate.

Edward Teller: Seth's effort received limited attention until Johnny von Neumann showed up in Los Alamos. Johnny von Neumann was so valuable, not only as a mathematician but in virtually every field, that he was welcome to work with us even for very short periods. He was allowed to come and go freely. Johnny gave a talk in which he proposed a method of assembly that involved shaped charges. He then came home to see Mici, meet Paul, and have dinner. Afterwards, as we sat in the living room, I told him about Seth Neddermeyer's approach. Johnny immediately got interested in a quantitative manner. Assuming, as was natural, that the fissionable material was incompressible, Johnny could easily calculate the spherical flow of material toward the center.

Nicholas Metropolis, *physicist, Los Alamos Lab*: Von Neumann was very quick in seeing all of the implications of a really good idea. He could just run through, like no one else could, the consequences that might ensue from any new idea.

Edward Teller: In the midst of this discussion, our furnace began a booming serenade so impressive that Johnny stopped talking and looked about with some alarm. When I told him that it was only the steam in the system, he responded, "I would never live it down if I were killed by a mere subcritical explosion at this particular project."

After a few more minutes work, Johnny found that, under Seth's proposal, pressures of hundreds of millions of atmospheres would develop. At that point, I was reminded of a fact I had learned at the George Washington University theoretical physics conference on geophysics: Iron in the core of the earth, under an estimated pressure of 5 million atmospheres, is compressed by about 30 percent. I pointed out that at the high pressures Johnny was talking about, the fissionable materials would be compressed. In that case, the critical mass would become much smaller. Needing less fissionable material for an explosion, particularly at the time when such materials were in short supply, seemed to us a splendid idea. At the same time, we could achieve a speed of assembly great enough that premature neutrons would not cause pre-detonation in plutonium—at least if the percentage of Plutonium-240 was not too high.

Robert Christy: Von Neumann had an idea that if you put a lot of explosive around a little shell of material, and hit it hard and drive it together symmetrically, not only will it assemble into a sphere but it will compress. You'll compress the metal into something denser than ordinary uranium. And it was known, of course, by everyone in the business, that if you had uranium at twice normal density, the critical mass would be a quarter as great, or something like that. So this meant that with a smaller amount of material you might be able to get a big explosion, by using this concept of compressing the metal.

Edward Teller: The next morning, Johnny and I presented our findings to Oppenheimer. He immediately grasped their implications. Within a week, magnificent administrator that he was, he had turned the direction of the research around. From then on, our main efforts were no longer devoted to a gun-assembled weapon but rather to the implosion assembly.

Robert Christy: It was an idea that everyone was taken with.

Emilio Segrè: As a consequence of this discovery, the Los Alamos project took a sharp turn.

Robert Bacher: The laboratory was completely reorganized early in July of 1944. The experimental physics division, of which I was the head, was split up and so was the weapons division, under Captain [William "Deak"] Parsons. Two new divisions were formed to replace the experimental physics division. We had some work on explosives. The other division that was set up was called G division—G stood for "gadget"; "gadget" was what we called the implosion bomb.

Charles L. Critchfield, *mathematical physicist, Los Alamos Lab*: George Kistiakowsky came here from Houston to head up the explosive work. He was the nation's most qualified person to direct the scientific approach to high-precision casting and machining of explosives, which was what was required. [Ordnance Director Capt. William S.] "Deak" Parsons got mostly interested in the delivery problem for the gun device, the one that was used on Hiroshima. The implosion work really fell into Kistiakowsky's hands, and I was transferred from Deak's division into Bacher's. Robert Bacher had been head of the Physics and Research Division, and Robert chose him to head up what they called the Gadget, or G, Division.

Edward Teller: Johnny began what proved to be his third extremely important contribution to the work on the atomic bomb during that same visit: He began persuading us to use computers, pointing out the usefulness that computers would have in our calculations. Johnny von Neumann brought the first computers to Los Alamos. The equipment, provided by International Business Machines, now known as IBM, was advanced only in the sense that it provided electrical connections to drive mechanical motions.

Robert Christy: IBM tabulating machines—these great big machines about four feet high and six feet long, where you feed a deck of cards into one end, and it will process the numbers punched into them—we could get it to do multiplication, actually—and then it spews out a deck of cards at the other end with this information on it. The advantage of this machine was that, although it's doing only one operation—multiply A by B and write down the answer—it does that for one item after another. So you could do that one operation on a whole sequence of things. And then you'd take the deck of cards over to another machine and it would go through and do another operation. It was the strangest sort of computation ever devised.

Edward Teller: But even those machines were a great help. They were promptly put to work for the numerical integration of the hydrodynamics of implosion.

Robert Christy: Feynman helped to organize the operation, to make things go. They devised this system, with a bunch of machines and people carrying decks of cards from one machine to the other, and everything humming and clacking away. That was the computation laboratory, a most amazing thing.

Edward Teller: Our next problem was how to produce a sufficiently spherical implosion. Johnny knew enough about explosives to propose the use of explosive lenses. Just as a beam of light changes its direction when it passes through water and can be focused by passing it through a glass lens, the direction of a shock wave produced by an explosive can be focused and redirected by passing it through different explosive materials. Explosive lenses consist of various pieces of explosive that are fitted together so that the detonation wave moves at different speeds as it passes through different portions in the explosive. Such a composite of explosives can thoroughly reshape the shock wave and, at least in theory, can produce the desired shock wave along the surface of convergent spheres.

George B. Kistiakowsky: I always lectured Von Neumann—if I may use that outrageous word with respect for him—on our attitude toward high explosives, that they were completely controllable, exact mechanisms; otherwise, it's just a blind, destructive force. It was because of that that Von Neumann began telling Oppenheimer that implosion was not a wild shot, but was something conceivable.

Luis Alvarez: George was certainly the most competent high-explosives expert in the United States. He had been director of the NDRC explosives laboratory at Bruceton, Pennsylvania, and was unhappy at first to be sent into the boondocks to work on a program he thought could not help win the war.

George B. Kistiakowsky: I didn't think the bomb would be ready in time and I was interested in helping to win the war.

Luis Alvarez: He soon changed his mind. He was a tall, vigorous Ukrainian, and the contributions he made were vital to the bomb program's success.

Robert Christy: Implosion is a very complicated hydrodynamic calculation, in which you ask, "What happens to all this material?" a tenth of a microsecond by a tenth of a microsecond. As the pressures build up and it gets closer and closer together, you have to follow that by calculations of what's going on throughout all the material. You have to follow every little bit of a layer.

George B. Kistiakowsky: When you design the charge in a clever way, you end up with a spherical wave traveling towards the center of the charge and centered on the plutonium sphere in the middle.

Luis Alvarez: To make implosion work, we thus required two inventions. The first was the explosive lens, which behaves much like an ordinary glass lens: it takes a spherical wave that is expanding from a point and turns it into a spherical wave that is converging on a point. The second invention was simultaneous detonation. I led the team that made the second invention.

George B. Kistiakowsky: The electric detonators then in existence had horribly poor timing, so that to explode them simultaneously looked to us at least absolutely impossible. Mind you, since detonation waves travel almost a centimeter per micro-second, the timing we were concerned about were fractions of a millionth of a second. Luis Alvarez in the summer of 1944 started experimenting with electric detonators and, I must say, completely to my surprise, found a way of setting them off in such a way that the simultaneity was very acceptable.

Luis Alvarez: One day I suggested to George Kistiakowsky the possibility of starting the detonation wave in a detonator by discharging a high-voltage capacitor—a device for storing electricity—through the detonator's bridge wire. George was skeptical but agreed I should give it a try. Larry Johnston, my former student, had just arrived at Los Alamos from MIT. He prepared to try out my idea.

Lawrence H. Johnston: Alvarez asked Kistiakowsky why they did not use thirty-two electric detonators fired simultaneously to do the job. Kistiakowsky said that electric detonators had an intrinsic delay of several milliseconds in firing which would spoil the simultaneity. Timing of all the lenses was required simultaneous to within less than one microsecond. Alvarez then decided there was no basic physical law which would require this amount of delay if you could put enough electrical energy fast enough into the right design of an electric detonator. So he gave me the job of designing a detonator and electric firing system that would have no substantial delays in initiating a high explosive.

At Los Alamos you could get things and services fast if you were working on a high priority project. Within two days, I had a portable building set up on lonely South Mesa, two miles from the main tech area. Also a big workbench, some stools, a gasoline driven generator, a few electric cords, an assortment of mechanical and electronic tools, an electronic power supply giving up to 5,000 volts DC, an assortment of high voltage capacitors, a large roll of primacord, a gasoline blowtorch, some chemical glassware, some matches, a box full of DuPont electric blasting caps of the usual kind, and an olive drab colored automobile to get me around.

Luis Alvarez: The detonators in Larry's first test fired simultaneously within less than one microsecond. In a few days he was firing independent electrical detonators with a timing spread of less than one-tenth of a microsecond, at which point he changed to more precise time measurements. In a few months my group, now abruptly enlarged, brought the timing spread for hundreds of detonators fired simultaneously to within a few billionths of a second. Now we had to develop our new detonators and devise methods for studying the time spread in hundredths of a microsecond between groups of thirty-two and even sixty-four detonators fired simultaneously.

George B. Kistiakowsky: Up to 25 tons of H.E. was trucked up the hill monthly during the most active period. The manufacture of the H.E. charges was really hard, tough and dirty work. A lot of people thought it was also very dangerous and because of that I went to S-Site very frequently and tried out new operations simply to show confidence in what we were preaching.

Luis Alvarez: Our South Mesa operation was different from any I had ever been associated with before. Some of our Army men were technically skilled; others served us as laborers. A large force of Spanish-American women imported from nearby towns loaded detonators behind armored shields. We used insensitive explosives and lost not so much as a finger. We experimented to decrease the timing spread, sorted different particle sizes, varied packing pressure, changed all the engineering variables we could think of. It was cookbook work more than scientific, but we knew it was important and pushed it hard.

George B. Kistiakowsky: We ended with a spherical charge of high explosives, almost five feet in diameter with a metallic pit in the middle. In the center of the pit was the plutonium fissionable material. Our job was to induce the pit and the plutonium to be compressed in an orderly fashion under the extreme pressure of a detonation wave, many millions of pounds per square inch, into something very much smaller than it normally was, whereupon it would become supercritical. A nuclear reaction would then spread and a big bang follow.

John H. Manley: In spite of many difficulties, the scheduling of the whole project was never held up by a weapons problem; it was always the production of materials for weapons that determined the time scale.

Brig. Gen. Leslie Groves: In September, it became clear that we would use both a gun-assembly bomb—the Little Boy—and an implosion bomb—the Fat Man. We decided to freeze the external shapes of the three models then existent—one Little Boy and two Fat Men—to permit completion of the necessary modifications to the B-29 [that would deliver the bomb].

Col. Kenneth D. Nichols: Our best guess at that time was that sufficient U-235 for one gun-type weapon would be available about August 1, 1945. Groves was determined to drive ahead with the implosion weapon with the objective to beat the U-235 bomb. He still hoped we might have a plutonium weapon ready between March and July 1945. Both Compton and Oppenheimer thought this was possible, but Conant was not so optimistic. At the same time, we continued to plan on the gun-type weapon instead of implosion for U-235, in spite of the larger quantities of U-235 needed because Oppenheimer felt more confident that the gun type would work. We wanted to be certain that we had at least one type of atomic bomb.

"It came like a bombshell"

HANFORD: LIFE IN A CONSTRUCTION CAMP

The Hanford Engineer Works had to build a city out of the desert in Washington State.

Long before the X-10 reactor in Oak Ridge had come online, DuPont and the Met Lab were at work designing a comparably giant version of the graphite reactor to refine plutonium at scale. Groves and the Manhattan Project seized some 400,000 acres along the Columbia River, displacing about 1,500 locals as well as native tribes. Major excavation work for the first Hanford reactors began in the fall of 1943, and as progress continued, the Hanford construction camp grew into the largest ever in the US, aiding a total workforce of about 45,000 personnel, and making it by war's end the fourth-largest city in Washington State. Like many aspects of the Manhattan Project, its construction was a lesson in sheer audacity, as it swallowed enormous quantities of industrial resources—just preparing the vast site, before even counting the first shovelful of dirt, piece of lumber, or drop of concrete, required building more than 300 miles of road, 700 miles of railroads, and erecting 11,000 utility poles to provide electricity.

Brig. Gen. Leslie Groves: Hanford was then a very small town.

Annette Heriford, *resident, Hanford*: We owned thirty acres of Jonathon and Winesap apple orchards. We had planned to switch to red delicious. Our place was located 3½ miles from Hanford and 4 miles from White Bluffs. We were called "the in-between people." When the government arrived, the combined population of Vernita, Cold Creek, Hanford, and White Bluffs was between 1,200 and 1,500 people.

Ray Derenleau, *resident, Richland*: We got notice from the government on March 6, a little before noon, in the mail. I was plowing a field and I came in for lunch and [my parents] were telling me about it. After I ate, I went back out and cranked up that tractor. I bet I hadn't been plowing an hour and a half and somebody called up and told them to get that tractor out of the field.

Annette Heriford: In March, 1943, when I was about twenty-two, we received a letter from the government saying that we would have to move in thirty days. It was a terrible shock. I can't describe it. It was unbelievable. The only thing that made it credible to us was because of the war. Our town had been chosen for the war effort. We were so patriotic. Although we could go along with that idea, it was still a terrible blow. Even to think about it now, I can't even describe it. In spite of our patriotism, I remember one man stood there with a shotgun and said they would have to move him.

Jay Perry, *town appraiser*: If a bomb had been dropped in the community it would not have caused any more uproar. I liken it to what happens when one kicks a hive of bees. Gradually it became known that the Government planned to acquire 400,000–500,000 acres in northern Benton County and across the Columbia River in Franklin County on which some kind of plant connected with the war effort would be built.

Lloyd Wiehl, ***attorney, Yakima*****:** It came like a bombshell. They announced they were taking the whole valley. For what? We didn't know.

C. Marc Miller, ***appraiser, Army Corps of Engineers*****:** The negotiators for the Corps of Engineers had great difficulty in negotiating for the acquisition of any of the land because of the very low appraisals. Much of it went into litigation.

Lloyd Wiehl: Charles Powell, later a federal judge from Kennewick, and I got together and we took most of these land cases to court and the verdicts were so much over the appraisals. We had them reappraised. It was so ridiculous that the government finally confessed that they were wrong. We settled nearly all of the cases out of court. If they'd gone ahead with that original deal and everybody had signed up, it would have been a tremendous injustice.

Kathleen Hitchcock, ***daughter of White Bluffs newspaper publisher*****:** My mother took the evacuation very hard, they had always expected to live there the rest of their lives. And it was pretty hard when the Army engineers came in and told them to, you know, get out. It was a pretty hard thing. Some of them ended up at Medical Lake [a state mental hospital], you know, couldn't quite face it. My mother never really adjusted to it.

Brig. Gen. Leslie Groves: Long before all this confusion in the courtroom began, the first DuPont employee, an engineer named Les Grogan, arrived in Hanford on February 28, 1943.

Bob Gilbert: Prisoners from McNeil Island were brought in to harvest the abundant crops remaining after the farmers were evicted. Living quarters were established for them at the north end of the Benton City Road on the west bank of the Yakima River. It was a large camp, upstream from the Horn Rapids Dam, where Indians maintain a fishing platform. It is a beautiful spot on the hillside and occupied several acres, all immaculately maintained by the inmates. This site is still referred to as Columbia Camp. Father Sweeney ministered to the inmates at this camp.

Frank Buck, ***age 16, member of Wanapum Tribe*****:** We used to live in the tules [reed huts] until spring, then we take them apart, put them away and we move.

First we move after the root feasts, clear up to Soap Lake and Waterville. Then down to Ellensburg. Horn Rapids for fishing. Naches Pass for berries and more fishing for several weeks. After this we come back to Priest Rapids, where our home was for winter. We just went over this year after year. We just circle the same way every time. When the Army came into Hanford, they said we can't go in there.

W. K. "Mac" MacCready, *project liaison*: The first shovel was stuck in the ground at Hanford in the early summer of 1943. All of the buildings, all of the facilities, all of the roads, railroads, all of the interim structures necessary to carry on construction, were built, the Hanford plant was finished, all of the temporary stuff was cleared out and construction gone by the 6th of February 1945. Three reactors were built, three major separations plants, and all of the affiliated stuff, all were built in less than two years.

Claude Rawlins, *farmer, White Bluffs*: We didn't hate the government over it, we hated DuPont. I remember never buying a DuPont product after that. If it said DuPont, we didn't buy it. There was the Japanese and the Germans and DuPont—those were the enemies.

* * *

Brig. Gen. Leslie Groves: At the time the design of Hanford was begun, plutonium had been separated from uranium only in infinitesimal quantities and by laboratory methods. The most feasible process was largely a matter of opinion and the equipment needed was even more conjectural.

Frank Mackie, *construction manager, DuPont Corporation*: Hanford was quite the largest plant DuPont ever built up to then, and other than dams and things of that sort in faraway places, I guess it was the largest thing anybody had ever built.

Bill Compton, *DuPont Corporation*: Soon, construction of homes began, including "A" homes, two story duplexes; "B" homes, one story duplexes; "H" houses, three bedroom single units; "E" houses, four bedroom single units; and "J" houses, two story, four bedroom single units. All were the same basic construction, but they were painted different colors. These homes were primarily for the operating personnel. A few were allocated to key construction people. There was a housing list, and the day you came to the Hanford Works your name was entered on the list. When your name came up, you were called and assigned a house based on the size of your family and your job position.

Leon Overstreet, *steamfitter, American Can Company*: I was the ninth fitter lured on the DuPont construction job and my brother Paul was the tenth. We came in together. I was working at the Sunflower Ordnance Works in Kansas, near Kansas City. I was a steamfitter. On a day in May 1943, I heard two laborers talking. They said, "Boy, there's a big job out at Walla Walla, Washington." I called after work that day to the union business manager at Walla Walla, Washington, and he said to come on out and bring all of them who are willing to work. He said he heard it was the largest construction job in the world. I got my brother and a welder I was working with interested, and we got all our coupons for gasoline and tires and came on out.

Harry Petcher, *head of box lunch department*: My wife and I got married in May, 1943, and I was managing a night club in Chicago at that time, and during the day I was working for the Army Signal Corps on Pershing Road in Chicago as a nomenclature clerk. My wife called me at work one day and said, "Honey, I just took a job for both of us at a place called Hanford, Washington." I said you gotta be kidding. What are we going to do there? She told me I would be a waiter and she would be a waitress. What's it going to pay? She told me 55 cents an hour. I said you gotta be kidding. They promised a 12-hour day, seven days a week, time and a half after eight hours. That was 85 cents an hour, room and board, big wages.

William J. Dowis: After a night at the Transient Quarters, I joined a group of new construction workers, waiting to be taken to the construction site. Our vehicle was a cattle carrier, or "cattle car," a long, covered flatbed. The wood floor bore the marks of cattle hooves and had a trace of straw. Two long benches were placed along the sides. This carrier had been pressed into service in lieu of a bus. The "car" filled up with about forty people, all men except for two young women. As we started moving, all one could see through the cracks in the side panels was frosty sagebrush on the desert.

Leon Overstreet: This fella we rode out there with, a carpenter or somebody, he said it was the largest construction job in the world. When we came over the hill and looked down on this Hanford site, all we saw were eight or ten frame buildings under construction. It didn't look very big to us. That was the 7th day of May, 1943.

Margaret Hoffarth, ***waitress, Hanford Mess Hall*:** People, including me, came out here thinking Washington was the Evergreen State, and got dumped in a desert.

Louise Cease, ***project spouse*:** When we first came here, it was wild. There was nothing here. The sand was knee-deep. We picked out our first house, a one-bedroom prefab.

Jesse Brinkerhoff, ***fireman, DuPont Corporation*:** There was no electricity out there, no inside facilities, an outside toilet. Our water was brought to us each day in a barrel with ice in it. We lighted with coal oil lamps. My wife washed clothes on the washboard. We used wood and coal for fuel in a stove.

Jerry Saucier, ***operator*:** I worked as many hours as I wanted to work, sometimes 52 hours a week or more, time and a half after 40 hours. We always had lots of problems, like leaks in the steam lines. The living conditions were good, for a barracks, the same as if you were in the service, like any army camp. They were built to standards, rough, but ample.

Betsy Stuart, ***secretary*:** We went down to dinner the first night at the Transient Quarters and the salad dressing was so wonderful. We pigged out on the salad, and we had diarrhea for days. They were making the salad dressing with pure mineral oil—you couldn't get regular salad oil. Everybody got a good case of diarrhea when they came to Richland.

Harry Petcher: The way the food was prepared was all family style. The waitresses or waiters would run with these big carts up to the front where the cooks were dishing this stuff into family pans, like fried chicken. They would heap these big pans with fried chicken and run down the aisle and scoot it on these tables where all these guys were sitting, banging their hands.

Francis J. "Frank" McHale, ***safety engineer and fire marshal, Army Corps of Engineers*****:** For $13.25 per week, each worker was provided a room in the barracks with three unlimited meals per day, and a lunch packed for carry out. Because of the shift work, the cafeterias were kept open around the clock. You could eat all day and all night.

Harry Petcher: We were making sandwiches for box lunches, putting them in a paper bag. The first day I made something like 500. The box lunch was about 1,500 calories. We had three sandwiches with three ounces of food in each sandwich. Cheese, beef, or ham or chicken. There was fresh fruit; every once in a while we had salad. We used to give them a cold baked potato—a potato is a good vitamin source. Another thing, we dropped in two salt tablets in the box lunch. Toward the end, we started putting in candy bars, chewing gum and cigarettes, a sample pack of four. Our lunch cost was about 38 cents. We charged 55 cents.

Francis J. "Frank" McHale: Initially church services were conducted in a big old worn out circus tent we purchased from the Ringling Brothers. If you poked your finger on the canvas when it rained, it leaked. Fortunately it did not rain much. It kept the sun off and it kept people happy.

Monsignor William J. Sweeney, ***project priest*****:** The circus tent was big—a regular three-ring circus tent. It was so big you couldn't see the people sitting in the back. It was a movie theater during the week.

Francis J. "Frank" McHale: Each week, 50,000 people were paid. Each worker was given a payroll number. There were 50 lines; the first line was labeled for payroll number 1 through 1,000. The second was for payroll numbers 1,001 to 2,000, and so forth. The accounting and payroll people worked around the clock. At first workers were paid with checks. Merlin True, a payroll truck driver and teller, noticed that no checks had been cashed by one of the workers. Merlin asked the worker why he did not cash his checks. The worker responded that he did not know what to do with his checks. After they found other workers were also having difficulty cashing checks, they paid cash; that worked out much better.

Robert E. Bubenzer, ***security supervisor, DuPont Corporation*****:** We had to bring cash in every payday for the bank. We had an armored car, and we had two cars in front of it and two cars behind it and an airplane overhead. We would bring it from the railroad station at Pasco. We were transporting between one and two million dollars in mail sacks. This was on a Friday, and every Friday we would have twelve armed guards at the bank.

Col. Franklin T. Matthias: We made up our minds when we first started that we would put people in barracks regardless of what they looked like. It wasn't more than a few weeks after we started getting people in our camp that I had a visit from a whole bunch of Black guys led by a Black minister who said they would rather have their own barracks. They hadn't had any real trouble, but they figured they would.

Luzell Johnson, *cement finisher*: Everybody played baseball together. The teams were Black and white.

Roger W. Fulling, *division superintendent, DuPont Corporation*: Baseball was a great source of relaxation and at Hanford each craft, like carpenters, fitters and so forth, had its own team and there was an organized league between the crafts. One craft in particular was not doing too well. The head of the craft, the superintendent, said he wanted some changes in the league standings. He instructed recruiters in that craft to do some screening in the selection of candidates for hiring. This craft superintendent, unnamed but known to me, told his recruiters to concentrate on the Pacific Coast League baseball players. As a result, the craft went from the bottom to the top of the league. DuPont corrected this method of recruiting labor.

Annette Heriford: Three shifts were employed around the clock to construct a big auditorium. Robley Johnson said it was completed after only ten days. A Quonset hut was set up for a youth center. I was the director in the youth center. I taught tumbling, dancing, and also swimming in a man-made lake. The new residents also enjoyed ping pong, pool, and a well-stocked library. Nothing was too good for the young people that were needed to keep the families happy.

Francis J. "Frank" McHale: We built a recreation hall at Hanford. We brought in big name bands. It had the longest bar in the world, but because of state regulations, no one could stand at the bar. Everyone had to sit at tables. A pitcher of beer with as many glasses as you needed was $1. The dance floor in the recreation hall was the biggest in the northwest at that time. Occasionally shows and acts were brought in to perform in the recreation hall.

Jerry Saucier: The beer hall was pretty good-sized—a long bar, about the longest I had seen. They had a special crew to take care of the beer and the ice. It was a popular place, all during the day people working different hours. It got pretty rough some nights. One night, I was in there and all of a sudden all hell broke loose. They had a riot squad with trucks and they backed it up to the door and a guy gets up there with a bullhorn and tells them to break it up. Finally, the cops started using clubs and throwing guys in the wagon. Things got back to normal again. It was like an old western town where Marshal Dillon came in and had to straighten things out.

Robert E. Bubenzer: At the peak, in July 1944, we had 1,395 patrolmen. We had our own kangaroo court, and our own jail. Every morning we would screen them and unless it was awfully serious, a pat on the back and "Don't do it anymore" was our theory. In some cases, we would terminate lawbreakers, but in most cases it was important that we got them back to work. We needed workers.

Harry Petcher: You would get up in the morning and walk through your barracks and there's about twenty more barracks that weren't there last night.

Vera Jo MacCready, *project spouse*: People got confused, what with the new streets and the way the houses looked a lot alike. Several times I would be in the kitchen and a man would come in the back door, and usually I would know him and knew he just got in the wrong house.

Sam Campbell, *patrol captain*: One of our busiest periods was keeping people from being run over there at shift change, primarily 4–6 in the afternoon.

Margaret Hoffarth: Everything out there was sheer hurrying.

* * *

While much of the work at the Hanford Engineer Works was unprecedented and carefully guarded, the plants also faced one threat unique among all US industry during the war: Direct attack by Japanese bombs. From November 1944 to the spring of 1945, the Japanese Army lofted thousands of "Fu-Go" balloon bombs into the Pacific jet stream in hopes the bombs would traverse the ocean and land and explode in North America, sparking forest fires and instilling panic in the homeland.

Leona H. Woods: Large flocks of geese flew across the Columbia to the dry-farmed grain fields and irrigated mint fields on the east side for breakfast and dinner and returned at night, sleeping somewhere on the reservation. Night after night, the Army Air Force detachment mistook the radar image of the geese flocks for attacking enemy planes, flew their planes out and searched fruitlessly. After a few such abortive alerts, we all became sky conscious, especially because Japanese fire-carrying balloons began to drift overhead in significant numbers.

Walter O. Simon, *operations manager, DuPont Corporation*: Japanese balloon bombs were a real worry. Everybody at the plant was always looking up because of the statistical chance of one falling. I remember seeing forty at one time going over. The Navy planes at Pasco chased them regularly but they had poor luck. Matthias and I went over to prod them about getting better protection. They never managed to shoot one down, although a number came down on the project, but away from the buildings. The bombs never went off, but the balloons blew around and the military were a great sight trying to round these up without being blown up themselves. The only balloon that caused any damage to Hanford was the one that landed on the power line from Grand Coulee Dam.

Leona H. Woods: One of them tangled on a power pole, shorted the transformer, and shut off power for the better part of a day.

Walter O. Simon: It knocked out the reactors very briefly. The only American war plant shut down by enemy action during the whole course of the war. We mentioned that to Groves and he said, "I suppose all you fellows will apply for the Purple Heart."

Leona H. Woods: At noon one day we stood outside staring at the sky while we ate our sandwiches. It wasn't long before someone spotted Jupiter in the daytime sky, a pale sphere about the apparent size of a high-flying balloon, and we called out the planes to shoot it down. A plane went up and up until it reached its ceiling, and the pilot returned to reprimand us for frivolity.

* * *

Thomas L. Hankins, ***professor, University of Washington*****:** The real achievement of the Manhattan Project was the organization of it. After the war there was this problem of espionage and the popular press seemed to indicate there was a secret to the bomb and these scientists had discovered a profound equation somewhere. That wasn't the case. What was needed was an enormous industrial effort—at Oak Ridge, at Hanford, and at Los Alamos. It was a very large industrial effort, a major effort that required a lot of very skilled engineering and designing.

Roger W. Fulling: The missing link in the Manhattan Project story is that the atomic bomb was a product of American industry. This story has not been told. I want people to understand, before I go, the importance of industry to this project.

"So complicated and so obscure"

HANFORD: MAKING PLUTONIUM EN MASSE

One worker thought the "Queen Marys" looked like ships built upside-down.

The Hanford Engineer Works has been traditionally overlooked in Manhattan Project histories—failing to capture the public imagination like Los Alamos with its larger-than-life personalities. But there is an argument made by Hanford historian Steve Olson and others that the Washington State site is actually the most important location of the nuclear age—its first full-size nuclear reactor is the parent of all reactors since, and plutonium, first created en masse in Hanford's pools, remains the basis for effectively every nuclear weapon since.

The main production facilities at Hanford consisted of a two-step process—the reactors, located in what was known as the "100 area," that produced the plutonium, and then, about ten miles away, three giant chemical separation facilities located in the "200 area." These enormous windowless buildings—about 800 feet long, 65 feet wide, and 80 feet tall—were nicknamed the "Queen Marys" after their resemblance to a giant ocean liner sitting in the Washington desert. There, the irradiated slugs from the reactor were chemically treated and dissolved to remove the uranium and retrieve the one-part-in-a-million that was plutonium. A third part of the site, known as the "300 area," housed the metal fabrication and testing facilities, where uranium was heated and extruded into tens of thousands of "slugs" for use in the reactors.

*The first reactor started operations September 26, 1944. It was a vastly more powerful one than the pilot plant that had been built in Oak Ridge; the X-10 reactor achieved about 4 megawatts, but the three reactors in Hanford—known as B, F, and D—were designed for 250 megawatts. D reactor was operational by December, and F followed in February, all beginning to churn out plutonium for the bombs.**

Leon Overstreet: We went out to 100-B—the first reactor—in May 1944. We were among the first steamfitters on the job. I was amazed. I couldn't figure it out. I looked at that thing we were working on—it had all kinds of tubes and pipes running through it, and graphite blocks that the other crafts were laying around the pipes. Nobody could understand what kind of a contraption it was. They had never seen anything like it. You can usually understand what you're doing. But boy that one floored us.

Joe Holt, *construction worker, DuPont Corporation*: We were the first carpenter crew out there at the first reactor, and everybody worked with the engineers driving stakes, and then they started bringing in equipment. Heavy equipment, cranes, there was a trainload a day. Some of those cranes were so big they sat right on the track, all kinds of heavy equipment. Everything they asked for, they got.

W. K. "Mac" MacCready: While the plant was being built, there were only two people in the construction organization on site that knew the purpose of this

* The Hanford plant area, which operated well into the 1980s, eventually left an environmental disaster for future generations; today, it's estimated that the decades-long cleanup effort might cost half a trillion dollars. The land seized by Groves in World War II may forever be too polluted to hand back to the public.

construction. We must never say anything that would give any inkling to any of the construction people of what the plant was for.

Walter S. Carpenter: This operation—it was so complicated and so obscure.

Brig. Gen. Leslie Groves: Security necessitated special handling of the multitude of drawings, reports and correspondence that passed between the various offices. To speed up construction, working drawings were broken down to disclose as little information on the overall project as possible. By this means, it was possible to treat many of them as unclassified. Such measures were particularly necessary when drawings were sent to subcontractors or used by construction workers at the site.

Blake Miller: I was commissioned to do drafting. l was assigned to an inner room constructed from concrete and with no windows. A patrol officer was stationed at the door. The room had only a drafting table. One day, my supervisor brought a gentleman in with an attaché case attached with a chain to the man's wrist. With two keys he opened the case, laid the blueprints on the table, and told me to go to work. Many copies were needed. The maps had symbols, large grooves from which they made the graphite for the piles. Security was so tight that I would walk out of the inner office accompanied by a patrolman. Patrol followed me all the way to the john and all the way back.

Dewitt "Bill" Bailey, *special material handler, B Reactor, DuPont Corporation*: No way did I have a notion of what we were doing during the war. I don't think anybody else did. They only had one guy who could look at the blueprints. A general foreman or superintendent would go in and get a pencil sketch off of the main blueprint.

Joe Holt: They started digging this hole for the reactor building, and it was like going down to China. They put in three different concrete mixers to pump the concrete. I don't know how deep that hole was—just for the base.

Brig. Gen. Leslie Groves: The complications were many. Many pieces of equipment weighing as much as 250,000 pounds each had to be assembled with tolerances more suitable for high-grade watchmaking.

Joe Holt: They got the first reactor building up and then started laying the graphite. I helped on that. It was wonderful—very precise work. The blocks were different lengths, but all had to be fitted to tolerances in the thousandths. We had to wear protective clothing, shoe coverings, so there wouldn't be any contamination of the graphite. There were guys running a vacuum cleaner all the time to keep anything loose off the graphite.

Roger W. Fulling: Initially, we had a hell of a time getting the graphite block program through Union Carbide. I had to go up to the Union Carbide New York offices and present the program to their senior executives as to how important this was, and why we had to have it in large quantity and on schedule.

Brig. Gen. Leslie Groves: It was through the assistance and the strength of the industrial companies of America that DuPont was able to solve the hundreds of difficult design and material problems that had to be mastered. It is hard now to realize how difficult some of our developmental problems were.

Roger W. Fulling: The graphite blocks were laminated with a very special composition of fiber board. The machining was very, very interesting and requiring very high precision. And the only people who could do this was Vermont Marble in Rutland.

Joseph O. Hirschfelder: In order to make the plutonium piles at Hanford so much carbon black was required that for a period there was a shortage of rubber tires in the United States.

Raymond P. Genereaux, *design project manager, DuPont Corporation*: I had engineers of every calling on my team, mechanical, electrical, civil, metallurgical, chemical. It was that combination of people and talent that you needed.

Frank Mackie: We had our design division in Wilmington, with a nucleus of a design group at Hanford. If we got into a problem one night, we'd try to have it solved by our construction and design groups by the next morning. We had quite a few design men at Hanford, and they were only a telephone away from the big group in Wilmington.

C. N. Gross, *construction consultant, General Electric*: The teletype between Hanford and Wilmington was going 24 hours a day on design changes.

Francis J. "Frank" McHale: I had been cautioned not to recruit people from Oklahoma or Arkansas, because they were a bunch of hillbillies who would not work and would not take orders. The "Oakies" and the "Arkies" are the people who built this project. They did the hard manual labor and attended our schools where they learned to be plumbers, steam fitters, and all the other trades.

Joe Holt: It didn't matter what, if a man had only one arm or one leg, if he wanted to come to Hanford he had a job. Most of the men were older than me, a lot of them were in their sixties. They needed help so bad. They were determined to build a plant at all costs.

Frank Mackie: As far as materials were concerned, Hanford had the highest priority for government work and we could almost pick and choose what we wanted and when we wanted it.

Dewitt "Bill" Bailey: There was no reason to run out of anything because they could tap into anything in the United States.

Brig. Gen. Leslie Groves: Before the Hanford works were finished, DuPont employed over ten thousand subcontractors.

Dewitt "Bill" Bailey: We were running three shifts. They had electricians, pipefitters, millwrights, and those people were working all around the thing. Everything was being done at practically the same time. And it was so engineered that when one phase finished out, all of it was about finished and it was ready to pull the switch. We would repeat the work on the other reactors.

Brig. Gen. Leslie Groves: When our needs grew even more pressing, we were unable to find enough pipe fitters to maintain our schedule. Investigation showed that there simply were not enough in the United States to fill the demands. The solution we adopted was to locate a considerable number of pipe fitters, all union members, who had been inducted into the Army. These men were given the opportunity to be furloughed to the inactive reserve on condition that they would accept employment at Hanford as civilians at the going rates of pay.

Joe Holt: The concrete was made right there—they had the gravel and sand, all they hauled in was the cement. They started pouring this concrete, and it got below zero, so they brought in steam locomotives. They must have had, I don't know, 10 or 15. They built the railroad, and run the steam locomotives in there. They took all the steam the engines could produce. They had the concrete covered with tarps and these steam locomotives was furnishing steam underneath to keep the wet concrete from freezing before it set. Steam was flying every place.

Brig. Gen. Leslie Groves: Originally eight separation plants were considered necessary, then six, then four. Finally, with the benefit of the operating experience and information obtained from the Clinton semi-works, we decided to build only three, of which two would operate and one would serve as a reserve. I should like to point out that these separation plants were designed when we only had sub-microscopic quantities of plutonium.

Raymond P. Genereaux: We called the main separations building a canyon. We built three canyons—T, U, and B—and used two. Two were 810 feet 6 inches long by 102 feet and 85 feet two inches from bottom to top. The other one was 65 feet longer because we added a lab for handling hot materials.

Leona H. Woods: One of my bosses took me on a tour of the Queen Marys, carrying with us blueprints of the construction and plumbing diagrams. These huge concrete canyons were positioned about 10 miles apart in the desert, taking advantage of low hills between for shielding from each other.

Raymond P. Genereaux: One day some workmen were at one of the 221 Buildings—our designation for the canyon buildings—and the building was just up to grade. The bottoms were about 50 feet into the ground, and one of the workmen said, "I don't understand anything about it." The other guy said, "Yeah, I think they're building it upside down."

Leona H. Woods: These were the processing units for solution of the irradiated uranium slugs in nitric acid and for separation of plutonium and uranium from the fission products and of uranium and plutonium from each other. The irradiated slugs were to be brought into the first vat of the canyon on railway cars, in large tanks of cooling water. We went along the empty and echoing balconies of the canyon, checking pipes and valves, going step by step through the process as yet tested only in pilot-plant stage—how does this effluent get removed, how is that precipitate carried into the next cell, and so on. We found only one mistake; it had already been discovered a day or so before by an independent checking team. It was a pipe that had been blocked off in a maze of pipes.

* * *

One of the most significant challenges for the reactor was the design and manufacturing of the uranium "cans" that would make up the reactor. As the building construction advanced in the 100 area, little progress had been made in the 300 area in perfecting how to clad the uranium in aluminum necessary for the reactor processes.

Maj. Gen. Leslie Groves: The aluminum tubes illustrate how complicated even the most simple item could become.*

Arthur Holly Compton: The task of soldering and enclosing the uranium billets in aluminum cans came critically close to holding up the entire project. The final stages of this task were accomplished in a development laboratory set up by DuPont for the purpose in the Hanford area.

Maj. Gen. Leslie Groves: Seven months of persistent effort, principally by the Aluminum Company of America, were required to perfect a metal of the proper characteristics so that a satisfactory tube could be produced in quantity.

Walter O. Simon: The summer of '44 was coming along and the reactor was shaping up and there would be nothing to put into it. It was a little terrifying because if we didn't have them it would stop the whole thing. The reactor would be ready on September 15 and we would have nothing to put into it.

* Groves was promoted in the spring of 1944 to a two-star general, in recognition of his leadership of the Manhattan Project.

Leona H. Woods: With ten days or so to go before start up, only a few percent of the required slugs were on hand and successfully processed.

Walter O. Simon: The uranium was held in an aluminum can, a slug, about eight inches long and an inch and five-eighths in diameter. The can had to fit very tightly with no air space or bubbles. They couldn't leak because if water got into the uranium it destroyed the ability to react. So the concept was that the scientific people would find out how to do this and give us instruction. They found out how to design it but they never made a slug in the laboratory that didn't leak.

Roger W. Fulling: Extrusion is an art. You would start with a stock and you would extrude at the right temperature, cooling atmospheric conditions had to be just right.

Walter O. Simon: We had a production superintendent at Hanford named Earl Swenson, who was a real dyed-in-the-wool production man. He said, "They'll never make one of these in the lab, even if they work on it for ten years. It's a statistical matter. Why don't we make a thousand a day—we'll examine each one and test them all, and the poor ones we'll strip the aluminum can off and save the uranium and the next day we'll make another thousand."

Roger W. Fulling: The welding of the uranium containers was intricate. The welders working on the aluminum cans to contain the uranium fuel were not like you would see welding a steel plate to a steel beam or two steel beams together. These men were artists. They were the top of the craft, like the old goldsmiths.

Walter O. Simon: The first day a thousand failed, but there were maybe 10 better than the others, and we tried to figure out why these 10 were better. The next day, maybe they had 18 that were better. They kept doing this and lo and behold after about three weeks there was one perfect can. Purely statistical. If you made a thousand a day for three weeks, you had made 20,000 until you got one good one. They made five good ones the next day, and 10 the next and after a while, out of a thousand, they were making 500 and then 600 a day that were all right.

William P. "Bill" McCue, Sr., ***project staff, B Reactor*****:** I think Earl Swenson canned 30,000 pieces before they finally got a successful one, without voids. Somebody said something about that and Earl said, "Well, if necessary, we'll can another 30,000, until we get it right."

Roger Hultgren, ***chemist, T-Plant*****:** The canning process was critical. If we had not been able to protect the uranium from corrosion by the coolant, it would not have been possible to operate the B Reactor. As it turned out, we successfully canned the uranium slugs in aluminum jackets, bonded and welded them, machined them to the correct dimensions, and tested them in high-temperature, high-pressure water in autoclaves as a final quality test. In early September 1944, I accompanied a shipment of fuel elements from the 321 Building to the B Reactor.

Walter O. Simon: The director of DuPont's plutonium effort, the TNX Division, was Roger Williams, and the success of the project was due to his skill and guidance. He was a genius. The books to date on the Manhattan Project rarely mention him. He was a modest man and avoided the limelight.

"A gram of plutonium per day"

HANFORD: THE B REACTOR

DuPont's overbuilding of the B Reactor ended up saving the reactor project.

The chemical separation process, developed by Glenn Seaborg at UC-Berkeley, took irradiated slugs from the nuclear reactor and dissolved them in chemical solutions inside the giant Queen Mary facilities, an intricate multistep procedure that eventually allowed the plutonium to be isolated and removed. The first irradiated uranium slugs were ready for the Queen Marys just after Christmas 1944 and the first plutonium shipments to Los Alamos began February 2, 1945, almost exactly a year after the reactor assembly began. The reactors consumed enormous quantities of water from the nearby Columbia River, equivalent to the needs of a million-person city. The functionally identical F and D Reactor complexes followed the creation of the first B Reactor and came online in November and February 1945, finally allowing Hanford to manufacture plutonium at a meaningful scale.

C. N. Gross: The design level for plutonium production per reactor was 250 grams a day when the power level was 250 megawatts. Each megawatt was supposed to produce a gram of plutonium per day.

Leona H. Woods: This was the first big reactor in the world. Here were all these bigshots, lining the walls, to watch the startup. The operators were all coached. They had manuals. They had been through the routine X-Y-Z times. So here comes startup. You can see the water getting hot, the readings going up on the recorders, you could hear it rushing in the tubes, you could see the control rods coming out and out and out.

Robert D. Miller: I remember the day we started B Reactor. I was on the 4–12 shift. When I got to work, Enrico Fermi was sitting in the office with an old mechanical hand-cranked Marchant calculator studying why the reactor had shut itself down several hours after being started.

Dale Babcock, *chemist, DuPont Corporation*: The first nuclear reactor at Hanford died almost right away.

Leona H. Woods: Something happened, and there was no more reactivity. The reactor went dead, just plain dead. People stood around and stared at each other.

Alvin M. Weinberg: The pile shut itself down after a few hours of operation: the entire plutonium project seemed to be turning into a fiasco! We in Wigner's group tried to figure out what was going on; could some impurity in the water be depositing on the fuel elements and absorbing neutrons?

Leona H. Woods: During the night, after we had gone home leaving John Wheeler and Don Hughes on watch, one of the operators pulled out the control rods and found that the pile was regaining reactivity. The operators followed the build-up of the neutron flux and then once again watched it die away.

Dale Babcock: John Wheeler decided it probably was caused by a fission product. He selected three pairs of decay products, and he decided we should calculate how these would behave. We divided into three teams. I certainly was low end on the totem pole as far as knowing how to do it was concerned. It so happened I was part of the group which had the fission product that caused the problem, but we were so slow John and Charlie Wende finished up their products and they came over and worked over our backs. It was the Xenon-135.

Edward Teller: The explanation was quickly identified. One of the radioactive fission products—iodine—decayed into radioactive xenon. Xenon, it turned out, was a fierce neutron absorber. At low power levels, the xenon had time to decay into harmless cesium before absorbing neutrons. But at high power levels, the only way to solve the problem was to destroy the xenon by providing it with extra neutrons.

Eugene Wigner: One problem we never foresaw: that some of the chain reaction's undesirable fission product would have an absorption large enough to stop the reaction. When the first large-scale chain reaction was attempted, this soon occurred. A fission product, Xenon-135, was produced, with an enormous cross section. It absorbed neutrons vigorously and the chain reaction halted.

Leona H. Woods: By the time Fermi and I arrived the next morning, Wheeler and Don Hughes had largely solved the problem. What remained was several days of hard work following mathematically the observed buildup and decay of reactivity of the pile, fitting it to coupled differential equations, and evaluating the absorption cross section. We did this with hand computation, using desk-top computers, step by step, in steps corresponding to intervals of about ten minutes.

Alvin M. Weinberg: In this instance DuPont's conservatism, which irked Wigner so, was sound.

Edward Teller: Crawford H. Greenewalt took a remarkably positive and imaginative approach. In planning the Hanford reactors, the Met Lab scientists insisted that only minimum-sized reactors were required. Making them as small as possible, they declared, would put them into production faster, thereby speeding up the collection of weapons-grade material. Greenewalt, whom we called Greenie, was concerned that the project was moving too fast; he believed the reactors were risky even with the inclusion of the safety factors on which he had insisted. Greenie insisted that the size of the reactors be increased.

Dale Babcock: We suggested enlarging each one of the 1,500 fuel assemblies so that they would contain more uranium and expanding the number of fuel assemblies to 2,004. The added fuel assemblies were what allowed us to overcome the later poisoning by xenon.

Edward Teller: Greenie, by cautiously building a bigger reactor than theorists wanted, had made it possible to increase the number of fuel rods and thus the power.

Dale Babcock: If we had not been able to add more fuel, I'm certain we would not have been able to produce plutonium at the rate we had calculated, which was 250 grams per day per reactor.

David Hall, *head of Reactor Division*: The DuPont people say their foresight provided for the unexpected, as in the case of the xenon poisoning. In fairness, and I am not criticizing DuPont, I think they may not have done what they had done if they had been in a competitive position. They were running at cost, and they did not get a profit, but there was no expense to them. For example, my wife and I, both with Ph.Ds, were hired to do really quite menial tasks, jobs that could have been done by people without training. It was over-kill, and it paid off.

Leona H. Woods: It was a victory for conservative DuPont engineering practice that the empty tubes were available. Fermi calculated that if all the extra holes of the reactors were loaded with uranium slugs, the reactors would have enough reactivity for successful operation. It was so done in the next few days, with the slug canning assembly line again working around the clock. The first plutonium production reactor again started up, this time with no drama. The baby-sitter shifts of physicists sat around the clock.

Dale Babcock: I'm biased, but I think John Wheeler's analysis of the xenon poisoning at Hanford was in the Nobel Prize category. The problem appeared, it was solved, and we were going again.

Leona H. Woods: Three months later, the first batch of irradiated slugs were pushed out, and were trucked on the short railway to the Queen Mary where they were dissolved in nitric acid and the metal separations carried out.

W. K. "Mac" MacCready: To run a batch through took about 12 hours, through 221-T building—the big rascal with the thick concrete walls—and 224 building, a more normal building of concrete blocks. By the time you ran through 221-T building, you had separated most all of the fission products as well as the uranium from the plutonium. By the time you got to 224, it was 99 percent-plus pure. The radiation exposure was very low, so they could run through the next stages of purification in a more normal building without all the shielding or the remote operation. Eventually, the product was a 99. 99 percent pure solution of plutonium as a nitrate salt in solution.

Leona H. Woods: When the Queen Marys began to function, dissolving the irradiated slugs in concentrated nitric acid, great plumes of brown fumes blossomed above the concrete canyons, climbed thousands of feet into the air, and drifted sideways as they cooled, blown by winds aloft. The plumes cooled and descended on the desert where the iodine vapor stuck to the artemisia leaves; these leaves were eaten by the rabbits, which in turn were eaten by the coyotes. The Army guards of the huge reservation, with nothing else in particular to do, were asked by the medical staff to procure some coyotes at regular intervals, and so they drove around in jeeps over the desert floor, bucking across arroyos and gravel residues of ancient high water, shooting a monthly quota of coyotes. From the carcasses, the increasing radioactive content of the coyotes' thyroids was regularly monitored.

John A. Wheeler, *nuclear physicist, Metallurgical Laboratory*: An observer from afar, looking upon the scene in 1944, would have been convinced that he was looking at one alchemist's dream inside another. It was preposterous enough to think that dead uranium, put into regularly-spaced crannies in tons of dead black graphite, would come alive. It was still more preposterous to imagine this life, this silent darting back and forth of invisible neutrons, as producing in the course of time not merely a few atoms of plutonium, but billions upon billions of them, the philosopher's dream of synthesizing a new element achieved in kilogram amounts.

Leona H. Woods: Less than two months later, the first batch of plutonium arrived at Los Alamos.

Walter O. Simon: There was extreme pressure to produce a certain specified number of grams of plutonium, which in retrospect must have been enough for a test bomb and the Nagasaki bomb.

Oswald H. Greager, *chemist, DuPont Corporation*: At the end, it was a semi-solid of jelly-like consistency and was put into a sample can, a strong spherical container of stainless steel. This was shipped to Los Alamos.

Walter O. Simon: We shipped it in a solution. It looked like brown molasses. We shipped enough by June that we were cleaned out.

Bill Compton: "Big" Simpson was in charge of picking up the plutonium nitrate and trucking it to Los Alamos.

2nd Lt. O. R. "Big" Simpson, *project courier*: It was May when we started the convoys. We had three panel trucks with a lead car and a rear car. The cars were ordinary Ford sedans. There would be two people in a truck and two people in each car. We drove directly through. Everybody was armed. We carried shotguns and .38-caliber revolvers, and we had a submachine gun for each vehicle. When we stopped for chow, one guy would stay with each vehicle while the other guy ate. We would go down through Idaho, from there we cut down into Utah into Fort Douglas in Salt Lake City. From here to there was something like 707 miles.

We tried to make the run all at once at first, all the way to Los Alamos. But we decided that was not the way to do it. So Los Alamos came to Fort Douglas to meet us. The Los Alamos crew would arrive a day ahead of us so they could get their rest. We switched vehicles, unloading our containers into their vehicles. It was the dullest thing in the world. It was the most routine deal I have ever run across in my life.

Walter O. Simon: I don't know how much plutonium we shipped. We were strictly forbidden to keep notes or diaries.

Cyril S. Smith, *metallurgist*: The plutonium we metallurgists received was actually a fluoride, a dry powder. It came to Los Alamos from Hanford as a kind of syrupy nitrate, which was treated by the chemists in a series of ingenious purification processes. The powder was kind of a pinkish color, a pale pink.

Oswald H. Greager: They converted it into plutonium metal and made the parts for a weapon.

Paul Numerof: Late one evening my concentration was interrupted by the sound of hurried footsteps. This had to be investigated. *Who was running? And why? Had there been an accident with the radioactivity scattered all around? Had there been a chemical explosion? Was there a fire in one of the laboratories in the building?* A thousand thoughts raced through my head.

I saw someone walking in the hallway and asked him if there was a problem. "No problem," he said, "they've just completed the plutonium reduction!" A small group of men were looking at two metal hemispheres. If placed together they would have been about the size of a large grapefruit. As it was, they were just two grey-black pieces of metal which were not of this world. They were manmade. In a few more days these two pieces of metal would destroy the city of Nagasaki, Japan. I couldn't help but contrast these two ominous pieces of metal with what I had seen a year before, when the first tiny piece of metallic plutonium had been produced. It was the size of a very, very small pea, and it sat in an inch-long glass test tube. Now this.

Leona H. Woods: Plutonium is a very dense metal. When you hold a lump of it in your hand, it feels warm, like a live rabbit.

John A. Wheeler: People at Los Alamos gave me a piece to hold. The marvelous thing about it was the temperature of it. Here, day in day out, producing enough heat to keep itself quite warm, not for 10 years, not for a hundred years, but for thousands of years. It gives you an immediate sense of energy capacity.

PART IV

READYING *the* BOMB

1944–1945

By the fall of 1944, progress on the atomic bombs had advanced to the point where the leaders of the Manhattan Project were ready to think about how they would deliver the still-on-the-drawing-board weapons to targets in Europe and the Pacific. Much like the rest of the project to date, the actual use of the atomic bomb necessitated creating an all-new elite military unit with specially modified planes and training it in never-before-imagined tactics that would allow the crews to survive the largest explosion ever.

"Hell is on us"

BOEING'S BOMBER

Col. Paul Tibbets recruited two WASPs, Dorothea Moorman and Dora Dougherty, to show what was possible with the B-29 Superfortress.

Getting the "Fat Man" and "Little Boy" bombs to their target safely proved its own enormous effort, one that ultimately relied upon a military advance even more expensive than the Manhattan Project itself: The B-29 "Superfortress" was a giant—it weighed around 140,000 pounds fully loaded, contained 55,000 parts and 600,000 rivets, had a tail as tall as a three-story building, and its wingspan of 141 feet was longer than the entire first flight by the Wright brothers. It was the Air Force's most advanced bomber and, with a development cost of $3.7 billion, the most expensive weapon system of the war.

The B-29 was the weapon, planners hoped, that would knock Japan out of the war. Its long range would allow the US to bomb the homeland directly from bases on the Asian mainland and from Pacific islands, captured at great bloody cost by the Marines. Time felt short—Germany had been under air assault by British and American bombs for nearly four years before Japan would suffer its first sustained raids, and now the Air Force felt enormous pressure to deliver devastating blows quickly.

Robert M. Robbins, *XB-29 test pilot, Boeing Company*: In late 1938 Boeing had started thinking about a superbomber—an airplane for which, at that time, there was no established military requirement and no money—also, an airplane which no one knew how to build. The Army talked about an airplane with a 5,000-mile range capable of hitting an enemy aircraft carrier when it was still at least two days offshore. The B-17 could strike a carrier that was only one day out—too close for comfort. By August 1939 there finally was a superbomber configuration that Boeing could be proud to propose to the Air Corps. It was called the Model 341. It would later grow into the Model 345 and eventually become the B-29. Support for a superbomber spread rapidly. On 5 February 1940 Boeing was one of several aircraft manufacturers to receive from the Army an invitation to bid on a high-altitude, high-speed bombardment airplane with a requirement for a 5,333-mile range with a 2,000-pound bomb load. A month later Boeing proposed the Model 341 with a gross weight of 85,000 pounds to meet the requirement.

Col. Paul W. Tibbets: Although designed as a replacement for the B-17, and built by the same company, it was much more than an overgrown version of the Fortress. It contained many innovations, including a fire control system that would permit mounted guns outside the airplane to be fired by a gunner who had no manual contact with the weapons. As a result, one man could control more than one of the five guns.

William E. Shine, *instructor, Base Communication and Radar School, Smoky Hill Army Air Base, Kansas*: The B-29 airplane was designed around a radar set—the AN/APQ-13. In all other airplanes, radar was an add-on modification but on the B-29 both bombing and navigation were performed using radar.

Col. Paul W. Tibbets: The B-29 was also pressurized, enabling the crew to get to the target in shirtsleeve environment, reducing the fatigue on long missions.

For me, it meant that I could puff on my pipe during the flight instead of having to wear an oxygen mask at high altitudes. In addition to carrying more and larger bombs, the B-29 could fly higher, faster, and farther than the B-17. These qualities were urgently needed if we were to wage a devastating aerial war against Japan.

Robert M. Robbins: Two of the very tough choices they made were to put the B-29 into production even before the engineering was completed and to commit them to combat before developmental testing could get them more fully debugged.

Gen. Henry "Hap" Arnold, *chief, Army Air Forces*: It was so large and complicated that it required about ten thousand drawings before it was possible to put it into production.

Maj. Gen. Curtis LeMay, *chief, Strategic Air Forces—Pacific*: Hap took the chances, cut the corners, and ordered this unique airplane into production before the prototype was even completed. Arnold took a calculated risk of unprecedented proportions—everything could have exploded in his face.

Col. Paul W. Tibbets: In Washington, where I reported for assignment to the B-29 program, I found that the big bomber project was a shambles. "I don't know whether we'll ever have a B-29," General Eugene Ewbank told me. Only the week before, on February 18 [1943], Boeing's chief test pilot, Eddie Allen, and ten top technicians had been killed at Seattle in the crash of a B-29 in a test flight.

Maj. Gen. Curtis LeMay: It was a test program disaster of unparalleled proportions.

Robert M. Robbins: Shortly after Eddie's accident, Brigadier General K. B. Wolfe was directed by General Arnold to take over all aspects of the B-29 program. One of his directives was that the Army Air Corps would take over the entire B-29 flight test program and that the #1 XB-29 flight test program would be done at Wichita where conditions were much more favorable. The weather was better, runways were longer and wider, approaches were clearer and good alternate fields were relatively close. The Boeing Wichita plant would provide support.

T/Sgt. Kenneth L. Eidnes, ***computer specialist, 393rd Bombardment Squadron*****:** As this aircraft was a new conception, there was much testing to be done and the Army Air Corps was assigned to do a lot of it. An officer was put in charge of testing and came to Boeing at this time. Paul Tibbets had just returned from England where he had completed a tour of combat flying B-17s. He flew many hours testing all the components of the aircraft, the fire control system, recommending changes to be made and testing the changes that were made. It is well known that the biggest problem was the engines.

Maj. Charles W. Sweeney: Once the military had ordered production of sixteen hundred B-29s even as the bugs were still being worked out, the need for flight instructors to train the pilots to fly them was pressing. General Armstrong assigned Tibbets to oversee the development of a flight instructors' school. I would identify and standardize all procedures for the operation of the aircraft.

Col. Paul W. Tibbets: After the excitement of combat over Europe and North Africa, my assignment in the States had been an emotional letdown. The war, which had been a day-to-day reality, now seemed remote. My contribution to this effort consisted of working sixteen hours a day testing B-29s and training crews to fly the big new planes. Because this bomber was being built for action in the Pacific, I was obliged to reorient my thoughts about the priorities in this global war. In Europe, it was easy to conclude that here was the primary theater of action.

Vice Adm. William "Bull" Halsey, Jr.: Europe was Washington's darling. The South Pacific was only a stepchild.

Maj. Charles W. Sweeney: The B-29 itself was getting a reputation among some pilots as being unreliable and dangerous. The psychological effect of the pilots' lack of confidence was feeding on itself.

Col. Paul W. Tibbets: I decided it was just another flying machine with characteristics that were not too different from those with which I was familiar.

There was plenty of open prairie around Wichita, and I didn't think it possible to get into serious trouble even if the plane developed one of the flaws for which it had already become famous. It would be easy to belly it in and walk back for another one and keep on testing. The flaws diminished during the next few months, and I like to think that my experimental flights helped to spot the troubles.

Col. Samuel R. Harris, Jr., *commander, 499th Bombardment Group*: This airplane has more bugs in it than a Tennessee mountain bed.

Maj. Gen. Curtis LeMay: As many bugs as the entomological department of the Smithsonian.

Maj. Charles W. Sweeney: A colonel who commanded a group of B-29s in training at Clovis, New Mexico, had called Tibbets to ask his advice about the growing hesitancy of his pilots to fly the airplane. Engine fires, in particular, had become commonplace. Tibbets had an idea.

Col. Paul W. Tibbets: I was confronted by a man from General Arnold's office in Washington with the fact that they were having trouble at Clovis, New Mexico trying to get college football heroes to fly the B-29. They said it was unsafe. Well, by that time I had about a thousand hours in that thing, and I just couldn't agree with that thesis. They said, "Can you think of any way we could cure it?" Didn't take me long to figure it out. I said, "Train two women to fly it."

Maj. Charles W. Sweeney: With the vast majority of men in uniform, most of them either in Europe or in the Pacific, the military had begun to more effectively use the skills of its women, who were not permitted by law to engage in combat. Pilots were needed for stateside duty to ferry aircraft from the plants to airfields and from one field to another. So the Women's Auxiliary Service Pilots (WASPs) was created under the leadership of Jackie Cochrane. Jackie, a famous aviatrix before the war and a pioneer in aviation, recruited both experienced women pilots and those who wanted to learn to fly. The WASPs flew in all kinds of conditions to carry out their assignments, and many lost their lives in the line of duty. Their contribution to the war effort has never been fully appreciated—or, for that matter, even known—by the public. Tibbets selected two WASPs in our unit and took them in a B-29 to an unused airfield in Anniston, Alabama.*

Col. Paul W. Tibbets: Eglin Field had a WASP detachment. Permission was granted, and the thing was arranged. I went down to the nurse's quarters.

Dora Dougherty, *WASP*: Didi Moorman was there—she was the only one of us not flying that afternoon. She and some of the nurses were sitting there in their shorts with their hair up trying to keep cool, and these two guys walked in their day room. When everybody started to vanish they said to Didi, "You're the one we want to talk to."

Dorothea "Didi" Moorman, *WASP*: I had a day off, and I was in the nurses' quarters, and these two gentlemen came in. The man said, "pardon me, but are you a WASP?" "Yes, yes, I am." "Well, I'm Colonel Paul Tibbets," and he said, "I'd like to talk to you." A colonel was to me a big rank then. And he said, "I'm looking for two WASPs who have no four-engine time." And I said, "Well, none of us have any four-engine time. We were not checked out in it." He said, "I'm having a problem. I'm the project officer on the B-29. I'm having a problem because we've had some engine fires, and we've had some pilots who are reluctant to fly it. My feeling is if I can check out two WASPs with no previous four-engine time in an eight-hour checkout, and check them in this aircraft and let them fly it, they'll have to fly it. It will be a matter of pride." It sounded like a good line of thought to me. He said, "I'll take you," and he said, "Now what are the other girls doing?" I told him Dora was checking out in the A-20. He said, "I'll take Miss Dougherty."

Maj. Charles W. Sweeney: It was important that word not get out. He trained them to fly the B-29.

* Although they worked alongside military personnel, flew military planes, and were specifically trained to "fly the Army way," WASPs were not technically considered part of the Army Air Forces and were classified as civilians. In the 1970s, when the Air Force began to admit women to pilot training, pressure rose to recognize the past contribution of WASPs. In 1977, legislation signed by President Carter granted them veteran status and, in 1984, they were officially granted World War II Victory Medals.

Col. Paul W. Tibbets: We worked at it three days. I worked the girls hard three days, we flew for seven hours a day.

Dora Dougherty: It just didn't seem possible to me, when they said that we were going to fly it. I didn't think I was strong enough. I didn't think my hand was big enough for four throttles.

Dorothea "Didi" Moorman: The way they handled this was we would trade off; first one of us in the pilot seat, the next one in the copilot seat, and the colonel always sat in the jump seat. His only reason for this was to prove his aircraft, and the aircraft was a beautiful piece of equipment.

Dora Dougherty: Didi and I would alternate every half-hour in the pilot seat, while Colonel Tibbets was our instructor pilot. I think all of the women of the WASP felt at all times as we did that day: We felt that we were representing all of the women pilots of the world, and that we had to do the very best that we could to uphold the reputation of women pilots. We were so intent on everything we did.

Maj. Charles W. Sweeney: When he was satisfied that they were ready, he sent them on their way with orders to land at Clovis.

Dorothea "Didi" Moorman: The colonel said we are going to go tour the B-29 bases. We went to Birmingham, went back down to Eglin. We landed at Tinker Tower, Oklahoma. We got off—and I had flown that leg—and this big lieutenant came up, and he looked at me, and he said, "did you fly that aircraft in? How did you manage that?" Then we went to Clovis, our first B-29 base. We came in there, and the base paper, of course, played it up. I'm sure they worked with the colonel on this because it said, these two bits of femininity brought this aircraft in. This went like wildfire—women flying the B-29! Oh, man, it was big news.

Col. Paul W. Tibbets: They were dumbfounded that two women would fly that airplane that way when they said it wouldn't fly. It was an amazing effect.

Harry McKeown, *director, Maintenance & Supply and base test pilot, Clovis Air Base*: From that day on we never had a pilot who didn't want to fly the B-29.

Col. Alva L. Harvey, *B-29 project officer*: In mid-summer 1943, the first of the B-29 bombardment wings was organized. B-29 bases were constructed in India and China for our combat operations against the Japanese. Movement to these bases began at the end of April 1944.

1st Lt. Fountain L. Brown, *B-29 copilot, 40th Bomb Group*: On 15 June 1944, we departed Hsinching, China, bombed the Imperial Iron and Steel Works, Yawata, Japan, and returned. Our crew flew one of the twenty aircraft that formed the first B-29 strike against the Japanese homeland. The importance of this mission was sufficient to draw eleven general officers and numerous war correspondents. Not that the bombing results were that good, but the Yawata mission was the beginning of the end for Japan.

Gen. George C. Marshall: The Japanese islands first came under bombardment of China-based B-29s on 15 June 1944. This assault was joined by Superfortresses based in the Marianas on 24 November 1944.

Kiyoshi Kiyosawa, *journalist, diary entry, December 27, 1944*: Today the enemy came in rows of silvery wings.

Marshal Adm. Osami Nagano, *adviser, Japanese government*: Hell is on us.

"Bleak and barren"

CODE NAME SILVERPLATE

Col. Paul Tibbets was not even thirty when he was tapped to build the 509th Composite Group.

The bomber wing that would ultimately be named the 509th Composite Group was unlike any other force in the US military—specifically created to deliver a single weapon, endowed with the highest priority levels, outfitted with the best machines and crews handpicked from across the Army Air Forces. Its commander had just months to train them for an unprecedented mission.

Maj. Gen. Leslie Groves: In employing the bomb in battle, the Army Air Force would obviously play a major role, provided, of course, that it could be airlifted. Consequently, I called on General Hap Arnold in the spring of

1944 and discussed the whole situation with him, including our prospects for success and the date upon which the bomb would probably be ready. I had decided it would be reasonable to plan on using the B-29 as the carrier plane, though we might have to make certain modifications—all of which appeared feasible—in the plane's bomb bay and bomb-handling equipment. General Arnold and I agreed at our first meeting that we should create an Air Force unit that would be self-sustaining; for that reason, Arnold decided to organize it as a composite group, built around a heavy bombardment squadron. Our first problem was the selection of its commanding officer.

Col. Paul W. Tibbets: One day [in September 1944] I'm running a test on a B-29, I land, a man meets me. He says he just got a call from General Uzal Ent [commander of the Second Air Force] at Colorado Springs. He wants me in his office the next morning at nine o'clock. He said, "Bring your clothing—your B4 bag—because you're not coming back." Well, I didn't know what it was and didn't pay any attention to it—it was just another assignment. I got to Colorado Springs the next morning perfectly on time. A man named Lansdale met me, walked me to General Ent's office and closed the door behind me. With him was a man wearing a blue suit, a US Navy captain—that was William Parsons, who flew with me to Hiroshima—and Dr. Norman Ramsey, Columbia University professor in nuclear physics. And Norman said: "OK, we've got what we call the Manhattan Project. What we're doing is trying to develop an atomic bomb. We've gotten to the point now where we can't go much further till we have airplanes to work with."

Maj. Gen. Leslie Groves: Tibbets had been the Operations Officer of the 97th Bombardment Group in the North African and European Theater of Operations, where he had flown the usual number of combat missions, and had then been returned to the United States. He was a superb pilot of heavy planes, with years of military flying experience, and was probably as familiar with the B-29 as anyone in the service.

Col. Paul W. Tibbets: General Ent laid out what was going on and it was up to me now to put together an organization and train them to drop atomic weapons on both Europe and the Pacific. My edict was as clear as could be. Drop simultaneously in Europe and the Pacific because of the secrecy problem—you couldn't drop it in one part of the world without dropping it in the other. And so he said, "I don't know what to tell you, but I know you happen to have B-29s to start with. I've got a squadron in training in Nebraska—they have the best record so far of anybody we've got. I want you to go visit them, look at them, talk to them, do whatever you want. If they don't suit you, we'll get you some more." He said, "Paul, be careful how you treat this responsibility, because if you're successful you'll probably be called a hero. And if you're unsuccessful, you might wind up in prison."

* * *

Col. Paul W. Tibbets: Although I came out of General Ent's office flattered by the importance of my new assignment, it wasn't until the next day that I became fully conscious of the terrible responsibility that was now mine. At the age of twenty-nine, I had been entrusted with the successful delivery of the most frightful weapon ever devised, one that had been developed at a cost of two billion dollars in a program that involved the nation's best scientific brains and the secret mobilization of its industrial capacity. My first job was to find a home for the outfit that I still had to organize. Of the three bases General Ent had offered me, I flew first to Wendover in northwestern Utah on the Nevada border.

Capt. Thomas L. Karnes, *personnel officer, Wendover Army Air Base*: The Army Air Corps established Wendover Field as an air base in 1940. Located on the edge of the Bonneville Salt Flats at the Utah, Nevada state line, its terrain and isolation provided a perfect location for the training of aerial gunners and bomb crews. Originally designed in 1941 as a depot to Ft. Douglas, the nearly 2 million acres of salt and scrub persuaded the Army Air Corps to make the place the world's largest bombing and gunnery base. In August 1941, the eleven men stationed there began setting up targets on the salt flats that had ruined the famous Donner party. At least fourteen bomb groups were trained there from April 1943 when I came until April 1944.

Cpl. Mont J. Mickelson, *machine shop, 603rd Air Engineering Squadron*: Wendover was a remote base where various aircraft—B-17, B-24, P-47, cargo, and other crews—received training.

Capt. Thomas L. Karnes: In August 1944, the last trainees left and only the permanent cadre and a half dozen administrative airplanes remained. The base no longer had any function and many of us wondered if the base were about to be closed. During this strange period, a lone B-29 arrived at the base and its pilot came to headquarters to declare his desire to inspect the general facilities.

Col. Paul W. Tibbets: As I approached Wendover from the air, I liked what I saw. It was remote in the truest sense.

Capt. Charles D. "Don" Albury, ***airplane commander, Crew C-15, 393rd Bombardment Squadron*****:** I flew in with Paul Tibbets to inspect the airport to see if it was usable for B-29s. Paul decided we could always take off to the south or the east and maybe use the west runway. On our flight to Wendover, Paul Tibbets asked if I would like to go overseas with the outfit he was going to form. I said, "Yes, of course" because I had a lot of respect for him and his abilities.

Capt. Thomas L. Karnes: Although only a captain, I was the ranking headquarters officer at the time, so it fell upon me to greet the visitor. He was Paul Tibbets. He asked a few questions, toured the base, thanked me and left.

Col. Paul W. Tibbets: I was so well satisfied with what I saw that I didn't even examine the other two bases.

Capt. Thomas L. Karnes: I gave the episode no particular thought until a few weeks later when Tibbets returned. He said he was organizing an unusual bomb group that would have a large number of men with rare qualifications, but he thought many of the base cadre could be utilized as the nucleus of the group. Paul Tibbets and I were about the same age. His air of quiet confidence impressed me immediately as it must have the generals who selected him to command the 509th and I was eager to work for him.

Cpl. Mont J. Mickelson: Suddenly, an air of secrecy filtrated the entire base. B-29 aircraft arrived. Three of us from the machine shop were asked to volunteer and join the mysterious newly formed group.

Cpl. Maurice C. Sullivan, ***criminal investigator, 1395th Military Police Company*****:** Suddenly, the base was flooded with all types of strangers working on various secret surveys. The Base Intelligence Office cooperated closely with the strangers. After a while, I, being an avid science fiction fan, began to form a minuscule idea of the mission of the 509th. To learn more of atomic theory, I checked a book from the base library entitled, *Atoms in Action*. Shortly thereafter, I was visited by a very curious CIC [counterintelligence corps] agent in my quarters. I played it cool. Later I was interviewed by his superior and others. To make a long story short, I realized my hope of transferring into the 509th. The only conditions were to keep quiet and do my job.

Col. Paul W. Tibbets: With the base selected, my next task was to round up the necessary personnel. I went over to Harvard, Nebraska, to take a look at the 393rd Bomb Squadron, which General Ent had offered me as the nucleus of my outfit.

Maj. Gen. Leslie Groves: The 393rd Heavy Bombardment Squadron was detached from the 504th Bombardment Group to form the nucleus of the new unit—the 509th Composite Group. The 393rd was picked because of the fine reputation it had gained during its training. The squadron was about to go overseas with its parent organization when the new orders were received.

Col. Paul W. Tibbets: I set up headquarters at Wendover on September 8, just one week after being given my assignment. The 393rd squadron personnel arrived with their airplanes three days later. They consisted of the flight and ground crews for 15 B-29s.

Lt. Jacob Beser, ***radar countermeasures officer, 393rd Bombardment Squadron*****:** On the afternoon of September 10, 1944, the commandant of Fairmont Army Airfield published general order no. 254. Paragraph 7 of that order was a bombshell. All personnel of the 393rd Squadron were ordered to depart not later than September 15th to Wendover Field, Utah, for temporary duty, complete with all organizational equipment. The inclusion of all organizational equipment and the statement that no per diem would be paid while at Wendover, and authorization for dependents to accompany were all clues to the fact that the 393rd was never going to rejoin the 504th.

Col. Paul W. Tibbets: With authority to draw upon the best available men in the air force, I set out to surround myself with people whose superior skills I recognized. From my old B-17 crew in Europe I summoned Tom Ferebee, the best bombardier who ever looked through the eyepiece of a Norden bomb sight; Staff Sergeant George Caron, my old tail-gunner; Dutch Van Kirk, navigator; and Staff Sergeant Wyatt Duzenbury, flight engineer. They would be assigned to my plane in the squadron and would be in charge of training their counterparts in the other aircraft.

I also called on Bob Lewis, who had been involved with me in B-29 testing and would serve as my copilot, often becoming commander of my aircraft when other duties prevented me from flying. In fact, he would fly the plane so often that he came to consider it his.

Other key people brought into the outfit, on the recommendation of those whose judgment I respected, included bombardier Kermit Beahan, navigator James Van Pelt, radar specialist Jacob Beser, and pilots Charles Sweeney and Don Albury.

Maj. Charles W. Sweeney: Captain Albury, Master Sergeant John Kuharek, and a few others and I were among a small nucleus who were the first arrivals of a group that was to become fifteen hundred men. What caught my attention immediately was that security at the base was pervasive. Restricted areas were set up and military police were posted everywhere. Barbed wire cordoned off sections of the field. Signs were prominently posted warning of the importance of secrecy. At one end of the flight line there was a missile-testing project, its missiles similar to the V-2 rockets being used by the Germans. Soon I would learn that this project was a cover. The true purpose of this base had nothing to do with rockets.

Sgt. Paul Metro, ***radar, 393rd Bombardment Squadron*****:** On Tuesday, September 12, we boarded a train for Utah. I don't remember much about the trip except we passed along the shore of the Great Salt Lake and entered barren desolate salt flats.

Lt. Jacob Beser: Friday, September 15, 1944, the troop train that carried the bulk of the men of the 393rd from Fairmont to Wendover had been sitting in a freight yard in Salt Lake City, Utah, adjacent to a load of Italian prisoners of war. Both trains were awaiting new engines and crew before proceeding further. As the men on both trains began to wake up, they began talking back and forth between the trains; many of the POWs were quite fluent in English, and some of our Brooklyn boys spoke the language of their fathers. One thing was obvious to us, as far as creature comforts were concerned, the train supplied to the POWs had it all over ours. Both trains had "kitchen cars" set up and the troops on either train prepared their own food. If you have never been involved in a large troop movement, you cannot appreciate the miracle of hot food. Uncle Sam, in those days at least, supplied good food and if the cooks didn't ruin it, one could eat reasonably well. This was nothing compared to the way those Italian boys were fed. The hot breakfast pastries that they were served made our hot GI bread almost medicinal. There was one redeeming circumstance, however, we had American cigarettes in quantity, and for these, the Italians would have traded their mothers. Their pastries were just superb. At about 1000 hours, a new engine was hooked to our train, we moved out of the yard, and once again headed west on the last leg of our trip for Wendover.

Col. Paul W. Tibbets: For morale purposes, we decided to let the married men bring their families to Wendover.

Capt. Charles D. "Don" Albury: We had just bought a 1939 Ford convertible coupe, dark green, in Pratt, Kansas. When my transfer came in, Roberta and I piled our entire possessions in the rumble seat and started for Wendover. At the outskirts of Salt Lake City, on our way to Wendover, we stopped for breakfast. Roberta being about three months pregnant, spotted waffles with strawberries and whipped cream and ordered it several times. We made that 125-mile trip for that same dish. At Wendover, just being the two of us, we were given housing, single room, single bed, at the civilian dormitories. What a deal—pregnant wife and me 155 pounds on a single bed.

Esther Bartlett, ***spouse of Albert Bartlett, 393rd Bombardment Squadron*****:** In order to be eligible for housing, I needed to get a job. So off I went to the PX to apply for a job, after figuring out how to get a pass to get on base. Luckily I was hired on the spot and was able to return immediately to the housing office with the required paperwork. I got to the station as the train was pulling in with my husband. Some of the other soldiers saw me and quickly told Albert that "his wife was already there!" I felt very proud of myself that by the time he arrived, I had a job and we had an apartment. Our life in Wendover had begun. Bright and early the next morning I began serving donuts and coffee at the PX. I learned how to make the batter and fry donuts. Empty coffee cups went into the dishwasher. Each night I went home smelling of fried dough and coffee.

Sgt. Joseph Ross, *radar countermeasures, 393rd Bombardment Squadron*: I remember my first view of Wendover as the troop train arrived at the base, it didn't look like much of an oasis at the end of the salt flats.

Sgt. Paul Metro: This was to be our home for the next 7–8 months.

Maj. Charles W. Sweeney: Wendover Field was desolate and primitive, all right.

Virginia P. Karnes, *military spouse*: The words bleak and barren come to mind.

1st Lt. Russell F. Angeli, *airplane commander, 320th Troop Carrier Squadron*: Desolate, God forsaken, you name it.

Capt. Charles D. "Don" Albury: My first impression of Wendover: What a desolate place this is.

Sgt. Gillon T. Niceley, *tail gunner, Crew C-11, 393rd Bombardment Squadron*: What a desolate place.

Cpl. Herbert D. Swasey, *603rd Air Engineering Squadron*: Desolate.

Cmdr. Frederick L. Ashworth, *director of operations, Project Alberta*: There was nothing separating the town from the North Pole but a barbed wire fence!

Dorothy Allen, *spouse of Raymond E. Allen, tail gunner, Crew C-12, 393rd Bombardment Squadron*: Wendover was a town located on the Utah/Nevada line with one hotel, one drug store, one grocery store, I'm sure a filling station or two, some house trailers, a few houses and a population of 103 which did not include the military people and their dependents on the base.

2nd Lt. Fred J. Olivi: Colonel Tibbets had said our quarters might be a bit "primitive." He was right. Not only were they primitive, they were almost "unlivable" tar paper shacks, more suited to house cattle or sheep than officers in the United States Army Air Corps! These ten-man, one-story wooden buildings were constructed about a foot off the ground with two-by-four frames, sheathed with thin plywood, and covered with tar paper. Inside there were five small cubicles, two men to each. An upper and lower bunk bed filled up most of the space in each cubicle; the ceiling was so low that the man sleeping in the upper bunk could barely sit upright.

Potbellied stoves burning soft coal stood at each end of these architectural nightmares. An enlisted man was assigned to keep them going twenty-four hours a day. I soon discovered, however, that the fierce winds blowing across the salt flats regularly blew out the fires, causing soot to fill the shack. I lost track of the number of cold mornings when I had to shake out my bed linen with soot all over the covering blanket.

Maj. Charles W. Sweeney: After I attended an early-morning mass on my first Sunday at Wendover, a uniformed security officer, Captain McClanahan, came to my quarters and invited me to take a ride with him. We drove out into the desert. The sun's glare bleached the landscape. The jeep slowed, he stopped. "Did you ever read about Einstein's theory of relativity?" he asked. I answered, "Yes." He reached down and picked up a handful of the brownish, grainy desert dirt and held it as he spoke. He told me that our scientists were working on a new weapon, a weapon using Einstein's theory. The weapon would be twenty thousand times more powerful than any existing bomb. He never took his eyes from mine as he spoke. He said, "One bomb will reduce an entire city to this." He tossed the handful of dirt into the air. I watched as it scattered in the wind. There are some moments in life that stay indelibly embedded in your memory. This was one of those moments. I knew I would not forget—not a single detail. One plane. One bomb. One city. I asked my first question. "How heavy is the bomb?" "Colonel Tibbets will brief you on the information you need to know. And never refer to it as a 'bomb.' Call it a 'gimmick' or a 'gadget,' but *never* a 'bomb.'"

Col. Paul W. Tibbets: One of our most important tasks was related to security. It was necessary to impress upon every man as he joined our outfit that he must not discuss the nature of our operation with anyone. We put the screws on very tight. It was awkward to explain to our people that they must not talk to outsiders about our mission. They themselves were in the dark, so how could they give away information they didn't possess? We explained that we didn't want them even to speculate or to give out a hint that our operation was different from any other in the military.

Maj. Charles W. Sweeney: The next day I met with Colonel Tibbets. I knew he could requisition any equipment, matériel, or personnel he wanted from any source anywhere, without any questions being asked.

Col. Paul W. Tibbets: If I ran into trouble, such as a refusal to make available some needed service or equipment, I was authorized to break the impasse by use of a code word, "Silverplate," which would be recognized even by those who had no knowledge of the project with which it was associated.

Maj. Charles W. Sweeney: This was unheard of for the military, with its rigid bureaucracy. What was even more incredible was that a lieutenant colonel had this power, which most generals only dream of.

Col. Paul W. Tibbets: We had the help of an efficient security organization attached to our group by the Manhattan District. It was commanded by William "Bud" Uanna, who had been sent to us by General Groves. He was accompanied by a small army of special agents, about thirty in number, whose job it would be to infiltrate every phase of our operation and literally spy on our people to be sure there was no information leakage. We worked out a plan to monitor the mail, the phone calls, and even the off-duty conversations of our men. In peacetime civilian life, this would have been an unthinkable invasion of privacy. In the military, and particularly in our supersecret operation, it was an essential precaution.

Dora Dougherty: Col. Tibbets arranged for me to fly cargo out of Wendover for him. My fellow WASP, Mary Helen Gosnell was with me. The nurses' barracks were to become our permanent Wendover home for the two months we would be stationed at Wendover. Next morning, we had our first daylight view of the base. The cold Utah mountain air greeted us and I saw my first mountain. There it was at the end of the runway, dark and brooding. We officially reported in and as we became acquainted with the base, we saw the warning sign: WHAT YOU HEAR HERE, WHAT YOU SEE HERE, WHEN YOU LEAVE HERE, LET IT STAY HERE!

Capt. Thomas L. Karnes: One early episode taught me the seriousness of our security measures. Paul directed me to arrange the transfer of one of our officers, a lieutenant colonel, to the Aleutians! He was on Tibbets' staff and his crime was talking too much in a bar. Rank meant nothing when it came to security.

Col. Paul W. Tibbets: Although we began training flights almost at once, a couple of months went by before our entire organization was complete. It was on December 17, 1944—by coincidence the 41st anniversary of the Wright Brothers' first flight in a powered aircraft at Kitty Hawk—that the 509th Composite Group was officially activated.

T/Sgt. Ralph C. Berger, ***aircraft technician, 603rd Air Engineering Squadron*****:** The thing [I remember] was the midnight Christmas Service, December 25, 1944, at the base chapel. Most of my friends had gone home for the holidays. When I came out of the chapel, it was a very cold and crisp night and I took a walk. The airbase was surrounded by mountains. They were playing Christmas Carols and the music was reverberating off of the hills. It was beautiful, but this was one time I was really homesick in the service.

"Dropping 10,000-pound bombs"

TRAINING THE 509TH

Bob Hope remarked that barren Wendover, Utah, was more aptly called "Left Over, Utah."

Ultimately, the 509th Composite Group would be made up of the 393rd Heavy Bombardment Squadron, which flew the B-29 bombers; the 320th Troop Carrier Squadron, which flew seven C-54 transport planes that kept the group supplied; and other supporting units, including the 390th Air Service Group, the 603rd Air Engineering Squadron, the 1027th Air Material Squadron; and a unique specialist-filled unit called the First Ordnance Squadron that would actually handle and load the atomic bombs.

The most pressing task for Paul Tibbets's 509th Composite Group in the beginning of 1945 was that it had to perfect loading, navigating, and dropping an all-new bomb shaped unlike anything any of them had ever seen—all with possibly just months to go before the bomb would be ready for their planes.

Maj. Charles W. Sweeney: Wendover Field was ill equipped for the massive influx of men and machines that was under way. The field and its ancillary services, designed for a small contingent of fighters, were unsuitable for the demands of a heavy bomber group. By December, over eight hundred officers and other personnel had crowded into the existing facilities, and by the end of January 1945 the number had ballooned to over fifteen hundred. Colonel Tibbets had to create an entire self-contained and self-sustaining unit overnight—security, communications, staff support, armament, weather, photography, personnel, intelligence, cooks, bakers, and candlestick makers. Supplies had to be brought in and maintenance and facility improvements had to be made on an ongoing basis. All of this quickly made getting the 509th into operational shape a monumental challenge.

Then, once the organization had been put into motion and staffed, Tibbets had to select the crews, develop unique tactics for delivering an untested weapon that might never come to be, train the crews in the new tactics—and in the B-29, which was still undergoing design changes—develop a strategy to get the weapon to a target, and coordinate with scientists who were unsure if a functioning weapon could be delivered in time.

Maj. Gen. Leslie Groves: The total authorized strength of the 509th Group was set at 225 officers and 1,542 enlisted men. It was a completely self-contained unit.

2nd Lt. Fred J. Olivi: The 509th Composite Group was unlike any Army Air Corps organization I had ever heard of.

Col. Paul W. Tibbets: There had been nothing like it in this or any other war. Some were to call it "Tibbets's Individual Air Force" because I was given the authority to requisition anything needed to carry out my assignment.

2nd Lt. Fred J. Olivi: Only fifteen B-29s made up the 393rd Squadron, five airplanes each in Flights designated as "A," "B" and "C." Three other B-29s were added to the squadron just prior to the time we left for Tinian Island.

In addition to the bomber squadron, the self-contained 509th also had its own "airline," the 320th Troop Carrier Squadron. This squadron flew seven C-54 four-engine transport planes and was affectionately called the "Green Hornet Airline."

Maj. Charles W. Sweeney: A small group of civilian technicians and scientists operating under the code name Project Alberta served as liaison between Silverplate and the Manhattan Engineer District.

2nd Lt. Fred J. Olivi: There was a constant stream of strangers at Wendover. These men were "inspecting" the B-29s, working with the engineering and ordnance people. Exactly who they were and what they were doing was not my business. I figured I would be told in the future—if they wanted me to know.

Philip E. Doane, *1st Ordnance Squadron, Special (Aviation)*: We did not question any of the reason for any activity that was occurring because it was obvious something pretty important was in the works.

Col. Paul W. Tibbets: There were a number of civilian scientists on the base at times. To explain the presence of these people in civilian clothes, I told Lucy they were sanitary engineers. When I came home one day, I found that she had called one of them to unplug a stopped-up bathroom drain. This Ph.D. didn't understand how he came to be asked to do the job, but he was a good sport and took care of the problem, for which his advanced degree in physics did not necessarily qualify him. He and I laughed about it later.

Maj. Charles W. Sweeney: Scientists and our personnel going from Wendover to Los Alamos or to Wendover from Los Alamos never traveled directly.

Lt. Morris R. Jeppson, *1st Ordnance Squadron, Special (Aviation)*: Sometime in the winter of 1944–45, I was ordered to make a trip to a place that proved to be Los Alamos, New Mexico. We arrived at Albuquerque where a car met us and drove off somewhere. The driver briefed us, "We will stop in Santa Fe where you will exchange your Air Force insignia for Army Ordnance.

Where you are going, people are not to know the Air Force is preparing to use weapons they are developing."

Col. Paul W. Tibbets: Great pains were taken to disguise the fact that air force personnel were at Los Alamos. The purpose may have been to keep from ruffling the sensitive feathers of a few scientists who didn't mind making a bomb but who were appalled by the thought that it might actually be used. I removed all Air Corps insignia from my uniform and substituted the gold castle emblem of the U.S. Army Engineers. Sometimes I would even change shirts so that the pinholes for the wings did not show, although I always wondered if those Ph.D.'s were knowledgeable or interested enough in military matters to make the necessary deductions.

Maj. Charles W. Sweeney: It became painfully obvious that we had a limited amount of time to perfect the tactics of delivery, even while the scientists were working feverishly to complete development of a functioning bomb.

Col. Paul W. Tibbets: With our newly modified airplanes, we began intensive training at once over the vast open spaces of the western desert from Utah and Nevada to California. My first concern was for accuracy in dropping the bomb, and my next, for a maneuver that would put us as far as possible from the point of explosion.

Maj. Charles W. Sweeney: We had three bombing ranges: Target A, at Tonopah, Nevada, near the California border; Target B, at the Salton Sea in Southern California, about one hundred miles east of San Diego, where a large white raft was anchored at the southern end of an oval-shaped lake that ran north and south; and Target C, an abandoned army air corps range near Wendover. Observation posts were set up at each range incorporating photographic cameras using high-speed film and motion picture cameras to record the arc and speed of the bombs' descent to the target.

Capt. James Price, *airplane commander, Crew B-7*: We were dropping 10,000-pound bombs. They were called "pumpkins." That was one reason I named my airplane *Some Punkins*. The Salt Lake City newspaper had a cartoon about two long legged girls. They were called "some punkins" and they looked like one of the girls we had painted on the airplane.

2nd Lt. Fred J. Olivi: It looked like a squat, misshapen pumpkin, and for our practice bomb runs to Muroc Lake, California, it even was painted a mustard yellow.

Maj. Charles W. Sweeney: We learned as we went. We had no ballistic tables for a bomb of this weight and shape. No carrying hooks to hold its ten-thousand-pound weight. No reliable fuses to trigger the complicated firing mechanism for a plutonium device.

2nd Lt. Thomas F. Costa, *bombardier, Crew 5-7, 393rd Bombardment Squadron*: The practice pumpkins did not contain high explosives but were filled with concrete to the right weight.

Maj. Charles W. Sweeney: The problem was: once the pumpkin was replaced by the bomb, would we have enough time to get out of there after we released? Without knowing the exact explosive force that would be unleashed or even the true nature of the explosion, the scientists at Los Alamos offered their best estimate.

Col. Paul W. Tibbets: The scientists had told me that the minimum distance at which we could expect to survive would be 8 miles. It takes a B-29 two minutes to fly 8 miles, whereas it would take the bomb only 43 seconds from the moment it left our airplane, flying at 31,000 feet, to the point of detonation less than 2,000 feet above the ground. The shock wave would race toward us at the speed of sound—about 1,100 feet a second—which meant that it would take approximately 40 seconds to travel 8 miles.

Maj. Charles W. Sweeney: Tibbets's answer to the problem was brilliant. The bomb, of course, would be released before we were over the center of the target. On release, it would initially travel at the same speed as the airplane, approximately 320 miles per hour ground speed, then fall in a trajectory toward the target. If, immediately upon release, we banked the B-29 into a sharp, rapid, diving 155-degree turn—going back in the same direction we came from in a tight arc—we could take the airplane eight slant-range miles or more away from the blast in forty-three seconds, even though the maneuver would reduce our altitude by about seventeen hundred feet.

Col. Paul W. Tibbets: I took the airplane up. I got myself to 25,000 feet, and I practiced turning, steeper, steeper, steeper and, I got it where I could pull it round in 40 seconds. The tail was shaking dramatically and I was afraid of it breaking off, but I didn't quit. That was my goal. And I practiced and practiced until, without even thinking about it, I could do it in between 40 and 42 seconds, all the time.

Maj. Charles W. Sweeney: It was a totally unheard-of tactic for bomber pilots trained to fly in tight formations into and away from the target. But once Tibbets had devised it, it was up to the pilots to execute it. There were no training schools or manuals on this one. We would have to train ourselves.

2nd Lt. Fred J. Olivi: [Pilot Charles D. "Don"] Albury surprised me by executing this hazardous and tricky maneuver on one of my first training flights, telling me to pay close attention because the 155-degree diving turn he was going to execute was "S.O.P." (Standard Operating Procedure) when dropping "The Pumpkin." He called over the intercom to the rest of the crew, "Hold on, Boys. Here we go!" Albury suddenly dropped the left wing and swung the B-29 into a sharp turn and dive. I felt the centrifugal force push me against the side of the aircraft as it banked and picked up speed.

At first I thought, "He's banked too hard. This plane wasn't designed to take this kind of stress. He'll kill us all." But as Albury brought the nose of the B-29 up and straightened out the flightpath, I saw he was laughing. "Crazy maneuver. But this ship can take it, Olivi, as long as you don't push it too far." It took me quite a few training sessions before I felt comfortable taking the B-29 into this dangerous maneuver. But I soon gained confidence, always remembering not to exceed the 155 degrees.

* * *

Maj. Charles W. Sweeney: Our actual B-29 missions could involve a three-thousand-mile round-trip flight over water, so navigational training became a high priority. Even a minute miscalculation could result in missing the intended destination by many miles, given the distances to target. By then it was pretty clear that if the mission were ever flown, it would be flown against the Japanese. The Germans were collapsing on both the western and eastern fronts in Europe.

Col. Paul W. Tibbets: Classroom work and lectures were helpful, but I was convinced that the crews wouldn't really understand and conquer the problem except by experience. Accordingly, I asked for and received permission to send crews to Batista Field near Havana, Cuba, where we could use the whole Caribbean for flying practice missions. There were dozens of islands of all sizes on which to make simulated bomb runs while practicing the transition from overwater to over-land flying. We sent five airplanes at a time to Cuba for training.

Capt. James F. Van Pelt, ***navigator, Crew 15, 393rd Bombardment Squadron*****:** Our group was originally designed to be self-sustaining. This was one of the main reasons we went to Batista, to test our ability to move quickly. We designed the group in such a way that we had our own service groups. We had our own metalsmiths. We could make a complete repair and almost build a ship; also had quite a few technicians. Everything was moved from Wendover to Batista. We carried the equipment in our airplanes, B-29s and C-54s. We moved in two days carrying crews, spare parts, crewchief stands, engines, bombing and navigating equipment, etc.

2nd Lt. John L. Downey, ***393rd Bombardment Squadron*****:** The flight training in Cuba was conducted in two phases, one consisted of both radar and visual bombing from 20,000 to 30,000 feet altitude. The second part was simulated combat missions, with formal briefings, against a simulated enemy target. All facets of planning and conducting a very realistic combat mission were followed. From the 15th to the 31st of January, the participating crews averaged 42 flight hours each in these training exercises. On one of these missions, we encountered a rain squall en route and were pretty much flying blind at a low altitude over the ocean heading east toward the island of Bermuda. Without any warning we broke out of the storm and thanks to Pete's (Bob Petrolli, Navigator) navigation we were right over the bay at Bermuda; it was late in the day and just getting dark. From the nose position, I could see a large ship below us that was busy turning on all their large red crosses, a hospital ship. At the same time, there was a Navy Destroyer along side the hospital ship and they were busy turning on their searchlights and illuminating us. Seems like they were as surprised as we were and weren't taking any chances on us being unfriendly.

Sgt. Paul Metro: I was able to visit Havana on three weekends, staying at the luxurious Hotel Nacional overlooking the sea. The first visit was a festive occasion; José Martí Day, [named for] Cuba's Liberator. There was a parade with huge crowds everywhere. We visited some of the tourist spots, had our picture taken at the famous Sloppy Joe's Bar, met a Cuban senator and had a wild taxi ride. I bought souvenirs; a pair of mahogany vases and cheap pair of castanets, saw the sights, took snapshots and had dinner in a restaurant in the Capitolio. Some of the guys went to see the cockfights in San Antonio.

2nd Lt. John L. Downey: Visiting Havana was quite an experience.

2nd Lt. Robert J. Petrolli, ***navigator, Crew A-2, 393rd Bombardment Squadron*****:** In Cuba, we had a lot of fun.

Maj. Charles W. Sweeney: This experience also had the benefit of solidifying a sense of pride among the men that they were part of the 509th Composite Group. Sprung from their penitentiary-style life at Wendover, now out and about in the general population, they saw themselves for what they were, a special and elite military unit. A corner had been turned in unit cohesion. The 509th now meant something to the men.

* * *

Maj. Charles W. Sweeney: The colonel asked my opinion about removing all the armament from the B-29—the turrets, guns, and ammunition—and leaving in just the 20mm cannon in the tail. He explained that the airplane would then be lighter by about seven thousand pounds, which would get us the increased speed, maneuverability, and altitude. This would be much more valuable to the safety of the crews than the guns. I told him I thought it was a terrific idea. Tibbets decided that new airplanes would have to be manufactured with the turrets removed and other design changes built in on the assembly line. As long as new airplanes were going to be ordered, he wanted them equipped with the new Curtis Electric reversible propellers that would allow the plane to stop in a shorter distance on landing, with pneumatic bomb bay doors that snapped open and shut, thus decreasing air drag on the airplane, and with fuel injection for better fuel economy. These changes would prove to be critically important in helping me successfully complete my mission over Nagasaki and in saving the lives of my crew and me.

Having made the decision, Colonel Tibbets invoked "Silverplate" and asked Dayton to order twenty-five brand-new redesigned B-29s from Boeing. Boeing selected the Martin plant in Omaha for this production. Engineers worked around the clock to design the changes. When they were completed, Boeing inserted the new design into its assembly line.

2nd Lt. Raymond P. Biel, ***pilot, Crew A-1, 393rd Bombardment Squadron*****:** The highlight at Wendover was to visit the Boeing assembly plant in Omaha and pick up a new aircraft specially equipped for a top secret mission; like driving a new Cadillac off the showroom floor.

Maj. Charles W. Sweeney: Each airplane was assigned to one crew. My crew was designated as C-15. Our assigned aircraft as delivered from the factory was Number 89, which was painted in block numbers on the nose of the fuselage. Later the fuselage would be painted with our name, *The Great Artiste*, and our logo, a debonair magician in tails. For the missions, however, all nose art would be removed. Our unit markings would also be changed prior to the missions to confuse the enemy about who we were and where we came from, in case they got to us with fighters.

2nd Lt. Fred J. Olivi: We were ordered to fly to Offutt Field at Omaha, Nebraska, where we exchanged our aircraft for a brand new one. Its serial number was 44-27353. Up to this moment, Albury and I had flown training missions at Wendover in any B-29 that was available and assigned to our crew. We switched from plane to plane. But now we had our own B-29. We flew it back to Wendover and went out on several "shake-down" training flights. I particularly liked the reversible propellers.

Capt. Frederick C. Bock, ***airplane commander, Crew C-13, 393rd Bombardment Squadron*****:** V-77: The *Bockscar* was the second of the fifteen modified Silverplate planes to be built at the Martin Plant in Omaha.

2nd Lt. Leonard Godfrey, ***navigator, Crew C-13, 393rd Bombardment Squadron*****:** Fred Bock was the most methodical, careful, thoughtful pilot you can imagine. We did a test flight in Omaha there as passengers with the factory crew and then flew it back to Wendover.

2nd Lt. Fred J. Olivi: The new B-29 was a signal, our "tip off" that something was going on, that our days at Wendover were almost over.

* * *

Col. Paul W. Tibbets: The winter was coming to an end and I knew we would have to be in place and ready to go long before the bomb was ready. The first and only test was scheduled for July, and plans called for us to drop the first bomb on an enemy target in early August.

Maj. Charles W. Sweeney: Colonel Tibbets sensed the stalling of momentum and seized the day. He knew that moving our personnel, equipment, and supplies overseas would be a time-consuming process.

Col. Paul W. Tibbets: I had just passed my thirtieth birthday and now wore the eagles of a full colonel on my uniform. A load of responsibility had been thrown on my shoulders and I decided to exercise the authority that went with it. Without asking anyone's advice or consent, I transmitted to Washington the code word that said, in effect, "Issue the orders for the 509th to be processed for overseas movement."

Maj. Charles W. Sweeney: On May 6, 1945, twelve hundred of our support personnel boarded the troop ship S.S. *Cape Victory* at Seattle and sailed west. They would arrive three weeks later at Destination. The C-54 transports would set down on May 18. Finally, at the beginning of June, our fifteen B-29s would touch down to join our fellow comrades.

Cpl. Mont J. Mickelson: We boarded *Cape Victory*, a Victory Class troop ship manufactured by Kaiser Steel. Bunks were layered seven high, canvas roped to steel pipe frames. Needless to say, the environment became extremely smelly and stale. The tranquil trip through Puget Sound was beautiful. Then high Pacific storm seas changed all that. Waves began crashing over the smaller Victory ship's bow. Many personnel became extremely seasick, whether psychological or not. Many relieved stomach contents over the rail for three days before subsiding. We docked at Honolulu, Oahu, Hawaii for three days, were not allowed to leave the dock but those beautiful and handsome local people entertained us with a typical show of music, singing and dance. Many of us were happy to purchase canned pineapple to enjoy a delicacy eaten without standing upright with the ship heaving and rolling from side to side.

2nd Lt. Jack Widowsky, ***navigator, Crew B-8, 393rd Bombardment Squadron*****:** We were all ready because I think we were tired of the intense training we received the past eight months.

Staff Sgt. William C. Drainer, ***radar, 393rd Bombardment Squadron*****:** Leaving Wendover was comparable to the time I left home and family in West Virginia in 1942. I had that same feeling as I looked down at the airfield and thought that life wouldn't be that nice again!

Sgt. Maj. Arthur J. Johnson, ***390th Air Service Group Headquarters*****:** I was a member of the advance party. We left Wendover on May 15, 1945, under secret orders and with a security agent through Hamilton AFB, California. When we left there, well before midnight, each of us was given a sealed envelope containing our secret orders and revealing our destination. We were not permitted to open them until we had passed the point of no return on our way to Hickam Field, Hawaii. At last we knew we were going to Tinian Island.

"You are the one in trouble now"

SPRING 1945

The death of FDR in the final months of the war shook the nation.

As the winter and spring of 1945 unfolded and the German military collapsed in Europe under unrelenting Allied pressure, the tempo of the Manhattan Project quickened across its various design and production facilities. By January, the calutrons at Oak Ridge were spinning away—on an average day, about 85 percent of the 864 Alpha calutrons were running and generating about nine ounces of uranium. There would be enough material for a bomb in about six months.

Since 1942, US Marines had steadily advanced through the Central Pacific, bloody island by bloody island, fighting the Japanese to the last man. On many islands, less than one percent of the Japanese defenders lived to see the end of the battle, with many committing suicide, sometimes in dramatic Banzai charges, rather than surrendering. The US Army had advanced through the southern Pacific, up through the Northern Solomons, then New Guinea, and finally back to the Philippines, where Gen. Douglas MacArthur had famously promised to "return" when driven away by Japanese advances in 1942. The fighting was hellish and supplies had been delivered across thousands of miles of the Pacific Ocean for each landing and resupply.

In mid-April, the nation experienced a surprise cataclysm: The death of the commander-in-chief who had led the US into and through the war, a development that thrust an inexperienced onetime Missouri haberdasher into the role of deciding the ultimate use of the atomic bomb—a development and invention that surprised him perhaps most of all.

Harry Truman, *Vice President of the United States*: During the first few weeks of Franklin Delano Roosevelt's fourth administration, I saw what the long years in the Presidency had done to him. He had occupied the White House during twelve fateful years—years of awful responsibility. He had borne the burdens of the reconstruction from the great depression of the 'Thirties. He shouldered the heavier burdens of his wartime leadership. It is no wonder that the years had left their mark. The very thought that something was happening to him left me troubled and worried.

Eleanor Roosevelt, *First Lady of the United States*: On the 1st of March, Franklin addressed the Congress, and I knew, when he consented to do this sitting down, that he had accepted a certain degree of invalidism. I found him less and less willing to see people for any length of time, needing a rest in the middle of the day. He was anxious to get away and I was pleased when he decided to go to Warm Springs, where he always gained in health and strength. He invited his cousins, Laura Delano and Margaret Suckley, to go down with him.

Adm. William Leahy, *chief of staff to the president, the White House*: It was apparent he needed a longer rest, so he finally heeded his medical advisers and decided to spend three weeks at his "second home" in Warm Springs, Georgia. When he left to take the train for Georgia, I walked with him from the office where we had been talking, to the south entrance of the White House. He was cheerful, as usual. That was the last time I saw Franklin Roosevelt alive.

Eleanor Roosevelt: On April 12, in the afternoon, Laura Delano called me to say that Franklin had fainted while sitting for his portrait and had been carried to bed. I talked to Dr. McIntire, who was not alarmed, but we planned to go down to Warm Springs that evening. He told me, however, that he thought I had better go on with my afternoon engagements, since it would cause great comment if I canceled them at the last moment to go to Warm Springs. I was at a benefit at the Sulgrave Club in Washington when I was called to the telephone. Steve Early, very much upset, asked me to come home at once. I knew that some thing dreadful had happened. Nevertheless, the amenities had to be observed, so I went back to the party and said good-by, expressing my regrets that I could not stay longer because something had come up at home which called me away.

I got into the car and sat with clenched hands all the way to the White House. In my heart I knew what had happened, but one does not actually formulate these terrible thoughts until they are spoken. I went to my sitting room and Steve Early and Dr. McIntire came to tell me the news. Word had come to them through Dr. Bruenn in Warm Springs, first of the hemorrhage, and later of Franklin's death.

I sent at once for the vice-president, and I made arrangements for Dr. McIntire and Steve to go with me to Warm Springs by plane that evening. Somehow in emergencies one moves automatically.

Harry Truman: Shortly before five o'clock, I went to the office of House Speaker Sam Rayburn. As I entered, the Speaker told me that Steve Early, the President's Press Secretary, had just telephoned, requesting me to call the White House. I returned the call and was immediately connected with Early. "Please come right over," he told me in a strained voice. I reached the White House about 5:25 p.m. and was immediately taken in the elevator to the second floor and ushered into Mrs. Roosevelt's study. I knew at once that something unusual had taken place. Mrs. Roosevelt seemed calm in her characteristic, graceful dignity. She stepped forward and placed her arm gently about my shoulder. "Harry," she said quietly, "the President is dead."

Eleanor Roosevelt: I could think of nothing to say except how sorry I was for him, how much we would all want to help him in any way we could, and how sorry I was for the people of the country, to have lost their leader and friend before the war was really won.

Harry Truman: For a moment I could not bring myself to speak. "Is there anything I can do for you?" I asked at last. I shall never forget her deeply understanding reply. "Is there anything we can do for you?" she asked. "For you are the one in trouble now." It seems to me that for a few minutes we stood silent.

James C. Forrestal, *Secretary of the Navy*: I was with the Secretary of State and the Attorney General at 5:45 p.m. when a message came for Mr. [Edward] Stettinius to go immediately to the White House. At 5:50 p.m. I received a message on the telephone asking Attorney General [Francis] Biddle and myself to go to the White House.

Harry Truman: Secretary of State Stettinius entered in tears, his handsome face sad and drawn. He had been among the first to be notified, for as Secretary of State, who is the keeper of the Great Seal of the United States and all official state papers, it was his official duty to ascertain and to proclaim the passing of the President. I asked Steve Early, Secretary Stettinius and [White House staffer] Les Biffie, who now also had joined us, to call all the members of the Cabinet to a meeting as quickly as possible.

James C. Forrestal: We went to the Cabinet room of the White House where there were gathered the Vice President, Secretary Wallace, Secretary Stimson, Secretary Morgenthau, Secretary Perkins, Secretary Wickard, Secretary Ickes, Leo Crowley and "Cap" Krug.

Adm. William Leahy: The constitutional provisions for succession to the Presidency were swiftly carried out. At 7:09 p.m. April 12, in the Cabinet Room of the White House, flanked by the heads of the executive departments and offices of the government, Truman was administered the oath of office by Chief Justice Harlan Stone. Truman stood at the north end of the big table in the middle of the room.

James C. Forrestal: Mr. Truman responded to the oath firmly and clearly. His only active omission was a failure to raise his right hand when he was repeating the oath with his left hand on the Bible. The Chief Justice had to indicate to him that he should raise his hand—under the circumstances it gave dignity and firmness.

Harry Truman's swearing-in.

Harry Truman: We were in the final days of the greatest war in history—a war so vast that few corners of the world had been able to escape being engulfed by it. In that war the United States had created military forces so enormous as to defy description, yet, now when the nation's greatest leader in that war lay dead, and a simple ceremony was about to acknowledge the presence of his successor in the nation's greatest office, only two uniforms were present, and these were worn by Admiral of the Fleet Leahy and by General Fleming, who, as Public Works Administrator, had been given duties that were much more civilian in character than military. So far as I know, this passed unnoticed at the time, and the very fact that no thought was given to it demonstrates convincingly how firmly the concept of the supremacy of the civil authority is accepted in our land.

Adm. William Leahy: One could hardly see at that time how the complicated, critical business of the war and the peace could be carried forward by a new President who was, in comparison, almost completely inexperienced in international affairs.

Sen. James F. Byrnes: The task of the President at that time was unusually heavy. President Roosevelt had years of experience in the office and had learned to live with his problems as they accumulated; in contrast, President Truman was facing without warning unfamiliar hazards both at home and abroad.

* * *

Paul Numerof: In all of the twenty-seven months of the project work never stopped. Only once was a special announcement made: President Franklin Delano Roosevelt had died. Then came a second announcement: There would be a moment of respectful silence. There was. Then the work continued.

Maj. Charles W. Sweeney: My generation had never known another leader. He had taken us through two back-to-back cataclysmic disasters unprecedented in American history—the Great Depression and World War II. With my Catholic upbringing, it seemed to me almost biblical that, like Moses, President Roosevelt would not be with his people in their moment of triumph. Later, my feeling of unease was not lifted when I heard the tinny Midwestern twang of a man the nation and I barely knew.

J. Robert Oppenheimer, *remarks at memorial service for President Roosevelt, Los Alamos*: When the world had word of the death of President Roosevelt, many wept who are unaccustomed to tears, many men and women, little enough accustomed to prayer, prayed to God. Many of us looked with deep trouble to the future; many of us felt less certain that our works would be to a good end; all of us were reminded of how precious a thing human greatness is.

We have been living through years of great evil, and of great terror. Roosevelt has been our President, our Commander-in-Chief and, in an old and unperverted sense, our leader. All over the world men have looked to him for guidance, and have seen symbolized in him their hope that the evils of this time would not be repeated; that the terrible sacrifices which have been made, and those that are still to be made, would lead to a world more fit for human habitation. It is in such times of evil that men recognize their helplessness and their profound dependence. One is reminded of medieval days, when the death of a good and wise and just king plunged his country into despair, and mourning.

In the Hindu scripture, in the Bhagavad-Gita, it says, "Man is a creature whose substance is faith. What his faith is, he is." The faith of Roosevelt is one that is shared by millions of men and women in every country of the world. For this reason it is possible to maintain the hope, for this reason it is right that we should dedicate ourselves to the hope, that his good works will not have ended with his death.

* * *

Harry Truman, *President of the United States*: That first meeting of the Cabinet was short, and when it adjourned, the members rose and silently made their way from the room—except for Secretary Stimson. He asked to speak to me about a most urgent matter. Stimson told me that he wanted me to know about an immense project that was under way—a project looking to the development of a new explosive of almost unbelievable destructive power. That was all he felt free to say at the time, and his statement left me puzzled.

Vannevar Bush: At the close, Mr. Stimson stayed on and told the President of the existence of the vast project from which a new weapon of unprecedented power was forthcoming. He gave President Truman the broad outlines of the endeavor and said that I could tell him the full story.

Harry Truman: It was later, when Vannevar Bush, head of the Office of Scientific Research and Development, came to the White House, that I was given a scientist's version of the atomic bomb.

Vannevar Bush: I sat down with President Truman, and gave him the detailed fine structure of the affair—a full account of the atomic bomb as it then stood. Subsequently this report was enriched and amplified by Mr. Stimson and General Groves, with special reference to the probabilities of the future as regarded our then current monopoly of the weapon and the prospect that other nations, notably the Soviet Union, would attain it. My own meeting with President Truman was the first time I had ever seen him.

Harry Truman: That so vast an enterprise had been successfully kept secret even from the members of Congress was a miracle. I had known, and probably others had, that something that was unusually important was brewing in our war plants. Many months before, as part of the work of the Committee to Investigate the National Defense Program of which I was chairman, I had had investigators going into war plants all over the country. I had even sent investigators into Tennessee and the state of Washington with instructions to find out what certain enormous constructions were, and what their purpose was.

At that time, when these investigators were sent out, Secretary Stimson had come to see me. "Senator," the Secretary told me as he sat beside my desk, "I can't tell you what it is, but it is the greatest project in the history of the world. It is most top secret. Many of the people who are actually engaged in the work have no idea what it is, and we who do would appreciate your not going into those plants." I had long known Henry L. Stimson to be a great American patriot and statesman. "I'll take you at your word," I told him. "I'll order the investigations into those plants called off."

Sen. James F. Byrnes: I have always regretted that President Roosevelt died without knowing definitely that the project was a success: It had been undertaken and carried to a conclusion solely because of his vision and courage in the days when the effort seemed hopeless.

"A solemn but glorious hour"

100 TONS OF TNT

The main observation bunker at Trinity.

With the end of the war in Europe nearing and the bomb work nearing completion, the first days of May 1945 saw dramatic events span two continents.

George B. Kistiakowsky: To test or not to test the plutonium bomb was a very hot issue. Oppenheimer and I were pleading with General Groves that there had to be a test because the whole scheme was so uncertain.

John H. Manley: We had never really intended to test the uranium bomb—it was a gun assembly, the components could be thoroughly tested, and we felt quite sure it would work. There was not enough fissile material to spend on a test anyway. This bomb had to go right into combat. However, the implosion scheme was so new and so complicated that a field test would be absolutely essential before combat use.

Sen. James F. Byrnes: Though it is sometimes said that for many months the success of the bomb was assured, another indication to the contrary is the fact that though we had but three bombs, and could not hope to possess another for many months, our scientific advisers felt it essential to devote one to a test firing.

Maj. Gen. Leslie Groves: By May 1945, we reached the conclusion that our estimates of being ready early in August were reasonable and that we should have accumulated enough material for one bomb by late July. July 24 was finally set as the deadline date. And by the end of that day, enough uranium—and a little bit more—had been shipped to Los Alamos for the manufacture of the first bomb to be dropped on Japan.

Herbert L. Anderson: It was recognized that no amount of experimental work would yield as much information as an actual explosion, and plans were made for such a test, under a code name of "Project Trinity."

J. Robert Oppenheimer: Why I chose the name [Trinity] is not clear, but I know what thoughts were in my mind. There is a poem of John Donne, written just before his death, which I know and love. From it a quotation: "As West and East / In all flatt Maps—and I am one—are one, So death doth touch the Resurrection." That still does not make Trinity; but in another, better known devotional poem Donne opens, "Batter my heart, three person'd God;—." Beyond this, I have no clues whatever.

Kenneth T. Bainbridge: Oppenheimer asked me to be Director of the Trinity Project. John Williams was appointed as Deputy Director to oversee that the installation and construction of facilities for instruments and shelters conformed to the scientific requirements and were completed on time. In succeeding months increasing numbers of scientists and Special Engineer Detachment soldiers from Los Alamos were assigned to the Trinity Test Project as confidence rose that the implosion method might be practicable and sufficient core material might be available in June or July.

Maj. Gen. Leslie Groves: Bainbridge had the unusual qualification of being a physicist with undergraduate training in electrical engineering. He was quiet and competent and had the respect and liking of the over two hundred enlisted men later on duty at Alamogordo. His first step, with the assistance of Oppenheimer, Major W. A. Stevens, who was in charge of construction activities at Los Alamos, and Major Peer de Silva, the head of security at Los Alamos, was to select a site.

Kenneth T. Bainbridge: The basic requirements for the Trinity test site were a flat area to facilitate measurements, a remote but accessible region which for security reasons could not easily be associated with Los Alamos, and an area which could be cleared of all inhabitants months before the test date. The area had to be remote from populated areas so that people could be evacuated in the event of a low-order detonation, which would distribute poisonous plutonium, or a high-level explosion, which would be accompanied by dangerous radioactive fallout.

The base camp at Trinity.

Maj. Gen. Leslie Groves: After looking at several other sites, the committee finally settled on Alamogordo as being entirely satisfactory. It was on an air base, but was far removed from the airfield itself. Arrangements were promptly made with Major General U. G. Ent, under whose control the base came, for us to use the Alamogordo area.

Kenneth T. Bainbridge: I was convinced that a rehearsal was imperative as there would be only one chance with the main test. A proposal was made to Oppenheimer for a test of 100 tons of explosive, to check our instrumentation and facilities, to calibrate gauges, and to determine weaknesses in the plans and organization.

Val L. Fitch: In May, 100 tons of TNT were exploded near the tower site as a calibration of some of the instrumentation.

Kenneth T. Bainbridge: The center of the 100-ton pile was 38 feet above the ground to scale effects to conform to the final implosion test bomb on a 100-foot tower on the basis of the then predicted yield. Kistiakowsky's division obtained special fast-acting explosives arrayed in the cylindric cubic structure of TNT to improve the speed and uniformity of the explosion. As Kisty told me, these explosives were not sensitive to mechanical shock, which was proven when some boxes fell off a truck transporting the explosives from the rail.

Joseph L. McKibben: It was also to be an exercise in using the cameras and other diagnostic equipment, and for that they needed the timing equipment to be in operation. We only had time to do a small amount of checking up on the operation of our equipment. The 100-ton test presented us with a few failures, but with such a tight schedule that was not unexpected.

Kenneth T. Bainbridge: The 100-ton rehearsal shot was detonated on May 7. The rehearsal shot had gone off ¼ second early due to electrical pick-up. This would have been costly in the final test where so many of the results depended on programmed timing down to the last millisecond. This provided one more reason to rule that after four weeks prior to the final test date no new experiments would be added to avoid new wiring with attendant pick-up hazards.

Val L. Fitch: I thought that 100 tons made an incredible explosion.

Kenneth T. Bainbridge: The night of the successful rehearsal shot was the one and only time at Trinity that I had an alcoholic drink until a few days after the final bomb test. Lieutenant Bush, John Williams and I relaxed at a poker game with John H. Anderson who joined us when he could. Anderson was a civilian security agent I was told. What his job was I never asked and he never volunteered to define. We were feeling good because the explosion had been satisfactory and no one was hurt.

Gretchen Heitzler, ***rancher, Three Rivers Ranch, Otero County, New Mexico*****:** We retired late one night after returning from a picnic at White Sands. We dumped the sleeping children in their beds and flopped into ours, and it would be hard to say who was snoring the loudest when we were all startled awake by a terrific explosion. We rushed outside. We fruitlessly searched the premises and then retired to the kitchen to make a pot of coffee and talk things over. Sleep was out of the question. "I know who did it," I muttered. "Our dear boys from the Base are at it again."

Then Porter put in his two bits. "They're doin' somethin' over ta' tha' bombin' range. Bert Apgar says that trucks has bin goin' over there from Oscuro."

Rusty had also heard rumors of unusual activity on the bombing range, but we hadn't given it much thought. I began to get wound up. "Those idiots were trying to hit us. I *know* they were. They dropped a bomb this time and it must have landed around here some place. We're going to be killed before it's all over." And on that cheerful note, we trudged back to bed.

In a few days we went to El Paso, and there we received the news that the war in Europe was over. Germany had surrendered to the Allies on May 8, 1945.

Capt. Lewis L. Strauss: V-E Day came. Germany's unconditional surrender was signed in U.S. Army Headquarters at Rheims.

Harry Truman, ***message announcing the surrender of Germany, May 8, 1945*****:** This is a solemn but a glorious hour. I only wish that Franklin D. Roosevelt had lived to witness this day. General Eisenhower informs me that the forces of Germany have surrendered to the United Nations. The flags of freedom fly over all Europe. For this victory, we join in offering our thanks to the Providence which has guided and sustained us through the dark days of adversity.

We must work to finish the war. Our victory is but half-won. The West is free, but the East is still in bondage to the treacherous tyranny of the Japanese. When the last Japanese division has surrendered unconditionally, then only will our fighting job be done. I call upon every American to stick to his post until the last battle is won.

Adm. William Leahy: At 1:00 p.m., with General Marshall and Admiral King, we made a brief broadcast on a hookup of all radio networks, in celebration of the surrender. I concluded: "Japan must be beaten into defeat, into unconditional surrender. The reconquest of the Philippines was a step in that direction. The remaining steps must and will be taken. We have no intention of relaxing until the eastern barbarian shares the fate of his partner. We have not forgotten Pearl Harbor. We know that the American people, with equal devotion and sacrifice, will support their sons and brothers, who will be fighting our savage enemies in the far Pacific until the final victory is won."

Emilio Segrè: While we were in the desert setting up the experiment, we received news of Hitler's suicide, of the surrender of Germany and of the end of the war in Europe. One of my reactions was: "We have been too late." For me Hitler was the personification of evil and the primary justification for the atomic bomb work. This feeling was shared by many of my colleagues, especially the Europeans.

"Black as far as the eye could see"

SELECTING THE TARGETS

The B-29 raids on Japan caused widespread devastation in the spring of 1945.

Total war arrived in Japan long before the Manhattan Project finished its work. In the Pacific, the naval noose around Japan was tightening—submarines, carrier-based bombers, and mines were exacting a crippling toll on Japanese shipping, which was critical to supplying Japan with almost all its oil and industrial supplies—and vast aerial attacks by US bombers began to reduce the country's major cities to ashes.

After months of lackluster high-altitude bombing by B-29 Superfortresses—the early B-29 missions were mostly failures, huge morale-boosting PR victories back home, but ones that delivered only glancing blows to the military manufacturing capacity of Japan—the arrival of the thirty-eight-year-old Maj. Gen. Curtis LeMay as the US's top air commander in the Pacific had transformed the strategy. LeMay noted that Japan's tightly packed wooden cities were particularly susceptible to fires. Tokyo officials had first ordered firebreaks cleared in January 1944, offering up tiny sums to homeowners as more than 200,000 buildings were demolished to create 120-foot-wide firebreaks—but the city's density and wooden construction meant it would burn easily still.

LeMay sent in giant formations of bombers at low altitude, setting fire to Japan night after night. In just a single mission in March, US bombers as part of Operation Meetinghouse firebombed Tokyo, using incendiary devices to ignite firestorms that reduced about sixteen square miles of the city to rubble and killed more than 100,000 in the blaze and explosions. The firebombing was every bit as deliberate and deadly as the atomic bombs would be months later—the US B-29s dropped 1,665 tons of incendiary explosives into just ten square miles, each square mile of which was home to more than 100,000 people apiece. It was death on an industrial level never before seen. It was clear that Japan would lose—but US planners still feared the bloody cost of a ground invasion of the home islands, which might cause more than a million US casualties.

Robert Guillain: The winter of 1944–45 was one of the clearest, and the coldest, Tokyo had experienced in twenty years. In the daylight raids, the beauty of our terrifying liberators made me want to cry out. When they rushed through the blue sky in the frozen light of those glittering afternoons, flying fairly low as they doubled back after their bombing runs—they banked down fast then and flew right over my head—they were translucid, unreal, light as fantastic glass dragonflies. In each of those machines were twelve free fighting men who had come to liberate us. They had flown 1,500 miles over the ocean to get here, or roughly the distance from New York to Chicago, and they had to do it again on the return. In 1944–45, such distances seemed fantastic.

Then it was March 9, 1945, a date Tokyo will remember as it remembers that of September 1, 1923, the date of the great earthquake. The wind, which had been rising since morning, turned gusty in the afternoon; that night it was almost as violent as a spring typhoon. The wind was to blame for the coming tragedy. A single thought haunted the city: it could be terrible if they come in such a wind. And at eleven o'clock that night, they did come.

Brig. Gen. Thomas S. Power, ***commander, 314th Bomb Wing (Very Heavy), 21st Bomber Command*****:** I watched block after block go up in flames until the holocaust had spread into a seething, swirling ocean of fire, engulfing the city below for miles in every direction. True, there is no room for emotions in war. But the destruction I witnessed that night over Tokyo was so overwhelming that it left a tremendous and lasting impression with me.

Robert Guillain: Inhabitants stayed heroically put as the bombs dropped, faithfully obeying the order that each family defend its own home. But how could they fight the fires with that wind blowing and when a single house might be hit by ten or even more of the bombs, each weighing up to 6.6 pounds, that were raining down by the thousands? As they fell, cylinders scattered a kind of flaming dew that skittered along the roofs, setting fire to everything it splashed and spreading a wash of dancing flames everywhere—the first version of napalm.

Hidezo Tsuchikura, ***factory worker*****:** When the bombers started to pour fire into Tokyo in the mass incendiary raid, I had absolutely no intention of remaining outside in an open space. I wanted something overhead to protect my two children and myself. The moment the bombs started to fall, we all ran to the school building. Refugees poured in steadily. I could see from the windows that the fires were advancing rapidly toward the school.

Koyo Ishikawa, ***police photographer, Tokyo*****:** Everywhere I looked there was only fire.

Seiichi Tonozuka, ***age 28, Tokyo*****:** The fire seemed like a wave crest approaching from beyond the ocean.

Hidezo Tsuchikura: With every passing minute the air became more and more foul. I made the drastic decision to go out to the roof. It meant breaking a lifelong obsession against staying out in the open. Without the children, however, I would never have made the move. On the roof it was like stepping into hell. Pieces of flaming wood and sparks rained down from the sky or shot horizontally through the air. The night was terribly hot, but even this was a tremendous relief over what we had been forced to breathe. I watched the children inhaling deeply and smiling for the first time in many minutes. It was worth it. We sat down near a water tank. I told the children to stay down and stood up to see what was happening. The rooftop was lit up much brighter than if it were broad daylight. Flames leaped high over the city, and the noise was a continuing, crashing roar. The great bombers were still coming over Tokyo in an endless stream.

Staff Sgt. LeRoy "Trip" Triplett, ***radarman, B-29*** **Gamecock,** ***504th Bomb Group*****:** As far as the eye could see, to the east and north, there was a sea of flame, a mass of roaring fire that seemed to cover the city like a boiling cauldron. How could this fire ever be put out? How could anyone possibly live through the sea of hell?

Martin Sheridan, ***reporter observer*****, Boston Globe,** ***aboard B-29*** **Patches:** I not only saw Tokyo burning furiously in many sections, but I smelled it.

Hidezo Tsuchikura: The entire building had become a huge oven three stories high. Every human being inside the school was literally baked or boiled alive in heat. Dead bodies were everywhere in grisly heaps. None of them appeared to be badly charred. They looked like mannequins, some of them with a pinkish complexion. The swimming pool was the most horrible sight of all. It was hideous. More than a thousand people, we estimated, had jammed into the pool. The pool had been filled to its brim when we first arrived. Now there wasn't a drop of water, only the bodies of the adults and children who had died.

Capt. Shigenori Kubota, ***commander, Number One Rescue Unit, Imperial Japanese Army Medical School*****:** The entire river surface was black as far as the eye could see, black with burned corpses, logs, and who knew what else, but uniformly black from the immense heat that had seared its way through the area as the fire dragon passed. It was impossible to tell the bodies from the logs at a distance. The bodies were all nude, the clothes had been burned away, and there was a dreadful sameness about them, no telling men from women or even children. All that remained were pieces of charred meat. Bodies and parts of bodies were carbonized and absolutely black.

Robert Guillain: But what is the point of continuing this catalogue of horrors?

Brig. Gen. Thomas S. Power: The 9 March fire-bomb raid was the greatest single disaster in military history. In that fire raid there were more casualties than in any other military action in the history of the world. From both a tactical and strategic point of view, it was a tremendously successful raid.

Maj. Gen. Curtis LeMay: We knew we were going to kill a lot of women and kids when we burned that town. Had to be done.

Hirohito, *Emperor of Japan*: Tokyo has been reduced to ashes.

Adm. William Leahy: The best psychological warfare to use on these barbarians [is] bombs.

Masuo Kato: For more than three years my small nephew Kozo Ishikawa, who was about five years old when the war began, held an unshakable faith in Japanese victory. To his small world it was unthinkable that the Emperor's armies could suffer defeat or that the Japanese Navy should endure any fate other than glorious victory. After his home was burned to the ground during a B-29 raid, destroying almost every familiar material thing that had made up his existence, he told me with great gravity: "We cannot beat the B-29."

In Tokyo, in the six days after the raids, officials cremated and buried 77,000 bodies. Then, in the weeks and months that followed, LeMay followed the same playbook to destroy city after city—not just the big cities, like Tokyo, Nagoya, and Osaka, but smaller cities that no one in America had ever heard of, places like Tsuruga, Hamamatsu, and Toyama, where more than 99 percent of the city of 128,000 was burned. (Hiroshima and Nagasaki escaped the early waves of firebombing because LeMay had been asked to focus on thirty-three urban areas with significant aircraft manufacturing facilities.) Within three months, more than 100 square miles of Japanese cities had been burned out in raids that killed hundreds of thousands of Japanese and made several million more homeless. It turned the country into one filled with refugees, as the homeless and evacuees alike fled urban areas. On a near-nightly basis, hundreds of LeMay's B-29s took to the skies carrying some

*5,000 aircrew to Japan for more destruction. All told, sixty-six Japanese cities were burned and bombed by LeMay's B-29s.**

Maj. Gen. Curtis LeMay: You've got to kill people, and when you kill enough of them, they stop fighting.

Gen. Hap Arnold, *March 7, 1945*: We must not get soft—war must be destructive and to a certain extent inhuman and ruthless.

Maj. Gen. Curtis LeMay: If we lose, we'll be tried as war criminals.

Just two days after President Truman and Secretary of War Henry Stimson met to discuss the atomic bomb, the Manhattan Project convened a "Target Committee" to help advise the military on where to drop the coming atomic bombs. Given the firebombing and strategic bombing of industrial centers already underway, a key part of the interim committee's work would—ironically—be to save certain Japanese cities from the onslaught of LeMay's bombers so that they could be "reserved" for the atomic bomb.

Maj. Gen. Leslie Groves: Our most pressing job was to select the bomb targets. I had set as the governing factor that the targets chosen should be places the bombing of which would most adversely affect the will of the Japanese people to continue the war. Beyond that, they should be military in nature, consisting either of important headquarters or troop concentrations, or centers of production of military equipment and supplies. To enable us to assess accurately the effects of the bomb, the targets should not have been previously damaged by air raids. It was also desirable that the first target be

* Modern scholarship has held that the firebombing campaigns, in addition to being simply barbaric, were largely ineffective. "By the time the Twentieth Air Force achieved the strength and competence to inflict major damage on the industrial cities of the enemy, Japan's war-making powers were in terminal decline from blockade," Max Hastings writes in his book *Retribution: The Battle for Japan, 1944–1945*. "Blockade and raw-material starvation had already brought the economy to the brink of collapse." And yet the firebombing undoubtedly created the permission structure to make the leap to the atomic bomb; as Lawrence Freedman and Saki Dockrill concluded in their 1993 book, *Hiroshima: A Strategy of Shock*: "Nobody involved in the decision on the atomic bombs could have seen themselves as setting new precedents for mass destruction in scale—only in efficiency."

of such size that the damage would be confined within it, so that we could more definitely determine the power of the bomb.

Brig. Gen. Lauris Norstad, *chief of staff, 20th Air Force*: The experts felt that the only way we were going to bring this war to a conclusion is by something very dramatic and effective. Even then it would probably have to be finished by a landing on the home islands and with the kamikaze attitude, the estimate of the experts was that it would cost us up to a million men.

Maj. J. A. Derry and Dr. N. F. Ramsey, *memorandum to General Groves, summary of Target Committee Meetings, May 10 and 11, 1945 [declassified: June 4, 1974]*: Dr. Stearns described the work he had done on target selection. He has surveyed possible targets possessing the following qualifications: (1) they be important targets in a large urban area of more than three miles diameter, (2) they be capable of being damaged effectively by a blast, and (3) they are likely to be unattacked by next August. Dr. Stearns had a list of five targets which the Air Forces would be willing to reserve for our use unless unforeseen circumstances arise. These targets are:

> (1) Kyoto—This target is an urban industrial area with a population of 1,000,000. It is the former capital of Japan and many people and industries are now being moved there as other areas are being destroyed. From the psychological point of view there is the advantage that Kyoto is an intellectual center for Japan and the people there are more apt to appreciate the significance of such a weapon as the gadget.
>
> (2) Hiroshima—This is an important army depot and port of embarkation in the middle of an urban industrial area. It is a good radar target and it is such a size that a large part of the city could be extensively damaged. There are adjacent hills which are likely to produce a focusing effect which would considerably increase the blast damage. Due to rivers, it is not a good incendiary target.
>
> (3) Yokohama—This target is an important urban industrial area which has so far been untouched. Industrial activities include aircraft manufacture, machine tools, docks, electrical equipment and oil refineries. As the damage

to Tokyo has increased additional industries have moved to Yokohama. It has the disadvantage of the most important target areas being separated by a large body of water and of being in the heaviest anti-aircraft concentration in Japan. For us it has the advantage as an alternative target for use in case of bad weather of being rather far removed from the other targets considered.

(4) Kokura Arsenal—This is one of the largest arsenals in Japan and is surrounded by urban industrial structures. The arsenal is important for light ordnance, anti-aircraft and beach head defense materials. The dimensions of the arsenal are 4100' X 2000'. The dimensions are such that if the bomb were properly placed full advantage could be taken of the higher pressures immediately underneath the bomb for destroying the more solid structures and at the same time considerable blast damage could be done to more feeble structures further away.

(5) Niigata—This is a port of embarkation on the N.W. coast of Honshu. Its importance is increasing as other ports are damaged. Machine tool industries are located there and it is a potential center for industrial despersion [*sic*]. It has oil refineries and storage.

(6) The possibility of bombing the Emperor's palace was discussed. It was agreed that we should not recommend it but that any action for this bombing should come from authorities on military policy. It was agreed that we should obtain information from which we could determine the effectiveness of our weapon against this target.

It was the recommendation of those present at the meeting that the first four choices of targets for our weapon should be the following:

a. Kyoto
b. Hiroshima
c. Yokohama
d. Kokura Arsenal

Maj. Gen. Leslie Groves: With these selections in hand, I prepared a plan of operations for General Marshall, recommending his approval. This report was in my office when I went to see Secretary Stimson about another matter. In the course of our conversation, he asked me whether I had selected the targets yet. I told him that I had and that my report was ready for submission to General Marshall. I added that I hoped to see the General the next morning. Mr. Stimson was not satisfied with this reply and said he wanted to see my report. I said that I would rather not show it to him without having first discussed it with General Marshall, since this was a military operational matter. He replied, "This is a question I am settling myself. Marshall is not making that decision." Then he told me to have the report brought over. I demurred, on the grounds that it would take some time. He said that he had all morning and that I should use his phone to get it over right away.

Col. Paul W. Tibbets: Secretary of State Henry Stimson struck Kyoto from the list, although it was the target most favored by General Groves at our previous meeting. Stimson, an expert on the Far East, pointed out that Kyoto was a city of great historical significance and that it contained many shrines that the Japanese held in deep reverence. By this time, as the result of a more detailed study, Niigata had replaced Kokura on the target list, and finally Nagasaki was substituted for Kyoto.

Maj. Gen. Leslie Groves: I particularly wanted Kyoto as a target because it was large enough in area for us to gain complete knowledge of the effects of an atomic bomb. Hiroshima was not nearly so satisfactory in this respect. I also felt quite strongly, as had all the members of the Target Committee, that Kyoto was one of the most important military targets in Japan. Consequently, I continued on a number of occasions afterward to urge its inclusion, but Mr. Stimson was adamant.

Henry Stimson: Although it was a target of considerable military importance, it had been the ancient capital of Japan and was a shrine of Japanese art and culture. We determined that it should be spared. I approved four other targets including the cities of Hiroshima and Nagasaki.

"The Army was determined to drop the bomb"

THE INTERIM COMMITTEE

The patrician Henry Stimson, born just two years after the Civil War, found himself the nation's key decision-maker on the bomb's use.

With the war in Europe over, scientists who had fled Hitler's fascism reckoned with the increasing likelihood that their invention would be used not against the Nazis but against the Japanese. Whatever objections the scientific community had about the weapon's morality, the US's military and political leaders believed the weapon was the best path to avoiding a direct assault on the Japanese homeland. By the spring of 1945, it was clear victory against Japan would come; the country's once-venerable naval and air forces had been decimated and rendered all but ineffective as a fighting force, its merchant fleet had been destroyed effectively in its entirety, and its economy and industrial capacity were collapsing as the US Navy strangled Japanese shipping and supply chains crumpled just as the full might of the US industrial advantage came to bear.

For every four tons of war supplies the US delivered to the Pacific, Japan mustered just two pounds, and by the winter of 1945, the US Navy had more destroyers than Japan did carrier aircraft; at home on the mainland, the population's daily average caloric intake had fallen to just 1,500 or 1,600 calories, barely more than half a healthy diet, with rice often now mixed with seaweed for extra sustenance. The empire's oil reserves had fallen to less than 200,000 barrels and not a single oil tanker would make it to Japan after March 1945, even though the country relied heavily on oil imports for energy. But even facing such a weakening foe, US leaders still feared the death toll, both US and Japanese, that final victory would surely require.

Each battle as US soldiers and Marines neared the homeland seemed to get even more brutal; the fight for Okinawa in late June had seen nearly 50,000 casualties, including 12,520 killed or missing—figures that accounted for nearly one of five of all the casualties sustained by the Navy and Marines in the entire war. Mounting reports of Japanese atrocities against POWs and civilians, including torture, rape, and executions—as well as some ingrained racism—had also led US leaders toward a darker view of their opponent in the Pacific and what it would take to bring them to defeat. US officials threw around casualty figures from 30,000 to 50,000 to 200,000 or more just to take the home island of Kyushu.

Maj. Gen. Leslie Groves: When we first began to develop atomic energy, the United States was in no way committed to employ atomic weapons against any other power. As time went on, and as we poured more and more money and effort into the project, the government became increasingly committed to the ultimate use of the bomb, and while it has often been said that we undertook development of this terrible weapon so that Hitler would not get it first, the fact remains that the original decision to make the project an all-out effort was based upon using it to end the war.

Arthur Holly Compton: It became clear to the men working on the project that if the atomic bombs were to be used it would be not against Germany but against Japan. Volney Wilson, now doubly troubled in mind, came to me in the earnest hope that we might avoid atomic attack on Japan. His reason was the straightforward one of Christian compassion. Could not some way be found to bring the war to a quick close without the ghastly destruction that we knew the bomb would cause?

Victor Weisskopf: Long before the great test, the political and moral implications of the bomb were in the foreground of interest.

Leo Szilard: In the spring of '45 it was clear that the war against Germany would soon end, and so I began to ask myself, "What is the purpose of continuing the development of the bomb, and how would the bomb be used if the war with Japan has not ended by the time we have the first bombs?" Initially we were strongly motivated to produce the bomb because we feared that the Germans would get ahead of us, and the only way to prevent them from dropping bombs on us was to have bombs in readiness ourselves. But now, with the war won, it was not clear what we were working for.

Eugene Wigner: Ever since the Second World War ended, people have asked me: *Knowing what I do now, would I again be willing to help build the world's first atomic bomb?* I would like to say that I regret working on the bomb, if only to please most of my questioners. But I cannot honestly say that I do, either intellectually or emotionally. In fact, I wish the bomb had been built sooner. If we had begun serious fission work in 1939, we might have had an atomic bomb ready by late 1943, when Stalin's army was still bottled up in Russia. By August 1945, when we first used the bomb, Russia had begun to overrun much of Central Europe. If we had held an atomic bomb in 1944, The Yalta Conference would have produced a document much less favorable to Russia, and even Communist China might have been set back. So I do not regret helping to make the atomic bomb.

On the other hand, I never wanted the bomb dropped on Japan. What a wrenching decision! Once Germany surrendered, I hoped the atomic bomb would be made public. I felt hiding it would only hinder our political transition to the day when such bombs were common. With Hitler decisively defeated, I wanted to see our leaders consult an international panel before using the bomb. I would have opposed using the bomb on Japan unless that panel had given their consent.

Emilio Segrè: Now that the bomb could not be used against the Nazis, doubts arose. Those doubts were discussed in many private conversations.*

Arthur Holly Compton: As the war progressed further and the bombs came closer to readiness, the question of their use became the matter of prime importance. After several conversations between General Groves and myself, the General brought to the attention of Secretary Stimson the concerns of the scientists about the immediate use of the bomb and about planning for the longer term development and control of atomic energy.

Sen. James F. Byrnes: Secretary Stimson suggested the appointment of an Interim Committee to consider and make recommendations to the President on such important questions of policy as the test of the bomb, its use in the war, and the postwar use of atomic energy. President Truman approved Mr. Stimson's suggestion and asked him to serve as chairman. The President requested me to act as his representative on the committee.

Col. Kenneth D. Nichols: I believe that Stimson realized that after the death of President Roosevelt, greater responsibility for making the recommendations or decisions concerning the use of the weapon as well as the postwar policy for domestic and international control of atomic energy fell on him. In my opinion, Stimson was the best-qualified individual in the United States to undertake this responsibility. He had the experience of having been secretary of state as well as the wartime experience of being secretary of war. He held the respect of the nation. Perhaps most important, he had direct knowledge of the atomic bomb project from the very beginning and so was completely familiar with the unique aspects of atomic weapons.

* Although the scientists didn't think about the bomb's use only against Japan until the winter of 1945, it's clear US policymakers were thinking that way far earlier. Even by September 1944, Churchill and Roosevelt were considering the bomb primarily for use against Japan. A memo in the FDR Presidential Library about a Hyde Park meeting in September 1944 reads, "The suggestion that the world should be informed regarding Tube Alloys, with a view to an international agreement regarding its control and use, is not accepted. The matter should continue to be regarded as of the utmost secrecy; but when a 'bomb' is finally available, it might perhaps, after mature consideration, be used against the Japanese, who should be warned that this bombardment will be repeated until they surrender."

Sen. James F. Byrnes: The committee also included Under Secretary of the Navy Ralph Bard; Assistant Secretary of State William L. Clayton; Dr. Vannevar Bush, Director of the Office of Scientific Research and Development; Dr. James B. Conant, President of Harvard University; Dr. Karl T. Compton, President of the Massachusetts Institute of Technology; and Mr. George L. Harrison, president of the New York Life Insurance Company and special consultant to Secretary Stimson. Mr. Harrison served as chairman in Secretary Stimson's absence. We were assisted in our work by a group of scientists who had been connected with the project. They were Dr. Arthur H. Compton, Dr. Enrico Fermi, Dr. E. O. Lawrence, and Dr. J. Robert Oppenheimer.

Leo Szilard: I was very unhappy about the composition of the committee, because many of the people had a vested interest that the bomb be used. You see, we had spent two billion dollars. Bush and Conant felt a responsibility for having spent two billion dollars and they would, I think, have very much regretted not to have something to show for it. The Army was determined to drop the bomb.

Henry Stimson, *opening statement, Interim Committee meeting, May 31, 1945, meeting minutes*: The Secretary [Stimson] expressed the view, a view shared by General Marshall, that this project should not be considered simply in terms of military weapons, but as a new relationship of man to the universe. This discovery might be compared to the discoveries of the Copernican theory and of the laws of gravity, but far more important than these in its effect on the lives of men. While the advances in the field to date had been fostered by the needs of war, it was important to realize that the implications of the project went far beyond the needs of the present war. It must be controlled if possible to make it an assurance of future peace rather than a menace to civilization.

Sen. James F. Byrnes: As I heard these scientists and industrialists predict the destructive power of the weapon, I was thoroughly frightened. I had sufficient imagination to visualize the danger to our country when some other country possessed such a weapon. Thinking of the country most likely to become unfriendly to us, I asked General Marshall and some of the others at the meeting how long it would take the Soviets to develop such a bomb. The consensus was that they would have the secret in two or three years, but could not actually produce a bomb in less than six or seven years. One or two expressed the opinion that Soviet progress would depend upon whether or not they had taken German scientists and production experts as prisoners of war for the purpose of having them work on such weapons. No one seemed too alarmed at the prospect because it appeared that in seven years we should be far ahead of the Soviets in this field; and, of course, in 1945 we could not believe that after their terrible sacrifices, the Russians would think of making war for many years to come.

Col. Kenneth D. Nichols: There was discussion concerning the advisability of giving the Japanese some form of harmless demonstration to convince them of the power of this new weapon. The many arguments against this also were considered. Oppenheimer could think of no demonstration sufficiently spectacular to convince the Japanese to surrender. In addition, the demonstration might be a dud, and probably most important, any harmless demonstration would result in losing the important shock effect of surprise.

Vannevar Bush: The decision was pretty well fixed, I think, in Stimson's mind before the convening of the Interim Committee. This committee was brought together in order that there might be various new points of view brought to bear on this thing. I think it was quite honestly an attempt to get fresh ideas and fresh analysis—not merely a matter of building up a record. The Interim Committee worked harmoniously and again went into everything with great care. Its decision was unanimous.

Henry Stimson: On June 1, after its discussions with the Scientific Panel, the Interim Committee unanimously adopted the following recommendations: (1) The bomb should be used against Japan as soon as possible. (2) It should be used on a dual target plant surrounded by or adjacent to houses and other buildings most susceptible to damage, and (3) It should be used without prior warning [of the nature of the weapon].

James B. Conant: As far as the advice of the Interim Committee is at issue, it must be remembered that on June 21, 1945, the date of our last meeting, the war did not appear to be coming to an end. The plans for an enormous invasion of Japan had been agreed on and the necessary steps were under way.

Gen. George C. Marshall: We had just gone through a bitter experience at Okinawa, preceded by a number of similar experiences in other Pacific Islands, down north of Australia. The Japanese had demonstrated in each case they would not surrender and they would fight to the death. Even their civilians would commit suicide rather than to be taken under the control of American forces. Resistance in Japan, with their home ties, would be even more severe. We had had the terrific bombing—we had had 100,000 people killed in Tokyo in one night by bombs—and it had had seemingly no effect whatsoever. It destroyed the Japanese cities, yes, but their morale was not affected as far as we could tell at all. It seemed quite necessary, if we could, to shock them into action.

Vannevar Bush: An invasion of Japan was already being mounted, that it involved several hundred thousands of estimated casualties, and that once rolling, it could not be stopped in its tracks. I also felt sure that use of the bomb, far less terrible in my mind than the fire raids on Tokyo, if it brought a quick end to the war, would save more Japanese lives than it snuffed out.

Gen. Holland M. "Howlin' Mad" Smith, *commander, V Amphibious Corps, US Marines*: At his headquarters in Manila, General Douglas MacArthur, Supreme Commander-in-Chief, was working on plans for the grand assault on the home islands of Japan. These plans involved two landings at intervals of several months. OLYMPIC, the code name given the first phase of the operation, provided for a landing on the southern coast of Kyushu, Japan's southernmost island, in November, 1945. Nagasaki, target of the second atomic bomb, is the principal city on Kyushu. CORONET, the second phase, involved a landing on Honshu, the main island, in February, 1946.

Gen. Douglas MacArthur: The Sixth Army would be employed for OLYMPIC, the Eighth, and the First Army from Europe, for CORONET. The substance of Japan had already been gutted, the best of its army and navy had been defeated, and the Japanese homeland was now at the mercy of air raids and invasion.

Brig. Gen. Lauris Norstad: That was also a factor earlier in the firebombing—that the firebombing should convey to the Japanese that we had it in our power to destroy anything in Japan at our will. It was our hope that that would at least contribute to a decision to end it. This certainly conveyed the idea that the war was over as far as they're concerned unless they wanted those islands pulverized and dumped into the Pacific.

Gen. Sir Thomas Blamey, ***commander, Australian Army*****:** Our troops have the right view of Japs. They regard them as vermin.

Ernie Pyle, ***war correspondent*****:** In Europe we felt our enemies, horrible and deadly as they were, were still people. But out here I've already gathered the feeling that the Japanese are looked upon as something inhuman and squirmy like some people feel about cockroaches or mice. I've seen one group of Japanese prisoners in a wire-fenced court-yard, and they were wrestling and laughing and talking just as humanly as anybody. And yet they gave me a creepy feeling and I felt in need of a mental bath after looking at them.

Russell Brines, ***correspondent, Associated Press*****:** American fighting men back from the front have been trying to tell America this is a war of extermination. They have seen it from foxholes and barren strips of bullet-strafed sand. I have seen it from behind enemy lines. Our picture coincides. This is a war of extermination. The Japanese militarists have made it that way.

Lt. Col. John Masters, ***chief staff officer,*** **19th Indian Infantry Division,** ***British Army, Burma front*****:** They are the bravest people I have ever met. In our armies, any one of them, nearly every Japanese would have had a Congressional Medal or a Victoria Cross. It is the fashion to dismiss their courage as fanaticism, but that only begs the question. They believed in something and they were willing to die for it, for the smallest detail that would help achieve it. What else is bravery? By 1944 the number of Japanese captured unwounded, in all theatres of war, probably did not total one hundred. Frugal, bestial, barbarous and brave, artistic and brutal, they were the enemy, and we now set about, in all seriousness, the task of killing every one of them.

Col. Harry F. Cunningham, ***intelligence officer, Fifth Air Force, writing on July 21, 1945*****:** The entire population of Japan is a proper military target. There are no civilians in Japan. We are making war and making it in the all-out fashion which saves American lives, shortens the agony which war is and seeks to bring about an enduring peace. We intend to seek out and destroy the enemy wherever he or she is, in the greatest possible numbers, in the shortest possible time.

Lt. Gen. Seizo Arisue, ***chief of intelligence, Imperial General Headquarters*****:** If we could defeat the enemy in Kyushu or inflict tremendous losses, forcing him to realize the strong fighting spirit of the Japanese Army and people, it would be possible, we hoped, to bring about the termination of hostilities on comparatively favorable terms.

Gen. George C. Marshall: We had to end the war, we had to save American lives. We had to halt this terrific expenditure of money which was reaching a stupendous total.

Vannevar Bush: There never was any question in the minds of the people who really understood the situation about what the decision would be.

Leo Szilard: The time approached when the bomb would be tested. I knew by this time that it would not be possible to dissuade the government from using the bomb against the cities of Japan, the cards in the Interim Committee were stacked against such an approach to the problem. Therefore all that remained to be done was for the scientists to go unmistakably on record that they were opposed to such action.

Col. Kenneth D. Nichols: Leo Szilard at the Met Lab drew up a petition on July 3, 1945, addressed to the president, requesting that the bomb not be used. In his cover letter of July 4, requesting scientists to sign the petition, Szilard wrote, "The fact that the people of the United States are unaware of the choice which faces us increases our responsibility in this matter since those who have worked in 'atomic power' represent a sample of the population and they alone are in a position to form an opinion and declare their stand."

James B. Conant: My own misgivings have never been about the use of the bomb. I think the decision was correct. What has often worried me is the thought that if only this or that had been different, the first bomb might have been dropped in May. The initial estimate of the S-1 group in the spring of 1942, it will be remembered, was to the effect that a few bombs would be ready by July 1, 1944. I also remember a conversation with Oppenheimer in the fall of 1944 in which we both looked forward to "bombs away by the first of May." I still recall my disappointment and frustration when I became convinced by Groves' figures that the summer of 1945 was the earliest possible date. I felt the difference between May 1945 and August 1945 was very large in terms of American casualties. And history proved that I was right.

Harry Truman: The final decision of where and when to use the atomic bomb was up to me. Let there be no mistake about it. I regarded the bomb as a military weapon and never had any doubt that it should be used.

"Accompany him on a fishing trip"

TRINITY

Loading the bomb's core at the McDonald Ranch.

Finally, in mid-July, all of the pieces of the massive Manhattan Project came together—a milestone literally marked by the assembly of the world's first atomic weapon, readied for a test in a remote corner of the New Mexico desert, a moment that the scientists and military hoped would mark the official beginning of the atomic age.

Boyce McDaniel: The feverish activities for the detonation of the Alamogordo shot got under way.

Val L. Fitch: Between May and the middle of July we made a number of trips between Los Alamos and Trinity. As little time as possible was spent at Trinity because the working and living conditions there were highly uncomfortable.

Leona H. Woods: People staying there in the living quarters got up at five o'clock in the morning, worked outside until the desert heat became intolerable, moved inside, returned to the test area when the afternoon cooled off, and after supper held planning sessions to report progress and decide on the priorities for the next day's jobs.

In the middle of May, on two separate nights in the same week, the Air Force mistook the Trinity base for its illuminated practice bombing target and dropped bombs on the carpenter shop and on another building, neither of which was occupied by people after dark.

Boyce McDaniel: There were, of course, a lot of rumors floating around Los Alamos about the shot, and some concern about its danger. In particular, the wives, most of whom were in more or less curious ignorance about the whole affair, were very worried about what was likely to happen. I remember my effort to reassure Jane before I left for the desert site. During the years that we had been up on the mesa at Los Alamos, we had made frequent trips to Santa Fe for shopping purposes. Since many people did not have cars, a shuttle service had been set up for such trips. The cars were driven by WACs and the rides up and down the switchbacks were sometimes quite exciting. I remember comparing the danger associated with the first bomb test as being no more dangerous than taking a trip to Santa Fe. Jane seemed to feel that that was a reasonable risk.

Arthur Holly Compton: In early July 1945, six days after enough plutonium had been received, the test bomb was ready. I had an invitation from Robert Oppenheimer to accompany him on a fishing trip. I knew what his invitation meant.

George B. Kistiakowsky: The assembly to be fired at Trinity had to be trucked through Santa Fe and Albuquerque and a lot of people outside the X Division thought that these assemblies were far more dangerous than ordinary iron aircraft bombs, which they really weren't at all. So I rather vividly remember that I got on a truck with a loaded assembly and drove it around the Los Alamos roads which were certainly worse than any roads we would encounter on the trip to the Alamogordo site, just to show that nothing would happen.

Ralph C. Sparks: Phil Morrison and [Chicago Met Lab chemist] Roy Thompson came into Gamma shop with a security guard. Roy asked if I could take a smooth stone and remove some rough spots on one of the central hemispheres. I opened the magnesium carrying case with my Allen wrench and Phil removed the top hemisphere. The plutonium hemispheres had been nickelplated to prevent oxidation. There were two or three small bumps on the nickel surface. I took out my 600-grit Indian honing stone and stoned the lumps away. The hemisphere was warm to the touch, about 110 degrees F, and would stay warm for several hundred years. As I lifted the piece of plutonium, I found it hard to believe the value of it—many millions of dollars. The Army security guard stood by to be sure the metal didn't get lost or stolen. Phil placed the thin gold disc between the hemispheres, and the carrying case was reassembled. That afternoon Phil delivered the carrying case and its contents to the McDonald ranch house at Trinity Site where final assembly would be done.

Boyce McDaniel: The plutonium core for the bomb had been sent down by a guarded caravan. I remember Phil Morrison rode down to the site with us. He was carrying the initiator with him. It was a spherical shell of beryllium containing polonium, which was to be mixed on implosion to produce the triggering neutrons.

Cyril S. Smith: We put the core together at the McDonald ranch house. The core ended up as a cylinder, as I remember it, approximately, four inches in diameter and 12 inches long with spherical ends because it was part of the larger sphere of uranium which had the explosive lenses around it. It was like a large Polish sausage with rounded ends.

Robert Bacher: We assembled the bomb core with a duplicate of a set of equipment that had already been sent overseas, so that we weren't using anything that they wouldn't have over there. When we found we needed something, it was immediately sent over[seas].

Boyce McDaniel: Finally, the moment came to carry the plutonium core, with its initiator, from our temporary assembly site in an abandoned farm house to the firing tower. With the proper initiator safely stowed away inside the core, and the core mounted in a cylindrical plug of uranium, we gingerly drove to the foot of the tower. There, in the center, under the 100 foot tower, we found a tent set up with the partially assembled implosion device inside. It was in the shape of a five-foot-diameter sphere, and was made up of explosive lens sectors shaped like watermelon plugs, all pointed toward the center.

The shell was incomplete, one of the lenses was missing. It was through this opening that the cylindrical plug containing the plutonium and initiator was to be inserted. In fact, it had to be inserted into a mating piece of uranium which had the shape of a small sphere with a cylindrical hole cut out of it just the size of the plug.

Cyril S. Smith: When the time came for the final assembly in the tent at the base of the test tower, the core wouldn't slide into place.

Boyce McDaniel: Imagine our consternation when, as we started to assemble the plug in the hole, deep down in the center of the high explosive shell, it would not enter! Dismayed, we halted our efforts in order not to damage the pieces, and stopped to think about it. The crisis passed. The plug had been in contact with the uranium shell during this period. This contact had managed to bring the temperature of the shell and the plug to the same value. The long period of standing in the hot shelter at the farm house, together with the ride in the car, had raised the temperature of the plug so much that the plug could not be inserted in the shell until they reached thermal equilibrium with each other. Finally, then, the plug was lowered gently home.

George B. Kistiakowsky: Bacher and his group inserted the plutonium into the pit, then Bradbury and a couple of SEDs replaced the high explosive castings, which had been taken out to be able to get into the pit. The bomb was hoisted to the top of the hundred-foot tower.

William L. Laurence: That the "survival of the eyewitness" could by no means be taken for granted, even at a distance of twenty miles, became evident to me from the nature of some advance material I was asked to prepare. One piece was a purely fictitious account to be used in the event of an unforeseen catastrophe following the first atomic explosion in the New Mexico desert, resulting in great damage over a wide area, including the sudden total disappearance without trace of a large number of the country' s outstanding scientists, not to mention a certain member of the journalistic fraternity.

The secret was to be kept at all costs, and so a plausible tale had to be ready for immediate release, minus by-line, of course, since by the time of publication the "eyewitness" also would most likely have been a highly turbulent radio-active ghost.

Edward Teller: The afternoon before the test, Oppenheimer sent a memorandum to everyone permitted to view the test of the implosion (plutonium) bomb, which was code-named Trinity. Because the test would take place before sunrise, we would be driven down in buses the evening before. Oppenheimer's memorandum contained advice about spending the night in the desert. Its most important message was, "Beware of the rattlesnakes!" I left the laboratory well after sundown and, as I was trying to find my way in the dark, I literally bumped into Bob Serber.

Knowing that he was also going to the test, I asked him how he planned to deal with the danger of rattlesnakes. He said, "I'll take along a bottle of whiskey." Then I remembered that Bob was one of the few people with whom I had not discussed the question of what unknown phenomena might cause a nuclear explosion to propagate in the atmosphere. Because I took that assignment seriously, and even though officially the project had been completed, I proceeded to dish out the arguments and counter-arguments that we had considered. I ended by asking, "What would you do about those possibilities?" Bob replied, "Take a second bottle of whiskey." Later that night, we boarded the bus that took us to the test site near Alamogordo in southern New Mexico.

Lawrence H. Johnston: We arranged [for our monitoring plane] to take off from Kirtland Air Force base near Albuquerque, but Oppenheimer called Alvarez at the last minute. He had cold feet about how big the explosion might be. If it was ten times what they had calculated, we might be in danger. He ordered us to be at least twenty miles away from the bomb when it exploded. Alvarez was very angry about this because it would make our measurements much weaker than would be expected. We took off before dawn on July 16 and flew around listening to the countdown coming from the main bunker at Alamogordo.

Joseph O. Hirschfelder: It was time to get ready for the explosion. There were 300 of us assembled at our post. These included soldiers, scientists, visiting dignitaries, etc. We were all cold and tired and very, very nervous. Most of us paced up and down. We all had been given special very, very dark glasses to watch the explosion.

Hugh T. Richards: I was at Base Camp, 9.7 miles from ground zero. The shot was scheduled for 4:00 a.m. July 16. However, around 2:00 a.m. a heavy thunderstorm hit the base camp area and on advice of the meteorologist, the test was postponed until 5:30 a.m. to let the bad weather pass the area.

George B. Kistiakowsky: The thing was ready to be fired. Just before the time counting came to zero I went up to the top of the control bunker, put on dark glasses and turned away from the tower. I was rather convinced that the physicists exaggerated what would happen from a nuclear point of view. Well, I was wrong.

Brig. Gen. Thomas F. Farrell: Dr. Oppenheimer held on to a post to steady himself. For the last few seconds, he stared directly ahead.

Maj. Gen. Leslie Groves: The blast came promptly with the zero count on July 16, 1945.

Kenneth T. Bainbridge: The bomb detonated at 5:29:45 a.m.

Brig. Gen. Thomas F. Farrell: In that brief instant in the remote New Mexico desert the tremendous effort of the brains and brawn of all these people came suddenly and startlingly to the fullest fruition.

Robert Christy: Oh, it was a dramatic thing!

Val L. Fitch: It took about 30 millionths of a second for the flash of light from the explosion to reach us outside the bunker at S-10.

William L. Laurence: There rose from the bowels of the earth a light not of this world, the light of many suns in one.

Joseph O. Hirschfelder: All of a sudden, the night turned into day.

Maj. Gen. Leslie Groves: My first impression was one of tremendous light.

Warren Nyer: The most brilliant flash.

Otto R. Frisch: Without a sound, the sun was shining—or so it looked. The sand hills at the edge of the desert were shimmering in a very bright light, almost colorless and shapeless. This light did not seem to change for a couple of seconds and then began to dim.

Emilio Segrè: In fact, in a very small fraction of a second, that light, at our distance from the explosion, could give a worse sunburn than exposure for a whole day on a sunny seashore. The thought passed my mind that maybe the atmosphere was catching fire, causing the end of the world, although I knew that that possibility had been carefully considered and ruled out.

Rudolf Peierls: We had known what to expect, but no amount of imagination could have given us a taste of the real thing.

Richard P. Feynman: This tremendous flash, so bright that I duck.

Joan Hinton, *physicist, Los Alamos Lab*: It was like being at the bottom of an ocean of light. We were bathed in it from all directions.*

Marvin H. Wilkening, *physicist, Los Alamos Lab*: It was like being close to an old-fashioned photo flashbulb. If you were close enough, you could feel warmth because of the intense light, and the light from the explosion scattering from the mountains and the clouds was intense enough to feel.

Kenneth T. Bainbridge: I felt the heat on the back of my neck, disturbingly warm.

* Hinton, a world-class skier who had been set to be part of the 1940 Olympics, had been studying physics at the University of Wisconsin when she joined Fermi's team at Los Alamos. She was not included in the group allowed to the Trinity Test Site and instead snuck to a hill about 25 miles away to watch the explosion. After the war, she grew disenchanted with the nuclear arms race—she later told a peace conference she regretted "helping build a bicycle when I didn't have control of where it was going to go"—and defected to China in 1948, where she lived until she died in 2010 at eighty-eight.

Hugh T. Richards: Although facing away from ground zero, it felt like someone had slapped my face.

George B. Kistiakowsky: I am sure that at the end of the world—in the last millisecond of the earth's existence—the last man will see what we have just seen.

Warren Nyer: I knew instantly that the whole thing was a success.

Lawrence H. Johnston: At count zero dropped our parachute gauges. There was a flash as the bomb went off and we prepared for the shock wave to reach our microphones hanging in the air from the parachutes to be recorded. The flash was pretty bright, even at twenty miles. The white light lit the ceiling of our plane, faded to orange and disappeared. My immediate reaction was *Thank God, my detonators worked!*

Joan Hinton: The light withdrew into the bomb as if the bomb sucked it up.

Maj. Gen. Leslie Groves: Then as I turned, I saw the now familiar fireball.

Boyce McDaniel: The brilliant flash of an ever-growing sphere was followed by the billowing flame of an orange ball rising above the plain.

Otto R. Frisch: That object on the horizon, which looked like a small sun, was still too bright to look at. I kept blinking and trying to take looks, and after another ten seconds or so it had grown and dimmed into something more like a huge oil fire, with a structure that made it look a bit like a strawberry. It was slowly rising into the sky from the ground, with which it remained connected by a lengthening grey stem of swirling dust; incongruously, I thought of a red-hot elephant standing balanced on its trunk.

Brig. Gen. Thomas F. Farrell: Oppenheimer's face relaxed into an expression of tremendous relief.

William L. Laurence: I stood next to Professor Chadwick when the great moment for the neutron arrived. Never before in history had any man lived to see his own discovery materialize itself with such telling effect on the destiny of man, for the immediate present and all the generations to come. The infinitesimal neutron, to which the world paid little attention when its discovery was first announced, had cast its shadow over the entire earth and its inhabitants. He grunted, leaped lightly into the air, and was still again.

Maj. Gen. Leslie Groves: As Bush, Conant, and I sat on the ground looking at this phenomenon, the first reactions of the three of us were expressed in a silent exchange of handclasps. We all arose so that by the time the shock wave arrived we were standing.

Val L. Fitch: It took the blast wave about thirty seconds. There was the initial loud report, the sharp gust of wind, and then the long period of reverberation as the sound waves echoed off the nearby mountains and came back to us.

William L. Laurence: Out of the great silence came a mighty thunder.

Edward Teller: Bill Laurence jumped and asked, "What was that?" It was, of course, the sound of the explosion. The sound waves had needed a couple of minutes to arrive at our spot twenty miles away.

Otto R. Frisch: The bang came minutes later, quite loud though I had plugged my ears, and followed by a long rumble like heavy traffic very far away. I can still hear it.

Robert R. Wilson: The memory I do have is when I took the dark glasses away, of seeing all the colors around and the sky lit up by the radiation—it was purple, kind of an aurora borealis light, and this thing like a big balloon expanding and going up. But the scale. There was this tremendous desert with the mountains nearby, but it seemed to make the mountains look small.

William L. Laurence: For a fleeting instant the color was unearthly green, such as one sees only in the corona of the sun during a total eclipse. It was as though the earth had opened and the skies had split.

Joseph O. Hirschfelder: The fireball gradually turned from white to yellow to red as it grew in size and climbed in the sky; after about five seconds the darkness returned but with the sky and the air filled with a purple glow, just as though we were surrounded by an aurora borealis. For a matter of minutes we could follow the clouds containing radioactivity, which continued to glow with stria of this ethereal purple.

Robert Christy: It was awe-inspiring. It just grew bigger and bigger, and it turned purple.

Joan Hinton: It turned purple and blue and went up and up and up. We were still talking in whispers when the cloud reached the level where it was struck by the rising sunlight so it cleared out the natural clouds. We saw a cloud that was dark and red at the bottom and daylight on the top. Then suddenly the sound reached us. It was very sharp and rumbled and all the mountains were rumbling with it. We suddenly started talking out loud and felt exposed to the whole world.

Joseph O. Hirschfelder: There weren't any agnostics watching this stupendous demonstration. Each, in his own way, knew that God had spoken.

Maj. Gen. Leslie Groves: Unknown to me and I think to everyone, Fermi was prepared to measure the blast by a very simple device.

Herbert L. Anderson: Fermi later related that he did not hear the sound of the explosion, so great was his concentration on the simple experiment he was performing: he dropped small pieces of paper and watched them fall.

Maj. Gen. Leslie Groves: There was no ground wind, so that when the shock wave hit it knocked some of the scraps several feet away.

Herbert L. Anderson: When the blast of the explosion hit them, it dragged them along, and they fell to the ground at some distance. He measured this distance and used the result to calculate the power of the explosion.

Maj. Gen. Leslie Groves: He was remarkably close to the calculations that were made later from the data accumulated by our complicated instruments.

Joseph O. Hirschfelder: Fermi's paper strip showed that, in agreement with the expectation of the Theoretical Division, the energy yield of the atom bomb was equivalent to 20,000 tons of TNT. Professor Rabi, a frequent visitor to Los Alamos, won the pool on what the energy yield would be—he bet on the calculations of the Theoretical Division! None of us dared to make such a guess because we knew all of the guesstimates that went into the calculations and the tremendous precision which was required in the fabrication of the bomb.

Berlyn Brixner: The bomb had exceeded our greatest expectations.

Kenneth T. Bainbridge: I had a feeling of exhilaration that the "gadget" had gone off properly followed by one of deep relief. I got up from the ground to congratulate Oppenheimer and others on the success of the implosion method. I finished by saying to Robert, "Now we are all sons of bitches." Years later he recalled my words and wrote me, "We do not have to explain them to anyone." I think that I will always respect his statement, although there have been some imaginative people who somehow can't or won't put the statement in context and get the whole interpretation. Oppenheimer told my younger daughter in 1966 that it was the best thing anyone said after the test.

Leona H. Woods: The light from Trinity was seen in towns as far as 180 miles away.

Luis Alvarez: Arthur Compton told of a lady who visited him after the war to thank him for restoring her family's confidence in her sanity. She had visited her daughter in Los Angeles and was driving home across New Mexico early one morning to avoid the midday heat. She told her family that she saw the sun come up in the east, set, and then reappear at the normal time for sunrise. Everyone was sure that Grandma had lost her marbles, until the story of the Trinity shot was reported in the newspapers on August 7, 1945.

Elsie McMillan: [At home in Los Alamos,] I had to try to get some more sleep. There was a light tap on my door. There stood Lois Bradbury, my friend and neighbor. She knew. Her husband [Norris] was out there too. She said her children were asleep and would be all right since she was so close and could check on them every so often. "Please, can't we stay together this long night," she said? We talked of many things, of our men, whom we loved so much. Of the children, their futures. Of the war with all its horrors. Lois watched out of the window. It was 5:15 a.m. and we began to wonder. Had weather conditions been wrong? Had it been a dud? I sat at the window feeding Ed's and my baby. Lois stood staring out. There was such quiet in that room. Suddenly there was a flash and the whole sky lit up. The time was 5:30 a.m. The baby didn't notice. We were too fearful and awed to speak. We looked at each other. It was a success.

Leona H. Woods: The most important problem given to Herb was to measure the yield of the Trinity test of the plutonium bomb. Herb converted some Army tanks with thick steel shielding to drive out into the desert after the Trinity explosion for scooping up samples of surface dirt. After the successful firing at Trinity, the tanks scooped up desert sand now melted to glass, containing and also covered with fallout.

Herbert L. Anderson: The method worked well. The result was important. It helped decide at what height the bomb should be exploded.

Brig. Gen. Thomas F. Farrell: All seemed to feel that they had been present at the birth of a new age.

J. Robert Oppenheimer: We knew the world would not be the same. A few people laughed, a few people cried. Most people were silent. I remembered the line from the Hindu scripture, the Bhagavad-Gita; Vishnu [a principal Hindu deity] is trying to persuade the prince that he should do his duty, and to impress him, takes on his multi-armed form and says, "Now I have become death, the destroyer of the worlds." I suppose we all thought that, one way or another.

George B. Kistiakowsky: I slapped Oppenheimer on the back and said, "Oppie, you owe me ten dollars" because in that desperate period when I was being accused as the world's worst villain, who would be forever damned by the physicists for failing the project, I said to Oppenheimer, "I bet you my whole month's salary against ten dollars that implosion will work." I still have that bill, with Oppenheimer's signature.

Maj. Gen. Leslie Groves: Shortly after the explosion, Farrell and Oppenheimer returned by jeep to the base camp, with a number of the others who had been at the dugout. When Farrell came up to me, his first words were, "The war is over." My reply was, "Yes, after we drop two bombs on Japan." I congratulated Oppenheimer quietly with "I am proud of all of you," and he replied with a simple "Thank you." We were both, I am sure, already thinking of the future.

J. Robert Oppenheimer: It was a success.

Joseph O. Hirschfelder: If atom bombs were feasible, then we were glad that it was we, and not our enemy, who had succeeded.

Edward Teller: As the sun rose on July 16, some of the worst horrors of modern history—the Holocaust and its extermination camps, the destruction of Hamburg, Dresden, and Tokyo by fire-bombing, and all the personal savagery of the fighting throughout the world—were already common knowledge. Even without an atomic bomb, 1945 would have provided the capstone for a period of the worst inhumanities in modern history. People still ask, with the wisdom of hindsight: *Didn't you realize what you were doing when you worked on the atomic bomb?* My reply is that I do not believe that any of us who worked on the bomb were without some thoughts about its possible consequences. But I would add: How could anyone who lived through that year look at the question of the atomic bomb's effects without looking at many other questions? The year 1945 was a melange of events and questions, many of great emotional intensity, few directly related, all juxtaposed. Where is the person who can draw a reasonable lesson or a moral conclusion from the disparate events that took place around the end of World War II?

Cmdr. Norris Bradbury: Some people claim to have wondered at the time about the future of mankind. I didn't. We were at war, and the damned thing worked.

Maj. Gen. Leslie Groves: We had prepared for an official release weeks before. Lieutenant W. A. Parish, Jr., had been provided with a release to be issued by the Commanding Officer at Alamogordo Base. Every word in this release was numbered, so that it was a simple matter to alter it without disclosing any secrets to an unauthorized listener-in. I telephoned to Parish and made the necessary deletions and insertions in the release, and told him to have it given out at once.

Col. William O. Eareckson, ***commander, Alamogordo Army Air Base, statement, July 16, 1945*****:** Several inquiries have been received concerning a heavy explosion which occurred on the Alamogordo Air Base reservation this morning. A remotely located ammunition magazine containing a considerable amount of high explosives and pyrotechnics exploded. There was no loss of life or injury to anyone, and the property damage outside of the explosives magazine itself was negligible. Weather conditions affecting the content of gas shells exploded by the blast may make it desirable for the Army to evacuate temporarily a few civilians from their homes.

Arthur Holly Compton: The Chicago newspapers carried an item telling of the explosion of a munitions dump in New Mexico with remarkable light effects. That evening a phone call came from Oppie: "You'll be interested to know," he said, "that we caught a very big fish."

Edward Teller: The sun was well up in the sky when our bus rolled up the slopes of the Los Alamos mesa. Mici, smiling, received me at the door: "Did you hear the news? A big ammunition dump in southern New Mexico exploded with considerable pyrotechnics. But no one was hurt." She obviously knew what had gone on even though I had not been allowed to tell her anything.

Phyllis K. Fisher: Later in the day, those who had witnessed the detonation at Alamogordo returned exhausted and drained. They could hold in their feelings no longer and began to speak of their experience. It was as though a dam had burst. Fever-pitch excitement held sway on our hill, as people went wild with the release of long-suppressed emotions.

Paul Numerof: I was the only one in the lab on that day until late in the afternoon. One by one, each man eventually appeared. All were quiet. Subdued. They spoke softly—it was hard to hear them. It seemed as though they sought support from each other, as though what they had seen was too much for any one man to carry, that the burden had to be shared. One man described his feelings as having seen the devil come up out of the earth and reach toward the sky as though to pull the heavens down. Others nodded in agreement.

Edward Teller: I lay down, but I was too excited to sleep. Finally, I went to my office. About eleven o'clock, young Mary Argo, eyes bright and shining, burst in: "Mr. Teller, Mr. Teller. Have you ever seen such a thing in your life?" An answer was impossible. We both laughed. Our laughter that day was not a response to the bomb but to our ridiculously inadequate reactions to it.*

Maj. Gen. Leslie Groves: My thoughts were now completely wrapped up with the preparations for the coming climax in Japan.

Luis Alvarez: After the test we drove back to Los Alamos, packed our footlockers, and flew to San Francisco, from which we staged for the B-29 base on Tinian, fifteen hundred miles from Japan.

Charles L. Critchfield: That famous saying that Oppenheimer made when the bomb finally went off—"I have become death, the shatterer of worlds."—it's always said that it's a quotation from the Gita, but of course it isn't, because it's in English. I looked through these three volumes of Gitas for that line and it's there. But it's very different from the way Robert says it. Chapter 11 is called "The Book of the Manifesting of the One and Manifold." In Verse 12 of that chapter, it says, "If a thousand suns should at once blaze up in the sky, the light of that mighty soul would be all their brightness"—the "mighty soul" being God, of course. In Verse 31 of that chapter, the soldier Arjuna says, "Tell me, you awful form, who are you?" Krishna says, "I am time, destroyer of worlds." The word "time" is the Sanskrit word "karma," which is used in a sense that means "Father Time" and, therefore, can be associated with death and with the Supreme Deity. I suspect Robert made up his own [translation] because he read Sanskrit. I wouldn't put it past him to have rehearsed this saying so that he'd be prepared to be dramatic, because he liked to be dramatic.†

* Mary Argo, a physicist on Teller's theoretical team working on the development of the "super," a fusion or hydrogen bomb, and the spouse of fellow physicist Harold Argo, was the only woman formally invited to attend the Trinity test.

† Oppenheimer's own copy of the *Gita*, now in the collection of the Los Alamos National Laboratory, is a 1929 translation by Arthur W. Ryder. That particular verse, verse 31 of the eleventh canto, is presented as, "Death am I, and my present task Destruction."

"'Babies satisfactorily born'"

POTSDAM WITH TRUMAN

The Trinity test hung over the Potsdam negotiations between Churchill, Truman, and Stalin.

The atomic bomb was always as much a political tool as it was a military weapon, and its arrival at Alamogordo in mid-July coincided with the high-stakes geopolitical bargaining between the US, the United Kingdom, and the Soviet Union at Potsdam, amid the rubble of the defeated German capital nearby in Berlin. There, the three powers found themselves simultaneously negotiating the end of the war while also beginning the posturing for the postwar world. When word arrived from Trinity of the success of the "gadget," Churchill and Truman saw the faint glimmer of hope that they could end the war in the Pacific more quickly than first imagined and without any Russian help. The sooner Japan surrendered, the better.

Harry Truman: Acting Secretary of State [Joseph] Grew had spoken to me in late May about issuing a proclamation that would urge the Japanese to surrender, but would assure them that we would permit the Emperor to remain as head of the state. Grew backed this with arguments taken from his ten years' experience as our Ambassador in Japan, and I told him that I had already given thought to this matter myself and that it seemed to me a sound idea. It was my decision then that the proclamation to Japan should be issued from the forthcoming conference at Potsdam. This, I believed, would clearly demonstrate to Japan and to the world that the Allies were united in their purpose. By that time, also, we might know more about two matters of significance for our future effort: The participation of the Soviet Union and the atomic bomb.

Sen. James F. Byrnes: While we were aboard the *Augusta* en route to Potsdam, the final preparations were under way in New Mexico for the crucial test. The day the greatest blast the world had yet known was reverberating over the sands of Alamagordo [*sic*], the President, Admiral Leahy and I were looking at the rubble that had been Berlin. When we arrived in Berlin, we learned that Marshal Stalin would be delayed a day. This gave us a chance to do a little sightseeing; the President, Admiral Leahy and I drove into Berlin. We were greatly impressed by the streams of people walking along the road. Despite all we had read of the destruction there, the extent of the devastation shocked us. It brought home the suffering that total war now visits upon old folks, women, and children, besides the men in uniform.

Maj. Gen. Leslie Groves: Mrs. O'Leary, my secretary, had been told the day before the test to be in the office to receive a message. I had left with her a special code sheet which I would use to pass on the results of the test either by telephone or by teletype. In addition, I made use of another code, of which only she and I had copies, so that I could safely talk to her over the telephone. In my message to her, I gave her the salient facts which should be reported by cable to the Secretary of War at Potsdam.

Harry Truman: The historic message of the first explosion of an atomic bomb was flashed to me on the morning of July 16th. As I read the message from Stimson, I realized that the test not only met the most optimistic expectation of the scientists but that the United States had in its possession an explosive force of unparalleled power.

Winston Churchill: On July 17, in the afternoon Stimson called at my abode and laid before me a sheet of paper on which was written, "Babies satisfactorily born." By his manner I saw something extraordinary had happened. "It means," he said, "that the experiment in the Mexican desert has—come off. The atomic bomb is a reality." Although we had followed this dire quest with every scrap of information imparted to us, we had not been told beforehand, or at any rate I did not know, the date of the decisive trial.

Maj. Gen. Leslie Groves: I wrote a full report and sent it over by courier to the Secretary at Potsdam. In Potsdam it was delivered to Colonel Kyle, Mr. Stimson's aide, who placed it in his hands at 11:35 a.m. on July 21.

Henry Stimson, *diary, July 21, 1945*: General Groves' special report was an immensely powerful document. It gave a pretty full and eloquent report of the tremendous success of the test and revealed far greater destructive power than we expected. At three o'clock I found that Marshall had returned from the Joint Chiefs of Staff, and to save time I hurried to his house and had him read Groves' report and conferred with him about it. I then went to see President Truman and read the report in its entirety. The President was tremendously pepped up by it.

Sen. James F. Byrnes: Prime Minister Churchill, whose co-operation with President Roosevelt had contributed so much to the success of the great gamble, was intensely interested in the reports.

Henry Stimson, *diary, July 22, 1945*: Churchill told me that he had noticed at the meeting of the Three yesterday that Truman was much fortified by something that had happened, that he had stood up to the Russians in a most emphatic and decisive manner, telling them as to certain demands that they could not have and that the United States was entirely against them. He said, "Now I know what happened to Truman yesterday. I couldn't understand it. When he got to the meeting after having read this report, he was a changed man. He told the Russians just where they got on and off and generally bossed the whole meeting." Churchill said he now understood how this pepping up had taken place and he felt the same way.

Winston Churchill: Up to this moment we had shaped our ideas towards an assault upon the homeland of Japan by terrific air bombing and by the invasion of very large armies. We had contemplated the desperate resistance of the Japanese fighting to the death with Samurai devotion, not only in pitched battles, but in every cave and dugout. I had in my mind the spectacle of Okinawa island, where many thousands of Japanese, rather than surrender, had drawn up in line and destroyed themselves by hand-grenades after their leaders had solemnly performed the rite of *hara-kiri*.

Harry Truman: In all, it had been estimated that it would require until the late fall of 1946 to bring Japan to her knees. This was a formidable conception, and all of us realized fully that the fighting would be fierce and the losses heavy.

Winston Churchill: Now all this nightmare picture had vanished. In its place was the vision—fair and bright indeed it seemed—of the end of the whole war in one or two violent shocks. There never was a moment's discussion as to whether the atomic bomb should be used or not. To avert a vast, indefinite butchery, to bring the war to an end, to give peace to the world, to lay healing hands upon its tortured peoples by a manifestation of overwhelming power at the cost of a few explosions, seemed, after all our toils and perils, a miracle of deliverance.

Sen. James F. Byrnes: As soon as we had studied all the reports from New Mexico, the President and I concluded we should tell Generalissimo Stalin that we had developed the bomb and proposed to use it unless Japan acceded promptly to our demand for surrender. The Soviet Government was not at war with Japan, but we had been informed of their intention to enter the war and felt, therefore, that Stalin should know.

Winston Churchill: An intricate question was what to tell Stalin.

Sen. James F. Byrnes: At the close of the meeting of the Big Three on the afternoon of July 24, the President walked around the large circular table to talk to Stalin.

Harry Truman: I casually mentioned to Stalin that we had a new weapon of special destructive force. The Russian Premier showed no unusual interest. All he said was that he was glad to hear it and hoped we would make "good use of it against the Japanese."

Sen. James F. Byrnes: I was surprised at Stalin's lack of interest. I concluded that he had not grasped the importance of the discovery. I thought that the following day he would ask for more information about it. He did not. Later I concluded that, because the Russians kept secret their developments in military weapons, they thought it improper to ask us about ours.

Winston Churchill: Eventually it was decided to send an ultimatum calling for an immediate unconditional surrender of the armed forces of Japan. This document was published on July 26.

Sen. James F. Byrnes: Two nights after the talk with Stalin, the Potsdam Declaration was issued. We devoutly hoped that the Japanese would heed our warning that, unless they surrendered unconditionally, the destruction of their armed forces and the devastation of their homeland was inevitable. But, on July 28, the Japanese Premier issued a statement saying the declaration was unworthy of notice. That was disheartening. There was nothing left to do but use the bomb. Secretary Stimson had selected targets of military importance and President Truman approved his plans. Shortly thereafter Secretary Stimson left for the United States.

Col. Kenneth D. Nichols: When Groves received word back from Potsdam of the decisions made there, the momentum of preparations for use of the bomb accelerated. On July 23, Groves prepared the final written directive governing the bomb operation on Tinian. Over the signature of General T. T. Handy, the acting chief of staff during General Marshall's absence in Potsdam, the orders stated to General Carl Spaatz that the 509 Composite Group, Twentieth Air Force was to "deliver its first special bomb as soon as weather will permit visual bombing after about 3 August 1945, on one of the targets: Hiroshima, Kokura, Niigata and Nagasaki. . . . Additional bombs will be delivered on the above targets as soon as made ready by the project staff."

PART V

UNLEASHING *the* BOMB

JULY–AUGUST 1945

"The whole island was alive"

AT TINIAN

The 509th's base camp at Tinian Island.

The 509th Composite Group had a roughly 6,000-mile journey from Utah to get to Tinian, in the Northern Mariana Islands, where it would be based for its looming atomic mission. Tinian, about 40 square miles large and just 1,500 miles from Japan, had been captured in the summer of 1944 amid typically bloody fighting—only about 300 of the 8,500 Japanese troops on the island survived or surrendered—and nearly a year later, there were still Japanese soldiers living wild in the island jungles.

2nd Lt. Fred J. Olivi: As we circled Tinian, waiting for clearance to land, I found myself staring at the four 8,500-foot-long parallel runways at the northern edge of the island. We had heard about these engineering marvels, constructed out of coral by the Navy Construction Battalions—the SeaBees—in less than a year. But I could hardly believe my eyes at the immensity of the project. Oriented east to west, the runways seemed to cover thousands of acres and ran from shore to shore. We landed and took off over water at North Field; there were no other options. And just across a three-mile strait lay the island of Saipan, also with long runways and hundreds of B-29s.

2nd Lt. Jack Widowsky: My first impression of Tinian was I couldn't believe so many planes and the large runways could be on such a small island.

Harold Agnew, *scientific observer, Project Alberta*: The first thing I remember seeing on Tinian and still have that picture in my mind was the cemetery with all the white crosses. I thought about all the Marines and Seabees who lost their lives taking that island and building the facilities while there were still Japanese soldiers on the island.

Luis Alvarez: Tinian resembles Manhattan in size, shape, and orientation.

2nd Lt. Fred J. Olivi: Tinian Island covers approximately 42 square miles and is about 10-1/2 miles long and four miles at its widest point.

Luis Alvarez: The Seabees who constructed its airfields noticed the resemblance and made it complete with signing; Tinian's southern tip became "The Battery," the road up the west side "Riverside Drive," the road from the Battery to North Field "Broadway," the headquarters at Forty-second and Broadway "Times Square."

Col. Paul W. Tibbets: Tinian Island became known as Manhattan in the Pacific, New York without subways. Then there were Park Avenue, Madison Avenue, and Riverside Drive. The section reserved for our 509th Composite Group was in the "Columbia University district."

Maj. Charles W. Sweeney: The address for the 509th was the corner of 125th Street and Eighth Avenue, formerly occupied by the Seabees. It pleased me to no end that someone had named the road that ringed North Field, Boston Post Road.

2nd Lt. Fred J. Olivi: In addition to North Field, there were runways located in the middle of the island, designated as West Field. The whole island was alive with B-29 bombers, and North Field had become the largest and busiest airfield in the world.

Luis Alvarez: In the last year of the war, flights of up to five hundred bombers departed two or three times a week from North Field, a second field to the southwest, another on Saipan, and a fourth on Guam to drop thousands of tons of incendiary and high-explosive bombs on Japan.

2nd Lt. Albert O. Felchlia, *navigator, 320th Troop Carrier Squadron*: Prior to starting overseas flights for 509th support, the 320th C-54s were decorated and received the nickname "Green Hornet Line." A green stripe was painted on each side of the fuselage starting aft near the tail as a point, growing to a width a little wider than the windows, continuing the length of the fuselage just past the front window. From this point was drawn a large wing that terminated in a circle containing a Walt Disney type winged Burro with saddle bags flying between two Pacific Atolls, under the Pilot's window. These decorations were unusual for the time and received considerable notice wherever our planes flew. A small black replica of the Burro was painted just forward of the logo each time the plane flew to Tinian and returned to Wendover. In addition, a small green winged circle with a white numeral was painted on the tail.

Luis Alvarez: When we arrived at Tinian, Larry Langer, one of my Los Alamos poker partners, met our Green Hornet transport plane and delivered us to the tents that would be our bedrooms for the next two months. Langer gave us a quick jeep tour and delivered us to the technical area, closely guarded Quonset huts at the northern edge of the airfield. Los Alamos had supplied our large Quonset hut with a primitive air conditioner, really a dehumidifier, which kept us comfortable even though the outside temperature was often over eighty degrees Fahrenheit and preserved our equipment from deteriorating in the salty, humid air.

Maj. Charles W. Sweeney: The compound was enclosed by a high fence with a main gate that was guarded around the clock by armed sentries. The perimeter of the fence was patrolled by heavily armed MPs. This area contained the only windowless, air-conditioned buildings in the Pacific, where the Alberta and Manhattan scientists and technicians and the First Ordnance personnel were laboring. Here the various components of the bombs would be assembled. The actual bombs' casings and electrical circuits were also kept in this area, awaiting the internal workings that would breathe life into the weapons—uranium and plutonium firing mechanisms and cores.

Sgt. Robert L. Shade, *1st Ordnance Squadron, Special (Aviation)*: Upon arrival, I was assigned a 6x6 truck containing a welder, compressor, drill press, lathe and shaper as my portable machine shop. Then I was assigned to fence in the work area with barbed wire. The Seabees had erected a large Quonset Hut to house a central machine shop and assembly building. I welded the steel girders and I-beams forming rails in the ceiling center to hold the traveling crane that moved the heavy bomb parts.

Maj. Gen. Leslie Groves: Because of the shipping jam, each vessel was required to wait its turn for unloading. This could mean a delay of as much as three months in the unloading of some of our vital equipment. It was a simple matter, through Purnell, to have [Chief of Naval Operations] Admiral [Ernest] King cable Nimitz that all of our material must be unloaded immediately upon its arrival at Tinian. This was quite upsetting to the normal operations on the island, but it was typical of the support that we unfailingly received from Admiral King, Admiral Purnell, and the entire Navy at all times.

Ensign John L. Tucker, *US Naval Reserve, Project Alberta*: We could not find our tools, inspection and test equipment sent by ship, but the tools I had sent by Green Hornet were there, and that is what we used. After Trinity, the rest of the Alberta people jumped on a plane and came to Tinian. We then did our thing and subsequently came home. After VJ Day, the lost tools and equipment were found very neatly packaged and cosmolined. They were beautiful kits, but our job was over and we had no use for them then. Before we went home, we loaded these kits and most of the other tools and equipment we had brought over, into a Landing Ship Tank, took it out to sea and dumped it overboard.

Maj. Charles W. Sweeney: One year earlier, as Marines stormed ashore and eventually took Tinian, hundreds of Japanese soldiers went into hiding in the caves, jungles, and hills around this tiny island. They continued to radio reports of our activities to neighboring islands still held by Japanese forces. We were warned not to venture too far out after dark. Not long after our arrival, in spite of the tight security surrounding our group, [the Japanese propaganda radio station] Tokyo Rose welcomed the 509th to Tinian and encouraged us to go home to our loved ones before we were killed. In later broadcasts, she assured us that Japanese fighter planes and antiaircraft gunners would take special aim at the mark on the tails of our airplanes, our distinctive arrowhead inside a circle. Although none of us would admit it, her broadcasts were a little unsettling.

William F. Roos, *construction engineer, Army Corps of Engineers*: One time an armed guard, who was protecting a tank farm erection crew, saw a chicken running out of the underbrush. Thinking it would look good in a stew pot, the guard gave the fowl a burst from his sub-machinegun. He completely missed the chicken, but to his surprise a white flag appeared above the bush and out came five gaunt and frightened enemy soldiers.

2nd Lt. Fred J. Olivi: The isolation of our group from everyone else, our aircraft with gun blisters but no guns, our unique tail insignia a black arrow in a circle, and our failure to take part in any of the normal combat bombing missions soon had the 509th marked as a "special" unit.

Cpl. Ralph Fry, *603rd Air Engineering Squadron*: We met men from other groups who asked about what we were doing, which was very much secret. We just didn't talk about it.

2nd Lt. Fred J. Olivi: During our indoctrination period with the 313th Wing, I was "quizzed" by a couple of co-pilots who wanted to know why our B-29s lacked gun turrets, and what kind of bombs we were going to drop, and how soon we would start dropping them? I think I finally said, "Look guys, I just can't answer your questions. Ask Colonel Tibbets!" That answer didn't satisfy them; but to tell the truth, I didn't know much more than they did!

T/Sgt. Kenneth L. Eidnes: The food that was served to us was top grade with plenty of it. The only time I would not eat was when Australian mutton was served. It had a terrible smell.

Sgt. Paul Metro: Whatever they did, they could not make the "mutton" we called goat meat very palatable. Many of us swore off lamb for the rest of our lives. One time, they made a valiant effort to make ice cream but it was a great milkshake. This was greatly appreciated anyway. Anything cold was a rare delight.

T/Sgt. Kenneth L. Eidnes: On the island, we were allowed one bottle of 3.2 beer a day and three cokes a week.

Cpl. Clyde L. Bysom, ***tail gunner, Crew B-7, 393rd Bombardment Squadron*****:** Life on Tinian had its ups and downs. It was hot, humid and clothes never dried. Green mold had to be scraped off our shoes and rain was almost a daily occurrence. Movies were outside and raincoats were needed at least one time during a movie. We enjoyed a super USO stage presentation of *South Pacific*. Another time, comedian Peter Lind Hayes brought a group from Saipan featuring a small band led by Joe Bushkin, piano and trumpet, and harmonica virtuoso Larry Adler to our group theater.

Capt. James Holmes, ***390th Air Service Group*****:** One of our least thankful jobs was censoring mail. Nobody seemed to like that. But there was one man who really loved it. And he was the one who was called over one day and asked, "Do you really want us to send these?" Because he had written two almost identical letters, one to his wife and the other to his girlfriend, and placed them in the wrong envelopes. I think the marriage was saved.

Maj. Charles W. Sweeney: After the bleak, dreary endlessness of Wendover, life on Tinian was lush.

* * *

2nd Lt. Paul Wayne Gruning, ***bombardier, Crew B-6, 393rd Bombardment Squadron*****:** July 4, 1945, we flew a practice bombing mission to the Island of Rota, between Guam and Tinian.

Maj. Charles W. Sweeney: After a series of runs we were authorized to bomb Truk and Marcus, where the Japanese had such limited antiaircraft batteries to throw up at us that they would have little or no effect. This provided our first combat conditions, even though these runs were still recorded as "practice" missions by the air force.

2nd Lt. Fred J. Olivi: Since it was only four hours away from Tinian, Truk became the "target of choice" for our B-29 crews. Truk was bombed daily almost around the clock, and surprisingly, they fired back at us. This was my first experience with ack-ack, which didn't even come close as we made our bomb run.

Maj. Charles W. Sweeney: On July 20 we were finally cleared to fly missions over Japan. The targets were Otsu, Taira, Fukashima, Nagaoka, Toyama, and Tokyo. It would be my first combat over enemy territory. At long last, we were in the war. We were dress-rehearsing for the big day.

Col. Paul W. Tibbets: Precision bombing would accustom the Japanese to seeing daylight flights of two or three bombers over their target.

Pfc. Richard H. Nelson, ***radio operator, Crew B-9, 393rd Bombardment Squadron, letter to parents, July 27, 1945, Tinian*****:** Dearest Mom, Dad and Loraine, Just another little note to let you know what is happening. Well I've now finished two missions over Japan. We are really getting our chance now. I'll tell you now they are really bombing hell out of Japan.

Col. Paul W. Tibbets: During the last half of July, our planes made twelve strikes with "pumpkins" on Japanese cities. The weather was not always cooperative during this period, and some of the bombs had to be dropped by radar sighting, even though it had been decided that when the time came, the atomic bomb would be released only under visual conditions. We learned that cloudy weather was typical for the Japanese islands during July, but long-range forecasts led us to expect some clear days soon after the first of August.

"20,000 rolls of sealed toilet paper for Douglas MacArthur"

MOVING THE BOMB

The USS *Indianapolis* raced the bomb's final parts to Tinian.

The vastness of the Pacific is hard to imagine—it represents nearly a third of the earth's surface (32.4 percent, to be exact) and is larger than all the land across the entire world put together. Supplying the US front lines as the war progressed swallowed up the vast resources US shipyards provided. The journey to Okinawa from California usually took between 26 to 30 days, and hundreds of Liberty- and Victory-class supply and troop ships were in constant motion back and forth; altogether, the US manufactured 2,700 Liberty ships and 1,000 Victory ships.

The transportation of the atomic bomb's most valuable piece, the uranium core, to the front lines of the Pacific War occasioned its own drama—and forever linked the Manhattan Project with the greatest US naval tragedy in its history.

The bomb's carefully shaped core at Los Alamos represented nearly all the uranium produced by the US government up until that moment. The end product of all the work at Oak Ridge and so many other places across the country, the cost of billions of dollars, and the labor of more than 100,000 people over more than three years, weighed a grand total of about 140 pounds, the size of a modest single person.

Transporting the final, finished parts of the atomic bomb fell to the USS Indianapolis, *a cruiser that happened to be back in the US for repairs after a kamikaze attack off Okinawa. The suicidal dives by kamikaze planes—named for a "divine wind" that had once helped save the Japanese empire from an invading fleet—had become the bane of sailors through the winter of 1945. Off Okinawa alone, Japanese pilots had launched hundreds of kamikaze attacks during the nearly three-month campaign to secure the island. By war's end, 2,550 kamikaze attacks would kill 12,000 Americans, wound 36,000, and sink 74 ships.*

Gen. George C. Marshall: The ferocity of the ground fighting was matched by frequent Japanese air assaults on our shipping in the Okinawa area. By the middle of June, 33 US ships had been sunk and 45 damaged, principally by aerial attacks. In the Philippines campaign US forces first met the full fury of the kamikaze or suicide attacks, but at Okinawa the Japanese procedure was better organized and involved larger numbers of planes; also the Baka plane appeared, something quite new and deadly. This small, short range, rocket-accelerated aircraft, carried more than a ton of explosives in its warhead. It was designed to be carried to the attack, slung beneath a medium bomber, then directed in a rocket-assisted dive to the target by its suicide pilot. It was in effect a piloted version of the German V-1. By the end of June we had suffered 39,000 casualties in the Okinawa campaign, which included losses of over 10,000 among naval personnel of the supporting fleet. By the same date, 109,520 Japanese had been killed and 7,871 taken prisoner.

Col. Kenneth D. Nichols: From the Trinity test onward, events moved rapidly.

Maj. Gen. Leslie Groves: We could now establish firmly that the first atomic bomb drop on Japan would be sometime around the first of August.

Luis Alvarez: The question of how to transport that extremely scarce nuclear material to Tinian had occasioned serious debate. The U-235 bullet came out by sea, along with the nonnuclear components of the Little Boy bomb; the three target rings were flown out on Green Hornets.

Maj. Gen. Leslie Groves: The major portion of the U-235 component for this bomb began its journey overseas on July 14 when a convoy consisting of a closed black truck, accompanied by seven cars with security agents, left Santa Fe for Albuquerque. From Albuquerque, the bomb was flown in an Air Force plane to Hamilton Field just outside San Francisco, where it was picked up and carried to Hunter's Point. The parts of the bomb, which were packed in a large crate and a small metal cylinder, were in the custody of Major Furman from my office, and Captain Nolan, a radiologist at the Los Alamos Base hospital.

Dr. James F. Nolan, *Project Alberta*: I was assigned to accompany the active material on the cruiser *Indianapolis*, after accompanying the material from Los Alamos to Kirtland Air Force Base by motor vehicle and then its transshipment by air to San Francisco where it was loaded at Hunter's Point. The *Indianapolis* debarked on the morning of July 17 when the Trinity Test was carried out. I did not hear any news concerning the test until arriving at Tinian Island.

Paul Murphy, *crew, USS* Indianapolis *(CA-35)*: Because we were fast and because we were available, we were chosen to make a speed run to the island of Tinian carrying a secret weapon. We didn't know what it was.

Cpl. Edgar Harrell, *US Marines detachment, USS* Indianapolis: The big USS *Indianapolis* was [my] home for the duration of the war. We were right in the middle of the conflict in the Pacific. I was at Eniwetok, Kwajalein Island, Saipan, Tinian, Guam, the sea battle of the Philippine Sea. I was down at Peleliu. I was at Iwo Jima, at Okinawa, three air strikes on Tokyo. After Okinawa, we had received the kamikaze plane. We had to come to the States for repair.

Soon after repair, we noticed out on the dock that there were all kinds of Marine and Navy brass out there. We noticed our crane was reaching over out on the dock, picked up a big crate—I mean some 12 or 15 feet long and four feet or so high and wide—and set that on the quarterdeck. My Marine captain said, "Harrell, station a guard in the port hangar deck." "Captain Parke, what are we guarding?" He said, "We don't know." There was a couple of supposed to be [Army] officers coming aboard, and they had a little canister in a metal cage with a padlock on it. That looked suspicious.

Paul Murphy: They secured the crate on the quarterdeck, and it was guarded by Marines 24 hours a day—very secret.

Brig. Gen. Leslie Groves: The only untoward incident during the voyage grew out of the fact that Furman and Nolan were traveling in the guise of field artillerymen, which led to some very searching and embarrassing questions by the ship's gunnery officers, which they were wholly unprepared to answer.

Cpl. Edgar Harrell: We proceeded on with our 5,300 miles from San Francisco to Tinian Island. We made that in ten days. All we knew was every day we could save going to Tinian, we might shorten the war that much. Scuttlebutt is rapid. We sailors made up stories of what we're carrying—the best story I heard about what we were taking to Tinian was 20,000 rolls of sealed toilet paper for Douglas MacArthur.

Norman F. Ramsey, *scientific/technical deputy, Project Alberta*: Although preliminary construction at Tinian began in April of 1945, intense technical activities did not begin until July. The first half of July was occupied in establishing and installing all technical facilities needed for assembly and test work. After completion of these preparations, a Little Boy unit was assembled. On 23 July, the Tinian base became fully operational for Little Boy tests with the dropping of Unit L1. In this test, the dummy Little Boy was fired in the air by the radar fuse with excellent results. The second Little Boy Unit L2 was dropped 24 July and a third Unit L5 on 25 July. The remaining Little Boy was part of a test to check facilities at Iwo Jima for emergency reloading of the bomb into another aircraft. On 26 July, the Little Boy U-235 projectile was delivered. The three parts of U-235 target inserts arrived in three separate, empty Air Transport Command C-54s during the evening of 28 to 29 July by 0200.

Maj. Charles W. Sweeney: On the morning President Truman announced the terms of the Potsdam Declaration, the cruiser *Indianapolis* arrived at Tinian. Also awaiting delivery was the plutonium core for the second bomb—the real "pumpkin." These additional components were en route from Hamilton Air Force Base in California aboard three B-29s, each carrying separate radioactive packages.

Luis Alvarez: The plutonium core of Fat Man, the Nagasaki bomb, occupied a shelf a few feet from where I worked once it arrived. A small sphere, plated with one-thousandth of an inch of nickel to absorb alpha particles, it was stored in an aluminum box with cooling fins to dissipate the heat generated by its alpha decay. Each of us on several occasions held this ball in our bare hands, feeling its warmth. An Army guard stationed beside the core protected it with his life. He obviously didn't know what he was guarding. It was good duty, sitting all day in an air-conditioned Quonset hut.

Frank Tarkington, *US Navy*: My group ran the Navy communications from [Tinian]. One of the physical points on the island was a small mountain called Mount Lasso. The Seabees had installed towers on top. I was put the chief in charge of the Navy radio station in a small Quonset hut on top of Mount Lasso. The transmitter site overlook[ed] North Field, where the bulk of the B-29s were. You could see everything going on. The *Indianapolis* had come into Tinian, and everybody knew something big was going to happen. Otherwise, why we would have had a big, heavy Navy cruiser in a little place like Tinian? We didn't know anything about what was going on.

Russ Harlow, *Project Alberta*: The *Indianapolis* arrived in the afternoon July 26, 1945 Tinian time. There was no dock so it was anchored inside the antisubmarine net in the harbor area. A small Navy boat went out to the *Indianapolis* to pick up cargo from Los Alamos Site Y.

Col. Paul W. Tibbets: The cruiser *Indianapolis* unloaded a 15-foot wooden crate onto the deck of an LST. Two men left the ship by ladder, struggling with a heavy lead bucket as they stepped into a waiting motor launch. The crate, containing the firing mechanism for the bomb, and the bucket, with a slug of uranium (U-235), were taken to the bomb assembly hut, where they would be fitted into one of the three casings that had previously been supplied.

Russ Harlow: The *Indianapolis* was at Tinian about 3½ hours, then left for Guam to refuel and give the crew a day of freedom.

Luis Alvarez: Sea delivery was assumed to be more reliable, but that assumption almost proved to be disastrously wrong.

Col. Paul W. Tibbets: Four days after departing Tinian en route to the Philippines, the *Indianapolis* was sunk by a Japanese submarine. Only a few of the 900 crewmen survived.

Paul Murphy: We left Tinian and went to Guam. We left Guam July 28, and we were about halfway across the Philippine Sea on July 29—which is Sunday. I had the 8-to-12 watch that night, eight till midnight, and I got off watch about ten minutes to 12, a little early. I retired to my quarters. About midnight, a Japanese submarine was surfaced about 15,000 yards ahead of us. He submerged immediately, turned his periscope 360 degrees, and saw that this ship was coming directly towards him unescorted. All he had to do was wait until we made a perfect target. He fired six torpedoes. Two of them hit us. The first one blew off about 40 feet of the bow. The second one exploded the first eight-inch gun turret in the powder room near the aviation gasoline. And it made a huge explosion and fire broke out.

Cpl. Edgar Harrell: It's really bedlam up above deck. We don't know what's happening down below, but with the bow of the ship off, we become a funnel. We're moving forward—those screws are still turning, we're pushing forward, and you could hear all of that water coming in. You knew the ship was doomed.

Paul Murphy: We took on water rapidly. In 12 minutes, the ship sank. I was knocked out of my bunk, quickly dressed, grabbed a life jacket. The deck immediately below me on the starboard side had five-inch guns normally on it, and they were all underwater. I just barely had time to step off of the ship. The water was covered with oil and black. I swam as fast as I could away from the ship so I wouldn't be sucked under. When I got out to about 200 feet, maybe 250, I found a group of men—you couldn't tell who was where or what or how many. All we could do was wait until the sun came up the next morning so we could see what our circumstances were. When the sun came up, we found that we had two life rafts in the group and three floater nets—a floater net is like a cargo net with cork discs on each side. We tied those three together with the life rafts, and we had about 250 or more men in this group.

Cpl. Edgar Harrell: That first night, we had boys that did not have lifejackets. Some were injured. They're hanging on to someone else. It's a rough time there—even the first night. We lost, no doubt, a dozen boys that first night. Then the first morning came, we had company—at any given time, you could look out, and you could see a big fan cutting through the water. And out of fairness to the sharks, they were not attacking us, but they were there, and that was enough. You could just only imagine the fright that they were causing.

Paul Murphy: Many had broken limbs or burned bodies, terrible shape, hurting very badly. We let the ones that were injured and burned use the life rafts. This way, they could take care of themselves and feel comfortable that somebody is with them. As the day went on, those men died. We had a doctor in our group. We'd call him over, and he would take their dog tags off and declare them dead, and we would let them fall to the deep. These were the ones that, of course, the sharks attacked first. That's Monday, but we were due into Leyte the next day, so we were very optimistic that help would be out to pick us up. In the second night and Tuesday morning, we were looking forward to being found. We had no food, no water. Sun was blistering hot. Many of us tore the shirt tails off our shirts and put them over our heads to keep from burning our skin any more than necessary.

Tuesday came. Sharks started to look us over, but nobody came to rescue us. Wednesday came, and still no change. Everybody was getting thirsty and hungry, starting to lose patience with our chances. We prayed every day, learned how to say the Our Father. I bet we said that prayer at least three to six times a day. I don't think we had an atheist in our group by this time, but we all were crying for help.

Cpl. Edgar Harrell: The boys are so thirsty—your lips are cracked open, they're bleeding, and you have all of that oil just all over you.

Paul Murphy: A lot of the men started to hallucinate. They would drink water, but it was salt water. In about two hours or so, their throat would swell, their tongue would swell, and they would just suffocate and go wild and just drown. Shark bait.

Cpl. Edgar Harrell: Third day by noon, there's only 17 of us. We started out with some 80. A kapok jacket [World War II life jacket] was good for 48 hours. Forty-eight hours are gone, and our kapoks are giving out. They do not have enough buoyancy to hold you completely out of the water. You're having to swim. You're having to do something to keep your head above water. We turn them upside down, and we sit in them—by sitting in them, now your head is out of the water, but you've got to keep swimming or else it'll pitch you. And if it pitches you now, you've got to struggle. You don't have the energy to get that kapok back down under you.

Paul Murphy: We had four days and five nights in the water. An airplane found us. We had eventually two PBYs flying over us.

Cpl. Edgar Harrell: As [PBY pilot] Adrian Marks came on the scene, he could see boys just scattered everywhere—some in life rafts, some on floating nets, some in groups, and then there were stragglers. He said he saw one place where there's more than 30 sharks attacking boys, and he knew that they were killing boys.

Paul Murphy: Marks decided that he was going to make an open sea landing—against all Navy regulations. He made an open sea landing and landed in eight- to twelve-foot walls of water, made a perfect landing—popped every rivet probably in his plane, and would not be able to take off. He picked up 56 men.

Lt. Cmdr. Adrian Marks, *pilot, PBY-5A Catalina, US Navy*: We would have to make heartbreaking decisions. I decided that the men in groups stood the best chance of survival. They could look after one another, could splash and scare away the sharks and could lend one another moral support and encouragement.

Cpl. Edgar Harrell: They pulled me over and pulled me in the plane, and they stacked us just like sacks of feed against each other.

Paul Murphy: He and the crew tied the men on the wings and tied them with parachute shrouds so they wouldn't fall off. When he found out that that was the men of the USS *Indianapolis*, and we'd been sunk, he realized that there was a vast amount of men in the water. He broke another regulation and contacted all ships in the area, gave them his exact location, and told them to proceed to pick up survivors. The first ship that came into the area was the USS *Doyle*. It was commanded by a man by the name of Graham Claytor—Graham Claytor was later the Secretary of the Navy under Jimmy Carter—he proceeded towards our location. When he got close, he shined his 24-inch searchlights against the bottom of the clouds so that the other ships could see it for a beam to head towards and also to let the survivors know that help was on the way.

Lt. Adrian Marks: Even though we were near the equator, the wind whipped up. We had long since dispensed the last drop of water, and scores of badly injured men were softly crying with thirst and with pain. And then, far out on the horizon, there was a light.

Paul Murphy: The *Bassett* was the second ship that came in. It was my favorite ship because it's the one that picked me up. They picked up 152 men out of the water, almost half of the survivors. When we later had reunions and invited crews of the rescue ships to visit us, we really found out really how bad a condition we really were in. Many of us never had any idea.

Col. Kenneth D. Nichols: The *Indianapolis* was the last major U.S. ship to be lost during the war and the greatest single disaster in the history of the Navy.

Luis Alvarez: If the *Indianapolis* had been sunk with Little Boy aboard, the war could have been seriously prolonged.

"There was complete quiet"

THE DAY BEFORE

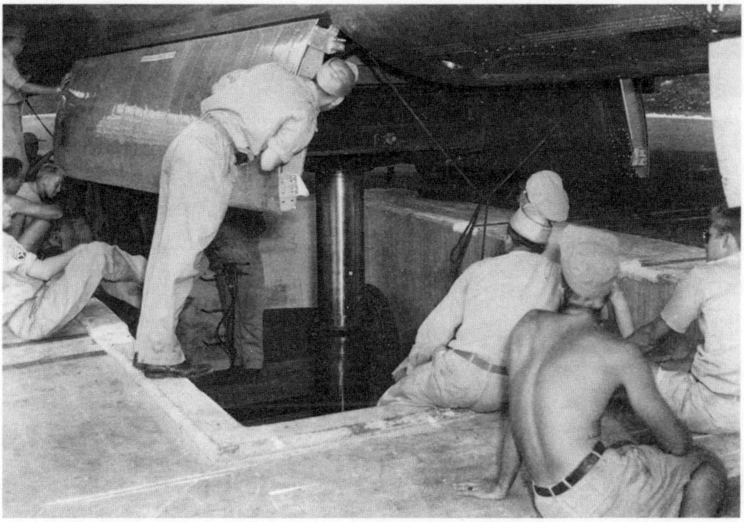

Loading "Little Boy" into the belly of the *Enola Gay*.

With the weather clear above Japan and the bomb pieces all safely arrived in Tinian at the start of August 1945, Generals Groves, LeMay, and Spaatz were ready to launch the 509th Composite Group on its inaugural atomic mission.

Adm. William Leahy: No one could foresee on the first day of August 1945 that Japan would be out of the war in less than two weeks.

Luis Alvarez: Time passed quickly for us. Little Boy was ready on July 31 and would have flown August 1 if a typhoon approaching Japan hadn't delayed it. For two nights the weather scrubbed the mission, and we all went to bed. By August 5 the typhoon had passed.

Maj. Charles W. Sweeney: Shortly after noon on August 1 Colonel Tibbets called me in and told me the mission would be carried out on August 6, weather permitting. He then briefed me on the specifics and my role.

Col. Paul W. Tibbets: In all, seven planes would be taking part in the mission. Two would accompany me, one with scientific instruments to measure the intensity of the blast and another with photographic equipment to make a pictorial record of the event. Then there would be a standby plane, which would land at Iwo Jima for use in case the bomb-carrying plane ran into mechanical trouble.

Maj. Charles W. Sweeney: Three airplanes would fly ahead to the potential targets one hour ahead of the strike force to report on weather at the targets—Claude Eatherly in *Straight Flush* to Hiroshima, John Wilson in *Jabit III* to Kokura, and Ralph Taylor in *Full House* to Nagasaki.

Tibbets would fly the strike airplane, as yet unnamed, carrying the bomb. After rendezvous over Iwo Jima, I would fly *The Great Artiste* in formation with him to the target and drop the instruments that would measure heat, blast, and radiation. It was unusual in a combat mission for instruments to be dropped. But the scientists had precious little data about the effects of a nuclear explosion, and this would provide them with at least some important information. Much of their theoretical projections depended on accurate measurements at the target.

George Marquardt had been assigned to pilot *Necessary Evil*, the photographic airplane, accompanying Tibbets and me to the aiming point to record the explosion and damage on the ground. The scientists, as well as the military, had to have photo information at the moment of explosion to assess the true destructiveness of the weapon.

Col. Paul W. Tibbets: Ever since examining aerial photos of the four cities on the reserved list, I had favored Hiroshima as the primary target. It was important industrially and militarily and had been spared from previous attack only because it was one of several that were being saved for atomic destruction. Several additional considerations went into the final decision. One was the report that prisoner-of-war camps might be located in two or three of the cities, but none was known to exist at Hiroshima. Not until after the war was it learned that 23 fliers who had been shot down in the area were housed in Hiroshima castle.

On the basis of the order received from Groves, I drafted a more detailed one and sent it to LeMay. On August 3, it came back in approximately the same form over his signature as the official order for Special Bombing Mission No. 13, designating Hiroshima as the target. In case the primary was clouded over, the secondary target was to be Kokura; the third, Nagasaki. The 12 previous "special missions" had been our flights to Japan with the nonatomic "pumpkins."

With the decision now made, Tom Ferebee and I studied a huge airphoto of the city and surrounding area. From this, he chose a geographical feature east of the city as the initial point, from which we would start our bomb run. As the aiming point, he put his finger on a T-shaped bridge near the heart of the city. There were many bridges across the deltaic branches of the Ota River, which divided the city into many sections, but this one stood out because of a ramp in the center that gave it the shape of the letter "T." To Hiroshimans, it was known as the Aioi bridge.

Maj. Charles W. Sweeney: The code name for our mission was Centerboard.

Sgt. Raymond Gallagher: About three o'clock on August 4th, we were sitting in our Quonset hut, just playing cards. A runner came along and opened the door to inform the crews that were in this Quonset that there would be a briefing at five o'clock that afternoon. This particular briefing seemed to be a little different from normal. In order to get into the Quonset which held the briefing, there was an MP at the door. Even though we knew him personally by name, he would not allow anyone inside unless they showed proper identification. There were six crews that were allowed, along with top brass from Washington and also, if you want to call it that, top brass from the Navy.

Maj. Charles W. Sweeney: The Quonset hut had been cordoned off by armed MPs. Everyone entering was carefully checked by security. Inside, each crew sat together on rows of straight-backed wooden benches on either side of an aisle leading to the front of the long, narrow hut.

Capt. Theodore "Dutch" Van Kirk: You knew it was going to be a big one—there are guys out there with Tommy guns and everything guarding you.

Sgt. Raymond Gallagher: When you got inside that Quonset, there was complete quiet.

Maj. Charles W. Sweeney: At the front, on a slightly elevated podium, were two large blackboards draped with white cloths. The rest of the area resembled any other briefing room, with maps of Japan and adjacent islands covering the walls. Tibbets explained that we were going to drop a bomb of unimaginable destructive force. The word atomic or nuclear was never uttered by him or any of the others who would shortly brief us. He told us this single bomb would be the equivalent of twenty thousand tons of TNT. That got everyone's attention.

He then introduced Captain [William "Deak"] Parsons, who motioned to a projectionist at the back of the room. The room went dark. In the thirty-five years that I have served in the military, I have never been at one briefing where they didn't screw up the projector. This briefing was no different. The film was not feeding onto the projector's sprockets. A single beam of light divided the darkness in the center aisle. Dust and insects fluttered in the beam. After some fumbling in the dark, the images started to flicker onto the screen before us. An intense flash erupted out of the darkness, and from the desert floor an angry, seething fireball exploded upward, blossoming into a mushroom-shaped cloud. We sat immobile, riveted by what we saw.

Lt. Morris R. Jeppson: Parsons brought the report of the Trinity test of the implosion and explosion of the Fat Man weapon to Tinian island.

Sgt. Raymond Gallagher: Capt. Parsons showed pictures of a bomb that had been recently exploded in New Mexico. The term that he used was "atom bomb." He tried to be as descriptive as he possibly could be in describing its effect in July, when this bomb was exploded. He tried to impress on us how important it was that this bomb be carried and dropped on its proper target.

Luis Alvarez: In July 1943 I had attended the briefing for the largest conventional bombing raid in history, the bombing of Hamburg by the British Royal Air Force. Now I was being briefed for an equivalent raid by a single plane. Then I had been a spectator; now I was a participant. The difference occasioned very different feelings.

Sgt. Raymond Gallagher: The lights flickered on. Tibbets resumed the briefing as Payette and Buscher unveiled the blackboards. Displayed were high-resolution reconnaissance photographs of Hiroshima, Kokura, and Nagasaki. These were the targets in order of priority.

Luis Alvarez: We for the first time learned the name of our target—Hiroshima.

Maj. Charles W. Sweeney: He explained the assignments for each of the seven aircraft and details on the flight plan. The expected date would be August 6, weather permitting.

2nd Lt. Fred J. Olivi: We were told that seven B-29s, led by Colonel Paul Tibbets, would participate in a highly secret mission to the Japanese Empire. Take-off would be early the morning of August 6th.

Maj. Charles W. Sweeney: The group meteorologist briefed us on the weather. He expected a clearing trend and that the targets should be improved by the sixth. Tibbets then closed the briefing by telling us that this bomb would end the war. He reminded us that the mission was still top secret. We were not to talk about it even to each other. He offered that anyone who did not want to take part could leave and there would be no questions asked. No one responded. The briefing was over, leaving each of us to his thoughts.

Col. Paul Tibbets: The word came Sunday morning, August 5. After three days of uncertainty, the clouds that had hung over the Japanese islands for the past week were beginning to break up. Conditions were "go" and tomorrow was the day.

Maj. Charles W. Sweeney: In the sterile bureaucratic language of the military, our operational orders were officially designated Field Order No. 13, Special Bombing Mission No. 13, Operations Order No. 35 of the 509th Composite Group.

2nd Lt. Fred J. Olivi: Our playtime was over. The 509th was about to change the course of the war!

ATOMIC BOMB MISSIONS, August 1945

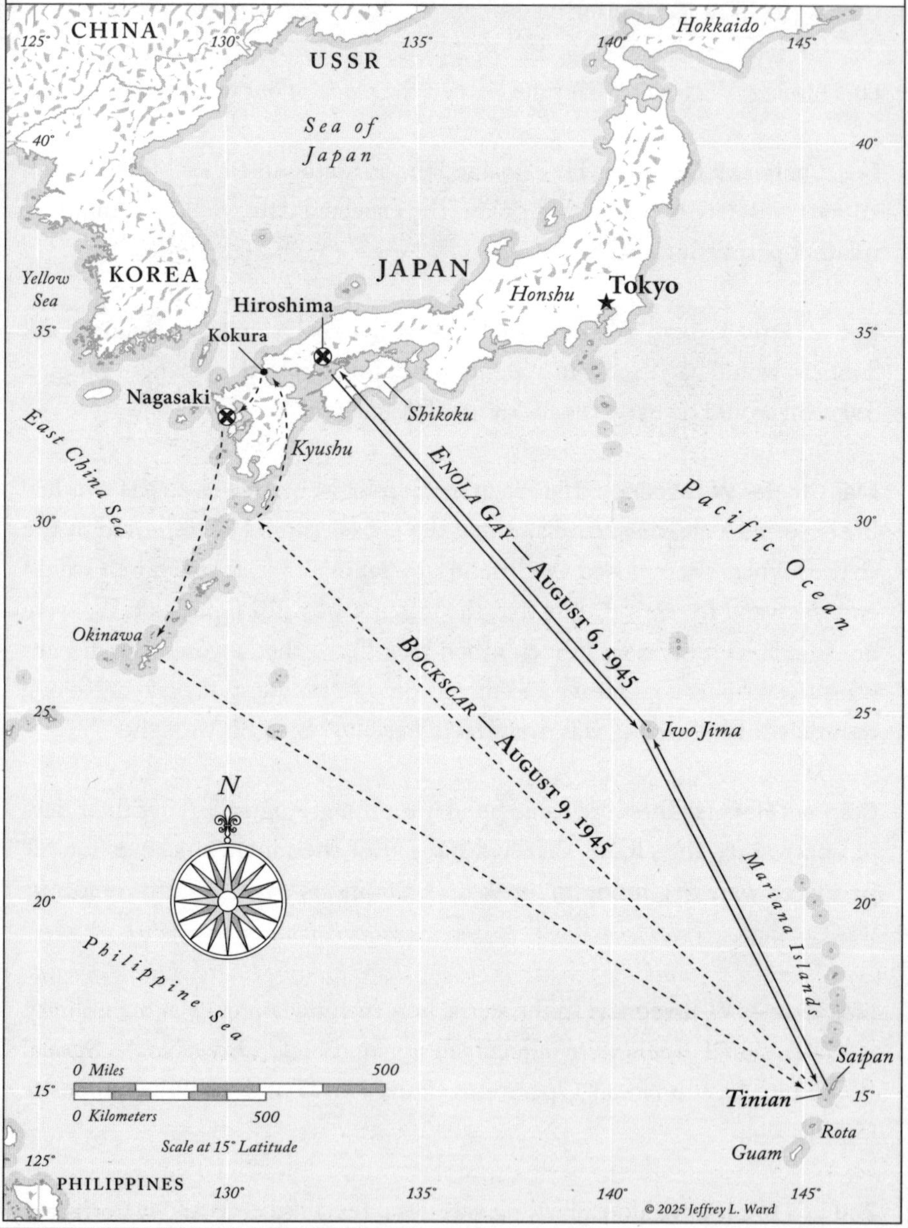

"'I've got all day to learn'"

CODE NAME CENTERBOARD

The final briefing before the 509th launched the first atomic mission.

Throughout August 5, preparations were underway on Tinian for the inaugural mission, and the crews selected for the historic mission readied themselves. As they flew the mission ahead, the crews aboard the strike aircraft recorded their logbook and notes in "Tinian time," known as Chamorro Standard Time, which was one hour ahead of Japanese Standard Time. Thus, their target drop-time of about 9:15 a.m. was 8:15 a.m. in Hiroshima.

Col. Paul W. Tibbets: As the time approached for the Hiroshima mission, I gave serious thought to a name for my plane. Considering the historical importance of the event, it seemed hardly fitting to announce that the world's first atomic bomb had been dropped from an unnamed B-29 bearing the number 82. The

B-17 I flew in Europe and North Africa was named the *Red Gremlin*. Most of the planes in the 509th had been given names such as Claude Eatherly's *Straight Flush*, Chuck Sweeney's *Great Artiste*, and Frederick Bock's *Bockscar*. My thoughts turned at this moment to my courageous red-haired mother. Her name, Enola Gay, was pleasing to the ear. It was also unique, for I had never heard of anyone else named Enola. It would be a fine name for my plane. Several of my crew members, who had become acquainted with mother on her visit to Wendover, gave hearty approval.

Sgt. Robert C. McClary, ***armament, 393rd Bombardment Squadron*****:** The nose art was painted by a tent mate, Bob Wells. He painted *Enola Gay*, *Bockscar*, *Straight Flush*, *Next Objective*, *The Great Artiste*, *Full House*, and *Strange Cargo*.

Harold Agnew: My first task was to start installing the equipment required in the back section of the plane assigned to us, *The Great Artiste* and was told our pilot would be Chuck Sweeney. Installing the equipment in the daytime inside that aluminum fuselage was a very very sweaty job. Our plan was to follow alongside the *Enola Gay* and when the bomb was dropped, release our blast gauges which were suspended by parachutes and receive a signal of the blast pulse and its duration and record it on film using standard gun cameras hooked up to an oscilloscope.

Lt. Morris R. Jeppson: Navy Captain Parsons was second in command of the military in the Manhattan Project. The Little Boy weapon was Parsons' design. He was greatly concerned that B-29s loaded with conventional bombs were crashing at the ends of runways on Tinian during take-off and that such an event could cause the U-235 projectile in the gun of the Little Boy to fly down the barrel and into the U-235 target. This could have caused a low-level nuclear explosion on Tinian.

Col. Paul W. Tibbets: Parsons, who knew just about all there was to know about the workings of our bomb, having participated in its development, was blunt and convincing as he spoke of the risks. "If we crack up and the plane catches fire," he said, "there is danger of an atomic explosion that could wipe out half of this island."

Lt. Morris R. Jeppson: On his own, Parsons decided that he would go on the Hiroshima mission and that he would load the gun after the *Enola Gay* was well away from Tinian.

Col. Paul W. Tibbets: That way, if we crashed, we would lose only the airplane and crew, himself included. The island would be saved. "Are you sure you can do it?" Farrell asked. "No," Parsons replied, "but I've got all day to learn."

Lawrence H. Johnston: On August 5th, we were alerted and got ready.

Col. Paul W. Tibbets: Shortly after noon, the tarpaulin-covered bomb was taken by trailer from the assembly hut to the loading pit. I watched every step of the operation as the *Enola Gay* was towed into position above the bomb. Looking at the huge bomb with its blunt nose and four tail fins, I wondered why we were calling it Little Boy. It was a monster compared with any bomb that I had ever dropped. Little Boy was 28 inches in diameter and 12 feet long. Its weight was a little more than 9,000 pounds. With its coat of dull gunmetal paint, it was an ugly monster. I watched as it was hoisted slowly into the bomb bay, which, like the other B-29s in our outfit, had been modified to accept this superweapon.

Lawrence H. Johnston: People gathered at the bomb pit where the Little Boy bomb was being loaded into the bomb bay of the *Enola Gay*. We were given opportunity to write messages on the bomb itself. I wrote, in black marker "To the people of Japan, from my friends in China" recalling the atrocities the Japanese Army had committed in its rape of Nanking. Army photographers were taking flash pictures of the loading and of the crew.

Col. Paul W. Tibbets: A number of our people stopped by to scrawl messages on the side of the bomb. One, addressed to Emperor Hirohito, was signed "From the Boys of the *Indianapolis*," implying revenge for the loss of those aboard the cruiser that had been sunk after delivering the material for this bomb.

Capt. James F. Van Pelt: At 1800, we had a briefing which lasted two hours. We were then instructed to go back to bed and relax. Things were really quiet around camp. We could feel the tension knowing this particular mission was different. We all realized the importance the outcome would have on the whole world.

Capt. Theodore "Dutch" Van Kirk: We had our briefings and then they told us to go back and get some sleep. How they expected to tell you you're going out and dropping an atomic bomb, then go get some sleep, I have absolutely no idea. I know I didn't sleep. Tibbets didn't sleep. We were all in the same poker game. That's how I know.

Lt. Jacob Beser: The general briefing for the Hiroshima mission was started at 2300 in the Combat Crew Lounge for the crews that would precede us to the Empire. These crews would proceed to three separate respective target areas to look at weather conditions. At about 0900, they would contact us in the strike aircraft while we were en route and give us the results of their observations.

Capt. Theodore "Dutch" Van Kirk: I found out later a lot of the scientists, when we left, were sorry to see us go because they didn't think we were coming back. I expected to come back, I'll tell you that.

Lt. Jacob Beser: The strike mission general briefing began at midnight and was a closed briefing. Only those directly involved were permitted to attend. Colonel Tibbets thanked everyone for their help and cooperation in getting us this far and that tomorrow the world will know the 509th helped end the war. Other details were covered by Operations and Intelligence; then Captain Parsons rose to speak. He said he had brought a movie of the weapon test in New Mexico which would give an idea of what to expect. The movie projector malfunctioned and we were not able to view the movie. He then gave us a tutorial lecture and chalk talk and drew a picture of a mushroom cloud describing the color display that would come with it.

Maj. Charles W. Sweeney: Everything was a go. The weather looked good; it would be a cloudless day over Japan. Intelligence reported no changes in air defenses at the three targets since the fourth. Air-sea rescue would be on station and ready. The Japanese had not surrendered. Recall codes were reviewed in the event we were ordered to return. Our call sign for the mission would be Dimples.

The intelligence officer stepped forward to synchronize our watches. On his instructions, we set our watches at 11:30, with the second hand at 12. He began, "Thirty seconds, twenty-five, fifteen, ten, nine, eight, seven, six, five, four, three, two, one, hack." In unison, we all pushed our winding stems in. The second hands began their sweep.

Lt. Jacob Beser: The briefing was over at 0030 and we headed for the mess. William Laurence of the *New York Times* had been loaned to the War Department to do all the releases on our project. He was short of stature, had a boxer's flattened nose and spoke with a very heavy Russian, Jewish accent. He was disappointed he could not go along on this trip, but was promised a spot on the next one. He just sat in the mess and marveled at the way we youngsters packed away our food.

Maj. Charles W. Sweeney: The three weather crews had already finished up and were being trucked to the runway, when, at about midnight, Tibbets came into the mess hall. Our three crews quieted down as he spoke. Again, without using the words atomic or nuclear, he told us we could end the war by dropping this very powerful bomb. He reminded us to do our jobs, the jobs we had trained so hard to do.

Capt. James F. Van Pelt: He only made three speeches the entire time on Tinian. One was before our first mission, one before the first atomic bomb mission, and one before the Nagasaki mission.

Col. Paul W. Tibbets: Bill Laurence, who took notes, has quoted me as follows: "Tonight is the night we have all been waiting for. Our long months of training are to be put to the test. We will soon know if we have been successful or failed. Upon our efforts tonight it is possible that history will be made. We are going on a mission to drop a bomb different from any you have ever seen or heard about. This bomb contains a destructive force equivalent to twenty thousand tons of TNT." The mention of this figure made an impression. The men sat there in shocked disbelief. Even though they had seen the Alamogordo pictures the night before, they were unable to imagine a single bomb with such explosive force. Frankly, neither could I, even though I had been exposed to detailed explanations by the scientists ever since being placed in command of the 509th.

Sgt. Joe Stiborik, *radar operator,* Enola Gay: We never did realize what we had.

Col. Paul W. Tibbets: Anyone who was still skeptical must have been given pause when goggles of the type used by welders, with adjustable Polaroid lenses, were passed out to each member of the three crews. All were warned to have the goggles ready for use as soon as the bomb was released in order to protect their eyes from a flash far brighter than the sun.

Maj. Charles W. Sweeney: Our heads bowed, the 509th's chaplain's deep, rich voice invoked the Lord's blessing for us and our mission. He beseeched Almighty God to deliver us safely so that we might bring the war to a speedy end.

Capt. William B. Downey, *Protestant chaplain, 509th Composite Group*: Almighty Father, who wilt hear the prayers of them who love Thee, we pray Thee to be with those who brave the heights of Thy heavens and who carry the battle to our enemies. Guard and protect them, we pray Thee, as they fly their appointed rounds. May they, as well as we, know Thy strength and power, and armed with Thy might may they bring this war to a rapid end. We pray Thee that the end of war may come soon, and that once more we may know peace on earth. May the men who fly this night be kept safe in Thy care, and may they be returned safely to us. We shall go forward trusting in Thee, knowing we are in Thy care now and for ever. Amen.

Capt. James F. Van Pelt: We finished our briefing about 2400 at which time we had a late snack at the mess hall including fried eggs, a rare occasion in the Pacific.

Col. Paul W. Tibbets: When we were about to leave the mess hall, flight surgeon Don Young came to my table and slipped me a small cardboard pillbox. "I hope you don't have to use these," he said, trying to be cheerful. The pillbox contained 12 cyanide capsules, one for each member of the *Enola Gay*'s crew.

Except for Deak Parsons and myself, no one on our flight knew about the suicide preparations. Nor would they know unless an emergency would occur forcing us to bail out over enemy territory.

Maj. Charles W. Sweeney: As each crew was ready, the three trucks proceeded to North Field and the assigned hardstands. It was now a little after one a.m. The weather airplanes were already conducting their final preflight checks and would be airborne in about half an hour.

Col. Paul W. Tibbets: Four of us jumped in a jeep and headed for the flight line, where a surprise awaited us. There stood the *Enola Gay*, bathed in floodlights like the star of a Hollywood movie. Motion picture cameras were set up and still photographers were standing by with their equipment. Any Japanese lurking in the surrounding hills—and there were still some who had escaped capture—had to know that something very special was going on.

Capt. James F. Van Pelt: They had two big sets of Hollywood studio lights consisting of a steel rack with about thirty lights on wheels so it could be moved around.

Capt. Theodore "Dutch" Van Kirk: I looked at it and said, "it looks like a Hollywood premiere!" Dick Nelson, our radio operator who came from Southern California, looked at it and he says, "looks like a supermarket opening to me."

Cpl. Armen Shamlian, *photographer, 390th Air Service Group*: I took photos of the crew, with the final shot being Colonel Tibbets looking out the window from the cockpit. I called out to him, "Colonel, please wave," so he did with a smile and the plane started rolling away to take off for Hiroshima.

Col. Paul W. Tibbets: I think the picture-taking would have continued all night if I hadn't called a halt shortly before two o'clock in order to complete preparations for takeoff.

Lawrence H. Johnston: Then we were told to pick up our protective gear: A parachute, an inflatable rubber life raft, a steel helmet, a vest with emergency supplies, eating rations, shark repellent, fishing line and a very heavy flak suit loaded with steel plates. We climbed up the ladder into our back compartment of the plane. We had Alvarez, Harold Agnew, and myself back there.

2nd Lt. Franklin K. "Ken" Wey, *bombardier,* Straight Flush, *Crew C-11, 393rd Bombardment Squadron*: On the August 6th mission, the ground crew, as usual, loaded a case of beer on the catwalk in the bomb bay so it would be cold when the plane returned. Fred Krug was a weatherman from the briefing team and a close friend to Buck and me. He wasn't scheduled to fly a mission and since we weren't carrying a bomb, we smuggled him aboard so he could tell his grandchildren he flew a mission over Japan.

Lt. Jacob Beser: Just prior to boarding the airplane for takeoff, Ed Doll handed me a small piece of rice paper, not much larger than a postage stamp, that had four radio frequencies on it. His instructions were to "eat it before you bail out." These frequencies were the measured operating frequencies of the modified APS-13s that were being used as proximity devices on the weapon, which was in the region of 400-420 MHZ.

Col. Paul W. Tibbets: Twelve of us climbed into the B-29 for the historic flight. The others were Captain Robert A. Lewis of Ridgefield Park, New Jersey, the copilot; Major Thomas W. Ferebee, Mocksville, North Carolina, bombardier; Captain Theodore J. Van Kirk, Northumberland, Pennsylvania, navigator; Lt. Jacob Beser, Baltimore, Maryland, radar countermeasures officer; Navy Captain William S. ["Deak"] Parsons, Santa Fe, New Mexico, weaponeer and ordnance officer; Second Lt. Morris Jeppson, Carson City, Nevada, assistant weaponeer; Sgt. Joe Stiborik, Taylor, Texas, radar operator; Staff Sgt. George R. Caron, Lynbrook, New York, tail gunner; Sgt. Robert H. Shumard, Detroit, Michigan, assistant flight engineer, Pfc. Richard H. Nelson, Los Angeles, California, radio operator, and Tech. Sgt. Wyatt E. Duzenbury, Lansing, Michigan, flight engineer. All of us wore the loose-fitting belted coveralls that were customary for bomber flight crews. With two exceptions, we wore the standard long-peaked flight caps. George Caron was wearing the Brooklyn Dodger cap that had become his trademark. He was a fanatical Dodger fan. A preflight picture shows Dutch Van Kirk in an ordinary overseas cap.

Capt. James F. Van Pelt: Our three weather ships commanded by Eatherly, Taylor, and Wilson took off an hour ahead of us, each to one of the three targets, Hiroshima, Kokura and Nagasaki. Complete radio silence was essential so we could listen to their radio broadcasting frequency. An hour from our turning point, we would receive weather reports from these three ships telling us which target was clear.

Maj. Charles W. Sweeney: As I idled on Runway B, I could see over to Runway A. At 2:45 a.m. Colonel Tibbets started his run.

Col. Paul W. Tibbets: More than a mile and a half of chipped coral runway stretched out before me in the darkness. The plane trembled and shuddered during the engine run-up. We were heavily loaded, with 7,000 gallons of gasoline and the 9,000-pound bomb. After eleven months of planning and practice, it was showdown time. "Dimples Eight Two to North Tinian Tower. Ready for takeoff on Runway Able."

Maj. Charles W. Sweeney: I saw him lift off and then lost sight of him in the darkness. We were using no running lights. Precisely two minutes after Tibbets's takeoff, I lifted off into the clear starry night, and precisely two minutes after me, George Marquardt lifted off. We would be staggered at about ten-mile intervals until we reached our rendezvous over Iwo Jima, the halfway mark on our journey.

Cpl. Armen Shamlian: I went back to the photo lab to develop and print the negatives. They looked good so I went to bed. I woke up about 7 a.m. wondering about the mission.

* * *

Maj. Charles W. Sweeney: I lit my Cuban Romeo y Julieta and settled back for the three-hour flight to the rendezvous. There was little chitchat. The crew tried to catch some shut-eye. The atmosphere on board was relaxed. Not loose, but tension-free. Relaxed in the way that any group of professionals is when its members are carrying out a job they're supremely trained to do and confident in their abilities.

Col. Paul W. Tibbets: We were only eight minutes off the ground when Parsons and Lt. Morris R. Jeppson lowered themselves into the bomb bay to insert a slug of uranium and the conventional explosive charge into the core of the strange-looking weapon.

Lt. Morris R. Jeppson: This was done, I believe at about 7,000 feet altitude.

Col. Paul W. Tibbets: Jeppson held the flashlight while Parsons struggled with the mechanism of the bomb, inserting the explosive charge that would send one block of uranium flying into the other to set off the instant chain reaction that would create the atomic explosion. Working in cramped quarters and handling tooled steel so sharp that it sometimes cut his fingers, as it had in practice the afternoon before, Parsons managed to put the incredible weapon in working order in just twenty-five minutes.

Lt. Morris R. Jeppson: After returning to the cabin I periodically monitored the circuits in the bomb.

Capt. Robert A. Lewis, *copilot, logbook, aboard the* Enola Gay: At forty-five minutes out of our base everyone is at work. Colonel Tibbets has been hard at work with the usual tasks that belong to the pilot of a B-29. Captain Van Kirk, navigator, and Sergeant Stiborik, radar operator, are in continuous conversation (on the interphone), as they are shooting bearings on the northern Marianas and making radar wind runs.

Col. Paul W. Tibbets: In the cockpit, I found it a good time to catch some sleep. After less than an hour of fitful but useful slumber, I was back at the controls. I resumed control of the plane. We ascended gradually from 4,600 to 5,500 feet. Then, at 5:34, I began our climb in earnest. Twenty minutes later, we reached our new cruising altitude of 9,300 feet. Through broken clouds ahead, the island of Iwo Jima came into view.

Maj. Charles W. Sweeney: It was about 5:45 a.m. when we caught sight of Iwo.

Lt. Jacob Beser: It was here we would rendezvous with the other two airplanes.

Maj. Charles W. Sweeney: Rising prominently above the island was Mount Suribachi. George and I slipped in behind Tibbets in formation on each of his wings as he circled Suribachi. As I looked to the east I saw the sun emerging above the horizon, a huge red ball rising up from the ocean.

Col. Paul W. Tibbets: As we took leave of Iwo Jima, we were slightly more than three hours away from our target. Our target? We weren't sure at this time where we were going. It would be one of three: Hiroshima, Kokura, or Nagasaki.

Lt. Jacob Beser: As we neared Japan, I began to detect the familiar Japanese early warning radar. Soon it was locked on us. Then another radar picked us up. At the same time, but on different frequencies that we shared with the Navy, I detected considerable activity off the coast. The Fifth Fleet was in full operation that morning and the radio chatter of the pilots made fascinating listening.

Lawrence H. Johnston: At altitude, Agnew and I started testing our equipment. Alvarez was very tired from burning the midnight oil. He soon climbed up into the padded tunnel and went soundly to sleep. Agnew switched the power on to the pressure gauges in the bomb bay. Before the drop, these gauges were powered from the plane's power system. When they were dropped out of the bomb bay, they would change over to their internal batteries for the few minutes they performed their task of telemetering their pressure data. I picked up the telemetering signals on the three FM receivers and tuned the receivers to the signals. I loaded film into the three movie cameras and checked their focus.

Luis Alvarez: That done, we watched our progress up the island chain on the radar repeater screen. By the time we saw the coast of Shikoku a hundred miles ahead, we had checked our radio transmitters and were seeing signals on our oscilloscopes. Approaching the coast, we donned flak suits and arranged flak mattresses to sit on. I decided not to wear a parachute; if we were shot down, I didn't want to be captured.

Col. Paul W. Tibbets: On this stage of the flight, I was smoking my pipe with a little more intensity than usual.

Capt. Robert A. Lewis, *logbook, aboard the* Enola Gay: After leaving Iwo we began to pick up some low strata and before very long we were flying on top of an undercast. At 7.10 the undercast began to break up just a little, but, outside of a high thin cirrus and the low stuff, it is a very beautiful day. We are now about two hours from Bombs Away.

Capt. Theodore "Dutch" Van Kirk: I could see the weather is perfect.

Maj. Charles W. Sweeney: The sky was crystal clear.

Capt. James F. Van Pelt: It looked to be a beautiful day, the weather was almost perfect. There were a few clouds over the water but I can't remember any day I spent in the Pacific when it was more perfect for flying than it was on August 6th.

Capt. Theodore "Dutch" Van Kirk: I could look out and see the coastline of Japan from probably a hundred miles away at that altitude. I could pick out the city of Hiroshima from 75 miles away at least.

Capt. James F. Van Pelt: We could see boats around Iwo with their hulls sticking out of the water, airplanes were taking off and landing. Chuck was still in radio contact with the Colonel submitting position reports to aid the operator every hour and a half in case of a ditching. We could see a few ships we had to classify, record their position, speed and direction of travel in the navigator's log.

2nd Lt. Franklin K. "Ken" Wey: I made two bomb runs over the target, on the same heading they would fly to drop the bomb, to make sure cloud cover would not interfere with the sighting. My message to the *Enola Gay* was "2/10ths cloud cover at 15,000 feet bomb primary." It was coded and radioed. We had been ordered beforehand not to stay.

Col. Paul W. Tibbets: The next hour was one of suspense as we droned toward the enemy homeland. Without waiting for the weather word, I climbed slowly toward what was to be our bombing altitude of 30,700 feet. We were almost at this level when, at 8:30, the awaited message came in code from Eatherly's *Straight Flush*, high over Hiroshima. As tapped out by Sgt. Pasquale Baldasaro aboard that plane, and taken down on his pad by our radio operator, Dick Nelson, the message consisted of these cryptic letter-figure combinations: "Y-3, Q-3, B-2, C-1." Bending over Nelson as he wrote, I translated the message to mean that the cloud cover was less than three-tenths at all altitudes. "C-1" was advice, quite unnecessary under the circumstances, to bomb the primary target.

Lt. Jacob Beser: The decision was made, then and there on the *Enola Gay* to go to Hiroshima.

Sgt. Gillon T. Niceley: On our trip to and from Hiroshima, we mostly listened to Tokyo Rose, discussed the mission, and, I being in the tail, watched for enemy planes or anything that didn't seem natural.

Col. Paul W. Tibbets: At 7:30, Deak Parsons made some adjustments on the console that controlled the bomb's intricate circuitry. He informed us that the bomb was armed and ready.

Lt. Morris R. Jeppson: There were three green electrical safety plugs inserted in the casing of the weapon. These prevented improper voltages going to the detonators of the gun charge. I reported to Parsons and Colonel Tibbets that everything was operating properly. I then returned to the bomb bay, removed the green safety plugs, and replaced them with three red plugs that had connections to enable the detonation of the gun by the fusing mechanism. The bomb was now armed.

Capt. Robert A. Lewis, *logbook, aboard the* Enola Gay: The bomb is now alive. It is a funny feeling knowing it is right in back of you. Knock wood.

Capt. Theodore "Dutch" Van Kirk: We went in across the island [Shikoku] across the inland sea to just west of Hiroshima where he turned on the IP—the initial point. We were supposed to drop at 9:15, so I thought, well, I'm gonna try to get as close as possible. I extended the IP a little bit to use up a little more time.

Capt. Robert A. Lewis, ***logbook, aboard the*** **Enola Gay:** It is 8.50. Not long now, folks.

Capt. James F. Van Pelt: The Colonel turned on course for a bomb run on Hiroshima. We were all getting very tense. The minutes seemed like hours.

Col. Paul W. Tibbets: Although I was sure this was our target, there were other cities in the area and I wanted my judgment corroborated. I remembered a pharmacist of my acquaintance who always required an assistant to verify the label on every bottle before mixing a prescription. "Do you all agree that's Hiroshima?" I asked the other crewmen. They promptly concurred.

Capt. James F. Van Pelt: Finally, the Colonel opened his bomb bay doors. We could see Hiroshima ahead and below us. It is located on the water front of Honshu Island with seven rivers and an old castle in the center very near our target.

Col. Paul W. Tibbets: The T-shaped bridge was easy to spot. Even though there were many other bridges in this sprawling city, there was no other bridge that even slightly resembled it.

Capt. James F. Van Pelt: A bombardier could not ask for a more perfect day.

Capt. Theodore "Dutch" Van Kirk: It's one of the easiest missions that I ever flew in my life—much easier than flying over Germany, cause the Japanese weren't shooting at us.

Capt. Robert A. Lewis, ***logbook, aboard the*** **Enola Gay:** There will be a short intermission [in the logbook] while we bomb our target.

* * *

Col. Paul W. Tibbets: At 17 seconds after 9:14 a.m., just 60 seconds before the scheduled bomb release, he flicked a toggle switch that activated a high-pitched radio tone. This tone, ominous under the circumstances, sounded in the headphones of the men aboard our plane and the two airplanes that were with us; it was also heard by the men in the three weather planes, which were already more than 200 miles away on their return flight to Tinian. Exactly one minute after it began, the radio tone ceased and at the same instant there was the sound of the pneumatic bomb-bay doors opening automatically.

Lawrence H. Johnston: We heard the wind rushing as the bomb bay doors on our plane opened.

Lt. Jacob Beser: At precisely 08:15:15 Hiroshima time, the tone signal stopped.

Col. Paul W. Tibbets: Out tumbled Little Boy, a misnamed package of explosive force infinitely more devastating than any bomb—or cluster of bombs—ever dropped before.

Lt. Jacob Beser: The bomb was on its way.

Col. Paul W. Tibbets: By my watch, the time was 9:15 plus 17 seconds. In Hiroshima, it was 8:15. We had crossed a time zone in our flight from Tinian.

Maj. Gen. Leslie Groves: The original scheduled time was 0915. Thus, in a flight of some seventeen hundred miles taking six hours and a half, Colonel Tibbets had arrived on target only one-half of a minute off schedule.

Lawrence H. Johnston: A continuous tone transmitted by the *Enola Gay* ended. Simultaneously, our bombardier dropped our parachute gauges which would slowly descend while the bomb dropped to its target, exploded and the pressure wave traveled up to our high altitude. The receivers needed constant tuning as the parachutes descended to slightly higher pressures.

Col. Paul W. Tibbets: With the release of the bomb, the plane was instantly 9,000 pounds lighter. As a result, its nose leaped up sharply and I had to act quickly to execute the most important task of the flight: to put as much distance as possible between our plane and the point at which the bomb would explode. The 155-degree diving turn to the right, with its 160-degree bank, put a great strain on the airplane and its occupants. I was flying this biggest of all bombers as if it were a fighter plane.

Capt. Theodore "Dutch" Van Kirk: We made the turn that we had practiced many, many times in how to get away from the bomb—155-degree turn and put the nose down, pushed the throttles forward, just run like the devil.

Luis Alvarez: The bomb took forty-three seconds to drop thirty thousand feet to its detonation point, our three parachute gauges drifting down above. For half that time we were diving away in a two-G turn. Before we leveled off and flew directly away, we saw the calibration pulses that indicated our equipment was working well.

Lt. Morris R. Jeppson: We had been cautioned not to look back at the bomb explosion and to wear welders' goggles. The plane jerked up as usual when the heavy Little Boy was released. I counted the seconds to myself. I believe I had calculated it would take about 43 seconds to reach either the ground or the planned detonation elevation above the ground. For a second I thought, "It didn't work; it must be a dud." I had been told by Ed Doll before the flight, "This bomb cost two billion dollars; don't lose it."

Luis Alvarez: Suddenly a bright flash lit the compartment. The pressure pulse registered its N-shaped wave on our screens.

Maj. Charles W. Sweeney: Suddenly the sky was bleached a bright white, brighter than the sun. I instinctively squeezed my eyes shut, but the light filled my head.

Lawrence H. Johnston: A white flash coming up through our small window made a bright disc on the ceiling of the plane that faded to orange.

Capt. James F. Van Pelt: Even with our goggles on, we could see a brilliant flash said to be brighter than the sun.

Capt. Theodore "Dutch" Van Kirk: Didn't hear anything—couldn't hear a thing over the roar of the motors—but you saw the bright flash.

Col. Paul W. Tibbets: Caron, the only man aboard the plane with an immediate view of the awesome havoc we had created, tried to describe it to us.

Suddenly he saw the shock wave approaching at the speed of sound—almost 1,100 feet a second. Condensing moisture from the heated air at the leading edge of the shock wave made it quite visible, just as one sees shimmering air rising from the ground on a hot, humid day.

Capt. Theodore "Dutch" Van Kirk: Very shortly thereafter, we got the very first shock wave. It felt like when you're flying over Europe—a very close flak burst right under the wing or something of that type. It was measured at about two-and-a-half to three Gs. That doesn't seem like much, but if you're a B-29 at 30,000 feet, it's a pretty damn good jolt.

Lawrence H. Johnston: We felt a double jolt as the shockwave hit our plane.

Harold Agnew: We realized the second slap was the reflection of the shock from the ground.

Col. Paul W. Tibbets: There was a startling sensation that I remember quite vividly to this day. My teeth told me, more emphatically than my eyes, of the Hiroshima explosion. At the moment of the blast, there was a tingling sensation in my mouth and the very definite taste of lead upon my tongue. This, I was told later by scientists, was the result of electrolysis—an interaction between the fillings in my teeth and the radioactive forces that were loosed by the bomb.

Maj. Charles W. Sweeney: My tail gunner, Pappy Dehart, began uttering gibberish over the intercom. In combat, a gunner has to report what he sees precisely, distinctly, and once, and then wait for the pilot's acknowledgment. Pappy, an experienced gunner, was now running over his own words, his alarm garbling what he was saying. I tried to break in. "Pappy, say again." I soon realized that Pappy was trying to describe a sight no human being had ever seen.

Harold Agnew: I wrote in my notebook, "It really went off, it really did."

Sgt. Raymond Gallagher: What all of us saw was something that I don't think we will ever see, and hope to never see, the rest of our life.

S/Sgt. George R. Caron, *tail gunner,* Enola Gay: Everything was burning. I saw fires springing up in different places, like flames shooting up on a bed of coals. I was asked to count them. I said, "Count them?" Hell, I gave up!

Maj. Charles W. Sweeney: Hiroshima now lay to the west, on the right side of my airplane. I looked down and saw a roiling, dirty brown cloud spreading out horizontally over the city. Out of it was emerging a vertical cloud that looked like it contained every color of the rainbow, and more. The colors were vivid—hard to describe—some I had never seen before.

Col. Paul W. Tibbets: The giant purple mushroom had already risen to a height of 45,000 feet, three miles above our own altitude, and was still boiling upward like something terribly alive. It was a frightening sight, and even though we were several miles away, it gave the appearance of something that was about to engulf us.

Maj. Charles W. Sweeney: As it gained altitude, a huge white mushroom shape formed at the top.

Col. Paul W. Tibbets: Even more fearsome was the sight on the ground below. At the base of the cloud, fires were springing up everywhere amid a turbulent mass of smoke that had the appearance of bubbling hot tar.

Capt. Robert A. Lewis: My God, what have we done?

Capt. Theodore "Dutch" Van Kirk: All we could see at the city of Hiroshima was black smoke, dust, looked like a pot of boiling oil covering a city. We flew around in the southeast quadrant of the city to see what we could observe. Couldn't see anything because of the smoke dust. So we turned around and went home.

Capt. Robert A. Lewis: Even when the plane was going in the opposite direction, the flames were still terrific. The area of the town looked as though it was torn apart. I have never seen anything like it—never seen anything like it. When we turned our ship so we could observe results, there in front of our eyes was without a doubt the greatest explosion man had ever seen. We were struck dumb at the sight. It far exceeded all our expectations.

Col. Paul W. Tibbets: If Dante had been with us in the plane, he would have been terrified! A feeling of shock and horror swept over all of us.

Capt. William S. "Deak" Parsons, ***ordnance director, Manhattan Project*****:** It was a terrific spectacle. The huge dust cloud covered everything. The base of the lower part of the mushroom, a mass of purplish-grey dust about three miles in diameter, was all boiling—the entire area was boiling. The purple clouds and flames were whirling around. It seemed as though the whole town got pulverized. If the Japs say a meteor has hit them, we can tell them we have more where this one came from.

Luis Alvarez: After we secured our equipment, we left our cramped quarters and looked out the window for the first time over Japan. By then Sweeney was heading back toward Hiroshima, and the top of the mushroom cloud had reached our altitude. I looked in vain for the city that had been our target. The cloud seemed to be rising out of a wooded area devoid of population. I thought the bombardier had missed the city by miles—had dumped Ernest's precious bomb out in the empty countryside—and I wondered how we would ever explain such a failure to him. Sweeney shortly dispelled my doubts. The aiming had been excellent.

2nd Lt. Russell E. Gackenbach, ***navigator, Crew B-10,*** **Necessary Evil,** ***393rd Bombardment Squadron*****:** There was almost complete silence on the flight deck. It was evident the city of Hiroshima was destroyed.

Capt. William S. "Deak" Parsons, ***coded message to Tinian base*****:** Clear cut results in all respects successful. Exceeded TR test in visible results. Normal conditions obtained in aircraft after delivery was accomplished. Visual attack on Hiroshima at 05231 5Z with only one tenth cloud cover. Flack and fighters absent.

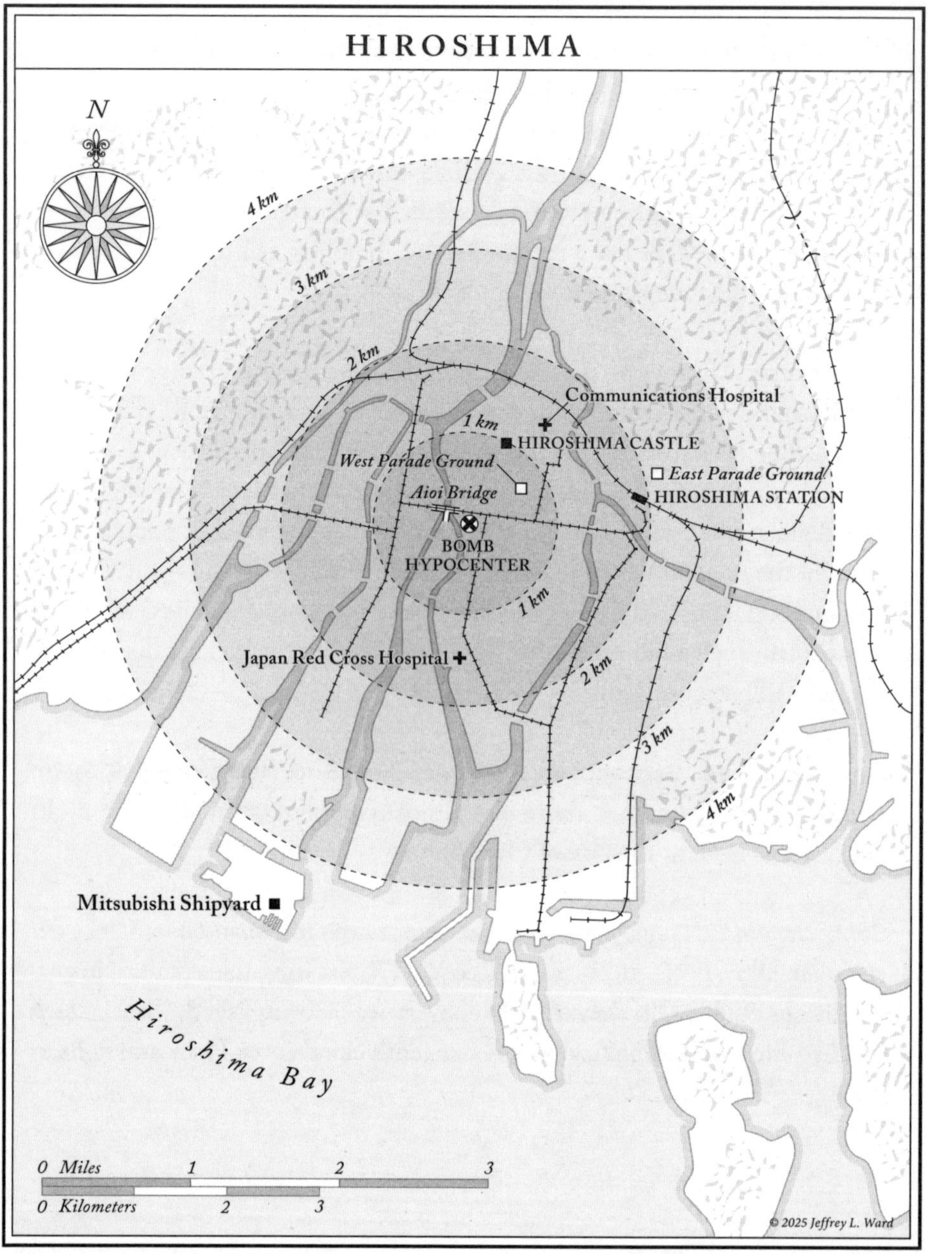
HIROSHIMA
N
4 km
3 km
2 km
1 km
Communications Hospital
HIROSHIMA CASTLE
West Parade Ground
East Parade Ground
Aioi Bridge
HIROSHIMA STATION
BOMB
HYPOCENTER
1 km
Japan Red Cross Hospital
2 km
3 km
4 km
Mitsubishi Shipyard
Hiroshima Bay
0 Miles 1 2 3
0 Kilometers 2 3
© 2025 Jeffrey L. Ward

"Pitch dark as a moonless night"

GROUND ZERO IN HIROSHIMA

The flash of the atomic bomb burned shadows into steel.

Hiroshima, the southern Japanese city and capital of Hiroshima Prefecture, had been founded on the Ōta River delta in the 1500s and in the 1800s grew into a major industrial center. The city, perched on the edge of Japan's critical Inland Sea, was shaped like a plump six-fingered hand, with the river tributaries emptying into Hiroshima Bay, and hundreds of bridges connected the city's five main islets, which rarely were more than a few hundred meters wide and a few kilometers long. Its name meant "City of Wide Islands."

Its castle, which dominated the city's landscape and psyche, had been built in the late sixteenth century, when a samurai warlord named Mōri Terumoto first settled there and began to rule over the surrounding area. With time, Hiroshima grew into a major military hub, especially during the First Sino-Japanese War in the 1890s when the emperor and the military located their main headquarters in the city. Mitsubishi factories and defense works grew up along the harbor. Through the 1930s and '40s, millions of Japanese personnel had departed for the battlefields of Asia and the Pacific, passing through the city's "Hall of Triumphal Return," and as the summer of 1945 unfolded, Field Marshal Hata Shunroku, commander of the Second General Army, was hard at work planning to defend the island of Kyushu from the looming US invasion.

By August 1945, local leaders anticipated that the city of about 350,000 residents—still mostly untouched by US bombing—would become a target imminently and had pressed thousands, including upward of 7,000 enthusiastic schoolchildren, primarily pulled from the seventh and eighth grade, into tearing down long stretches of the city's mostly wooden buildings to form large firebreaks that they hoped would save it from the fate of the vast burning experienced by cities like Tokyo.

Even though the city had mostly escaped bombing damage, its air raid sirens sounded whenever US bombers were nearby, and that night of August 5 into the morning of the sixth, the city's sleep had been interrupted twice by US air raids on neighboring regions. Ironically, when the Enola Gay *arrived overhead, the city's air defense team failed to send an alert amid some confusion in the command center.*

Many residents noticed the sound of Colonel Tibbets powering the Enola Gay *through its steep post-drop turn, and the bomb armed itself at around 6,000 feet before detonating at about 1,800 feet. The explosion of "Little Boy" unfolded in about a tenth of a second; in fact, by the time the residents of Hiroshima first perceived the explosion, all the interesting atomic science that had so consumed the scientists and physicists at the Manhattan Project was over. Effectively, all humans registered was the bomb's aftershocks, which hit the ground at about twice the speed of sound. The* Enola Gay *crew had aimed the bomb at the city's T-shaped Aioi Bridge, and it missed that target by the length of three football fields, falling about 240 meters away. Its "hypocenter"—point of explosion—was directly above the Shima Surgical Clinic, a spot now located at 1-5-25 Ote-machi, Naka-Ku in modern-day Hiroshima. The exact size of the explosion remains uncertain; only about one kilogram of the bomb's 64 kilograms of Uranium-235 turned supercritical as intended, and it was believed at the time to have detonated with the force of about 18,000 to 20,000 tons of TNT, but subsequent analysis holds it might have been closer to 13,000 to 15,000 tons. Regardless, the devastation was enormous, as a fireball and pressure wave of about 11 tons per square meter exploded outward. Contrary to popular belief, no one truly died instantly. As historian M.G. Sheftall writes, "The bombs' six-hundred-meter detonation heights—calculated for maximum blast effects over the targets—guaranteed that every one of their victims suffered at least a second or so of (literally) searing agony." Even up to two kilometers away, the fireball and heat were sufficient to deliver third- and fourth-degree burns. The outer layers of granite heated to the point of boiling and turned to sand.*

Tetsuo Miyata, ***assistant teacher, Kakogawa Village, Hiroshima Prefecture*****:** As the result of the incendiary raids that had occurred time after time since March, the cities of Japan had been reduced to ashes one by one.

Kimura Yasuko, ***schoolchild*****:** Hiroshima was a military capital, full of army and navy facilities. Children in that town were all like minisoldiers. Everything was done to orders.

Tetsuo Miyata: How many times did we resign ourselves to the thought, "This will be the night for Hiroshima to catch it"? At that time Hiroshima was the seventh city of Japan and in spite of the tense atmosphere it was full of a bustling activity. While other smaller cities were being demolished one after another, why was only Hiroshima being left out? It gave rise to a wildly selfish rumor that Hiroshima, by some special grace of God, would suffer absolutely no war damage.

Shigeru Tasaka, ***third grader*****:** The people of Hiroshima were perplexed to understand why Hiroshima was left almost without a scratch. And there were even some people who were thinking that perhaps this was because Hiroshima was being saved as some kind of testing ground. Unhappily, this expectation was confirmed. It was indeed so. The fateful day of August 6th was waiting for Hiroshima. I was only eight at the time but even now I remember clearly what happened.

Shintaro Fukuhara, ***fourth grader*****:** One thing I can never forget is the morning of the 6th of August, 1945.

Johannes Siemes, ***German Jesuit priest*****:** August 6th began in a bright, clear summer morning. I am sitting in my room at the Novitiate of the Society of

Jesus, approximately two kilometers from Hiroshima, halfway up the sides of a broad valley that stretches from the town at sea level into the mountains.

Tohru Hara, *sixth grader*: The sky of Hiroshima on that day was clear, it was splendid weather for A-Bomb No. 1, and it seems as if even by begging they couldn't have got better conditions.

Yohko Kuwabara, *sixth grader*: That was a fine, swelteringly hot morning. The midsummer sun seemed to be blazing down from the whole sky, so that one's eyes felt pricked with its brilliance.

Yokihisa Tokumitsu, *sixth grader*: The day was beautifully clear and hot.

Yuriko Yamamura, *third grader*: The height of the summer heat.

Yasuo Fujita, *age 5*: Rather sticky days had followed one another for a long time.

Setsuko Sakamoto, *junior college student*: On the 6th of August of 1945, we were ordered to help clear up after the demolition squads working on the Clearance Project. The ground almost blistered our feet from day after day of burning hot weather, but we cheerfully began the work of carrying away the roof tiles, chanting bravely in unison as we passed them along from one to another.

Hideko Tamura Snider, *student, age 10*: I was very relaxed when the air raid warning siren went off around 7:15 a.m. or thereabouts. It was a familiar sound by then, but I turned on a radio to find out what it could be all about anyway. A casual warning was being issued, stating three enemy planes were en route towards our city. "Only three?" I shrugged. It was hardly worth being warned about. *Hundreds maybe, but three?* A simple announcement came on a little later around 7:30 a.m., that the planes had turned around. The warning signal was cancelled.

Yuriko Yamamura: The all-clear had sounded. Everyone was relieved and had come out of the shelter.

Takuo Matsumoto, *President, Hiroshima Jogakuin*: At the time of the atomic bombing of Hiroshima I was serving as chancellor of Hiroshima Jogakuin. This school included a junior and senior high school as well as a college. That day, August the 6th, 1945, the senior high and college girls, about 500 of them, marched off early in the morning to work in a large factory outside of the city limits. The freshman students of the college were at school for orientation courses of study and were having their worship service that morning. The little girls of the junior high, more than 300 of them, were gathered together on the school grounds, ready to go out for the day's work. During the war years all the young people were required to do some sort of service for the country. I went out to greet them and talked to them about the work they had been asked by the government to do, gave them words of encouragement followed by a tearful short prayer, and sent them off.

Futaba Kitayama, *housewife*: The day was burning hot already in the morning. It was my turn that day in my Neighborhood Association to donate labor for the work of making air-raid defense fire lanes. Our group assembled at 7:30. Almost all of them were women, including some ladies who were more than sixty years old. After crossing the Tsurumi Bridge, I suddenly heard very clearly the engine of a plane. Its silver wings were shining brilliantly in the dazzling sunshine. The plane looked very small—small enough to be held in my hands. Then someone shouted, "Oh, that's a parachute! A parachute is coming down!" I responded by turning in the direction she pointed.

Yamaoka Michiko, *schoolchild, age 15*: I heard the faint sound of planes as I approached the river. I put my right hand above my eyes and looked up to see if I could spot them.

Setsuko Sakamoto: The rolling drone of a B-29 engine came echoing from a distant part of the sky. Shortly after the voice of our teacher, saying, "Oh, there's a B! There's a B!" made us look up at the sky.

Tohru Hara: And then it was eight-fifteen.

Yamaoka Michiko: That was the moment.

Shigehiro Naito, ***age 6*****:** I and Mother and my little sister Naoko were eating breakfast together.

Tokiko Wada, ***age 5*****:** I was just about to eat breakfast.

Kiyoko Tsuga, ***age 3*****:** At that time I was eating breakfast.

Sanae Kanae, ***age 4*****:** We were just about to put our chopsticks into our mouths—

Iwao Nakamura, ***fifth grader*****:** It was just as I was putting my chopsticks to my second bowl of rice.

Eiko Matsunaga, ***fifth grader*****:** I was eating breakfast, facing my mother. I was holding my rice-bowl in my left hand and my chopsticks in my right, and was just about to put some rice in my mouth when at that second it became suddenly bright before my eyes and an indescribable orange light came thrusting in. Automatically I put the rice into my mouth, laid down my rice-bowl and chopsticks, and ran four or five steps. I don't know what happened after that.

Kiyoharu Koike, ***age 4*****:** Just as I was eating some little clams there was a flash and in that instant the house broke apart; the glass broke, the kitchen cabinet fell over and everything was in a mess.

Yukiharu Suzuki, ***age 5*****:** I was eating some canned tangerines when there was a great flash and a bang and my Uncle Saito went flying outside.

Hisato Itoh, ***fifth grader*****:** Suddenly from outside the front entrance an indescribable color and light—an eerie greenish-white flash—came thrusting in.

Setsuko Yamamoto, ***first grader*****:** From no particular place there was a bright flash.

Chizue Sakai, ***third grader*****:** Our eyes were struck by a flash like a dazzling bolt of lightning.

Shigeko Hirata, ***age 5*****:** Suddenly there was a burst of yellow smoke and an indescribably loud noise.

Yoshiaki Wada, ***age 6*****:** Instantly a stupendous noise.

Shin Bok Su, ***civil defense volunteer*****:** "PIKA!"—a brilliant light—and then "DON!"—a gigantic noise.

Yamaoka Michiko: I felt colors. It wasn't heat. You can't really say it was yellow, and it wasn't blue. I simply fainted. I remember my body floating in the air. That was probably the blast, but I don't know how far I was blown.

Futaba Kitayama: I do not know how to describe that light. I wondered if a fire had been set in my eyes. It was something like an ominous purple-like color of sparks caused by a streetcar at night—only some billion times stronger. I don't remember which came first—the flash of light or the sound of an explosion that roared down to my belly. Anyhow, the next moment I was knocked down flat on the ground.

Kenshi Hirata, ***accountant, Mitsubishi Shipbuilding Corp.*****:** As I was about to enter the office, I saw through an open window what looked like a golden lightning flash that had blown up out of the earth. The weird light was everywhere. I immediately thought of an air-raid, and hurled myself prostrate in the passage.

Junko Fujimoto: I was a student worker just transferred from Toyo Kogyo where they manufactured guns, to the Second General Army Headquarters Secret Code Team. After breakfast I picked Soseki Natsume's work, "Kusamakura," out of my bookshelf and went out to the verandah. Just at that moment, the garden turned bright with abnormal white and I was covered with broken wall, ceiling panels and pieces of broken glass, and I was screaming "Mother," clinging to a pole. Even now, I still remember the noise of the wall falling.

Hideko Tamura Snider: Without any warning, an immensely blinding flash crossed my eyes, riveting my attention. Instantly, I saw a huge band of white light plummeting past the trees and the stone lanterns to the ground, with a swift swishing sound like a massive gushing waterfall. There was nothing in my memory that corresponded with the terrifying image.

Almost simultaneously, a thunderous, deafening explosion jolted the air with an immediate violent quake, shaking the very foundation of the earth and everything that stood on it. The end of the world must have come, I thought to myself as I instinctively jumped to my feet with the memory of Mama's voice echoing in my head, "Find something strong to hold onto."

Iwao Nakamura: It felt as though a magnesium flare of green-ish-white light had hit my face and then there was an ear-splitting roar and simultaneously everything became so dark that I couldn't see an inch ahead.

Tsutomu Yamaguchi, ***shipyard engineer, Mitsubishi Shipbuilding Corp.*****:** As I prostrated myself, there came a terrific explosion.

Matsushige Yoshito, ***photographer,*** **Chugoku Shimbun** ***newspaper*****:** I heard a tremendous cracking noise, like trees being torn apart, and at the same instant there was a brilliant flash of immaculate white, like the igniting of the magnesium we used to use for taking photographs. I couldn't see a thing. I sensed an explosive wind like needles striking me.

Yasu Tsuchida, ***elementary school teacher*****:** It was like being hit from behind by a large pole. The pressure was so intense that I felt I was throwing up my internal organs, such as my stomach, intestines and liver. I lost consciousness for a while though I did not know how long.

Johannes Siemes: The windows are broken in with a loud crash. I am sprayed by fragments of glass. The entire window frame has been forced into the room. I am bleeding from cuts about the hands and head.

Susumu Kimura, ***fifth grader*****:** Everything instantly became pitch dark.

Iwao Nakamura: Pitch dark as a moonless night.

Hideko Tamura Snider: It was dark all around me, as if the sun itself had disappeared, and the exploding earth raged in the thick black air and swirling wind.

I could no longer see, but just felt the motion and the terror. So this is dying in the war. I didn't know how it would happen or what would happen next, but I expected to be broken in pieces and blown up in bits along with my house.

Shin Bok Su: I couldn't see anything. It was pitch black. I heard Grandma's voice shouting. "Help, help!" "Where are you?" I called. "I'm in the living room. I'm suffocating!"

Tsutomu Yamaguchi: I looked toward the city and saw a huge, mushroom-shaped cloud rising high into the sky. It was an immense, evil-looking pillar. It seemed to be reflecting every shade in the spectrum, turning first one color and then another.

Yōko Ōta, *writer*: I just could not understand why our surroundings had changed so greatly in an instant. I thought it might have been something which had nothing to do with the war, the collapse of the earth which it was said would take place at the end of the world, and which I had read about as a child.

* * *

In the minutes after the bomb's detonation, the occupants of Hiroshima tried to make sense of what had happened to them. Nearly everything within a kilometer of the bomb's hypocenter had been instantly vaporized, with temperatures reaching approximately 3,000 to 4,000°C and the blast's wind speed is estimated to have neared 1,000 miles per hour across the inner city. Only a small handful of people are known to have survived within a radius of a thousand meters. Across the city, as much as 60 percent of all of Hiroshima's buildings were destroyed and about four square miles of the city were aflame. (A later official count held that the devastation was even worse for the residential areas: 70,147 of the city's 76,327 homes were destroyed.) Black rain fell as water vaporized in the explosion across the city, rose in the mushroom cloud in the stratosphere, cooled, and collected soot and debris from the boiling cloud as it dropped back to earth. For hours—and days—afterward, fires raged in the city, all but unstoppable. Just three of the city's firefighters survived the blast. Early casualty figures estimated about 66,000 died in the initial blast and about 140,000 died by the end of the year, meaning roughly half the city's residents perished from the bomb. The precise toll remains unknown.

Tazu Shibama, ***schoolteacher, Hiroshima Jogakuin*****:** I sat in the darkness for about ten minutes, and then I heard somebody moving near me. It was my neighbor. He had been standing in his garden, about 50 yards away. Instantly the blast threw him down and buried him in the same place where I was, under my broken house. He was strong enough to make his way out, and he pulled me out. I was saved before the fire came. Many, many people were not killed instantly, but buried under their houses and burned to death—burned alive. My neighbor went back to his house. All the houses were burning. He tried to save his wife and two daughters, but he was unable to save any of them. He stayed there for about a week. We did not know anything about the poison that spread in the air. My neighbor drank the poisoned water and breathed the poisoned air. He died after two weeks. So all his family was lost.

Dr. Michihiko Hachiya: Moving instinctively, I tried to escape, but rubble and fallen timbers barred the way. By picking my way cautiously I managed to reach the porch and stepped down into my garden. A profound weakness overcame me, so I stopped to regain my strength. In my surprise I discovered that I was completely naked. How odd! Where were my drawers and undershirt? What had happened? All over the right side of my body I was cut and bleeding. A large splinter was protruding from a mangled wound in my thigh, and something warm trickled into my mouth. My cheek was torn, I discovered as I felt it gingerly, with the lower lip laid wide open. Embedded in my neck was a sizable fragment of glass which I matter-of-factly dislodged, and with the detachment of one stunned and shocked I studied it and my blood-stained hand. *Where was my wife?* I began to yell for her: "Yaeko-san! Yaeko-san! Where are you?" Yaeko-san, pale and frightened, her clothes torn and blood-stained, emerged from the ruins of our house holding her elbow. Seeing her, I was reassured. My own panic assuaged, I tried to reassure her. "We'll be all right," I exclaimed. "Only let's get out of here as fast as we can."

Hiromu Morishita, ***ninth grader*****:** It was just like being thrown into an iron melting pot. My face was burned and I jumped into the river. One of my friends found me and asked me how his face looked. The skin was hanging down from his face like a rag. I was too scared to ask him about my own face.

1

The explosion at Trinity.

2

"Little Boy."

3

"Fat Man," being loaded in Tinian.

4

Luis Alvarez and an MP hold the "Fat Man" core.

5

The *Bockscar* crew.

6

7

Hiroshima, before and after.

8

Hiroshima, near ground zero.

9

Survivors walk amid the rubble of Hiroshima.

10

Nagasaki in October 1945.

11

Nagasaki seen from the air.

12

An injured Japanese mother and son receive relief food at Nagasaki, August 10, 1945.

13

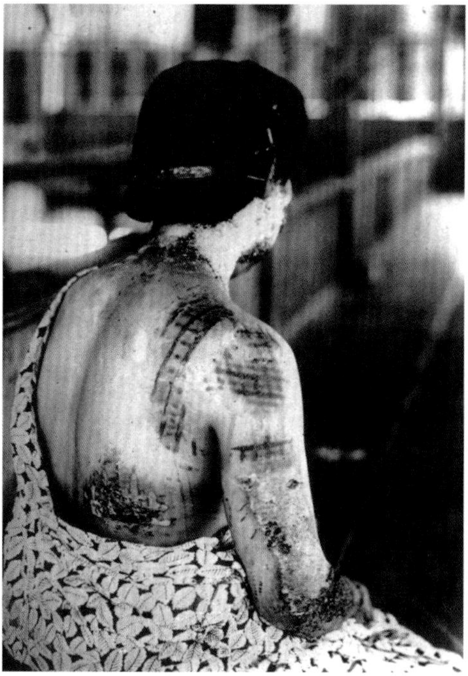

A woman's kimono pattern was burned into her back by the flash.

14

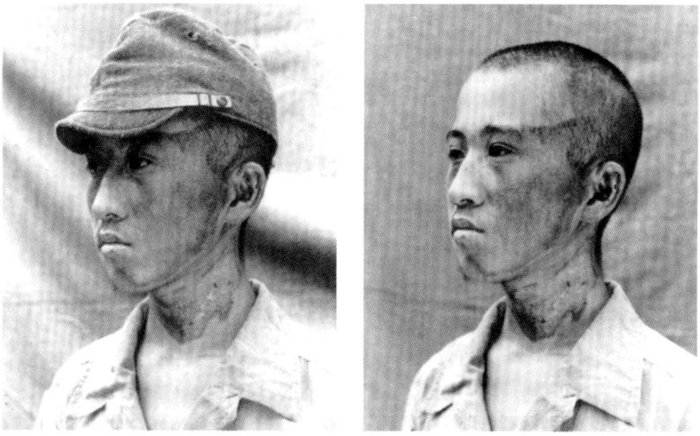

A soldier shows flash and burn marks on his face.

15

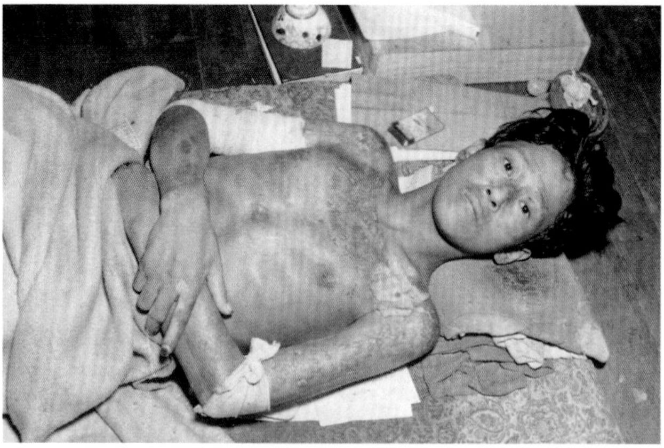

A Nagasaki victim awaits treatment.

16

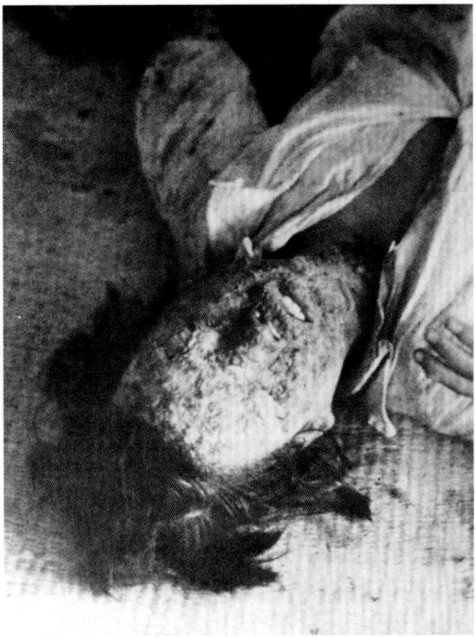

The body of a mobilized schoolgirl at Hiroshima hospital.

17

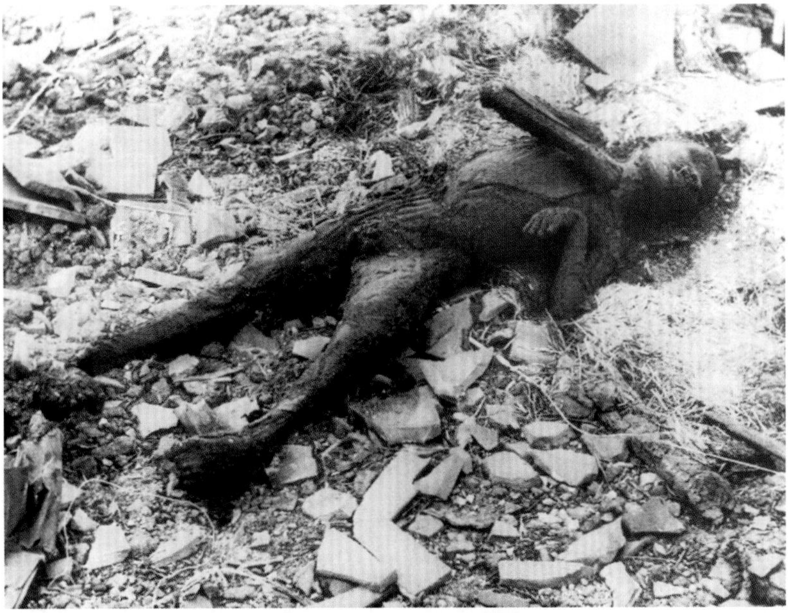

This photo by Yōsuke Yamahata, of a charred corpse in Nagasaki, was tentatively identified by forensic experts in 2016 as thirteen-year-old Shoji Tanisaki.

18

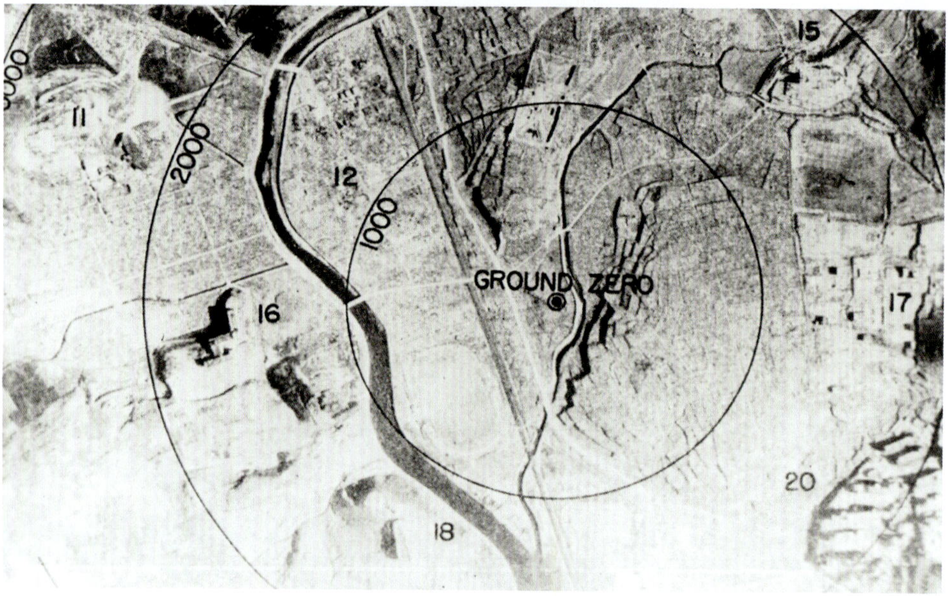

Nagasaki, before and after.

19

The *Enola Gay*, now on display at the Smithsonian.

Hideko Tamura Snider: Along the river, we saw a young school girl slowly walking, with pieces of skin hanging from her arms. Someone said that she was trying to cool her burned skin, but as she rubbed the water on, her skin came off. She was crying out in pain. A Catholic sister who ran a nursery school in the same area told me that some of the small children had been so burned that it was difficult to tell which side of their faces were which. She said that the way she could tell, finally, was to look down to their shoes and see which direction the shoes were pointing in. The little children were crying and wandering around. We could not stop. We moved on like a herd with a will of its own.

Yamaoka Michiko: Nobody there looked like human beings.

Dr. Michihiko Hachiya: We stood in the street, uncertain and afraid, until a house across from us began to sway and then with a rending motion fell almost at our feet. Our own house began to sway, and in a minute it, too, collapsed in a cloud of dust. Other buildings caved in or toppled. Fires sprang up and whipped by a vicious wind began to spread. It finally dawned on us that we could not stay there in the street, so we turned our steps towards the hospital. I was still naked, and although I did not feel the least bit of shame, I was disturbed to realize that modesty had deserted me.

Yasu Tsuchida: When I was in first grade, the Great Kanto Earthquake of 1923 hit the Tokyo region when I was there. During the earthquake, which measured 7.8, the ground had shaken vertically and violently. Wooden houses collapsed easily by such a large earthquake. However, in an earthquake some people like me could save oneself because there was a little time to escape before the house collapsed. When the A-bomb had exploded, the houses collapsed in a different manner. The houses were crushed with immense pressure from above. It was tremendous pressure as if a dinosaur had flattened a city with his feet.

Hideko Tamura Snider: The houses were caved in, crooked, and barely standing. Small flames were starting to spread like torches, and the wind fanned them swiftly into larger fire balls, terrorizing the fleeing people. I thought I heard cries of people asking for help—perhaps help pulling someone out of a crumbled house, someone who was still trapped. But there was no more time nor power in my body.

Takuo Matsumoto: How utterly amazed I was to see the entire city reduced to flat piles of demolished houses and broken branches of trees everywhere! Fires were already spreading in many parts of the city, and mobs of half-naked, burned, bleeding, groaning people were wandering aimlessly, being utterly lost as to what to do or where to go. Fire soon overtook our shattered high school building and reduced it to a pile of ashes, only fifteen minutes after I had crawled out of it. Fire overtook the college building too, and over a hundred of the girls who could not be pulled out were burnt to death.

Hirokuni Dazai, *chief of police*: The city was afire and the mountains were in flames. Everything was scorched to the ground. Every living thing was blackened and dead—or waiting to die.

Kazuo Chujo, *high school student and military truck driver, age 19*: Those who were outdoors within one kilometer of the hypocenter died instantly. The heat all but incinerated their internal organs, and on top of that there was the effect of the bomb blast. Some people within the two-kilometer area managed to get to river banks, parks, air raid shelters and schoolyards which had been turned into temporary rescue stations, but almost all of those who had not been under some sort of cover died within a few days.

Matsushige Yoshito: I approached the City Hall, about one kilometer from the hypocenter. Both it and the Western Fire Station were in flames. It was a sea of fire. I couldn't make my way to the newspaper office, so I returned to the western side of the Miyuki Bridge and tried to head towards the city center by passing along the bank of the river. But fireballs were rolling down the road. There was nobody to be seen. If I hang around here, I thought, I'll be swallowed up in these fires, so I returned to the bridge. You had to weave through the streets avoiding the bodies. People's bodies were all swollen up. Their skin, burst open, was hanging down in rags. Their faces were burnt black. I put my hand on my camera, but it was such a hellish apparition that I couldn't press the shutter. I hesitated about twenty minutes before I finally pushed it and took the first picture.

Kenshi Hirata: There was not a house standing as far as I could see. Everything had burned down, or collapsed in the blast. Although I knew the city well, it was actually difficult to find my way, for all the familiar landmarks were gone, and the streets I had often walked were now buried in debris and ashes. It was not like walking in streets at all; it was more like crossing a big burnt field.

Akira Iwanaga, *shipyard engineer, Mitsubishi Shipbuilding Corp.*: The whole city was flat. I could see only burning sewing machines, safes, burned bicycles, a few concrete structures, and corpses everywhere. Also dead horses. As I passed along the bank of the river, I saw a woman carrying the dead body of a child on her back. She was screaming loudly, evidently gone insane from shock.

Dr. Michihiko Hachiya: Others moved as though in pain, like scarecrows, their arms held out from their bodies with forearms and hands dangling. These people puzzled me until I suddenly realized that they had been burned and were holding their arms out to prevent the painful friction of raw surfaces rubbing together.

Johannes Siemes: A procession of people begins to stream up the valley. The crowd thickens continuously. Many are bleeding or have suffered burns. We give them first aid and bring them into the chapel. A few display horrible wounds. The least injured drag the more seriously wounded.

Setsuko Sakamoto: Making their way together are three high school girls who looked as though they were from our school; their faces and everything were completely burned and they held their arms out in front of their chests like kangaroos, with only their hands pointed downward; from their whole bodies something like thin paper is dangling—it is their peeled-off skin which hangs there, and trailing behind them the unburned remnants of their puttees, they stagger exactly like sleepwalkers, and yet they are encouraging and helping each other as they walked along searching for water.

Hideko Tamura Snider: With heart racing, I headed towards the Ota River, limping and dragging my right foot. Soon, more injured people were moving together in a silent march in the general direction of the outer limits of the city. Their bloodstained clothes were torn or singed black. Some were even bare. I did not know where all of these people were coming from. I tried to look for people I recognized so I could flee with them. There were no familiar faces. In the moving sea of horribly hurt people, no one seemed to notice a frightened, lost child. The once familiar call of Ojo-san, greeting me, never came. I was truly alone.

Futaba Kitayama: What happened to the sky that had been such a clear blue one only a moment ago? It was now dark, like dusk. Everything was vague and hazy, as if mist covered up my eyes—I wondered if I had lost my senses. I looked around trying to figure out what happened. I saw on the bridge something like a human figure, running. "Oh, yes! That must be the Tsurumi Bridge. I must hurry to cross it; if not, there will be no way to escape." I ran like mad toward the bridge, jumping over the piles of debris.

Tsuitaro Doi: In the fires there had been no place but the rivers for refuge. Heat and thirst drove all toward the water, and many jumped in just to escape the fearful heat.

Futaba Kitayama: Hundreds of people were squirming in the stream. I couldn't tell if they were men or women. They looked all alike. Their faces were swollen and gray, their hair was standing up. Holding their hands high, groaning, people were rushing to the river. I felt the same urge because the pain was all over the body which had been exposed to a heat ray strong enough to burn my pants to pieces. I was about to jump into the river only to remember that I could not swim. I went back up to the bridge. There, school girls, like sleepwalkers, were wandering about in confusion. I encouraged them to cross the bridge, "Hurry up, hurry up!" Upon crossing it, I looked back and found that the Takeyacho-Hatchöbori area suddenly had burst into flame. I had thought that the bomb hit only the area where I was.

Yasu Tsuchida: Hiroshima was a city that had developed in the delta region of the Ota river which had seven tributary rivers. Everywhere you go, you will come across a river. In peace time, there were boats of oyster-restaurant in the rivers and it was called the city of water, keeping a very charming air. However, at this time, the rivers became a great obstacle. When people came to the edge of a river, they would have to stop. Bridges had been burnt down by the fire and could not be crossed. And unfortunately, the river was high tide and swollen with water. Whether one was injured or not, he had to cross the river and get to safety on the other side.

When I came to the edge of a river near the famous garden which was called the Shukkeien, the garden of Duke of Asano, I could neither move forward nor retreat there. The only one choice I had, though, was to go in the river. I think I had been a good swimmer, but because of my injuries, I was not confident that I could swim across. Still, I had to take my chance. I pulled out one of the poles in the river bank, put it instead of a buoy under my left arm, and decided to cross the river. I saw many bodies flowing down from upstream, including animals such as horses, cows, cats, and dogs.

Sanae Kanae: When we came to the river there was a man who was really suffering; he was black all over and he kept saying, "Give me water, give me water." I felt so sorry for him I could hardly bear it.

Jiro Shimasaki: While crossing the bridge, many people yanked at my legs, demanding water and saying, "Give me water, give me water."

Yasu Tsuchida: When I reached the other side, it was full of people who were there before me, including a group of young female volunteer corps. "Please give me water!" "Could you bring me water!" they were asking the other people. Most of them were injured badly and in death agony.* Later I was told that their thirst was not only due to the heat or loss of blood, but also because of the destruction of their tonsils by radiation. I think now, their asking was a plea more painful than death. If I had been in good condition, I could have brought them some water from the river. But to my most reluctance, I had no strength to move because I had used up all my energy to cross the river.

Masayuki Hashimoto: People whose whole bodies were covered with burns were screaming, "Give me water, give me water!"

* There was a mistaken belief in Japanese military medicine at the time, drilled into the civilian population as well through civil defense drills, that giving water to already badly injured people might prove fatal, an impression that left many of the dazed atomic bomb survivors facing an agonizing choice to provide much-needed water to victims.

Tsuitaro Doi: Streams of men, women and children, many of them burned black, some with their skin peeled completely off, begging for water.

Yamaoka Michiko: Voices crying, "Help! Water!"

Matsushige Yoshito: "Please Mister Soldier, give me some water," they'd call out faintly.

Kazuo Chujo: I saw a young girl with grossly swollen lips: "Water—please," were the only words she could force from her throat.

Setsuko Yamamoto: I hadn't eaten anything after breakfast and hadn't had a drop of water to drink. I gave up from thirst and hunger and sat down exhausted beside the road. As I was crying there, a man who was passing put my hands around a bag of hardtack and gave me a drink of water from his canteen. Even now I can't forget the comfort of that moment.

Futaba Kitayama: I found myself squatting on the center of the Parade Ground. It must not have taken me more than two hours to get from Tsurumi-cho to the East Parade Ground, no matter how I wandered around. The darkness of the sky lessened somewhat. Still, the sun, as if covered with a heavy cloud, was dim and gloomy. My burns started paining me. It was a kind of pain different from an ordinary burn which might be unbearable. Mine was a dull pain that was coming from somewhere far apart from my body. A yellow secretion oozed from my hands. I imagined that my face also must be in this dreadful shape. By my side, many junior high school students, both boys and girls who were members of the volunteer corps, were squirming in agony.

Kazuo Chujo: Flames were closing in from all sides. All of a sudden, I realized that I was in serious trouble. The grounds of Hiroshima College was a few hundred meters away, and I knew that once there, I would be safe from the blaze, no matter how fierce. There was nobody around. Not a voice was to be heard. Stuck in that tiny clearing, all alone, I felt like the sole human being stranded in some remote corner of the earth. And it was most painful to watch my home, filled with memories, being consumed by fire. Everything was burning. I don't know how many hours I remained there. Many times, I attempted to get away, but the ground was scorching hot.

Takuo Matsumoto: I ran through the burning streets, to the spot in the heart of the city where our little junior high girls were about to do their required work. They had been fully exposed to the blast and the searing rays. When I reached the spot, hardly any of them were to be found there. Scores of them had been annihilated by the terrific blast. Others, having been blinded by the sudden flash, wandered about, not knowing which way to turn. Many of them had been taken outside the city limits and laid in rows, like logs, in all available large rooms of schools, hospitals and barracks in the neighborhood. 352 of our school girls, and twenty of our faithful teachers were killed outright. Not a single building in the heart of the city remained intact.

Matsushige Yoshito: I saw a burned trolley car at a curve. It looked like people were still on it, so I approached, put my foot on the step and peered inside. Fifteen or sixteen people were there, all dead. Kamiyacho had been only two hundred and fifty meters from the hypocenter. They probably died instantly when the pressure of the blast wind caused their internal organs to rupture. Then they burst into flame and burned, together with the car. All of them were naked. I had my foot on the rear doorstep. I didn't really stare at them, but recoiled in shock. The doors and windows were charred. Only the skeleton of that train remained. I don't remember if it was hot or not. I don't think I grasped the doorframe when I looked in. I thought about taking a picture. I even put my hand on the camera. But it was so hideous I couldn't do it.

Futaba Kitayama: How in the world could such a cruel thing happen? I wondered if the Hell that my grandmother had told me so much about in my childhood had fallen upon the earth.

Shigeko Hirata: To this very day if I close my eyes I remember all those sights that I saw then and I feel as if I were trembling again.

Hiromu Morishita: Climbing up Hijiyama hill, standing at the top, I looked around the city. But there was nothing. All the buildings were in pieces, and fires burned here and there all over the area. I felt numb. A group of soldiers walked by. All of them had been burned and they were holding their arms out in front of them. They looked like marching ghosts. An old lady began chanting a Buddhist prayer when she saw them. I tried to reach my home, but on the way the air was so hot, it seemed like an invisible wall in front of me, and I couldn't go any further. Instead I went up to the top of another hill to sit and wait for the fires to cool down.

Kazuo Chujo: That August day I stared, stupefied, at what had once been my beautiful Hiroshima—a city of lush greenery and clear waters where I had grown up. It took just one atomic bomb to wipe away everything beautiful and precious, to replace it with a scene of total carnage. Chaos is not accurate enough a word to describe it. Survivors like myself say that they saw Hell. I say I witnessed Doomsday, for that will be the picture, I am sure, of the human race on the day it annihilates itself.

Dr. Michihiko Hachiya: The streets were deserted except for the dead. Hiroshima was no longer a city, but a burnt-over prairie.

This photo, by Yoshito Matsushige, taken around 11 a.m., is one of the few taken in Hiroshima the day of the bombing.

"A picture-perfect mission"

LANDING AT TINIAN

The *Enola Gay* returns, triumphant, to Tinian.

The Enola Gay *and other strike aircraft found themselves transformed into celebrities when they arrived back in Tinian, even as the fires burned 1,500 miles away in Hiroshima.*

Capt. Theodore "Dutch" Van Kirk: You could still see that cloud 267 miles away when we were about 15,000 feet. That's how high the white cloud went that day.

Capt. Robert A. Lewis: It kept changing its weird colors until we lost sight of it.

Col. Paul W. Tibbets: It had been an easy mission, one of the most routine I had ever flown.

Maj. Charles W. Sweeney: A picture-perfect mission from beginning to end.

Capt. Robert A. Lewis: I had a strong conviction that it was possible, by the time we landed, that the Japs would have thrown in the sponge. Because of the total destruction, I didn't feel there was room for anything but complete surrender.

Luis Alvarez: I used the time to write a long letter to my four-year-old son, Walt, for him to read when he was older. I was thinking about the consequences of the bombing I had just witnessed: "The days of large bombing raids, with several hundred planes, are finished. A single plane disguised as a friendly transport can now wipe out a city. That means to me that nations will have to get along together in a friendly fashion, or suffer the consequences of sudden sneak attacks which can cripple them overnight. What regrets I have about being a party to killing and maiming thousands of Japanese civilians this morning are tempered with the hope that this terrible weapon we have created may bring the countries of the world together and prevent further wars. Alfred Nobel thought that his invention of high explosives would have that effect, by making wars too terrible, but unfortunately it had just the opposite reaction. Our new destructive force is so many thousands of times worse that it may realize Nobel's dream."

Col. Paul W. Tibbets: It was 2:58 p.m. when we touched down on the long runway from which we had taken off with such apparent effort twelve hours before.

Maj. Charles W. Sweeney: While we made our final approach to North Field, Colonel Tibbets had already landed and was taxiing in. As I touched down on Runway B, I saw a throng of people who had massed on the area near Tibbets's hardstand. The hundreds of cheering men was a sight to behold. As we rolled down the taxiway past Tibbets's airplane, it was clear that a full-scale celebration was under way.

Lennie R. Morrison, *1395th Military Police Company*: I was an MP guarding the planes at the airport. When they returned, Brig. General Davies, Wing Commander, called him to attention. Close behind was General Carl Spaatz, Commander of the USA Army Strategic Air Forces. There was a huge crowd.

It became still. General Spaatz faced Col. Tibbets and said a few words of congratulations. Then he pinned the Distinguished Service Cross on his chest, giving special recognition of the great job he and his men had done.

Col. Paul W. Tibbets: If I had given it any thought, I would have known that our arrival would be the occasion for some sort of ceremony. Although I managed quickly to palm the pipe I was smoking, I was hardly ready for the formality the occasion demanded, but no one seemed to mind. One after another shook my hands or slapped my back, jubilant over the success of our mission and wanting to hear more about the bomb and the destruction it had caused. Silver Stars were later presented to other members of my crew and to the crewmen from the other planes that took part in the mission.

Colonel Tibbets hides his pipe while being presented with a decoration for his historic flight.

Sgt. Paul Metro: As the *Enola Gay* was homeward bound, we on Tinian were celebrating the end of the war. We felt sure that Japan would surrender. There was a double ration of free beer, Coke, and a flatbed truck with a band where guys could jitterbug with each other since there were no women around. There were pie eating and egg tossing contests. Another contest was a three-man race in which the legs of the center man facing backwards were tied to the legs of the outside men.

Cpl. Armen Shamlian: Most of the 509th were celebrating with a "The End of the War" picnic. I photographed General Spaatz pinning the Distinguished Service Cross on Colonel Tibbets' flight suit along with photos of the debriefing at the Officers' Club.

William L. Laurence: There was no time lost in getting the fliers to the Quonset that served as the 509th Officers' Club for interrogation. As the fliers were questioned one by one, the story sounded more and more fantastic and awesome, more terrifying than any horror tale in fiction.

Col. Paul W. Tibbets: It was soon apparent that the interviewers were skeptical of our descriptions. Surely, they thought, we must be exaggerating the size of the mushroom cloud and the fact that the whole city was almost instantly obliterated from sight by the boiling mass of smoke and fire. We knew how Marco Polo must have felt when he returned from Cathay and found people of his native Venice unwilling to believe his descriptions of the Far East and its riches.

Pfc. Richard H. Nelson: Dearest Mom, Dad and Loraine, Well I've had four missions now. The last one was yesterday. It was a good one, just like all the rest of them are. I hope we get the rest of them in fast. I'm already in the mood to come home. You can see on the envelope they finally made me a Pfc. Two years in the Army and I finally got a promotion. As a Pvt, I was making about $40 a month and now I'll get about $7.20 more and maybe next month, I'll get Corporal stripes. I have so much to tell you but none of it will go through, so I might as well save it until I get home. Part of it you might find out in the newspaper and radio before I'm home but I still have a lot to talk about. I hope all of you are well and happy. I miss you all. Love, Rich

"Living or dying made no difference"

HIROSHIMA BURNING

Fires devastated downtown Hiroshima after the blast.

The later hours of August 6 in Hiroshima found the city devastated beyond recognition. Fires continued everywhere. Refugees and victims began the long quest to find missing family members, searching what used to be familiar neighborhoods now turned into scenes from Dante, and struggled to escape the burning carnage, usually on foot. Organized rescue missions were small and few, and hospitals were overwhelmed. Rivers were clogged with bodies, most burned beyond recognition—only with time would rescue crews realize that due to differences in body buoyancy, women floated faceup while male corpses floated facedown.

Throughout the wreckage, individual survivors—people like Kenshi Hirata, a twenty-six-year-old accountant for Mitsubishi Shipbuilding Corp., who had been married in July to a twenty-two-year-old woman from Nagasaki, Setsuko, and who had only been in their company-owned Hiroshima house for ten days as of August 6—tried to figure out what to do and how to reunite with the ones they loved.

Kenshi Hirata, ***accountant, Mitsubishi Shipbuilding Corp.*****:** First I decided to search for my wife along the river. I went to the river and looked over the stonewall that goes down to the water. Then I started for the hospital. When I reached the hospital I came upon a surprising and shocking scene. Numbers of people, burned red and black, were lying on the ground. Dead bodies were floating in the big pond in the center of the garden, which used to belong to Prince Asano. They must have jumped into the pond because of the unbearable heat. Some were dead with their hands clutching at the brink of the pond. Some were half sunken in the water. I could see that there were many more bodies sunk at the bottom of the pond. I walked from one corner of the garden to the other, looking at every woman who seemed to be about the age of my wife. I searched in the pond and in the trees, but I was unable to find her. As I made my way through the ranks of horribly burned people with their skin hanging in shreds, men, women and children crawled toward me with their hands stretched out, asking for water, water. I am haunted by their dying countenances as I had to push away their hands and continue the search for my wife.

After I got back to the neighborhood of my house, I found many people lying at the foot of the stonewall along the river where only the three had been before. I peered into what looked like the faces of young women, one after another, but they were so badly burned I could not discern their features. Finally, in desperation, I shouted loudly, "Setsuko, Set-suko!" An answer came from among the people along the wall, "Here is Setsuko-san!" I leaped for joy at hearing an answer and rushed to the group at the wall. Then my heart sank, for it was another woman with the same name as my wife's. For a while I paused to watch the sad sight of fathers and brothers carrying along the dead bodies of their daughters and sisters on stretchers. These were all high school girls who had been mobilized in war industries and brought to Hiroshima from the neighboring counties. When the city was destroyed, the men rushed to Hiroshima from everywhere around that day and found their sisters and daughters tragically burned to death.

Hakuzo Iwamoto, ***chauffeur*****:** A boy of about ten years old, with his face burnt and body all naked and blood-stained, followed me saying, "Help me, mister! Help me!" I could not help him at all. While wandering around he dropped out of my sight. Maybe he died somewhere. The fire spread out increasingly and the whole city seemed to be on fire. Then, all of a sudden, a strong northerly wind blew and turned the flames into a fire cyclone. The cyclone went around burning leaves of trees at the edge of the pond, even pulled out small trees, throwing them into the sky and then back to the pond.

Futaba Kitayama: Steadily, my face became stiffer. I put my hands carefully on my cheeks and felt my face. It seemed to have swollen to twice its size. Now I could see less and less. Alas, I would not be able to see at all soon. After all the effort, was I destined to die? I kept walking and, by following the hill footpath, reached Hesaka village. I saw on the street many victims being carried away by stretcher.

Hakuzo Iwamoto: I came to the place where my house was supposed to be standing. I found my wife lying down on the street almost without breath. She barely managed to tell me—she was hit by the falling house and could not walk; she had crawled into a water hole dug out near our house and stayed in the water until the house was completely burnt up. As far as I could see, it was nothing but a devastating scene of destruction. I felt an utter loneliness. I looked into the water tank and found that a half dozen burned bodies were floating. I pulled myself up and set out carrying my wife, who was almost dead. I headed toward the old Public Auditorium and had to rest three times to walk only 300 meters. She asked me every time for water. I found a broken cup on the street and gave her water with it from the hand fire pump. I finally got to the Auditorium and laid her down on the stone step. While we were resting the city official brought hard biscuits in a bucket. We were given a handful and ate them there.

Kazu Kishimoto, ***mother of Taeko Kishimoto, eighth grader at Hiroshima Jogakuin*****:** I began to worry about my daughter in the late afternoon and left for Zakoba-cho about 3:00 p.m. to find her. Black smoke covered the sky over the station, which had burst into flames. I took a round-about way to the foot of Mt. Futaba, and went across Tokiwa Bridge to come out to the street-car road of Hakushima. I prayed for many college students who had been burned to death in front of Kirin Beer Hall in Shintenchi by a big water tank while holding out their hands for help.

As far as the eye could see, Hiroshima City had turned into a burned barren field. I finally reached Zakoba-cho by aiming at the Chugoku Electric

Power Supply Company. There I examined each dead body lying one after another in the narrow street, but I couldn't find my daughter, Taeko. A burned lunch box and a flask left on a slightly elevated spot looked mournful to me. On both sides of the Red Cross Hospital entrance dead bodies were lying one upon another. I guessed that they passed away filled with relief because they had finally reached the hospital. Taeko wasn't there, either.

Sunao Kanazaki, *factory worker*: I came to Asahi Bridge. My hometown was just on the other side. Crowds of people burned beyond recognition were lying in piles at the foot of the bridge. The railing had been blown away. Lots of boards were missing and flames were licking up all over it. In desperation, I jumped and ducked my way to the other side. My house was flattened completely. Calling their names over and over, I searched for my wife and children, tossing aside whatever debris came to hand. But I couldn't find them. The riverbank was covered with people so totally transformed that I couldn't tell who was who. Still I went from one to the next, checking. The survivors wandered throughout the city. We ate anything we could put in our mouths, unaware that it was poisoned by radiation. Most of us came down with high fevers and diarrhea. Some died. Truly, living or dying made no difference. It was all hell.

Toyoko Sugano, *factory worker*: The fire was coming towards me. I crawled into the river. The water was so hot! I lowered my head in the water and then I put my face up. There was a wind blowing with the fire and my hair was all burned. So I had to put my head down into the water again. Something was touching my face. Then I looked up and saw many dead bodies floating. I don't know whether they were men or women or children. Those still alive were moaning and groaning, floating in the river. I thought I was going to die. I was so hot, so I put my head into the water again. When I looked up, it was already evening. When the fire had burned down somewhat, I climbed to the riverbank and fainted again.

Yasu Tsuchida: I had been afflicted by the radiation and had lost a lot of blood. Though it was very hot, owing to the heat of great fire and to high temperature in August, I was shivering to feel coldness, for a fever above forty degrees. I was so cold and tired that I could not stand still. Then, I have laid there shaking, covered myself with the burnt sand on the river bank. After a while, perhaps the fire would bring on rain. The sky suddenly clouded over and it began to pour. It was radio-active rain. Later, I heard this rain described as black rain, but at the time, I could not distinguish whether it was black or clear. I only had known that the rain made my wounded body tingle with pain.

Tazu Shibama: I walked all day long because there were no trains or busses, nothing to ride. I came to a wooden bridge near Hiroshima station. It was burning. I was barefoot and it was so hot. I had to run across the burning bridge. Water was running underneath the bridge, but still the bridge was burning. Hundreds and hundreds of people were exposed to radiation in the streets. They were already burned, their faces with skin hanging, their clothes all gone, walking just like ghosts. Their shock was so great, they lost words, they couldn't speak. Even little children did not cry. They just walked quickly to get out of this terrible place.

The Hiroshima train station and train tracks out of the city became a major destination and thoroughfare for the evacuating victims, and as the day progressed, trains would begin to ferry refugees out to communities better equipped to provide aid. Takejiro Nishioka, the publisher of Nagasaki's main newspaper, had been journeying to Tokyo that morning and his train had been on the outskirts of Hiroshima when the bomb exploded. The train stopped and the passenger cars were decoupled so the locomotive could venture forward and investigate the situation in Hiroshima. Given his position, Nishioka climbed into the locomotive too.

Takejiro Nishioka, *publisher,* Minyu (People) *newspaper*: Pretty soon, the locomotive had to stop because the track was jammed with numberless victims of the blast, leaving the city on foot. The line seemed to be endless, and it was a sight horrible beyond description. Many of the victims had the skin peeled from their faces and arms. From time to time one would fall to the ground, while the others kept slowly walking, many of them murmuring in a low voice, "water, water!" As we came closer to the smoke-shrouded city, the ground all around spouted little flickering jets of fire, as of tiny bits of burning material like sulphur. The little flames could have been extinguished easily by stepping on them, but no one wanted to do that.

At length I managed to make my way through the burning city, and found Field Marshal Hata's headquarters below a red shrine on top of a hill.

The field marshal's house was not damaged outside, as it was sheltered by the hill from the full effect of the concussion. At the entrance, an elderly officer answered in a despairing manner, "I don't know if the field marshal is alive or dead!" This officer added that he thought Hiroshima had been hit by an atomic bomb. I myself had a vague idea that such a weapon might be used; our scientists were well acquainted with atomics. I decided to walk back to the station and try to take a train to Nagasaki, for it was plain that there was nothing I could accomplish under the circumstances in Hiroshima. The walk back, among innumerable dead and dying, the bleeding and skinless people, groaning and calling for water, was the most horrible, pitiable sight I have ever seen even in a drawing of hell!

Keiko Hatta, *age 14*: When I reached Tenma Bridge, it was destroyed. I was obliged to walk on a railway bridge, looking down the river, where many dead bodies were floating. I finally got to Koi Station. Fortunately, a freight train was just about to start, so I got on it. From the window I saw truck after truck of rescue parties coming into the city. It took longer than usual to get to my town, Hatsukaichi. A last the train reached my station. As soon as my family saw me, they couldn't speak and acted as if they were seeing a ghost. They told me that my father had just gone out to find me, carrying a rucksack in which he had put ointment for burns and an instrument for gathering my ashes in case I was dead. After I came home, I suffered from diarrhea for a long time, and for many days I felt languid and weakened. My mother's nourishing meals must have worked, for I got well about three months later.

Tetsuo Miyata: The first refugee train from Hiroshima arrived in the evening of that day. The sight of that lady, wearing a blood-soaked excuse for a bandage, with the torn remnants of her dress draped about her, shuffling uncertainly in her bare feet, but even so holding firmly onto the hand of a screaming child. The man, limping as he walks, himself covered all over his body in every conceivable spot with cuts, carrying on his back a child whose whole face is swollen from burns so that he cannot see. An old woman comes along. Under her arm she carries a little bundle, and with her hand she repeatedly wipes away the sweat, turned brown with blood and dust, that is continually getting into her eyes. She has one foot stuck into a sandal that she must have picked up somewhere, and she is muttering to herself as she walks along, but suddenly she staggers and sits down flat on the ground, and scratching at the earth she looks up at the sky and bursts out crying in a loud voice like a baby's.

On that day several hundred refugees were taken into this school. We spread thin matting on the floor of the classrooms and made them into temporary first-aid stations. The few uninjured ones, with bloodshot eyes and flushed with hysteria, walked back and forth along the halls crying in shrill voices. A high school girl whose burned face was swollen up like a comic mask came in with her mother leading her by the hand. It seems that she had encountered the bomb at school, and then limped a mile and a half back to her home through the flames and smoke. As she lay down on the mat, still holding her mother's hand, she asked in a faint voice, "Where is this?" The poor thing was quite blind.

* * *

Dr. Michihiko Hachiya: Our progress towards the hospital was interminably slow, until finally, my legs, stiff from drying blood, refused to carry me farther. The strength, even the will, to go on deserted me, so I told my wife, who was almost as badly hurt as I, to go on alone. Yaeko-san looked into my face for a moment, and then, without saying a word, turned away and began running towards the hospital. Once, she looked back and waved and in a moment she was swallowed up in the gloom. It was quite dark now, and with my wife gone, a feeling of dreadful loneliness overcame me.

Sunao Kanazaki: The whole city was engulfed in white and black smoke. I couldn't help running. Soon I saw a military truck coming out from town. In that instant, my anxiety turned to terror. The truck was packed full of blackened human beings that looked more like charred lumber. *What about my wife and children?* I fought to banish that thought and kept running.

Takuo Matsumoto: Later in the evening of that fateful day of the explosion, I hurried to the park where I had left my wife and daughter early in the morning. It was extremely difficult for me to recognize them among the hundreds of refugees there. After having searched throughout the park for about an hour, I was on the point of giving up in despair, when suddenly I heard a girlish cry saying "Mother is here. Come and help me!" It came from the river which ran along the park. I looked down, and there I saw my own daughter crying for help. I shouted "Oh, Yuko," and then I jumped down into the river. There I found my dear wife floating in the water. According to what my daughter told me then, the ferocious flames of fire, which toward the evening enveloped the entire city, had created such a fearful noise that it startled the refugees and led them to imagine another attack by enemy planes. In order to escape this imagined attack, they rushed to the river bank and in so doing crowded against my wife and daughter, who were sitting there, earnestly praying together for their unfortunate fellow sufferers and for peace in the world. Thus my wife and daughter were pushed down into the river seven feet below and that was enough to kill my wife whose weak heart had been strained beyond endurance by the successive tragic events of the day.

Dr. Michihiko Hachiya: All who could were moving in the direction of the hospital. I joined in the dismal parade when my strength was somewhat recovered, and at last reached the gates of the Communications Bureau. Familiar surroundings, familiar faces. There was Mr. Iguchi and Mr. Yoshihiro and my old friend, Mr. Sera, the head of the business office. They hastened to give me a hand. My friends passed me through an open window into a janitor's room recently converted to an emergency first-aid station. The room was a shambles: fallen plaster, broken furniture.

Yasu Tsuchida: I walked and rested for a while and then started to walk again. In this way, I could make my escape from the flames. I spent the night in a forest of pine tree in the Training Field. After walking around in hell about two kilometers for a day, I dropped down, utterly exhausted and could not move an inch. In the sky over Hiroshima, there were no birds, not even the sound of insects. I only heard the voices of people calling out the names of relatives, and the creaking of the cartwheels.

Kazuo Chujo: Night descended ominously. I remained on the university grounds. As if all insects had also died, there was not even one mosquito on that summer night. A pitch black world spread far and wide. Once in a while, flames shot up here and there. I could not even doze off; sleep refused to come.

Kazuo Chujo: Occasionally, human shadows moved in the darkness. They were searching for their relatives, apparently reluctant to give up the search and leave. Nobody spoke a word, too numb from the sudden blow dealt by fate.

Kenshi Hirata: Finally, about nine o'clock, I again turned my feet back toward my house, completely exhausted. Even in midsummer, night fell before nine o'clock. Though the whole city of Hiroshima was burned down now, a large part of the ruins were still blazing. The sky had turned red, reflecting the flames below. I thought, *if she is dead, she may feel lonely by herself. I will sleep together with her overnight here.* As I lay alone on the ashes of my home, I felt neither sorrow nor loneliness. Finally, because of the fatigue from the day's labor, I fell into deep slumber. It might have been around four in the morning when I was awakened by somebody poking me with what seemed like a bar. As I opened my eyes, I saw five or six soldiers surrounding me. They were carrying stretchers. One of the soldiers said, "Look! He is still alive." He continued, "How do you feel?" I answered. "This is the site of my house. When I got back from the company, I found that everything was gone, as you see here now. I thought my wife was probably dead underground here, and I decided to sleep with her overnight here. Therefore, I have been sleeping here." Hearing this the soldiers said, "We are very sorry," and went away.

Teiichi Teramura, ***field officer, 52nd Ship Construction Battalion, Murotsu (45 miles from Hiroshima)*****:** I was at the battalion headquarters in the early afternoon of August 6 when a telegram arrived from our commander informing us that a bomb of an unknown type had fallen on Hiroshima that morning and caused great destruction. I was ordered to the stricken city to provide emergency relief. Tormented by an ominous foreboding, I set out by a fast boat. Night had fallen by the time I reached the port of Ujina in Hiroshima. As I stepped onto the jetty, I involuntarily came to a halt. I could see nothing clearly in the darkness, but the air around me reeked of blood and death. Then moaning assaulted my ears and made them ring as if a vast number of scales were being played together. I realized to my horror that all around me were thousands of wounded people, lying on the cold concrete waiting for death. They had been placed there because there was nowhere for them to go, and none of them were receiving any medical attention. They were living corpses in a hell on earth, with only the peace of death to hope for. Though I wanted to do something for them, I realized bitterly that nothing could help them now.

Naoko Masuoka, *junior college student*: I was loaded into the car of a rescue squad that happened to come along just then, and taken to Ujina, where I was given careful first aid treatment and then sent by boat to Ninoshima. In the boat there was one woman who was completely naked and burned all over, and she was writhing her body around in agony as if she were out of her mind. We arrived at Ninoshima and there began five days of life that I shall never be able to forget as long as I live. We lie on a blanket spread over a straw mat on the board floor. On this side and on that, the people who see dying every day can hardly be distinguished from the living. A person who was talking cheerfully yesterday is a cold dead body this morning. Can the dying of a person be such an ephemeral thing?

Nakaichi Nakamura: I was with one of the first relief teams to enter Hiroshima. Fires were raging, and the earth was as hot as if it had been baked. A scene terrible beyond description spread before my eyes. It was hell re-created on earth. Our work began with aid to the injured. As dawn approached, appeals for protection against the cold arose from all sides. We covered people with all the blankets we had, but even so, when morning came at last, we discovered that half were already dead. Smeared with blood and dirt, we picked up the bodies that lay wherever we looked, hoisted them on our backs, and loaded them onto whatever boards we could find that had escaped the fires. The collection of corpses continued until late at night.

When we found a suitable vacant lot, we dug a huge hole and lined the bottom with pieces of wood. Onto these we gently lowered about fifty bodies, swollen, stomachs gaping open, eyeballs gone, many the torn bodies of young children—and set fire to them. We stood around them as they burned and did not move until the flames had died away.

Yasu Tsuchida: The red-blazing fires in the sky at night, and the faint breathing of people who would be hovering crisis between life and death, seemed to represent the last day of the earth.

"'The greatest thing in history'"

REACTION TO THE BOMB

The Knoxville News-Sentinel

Served by United Press, Scripps-Howard Alliance, Chicago Daily News Foreign Service, NEA Service, Acme Telephoto and Newspictures, Associated Press Daily.

ESTABLISHED 1886—ISSUE No. 18,595 KNOXVILLE (101), TENNESSEE, MONDAY EVENING, AUGUST 6, 1945

SECOND EXTRA EDITION Price Five Cents

Oak Ridge Has Over 425 Buildings

ATOMIC SUPER-BOMB, MADE AT OAK RIDGE, STRIKES JAPAN

WASHINGTON, Aug. 6—The United States has unleashed against Japan the terror of an atomic bomb 2000 times more powerful than the biggest blockbusters ever used in warfare.

President Truman revealed this great scientific achievement today and warned the Japanese that they now face "a rain of ruin from the air the like of which has never been seen on this earth."

More and more of these devastating bombs, unlocking the vast hidden energy that lies within the atom, will tumble on Japan if they continue to reject the Potsdam surrender ultimatum.

The new atomic bomb was used for the first time yesterday. An American plane dropped one on the Japanese army base at Hiroshima.

Its use marked victory for the Allies in the greatest scientific role in history. We put $2,000,000,000 and the work of 125,000 persons into the project.

A single bomb has more power than 20,000 tons of TNT. It has more than 2000 times the blast power of the British "grand slam" volcano bomb, the largest ever used previously in the history of warfare.

Secretary of War Henry L. Stimson disclosed that an improved bomb would be forthcoming shortly that would increase by several-fold the present effectiveness of the new weapon.

Thick Cloud Obscures Target Area

The War Department said it was not yet able to make an accurate report of the damage caused by the first bomb.

"Reconnaissance planes state that an impenetrable cloud of dust and smoke covered the target area," an announcement said. "As soon as accurate details of the result of the bombing become available, they will be released by the secretary of War."

Development of the bomb, a victory of American scientists in a desperate race with Germany, is "the greatest achievement of organised science in history," Mr. Truman said in a statement released at the White House.

The United States, he added, is now prepared "to obliterate more rapidly and completely every productive enterprise the Japanese have above ground in any city.

Japan Warned in Potsdam Ultimatum

He revealed that the July 26 ultimatum issued to Japan was made "to spare the Japanese people from utter destruction."

When the ultimatum was rejected, the atomic bomb was sent into action.

"If they (the Japanese leaders) do not now accept our terms, they may expect a rain of ruin from the air, the like of which has never been seen on this earth," he said.

Mr. Truman revealed that "two great plants and many lesser works" employing more than 65,000 workers are producing the new atomic bomb. Even more destructive bombs are being developed, he said.

Mr. Truman said that Secretary of War Henry L. Stimson, who has kept in personal touch with the atomic developments, would make public further details. Stimson's statement, the President said, will give "facts" concerning the atomic production centers at Oak Ridge, near Knoxville, Tenn.; at Richland, near Pasco, Wash.; and near Santa Fe, N. M.

Oak Ridge One of Three Centers

Production centers are located at Oak Ridge, near Knoxville, Tenn.; at Richland, near Pasco, Wash.; and near Santa Fe, N. M.

Mr. Truman's statement, released while he still was en route home by cruiser from Potsdam, lifted the secrecy from one of the most closely-guarded enterprises of the war. No mention of atomic power or any possible use of it in warfare has been allowed under the newspaper and radio code of the Office of Censorship.

Mr. Truman did not reveal the effects of the first bomb used against Japan. He said, however, that despite the vast multiplied potency of the bomb, "the physical size of the charge is exceedingly small."

"It is an atomic bomb," he said. "It is a harnessing of the basic power of the universe."

"The force from which the sun draws its power has been loosed against those who brought war to the Far East."

Uranium Ore Used for Bombs

Stimson revealed that uranium is the essential ore in the production of the bombs. He added that "steps have been taken and will continue to be taken to insure adequate supplies of this mineral."

(See full page of Oak Ridge pictures on Page 17, and further details on Pages 2 and 18.)

(Uranium is a "radioactive" chemical element. It belongs to the same family as radium. In radioactive elements the atoms slowly disintegrate by radiating energy, and in course of centuries one element is transferred into another.)

Stimson said "We are convinced that Japan will not be in a position to use an atomic bomb in this war."

"It is abundantly clear that the possession of this weapon by the United States, even in its present form, should prove a tremendous aid in the shortening of the war against Japan," Stimson said.

Stimson praised highly the scientists who had developed this atomic power.

"Behind these concrete achievements lie the tremendous contributions of American science," he declared. "No praise is too great for the unstinting efforts, brilliant achievements and complete devotion to the national interest of the scientists of this country. Nowhere else in the world has science performed so successfully in time of war."

The first atomic bomb presumably was devoted from a

Story of Secret Officially Told

Even Plant Chiefs Didn't Know What Work Others Did

Two Views of Giant Oak Ridge Production Plant

The news of the atomic bomb lifted the curtain on the secret locations of the Manhattan Project.

Word of the bomb's use and the devastation of Hiroshima remained under wraps until President Truman officially announced the news to a country and a world that was, for the most part, simply confused and unable to grasp the awesome size of the new weapon.

Harry Truman: On August 6th, the fourth day of the journey home from Potsdam, came the historic news that shook the world. I was eating lunch with members of the *Augusta*'s crew when Captain Frank Graham, White House Map Room Watch Officer, handed me the following message: "Following info regarding Manhattan received. 'Hiroshima bombed visually with only one tenth cover at 0523 15A. There was no fighter opposition and no flak. [Capt. William S. "Deak"] Parsons reports 15 minutes after drop as follows: Results clear cut successful in all respects. Visible effects greater than in any test. Conditions normal in airplane following delivery.'" I was greatly moved. I said to the group of sailors around me, "This is the greatest thing in history. It's time for us to get home."

Sen. James F. Byrnes: Ten minutes later Captain Graham was back with a second message, this time from Secretary Stimson. His report indicated that the results of the bomb were even more successful than the test had led us to expect. The President read the message aloud to me, and then stood and asked the crew to listen for a moment.

Harry Truman: I then told the crew of the dropping of a powerful new bomb, which used an explosive 20,000 times as powerful as a ton of TNT. I went to the ward room where I told the officers, who were at lunch, what had happened. I could not keep back my expectation that the Pacific War might now be brought to a speedy end. A few minutes later, the ship's radio receivers began to carry news bulletins from Washington about the atomic bomb, as well as a broadcast of the statement I had authorized just before leaving Germany. Shortly afterwards, I called a press conference of the correspondents on board and told them something of the long program of research and development that lay behind this successful assault.

Col. Paul W. Tibbets: The best-kept secret of the war was no longer a secret. Over the radio came word that President Truman, then on his way home from Potsdam, had announced the dropping of an atomic bomb. It was electrifying news in all corners of the world.

Maj. Gen. Leslie Groves: At the White House, everything was rather humdrum that morning. The press had been informed that there would be an important announcement by the President at eleven o'clock. White House correspondents are accustomed to such notices, and this one did not particularly arouse their interest. Many of them did not bother to go themselves, but sent assistants. Everything changed, however, when the President's Press

Secretary arose and read the first few sentences. As the words "more than twenty thousand tons of TNT" came out of his mouth, there was a tremendous rush of reporters.

Harry Truman, ***prepared statement announcing the bomb, released from Washington by Henry Stimson*****:** Sixteen hours ago an American airplane dropped one bomb on Hiroshima, an important Japanese Army base. That bomb had more power than 20,000 tons of TNT. It is an atomic bomb. It is a harnessing of the basic power of the universe. The force from which the sun draws its power has been loosed against those who brought war to the Far East. . . .

But the greatest marvel is not the size of the enterprise, its secrecy, nor its cost, but the achievement of scientific brains in putting together infinitely complex pieces of knowledge held by many men in different fields of science into a workable plan. And hardly less marvelous has been the capacity of industry to design, and of labor to operate, the machines and methods to do things never done before, so that the brain child of many minds came forth in physical shape and performed as it was supposed to do. What has been done is the greatest achievement of organized science in history. It was done under high pressure and without failure.

Luis Alvarez: When the President announced the bombing, Tinian was delirious. The 509th had been a black-sheep bunch to most of the other aircrews, commanding the best aircraft and the highest priorities and seemingly doing nothing more to earn them than drop odd-looking 10,000-pound bright-orange bombs. Now there was nothing but praise. Men who had been dreading the thought of the inevitable invasion took heart that the tools with which to end the war were at hand.

Gen. Robert L. Eichelberger, ***commander, US Eighth Army, Philippines*****:** When the atomic bomb was dropped on Hiroshima—it was as much a surprise to me as to my newest recruit—I was at my Leyte headquarters. I flew at once to Manila. All of us had been working on plans for the main strike against the Japanese homeland; we then called it Operation CORONET. In Manila there was a cheerful atmosphere. General MacArthur told me at once that he believed Japan would surrender as a result of the atomic bombing and because of the prospective entrance of Russia into the Pacific War.

Cpl. Edgar Harrell: On August 6, I'm in Guam, stretched out on a cot, my arms fastened, so I can't move, my legs fastened, I'm wrapped in Vaseline gauze, a bloody mess, but they're having trouble keeping the blood from flowing. And there's a gentleman that came in with the *Louisville Courier-Journal* and said, "Hey, Marine, do you know now what that was that you were guarding?" No, we didn't know. He said, "Well, you know today—Hiroshima!"

Maj. Gen. Leslie Groves: General Marshall expressed his feeling that we should guard against too much gratification over our success, because it undoubtedly involved a large number of Japanese casualties. I replied that I was not thinking so much about those casualties as I was about the men who had made the Bataan death march. When we got into the hall, Arnold slapped me on the back and said, "I am glad you said that—it's just the way I feel."

Luis Alvarez: When we developed our oscilloscope film, we found we had obtained only one good record, but it was exceedingly good. Before we could calculate the bomb yield, however, President Truman announced from Washington—without evidence so far as I know—that the yield was equivalent to 20,000 tons of TNT. In 1953 I learned from a theorist at Los Alamos, Fred Reines, that the damage done at Hiroshima couldn't be reconciled with the canonical 20 kilotons. I gave Fred the records from my personal files. With them he calculated an energy release of 12.5 kilotons, plus or minus one KT.

Walter Cronkite, *correspondent, United Press*: We received our first bulletin from Paris. In French it reported that the Americans had dropped on Japan a bomb the equivalent of 20,000 tons of TNT. Clearly, I thought, those French operators have made a mistake. So I changed the figure to 20 tons before sending the story along to our Belgian clients. With further adds on the story, my mistake became abundantly clear. It also turned out that at that time the world's only known supply of uranium was the Belgian Congo, and Belgium's Union Minière company sat on all of it. I went around to Union Minière's headquarters. Those officials in Brussels seemed to have no advance knowledge of the use to which their precious metal had been put. They were pale and almost trembling with fright when they heard the news that, thanks to their monopoly, they held the world's future in their hands—in war and, perhaps, in peace. The revelation seemed to have gotten their tongues. I might as well have tried to interview zombies.

Dr. Tatsuichiro Akizuki, ***Urakami Hospital, Nagasaki*****:** On the morning of 7 August I unfolded the newspaper as usual. It was a small tabloid that hardly deserved the title of newspaper. I glanced at it, muttering to myself: "Now, which part of the country was bombed yesterday?" And then the headline caught my eye: "New kind of bomb dropped on Hiroshima—Much damage done." This greatly alarmed me. The newspapers and the radio in those days were in the habit of saying 'some slight damage,' when referring to the ravages wrought on us both at home and in the various war zones. Now the newspaper openly said "much damage done," which seemed like a portent of some evil.

Hanson W. Baldwin, ***correspondent,*** **The New York Times,** ***writing on August 7, 1945*****:** In war—particularly this war—it is almost useless to talk of the "rules" of war. And quite clearly our development of an atomic explosive was in the nature of a race for survival. Its use will probably save American lives, may shorten the war materially, may even compel Japanese surrender. Yet when this is said, we have sowed the whirlwind. Much of our bombing throughout this war—like the enemy's—has been directed against cities, and hence against civilians. Because our bombing has been more effective and hence more devastating, Americans have become a synonym for destruction. And now we have been the first to introduce a new weapon of unknowable effects which may bring us victory quickly but which will sow the seeds of hate more widely than ever. We may yet reap the whirlwind. Certainly with such God-like power under man's imperfect control we face a frightful responsibility. Atomic energy may well lead to a bright new world in which man shares a common brotherhood or we shall become—beneath the bombs and rockets—a world of troglodytes.

* * *

Word of the "gadget's" use against Japan spread quickly through the labs and facilities of the Manhattan Project in Chicago, Oak Ridge, Hanford, and Los Alamos, where the presidential announcement marked an end to years of secrecy and obfuscation and came as a surprise to many of the participating personnel and the families who had lived alongside the work for years.

Doris Reynolds, *project spouse, Oak Ridge*: My husband was just finishing taking a shower and this news came and he had a radio on. Suddenly he came flying out of the bathroom with nothing on but his shorts, like a lunatic, and he said, "We did it! We did it! We did it!" and I said, "What did we do?" He said, "We dropped the bomb!" I said, "What bomb?"

William Reynolds, *worker, Oak Ridge*: That was the first she knew.

Doris Reynolds: I didn't know what we were doing here and "We did it! We did it!" I won't forget that day. Then we began to hear the whistles and the bells ringing. My neighbor down the street came running up into the yard, and everyone was just hugging and kissing. We were just so darn glad to find out what we were here for.

Waldo E. Cohn: Immediately it was a plant-wide holiday.

Charmian Cohn, *project spouse, Oak Ridge*: It was fantastic.

Waldo E. Cohn: We all took off. We drove around the town, randomly around town.

Charmian Cohn: Open cars screaming words.

Waldo E. Cohn: "Uranium!" "Plutonium!" All these words that we kept down here for all these years.

Charmian Cohn: "237!"

Waldo E. Cohn: We were like a bunch of school kids. It was really, really funny. I remember we had a chemistry section group leaders meeting up that night and we got drunk—good Lord. The wives this time could come along and we could tell them about it.

Charmian Cohn: We were all going, "Now we know what this is all about," you know. What a relief!

Waldo E. Cohn: Now we could talk about what we were doing and communicate with the outside world about it because we were real pleased. I mean, we had hundreds of papers ready to write. We couldn't break any of them loose.

Tom Dunigan, *Army Intelligence*: I think for Oak Ridgers, it was a more exciting day than even the end of the war.

Edward S. Bettis: Yes, it was. Everyone felt that their efforts had finally amounted to something, and I think without exception the general feeling was, well, now the war will end. This will be the end of the war.

Arthur Holly Compton: I was in Chicago when news of the atomic bomb was flashed over the radio and appeared in the newspapers. The members of the Metallurgical Laboratory were called together, and I told them what details I knew. Some learned then for the first time what the task was on which they had been working. For the most part it was a day of wonder.

Leona H. Woods: I certainly do recall how I felt when the atomic bombs were used. My brother-in-law was captain of the first minesweeper scheduled into Sasebo Harbor. My brother was a Marine, with a flame thrower, on Okinawa. I'm sure these people would not have lasted in an invasion. I have no regrets. I think we did right, and we couldn't have done it differently.

Juanita Cardwell, *project spouse, Oak Ridge*: We were shocked. We were thrilled. We did not feel guilty. We were happy because we thought that the end certainly justified the means. I had two brothers in the Pacific. One of them was a Marine ready to assault Japan. So that took care of my conscience.

* * *

Phyllis K. Fisher: For many of us on our hill, August 6, 1945, started off like any other day. A dazzling sun in a clear sky and a soft, warm breeze from the desert below gave little indication of the sudden thunderstorm that was to gather in the afternoon. Our scientific-military population started to work very early, as they usually did. The wives and the children on the hill, used to coping with the now-sandy, now-muddy temporary environment, went about their usual activities.

T/3 Eleanor "Jerry" Stone: On August 6, I was on paging when Nellie brought an announcement to be broadcast. "The first atomic bomb has been dropped on Hiroshima," it began. Well, here it was. Mostly, we felt excited. We were proud that Los Alamos had been able to develop the bomb and happy that the secrecy was over. Most of all, we anticipated the war's end. Nellie had asked me to call the outlying sites, which had no paging system, and the orderly rooms. All responded satisfactorily until I reached the MP non-com on duty. "How's that again? A what? Spell that name, will you?" Obviously, security had really been tight with respect to at least one individual!

Otto R. Frisch: We didn't know when the bomb would be dropped in earnest or where it would be dropped. One day, some three weeks after Alamogordo, there was a sudden noise in the laboratory of running footsteps and yelling voices. Somebody opened my door and shouted "Hiroshima has been destroyed!"; about a hundred thousand people were thought to have been killed. I still remember the feeling of unease, indeed nausea, when I saw how many of my friends were rushing to the telephone to book tables at the La Fonda hotel in Santa Fe, in order to celebrate. Of course they were exalted by the success of their work, but it seemed rather ghoulish to celebrate the sudden death of a hundred thousand people, even if they were "enemies."

Walter S. Carpenter: I was a member of the board of General Motors. I was over at the General Motors finance committee that morning. I got a long-distance call from Washington. There was General Groves on the phone. He started in about explaining about how grateful he was to the DuPont Company for all that they had done in connection with this program. I thought, *Well now, the boy's been drinking.* He appreciated everything that we had done and now that we could see what the realization was of all of our work and so on. I said "General, that's fine, but why do you call me up to tell me about that at this time?" He said, "Well haven't you seen any of the papers?" We'd been in committee for about three hours now. I hadn't seen the paper or anything. I said, "No. I have not." He says, "Well you get the papers and read them, and you'll find out what I'm talking about." I went downstairs immediately and got my papers. That was the first I'd heard of it.

2nd Lt. Carl G. Ackerman, ***pilot, 393rd Bombardment Squadron*****:** I never heard or knew anything about the atomic bomb until President Truman announced it publicly.

Walter M. Gorecki, ***rail transportation officer, 390th Air Service Group*****:** I can truthfully say that I was not aware that our group was to drop an atomic bomb on Japan. I always thought they were to be some sort of missiles that would end the war. This was the best kept secret.

James M. Dugger, ***1st Ordnance Squadron, Special (Aviation)*****:** I did not know we had an atomic bomb until after the first one was dropped.

Bernice Brode: My boys and I were boarding a Navy bus in Pasadena to visit the China Lake Naval Weapons Center in California when we read the headlines. Bill, my older boy, said very quietly, "This is Papa's bomb, you know, Mama." My eyes quickly caught the words from the paper: *atomic bomb, Hiroshima, Los Alamos*. The first two I had never heard of, but the last one, the forbidden name we had not dared utter in our letters home for more than two years, was now, incredibly, staring at me from a newspaper. So that was what we were making up there! A lady in front of me asked what an atomic bomb was and what was this place called Los Alamos. I did not know how to answer.

"A city of death"

THE DAY AFTER IN HIROSHIMA

The sun rose Tuesday, August 7, over a Hiroshima transformed by the atomic blast and the fires. Uncoordinated relief missions were underway, but the city's devastation was so complete—and so unexpected—that much of Japan did not realize yet what had transpired, nor, especially, did the government in Tokyo appreciate the scale of the US's new weapon.

Toyoko Sugano: When I woke up it was morning. I was so thirsty, craving for water. Then I noticed that black rain had fallen all over me. I was all black. I wanted to drink something, but I didn't have the courage to go down to the river. I drank muddy water and then I fainted again. The next time I opened my eyes I was at a grammar school in Hiroshima. I was bloody and burned all over my body. A man came with a rice bowl and gave some rice to me. I was very hungry, so I extended my hand and took the rice and then tried to put it into my mouth. But I couldn't eat.

Fumiko Sasaki, *eighth grader*: Under the direction of the soldiers, I hurried home the next morning. On the way, heaps of the dead and the burned lying about horrified me. The sea of flames the previous night, which had a weird beauty, licked up the whole city and made it barren. As far as the eye could see, nothing was left standing. Therefore I had no idea where my house had been. I hunted around and found the remains of Fukuya Department Store, but wondered where my house, which was near Fukuya Department Store, had gone. Nothing and none of my family were to be seen. I couldn't find my family at my acquaintances' either. Two days later I went back to the place again where my house had been and found the site had been cleared out by my relatives. They had dug up some dead bodies there, which were just bleached bones. I didn't want to believe these were my father's and mother's bodies. Four dead bodies were lying there like baked potatoes. Everyone in my family died, leaving me behind. I stood there alone, speechless in surprise.

Tohru Hara: Hiroshima, burning steadily for a day and a night, presently became a city of death. All that was left was a hell. People who had lost the last energy to live were lying with the railroad tracks for their pillow.

Dr. Michihiko Hachiya: In the space of one night patients had become packed like the rice in sushi, into every nook and cranny of the hospital. The majority were badly burned, a few severely injured. All were critically ill. Many had been near the heart of the city and in their efforts to flee managed to get only as far as the Communications Hospital before their strength failed. Others, from nearer by, came deliberately to seek treatment or because this building, standing alone where all else was destroyed, represented shelter and a place of refuge; they came as an avalanche and overran the hospital. There was no friend or relative to minister to their needs, no one to prepare their food. Everything was in disorder. And to make matters worse was the vomiting and diarrhea. Patients who could not walk urinated and defecated where they lay.

Those who could walk would feel their way to the exits and relieve themselves there. Persons entering or leaving the hospital could not avoid stepping in the filth, so closely was it spread. The front entrance became covered with feces overnight, and nothing could be done for there were no bed pans and, even if there had been, no one to carry them to the patients.

Kazu Kishimoto: The next day I heard there were lots of students taken to Ninoshima Island. So my older brother, a second lieutenant at that time, went to Ninoshima Island to find [my sister]. There he found Taeko's teacher and three of her classmates, but no Taeko. They were seriously wounded, but their memory was good. They told him that when they had been carrying roofing tile, there was a big flash and a sound. The house was completely crushed. They didn't see Taeko when they were taken almost naked to Ninoshima Island by car. Maybe Taeko couldn't run away, having been blinded while on the roof, and died there suffering and calling to her mother for help. Imagining a scene like that breaks my heart. Still I looked for her for another week in vain, hoping and praying that she took refuge somewhere.

Setsuko Tanaka, ***mother of Etsuko Tanaka, seventh grader at Hiroshima Girls School*****:** My husband searched for her for three or four days in the summer heat. He walked over countless dead bodies, crossed areas where there used to be houses. However, my daughter was nowhere to be found. Where and how did she escape? She must have suffered a lot. She must have died crying, "Mother, I'm hot, I'm hot." She only ate a poor porridge of corn that morning, which adds to our pity and sorrow, and we cannot help shedding tears. I don't want to remember anything now. I only hate war and pray for peace.

Kenshi Hirata: I decided to go back to the site of my burned house, and borrowed the services of some ten men to dig in the ashes. We dug all over the site about one foot deep, but not a bone of a human being came out. A new hope rose in my heart. "She is still alive somewhere," I said to myself. In order to make sure, we dug a bit deeper. What looked like a piece of shell was unearthed. I said it was a bit of shell, but the workers insisted it was a section of human bone. Suppressing my uneasy feeling, I helped dig around the place from where the "bone" was unearthed. At the spot upon which our living room had stood, the diggers found white bones in pieces, in a form that indicated that she was sitting. It was such a terrific shock to me that I was unable to shed a drop of tears. As we continued to work under the broiling sun of midsummer, sweat flowed like waterfalls and our trousers were soaked. From the spot where the kitchen was came a washing basin. I thought, since she came all the way from Nagasaki to die here, I shall put her bones in this washing basin and take them back. Only ten days ago we had brought this washing basin and other things with much difficulty in the crowded train from Nagasaki.

Kazuo Chujo: For three days after the bombing, I camped out on the Hiroshima University grounds. I was convinced that my parents—if alive—would return to the ruins of our house. I waited. Acquaintances exchanged news of their families, but I got no news of my parents. Fearing that we might miss each other on the way, I made a point of returning to the site of our house every few hours. I also expanded my area of search gradually. There were heaps of corpses wherever I went. The bodies I examined, poking them with a stick, were simply beyond count. By the river, there were those who were still alive. They were begging for water. In front of an air-raid shelter on the side of Hijiyama (Mount Hiji), I was shocked out of my wits by the sight of a stark-naked woman. Her face was bloated beyond recognition, and every shred of clothing had apparently been burnt off. She screamed for help, and then disappeared into the shelter. I can still hear her screams.

Hideko Tamura Snider: The stories from others who went to look for their relatives were most disturbing. We had heard that the dead and the dying were left on the ground where they fell. Rotting corpses were said to be everywhere. Those who had severe burns on their faces were hard to identify, even when they somehow survived long enough to reach a rescue station. The so-called "rescue" stations were filled to their capacities with injured but lacked medicine or aid. Since the injured people had fled in all directions, and the city no longer existed, there were no clues even as to where to start. The newspaper informed us that the horrific destruction was accomplished by a single bomb. It said that this bomb was so lethal that Hiroshima would not be fit for habitation for the next seventy-five years. The news did not stop anyone from going back into Hiroshima, however. People looked for their family, children, mothers, fathers, aunts and uncles, and brothers and sisters. No one could stay away, knowing that their child or mother may be dying without their comfort or help. The few lucky people who did find their relatives grieved even more deeply, since they were unable to save or relieve the suffering of the dying family members.

Hakuzo Iwamoto: A student in our neighborhood told me that my son Shiro had been spared. It was almost unbelievable. He told me that Shiro was at a burnt house near Shinbashi. I went there and found my son sitting naked looking out the other way. A lady was taking care of my son, and she told me, "Before the fire spread around some gentleman nearby brought your son over to the Motoyasu River. They stayed with us all night in the river. That's why he was saved. We have been taking care of him since. His burns are not so serious. He will soon be all right." I examined him and found that his left hand from the elbow to the finger and upper half of his head above his nose were burnt. I too felt that he would be all right soon. I thanked her and carried him on my back to the hospital. It was around six o'clock in the evening of August 7. Next day I moved my wife and son to a shelter behind the hospital.

Dr. Michihiko Hachiya: During the day, an effort was made to sort and rearrange the patients according to the nature and severity of their injuries, and not a few dead were found among the living, though fewer than yesterday. It irritated me when I heard the report, for I felt that the dead should be moved with greater dispatch in order to make room for the living. This is another example of my changed outlook. People were dying so fast that I had begun to accept death as a matter of course and ceased to respect its awfulness.

Hakuzo Iwamoto: My son started a high fever. I asked a nurse to give an antifebrile for him. But she said no drug was available. So I could do nothing but watch him. With us in the shelter there were about twenty soldiers who were patients of the Red Cross hospital. At about four in the afternoon, Shiro threw up some stuff which was as dark as coffee several times and passed away in two minutes. An hour later, I thought it would be a nuisance for our shelter-mates to leave a dead body there. At the gate of the hospital, soldiers were cremating many dead bodies. I wrapped up the body of my son with a bloodstained kimono which somebody had thrown away and brought it to the gate. I asked a sublieutenant who was directing the operation to cremate my son. He took my son's name, age and address and gave an order to a soldier. The soldier, in turn, took out some crude oil and poured it on the belly of my son. Then, immediately, two soldiers grabbed my son's body at his hands and legs and, over a good three meter distance, threw it into the flame.

Yokihisa Tokumitsu: At that hospital there were three or four funerals every day. Not many people left the hospital because they got well—the reason the number of patients gradually got smaller was because of the funerals. I didn't feel anything special about those people. It must be because I did not have enough strength left to think.

Hakuzo Iwamoto: Next day, I picked up some ashes where he was cremated. We went back to the hospital next day. I secured a space for my wife at a corner of a large room. The passageway of the hospital was all occupied with the people who were heavily burnt. At night they asked the nurses for water, crying "Give me water! (Mizu o kudasai.)" I could not sleep because of their cries. The victims filled even the ground around the hospital, and every day they died by the dozens. On the morning of August 14, I went to our burnt home. I found all of our goods were burnt up. I came back to the hospital. My wife was dead and cold.

Kimura Yasuko: When they could assemble a group of thirty or forty children who had received word, they sent them back by truck and handed them over to relatives who met them in the burned-out ruins of Hiroshima. I got word that my father had survived. Finally it was my turn to go home. We arrived in the early evening. The city didn't look as if it had been burned. It was flattened. In the middle of the ruins two buildings, a department store and the newspaper, stood alone. There, my father met me. When I was taken to a relative's house, there was a round flower vase with a piece of writing paper tied with packing twine. "This is Mother," Grandmother told me.

Kazuo Chujo: On the third day after the bombing, I finally located my mother's whereabouts after all that frantic searching. A neighbor told me that he had seen her name on the list of people evacuated to an island called Ninoshima. I was concerned about my father, but it was imperative that I get to Ninoshima. I ran to Ujina as fast as my legs could carry me. I played soccer in those days, so I was a very good runner. The port of Ujina was a pandemonium of people like me. The local fishermen were fully mobilizing their boats, ferrying people free of charge. I boarded a small craft powered by a hot-bulb engine, thanking the skipper. About thirty people boarded the vessel, sinking the gunwale almost to the water level. On the small boat bound for Ninoshima, I felt terribly lost and restless. I was anxious about my mother's injury, and wondered what sort of place she had been taken to.

Dr. Michihiko Hachiya: I considered a family lucky if it had not lost more than two of its members.

Kazuo Chujo: The whole of Ninoshima groaned. Groans and moans rose from hundreds of men, women and children suffering from horrible burns. And the stench of death rose from numerous bodies strewn, as if casually, all over the place. The injured who could not be accommodated in the quarantine buildings were laid out in open air on the concrete ground. I discovered my mother, after quite a search, in a building that looked like a barracks. There she was, among rows and rows of patients. She was in a semi-reclining posture, staring into space. I called to her, but she did not recognize me at first. In fact, both of us were caked with mud and quite disheveled, hardly any resemblance to what we used to look like. Distressingly, I have no memory whatsoever of my conversation with my mother, no matter how hard I try to recall it.

When I saw her back—one glance was enough; I instinctively shut my eyes. From her surprisingly thin shoulders to the hips, the skin was a reddish purple color, revealing a most hideous mess of a mosaic of bloody pus and bits of burnt flesh. Her head had been injured, probably by a flying roof tile. *Could such wounds ever heal?* My mother and I remained in the vast straw-matted barracks. Somebody had to be treating the wounded somewhere, but it seemed doubtful that my mother would ever get her turn.

Toshio Miyachi, ***Artillery Supply Corps (111th Chugoku Unit), Chugoku Regional Military District*:** At the West Parade Ground, approximately ninety soldiers who had survived the A-bombing were assembled. I and the other soldiers were engaged in cremating corpses. A tremendous number of corpses had to be cremated, like 250 one day and 300 the next. Especially memorable in that operation was two American soldiers who were lying dead on the steps of Hiroshima Castle. They must have been two POWs from the U.S. forces who were held in a building near Hiroshima Castle in those days.

Kazuo Chujo: Long rows of unclaimed bodies lined riverbanks and sidewalks. Their scorched flesh on which maggots crawled was spattered with blood and mud. If you tried to lift a body, the skin peeled off like an overripe peach. The remains had to be hauled away on a hook, like large fish, to be dumped into a trench for cremation. Each time a body fell into the trench, the torso hit the ground first and made a startlingly loud thud. The limbs bounced in exaggerated gestures, as if alive. One body was curled up tightly in a fetal position, with both elbows rigidly bent at right angles. The face was bloated to twice its normal size. It was cruel testimony to the ferocious intensity of the heat of the blast. On the river, bloated masses of dark reddish flesh bobbed with the tide like rafts.

Kenshi Hirata: On the morning of August 8, I went to the factory for a short while to make arrangements for my return to Nagasaki and to settle other matters. As I heard that the first train for Nagasaki would leave Koi, the next station, at about three in the afternoon, I left carrying my wife's bones with me in the washing basin. On the way to the station I threw the offerings of rice and flowers into a river, in accordance with Buddhist practice. As I was walking toward the station, there came along a man of about forty years old, loudly crying like a child. He was wearing only a shirt. I pitied him, thinking he also must have lost all his family and been left alone. I wondered how I was going to broach the death of my wife to her parents.

"A one-two punch would be lost"

MISSION #16

Project Alberta's Harold Agnew, Luis Alvarez, Lawrence Johnston, and Bernard Waldman on Tinian, with one of their parachute-borne pressure gauges.

Three days after the Hiroshima bombing, with little apparent progress on the peace front, the second atomic mission followed the pattern of the first—but from the start one screw-up after another unfolded as the planes took to the skies, mistakes and decisions that ultimately came close to ruining the mission and even costing the crew of the strike aircraft their lives. That Thursday morning on the Japanese island of Kyushu, the 180,000 residents of Kokura—the primary target of the 509th's sixteenth mission from Tinian—didn't realize how close their city came that morning to infamy.

Col. Paul W. Tibbets: Back on Tinian, the second atomic bomb was being assembled even as the world was learning about the first. It was altogether different in looks as well as explosive content. This was the shape with which we were most familiar—a "pumpkin" like those we had been dropping in practice. Unless the Japanese capitulated in the meantime, as some optimistically thought they would, we had scheduled the second bomb drop for Thursday, August 9. The Hiroshima flight had occurred on Monday. We made this decision Tuesday morning at a conference on Guam. Accompanying me to the meeting with Generals Spaatz and LeMay were Admiral Purnell, Captain Parsons, and Major John F. Moynahan, the 509th's public information officer.

Lawrence H. Johnston: We naively assumed that Japan would now surrender and the war would be over. Would we need to deliver another bomb? That question was soon answered when we were alerted to get ready for another mission August 9th.

Col. Paul W. Tibbets: On Tinian the next day, I went ahead with the plans for the second atomic mission. LeMay assumed that I would be flying this one also, but I had decided otherwise. I told him that Chuck Sweeney would drop the second bomb.

Maj. Charles W. Sweeney: It was up to me to live up to his expectations for this crucial second mission. I had to succeed. "We must make the Japanese believe we can keep them coming every few days until they surrender," the colonel had told me.

2nd Lt. Fred J. Olivi: I was elated, to say the least, to learn that I was to be a member of the crew which had been selected to drop the second A-Bomb on the Japanese Empire. It was important to let the Japanese know we had more of the devastating bombs that we dropped on Hiroshima.

Maj. Charles W. Sweeney: In truth, there was no third bomb behind us ready to go.

Col. Paul W. Tibbets: If indeed a third had been necessary, there was serious discussion of making Tokyo the next target. Although much of that city had been burned out by incendiaries, it was still the seat of government and the center of the empire's military planning.

Lt. Jacob Beser: Wednesday 8 August 1945 was to be a day of worries for everyone concerned with the mission due to depart at 0330 the next morning. The weather over Japan had deteriorated in the past forty-eight hours and the forecast for the next twenty-four hour interval was somewhat "iffy."

Lawrence H. Johnston: Alvarez remarked that if I went this time, I would be the only person who had witnessed all three of the wartime bomb explosions. We knew this was the only remaining bomb on the island and no more were scheduled to arrive soon from Los Alamos.

Luis Alvarez: On the evening of August 8 Bob Serber, the theoretical physicist Phil Morrison, and I sat in the officers' club discussing the forthcoming mission and wondering what we could do to help shorten the war. I remembered that our former Berkeley colleague Ryokichi Sagane was a professor of physics at the University of Tokyo and suggested we send him a message. It would appeal to him to inform the Japanese military that, since two atomic bombs had been dropped, it was obvious that we could build as many more as we might need to end the war by force. I drafted a letter that Bob and Phil edited. I wrote out an original and two carbon copies.

***Letter to Prof. R. Sagane, from three colleagues at Atomic Bomb Command Headquarters, August 9, 1945*:** We are sending this as a personal message to urge that you use your influence as a reputable nuclear physicist, to convince the Japanese General Staff of the terrible consequences which will be suffered by your people if you continue in this war. You have known for several years that an atomic bomb could be built if a nation were willing to pay the enormous cost of preparing the necessary material. Now that you have seen we have constructed the production plants, there can be no doubt in your mind, all the output of these factories working twenty-four hours a day, will be exploded on your homeland. Within the space of three weeks, we have proof fired one bomb in the American desert, exploded one in Hiroshima and fired the third this morning. We implore you to confirm these facts to your leaders and to do your utmost to stop the destruction and waste of life which can only result in the total annihilation of all your cities if continued. As scientists, we deplore the use to which a beautiful discovery has been put, but we can assure you that unless Japan surrenders at once, this rain of atomic bombs will increase manyfold in fury.

Lawrence H. Johnston: Alvarez wrote the final draft and we taped a copy in his handwriting onto each of the three canisters which would be dropped along with the bomb.

Luis Alvarez: [We found out later that] the letter was quickly found, delivered to the military, and discussed at length, but Sagane wasn't contacted and saw it only after the war. Through his courtesy I have the one surviving letter and the Panofsky pressure gauge to which it had been attached.

2nd Lt. Fred J. Olivi: Our mission brought about a change in aircraft. In order to drop instruments over Hiroshima special electronic equipment had been installed in the bomb bay of *The Great Artiste* to measure radiation and other data occurring at the time of the A-Bomb's explosion. When it became apparent that it was going to take at least a day to re-install the special "hanger" essential for carrying the Fat Man, a quick decision had to be made. We couldn't wait. Colonel Tibbets and his superior officers decided that the crew of *The Great Artiste* would carry Fat Man in another B-29 called *Bockscar*, named for its pilot, Captain Fred Bock. Bock and his crew would fly our B-29, *The Great Artiste*, and drop the instruments. A simple switch of crews from one B-29 to another. It happened all the time in the 509th depending on available aircraft for scheduled missions.

Capt. Frederick C. Bock: The intended strike formation consisted of three Silverplate B-29s manned by regular crews and others of the 509th plus members of Project Alberta and official observers. V-77 *Bockscar* carried the Fat Man Plutonium Bomb; V-89 *The Great Artiste* was equipped with instruments to detect and record the shock waves from the explosion; V-90 *Big Stink* was equipped with a special Fastax Camera for photographing the detonation of the bomb and the early growth of the fire ball.

Maj. Charles W. Sweeney: I had no idea exactly how prophetic and fitting it was that [Maj. Jim] Hopkins would be piloting the *Big Stink*.

Capt. Frederick C. Bock: On board with us were Lawrence Johnston and Walter Goodman of Project A, also William Laurence, science writer for *The New York Times* and special consultant to the Manhattan Project. There were three instrument canisters containing pressure gauges and radio transmitters in the bomb bay of V-89 to be dropped with deployable parachutes at the same time as the Fat Man bomb.

Lawrence H. Johnston: For this mission, there was no lack of important people who wanted to fly on the third plane, the observation plane, since things had gone so smoothly on the Hiroshima flight. On board were two distinguished Britons, Sir William Penney and Group Captain Leonard Cheshire of the Royal Air Force.

Maj. Charles W. Sweeney: Hours before the bomb was to be transported to the loading area, the assembly crew encountered a snag that would have been comical except for the circumstances. It was discovered that holes on the bomb casing and the tail section had been improperly drilled, making it impossible to align the two components and bolt them together. Many a father had confronted similar problems on Christmas Eve when trying to assemble cheaply made toys for his children. However, this was no toy, and it had cost two billion dollars. Without missing a beat, a technician with a metal file labored to scrape away enough of the aluminum plating on the fins to enlarge the holes so that the sections could be joined by the bolts.

Ens. Donald F. Mastick: I recall seeing Art Machen, Project A, sitting on the back of the Nagasaki bomb late at night with a rattail file to align a bolt hole to get a secure fitting of the tail assembly.

Maj. Charles W. Sweeney: Because the entire assembly was so complicated, the plutonium bomb would have to be armed and live when it was loaded onto the airplane. There would be no way to arm it in flight, as Captain Parsons had armed Little Boy on the Hiroshima mission. Thus, my crew and I would be rolling down the runway with a live, 10,300-pound plutonium bomb, and because of its weight, there would be just barely enough runway to gain the proper airspeed. If we crashed on takeoff, we could obliterate the island.

2nd Lt. Fred J. Olivi: I got my first close look at America's second atom bomb when members of the flight crew were invited to sign our names, or some sort of personal message, on Fat Man. The huge bomb had just been pulled out of the highly guarded assembly area and was ready to be slowly moved to the special loading pit. I had seen "Pumpkins" up close before, but this one somehow looked different. It was painted a dull, mustard yellow and looked ominous as it sat on its cradle.

Maj. Charles W. Sweeney: We were reminded in no uncertain terms to drop only visually, which was a natural introduction to the weather report. Because of the bad weather at lower altitudes and our proximity to the Japanese mainland, the rendezvous would be at 30,000 feet instead of at 8,000, as on the Hiroshima mission. This meant we would be flying through some turbulent weather for about five hours in complete radio silence.

Sgt. Raymond Gallagher: We were instructed to go to a small island off the coast of Japan, about twenty-five miles off the coast, and its name was Yakushima. At that point, we would rendezvous with the other two ships.

Maj. Charles W. Sweeney: The final briefing commenced at midnight. Our weather airplanes would precede us by an hour to the two possible targets. Charlie McKnight would fly number 95 to Nagasaki, and George Marquardt would fly number 88 to Kokura. Weather forecasts remained the same, clear at each target.

Added to my crew for this mission were three more officers, specialists in their fields: Lieutenant Jake Beser, who had been aboard the *Enola Gay* and would be responsible for monitoring radar frequencies in the event the Japanese tried to jam our radar and possibly detonate the radar fuse on Fat Man; Navy Commander Fred Ashworth, the weaponeer in charge of the bomb itself; and Lieutenant Philip Barnes, who would assist Commander Ashworth in monitoring a device connected to the bomb's fuses.

Chaplain Downey offered a prayer beseeching the Lord to see us safely through the mission.

Capt. William B. Downey: Almighty God, Father of all mercies, we pray Thee to be gracious with those who fly this night. Guard and protect those of us who venture out into the darkness of Thy heaven. Uphold them on Thy wings. Keep them safe both in body and soul and bring them back to us. Give to us all courage and strength for the hours that are ahead; give to them rewards according to their efforts. Above all else, our Father, bring peace to Thy world. May we go forward trusting in Thee and knowing we are in Thy presence now and forever. Amen.

Maj. Charles W. Sweeney: I settled down into the leather seat, strapped myself in, and began my checklist with my copilot, Don Albury. We were at the point of "Start engines." I prepared to give [John] Kuharek, the flight engineer, the command when he leaned around toward me and said, "Major, we have a problem. The fuel in our reserve tank in the rear bomb bay bladder isn't pumping. We've got six hundred gallons of fuel trapped back there." "How long to fix it?" I asked. "With all the special precautions, several hours," he responded. This left me with 6,400 gallons total for the flight instead of 7,000.

Sgt. Raymond Gallagher: The engineer learned that the pumps that would take the gas out of our rear bomb bay tanks were inoperative. The pilot conferred with a few of the higher-ranking men that had come to see us off.

Maj. Charles W. Sweeney: Our window of opportunity was rapidly closing on us. If we didn't take off soon, the mission would be scrubbed. The entire psychological impact of a one-two punch would be lost, and with it any real prospect of a quick end to the war. Tibbets, as was his style when he gave a man a job, said, "It's your call, Chuck." Rolling all the factors around in my mind, I determined that I had more than enough fuel to make it to target. The problem was, if I encountered any delays, the likelihood of making it back to Tinian was zero, and getting back to any American-held base would be problematic at best. I would have to ditch in the ocean. I looked at Colonel Tibbets and said, "The hell with it, I want to go. We're going." With all engines turning, we rolled to the taxiway and proceeded to Runway A.

2nd Lt. Fred J. Olivi: Sweeney held *Bockscar* on the runway a long, long time, taking full advantage of every precious foot. We were heavy. Almost too heavy, I thought. And one miscalculation, or an engine failure, would be a one-of-a-kind disaster. As first the nose wheel came off the concrete and then the main landing gear broke contact with the ground *Bockscar* was filled with a collective sigh of relief. Our first big obstacle—take-off—was behind us. We settled in and started to make the aircraft ready for our long mission—longer than we expected!

Maj. Charles W. Sweeney: It was about 2:45 a.m., slightly behind schedule. But we were on our way.

Luis Alvarez: Under the blackout conditions after the briefing, I went with Bob Serber to the equipment room to pick up his flight gear, delivered him to his plane, shook our several friends' hands, and wished them a good trip over the empire. Harold Agnew and I watched the planes take off from a hill south of the field, where I managed to give myself a thorough fright imagining I heard Japanese soldiers—some were still at large on the island—stalking us through the sugar cane. Back at the 509th area I stopped at my tent to find a dejected Bob Serber sitting on the stoop. There had been a parachute check at the end of the runway, Bob said, before his plane took off. He discovered he had picked up an extra life raft instead of a parachute, and the pilot had ordered him out—although Bob and his Fastax camera had been the only reason this third plane was flying. That snafu proved to be prophetic of the Nagasaki mission, as abominably run a raid as any in the history of strategic warfare. Everyone connected with it must have been horrified by its confusion.

* * *

2nd Lt. Fred J. Olivi: It was about 4:00 a.m. that Commander Ashworth opened the small hatch to the bomb bay and crawled inside. I recall that he was in the bomb bay about 15 or 20 minutes. Lieutenant Barnes stood by, but poked his head inside several times to talk with Ashworth. I asked Barnes what they were doing and Barnes replied they were changing the "green plugs to red" before the B-29 was pressurized. I wondered aloud if this meant that Fat Man was now set to explode, and I recall either Ashworth or Barnes replied, "Yes, if it goes below 5,000 feet, it'll detonate."

Lt. Jacob Beser: The weather en route to Japan was somewhat worse than forecast, although expected to clear by the time we reached our target area. We reached our rendezvous at 0900.

Maj. Charles W. Sweeney: Yakushima was visible through breaks in the clouds. We had been flying for almost five hours through bad weather in complete radio silence. Within moments, Fred Bock appeared on my right wing. A few minutes passed, but there was no sign of Hopkins.

Lt. Jacob Beser: Yet to arrive was Major James Hopkins in V-90.

Maj. Charles W. Sweeney: My orders were to wait fifteen minutes and then leave for the target, but the mission brief also called for three airplanes to proceed to target. The photographic airplane was vital to fulfill the mission plan. I decided to give Hopkins a little more time.

William L. Laurence: We kept on circling, waiting for the third ship in our formation.

Cmdr. Frederick L. Ashworth: It doesn't take much imagination to see that there was something definitely wrong here. We were using up precious fuel and after all the facts were in, it was clear that this nearly caused us to lose the mission.

Sgt. Raymond Gallagher: At a quarter to ten, because of our gas situation and waiting around for forty-five minutes, the pilot tipped his wing, which indicated to the ship on our right that we are going to head on in.

Lt. Jacob Beser: The weather reports had been received from Charles McKnight and George Marquardt and were about the same for both Kokura and Nagasaki. Since the Industrial Center at Kokura was briefed as our Primary Target, we proceeded there.

Maj. Charles W. Sweeney: Also unknown to me until after my return to Tinian was that when Hopkins failed to make the rendezvous and couldn't find us, for some inexplicable reason he broke radio silence and radioed back to Tinian: "Has Sweeney aborted?" The message got garbled in transmission and was received on Tinian as "Sweeney aborted." This inexcusable break in procedure not only could have given away our position to the Japanese, it also panicked the command on Tinian about the status of the mission. A consequence of Hopkins's transmission was that the air-sea rescue operation intended to pluck us out of the ocean if necessary was canceled. If we had to ditch in the ocean, no one would be there to pick us up.

Walter Goodman, ***engineer, Special Engineer Detachment***: Something that stays with me—that I still remember so clearly—for anyone who has any thought that we did something wrong or that another alternative was available to us, as we're crossing the ocean to Japan, [we] could look down on the sea around Japan and see the extent of our preparation for landing. It was breathtaking. As far as you can see in every direction were ships. I didn't think there were that many ships in the whole world. There were aircraft carriers, and battleships, and cargo vessels, and troop vessels. From that altitude, it looked so dense that you could probably walk from one ship to another without getting your feet wet. If this was going to be the intent or the difference between using the weapon and not using the weapon, there wasn't any question.

* * *

Lt. Jacob Beser: When we arrived in the target area, it was obvious that visual bombing was going to be a problem. Yawata, the steel industry center for Japan, had been fire bombed the night before and was still burning. Situated a few miles west of Kokura, it was sending smoke and haze over our target.

Capt. Kermit B. Beahan, ***bombardier, Crew C-15,*** **Bockscar,** ***393rd Bombardment Squadron***: Kokura, site of the largest arsenal in Japan, was completely obscured by clouds and industrial haze. We had strict orders the bomb must be released visually—that is the Bombardier must be able to sight the target through his bombsight.

2nd Lt. Fred J. Olivi: As we got into our first run, bomb bay doors open, Bombardier Kermit Beahan kept muttering about not being able to see the ground.

Sgt. Raymond Gallagher: Beahan opened the bomb bay doors. The ship on the right, who had the scientists, they immediately opened their bomb bay doors. Their jobs were to drop three instruments into the blast, which would come off of the bomb, which we would drop on Kokura.

Lt. Jacob Beser: We heard Kermit say "no drop." He could not get a clear sight of his briefed aiming point. We circled the area to try a second run.

Capt. James F. Van Pelt: We went back to our IP and made another run without success in seeing the target.

Lt. Jacob Beser: This time we not only didn't drop, but we were now receiving antiaircraft fire.

Sgt. Raymond Gallagher: We began to get flak from the ground from a town called Urata, which would be similar to our steel mills here in Gary. They have very good gun emplacements by their Navy.

William L. Laurence: We noticed black puffs of smoke coming through the white clouds directly at us.

Maj. Charles W. Sweeney: Tail gunner Pappy Dehart yelled, "Flak! Wide but altitude is perfect."

Lt. Jacob Beser: There was considerable conversation on the flight deck concerning fuel remaining and alternate flight plans. It seemed to me that Chuck and the Flight Engineer had a difference of opinion as to what the alternatives should be.

2nd Lt. Fred J. Olivi: As Sweeney once again began to circle our B-29, there was a great deal of animated conversation in the cockpit area regarding what to do next. Our Flight Engineer, Kuharek, seemed to disagree with what Sweeney was planning, and even Navy Commander Ashworth got into the discussion.

Lt. Jacob Beser: But a cool head prevailed; I heard Fred Ashworth very clearly enunciate what he felt we should be doing and especially not doing. There was no time for lengthy debate.

Capt. Kermit B. Beahan: We made three approaches from different directions hoping to sight the target from a different angle of view.

Cmdr. Frederick L. Ashworth: Again no success. Fifty-five minutes of precious fuel had been expended.

Maj. Charles W. Sweeney: Kuharek reported that our fuel situation was very critical. We had enough to get to our secondary target, Nagasaki, and make one run. But we wouldn't make it back to Okinawa, the closest American base. We would fall short by about fifty miles.

2nd Lt. Fred J. Olivi: The hour we spent over Kokuru, trying to drop Fat Man, seemed to last an eternity.

Maj. Charles W. Sweeney: I again banked sharply to set us on a southerly direction toward our secondary target. The quick maneuver caught Fred Bock by surprise. By the time I'd completed my turn, he was on my left wing. Not seeing *The Great Artiste* on my right, I asked, "Where's Bock?" Unknown to me, my elbow had hit the selector button, changing the intercom function to the transmit command function, sending my words spilling out over the empire. To my disbelief, Hopkins, somewhere out there, replied excitedly, "Chuck? Is that you, Chuck? Where the hell are you?" I don't know whether I was more upset by my carelessness or at hearing from the long-lost Major Hopkins. *What did he want me to do, broadcast my position?* I flipped the selector back to intercom, bit my lip, regained my composure, and calmly directed our navigator, "Jim, give me the heading for Nagasaki."

William L. Laurence: On we went to Nagasaki, a prayer in everyone's heart for a change in luck. Our radar soon told us we were approaching the city and the nearer we came, the greater grew our dejection. Like my friend Luis Alvarez, I had an Adjutant Generals Office (AGO) card on my person specifying it was valid only if captured by the enemy and informing the enemy I was entitled to the privileges of a colonel. I said to myself, any minute now, you may become a colonel.

* * *

Capt. Kermit B. Beahan: Fuel supply was now becoming a matter of concern. We proceeded to take a direct course to the secondary target, Nagasaki.

Maj. Charles W. Sweeney: I was now an hour and a half behind schedule. Turning to Don Albury, I said, "Can any other goddamned thing go wrong?"

Lawrence H. Johnston: We approached Nagasaki by the shortest path from Kokura and not along the planned bombing approach. We again prepared our instruments in *The Great Artiste*.

Maj. Charles W. Sweeney: I couldn't believe my eyes. Nagasaki was obscured by 80 to 90 percent cumulus clouds at 6,000 to 8,000 feet. A visual drop was improbable. We were approaching from the northwest and would arrive at the initial point in a few minutes. Kuharek confirmed again—we had enough fuel for a single bomb run. I called Commander Ashworth forward and laid out the situation. He was in charge of the bomb; I was in command of the aircraft. If we didn't drop, we were out of options. If we didn't get a visual on our first run and then depart, we'd have to dump the bomb into the ocean. I summed up quickly, "We haven't got the time or the fuel for more than one run. Let's drop it by radar. I'll guarantee we come within five hundred feet of the target."

Capt. Kermit B. Beahan: The decision was made, if necessary, we would drop the bomb by radar in spite of the edict stipulating visual release only.

Walter Goodman: They made one pass. Again, it was about eight-tenths covered.

Maj. Charles W. Sweeney: From the IP, Van Pelt and Buckley started to coordinate the approach to the aiming point. The outline of the city appeared on the scopes in front of Van Pelt and Buckley. Buckley called out headings and precise closure rates to Beahan, who fed the data into the bombsight, all the while hoping for a break in the clouds.

William L. Laurence: It was 12:01.

Capt. Kermit B. Beahan: We proceeded on the bomb run under radar control until about twenty to thirty seconds from bomb release when I saw a hole developing in the clouds over the target area. I took control of the aircraft and selected an aiming point in the Nagasaki industrial valley. Fortunately, the radar team had made an excellent initial bomb approach and in the very brief time remaining, I was able to synchronize the cross-hairs of the bombsight on the target and released the bomb visually with good results being achieved. It was as if a great weight had been lifted from our shoulders since we did succeed in following the order "visual drop only!"

Cmdr. Frederick L. Ashworth: Captain Beahan, the bombardier, was under fantastic pressure. It was imperative that we drop the bomb on the first approach.

Lt. Jacob Beser: The last fifteen seconds over Nagasaki I heard the bombardier say, "I've got a hole, I've got it."

Luis Alvarez: Ostensibly a hole opened in the 80 percent cloud covered target in the last moments of the run. I've always taken this hole in the clouds with a grain of salt, since Beahan, one of the best bombardiers in the Air Force, missed his target by two miles, a reasonable radar error in those days.

Lawrence H. Johnston: We heard the tone start which meant we were on a bombing run and we opened our bomb bay doors. The tone stopped, the bomb had been dropped and so had our parachute gauges.

2nd Lt. Fred J. Olivi: Beahan shouted in his Texas drawl, "Bombs away! Uh—that's *bomb* away." *Bockscar* suddenly leaped upwards as the 10,000-pound Fat Man dropped away.*

Maj. Charles W. Sweeney: Time seemed suspended.

* It took some time for *Bockscar* to claim its rightful place in history. The *Times'* Laurence, who didn't know about the last-minute aircraft swap between Sweeney and Fred Bock, assumed that since he was flying on the observer plane with Bock, that the bomb plane was *The Great Artiste*, a mistake he repeated both in his original dispatches as well as in his book a year later.

Lawrence H. Johnston: We saw the white flash come in through our window. *My detonators must have worked again!*

2nd Lt. Fred J. Olivi: The light of a thousand suns illuminated the cockpit. Even with my dark welders' goggles, I winced and shut my eyes for a couple of seconds.

Capt. James F. Van Pelt: We saw a purplish, white, brilliant flash the scientists claim is nine times greater that the intensity of the sun.

2nd Lt. Fred J. Olivi: A few seconds later, *Bockscar* was buffeted by three sharp shock waves, the first hit with far more force than the last. We had been told to expect shock waves. I felt three. The first one was quite severe, and the aircraft shook violently. For a moment I wondered if any damage had been done to our B-29. Thankfully it just gave us a real jolt, and all we could do at the time was to look at each other and hope there would be no structural damage to the aircraft. Neither of the next two shock waves were as violent as the first, they just shook us up a bit.

Cmdr. Frederick L. Ashworth: The evidence of these shock waves was more one of noise than anything else. I have always characterized it as if someone had struck an empty metal trash can with a baseball bat. There was a minor movement of the plane, no worse than a sharp bump frequently experienced when flying in a commercial aircraft in clear air turbulence.

Capt. Frederick C. Bock: We observed the boiling mass rise up. Our tail gunner, Robert Stock, took many photos as well as a movie. Within two minutes, the cloud was beyond our altitude of 30,000 feet. In three to four minutes, it was beyond 50,000 feet.

William L. Laurence: It was no longer smoke, or dust, or even a cloud of fire. It was a living thing.

Luis Alvarez: Fat Man exploded above a narrower stretch of the Urakami River valley than it had been targeted for; its yield was twenty-two kilotons, but it caused less damage than Little Boy, though damage enough to serve its grim purpose. The Mitsubishi factory almost directly below the point of explosion had made the torpedoes that devastated Pearl Harbor.

Sgt. Abe Spitzer, ***radio operator,*** **Bockscar:** For a second was time suspended for them below as it was for us above them? What were those tens of thousands of people doing when they died? I did a lifetime of wondering in that fragment of a moment when we waited for the blast. And I've wondered since.

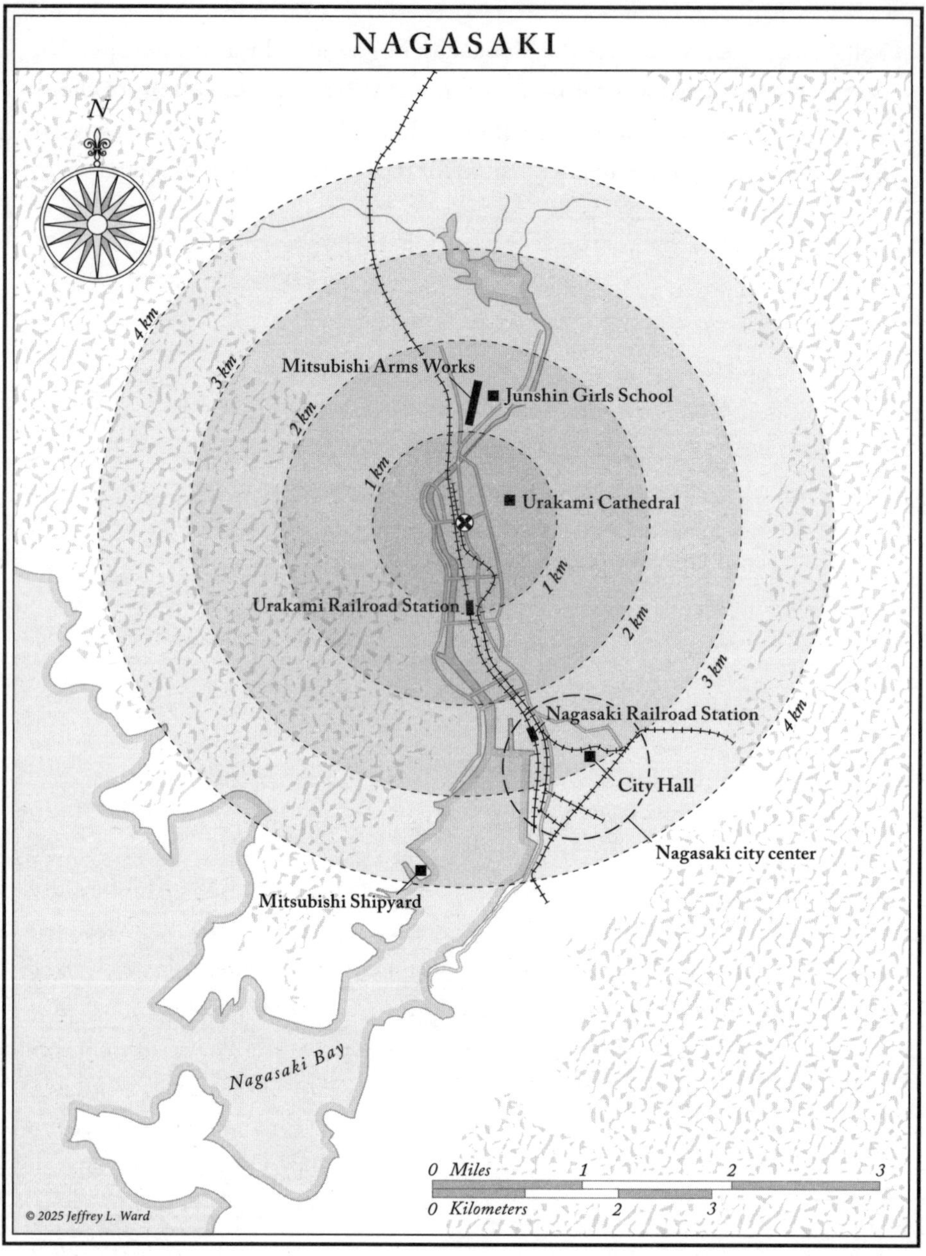
NAGASAKI
N
4 km
3 km
2 km
1 km
Mitsubishi Arms Works
Junshin Girls School
Urakami Cathedral
Urakami Railroad Station
Nagasaki Railroad Station
City Hall
Nagasaki city center
Mitsubishi Shipyard
Nagasaki Bay
0 Miles 1 2 3
0 Kilometers 2 3
© 2025 Jeffrey L. Ward

"Nothing else I could do"

GROUND ZERO AT NAGASAKI

Survivors walk amid the rubble of Nagasaki.

The port city of Nagasaki—on Kyushu, the southernmost of Japan's four main islands—was founded by the Portuguese in the 1500s and used for three centuries as the sole trading exchange between Europeans and the isolationist empire during what was known as the Sakoku system. That rich, romanticized interchange of cultures is what led Puccini to set his opera Madama Butterfly *in Nagasaki. The region had deep ties to the Jesuits, who were a key part of the Portuguese trade, and, as such, contained the largest population of Christians anywhere in Japan and was historically considered the most Western of Japanese cities. Following the forced reopening of Japan by US Navy Commander Matthew Perry in the 1850s, Nagasaki grew into a major industrial city and naval hub. By 1945, Mitsubishi Heavy Industries accounted for the majority of the city's employment, with thousands of workers in its sprawling network of shipyards, steel, and armaments plants.*

Its population in August 1945 was about 260,000, including large numbers of conscripted Korean workers and about 400 Allied POWs. The city, like Hiroshima, had largely escaped US bombing except for a handful of raids that had targeted the naval shipyards.

The bomb's hypocenter was in the northern end of the city, a few hundred yards from the Cathedral of Our Lady of the Immaculate Conception, known as Urakami Church, the largest Roman Catholic cathedral in Asia. About 35,000 were killed in the initial blast. Final casualty estimates range from 60,000 to 90,000 killed.

Dr. Tatsuichiro Akizuki: On Thursday, 9 August, the boundless blue sky, the loud shrilling of cicadas, promised another day as hot and as sultry as the day before.

Dr. Masao Shiotsuki: I was stationed nineteen kilometers away from the hypocenter at Omura Naval Hospital. I was twenty-five years old at the time and had been posted to Omura exactly one month earlier, on July 9, as a doctor in training fresh out of Navy Medical School. Omura Naval Hospital (or Omura National Hospital, as it is now called) in those days had an inpatient capacity of 2,000 and boasted some of the finest facilities and equipment in the navy. I will never forget how bright it was. The windows of the consulting room were wide open, and it was a hot midsummer day. The sky was clear and bright as it often is in Kyushu, especially by the sea, when suddenly an even brighter, more dazzling light flooded in on us. The strangeness of this light was enough to make anyone afraid, and both the director of the Navy Medical School and the director of the hospital seemed half-paralyzed with fear.

Dr. Tatsuichiro Akizuki: And the next moment—*Bang! Crack!* A huge impact, like a gigantic blow smote down upon our bodies, our heads, and our hospital. I lay flat—I didn't know whether or not of my own volition. Then down came piles of debris, slamming into my back. *The hospital has been hit*, I thought. I grew dizzy, and my ears sang. Some minutes or so must have passed before I staggered to my feet and looked around. The air was heavy with yellow smoke; white flakes of powder drifted about; it was strangely dark.

Taeko King, *age 15*: When the bomb hit Nagasaki, I was a fourth-year student at the prefectural Nagasaki Girls' High School. Under the so-called wartime student mobilization program, I was dispatched to the Mitsubishi Arms Factory in Morimachi. When I was working on the second floor, I saw a flash light. I then felt severe pain on all of my body as if I had been stuck by a thousand threads. After a while, I came to myself and found me under the collapsed factory building. I managed to creep out of the debris, pulled out a friend lying nearby, and left there in a hurry with her. I took her to her home in Inasa. After I left here there, I then began going to Shiroyama, where my home was. As I suffered burns in my face and the skin around my eyes sagged, my view was much limited. I went forward to the direction of my home as if creeping. When I managed to return to my home, which was located below the Shi-royama Primary School, all area around the house was burnt down. Or, I'd say, it looked gray all over—there was nothing there.

Etsuko Nagano, *age 16*: At around eleven o'clock on the morning of August 9, we saw a flash and it became dark a split second later. We heard tin roofs and roofing tiles fly through the air outside. The windows of the gym were blown out with the blast, and clouds of dust came in. I covered my eyes and ears with my hands, but I felt dust in my mouth. I lay down on the floor. The blast was so strong I couldn't open my eyes. After a while I fled to an air raid shelter nearby. I stayed there for a few hours, and then a factory worker came to me and asked if I was from the Urakami district. He heard that the whole town was destroyed, so I should go check on my family. The factory that I was working in at that time was behind some hills, so we didn't have such severe damage there. I hurried to check on my family who were all much closer to the explosion.

When I got to Nagasaki train station, I could look out over the neighborhood, and I saw scorched fields, burnt-out ruins, debris everywhere. All the buildings and houses were burned down or destroyed. I couldn't walk straight to my house, so I decided to follow a railroad track to get home. I walked about a mile following the railroad track, and then I came to a point where I should make a right turn. My house was ten minutes away. But there was no way to go there because the streets were covered with debris.

Dr. Tatsuichiro Akizuki: Near the center of the city, I was confronted immediately after the blast with a horrible sight: people with their skulls cracked open by the blast, children with their stomach walls torn open leaving their intestines exposed, and others covered with blood after being pierced all over their bodies with fragments of glass and splinters of wood driven into them by the force of the bomb's explosion. These and others like them had managed to totter and crawl to the yard of our sanatorium, only to collapse there. The glass and wood fragments had been blown deep into their bodies, even penetrating their internal organs. Some had fallen under collapsing homes or walls and been burned black underneath the flaming rubble; even those who somehow managed to escape burning to death under roof tiles or other materials and had escaped from the inferno suffered broken bones and spinal contusions and were unable to walk. Some had their limbs severed in the blast or the destruction that followed. There was nothing we could do for any of them.

The Nagasaki Medical College Hospital, the major medical facility in the area, was located only 600 meters from the hypocenter and had collapsed, producing a great number of casualties. As a result, no treatment was available to most of the atomic bomb victims. Relief squads arrived in the city from other parts of the prefecture and other prefectures, and they set up temporary headquarters in elementary schools throughout the city that had escaped destruction. Though they did their best to offer treatment to the victims, they were overwhelmed by the number of patients and the severity of their injuries.

Hideo Matsuno, *reporter*: I remember a house where the sole survivor was a child who was watching the dead bodies of his parents and crying. The child was holding a rice ball given by a passerby—the grains of rice stuck to his hand really made an impression on me. I wonder what happened to that poor kid.

Etsuko Nagano: Humans and animals were dead, everywhere. Many people roamed the streets, some of them had skin hanging down in shreds from the burns. I saw a man whose skin was hanging from his fingers, and he was lifting his arms out in front of him so that it was less painful. My father and I were probably the only people there who were not harmed. I also saw some people whose eyes had popped out. People had burns all over. People roaming on the streets staggered towards us and said, "please give us some water, please help us," but I didn't have a canteen or anything with me, so we couldn't help them. They were dying right in front of me. I saw thirty or forty people die on the spot.

Hideo Matsuno: The rescue train came in that same day, and when they blew the whistle people who looked as if they were dead—these were people who weren't moving at all, I don't know where they found the energy to go—but they all got up and made it down to the train. When we were getting on to the train people helped us by lifting our elbows but the handrail was greasy with blood and oil. My sister distinctly remembers wiping her hands on the seats to get it off.

Dr. Masao Shiotsuki: The relief mission led by Lt. Jinnai loaded drugs and medical supplies onto a navy bus and drove out the hospital gates.

Yasumasa Iyonaga, *chief orderly, Omura Naval Hospital*: As the relief squad bus drew closer and closer to Nagasaki, an indescribably horrible spectacle began to unfold before our eyes. The trees that remained were only bare branches; though it was midsummer, the landscape looked like a mountainside in winter. Those buildings still standing had all tumbled over to one side, but as we approached the center of the explosion, they had been pressed down from above and crushed completely out of shape. Reinforced concrete buildings had collapsed as though they were paper boxes.

Everywhere one looked were bare trees, piles of debris, and splinters of wood—the landscape of hell. The area had met with a truly formidable bombardment, that was obvious. I do not know how many dead bodies we saw along the way. Most of them were charred black, almost carbonized. We repeatedly encountered long lines of people fleeing the city. Their clothes were in rags and had turned completely black as though painted with coal tar, and their hair had burned off so it was difficult to tell the men from the women. I do not know whether they were searching for aid stations or looking for water, but they all plodded wearily forward. They did not hold their arms by their sides but let them dangle in front of them, like ghosts. None of them said a word.

Akira Nagasaka, *age 16*: All the trees on the hillside had been uprooted and were lying flat on the ground facing in the same direction. I picked my way through the fallen trees in a daze. A woman, probably in her mid-thirties, was lying on the ground, her hair wild, her clothes in tatters, her face red with blood. She was putting all the strength that remained in her to raise her head and murmur, "Water, water." I scooped some dirty water out of a nearby ditch and gave it to her. She drank it as if it were the most delicious thing ever to pass her lips, but most of it merely trickled down her chin onto her breast. "More, please," she begged, but she could do no more than gasp for breath when I brought it, having no strength left to drink. A few moments passed in silence. Then she looked up at me and asked me to take her home. I did not know what to do. I desperately wanted to find my mother. I did not see how I could cope with an unknown woman on my back. I spun around and ran away. As I fled, I told myself that there was nothing else I could do.

* * *

Through terrible acts of fate, luck, and chance, several hundred people—the exact figure is lost to history—who had been present in Hiroshima on August 6 fled or traveled to Nagasaki and were there when Bockscar *arrived in the sky around 11 a.m. on August 9. About 300 of them are believed to have journeyed to Nagasaki on two trains from Hiroshima on August 6. Many of those 300 died in the subsequent bombing, but there were about 160 people ultimately survived both bombings. In Japan, they came to be known as "Niju hibakusha"—twice-bomb-affected people. Tsutomu Yamaguchi, a 29-year-old engineer for Mitsubishi, is the only person who was officially recognized by the Japanese government as surviving both the Hiroshima and Nagasaki atomic bombings; the Nagasaki resident had been working in the Mitsubishi shipyards during the summer of 1945 with two colleagues from Nagasaki, Kuniyoshi Sato and Akira Iwanaga. Kenshi Hirata, the recently married and now widowed accountant, had arrived back in the city only the day before.*

Yamaguchi had been treated on August 8 at the company hospital for his burned face.

Tsutomu Yamaguchi: By chance I met an eye specialist who had been my senior at school. At first he didn't recognize me. I told him I had been injured at Hiroshima by some special type of bomb. He looked at my burned face and arm, and took me at once to his operating room. There he began to cut away all the burned skin with scissors. It was a slow job, because we had to stop and go to the air-raid shelter three times while he was trying to treat me. This doctor, whose name was Sato, was the first to treat an atomic bomb victim in Nagasaki, although he didn't know it at the time. When the burned skin was all removed, the flesh below was a bright, raw red—"like whale meat," Dr. Sato said. He fixed up the wounds with oils, and bandaged them, and I went home, not dreaming that the next day I was going to be an atomic bomb victim again!

[When I saw my mother that day,] for a moment, she thought I was a ghost, with my face hidden by the bandages and my feet under me. In Japan, ghosts do not have feet. She didn't dare come in the room, but finally asked me timidly, "Have you got feet?" I showed her my feet, to reassure her that I was alive and not just the ghost of her son, before she would come in. My family knew about what had happened to Hiroshima. They said there had been an announcement on the radio that Hiroshima had suffered heavily from a new type of bomb. My mother and father thought I must surely be dead, when they heard this, since I had sent them a telegram very early on the sixth, before the bomb fell, saying I would be home the next day. When I didn't appear, there was a great family discussion. Mother said someone should go to Hiroshima and recover my ashes. But my father argued, how could my ashes be recovered when no one knew just where I was? And then I appeared, looking like a ghost.

The next morning, promptly, Yamaguchi appeared back at work at Mitsubishi in Nagasaki. He, and many of the other soon-to-be "Niju hibakusha" faced disbelief from people in Nagasaki when they recounted the horror they'd seen in Hiroshima.

Tsutomu Yamaguchi: I reported to the director who had sent me to Hiroshima and he asked me what was going on there. I said that I didn't know what kind of bomb it was but that a single one had destroyed the entire city. I told him that I had come back with Iwanaga, but that I failed to come back with Sato, although I knew he was alive. Well, the director was angry. He reproached me for losing Sato. He said: "A single bomb can't destroy a whole city! You've obviously been badly injured, and I think you've gone a little mad." At that moment, outside the window, I saw another flash and the whole office, everything in it, was blown over. We were both on the ground. The director was shouting, "Help me! Help me!" I realised at once what had happened, that it was the same thing as in Hiroshima. But I was so angry with the director. I climbed out of the window and got away because I had to help myself.

Kuniyoshi Sato: People were asking me what happened in Hiroshima, because they had heard rumours. I was just explaining when I saw the flash of light. Instinctively I knew what was happening, so I jumped immediately into the water.

Kenshi Hirata: On the way to my wife's home with her bones under my arm, that golden-color ray whose memory was so vivid in my brains flashed in front of my eyes for the second time. I shouted to my aged father at the top of my voice: "This is the very flash!" Unconsciously, I shouted again to him, "Lie face downward!" In the immediate moment I was expecting that terrific explosion blast and roar. However, they were not so terrible as those in Hiroshima. I later learned that the spread of the explosive blast was checked by Konpira Hill, and that the districts on the side of the hill where my father and I were then did not suffer the most serious damage. But in two or three minutes, I saw people running out of their houses, holding their hands over injuries on their heads, faces and bodies. Most of these were wounds caused by flying pieces of glass.

When I reached the home of my wife, the house was in confusion. The floor had fallen in, the ceiling was down, and all the paper-covered sliding doors. It was not difficult for me to imagine the misery in those districts, hit by the bomb. The same tragedy and distress that I had seen in Hiroshima was now being repeated in Nagasaki, my home. I wished fervently that I would never see such sights again.

Tsutomu Yamaguchi: On August 9, the devil's column of fire stood even taller than before, as if mocking me with laughter because I thought I had escaped with my life from Hiroshima to Nagasaki. I felt as though it were a sentient beast that had literally chased me down.

Tsuitaro Doi: During the afternoon, wild rumors spread throughout Nagasaki that the city was marked for a second attack by the same type of bomb. Since about half the city was left unburned, I was inclined to believe these rumors, so I decided to evacuate my family immediately. Toward evening, carrying only what rice we could get, we started on foot for a fishing village about five miles out of town, where I thought we would be safe. The road to the village passed directly through the bomb center, hence was blocked by fire, so we had to take a long route over the mountains and didn't reach the village until two or three o'clock the next morning.

Takejiro Nishioka: There was a striking difference between the official accounts of Hiroshima and Nagasaki. In the case of Hiroshima, details on the effect of the bomb were made public immediately, perhaps by the prefectural authorities. But in the case of Nagasaki, the first announcement said merely that there had been "an attack by a new-type bomb, and the damage was slight." The details of the effect on Nagasaki were made public in many stages. First, it was "slight." Then there had been "some injuries." Casualties were placed first at 100, then 500, and so on, so that it took the country some time to get the picture. That is the reason why an impression has been created abroad that Nagasaki suffered little damage from the atomic bomb. But when Hiroshima was hit, word of serious damage spread all over the world without delay.

Tsutomu Yamaguchi: I believe that I had some idea that all my relatives and family must have perished in the blast, for my house was within a mile and a half of the explosion center.

* * *

The atomic bomb exploded just about a mile from Branch 14 of the Fukuoka Prisoner of War Camp, located in Saiwai-machi, which held about 200 to 300 Dutch, Indonesian, Australian, British, and other Allied prisoners who were forced to work at the Mitsubishi shipyard and other facilities. That, combined with other local prisoner of war camps—including Fukuoka Camp No. 11 about four miles away from the hypocenter—meant hundreds of Allied prisoners got what one called a "ringside view" of the bombing; nearly a dozen POWs would perish in the blasts.

Charles Barkie, *Dutch soldier, captured in Java in 1942*: On the fateful morning of August 9, alongside nine other captives, I had to do a special job for the Japanese. The rice warehouse, which later avoided destruction from the bombing, stored all the rice in straw bags weighing 100 kilograms each. This warehouse was a hole underground, which prevented it from catching on fire, and it was made with a firm, thick beam, and resembled a short Greek shrine. Our job was to put soil in a basket, bring it to the warehouse, and put it on the roof. We worked busily for many days, until the warehouse was almost completely hidden beneath a mound of soil. This was fast, sloppy work, and the Japanese let us work continuously for twelve hours; we even worked during the air-raid alarms.

At 10:45 a.m., an air-raid alarm sounded. Outside, we calmly continued working at a slow pace. Everybody said to one another, "I heard the sound of the airplane." With soil in my basket, I headed towards the rice warehouse. I wore shorts, an overcoat, and a hat atop my head. At 11:00, hell began.

Peter McGrath-Kerr, *Australian POW*: I was with a work party of six men repairing a bridge, over the Mifune canal, which had been blown up in an air-raid on 1 August. About 10 a.m., the soldier guarding us took us back to camp for a rest, although normally we would have worked on for a few more hours. About 11 a.m. I was lying on my bunk, reading a book. Three others—Miller, Prendergast and Jobling—were in the room. We heard a plane approaching but since there was no air alarm, took no notice. From here on I remember nothing until five days later after I was rescued from beneath the wreckage of our living quarters. The first thing I remember was waking up lying on a stretcher and seeing that everything in sight was flattened.

Charles Barkie: Suddenly, we were surrounded by a sea of flames. Because the golden flames which flared up were so scathing, everything it hit disappeared. The things around me lost their shapes and shadows. After the flash, the flames flared up and glared furiously down at everything. Everything happened with an ominous groan. The heat was terrible, and I felt dizzy and nauseous. I thought that I was only two or three meters away from the entrance of the warehouse and staggered to its entrance. Vibrations surrounded me and the sound hit me, almost tearing my ears apart. I lost all of my energy and felt that I might really die. Everything became dark. I don't know how long I was unconscious.

Jurgen Onken: After that, was darkness—darkness that was deeper than the night. It became harder and harder to breathe. The heavy crashing sound of collapsing buildings and the sound of splitting building beams echoed all around.

Jack Johnson: Then came the blast with a deafening bang and I felt as though I had been kicked in the guts. I found myself gasping for breath, pinned under a lot of rubble and unable to see. The world was black. Very gradually the dust started to thin out and I was able to wriggle from under the beams that had me pinned down.

Joseph Valencourt, *POW from Lawrence, Massachusetts*: After the atomic bomb I saw a cloud lit up like a sunset over Nagasaki.

Warrant Officer James MacIntosh, *POW from Invercargill, New Zealand*: It started as a white puff of smoke, swelling and growing to a mushroom shape, and suddenly lit up inside. It was terrifying, as if clouds had caught fire.

Sgt. Norman Jones, *POW from Hartlepool, England*: A huge white cloud, intermingled with orange flame spurting in all directions. I felt completely dumbfounded.

Cpl. Gerald Wilson, *POW from Clovis, New Mexico*: The atomic bomb cloud looked like a giant thunderhead. It kept boiling, getting larger.

Warrant Officer Eddie Kuhn, POW from *Wellington, New Zealand*: After a few minutes it became completely red-tinged, as if reflecting some huge city fire on the ground below. I was bewildered at this new horror.

Cpl. Richard Burke, *POW from Chicago, Illinois*: The atomic bomb cloud seemed to me like the dying embers of a sunset, but all in one spot.

Capt. Douglas Wilkie, *POW from Fairlight, England*: It seemed like a huge, ever-swelling mushroom-shaped whiteish cloud, with a glowing center and stem reaching to the earth. I was queerly uneasy and very puzzled, and thought it was perhaps a new type of incendiary bomb.

Lt. William Miller, *POW from Glasgow, Scotland*: The bomb appeared like a growing ball of white smoke, with a red ball inside, giving me an impression of vague terror as an unaccountable phenomenon.

Warrant Officer Richard Ranger, *POW from Auckland, New Zealand*: It gradually grew larger, with sheet lightning in the middle.

Staff Sgt. George Duke, ***POW from Lahore, India*****:** After a flash, white smoke expanded to the shape of an enormous parachute with an orange glow in the center. It gave me an empty feeling in the pit of my stomach.

Pvt. Thomas Jones, ***POW from Newport, Wales*****:** Following the explosion I saw a beautiful pure white cloud, which changed to red inside and commenced expanding. I thought it was a bomb raining red hot stuff down like a volcano.

Vernon Benjamin, ***POW from Natte Yallock, Australia*****:** Glowing clouds of smoke billowing up like a huge volcanic eruption.

J. H. C. DeGroot: The moment when the atomic-bomb exploded, I was sleeping in the upper part of a bunk bed. So I fell from the bed and had my left leg caught in between beds. Then I could not budge from there. For a little while I lost consciousness. If it was thirty seconds, a minute, or two minutes nobody knows. I do not think it was such a long time. When I became conscious, somebody was shouting.

Charles Barkie: I regained consciousness and became clear-headed again a little later. I felt my fingers trembling against the stones. I thought, "I'm not dead," and opened my eyes after a while. The area was pitch-black. I couldn't see anything at all. I thought I had lost my eyesight, and was taken by despair. However, fortunately, I didn't become blind. The darkness gradually faded away. I was going to stand up, but couldn't. My shoulders were badly injured, and my arms seemed to be dislocated at the elbows. Two or three of my friends were gathered together. One of them that was bulkier than the others called out for his mother while crying.

Jurgen Onken: Then there was silence; the silence of death. We were buried alive under the rubble of the city of Nagasaki. It was as if someone had trampled on an ant's nest with their foot. The air was getting thicker. As I breathed, my chest and throat hurt badly. I couldn't think at all. I just kept feeling myself struggling more and more to breathe. Instinctively, I tried to crawl out from the rubble. Finally, I was able to breathe easily again.

Richard Downie: As the dust settled, we could see further and you could not imagine what had caused such destruction. Looking back towards the industrial area, there was nothing still standing—an area of ½ to ¾ mile radius absolutely flattened. As far as you could see the place was burning.

Charles Barkie: I looked everywhere, but the town had vanished. Everything was flat and had collapsed. A fire had already begun to blaze in various places. One young Japanese factory girl cried hysterically and embraced me. What had actually just happened? Had there been a natural disaster? Could all this possibly have been the result of an unknown new weapon? Everything caught fire and hindered our search, which became virtually impossible later. Our Dutch Captain, Commander Alders, suffered a serious wound and, amid mountains of debris, fell to the ground. Because of this, he died a few days later. We had begun to pull some dead people from a pile of debris. Together, we carried a dead person and an injured person to safety, away from the dangerous fires. There were thirty-five severely wounded people in all. Ten of these people were in serious condition. The fire consumed everything and was very dangerous.

J. H. C. DeGroot: Besides Captain Alders, eight more people died; 192 people survived.

Jack Johnson: After emerging from beneath the debris, I joined some others of our group to search along the section we had occupied and there I found Peter McGrath-Kerr buried under a lot of fallen timber. He had been knocked out and apparently concussed. We freed him and took him to a clear area where a Dutch medical orderly was attending to some others who had been injured. We left him there and continued to search through the ruins until it seemed that further searching was useless. Small fires were starting in the area and everyone in sight was heading towards the hills.

Charles Barkie: Finally, the time came when we had no choice but to escape. Having a hard time, we advanced slowly and saw what had happened to people along the way. There were dead people in addition to people who'd been injured and burnt a crisp shade of black. People were dying everywhere. We followed one steep, rocky pathway alongside the edge of the valley.

J. H. C. DeGroot: We went across roads and the railroad, and crossed a bridge. Then we ran away towards Mount Konpira.

Charles Barkie: We climbed to the top while panting and drenched in sweat. Because the injured people had to be carried to the top, it took a long time and was difficult. The plants on the slope's field died due to severe heat and had already become a yellowish-brown. The houses built along the hillside had all been flattened. We looked, and there were victims there as well. We arrived at a cool clump of bamboo, where we were able to take refuge, and decided to sleep there.

Jurgen Onken: The city had disappeared. As far as I could see around me, there were only vast ruins of former towns. The hill that used to be covered with pine trees was barren. The shipyard, the harbor, a munitions factory, everything had been destroyed to death. The metal electric poles (for the train) were twisted and bent by the extreme heat. I was flabbergasted. I don't remember how long I stood there. I began to panic and screamed out of sheer terror.

Charles Barkie: We overlooked the city district from our position. The fire had not yet subsided. The reason is because most of the buildings in Nagasaki were made of wood. I thought about Nero. He'd set fire to Rome and burned it. I looked down at the now-burning city of Nagasaki and couldn't deny that I felt it was a beautiful scene. I truly felt that way. At last, I'd been freed from my life of servitude after falling into enemy hands almost four years prior. Unfortunately, it was too late for some of the injured people. They died on the verge of liberation.

Jurgen Onken: Other friends looked for food. It was a very smart thing to look for food and we were more than lucky to be able to find some. For the next several days, we had to catch and eat small birds or seagulls to survive. We could catch them easily because their wings were burnt and they couldn't fly.

* * *

In both Hiroshima and Nagasaki, thousands of Koreans had been brought from occupied Korea as conscripts or forced laborers. Like the POWs, their own misery and injury amid the destruction was mixed with joy that the war might be coming to an end—and that Japan was losing.

Kisang Lee, *age 29*: At that time, there were five or six thousand Koreans housed in temporary bunkhouses in Nagasaki city alone, including those taken from Korea by force and those drafted in Japan like myself. The barracks had no mats or rugs on the wooden floor. At night, all we could do was wrap ourselves in a ragged blanket and sleep crowded together. Our main job in the workplace was to build roads and air-raid shelters. We were usually supervised by a Japanese army employee in uniform but sometimes we were under the command of a soldier. The staple meal consisted of one third of rice and two thirds of wheat and corn at first, but toward the end of the war, we had to satisfy our hunger by a thin gruel three times a day.

In those days, I often tried some way or other to sneak away from my work because I was getting weaker every day with hunger and hard labor. On August 9, my coworker Han-san and I slipped away from the workplace. We managed to get through the inspection by the gatekeeper at the pier saying that we had to visit our friend in Nagasaki and we could take a boat to Nagasaki. In the city, we were waiting for a streetcar. Then we heard a strange roar of a plane.

Soongil Kim, *age 23*: The B-29 made a very quick U-turn and flew away. I was buried under a heap of rubble and lost consciousness. I woke up after a while, and saw the sky between the broken building materials above me and saw a giant octopus climbing up in the sky, spread out and turn into a big fire ball. I lost consciousness again.

Kisang Lee: No sooner had we run for shelter a few yards toward Oura-machi, we saw a blinding flash of light. "We'll be killed," I shouted and threw myself on the railroad tracks, or so it seemed. For I lost consciousness and couldn't remember exactly what happened. Ten minutes or so later, Han-san was calling my name. Trying to shake me awake, "Lee-san, Lee-san, what's the matter? What's the matter with you?" I came to and sat up on the tracks, to see the whole town wrapped in a cloud of dark red dust and smoke.

Jonghwon Kim, *age 25*: I was drafted as a laborer by the Japanese army and I came to Nagasaki on January 2, 1942. On that day I was digging a cave. Most of the workers were taking rest under a camphor tree in front of the cave. But I wanted to finish my task before lunch, so I went into the interior of the cave. When I took up my hammer and chisel, I felt a white flash and all the light-bulbs in the cave burst. I said "What happened?" The next moment a strong blast came in. By the blast I was thrown against the wall of the cave. I managed to stand up and after a while I went out of the cave. It was very dark and I could hardly breathe due to the lingering dust. With the dust settled, I found all the workers under the tree were blown away and even the camphor tree had been torn out by the roots.

Kisang Lee: We ran away for dear life following other people seeking shelter in the graveyard area on the hillside opposite the station. On the way we saw wounded people lying on the ground in a sea of blood coloring everything red. A massive pine tree had been uprooted and almost all the tombstones had been blown down. About thirty people, who had come to the graveyard, had nothing but their clothes. Their wounds and burns were beyond description. Soon I began to feel severe pain I had not experienced so far. So I cried, "Aigoh, Aigoh, Aigoh!" Then, somehow, the Japanese people around me began to move away from us. I hurried to look closely at myself. One side of my body—from the face under my field-service cap down to the hip—was badly swollen dark red with burns. My arms were double the size it should be. Around seven o'clock in the evening, we were told to move to a first-aid center at Katsuyama Elementary School. We walked staggering to the center a mile away. People seriously wounded were all carried on a stretcher, so we asked the staff to carry us the same way, but they refused and said, "You are young enough to walk." We had to grit our teeth and keep walking.

"'Start firing the flares'"

THE RETURN OF *BOCKSCAR*

The mushroom cloud was visible for hundreds of miles.

With its mission only barely completed, the crew of Bockscar *gritted their teeth as they wondered whether they would make it home after the Nagasaki bombing.*

Maj. Charles W. Sweeney: The mushroom cloud towered above us. Satisfied that we could make a preliminary strike report to Tinian, I told Abe Spitzer to transmit Beahan's report, "Nagasaki bombed. Results good." John Kuharek reported that we had barely 300 gallons of usable fuel left. Not enough to make it to Okinawa, almost 350 miles away. I had already done the math in my head when Kuharek confirmed, "Even if we slow down our rate of consumption, the best we can do is get within seventy-five, maybe fifty, miles of Okinawa."

2nd Lt. Fred J. Olivi: Jim Van Pelt once more turned to his charts and gave Major Chuck Sweeney a course for Okinawa and its Yontan airfield. Sweeney throttled back our B-29 engines and put *Bockscar* on the step, the maneuver we had practiced so many times before at Wendover designed to obtain maximum range using a minimum amount of fuel.

Maj. Charles W. Sweeney: Paul Tibbets had taught me a technique called "flying on the step." If you kept the power settings steady and took the aircraft into a gradual descent, the airplane would pick up a fraction more airspeed without using more power and fuel. The pilot would then level off. To retain that increased airspeed and perhaps even supplement it a bit more, you would start down another step and then another step, and so on. You could milk only a little bit more speed and fly a little farther without consuming more fuel, but that was all I needed—a little bit more. I had the advantage of being at 30,000 feet, so I started my way down the staircase.

Capt. James F. Van Pelt: As we were leaving the coast, the crew took off their flak suits, goggles, parachutes and C-1 vests. I then realized I was thirsty and none of the crew had eaten or drunk anything for hours before arriving on the coast of Japan. The canteens were all very cold from being on the floor. Then the crew went into a relieved, happy, carefree mood, laughing and congratulating everyone else.

Maj. Charles W. Sweeney: I told Spitzer to call for air-sea rescue. Spitzer reported, "Major, I'm getting no response." None of us, of course, knew that after Hopkins's transmission to Tinian, the brass had thought the mission had been aborted. Everyone in the air-sea rescue system resumed normal posture. If we dropped into the ocean, there was no guarantee that anyone would be there to get us.

2nd Lt. Fred J. Olivi: As we neared Okinawa, Sweeney radioed Yontan airfield asking for emergency clearance to land. I only heard his end of the conversation, but his actions told me what was happening at the other end. There was no reply! He kept trying time after time to contact the Yontan tower before our gas was used up. Our situation was critical. Kuharek told Sweeney, "Major, we're just about out. There's nothing left in the tanks!" I think everyone in *Bockscar* started to sweat. This was a real emergency, and far more frightening than anything that had happened thus far on the mission.

Lt. Jacob Beser: As we neared Okinawa, the radio traffic was horrendous. They had a raid of B-24s returning from Japan along with their fighter escorts. Chuck broadcast a "Mayday" distress signal which theoretically should have cleared the air, but it didn't.

Maj. Charles W. Sweeney: No answer from the field. The air traffic continued to come and go. They were either ignoring us completely or plain didn't see us, which was remarkable, as this massive silver B-29 lumbered toward them. "Mayday! Mayday! Yontan. Dimples 77," I yelled. I could hear the tower talking to other airplanes. But not to me.

Lt. Jacob Beser: He told the navigator to fire the appropriate flare with the Very Pistol.

2nd Lt. Fred J. Olivi: Suddenly Sweeney turned to me and yelled, "Olivi! Start firing the flares." I grabbed the flare gun and took out a flare marked "Red." It meant "Wounded on board." The procedure for firing a flare out of a B-29 was something we had all been trained to do back at Wendover. However, we had just practiced opening up the small, round hatch in the ceiling behind the pilot and co-pilot. We had practiced opening the flare gun, inserting a flare into the barrel, and finally pushing the gun up into the hole. But we never fired a real flare. It was considered too dangerous. We just rehearsed the procedure. But this was no rehearsal.

Lt. Jacob Beser: This brought no results either. In desperation, he told the navigator to fire everything.

2nd Lt. Fred J. Olivi: To this day, I have no idea, other than that first one, which colors I fired. It was: stick the gun in the hole, fire, remove, reload as fast as I could. Red blue pink green yellow white—all the colors of the rainbow. One after the other.

Maj. Charles W. Sweeney: We must have looked like the Fourth of July. But it sure as hell got their attention. The multiple flares signaled not only "aircraft out of fuel" but "prepare for crash," "heavy damage," "dead and wounded on board," and "aircraft on fire." It was a potpourri of disaster warnings. On reflection, any one or all could have been true, depending on what happened next. The smell of gunpowder from the Very Pistol that fired the flares filled the forward compartment.

Lt. Jacob Beser: This had two results; in the back of the plane, we thought a major fire had broken out from the amount of smoke coming out of every duct and two, some pilot in the traffic pattern sensed we were in trouble and peeled off. Those in the pattern behind him followed suit and we were able to land.

Capt. Kermit B. Beahan: We made a bee line to our emergency landing site in Okinawa. We landed OK and as we taxied to the airfield ramp both outboard engines sputtered to a stop—fuel starvation! It was really a "sweat job."

2nd Lt. Fred J. Olivi: Before we left the aircraft, I distinctly remember Sweeney saying, "Let's not mention where we came from or anything about what we did. They're not supposed to know anything about it. We're just a B-29 looking for gas to get home after a mission." Those may not have been his exact words, but he was very specific about maintaining security.

Sgt. Raymond Gallagher: We stayed on the island for two hours. We fueled up, topped our tanks off. Crews went and had chow, came back, loaded up, and we headed on back to Tinian.

2nd Lt. Fred J. Olivi: I don't recall much in the way of chit-chat on our flight back to Tinian. I'm sure each of us was deep in his own thoughts. I don't think any of us had any regrets. We had done the job we were trained to do: fly an atomic bomb nicknamed Fat Man to a targeted city in the Japanese Empire, drop it, then return to our home base on Tinian. It had been a very long day, and a very long and harrowing mission.

"'Do your best'"

AFTERWARD IN NAGASAKI

In one of the most famous images of Nagasaki, a young boy waits to turn his brother's body over to be cremated.

Nagasaki reeled from the bombing for days—and then, just as had happened in Hiroshima, a strange new disease started to take its toll.

Dr. Masao Shiotsuki: About five o'clock that evening, a telephone call came in from the mayor of Omura asking the head of the naval hospital for his assistance in treating bomb casualties. The number of dead and wounded in Nagasaki was beyond calculation. Nagasaki Medical College and all the treatment centers both within the city and on its periphery had been demolished. The mayor was asking us at Omura Naval Hospital to accept at least a thousand casualties. They would be put on board a specially prepared train at Urakami, then carried by trucks and other available transport from Omura Station to the hospital. The first train was scheduled to arrive at eight or nine that evening. Finally automobile horns sounded in the darkness and the truck and military transports arrived. The military transports were filled to capacity with patients, but the truck was even worse. In the open loading compartment, people had been stacked until there was no space left, and the living were indistinguishable from the dead. The sight was so horrifying that unthinkingly I cried out in dismay.

Ayako Okumura, ***third-year primary school student*****:** I knew that the most important thing was to find my mother. I went to the places where I thought she might be, like the fields where she helped out with the farming work, but I didn't come across her. I spent the night of August 9th in the air-raid shelter with my brother and my neighbors. People from other families were rejoicing, happy to be reunited with each other, and saying things like, "It's so good to see you survived!" and "After all that, you still look well!" I kept waiting for my mother and father to return, but they never did. None of my siblings came back either. I remember what happened up until that point, but from then on my memory is a blank. Maybe it was the shock of the atomic bombing, or maybe it was the misery I felt at losing everyone in my family except my little brother; whatever the reason, I came down with amnesia. Apparently I went to live with my aunt and cousins, but I have no recollection of that whatsoever.

Jungo Kawanami, ***age 11*****:** People were dying in the shelter one after another, without receiving any treatment or being given any food. There was no light either, just the dark of night. I trembled with fear as I waited for my father. Late at night, I don't know exactly what time it was, my father came crawling back to the shelter from Urakami, which was the bombing hypocenter. His burned body was covered with a wet cloak he had probably picked up on the way. As soon as he saw my face, he fell to the ground, without saying even a single word. He never woke up again, and a week later he died. He was thirty-seven years old. I was so overwhelmed by sorrow that I couldn't even cry. I just collected scrap pieces of wood and used them to cremate my father's body. The body of a man does not burn easily.

Dr. Masao Shiotsuki: Confronted with a reality in which nothing I had learned from medical textbooks was of the slightest avail, all I could do was grit my teeth and try in some way to relieve their pain. To patients crying for water, I brought water and let them drink their fill. For many this was the last drink. It is common knowledge that patients who can respond to treatment should not be allowed to drink water, because they might suffocate or go into shock. But how could I refuse water to these people who wanted it so desperately, knowing as I did that they were going to die? The same feelings led me to give morphine to patients whose suffering was unbearable, so that they could forget their agony even for just a little while. I also gave the nurses and orderlies permission to administer morphine without waiting for a doctor's orders. As a result, I assisted in committing euthanasia. Or to put it another way, I was a mercy killer. Those people died peacefully, I believe, their pain and agony relieved. But even today I myself feel terrible pain and agony that as a doctor I could not help them to live but could only send one after another of them to a painless death. My own torment will continue until the moment I too lose consciousness in death.

Namio Sakamoto, ***age 15, at Mitsubishi Electric manufacturing at the time of the bombing*****:** At dawn a rescue team came and led us in pulling the dead bodies of our classmates out from under the collapsed roof. We carried these to an open area by the training facility and laid them on the mats of summer cypress. We then made funeral pyres out of scrap wood and placed the dead bodies on top of them. We stacked the wood in three layers and put wood boards and chips around them. Then, we set them alight and bowed down in prayer. We stood transfixed as the bodies of our friends and elders collapsed in the rising flames. During the three days and nights we worked, we also helped collect the ashes of the dead from the burned dormitory. The ashes of about 150 victims from the dormitory and the training facility were put into plain wood cases that the company provided and stored in a meeting room until the end of the war.

Dr. Tatsuichiro Akizuki: Shortly after noon [on Sunday, August 12, three days after the bombing], a civilian patrol arrived at the hospital. Its leaders were two assistant police inspectors. The patrol consisted of about thirty people, most of whom came from the Kawanami Shipyard on the edge of the harbor. I was poor-looking and small, and my navy-blue suit was moreover stained with mercurochrome, blood and dirt. *Who would have thought that such a figure could be the doctor in charge?* In addition to the thirty members of the patrol, more than a hundred others now arrived as reinforcements, volunteers from the Kawanami Industry Company. The first group entered the hospital ruins and began to put the first floor in order. The second group went down into Motohara town. After a while they came back, carrying whatever injured people they could find. I was appalled to see how many people had hidden away in the shelters. Towards three o'clock, when nearly 200 patients had been brought to the hospital, one of the volunteers, standing at attention, informed the group leader that their work was finished. He answered: "Thank you very much." I went up to him and demanded: "Who's to take charge of this first-aid hospital? Where will the medicines come from?" The leader said: "You're a doctor, aren't you? Do your best."

They had brought in large quantities of straw from neighboring farms and scattered it on the floors. Upon the straw more than 200 severely wounded people now lay. The groans and lamentations of the injured echoed loudly in the ruined rooms. With the help of a nurse, I began to provide such treatment as I could as it began to get dark.

Sachiko Yasui, ***age 6*****:** Life after the atomic bombing was misery itself. We would collect nails, steel and wood from the scorched debris and use them to build what were more like shacks than real houses. Food supplies were extremely scarce, and we put up with our hunger by picking potato vines or anything else edible that was within reach and putting it in our mouths. The atomic-bombing survivors who had been left naked didn't even have clothes that they could use to trade. On rainy days the rain would leak everywhere, and when the wind was strong it would always seem like the shacks were about to be blown over. There were a lot of nights when we were full of anxiety, for it wasn't until some years later that properly-built houses were constructed.

"I swallow my own tears"

V-J DAY

Japan's surrender was celebrated wildly in Oak Ridge.

The twin atomic bombings, just three days apart, seemed finally to spark movement toward surrender by the Japanese government. At the same time, Russia's declaration of war and its invasion of Manchuria, where a million Soviet troops began to roll back the once-famed Kwantung Army, further tipped the balance toward surrender. But even at the last minute, as the emperor readied an unprecedented and historic radio address, hard-liners in the government tried to derail the surrender—sending soldiers charging through the Imperial Palace in a coup to find and destroy the recording of the emperor's surrender before it could be aired. Ultimately, though, the coup failed and the surrender proceeded, bringing an end to the greatest conflict in world history.

Gen. George C. Marshall: The destruction at Hiroshima was so complete that there was no communication at least for a day I think and maybe longer and it was not until the second destruction took place at Nagasaki that the Japanese were really aware of what had happened in the earlier bomb explosion. Quite evidently, they were shocked into action, because as nearly as they could guess they didn't know how many bombs we had. They didn't know the full details, but they knew that the destruction had been terrific from a single bomb. The Japanese could see Tokyo probably being wiped out next. We would have had a terribly bitter [time] and frightfully expensive in lives and treasure, etc. if we had to proceed with a landing in Japan. There were supposed to be nine more bombs completed in time for the first landing in the southern tip of Japan.

There were to be three bombs for each corps that was landing. One as a preliminary, then the landing, then another one further inland against the immediate supports, and then the third one against any troops that might try to come through the mountains from up on the Inland Sea. That was the rough idea in our minds.

Maj. Gen. Curtis LeMay: Hiroshima brought no instantaneous prostration of the Japanese military; nevertheless it was a startlingly rapid disintegration. Meanwhile we were still piling on the incendiaries. Our B-29s went to Yawata on August 8th, and burned up 21 per cent of the town, and on the same day some other 29s went to Fukuyama and burned up 73.3 per cent. We kept on flying.*

Sen. Richard B. Russell (D-GA), *telegram to Harry Truman, August 7th*: Permit me to respectfully suggest that we cease our efforts to cajole Japan into surrendering in accordance with the Potsdam Declaration. Let us carry the war to them until they beg us to accept the unconditional surrender.

Harry Truman, *response to Russell, August 9*: I know that Japan is a terribly cruel and uncivilized nation in warfare but I can't bring myself to believe that, because they are beasts, we should ourselves act in the same manner.

* Illustrating the ongoing cost of the air war, LeMay's B-29 raids from August 10 to August 14 killed roughly another 15,000 Japanese.

Adm. William Leahy: Moscow announced on August 8, 1945, that a state of war existed between the Soviet Republics and Japan. We presumed that a Russian invasion of Manchuria probably was under way, and I felt that hereafter we would be required to share both the military efforts against Japan and the rewards therefrom. More details were coming in on the atomic attack on Hiroshima. The Japanese Government leveled charges of cruelty and barbarism, claiming that the attack had been effective principally against noncombatant women and children. Although Hiroshima was a naval base, it did appear probable that the destruction of civilian life had been terrific.

Norman F. Ramsey, *scientific/technical deputy, Project Alberta*: On the day following the Nagasaki mission, the Japanese initiated surrender negotiations.

Kantarō Suzuki, *prime minister of Japan*: The Supreme War Council, up to the time the atomic bomb was dropped, did not believe that Japan could be beaten by air attack alone. They also believed that the United States would land and not attempt to bomb Japan out of the war. The Supreme War Council had proceeded with the one plan of fighting a decisive battle at the landing point until the Atomic Bomb was dropped, after which they believed the United States need not land when it had such a weapon; so at that point they decided that it would be best to sue for peace.

Hirohito, *internal cabinet discussion, August 9*: I have given serious thought to the situation prevailing at home and abroad and have concluded that continuing the war can only mean destruction for the nation and prolongation of bloodshed and cruelty in the world. I cannot bear to see my innocent people suffer any longer. Ending the war is the only way to restore world peace and to relieve the nation from the terrible distress with which it is burdened. The time has come when we must bear the un-bearable. I swallow my own tears and give my sanction to the proposal to accept the Allied proclamation on the basis outlined by the Foreign Minister.

Maj. Charles W. Sweeney: The days immediately following our mission were mixed with hopeful anticipation and nagging dread.

Col. Kenneth D. Nichols: Even after we had dropped the plutonium bomb on Nagasaki, we received no immediate indication that Japan would accept our peace terms. Groves sent the following memo to General Marshall on August 10: "The next bomb of the implosion type had been scheduled to be ready for delivery on the target on the first good weather after 24 August 1945. We have gained 4 days in manufacture and expect to ship from New Mexico on 12 or 13 August the final components. Providing there are no unforeseen difficulties in manufacture, in transportation to the theatre or after arrival in the theatre, the bomb should be ready for delivery on the first suitable weather after 17 or 18 August." Anticipating Japanese acceptance of peace terms, Marshall wrote on the memo: "It is not to be released over Japan without express authority from the President." Meanwhile, Los Alamos was preparing for their next shipment.

Robert Bacher: This work on checking out the cores of the bomb was done in a room across from my office, because I was directly responsible for it, and I darn well wanted to see that I went over some of these things myself. We had just finished the check-out of another core of a bomb, and there was a car waiting out front to take it down to the Albuquerque airport and a plane was ready to fly it over to Tinian, when Robert Oppenheimer came running down the hall and said he had a hold order from Washington. We knew that meant this was the end.

Adm. William Leahy: Japan announced over their government radio in Tokyo early in the morning of August 10, 1945, in plain language, that they were prepared to accept the proposal of the United States, the United Kingdom, and China issued at Potsdam. They were ready to surrender in accordance with the terms of that declaration on one condition: that no demand be made for the end of the authority of the Emperor to rule Japan. It appeared certain that the great World War was about to come to an end. While waiting for the Japanese Government to make its decision, the war against Japan was pressed with all possible vigor.

2nd Lt. Fred J. Olivi: On August 14th, we were informed there was to be yet another mission to the Japanese Empire. Peace had not yet come to the Pacific, and apparently it was decided to let the Japanese know we still had a lot of bombs left.

Maj. Charles W. Sweeney: On August 14, General Spaatz ordered into the air just about every aircraft in the theater—bombers, fighters, B-29s, B-24s, B-25s, B-26s, P-38s, you name it, anything that could fly and carry ordnance, strafe a target, or fire a rocket—for one massive show of force to push the Japanese to surrender. Eight of our airplanes would take part in this final assault.

Adm. William Leahy: Early Tuesday morning, August 14, 1945, there was a radio report from Japan, unofficial, that the Allied demand for surrender had been accepted by the Japanese Government.

Hirohito: Thinking of the people dying endlessly in the air raids / I ended the war / Having no thought of my own fate.

Cmdr. Tadashi Nakajima, *Imperial Navy*: Japanese forces everywhere had been alerted for a noon broadcast from the Emperor. It had been sadly rumored that the subject would be a rescript of surrender. Reception was very poor and many parts of what was said were not clear. Enough came through, however, to make it plain that we had been told to surrender.

***Imperial Rescript of the Termination of the War, August 15, 1945*:** To Our good and loyal subjects: After pondering deeply the general conditions of the world and the actual conditions obtaining in our Empire today, We have decided to effect a settlement of the present situation by resorting to an extraordinary measure. We declared war on America and Britain out of Our sincere desire to assure Japan's self-preservation and the stabilization of East Asia, it being far from Our thought either to infringe upon the sovereignty of other nations or to embark upon territorial aggrandizement. But now the war has lasted for nearly four years. Despite the best that has been done by everyone—the gallant fighting of military and naval forces, the diligence and assiduity of Our servants of the State and the devoted service of Our one hundred million people, the war situation has developed not necessarily to Japan's advantage, while the general trends of the world have all turned against her interest. Moreover the enemy has begun to employ a new and most cruel bomb, the power of which to do damage is indeed incalculable, taking the toll of many innocent lives. Should We continue to fight it would not only result in the ultimate collapse and obliteration of the Japanese nation, but also it would lead to the total extinction of human civilization.

Cpl. Uno Shintaro, ***intelligence officer, 41st Regiment*****:** I never dreamed the Emperor would throw in the towel. Radio reception was poor, so that all we caught were snatches from the Imperial announcement of surrender. I'd heard that an unprecedentedly powerful bomb had been dropped, but I still believed that in the battle on the beaches Japan would be strong. We would hit back then!

Hideko Tamura Snider: On the afternoon of August 15, the refugees from Hiroshima listened to the static-ridden, recorded radio announcement from the Emperor. Their heads were bowed to the tatami mats for the sound of his "holy" voice. I could not make out the words or understand them. The adults who did understand told me that the war had ended. We had all been told to endure and keep our heads up, for the suffering would end upon the news of victory. The new suffering, however, had only just begun.

Dr. Masao Shiotsuki: We were informed of the war's end, as were most civilians, by the emperor's radio broadcast, but I felt no emotion whatsoever as I listened. When I had seen the piles of bomb victims carried in by truck on that first night I had thought to myself, "The war is over."

Taeko King: I stayed in the shelter in my hometown for a while. A teacher at my school came to the shelter to look for school students and spotted me. But the teacher probably thought I was hopeless, so left me behind again. I couldn't move. It was hot. No water and food. Nobody to talk with. I thought I'd rather die at the time. Later, fortunately I was rescued by an acquaintance of my family and sent to the hospital of Kawanami Shipyard, where my sister was sent earlier. I was laid next to her bed. She had already been unconscious. On Aug. 15, the day the war was over, she died with her hand held by me. Many people died at the hospital one after another. They all mustered their last bit of strength and hailed to the Emperor.

Kazuo Chujo: Japan was defeated. My parents were dead. Yet, the sun continued to rise and set.

Farr L. Hurst, *machinist, 603rd Air Engineering Squadron*: We were watching a movie, *From Pillow to Post*. The film stopped and the operator announced over the loudspeaker the Japanese had unconditionally surrendered! Boy, everything on the island broke loose! Everyone was celebrating. People were running, driving Jeeps around, drinking and shooting flares all over the beach fronts. It was finally over.

Sgt. Abe Spitzer: It wasn't until the Japs sued for peace that I knew we really had shortened the war by six months or more with our "gimmick." And it wasn't for about two weeks, when I began seeing the photos of the atomic bomb damage at Hiroshima and Nagasaki and began reading the newspaper accounts of what those two bombs had done that I realized what kind of history we'd made.

George B. Kistiakowsky: It was a big bash after V-J Day when I got fairly soused at the party given by Robert Bacher. Those around me egged me on and so I went to the explosive stores and got out twenty-one fifty-pound boxes of TNT and with the help of a young man—since I was rather far gone—fired them off in a field and came back. The bastards told me I fired twenty-two. And then I went to sleep in my little house, which was across the street from Bacher's house. And then as a last thing they created a fantastic pile of empty bottles—beer, whiskey, tequila—in front of my only door, so I was really stuck for a while.

Herbert Pomerance, *research associate, Met Lab, Chicago*: V-J Day was, I think it was the only time I ever threw up from drinking liquor. That's when you went around to everybody's house, and I don't know what, and rang the siren in the dorm and worked the fire extinguishers. I don't know, did anything you wanted to. That was V-J Day. That was the big celebration.

Gen. Robert L. Eichelberger: The formal Japanese surrender took place on September 2, Tokyo time. From the very moment my plane left Luzon I had the eerie feeling that all of us were walking through the pages of history, the ceremony aboard the battleship *Missouri* surely did nothing to dispel this compelling sense of drama. From the steel deck of the *Missouri*, as hot in the sunlight as the top side of a kitchen range, I could see in Tokyo Bay the gleaming might of the greatest armada of all time.

Cmdr. Edwin Layton: Gray clouds swirled over the long lines of Allied naval vessels that crowded Tokyo Bay. The waters of the great bay were eerily still and black, dancing with reflections of the lean hulls of 260 assembled warships, an awesome demonstration of the military might that had been marshaled to defeat Japan. At the appointed hour of 0900, an American destroyer bearing the eleven-man Japanese delegation closed the battleship's starboard side. The emperor's burden of capitulation appeared to weigh heavily on the shoulders of the foreign minister.

Toshikazu Kase, *foreign minister, Japan*: The Supreme Commander invited the Japanese delegates to sign the instrument of surrender.

Cmdr. Edwin Layton: The final surrender document had been laid out before the Japanese delegation on an old mess table.

Toshikazu Kase: It was eight minutes past nine when MacArthur put his signature to the documents. Other representatives of the Allied Powers followed suit in the order of the United States, China, the United Kingdom, the Soviet Union, Australia, Canada, France, the Netherlands and New Zealand. When all the representatives had finished signing, MacArthur announced slowly: "Let us pray that peace be now restored to the world and that God will preserve it always. These proceedings are closed." At that moment, the skies parted and the sun shone brightly through the layers of clouds. There was a steady drone above and now it became a deafening roar and an armada of airplanes paraded into sight, sweeping over the warships. Four hundred B-29s and 1,500 carrier planes joined in the aerial pageant in a final salute. It was over.

Gen. Douglas MacArthur, *broadcast to the American people*: Today the guns are silent. A great tragedy has ended. A great victory has been won. The skies no longer rain death—the seas bear only commerce—men everywhere walk upright in the sunlight. The entire world is quietly at peace. The holy mission has been completed. And in reporting this to you, the people, I speak for the thousands of silent lips, forever stilled among the jungles and the beaches and in the deep waters of the Pacific which marked the way. I speak for the unnamed brave millions homeward bound to take up the challenge of that future which they did so much to salvage from the brink of disaster.

A new era is upon us. Even the lesson of victory itself brings with it profound concern, both for our future security and the survival of civilization. The destructiveness of the war potential, through progressive advances in scientific discovery, has in fact now reached a point which revises the traditional concept of war.

Col. Paul W. Tibbets: After the signing of the peace treaty aboard the battleship Missouri in Tokyo harbor on September 2, scientists from the Manhattan Project were anxious to get into Japan to check on the result of our bomb drops on Hiroshima and Nagasaki.

Robert R. Furman, ***engineer, Manhattan Engineer District*****:** After the two bombs were dropped and the Emperor of Japan declared the war was over, General Groves ordered three investigative teams be formed principally from the personnel already on Tinian. One team went to Hiroshima, one team to Nagasaki and the third team to visit all universities, government bureaus and corporations that might be engaged in nuclear research in Japan or Korea. I headed up the third team consisting of scientists and interpreters.

Col. Paul W. Tibbets: I took two C-54s and went to Okinawa to join the big parade of planes that were flying occupation forces into Japan. We learned that we could fly to a field near Nagasaki, but that the runways at the Hiroshima air base were in no condition to handle a C-54. Flying to Nagasaki, we landed at a naval base about 16 miles from the heart of the city.

Maj. Charles W. Sweeney: The valley floor was a stretch of rubble dotted by grotesquely twisted lumps of steel beams and columns. A brick chimney rose here and there amid the wreckage where the munitions plants had once stood. From a distance, the destroyed armaments plants looked like erector sets a child had twisted and bent and carelessly tossed away. I walked alone along a brick sidewalk to a point I estimated was where ground zero would have been. On one corner I peered down into the cellar of what had been a fire station. It was then that I was struck by the significance of our weapon. In the cellar was a fire truck that had been crushed flat, as if a giant had stepped on it. In fact, the entire infrastructure of the city was flat—no water, no emergency facilities, no firefighters. Everything was gone.

Col. Paul W. Tibbets: Ferebee, Van Kirk, and I walked around the city during the three days we spent there and were amazed at the extent of the destruction. Block after block had been flattened, as if by a tornado. All of us were deeply impressed by what we saw at Nagasaki and what we knew had occurred at Hiroshima. Chuck Sweeney went on a lecture tour after returning home, describing the bombings. He sent the profits to an orphanage in Hiroshima. Bob Lewis helped raise money to provide medical treatment for the so-called "Hiroshima maidens," girls who were disfigured by the blistering heat from the bomb.

J. Robert Oppenheimer: During the week when Hiroshima and Nagasaki were being bombed, we met at Los Alamos to sketch out a prospectus of what the technical future in atomic energy might look like—atomic war heads for guided missiles, improvements in bomb designs, the thermonuclear program, power, propulsion, and the new tools available from atomic technology for research in science, medicine, and technology. This work absorbed much of my time, during September and October; and in connection with it I was asked to consult with the War and State Departments on atomic-energy legislation, and in a preliminary way on the international control of atomic energy. I resigned as director of Los Alamos on October 16, 1945.

Maj. Gen. Leslie Groves: We had solved the immediate problem of ending the war, but in so doing we had raised up many unknowns. Our feelings at this time were eloquently summed up by Oppenheimer when, on October 16, 1945, I presented the laboratory with a Certificate of Appreciation from the Secretary of War.

Alice Kimball Smith: Under a brilliant New Mexico sky, virtually the entire population of the mesa assembled for the outdoor ceremony.

J. Robert Oppenheimer, *remarks upon receiving certificate of appreciation, October 16, 1945*: It is with appreciation and gratitude that I accept from you this scroll for the Los Alamos Laboratory, for the men and women whose work and whose hearts have made it. It is our hope that in years to come we may look at this scroll, and all that it signifies, with pride. Today that pride must be tempered with profound concern. If atomic bombs are to be added as new weapons to the arsenals of the warring world, or to the arsenals of nations preparing for war, then the time will come when mankind will curse the names of Los Alamos and Hiroshima.

Lawrence H. Johnston: I soon left Los Alamos for Berkeley to resume my graduate studies and get on with my career.

Frederic de Hoffmann: Los Alamos in the early 1940s was not only a project to end a world war, it was also the beginning of a new technological era. This I am sure is the way we all want to remember those days.

William Reynolds, *worker, Oak Ridge*: After the war ended, they laid off—well, we were 75,000 people here when the bomb was dropped and four months later there were 40,000 and the year after that there were 35,000. It went from expansion to nothing.

Maj. Charles W. Sweeney: On November 14, I lifted off from the runway at Tinian for the last time. The entire 509th was being rotated back to the United States lock, stock, and barrel. Our new base would be at Roswell, New Mexico. I brought *The Great Artiste* around for one last look and then headed to Kwajalein, on to Hawaii and then to Sacramento on our three-day hopscotching route back to the West Coast.

Pfc. James P. Patterson, *390th Air Service Group*: I was one of the last of the group to leave Tinian and was assigned to return as a passenger on the B-29 piloted by Capt. Lewis which was the *Enola Gay*. We flew, via Hawaii, to Mather field, CA, and finally to Roswell Army Air Field.

Maj. Charles W. Sweeney: The rest of my life lay ahead of me and I was anxious to get started.

Tsutomu Yamaguchi: I could have died either of those days. Everything that follows is a bonus.

Stanislaw Ulam: Life would never be the same.

Bernice Brode: The grand finale of our association with the Indians took place on a cold December night in 1945, when the square dance group from the hill was invited to a party at San Ildefonso. It was a joint affair arranged in detail by Po and a committee from our dance organization. It was Po's brainchild to celebrate the atomic age in general and the new relationship with their Anglo-scientific friends in particular. Four Indians opened festivities with a Comanche war dance accompanied by drums and a chanting chorus of men led by Montoya, our janitor from the Big House. Next Po called on us to put on a demonstration of a square dance. We used our most seasoned dancers to make a big impression. After a short interval some of the Indian men, Cokes in hand, began to shuffle to the drums that had started up. At the height of this excitement, with yells and shouts, Montoya, who was playing the drum, got up on a chair and shouted above the din, "This is the atomic age, this is the atomic age!"

"The atmosphere in the hospital changed completely"

THE SICKNESS

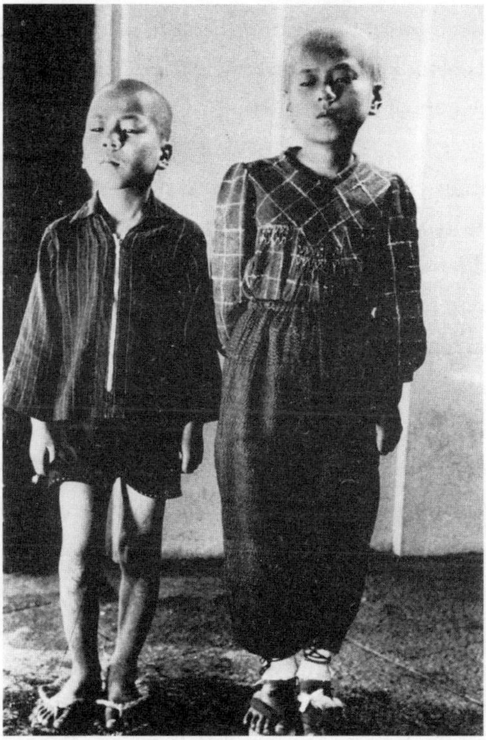

Two siblings, Toru and Aiko, victims of radiation poisoning.
The brother (*left*) died in 1949. The sister in 1965.

In 1945, few people understood the effects of radiation exposure—not even the Manhattan Project scientists understood the risk that came from atomic bombs. Families and doctors in Hiroshima and Nagasaki were even less prepared for the surprise illness that began to manifest in bombing victims—even those with seemingly slight injuries from the blast and fires—over the weeks of August 1945 and the fall and winter that followed. At first, doctors imagined they were dealing with some deadly new special infection or germ.

Kazuo Chujo: One does not get burnt by radiation. But radioactivity penetrates the tissues, contaminates the blood, and destroys, surreptitiously and steadily, the hematogenous tissues, pituitary gland and digestive organs. It is said that every one of those who escaped the heat and force of the bomb blast but were inside wooden buildings within 1.4 kilometers from the explosion site died within one month. The terrible thing about radiation is that none of the five senses registers anything when one is exposed to it. Furthermore, a nuclear blast also causes secondary radiation, through fallout. Many people became victims of secondary radiation when they entered Hiroshima a few days after the bombing in search of their relatives.

Tohru Hara: Another terror came to attack these people who had narrowly escaped with their lives. Radiation sickness. The radiations from the uranium atoms which had been used to make the atom bomb permeated deep into the bone-marrow of people whose bodies seemed to have received no injury. Their hair fell out, their gums bled, and finally their whole bodies became covered with purple spots and they died one after another.

Dr. Michihiko Hachiya: None of the patients had any appetite and one by one they were beginning to vomit and have diarrhea. *Did the new weapon I had heard about throw off a poison gas or perhaps some deadly germ?* I asked Dr. Hanaoka to confirm if he could the report of vomiting and diarrhea and to find out if any of the patients looked as if they might have an infectious disease. He inquired and brought word that there were many who not only had diarrhea but bloody stools and that some had had as many as forty to fifty stools during the previous night. This convinced me that we were dealing with bacillary dysentery and had no choice but to isolate those who were infected. Dr. Koyama, as deputy director, was given the responsibility of setting up an isolation ward. He chose a site on the grounds beyond the south side of the hospital, and with the help of some soldiers who happened along he managed to construct what amounted to a crude outdoor pavilion. What we were trying to do probably was not worth much, but it helped our morale to think we were doing something.

Dr. Masao Shiotsuki: One of the most horrifying symptoms for the atomic bomb victims was the loss of hair. This symptom became apparent among some of our patients on the afternoon of the third day after their admission. I first learned about this condition from Iyonaga: "Something odd has just begun to happen. The patients' hair is falling out. All you have to do is touch it and it comes out in clumps. The same thing is happening to men and women."

It soon became clear that loss of hair occurred in combination with several other symptoms. From that point on the atmosphere in the hospital changed completely. Up until now the severely burned and injured had lapsed into critical condition and died one after another. Now we looked on helplessly as even those who at first glance seemed to have only minor injuries and were on the road to recovery were suddenly stricken. Loss of hair, dark purple skin after an injection, small spots like pin pricks appearing on the skin and gradually growing larger, bleeding from the gums—these were the telltale symptoms, and if they occurred in combination, we knew the patient would die. We still did not know then that the "special bomb" that had fallen on Nagasaki was the atomic bomb, but if we had known, I doubt that even the specialists would have realized the extent of its radioactivity. And, of course, it completely transcended the imagination of a novice doctor in training like myself.

Yoshiko Uchimura, ***sixth grader*****:** My mother and older sister had cuts from broken glass all over their backs, but my father and little sister did not have a single scratch. The next day they went to Mother's place in the country and rested quietly there, but on about the 20th of August my little sister's hair suddenly began to fall out, bright red spots appeared all over her body, and suffering torment she departed from this world a week later. From about then on, my father and mother and sister were all three confined to their beds. My father and sister got suddenly worse, and it was said to be just a matter of time. When my aunt came to the country and took me back with her, my father no longer had enough energy to speak. My mother and sister too—whenever I combed their hair for them it came out in bunches and I was at my wits' end to know what to do. But although my mother and sister had breathed the poison, perhaps because they had so many cuts, they grew stronger day by day and their hair grew back, a little frizzled at first, but it straightened out all right.

Noriko Iwata, ***fifth grader*****:** Three or four days later an uncle who came to see us told us that Grandfather and Grandmother had escaped to Grandmother's old home, and both of them were uninjured. Then Grandmother's and my little sister's hair began to fall out, and they both lost their appetites. Their hair that had come out was scattered around on their pillows, and if you just touched their heads about fifty hairs came out in a bunch. Grandfather, too, suddenly said his head hurt and took to his bed.

Shin Bok Su: My husband had only gotten a small scrape on his knee. I thought we were lucky. But from the twenty-fifth of August his hair started falling out. He went to the hospital and got some medicine, but his mouth turned black. He died. His body had turned black.

Takuo Matsumoto: It was my daily, self-imposed task for the following months to walk to those places where the injured students were supposed to have been taken, and try to help them as best I could. Due to the effects of radiation, their faces and bodies were swollen, like those of lepers, and I could not distinguish them from hundreds of fellow sufferers who had been placed in the same rooms. I would therefore stand in the middle of a room and shout at the top of my voice: "Is there a student of Hiroshima Jogakuin in this room?" A small feeble reply would often be heard from a corner, "Yes, here I am!" I would then walk up to her, ask her name and address, assure her that I would try my best to contact her parents or relatives, offer a short prayer for her, leave words of encouragement, and then go off to another room, in continuing my hunt for other students. When, a couple of days later, I went back to them, they would often be gone, dead. It was heartbreaking for me to have to see them die one after another in this way day after day.

Emiko Okada: There were no medicines, so my grandmother gave us drinks made from boiled weeds and herbs to try to get rid of the poisons, even though we didn't know what they were.

Noriko Iwata: Our whole village was seized with fear. People who had escaped from Hiroshima without a single scratch lost their hair and developed spots and finally they died. There wasn't a thing that the doctors could do to help them.

Dr. Tatsuichiro Akizuki: One of the greatest cruelties of radiation poisoning is that victims may seem to recover or at first not even show symptoms of affliction, only to suffer from the disease at a later point. This forces the victims to live in constant fear and anxiety. Among the symptoms that may eventually occur are keloids, genital disorders, congenital disorders in infants exposed to radiation while in the womb, optic and blood disorders, and malignant tumors.

Yamaoka Michiko, *schoolchild*: I spent the next year bedridden. All my hair fell out. When we went to relatives' houses later they wouldn't even let me in because they feared they'd catch the disease. There was neither treatment nor assistance for me: Those people who had money—people who had both parents, people who had houses—they could go to the Red Cross Hospital or the Hiroshima City Hospital. They could get operations. But we didn't have any money. It was just my Mom and I. Keloids covered my face, my neck. I couldn't even move my neck. One eye was hanging down. I was unable to control my drooling because my lip had been burned off. I couldn't get any treatments at a hospital, so my mother gave me massages. Because she did that for me, my keloids aren't as bad as they would have been. My fingers were all stuck together. I couldn't move them. The only thing I could do was sew shorts, since I only needed to sew a straight line. I had to do something to earn money. The Japanese government just told us we weren't the only victims of the war. There was no support or treatment.

"No A-bomb must ever fall again"

EPILOGUE

MacArthur's occupation after the Japanese surrender kept secret the fallout of the atomic bombs for years.

In the months after the end of the war, the US went to great lengths to cover up the truth about what happened in Hiroshima and Nagasaki and hide the horror from the American people. Even while the rough enormous casualty figures were public, the specifics of the destruction and the experiences of those in Hiroshima and Nagasaki emerged only slowly. Japanese-American correspondent Leslie Nakashima, who had spent the war in Japan, traveled to Hiroshima in late August to search for his mother and filed a dispatch with United Press on August 27, 1945, that was the first widespread report about the scale of devastation.

Leslie Nakashima, *correspondent, United Press*: That the atomic bomb, more than Russia's entry into the war, compelled Japan to surrender as she did on

August 15 instead of waging a showdown battle on the Japanese mainland is a justifiable conclusion drawn after one sees what used to be Hiroshima city. I've just returned to Tokyo from that city, which was destroyed at one stroke by a single atomic bomb thrown by a super flying fortress on the morning of August 6. There's not a single building standing intact in the city—until recently of 300,000 population. The death toll is expected to reach 100,000 with people continuing to die daily from burns suffered from the bomb's ultra-violet rays.

On Friday, August 31, 1945, a brief version of Nakashima's story ran in The New York Times *with an editor's note appended: "United States scientists say that the atomic bomb will not have lingering after-effects in a devastated area." Below, on page 4 of the newspaper in the same column, a short story datelined Oak Ridge, TN, announced "Japanese Reports Doubted."*

New York Times *brief*: Japanese reports of deaths from radioactive effects of atomic bombing are pure propaganda in the opinion of Maj. Gen. Leslie R. Groves, commanding general of the Manhattan District. Studies by scientists in this country do not bear out the death reports, General Groves said at a press conference here today. "The atomic bomb is not an inhuman weapon," General Groves told workers and military personnel in a surprise visit to the project yesterday. "I think our best answer to anyone who doubts this is that we did not start the war, and if they don't like the way we ended it, to remember who started it," he said.

In early September 1945, Australian correspondent Wilfred Burchett was the first outside newsman to make it to Hiroshima.

Wilfred Burchett, *article, "The Atomic Plague,"* Daily Express, *September 5, 1945*: In Hiroshima, 30 days after the first atomic bomb destroyed the city and shook the world, people are still dying, mysteriously and horribly—people who were uninjured by the cataclysm—from an unknown something which I can only describe as atomic plague.

Hiroshima does not look like a bombed city. It looks as if a monster steamroller had passed over it and squashed it out of existence. I write these facts as dispassionately as I can in the hope that they will act as a warning to the world. In this first testing ground of the atomic bomb I have seen the most terrible and frightening desolation in four years of war. It makes a blitzed Pacific island seem like an Eden. The damage is far greater than photographs can show. When you arrive in Hiroshima you can look around and for 25, perhaps 30, square miles you can hardly see a building. It gives you an empty feeling in the stomach to see such man made devastation.

My nose detected a peculiar odour unlike anything I have ever smelled before. It is something like sulphur, but not quite. I could smell it when I passed a fire that was still smouldering, or at a spot where they were still recovering bodies from the wreckage. But I could also smell it where everything was still deserted. They believe it is given off by the poisonous gas still issuing from the earth soaked with radioactivity released by the split uranium atom. And so the people of Hiroshima today are walking through the forlorn desolation of their once proud city with gauze masks over their mouths and noses.

George Weller, *correspondent,* Chicago Daily News: I entered Nagasaki on September 6, 1945, as the first free westerner to do so after the end of the war. When I walked out of Nagasaki's roofless railroad station, I saw a city frizzled like a baked apple, crusted black. I saw the long, crumpled skeleton of the Mitsubishi electrical motor and ship fitting plant, a framework blasted clean of its flesh by the lazy-falling missile floating under a parachute. Along the blistered boulevards the shadows of fallen telegraph poles were branded upright on buildings, the signature of the ray stamped in huge ideograms.

In the battered corridors of these hospitals, already eroded by man's normal suffering, there was no sorrowful horde. The wards were filled. There was no private place left to die. Consequently the dying were sitting up cross-legged against the walls, holding sad little court with their families, answering their tender questions with the mild, consenting indifference of those whose future is cancelled. The atomic bomb's peculiar "disease," uncured because it is untreated and untreated because it is undiagnosed, is still snatching away lives here. Men, women and children with no outward marks of injury are dying daily in hospitals, some after having walked around for three or four weeks thinking they have escaped. The doctors here have every modern medicament, but candidly confessed that the answer to the malady is beyond them. Their patients, though their skins are whole, are simply passing away under their eyes.

While Weller's report from Nagasaki never made it past the US censor—and was ultimately lost for decades—Burchett's story created a stir, and a few days later, in an effort to combat the worrisome reporting, US military and Manhattan Project leaders spoke with William Laurence, now back at his post at The New York Times, *to downplay the fears of radiation.*

Maj. Gen. Leslie Groves, *quoted by William Laurence in* The New York Times, *September 12, 1945*: The Japanese claim that people died from radiations. If this is true, the number was very small. Any deaths from gamma rays were due to those emitted during the explosion, not the radiations present afterward. While many people were killed, many lives were saved, particularly American lives. It ended the war sooner. It was the final punch that knocked them out.

Within days, the US government sent out a notice to US editors asking them to restrict further reporting on the bomb and its effects in Hiroshima and Nagasaki and to submit further articles to the War Department for review as an issue of "the highest national security" to avoid details of the bomb becoming public. In Japan, the US occupation run by Supreme Commander of the Allied Powers (SCAP) Gen. Douglas MacArthur set even stricter ground rules.

Dr. Tatsuichiro Akizuki: As one of the major policies of General Douglas MacArthur's occupation, Japan was placed under a press code. The reasons for this were to preserve the peace under the allied occupation and to protect military security and the secrets of the atomic bomb. The occupation was afraid of the criticism that would be directed at the United States if the story of the tremendous cruelty of the atomic bomb were to become known in Japan and throughout the world.

Hideo Matsuno: Because of censorship orders from the military and the post war occupation government, articles couldn't be written directly from the information collected by reporters. We couldn't write articles detailing the misery. They just didn't permit us to write pieces describing too much of the atrocity. Instead, there were articles that justified the atomic bomb, saying it was inevitable. Even on the anniversary of the bombing, at first, we couldn't even provide extensive coverage on that day. The bomb was dropped on the northern part of Nagasaki in the Christian District. So people in the central part of the city tended to think that this was something that had nothing to do with them—they just wanted to forget everything bad that had happened as quickly as possible. The ruins of the Urakami Catholic Church were cleared right away.

It was only in 1946 that New Yorker *correspondent John Hersey traveled to Hiroshima and explored the wreckage and the tales of survivors in detail; the result of his reporting ran as a 30,000-word article that took up the magazine's entire issue in late August 1946. Hailed as an instant masterpiece, the magazine sold out on newsstands in minutes and was read aloud in its entirety on national radio.*

***Editors' Note,* The New Yorker, *August 31, 1946*:** *The New Yorker* this week devotes its entire editorial space to an article on the almost complete obliteration of a city by one atomic bomb, and what happened to the people of that city. It does so in the conviction that few of us have yet comprehended the all but incredible destructive power of this weapon, and that everyone might well take time to consider the implications of its use.

John Hersey, *article, "Hiroshima,"* The New Yorker, *August 31, 1946*: A hundred thousand people were killed by the atomic bomb, and these six were among the survivors. They still wonder why they lived when so many others died. Each of them counts many small items of chance or volition—a step taken in time, a decision to go indoors, catching one streetcar instead of the next—that spared him. And now each knows that in the act of survival he lived a dozen lives and saw more death than he ever thought he would see. At the time, none of them knew anything.

Lewis Gannett, *literary critic,* New York Herald Tribune, *August 29, 1946*: When headlines say a hundred thousand people are killed, whether in battle, by earthquake, flood, or atom bomb, the human mind refuses to react to mathematics. You swallowed statistics, gasped in awe, and, turning away to discuss the price of lamb chops, forgot. But if you read what Mr. Hersey writes, you won't forget. Mr. Hersey is the first writer to tell about Hiroshima with his feet on the ground, dusty with the ashes of atomized Hiroshima.

* * *

The effects of the bombs on the "Hibakusha" from Hiroshima and Nagasaki lasted for months, then years, and ultimately decades, following many of them the rest of their lives and hastening many of them to early deaths from cancer. The very adoption of the term "Hibakusha" was meant as a political statement amid the era of American occupation, a studiously and artfully neutral term that didn't imply a "victim" or even a "survivor," merely a "bomb-affected person."

Futaba Kitayama, *housewife, age 33*: My eyesight came back rather soon and in some twenty days I was able to see the faces of my children vaguely. But the burns on my face and hands did not heal up accordingly. The summer went and autumn came, but the wounds were still pulpy, like a rotten tomato. In early October, I could merely rise on the bed, and only in December could I manage to walk. After January passed, I could finally remove my bandages, only to find that my face as well as my hands would never be the same.

Sumiteru Taniguchi, *age 16, bike messenger*: For about two years, I lay in a sick bed. I couldn't move. I lay face down, motionless. Since my body was full of agony and pain, I cried and shouted at the medical doctors to kill me. Even a few doctors who were treating me gave up their attempts to save my life and were surprised to see me alive every time a new day arrived. Four years after the bombing, I was in better condition and could move a little bit. The wounds on my back were only half healed when I was discharged from the hospital. Finally after many years I recovered from my wounds and regained my health. I decided to have a major operation to remove all the scars on my back and elsewhere. I was afraid my health was not so good because my rotten flesh had been infested with maggots. Though I was still alive, a couple of times I stopped breathing. I thought death would relieve me from everything. When I started feeling pain, this pain gave me tremendous joy because I knew that I was alive. My body was badly burned and the scars on my body do not perspire. On a very hot summer's day, since I cannot perspire, it feels like I'm carrying a great burden made of raw cotton.

I noticed that a part of my wound had formed a tumor. The tumor broke and was about to become a cancer. I had an operation and that particular cancer was removed. The wound did not heal. Therefore it was necessary to graft the skin from another part of my body. I have to go to the atomic bomb hospital at least once a month to see if the tumor is behaving all right. This has been my life for more than sixty years. Psychologically, mentally, this life of mine has been a life of agony. I have not had much pleasure in living. I have not enjoyed life like every young man or woman is entitled to.

Tsunematsu Tanaka, ***Chugoku Power Distribution Company*****:** When I arrived in Wada Village, pieces of glass were still stuck in my back. Every day, I went down to the river to have my wife wash my back. The blood coagulated and clung to my back like coal tar. When my wife removed the blood clots with a needle, fragments of glass came off with the clots. She removed the blood clots and pieces of glass from my back for a week or ten days. Even when I assumed they were all removed, my back festered with remaining glass pieces during the 1950s and early '60s. I went to a surgical hospital in Sakai-machi to get all the pieces of glass removed.

Atsuko Tsujioka, ***junior college student*****:** Even now the scars of those wounds remain over my whole body. On my head, my face, my arms, my legs and my chest. As I stroke these blackish-red raised scars on my arms, and every time I look in a mirror at this face of mine which is not like my face, and think that never again will I be able to see my former face and that I have to live my life forever in this condition, it becomes too sad to bear. At the time I lost hope for the future. Not for a single moment could I get rid of the feeling that I had become a cripple. Naturally, for that reason I hated to meet people.

One of the most lasting stories to emerge from the ruins of the atomic bomb is the story of Sadako Sasaki, who was just two years old in 1945 and about two kilometers from the hypocenter in Hiroshima and became a victim of radiation poisoning only years later.

Shigeo Sasaki, ***father of Sadako*****:** In the winter of 1954–55, when she was in the sixth grade of elementary school, Sadako came down with a cold. She had never had any kind of illness until then. At first we assumed that it was only tonsillitis. However, two months later she was still unwell. We were told to take her to the Hiroshima Red Cross Hospital. She immediately had her blood tested there, and was diagnosed with acute malignant lymph gland leukemia, and was told that she had between three and six months to live. She was hospitalized there right away. The complications of this serious disease include bleeding, purpura, swollen organs, high fever, and pain. Her white cell count was extraordinarily high, four to five times higher than normal.

After two days in the treatment room, she was moved to another room where her roommate was a junior-high student two years older than she. It was she who told Sadako about the legend that your wish could come true if you folded one thousand paper cranes; and she kindly taught Sadako how to fold them. From then on, Sadako folded cranes constantly. Having been hospitalized just before she was to graduate from elementary school, her wish was to leave the hospital as soon as possible in order to enter middle school.

Smoothing wrinkles in the paper carefully with the palms of her hands, she folded and folded and folded cranes every day. She used many kinds of wrapping paper such as that which comes with medicine, candies, or gifts. Sometimes she folded them exquisitely making a wish on those cranes that she might get well and return to school. Every time I said to her, "Don't work so hard folding cranes, Sadako," she would always say very firmly, "It's all right. Don't worry about me, Dad. This is my own idea." Occasionally she made very tiny cranes as small as a grain of rice, using a needle. Her wish was so urgent that she endured the pain and devoted herself to folding cranes.

In October, 1955, the joints of her arms and legs became swollen and purple, and her appetite became weak. Then her body and legs swelled up, and she became unable to walk or go to the bathroom by herself. Her mother would carry her on her back to the restroom, and she was sad to find that Sadako had become as light as an infant. Still she kept folding cranes even in that devastated condition with her skinny arms outstretched, lying in bed. I often said, "Don't try so hard, my dear." "Don't worry, Dad," she would answer. Many strings of paper cranes were dangling from the ceiling of her sickroom, and there were countless cranes in the box as well.

Fujiko Sasaki, *mother of Sadako*: Her eyes were shining while she was folding the cranes, showing that she wanted to survive by all means.

Masahiro Sasaki, *brother of Sadako*: There was very little income for anyone in those times. Even the doctors were poor. They and the nurses gave my sister everything they could—including vitamin B injections and anti-inflammatory arthritis drugs that kept the swelling of Sadako's body under some kind of control. But all of the nurses and all of the doctors could not fund the blood transfusions beyond a monthly donation of their own blood—and there were many other leukemic children in the wards. So, my parents had to pay people for the blood transfusions. Father was making a living by cutting hair, and in order to fund each transfusion, he would have to serve five customers.

Shigeo Sasaki: On the morning of October 25, 1955, I got a telephone call from my wife Fujiko, saying, "Sadako is in critical condition." I contacted my other children, and rushed to the hospital by taxi. "I like to eat Ochazuke [rice in green tea]," she said. I went out right away to buy some cooked rice and pickles at a restaurant nearby. We gently fed her a spoonful. She faintly and slowly murmured just one word, "Tasty!" That was the last thing she ever said. Then she closed her eyes and lost consciousness. That day, at about ten a.m., she began her eternal journey. With her paper cranes, she expressed her ardent wish to live.

Particularly in the early years after the war, when radiation remained little understood, the Hibakusha faced intense discrimination in Japan. Only in the wake of the end of the US occupation in the early 1950s did survivor accounts become widely read. In 1954, a US test on Bikini Atoll in the Marshall Islands—the first test of a thermonuclear or hydrogen bomb—proved far more powerful than anticipated, and the 15-megaton explosion spread fallout over a vast region, including poisoning twenty-three crew of a Japanese fishing vessel, "Lucky Dragon No. 5," one of whom faced an agonizing and much-covered death. The resulting controversy drew renewed attention to the plight of the World War II Hibakusha. In 1955, a medical mission brought twenty-five survivors, known in the press as the "Hiroshima Maidens," to the US for plastic surgery and treatment, where in a literally made-for-TV moment, they met Enola Gay *copilot Robert Lewis for an episode of* This Is Your Life. *In 1957, the Japanese government began offering free comprehensive medical care to Hibakusha, recognizing the ongoing medical struggles, and the government issued "Atomic Bomb Survivor's Certificates" to those affected by the bombings. All told, the government has recorded about 650,000 Hibakusha, including both victims of the initial blast as well as those who were exposed to dangerous radiation in the two weeks following the bombings. As of 2024, there are about 106,000 left alive.*

Toyoko Sugano: For four years I was completely blind. I couldn't do anything, just lie in bed or occasionally sit up. Every morning it was so painful, I felt sad that I'd lived another day. When I was twenty-seven, my left eye suddenly became clear and I could see light. I couldn't get married. I didn't have my youth. When I was around thirty years old, an arranged marriage was offered to me. The man who had arranged the marriage asked me if I had been exposed to the A-bomb. And since I was quite innocent, I told him yes. He said the A-bomb is infectious and he ran away from the scene. He just stood up and left!

Hiroko Kawaguchi, ***third grader*****:** In the old days, many people hid their identity as A-bomb victims. Many women especially did not even apply for the atomic bomb victim's handbooks, hiding the fact that they were A-bomb victims, in order to attain their goal of getting married. Although I am currently grateful for the handbook, it took me a while to actually apply for it. Regarding marriage, I believed that I would marry someone whom my aunt and uncle would find for me. I eventually got married through a marriage interview. Fortunately, my new husband didn't care about my being an A-bomb victim. After getting married, I worried about my future children. I suffer from thyroid cancer. My elder brother and cousin also suffer from cancer. My daughter has an acoustic nerve tumor. I wonder if my daughter's illness can be attributed to the A-bombing.

* * *

Asaichi Okano, ***father of Kinue Okano, student at Hiroshima Jogakuin*****:** We received the news of my daughter's death, but, as her ashes and articles left behind were never found, I did not know how to believe or how to convince myself that she had died. I never lost hope that she must be alive somewhere, having escaped from danger by hiding behind something. But as I came to know the great power of the atomic bomb, little by little, I was obliged to lose hope that she was alive. Those days we tried to comfort ourselves by thinking that she died for the sake of our motherland. Now every time August 6th comes round I remember my daughter in her school uniform which she must have been wearing on the day of her death. I can't remember her in any other clothes.

Tsutomu Yamaguchi: I felt that my life ended in August of 1945, and that whatever might come after was my second life. I left the Mitsubishi company in February, 1946, when a great number of employees were discharged because there was no work for the shipyard. Then I decided that my second life, as I chose to regard it, should be spent in a way that would make a contribution to the people, and I took up educational work. I became a teacher of English in a junior middle school for the next nine years.

Ikuko Wakasa, *age 5*: I really hate to think about war and I hate to remember the day when the atom bomb fell. Even when I read books I skip the parts about war.

Tazu Shibama, *schoolteacher, Hiroshima Jogakuin*: Seeing Hiroshima today is like a miracle to me, because when I stood in front of that smashed railroad station, all I could see was the hill on the other side. All the houses and factories were gone. I thought it never would be rebuilt, because people said that when the A-bomb destroyed a city then nothing could live or grow for seventy-five years. But strangely enough, when spring came the next year, flowers started blooming and I saw green grass everywhere. That gave us hope to live.

Takuo Matsumoto: We feel we must appeal to all the nations and leaders of the world not to repeat such folly under any circumstances.

Jiro Shimasaki, *high school factory worker, Mitsubishi*: I would be happiest if I can talk about what happened to me to younger generations, including small children and elementary school students once a week, if possible, until I have no regrets before going to my death bed.

The dead await peace too: In Hiroshima's Peace Memorial Park, there are more than 800 identified remains of bomb victims from August 1945 waiting for any next of kin to claim them. A memorial for the Hiroshima girls' school, placed near where so many of them were working that day, features a carving of girl workers and a simple inscription: $E = MC^2$.

The 2024 Nobel Peace Prize was awarded to the survivor group Nihon Hidankyo "for its efforts to achieve a world free of nuclear weapons and for demonstrating through witness testimony that nuclear weapons must never be used again."

Terumi Tanaka, ***Nobel Peace Prize acceptance speech, December 10, 2024*****:** We established Nihon Hidankyo, the Japan Confederation of A- and H-Bomb Sufferers Organizations, in August 1956. Having ourselves survived the inhumane impacts of the atomic bombings, damage unprecedented in history, we launched this movement to ensure such suffering would never be repeated, with two basic demands. The first demand is that the State which started and carried out the war should compensate victims for the damage caused by the atomic bombs, in opposition to the Japanese government's assertion that, "the sacrifice of war should be endured equally by the whole nation." The second is to demand the immediate abolition of nuclear weapons, as extremely inhumane weapons of mass killing, which must not be allowed to coexist with humanity.

Our movement has undoubtedly played a major role in creating the "nuclear taboo." However, there still remain 12,000 nuclear warheads on the Earth today, 4,000 of which are operationally deployed, ready for immediate launch. Please try to imagine—there are 4,000 nuclear warheads, ready to be launched immediately. This means that damage hundreds or thousands of times greater than that which happened in Hiroshima and Nagasaki could happen right away.

Maj. Peer de Silva, ***security director, Manhattan Project*****:** Those bombs are now referred to as the Model Ts of their time.

Rudolf Peierls: It is not the scale of destruction that gave war a new dimension with the introduction of the atom bomb; what was new was the ease with which the weapon can be used, with a single plane creating the kind of destruction that could previously have been accomplished only by a massive military operation. We knew the destructive powers of the bomb, and its radiation effects, and Frisch and I pointed this out in our first memorandum. We knew the ease with which it could be used, and therefore the terrible responsibility it would impose on the political and military leaders who would have to decide whether and when to use it.

J. Robert Oppenheimer, ***remarks to Los Alamos scientists, November 2, 1945*****:** We did this job because it was an organic necessity. If you are a scientist you cannot stop such a thing. If you are a scientist you believe that it is good to find out how the world works; that it is good to find out what the realities are; that it is good to turn over to mankind at large the greatest possible power to control the world and to deal with it according to its lights and its values.

Lewis L. Strauss: The decision to use the atomic bomb to accelerate the end of a war already won was not the same as the one five years earlier when a decision had been taken to make the bomb. Yet both were decisions by compassionate men within the finite limits of human judgment. Both were decisions made by our chosen representatives. All of us in some degree shared an inescapable responsibility which will be judged, as Churchill has said, "in the after-time."*

Adm. William Leahy: It is my opinion that the use of this barbarous weapon at Hiroshima and Nagasaki was of no material assistance in our war against Japan. The Japanese were already defeated and ready to surrender because of the effective sea blockade and the successful bombing with conventional weapons. In being the first to use it, we had adopted an ethical standard common to the barbarians of the Dark Ages. I was not taught to make war in that fashion.

Edward Teller: I have been asked again and again, if I have regrets. Will you please excuse me, this is one of the most idiotic questions, except for the fact that apparently others do have regrets. I may suffer from some moral insufficiency, but I don't have regrets. I didn't put the world together and if you had the choice that something simple that was in the long run unavoidable should be first done by the United States or the Nazis or by the Soviets or by someone else, would you have regrets to make sure we did it first?

Col. Paul W. Tibbets: For years, the anniversary of Hiroshima would bring telephone calls from news media all over the country, ostensibly to request interviews but actually, and not so subtly, to inquire about my health and

* Strauss, a wealthy businessman and philanthropist, would go on to have a key role in the postwar Washington establishment, as one of the first members of the Atomic Energy Commission, where he would famously have a showdown with Oppenheimer later. During the war, he worked at the Bureau of Ordnance and then founded the Office of Naval Research, eventually rising to the rank of rear admiral in the reserve. His nomination to be commerce secretary in the Eisenhower administration erupted into one of the most bitter confirmation fights in modern history.

mental conditions. Always, the reporter seemed surprised and a bit disappointed to learn that I was leading a perfectly normal life and had no intention of repudiating my role in the historic event. Today's controversy over the use of the atomic bomb is interesting in view of the fact that in 1945, Americans were almost unanimously thankful that such a miracle weapon had been developed. The A-bomb ended the war and brought the boys home, and that was what counted.

Lise Meitner: What still gives ground for anxiety, of course, is what mankind will make of this newly won knowledge, which could come to be used for destruction on a tremendous scale.

C. P. Snow: Mark Oliphant said sadly, when the first atomic bomb was dropped: "This has killed a beautiful subject."

Alvin M. Weinberg: We nuclear people have made a Faustian bargain with society. On the one hand we offer, in the breeder, an inexhaustible source of energy. Moreover, this source of energy when properly handled is almost nonpolluting. Whereas fossil-fuel burners emit oxides of carbon, nitrogen, and sulfur, there is no intrinsic reason why nuclear systems must emit any pollutant except heat and a trace of radioactivity. But the price that we demand of society for this magical source is both a vigilance from and a longevity of our social institutions that we are quite unaccustomed to.

Maj. Charles W. Sweeney: One day, those of us who fought the war—who were eyewitnesses to it—will no longer be here to set the record straight. What, then, will future generations be told about America's role in the war in the Pacific? Who will be left to give an accurate firsthand account?

Hideo Matsuno, *reporter*: With more and more time passing by, it is essential that these things be recorded in books or passed down orally. We need to make sure that such an atrocity doesn't happen again.

Etsuko Nagano, *Hibakusha*: Please help us be the last victims of the atomic bombs. We don't want anybody in this world to suffer the agony that we have been experiencing.

Sunao Kanazaki, *Hibakusha*: No A-bomb must ever fall again. We don't need any more survivors.

Shigeko Hirata, *Hibakusha*: Let us live happily like little song-birds.

Kazuo Chujo, *Hibakusha*: Once a war is started, it cannot be stopped easily. Before the rock starts hurtling downhill, I insist each of us try to curb any sign that might lead to war. Once the rock starts rolling, humanity will witness another Hiroshima. The holocaust will be for once and for all.

Albert Einstein: I do not know how the Third World War will be fought, but I can tell you what they will use in the Fourth—rocks.

ACKNOWLEDGMENTS

In the summer of 2016 in a dusty antique store near Gloversville on the way to a friend's wedding in upstate New York, I found in a forgotten corner a framed newspaper touting the first atomic bomb. It was the August 7, 1945, edition of the Fulton County *Morning Herald* with a giant banner headline: "New Weapon May Lead to a New Ultimatum." I immediately knew I wanted it, but it had no price tag on it, and as I asked the clerk, I remember trying to do the mental calculation of what my upper limit for the artifact was. *$60? $100?* When the reply came of just "$10," it was a no-brainer. It's hung every day since on my office wall. The paper is an incredible time capsule of the moment—the stories all betray the befuddlement of that first-day news coverage about this new weapon. The sub-headlines read "US, Britain Pooled Atomic Facts"; "Sun Power Loosed on 'Setting Sun'"; "America's Atomic Bomb May Speed World Peace"; "It May Open Up a New Science"; and "Allies Possess 'Monster'—Withheld 'By God's Mercy' from German Scientists." And, if you look closely, there's another headline in the lower right corner hinting at the Cold War to come, "Illuminate 'Mystery Areas' Vandenberg Asks of the 'Big 3,'" warning of the descending blackout across Poland and other areas of Eastern Europe—what Churchill would label in a few years the "Iron Curtain"—and showing how even that August the world was lurching toward a new reality.

The work of the Manhattan Project and the invention of the atomic bomb changed everything about our politics, geopolitics, and science since, a simple fact that I feel ever more intensely as a historian and journalist given that this is now my second book on the history of the US and nuclear weapons. Before and in between, I've now spent two decades covering the US government, national security, and history—in newspaper columns, magazine articles, podcasts, TV documentaries, and a total of ten books—and I've come to think of my work as encompassing its own "historical cinematic universe," akin to my personal Marvel Cinematic Universe or DC Universe, where all the comic heroes and villains live and interact. My work comprises a living cinematic universe of our time, where all of the books and stories reflect and interact with each other and the "characters" cross from one book to another. If you lined them all up Carrie Mathison–style on a bulletin board you'd end up with quite the fascinating crazy spiderwebs with all the connections.

Dwight Eisenhower, one of the stars of my D-Day oral history, has been a major "character" in two of my other books, including *Raven Rock*—about the Cold War nuclear war plans and all that comes after August 7, 1945—and *Watergate*, where he chooses and promotes a young Richard Nixon as his vice president. Similarly, a young Elliot Richardson appeared in my D-Day oral history, *When the Sea Came Alive*, and reappears in *Watergate* talking of that same experience on June 6, 1944, as he faces the pressure of the Saturday Night Massacre. Bill Cooper, one of the leading UFO conspiracists of the 1980s, was a star character in my *Long Shadow* podcast on the rise of the Far Right, as his talk radio show helps inspire a young Austin public access host named Alex Jones. No book I've written so thoroughly webs across my "historical cinematic universe" as this one. The atomic bomb not only changes almost everything as a "what" but the "who" who would found the atomic age are some of the biggest players in what follows. The 509th Composite Group relocating post-Tinian at the end of the war sets them up for the starring role in the still-mysterious Roswell incident, where the wreckage of *something* ending up on the office floor of Col. William Blanchard kicks off my *UFO* book. Enrico Fermi, during a postwar lunch at Los Alamos, asks the most famous question in extraterrestrial studies: If life is so common across the universe, he ponders, *where are they*? That "Fermi Paradox" gets its own chapter in that *UFO* book. Similarly, Vannevar Bush, Lewis Strauss, Curtis LeMay, and many others from this book go on to starring roles in the postwar DC establishment that has been the focus of much of my writing. I write in *Raven Rock*, too, how the Mosler Safe Company gets the government contract to build the bunker doors for the US government's doomsday facilities after its bank safes are found to be one of the few surviving structures in the wake of the bombing of Hiroshima. And so forth and so on. Much of the fun of learning history to me has always been understanding why the world is today the way that it is.

Similarly, I find every new book project a wonderful opportunity to step into a new "cinematic universe" built by and inhabited by all the historians, researchers, and journalists who have also excavated that subject over the years. This subject was a particularly rich experience in that sense, as I've been able to rely on enormous work by previous researchers who had the chance to speak with these players during their lives—the insightful quotes from George C. Marshall mostly come from interviews with Forrest Pogue, for instance—and groundbreaking historians like Stephane Groueff, Richard Rhodes, Joseph Papalia, and others, who first uncovered the mysteries of the Manhattan Project. Many of their interview transcripts have been archived by the Atomic Heritage Foundation in a tremendous trove for future researchers, and I deeply appreciate the work of the AHF to keep these stories alive; its online resources are a researcher's blessing, including not just voluminous oral histories but personnel listings and ranks that I relied on to help fill out the IDs for this book. Every historian who ever touches this story will owe a giant debt to Robert Krauss, whose work and curation is responsible for much of what we will know about the stories of the 509th today and forevermore, and the stories of Los Alamos live on in no small part thanks to the work of Jane Wilson, Charlotte Serber, and others, including the decades of work by the Los Alamos Historical Society, who keep watch over a fabulous little museum just off Bathtub Row atop the mesa today. Similarly and specifically, I am enormously grateful to the many translators, Japanese, American, and others, past and present, who all helped bring the stories of Hibakusha to American ears. (Given that I was working off English translations already, I have purposely left all Japanese names in the form that they were rendered by the translator.)

I owe a huge intellectual debt to a host of canonical books about the Manhattan Project and the Pacific War, including the biography by Kai Bird and Martin Sherwin, *American Prometheus*, which became the big-screen hit *Oppenheimer*, as well as Richard Rhodes's *The Making of the Atomic Bomb*, Richard Franks's *Downfall: The End of the Imperial Japanese Empire,* Max Hastings's *Retribution: The Battle for Japan 1944–45*, as well as more recent works like James M. Scott's *Black Snow: Curtis LeMay, the Firebombing of Tokyo, and the Road to the Atomic Bomb*, Paul Ham's *Hiroshima Nagasaki*, and M.G. Sheftall's *Hiroshima: The Last Witnesses*. Hands down the most fun book I read for this project was Craig Symonds's *Nimitz at War: Command*

Leadership from Pearl Harbor to Tokyo Bay. Rhodes's book, which I've now read multiple times over the years, is as close to poetry as anything a historian can write. Just gaze upon the beauty of this onrushing sentence as it unfurls before you: "Condon pulled from a bookshelf a copy of Shakespeare's *The Tempest* and skimmed it for speeches meant for Prospero's enchanted island that might play contrapuntally against Oppenheimer's high and dry and secret mesa where no one had a street address, where mail was censored, where drivers' licenses went nameless, where children would be born and families live and a few people die behind a post-office box in devotion to the cause of harnessing an obscure force of nature to build a bomb that might end a brutal war."

Los Alamos captured the romance of the Manhattan Project and has been enormously well-documented over the years—I compiled dozens of previous works on life atop the mesa for this project—so I'm particularly indebted to three major efforts that helped preserve the less well-known stories of Hanford and Oak Ridge: S. L. Sanger's book *Working on the Bomb: An Oral History of WWII Hanford* and William Compton's *Memories of Early Atomic Pioneers*, both of which were invaluable, as was a giant effort by the Oak Ridge Public Library to compile video and written oral histories, all now available online. The latter project is a reminder of how libraries are the lifeblood of so many of our communities and such an incredible part of our civic fabric and national memory and why all of us owe them our thanks and defense as libraries and librarians face unprecedented attacks and challenges in the modern environment.

Similarly, every historical project I undertake leads me to wonder at the marvels that we've created in the National Archives, Library of Congress, and the presidential library system here in the US. The knowledge and records that they contain—often online and always free!—is astounding. For this project, I relied on at least three presidential libraries—Franklin Roosevelt, Harry Truman, and Dwight Eisenhower—and found their resources rich and staff helpful whenever needed. I am also deeply grateful to a whole host of other archivists and research librarians I worked with across the country in exhuming relevant materials, oral histories, photos, and more—including Director of Collections Management Toni M. Kiser at the National World War II Museum in New Orleans, who once again fielded a huge document request for me, Laura Santoyo at the American Academy of Pediatrics, Miriam Camacho Cabrera at the Special Collections & Archives for UC San Diego,

Sheila Bickle at the Woman's Collection at Texas Woman's University, and the team at the American Institute of Physics, as well as Olivia Fermi, who helped me track down photos of her grandparents. The Internet Archive allowed me to peruse a whole pile of long-out-of-print books that would have been nearly impossible to source otherwise.

To help sort through it all I am deeply, deeply grateful to four people for helping with the extraordinarily wide-ranging research for this project, which stretched across continents and centuries: Will DiGravio, Emily Piche, Nina Howe-Goldstein, and Gaelen Kilburn. This is my third book project with Will, who as before did yeoman's work on gathering quotations, source notes, references, and locating obscure documents. Emily Piche was a huge help in the final press of the book and with gathering the first-person stories of the Hibakusha, a uniquely traumatizing set of experiences, and I appreciate her willingness to wade into them. Every oral history project I do also owes a tremendous moral debt to Jenny Pachucki, my friend and collaborator on my original 9/11 oral history project, who taught me so much about this tradition.

At Avid Reader Press, this was the sixth book I started with the incredible duo of Jofie Ferrari-Adler and Julianna Haubner. I was terribly (*terribly!*) sorry when Julianna departed mid-project, but am forever grateful to her for all that she's done to shape me as a writer. Carolyn Kelly stepped in midstream and provided some incisively thoughtful suggestions.

I've done enough book projects to understand that "writing" the book is in many ways one of the smaller slices of what makes a project successful, and for all of the other slices, I owe thanks to my literary agent Howard Yoon and the team at WME—including Gail Ross, Dara Kaye, Jennifer Manguera, and the rest of the Ross Yoon team—as well as all the people who stand behind and around Jofie at Avid Reader Press and Simon & Schuster, including not least copy chief Jonathan Evans and copyeditor Fred Chase—both of whom I pressed to the limit with the project. (Sorry? And THANKS.) Fred, as always, saved me from a handful of bumbling errors that would have forever haunted me—and for the remainder of the as-yet-unidentified bumbling errors that will be the ones that in the end haunt me forever, I apologize to you, dear reader! Art director Alison Forner and book designer Kyle Kabel have done much to turn what you're holding in your hands into a full, living experience, from the cover to the interior design to the photos. I'm grateful, too, as always, to my longtime book-partners publicist David Kass and marketing leader

Meredith Vilarello, and Avid's other team members, including Eva Kerins and Katya Wiegmann, and many more. (For the full list, see the box at the back of this book, which underscores how many people touch a project like this and how many different "publishing" careers there can be!) Jon Karp remains a great champion for my work, and I'm proud to be in his S&S stable.

In the UK, I'm thankful for the help and guidance, too, of my editors and publishers there at Monoray Books, Jake Lingwood and especially Mala Sanghera-Warren, who helped drive us toward the title for this project.

At The Aspen Institute, I'd also like to thank Vivian Schiller, the world's greatest boss™, for giving me the freedom to tackle "hobbies" like books, and my colleagues at Aspen Digital, especially Beth Semel, Jeff Greene, Sasha O'Connell, and Chris Krebs, as well as my wider web of professional colleagues, including Ryan Sweikert and John Patrick Pullen at Long Lead and Michael Duffy and Mark Lotto at the *Washington Post*, who all let me pursue such fascinating stories in this modern-day cinematic universe. More broadly, I'd like to thank my corps of friends who feign interest in my latest endeavor and have kept me company spiritually during this incredibly challenging time in our world, including Mary Sprayregen, Dave Schilling, Katie and Rich Van Haste, Dan Reilly, Tam and Julie Veith, Jon and Vonnie Murad, Meg Little Reilly, Libby Franklin, Elizabeth Ralph, Nicco Mele, J.P. Fielder, Erin Delmore, Zach Dorfman, and Shane Harris. Here I deeply miss Savilla Pitt and Blake Hounshell too. I owe a special thanks, amid these particularly strange times, to my trio of cyber friends David Lashway, Sandra Joyce, and Geoff Brown, who have done so much to keep my spirits high and taught me so much about how to live a life well-lived. I owe a very special thanks, too, to Joe de Feo, whose painting *Meanwhile* kept me company for much of this project and provided daily inspiration.

In every one of my books, I thank an ever-growing list of people who have touched my life and been critical to me being who and where I am today. Among those who shaped my life path: Charlotte Stocek, Mary Creeden, Mike Baginski, Rome Aja, Kerrin McCadden, and Charlie Phillips; John Rosenberg, Peter J. Gomes, Richard Mederos, Brian Delay, Stephen Shoemaker, and Jennifer Axsom; Kit Seeyle, Pat Leahy, David Bradley, Rusty Greiff, Tim Seldes, Jesseca Salky, Paul Elie, Tom Friedman, Jack Limpert, Geoff Shandler, Susan Glasser, John Harris, David Shipley, and, not least of all, Cousin Connie, to whom I owe a debt that I strive to repay each day. My parents, Chris and Nancy Price Graff, have encouraged me to write since an early age, instilling in me a love of history and research and an intellectual curiosity that benefits me daily, and my marine biologist sister Lindsay has always been my biggest fan—and I hers. I am especially grateful for the more routine support as well that they've lent us as grandparents and aunt over the last seven years as I've written alongside parenting, from French toast bake to time at camp and the beach.

At home, our nanny Renèe Hallowell has given me the time and space to write for more than five years now, and I'm forever grateful for her calm and caring presence in my family's crazy and chaotic life, as I am for the extra help we get from Katey, Lexie, Lily, and Ty, who together help us balance, as best we can, that never-quite-right line of parenting and work. I continue to owe a daily debt to my friend Mary Louise Kelly, whose book *It. Goes. So. Fast.* changed my whole mental approach to parenting and gives me strength and vigor when I am most tired and impatient. And, of course, KB: Thank you.

—Garrett M. Graff
Burlington, VT
April 13, 2025

A NOTE ON SOURCES

The bulk of the 500 or so voices in this book are pulled from large-scale oral history projects, including efforts housed at the American Institutes of Physics, the Atomic Heritage Foundation and the National Museum of Nuclear Science & History, the Oak Ridge Public Library, and elsewhere, as well as from first-person participant memoirs and autobiographies published across the eight decades since World War II.

The main primary sources for these quotations are listed below, arranged by archival repository or publication. Some collections are available online, in which case the web address is noted. Other, more limited or atypical sources—including books, magazines, and videos—are noted in specific endnotes that follow. In some cases, like Leslie Groves or Paul Tibbets, quotations have been drawn from multiple locations. In those situations, the primary source responsible for the majority of that individual's quotations is listed below and exceptions, gleaned from other interviews with journalists or historians or documents published over the years, are noted specifically as exceptions in the endnotes that follow.

ORAL HISTORY COLLECTIONS

Oak Ridge Public Library

Available online at: https://cdm16107.contentdm.oclc.org/

R. L. Ayers
Hubert Barnett
Edward S. Bettis
Colleen Black
Connie Bolling
Juanita Cardwell
Charmian Cohn
Waldo E. Cohn
J. Nash Copeland
Tom Dunigan
Paul Elza
Hetty Horton

James Reagan Justice
Louise Keaton
Christopher Keim
Marjorie Ketelle
Ernest M. Lees
Mike Linden
John Michel
Mary Michel
Karl Z. Morgan
Charles E. Normand
Leta Orrison
Doris Reynolds
William Reynolds
John Shacter
Meyer Silverman
Donald Trauger
Marjorie Walls
Horace V. Wells, Jr.
Graydon Whitman
William Wilcox
Hal Williams

Japanese Ministry of Foreign Affairs, Testimony of Hibakusha

Available online at: https://www.mofa.go.jp/policy/un/disarmament/arms/testimony_of_hibakusha/

Chitoshi Honda
Hiroko Kawaguchi
Jungo Kawanami
Toshio Miyachi
Ayako Okumura
Namio Sakamoto
Jiro Shimasaki
Tsunematsu Tanaka
Sachiko Yasui

Eisenhower Center / National World War II Museum

New Orleans, La.

Edgar Harrell
Paul Murphy
Frank Tarkington

FIRST-PERSON MEMOIRS, AUTOBIOGRAPHIES, ESSAYS, AND HISTORIES

Tatsuichiro Akizuki, *Nagasaki 1945* (Quartet Books, 1981)
Luis W. Alvarez, *Alvarez: Adventures of a Physicist* (Basic Books, 1989)
Bernice Brode, *Tales of Los Alamos: Life on the Mesa 1943–1945* (Los Alamos Historical Society, 1997)
Vannevar Bush, *Pieces of the Action* (Morrow, 1970)
James F. Byrnes, *All In One Lifetime* (Harper & Brothers, 1958)
Kazuo Chujo, *The Nuclear Holocaust: A Personal Account* (Asahi Shinbunsha, 1983)
Winston S. Churchill, *The Second World War: The Hinge of Fate* (Houghton Mifflin, 1950)
James Conant, *My Several Lives: Memoirs of a Social Inventor* (Harper & Row, 1970)

Arthur Holly Compton, *Atomic Quest: A Personal Narrative* (Oxford University Press, 1956)

Peer de Silva, *Sub Rosa: The CIA and the Uses of Intelligence* (Crown, 1978)

Robert L. Eichelberger, *Our Jungle Road to Tokyo* (Zenger Pub. Co., 1982)

Laura Fermi, *Atoms in the Family: My Life with Enrico Fermi* (University of Chicago Press, 1995)

Richard P. Feynman, *Surely You're Joking, Mr. Feynman!* (Norton, 2010)

James C. Forrestal, *The Forrestal Diaries* (Walter Millis, ed.) (Viking Press, 1951)

Otto R. Frisch, *What Little I Remember* (Cambridge University Press, 1980)

Joseph C. Grew, *Report from Tokyo: A Message to the American People* (Simon & Schuster, 1942)

Leslie Groves, *Now It Can Be Told: The Story of the Manhattan Project* (Harper, 1962)

Robert Guillain, *I Saw Tokyo Burning: An Eyewitness Narrative from Pearl Harbor to Hiroshima* (Trans. by William Byron) (Doubleday, 1981)

John Gunther, *Inside Africa* (Harper & Brothers, 1955)

Hanoch Gutfreund and Jürgen Renn, eds., *Einstein on Einstein: Autobiographical and Scientific Reflections* (Princeton University Press, 2020)

Michihiko Hachiya, *Hiroshima Diary: The Journal of a Japanese Physician, August 6–September 30, 1945* (University of North Carolina Press, 1995)

Otto Hahn, *Otto Hahn: My Life* (Trans. by Ernst Kaiser and Eithne Wilkins) (Herder and Herder, 1968)

Werner Heisenberg, *Physics and Beyond: Encounters and Conversations* (Harper & Row, 1972)

Gretchen Heitzler, *Meanwhile, Back at the Ranch* (Hidden Valley Press, 1980)

Masuo Kato, *The Lost War: A Japanese Reporter's Inside Story* (Knopf, 1946)

Ernest J. King and Walter Muir Whitehill, *Fleet Admiral King: A Naval Record* (W. W. Norton & Company, 1952)

Kiyoshi Kiyosawa, *Diary of Darkness* (Eugene Soviak, ed., trans. by Eugene Soviak and Kamiyama Tamie) (Princeton University Press, 2008)

William L. Laurence, *Dawn Over Zero: The Story of the Atomic Bomb* (Knopf, 1946)

Edwin Layton, with Roger Pineau and John Costello, *"And I Was There": Pearl Harbor and the Midway—Breaking the Secrets* (William Morrow and Company, 1985)

William D. Leahy, *I Was There: The Personal Story of the Chief of Staff to Presidents Roosevelt and Truman Based on His Notes and Diaries Made at the Time* (Whittlesey House, 1950)

Curtis LeMay, *Mission with LeMay* (Doubleday, 1965)

Leona Marshall Libby (Leona H. Woods), *The Uranium People* (Crane, Russak, 1979)

Douglas MacArthur, *Reminiscences* (McGraw-Hill, 1964)

George C. Marshall, "Interviews and Reminiscences for Forrest C. Pogue," George C. Marshall Foundation, available at: https://www.marshallfoundation.org/life-legacy/pogue-interviews/

Kurt Mendelssohn, *The World of Walther Nernst: The Rise and Fall of German Science 1864-1941* (University of Pittsburgh Press, 1973)

Kenneth D. Nichols, *The Road to Trinity* (Morrow, 2009)

Paul Numerof, *In August 1945* (Los Alamos Historical Society, 2007)

Mark Oliphant, "The Beginning: Chadwick and the Neutron," *Bulletin of the Atomic Scientists* (38:10, 1982)

Fred J. Olivi, *Decision at Nagasaki: The Mission That Almost Failed* (Self-published, 1999)

J. Robert Oppenheimer, *Letters and Recollections* (Alice Kimball Smith and Charles Weiner, eds.) (Harvard University Press, 1980)

Abraham Pais, *Subtle Is the Lord: The Science and the Life of Albert Einstein* (Oxford University Press, 2005)

Rudolf Peierls, *Bird of Passage: Recollections of a Physicist* (Princeton University Press, 1985)

Ernie Pyle, *Ernie's War: The Best of Ernie Pyle's World War II Dispatches* (David Nichols, ed.) (Random House, 1986)

I. I. Rabi, Robert Serber, Victor F. Weisskopf, Abraham Pais, and Glenn T. Seaborg, *Oppenheimer* (Charles Scribner's Sons, 1969)

Eleanor Stone Roensch, *Life Within Limits* (Los Alamos Historical Society, 1993)

Eleanor Roosevelt, *The Autobiography of Eleanor Roosevelt* (Harper & Bros, 1961)

Glenn T. Seaborg with Eric Seaborg, *Adventures in the Atomic Age: From Watts to Washington* (Farrar, Straus, and Giroux, 2001)

Emilio Segré, *A Mind Always in Motion* (University of California Press, 1993)

Masao Shiotsuki, *Doctor at Nagasaki: "My First Assignment was Mercy Killing"* (Kōsei Publishing Co., 1989)

Holland M. Smith, with Percy Finch, *Coral and Brass* (Charles Scribner's Sons, 1949)

Hideko Tamura Snider, *One Sunny Day: A Child's Memories of Hiroshima* (Oregon State University Press, 2023)

C. P. Snow, *Variety of Men* (Alfred A. Knopf, 1967)

Ralph C. Sparks, *Twilight Time: A Soldier's Role in the Manhattan Project of Los Alamos* (Los Alamos Historical Society, 2000)

Lewis L. Strauss, *Men and Decisions* (Doubleday, 1962)

Charles W. Sweeney, with James A. Antonucci and Marion K. Antonucci, *War's End: An Eyewitness Account of America's Last Atomic Mission* (Avon Books, 1997)

Leo Szilard, *Leo Szilard: His Version of the Facts* (Spencer Weart and Gertrud Weiss Szilard, eds.) (MIT, 1978)

Edward Teller, *Memoirs: A Twentieth-Century Journey in Science and Politics* (Basic Books, 2002)

Paul W. Tibbets, *Flight of the Enola Gay* (Buckeye Aviation Book Co., 1989)

Harry S. Truman, *Memoirs by Harry S. Truman: Year of Decisions* (Signet Classics, 1965)

Yasu Tsuchida, *A Witness of Hibakusha (Hiroshima in Summer, 1945)* (The Campaign Popularizing "A Witness of a Hibakusha," 1988)

Alvin W. Weinberg, *The First Nuclear Era: The Life and Times of Nuclear Fixer* (American Institute of Physics, 1994)

John A. Wheeler, *Geons, Black Holes, and Quantum Foam: A Life in Physics* (W. W. Norton, 1998)

Eugene Wigner, *The Recollections of Eugene P. Wigner: As Told to Andrew Szanton* (Basic Books, 2003)

THIRD-PARTY HISTORIES, ORIGINAL INTERVIEWS, AND COLLECTED FIRST-PERSON MEMORIES

The 509th Remembered: A History of the 509th Composite Group as Told by the Veterans that Dropped the Atomic Bombs on Japan
Edited by Robert Krauss and Amelia Krauss, 509th Press, 2005

Harold Agnew	Dorothy Allen	Esther Bartlett
Charles D. "Don" Albury	Russell F. Angeli	Kermit B. Beahan

Ralph C. Berger
Raymond P. Biel
Frederick C. Bock
Clyde L. Bysom
Thomas F. Costa
Philip E. Doane
John L. Downey
William C. Drainer
Kenneth L. Eidnes
Albert O. Felchlia
Ralph Fry
Russell E. Gackenbach
Raymond Gallagher
Leonard Godfrey
Paul Wayne Gruning
Russ Harlow
James Holmes
Morris R. Jeppson
Arthur J. Johnson
Lawrence H. Johnston
Thomas L. Karnes
Virginia P. Karnes
Donald F. Mastick
Robert C. McClary
Paul Metro
Mont J. Mickelson
Lennie R. Morrison
Richard H. Nelson
Gillon T. Niceley
James F. Nolan
Robert J. Petrolli
James Price
Norman Ramsey
Joseph Ross
Robert L. Shade
Armen Shamlian
Maurice C. Sullivan
Herbert D. Swasey
John L. Tucker
James F. Van Pelt
Franklin K. "Ken" Wey
Jack Widowsky

S. L. Sanger, *Working on the Bomb: An Oral History of WWII Hanford*
Portland State University, Continuing Education Press, 1995

Dale Babcock
Dewitt Bailey
Jesse Brinkerhoff
Robert E. Bubenzer
Frank Buck
Sam Campbell
Roger W. Fulling
Raymond P. Genereaux
Oswald H. Greager
David Hall
Annette Heriford
Norman Hilberry
Kathleen Hitchcock
Margaret Hoffarth
Joe Holt
Luzell Johnson
Vera Jo MacCready
Frank Mackie
Franklin T. Matthias
Frank McHale
C. Marc Miller
Meta Newson
Warren Nyer
Leon Overstreet
Harry Petcher
Jerry Saucier
Walter O. Simon
O. R. "Big" Simpson
Betsy Stuart
William J. Sweeney
Lloyd Wiehl
Marvin H. Wilkening

Children of the Atomic Bomb: Testament of the Boys and Girls of Hiroshima
Complied by Arata Osada, translated by Jean Clark Dan and Ruth Sieben-Morgen, Uchide Rokakuho Publishing House, 1989

Shintaro Fukuhara
Tohru Hara
Masayuki Hashimoto
Shigeko Hirata
Hisato Itoh
Noriko Iwata

Susumu Kimura
Kiyoharu Koike
Yohko Kuwabara
Naoko Masuoka
Eiko Matsunaga
Yamaoka Michiko
Tetsuo Miyata
Shigehiro Naito
Iwao Nakamura
Chizue Sakai
Setsuko Sakamoto
Yukiharu Suzuki
Shigeru Tasaka
Yokihisa Tokumitsu
Kiyoko Tsuga
Atsuko Tsujioka
Yoshiko Uchimura
Tokiko Wada
Yoshiaki Wada
Ikuko Wakasa
Setsuko Yamamoto
Yuriko Yamamura

George Weller, *First into Nagasaki: The Censored Eyewitness Dispatches on Post-Atomic Japan and Its Prisoners of War*
Crown Publishers, 2006

Vernon Benjamin
Richard Burke
George Duke
Norman Jones
Thomas Jones
Eddie Kuhn
James MacIntosh
William Miller
Richard Ranger
Joseph Valencourt
George Weller
Douglas Wilkie
Gerald Wilson

Behind Tall Fences: Stories and Experiences About Los Alamos at Its Beginning
Compiled by Mary E. Mann, edited by John C. Allred, Los Alamos Historical Society, 1995

Berlyn Brixner
Charles L. Critchfield
L.D.P. King
Joseph L. McKibben
Nicholas Metropolis
Hugh T. Richards
Robert Serber

Standing By and Making Do: Women of Wartime Los Alamos
Edited by Jane Wilson and Charlotte Serber, Los Alamos Historical Society, 1988

Jean Bacher
Shirley B. Barnett
Kathleen Mark
Ruth Marshak
Charlie Masters
Dorothy McKibbin
Charlotte Serber
Alice Kimball Smith
Jane S. Wilson

William M. Compton, *Memories of Early Atomic Pioneers: Memories of Early Pioneers of the Atomic Energy Commission Hanford Engineering Works*
Reach Museum, 2015

Obie Amacker
Bill Compton
Bob Gilbert
Annette Heriford
William (Bill) P. McCue, Sr.
W. K. MacCready
Frank J. McHale
Blake Miller

Haruko Taya Cook, *Japan at War: An Oral History*
The New Press, 1992

Nogi Harumichi
Yamaoka Michiko
Noda Mitsuharu
Uno Shintaro
Tominaga Shozo
Shin Bok Su
Kimura Yasuko
Matsushige Yoshito

Summer Cloud: A-Bomb Experience of a Girls' School in Hiroshima
Edited by Hiroshima Jogakuin Jr. & Sr. High School English Department
Sanyusha Shuppan, 2016

Junko Fujimoto
Keiko Hatta
Kazu Kishimoto
Takuo Matsumoto
Asaichi Okano
Fumiko Sasaki
Setsuko Tanaka

All in Our Time: Reminiscences of Twelve Nuclear Pioneers
Edited by Jane Wilson, Bulletin of the Atomic Scientists, 1975

Philip B. Abelson
Herbert L. Anderson
Kenneth T. Bainbridge
Val L. Fitch
Boyce McDaniel
Albert Wattenberg
Robert R. Wilson

Reminiscences of Los Alamos, 1943–1945
Edited by Lawrence Badash, J. O. Hirschfelder, and H. P. Broida, Springer, 1980

Norris Bradbury
John H. Dudley
Joseph O. Hirschfelder
George B. Kistiakowsky
John H. Manley
Edwin M. McMillan
Elsie McMillan

Nagasaki: Voices of A-Bomb Survivors
The Nagasaki Testimonial Society, Self-published, 2009

Charles Barkie
J.H.C. DeGroot
Jonghwon Kim
Soongil Kim
Kisang Lee
Jurgen R. Onken

Robert Trumbull, *Nine Who Survived Hiroshima and Nagasaki: Personal Experiences of Nine Men Who Lived Through Both Atomic Bombings*
E. P. Dutton, 1957

Tsuitaro Doi
Kenshi Hirata
Akira Iwanaga
Sakairo Mishima
Takejiro Nishioka
Tsutomu Yamaguchi

Diana Wickes Roose, *Teach Us to Live: Stories from Hiroshima and Nagasaki*
Intentional Productions, 2007

Sunao Kanazaki
Hiromu Morishita
Tazu Shibama
Toyoko Sugano
Sumiteru Taniguchi

Nowhere to Remember: Hanford, White Bluffs, and Richland to 1943
Edited by Robert Bauman and Robert Franklin, Wayne State University Press, 2018

Ray Derenleau
Jay Perry
Claude Rawlins

Give Me Water: Testimonies of Hiroshima and Nagasaki
A Citizens' Group to Convey Testimonies of Hiroshima and Nagasaki, Self-published, 1973

Hakuzo Iwamoto
Futaba Kitayama

SOURCE NOTES

Author's Note

xvii *"Robert Furman, an":* Robert Furman, interview by Finn Aaserud, March 7, 2002, Niels Bohr Library & Archives, American Institute of Physics, College Park, Maryland, https://www.aip.org/history-programs/niels-bohr-library/oral-histories/25565.

xxi *"the question of morality":* James D. Hornfischer, *The Fleet at Flood Tide: America at Total War in the Pacific, 1944–1945* (Bantam Books, 2016), xviii.

Foreword: Dawn at Trinity

xvii *"For some hectic":* Department of the Army Files, "No. 1305 The Commanding General, Manhattan District Project (Groves) to the Secretary of War (Stimson)," July 18, 1945, https://history.state.gov/historicaldocuments/frus1945Berlinv02/d1305.

xvii *"The scene inside":* Ibid.

xxx *"As the time":* Ibid.

Particles Unseen

4 *"In the beginning":* Albert Einstein, "Autobiographical Notes," in *Albert Einstein, Philosopher-Scientist*, ed. P. A. Schilpp (MJF Books, 1970), 19.

4 *"Besides, the clothes":* Lucretius, *De Rerum Natura*, ed. William Ellery Leonard (Perseus Digital Library, 1916), https://www.perseus.tufts.edu/hopper/text?doc=Perseus%3Atext%3A1999.02.0131%3Abook%3D6%3Acard%3D470.

4 *"Democritus' opinions are":* Diogenes Laërtius, *Lives of the Eminent Philosophers*, trans. R. D. Hicks (Loeb Classical Library, 1925), https://penelope.uchicago.edu/Thayer/E/Roman/Texts/Diogenes_Laertius/Lives_of_the_Eminent_Philosophers/9/Democritus*.html.

4 "*All these things*": Isaac Newton, "from Query 31," *Opticks*, 1704, https://web.lemoyne.edu/giunta/newton.html, accessed April 7, 2025.

4 "*If the matter is worked back*": Ruggero Giuseppe Boscovich, *Theoria Philosophiæ Naturalis*, 1763, translated and published as *A theory of natural philosophy* (Open Court Publishing Co., 1922), 37, https://archive.org/details/theoryofnaturalp00boscrich/page/n5/mode/2up, accessed March 10, 2025.

4 "*Matter, though divisible*": *Dalton's Manuscript Notes*, Royal Institution Lecture 18 (Jan. 30, 1810) in Ida Freund, *The Study of Chemical Composition: An Account of its Method and Historical Development* (Cambridge University Press, 1904), 288.

5 "*Though I may*": Lise Meitner, "Looking Back," *Bulletin of the Atomic Scientists* 20, no. 9 (1964): 2–7.

5 "*Of what nature the rays*": Emilio Segrè, *From X-Rays to Quarks: Modern Physicists and Their Discoveries* (Dover Publications, 1980), 24.

6 "*Antoine Becquerel discovered*": Pierre Curie, "Radioactive Substances, Especially Radium," Nobel Lecture, June 6, 1905, https://www.nobelprize.org/uploads/2018/06/pierre-curie-lecture.pdf.

6 "*For more than*": Otto Hahn, "From the Natural Transmutations of Uranium to Its Artificial Fission," Nobel Lecture, December 13, 1946, https://www.nobelprize.org/uploads/2018/06/hahn-lecture.pdf.

6 "*Uranium emits very*": Pierre Curie, "Radioactive Substances, Especially Radium."

6 "*In making measurements*": Ibid.

6 "*All the elements*": Marie Curie, "Radium and the New Concepts in Chemistry," Nobel Lecture, December 11, 1911, https://www.nobelprize.org/prizes/chemistry/1911/marie-curie/lecture/.

7 "*If it were ever*": Ernest Rutherford, *Radio-activity* (2nd ed.) (New York: Juniper Grove, 2007), 336–38.

7 "*Einstein's work on*": Quoted in Abraham Pais, *Subtle Is the Lord—The Science and the Life of Albert Einstein* (Oxford University Press, 2005), 192.

8 "*In 1912 Niels*": Mark Oliphant, "The Beginning: Chadwick and the Neutron," *Bulletin of the Atomic Scientists* 38, no. 10 (1982): 14–18.

8 "*It could be*": Richard Rhodes, *The Making of the Atomic Bomb* (Simon & Schuster, 1986), 69.

8 "*Abstract thinking, which*": Niels Bohr, Nobel Banquet Speech, December 10, 1922, https://www.nobelprize.org/prizes/physics/1922/bohr/speech/.

9 "*Lord Rutherford suggested*": H. Pleijel, "Nobel Prize Award Ceremony Speech," December 10, 1935, https://www.nobelprize.org/prizes/physics/1935/ceremony-speech/.

10 "*Joliot and Irène*": Enrico Fermi, "Artificial Radioactivity Produced by Neutron Bombardment," Nobel Lecture, December 12, 1938, https://www.nobelprize.org/uploads/2018/06/fermi-lecture.pdf.

11 *"We not only believe":* Niels Bohr, "The Structure of the Atom," Nobel Lecture, December 11, 1922, https://www.nobelprize.org/uploads/2018/06/bohr-lecture.pdf.

11 *"If, in some cataclysm":* Richard Feynman, "Atoms in Motion," the Feynman Lectures, California Institute of Technology, https://www.feynmanlectures.caltech.edu/I_01.html, accessed April 8, 2025.

Darkness Falls on Europe

15 *over the course of 1923:* Rhodes, *The Making of the Atomic Bomb*, 18.

16 *"out of the prospering":* Ibid., 106

16 *"Antisemitism is strong here":* Ibid., 168.

17 *"We are moving":* Peter Gay, *Freud: A Life for Our Time* (Norton, 1998), 553.

17 *"How did Hitler come to power":* Louis Fischer, "The Road to Hitler," in *They Were There: The Story of World War II and How It Came About*, ed. Curt Riess (G. Putnam, 1944), 8.

18 *"The night of February 27, 1933":* John Gunther, "The Fire," in *They Were There*, 20.

19 *"The elimination of":* Edgar Ansel Mowrer, "Persecution of the Jews," in *They Were There*, 25.

19 *"I didn't take":* Otto Frisch, interview by Charles Weiner, American Institute of Physics, New York, New York, May 3, 1967, https://www.aip.org/history-programs/niels-bohr-library/oral-histories/4616.

19 *"Stringent new laws":* Ralph W. Barnes, "The Shame of Nuremberg," in *They Were There*, 43.

19 *"We must preserve":* Ibid., 45.

20 *"Breslau, where I":* Kurt Mendelssohn, *The World of Walther Nernst: The Rise and Fall of German Science, 1864–1941* (University of Pittsburgh Press, 1973), 164.

21 *"[Rutherford] did a":* Rhodes, *The Making of the Atomic Bomb*, 195.

22 "'Physics as soma'": Giuseppe Bruzzaniti, *Enrico Fermi: The Obedient Genius*, trans. Ugo Bruzzo (Springer, 2007), 90.

Fleeing Fascism

27 *"At the Dutch":* George Axelsson, "Is the Atom Terror Exaggerated?," *Saturday Evening Post*, January 5, 1946.

28 *"Lise Meitner was the intellectual":* Ruth Lewin Sime, *Lise Meitner: A Life in Physics* (University of California Press, 1996), 241.

29 *"Frisch looked up":* Richard Rhodes, *The Making of the Atomic Bomb* (Simon & Schuster, 1986), 263.

31 *"When fission was discovered":* Ibid., 274–75.

Adjusting to the New World

33 *"The murder of Czechoslovakia":* Edward W. Beattie, "The Protector," in *They Were There: The Story of World War II and How It Came About*, ed. Curt Riess (Putnam, 1944), 126–29.

36 *"I felt it was":* Alexander Sachs, "Opening Testimony: Background and Early History Atomic Bomb Project in Relation to President Roosevelt," Hearing Before the Special Committee on Atomic Energy, United States Senate, Seventy-Ninth Congress, First Session, November 27, 1945, http://www.fdrlibrary.marist.edu/_resources/images/ergen/ergen903.pdf.

37 *"I was quite young":* Letter from Janet Coatesworth to Gertrud Szilard, August 29, 1964, Box 85, Folder 5, Leo Szilard Papers, UC–San Diego Special Collections & Archives.

38 *"I sought and waited":* Sachs, "Opening Testimony."

39 *"I brought the material":* Ibid.

41 *"You who are scientists":* Franklin Delano Roosevelt, "Radio Address Before the Eighth Pan American Scientific Congress, Washington, D.C.," May 10, 1940, The American Presidency Project, https://www.presidency.ucsb.edu/documents/radio-address-before-the-eighth-pan-american-scientific-congress-washington-dc.

The M.A.U.D. Committee

47 *"I was asked if":* James Chadwick, interview by Charles Weiner, April 20, 1969, Niels Bohr Library & Archives, American Institute of Physics, College Park, Maryland, https://www.aip.org/history-programs/niels-bohr-library/oral-histories/3974-4.

50 *"[The Nazis] have":* Herbert Childs, *An American Genius: The Life of Ernest Orlando Lawrence* (Dutton, 1968), 303.

52 *"I was brought in":* George Kistiakowsky, interview by Richard Rhodes, January 15, 1982, Cambridge, Massachusetts, Voices of the Manhattan Project, Atomic Heritage Foundation, https://ahf.nuclearmuseum.org/voices/oral-histories/george-kistiakowskys-interview/.

December 7, 1941

53 *"It was only":* R. Gordon Arneson, interview by Niel M. Johnson, June 21, 1989, Washington, D.C., Harry S. Truman Presidential Library, https://www.trumanlibrary.gov/library/oral-histories/arneson.

57 *"A general war in the Pacific":* Henry C. Wolfe, "MacArthur," in *They Were There*, ed. Curt Riess, 403.

60 *"We grew up in a world":* Max Hastings, *Retribution: The Battle for Japan, 1944–45* (Knopf, 2008), 332.

61 *"December 7, 1941—Mama":* Edwin Nakasone, interview by Russell Nakaishi, June 25, 2005, Go for Broke National Education Center, Japanese American Military History Collective, https://ndajams.omeka.net/items/show/1051456.

62 *"It was shocking":* Frances Perkins, interview by Dean Albertson, 1951–1955, Notable New Yorkers, Columbia University Libraries Oral History Research Office, http://www.columbia.edu/cu/lweb/digital/collections/nny//perkinsf/transcripts/perkinsf_8_1_66.html.

63 *"A democracy has":* George C. Marshall, interview by Forrest C. Pogue, February 15, 1957, Forrest C. Pogue Interview Tapes, The George C. Marshall Foundation, https://www.marshallfoundation.org/wp-content/uploads/2014/05/Marshall_Interview_Tape16.pdf.

Setting Up the Met Lab

68 *"We have taken a tremendous wallop":* Craig L. Symonds, *Nimitz at War: Command Leadership from Pearl Harbor to Tokyo Bay* (Oxford University Press, 2022), xvi.

68 *"Before we're through":* Bob Drury and Tom Clavin, *Halsey's Typhoon: The True Story of a Fighting Admiral, an Epic Storm, and an Untold Rescue* (Grove Press, 2007), 6.

71 *"When we went":* Albert Wattenberg, "December 2, 1942: The Event and the People," *Bulletin of the Atomic Scientists* 38, no. 10 (1982): 22–32.

72 *"The exponential piles":* Ibid.

FDR's OK

75 *"We were told to prove":* Norman Hilberry, interview by Stephane Groueff, March 7, 1965, Voices of the Manhattan Project, Atomic Heritage Foundation, https://ahf.nuclearmuseum.org/voices/oral-histories/norman-hilberrys-interview-1965-part-3/.

76 *"One of the most":* Vannevar Bush, interview by Eric Hodgins, 1964, MIT Libraries, https://dome.mit.edu/handle/1721.3/190108.

77 *"On June 17, 1942":* This and subsequent James C. Marshall quotes from James C. Marshall, interview by Stephane Groueff, November 4, 1965, Voices of the Manhattan Project, Atomic Heritage Foundation, https://ahf.nuclearmuseum.org/voices/oral-histories/colonel-james-c-marshalls-interview/.

78 *"Somervell and Styer":* Leslie Groves, interview by Stephane Groueff, January 5, 1965, Voices of the Manhattan Project, Atomic Heritage Foundation, https://ahf.nuclearmuseum.org/voices/oral-histories/general-leslie-grovess-interview-part-1/.

82 *"Oppenheimer understood the":* I. I. Rabi, "Introduction," in *Oppenheimer*, eds. Robert Serber et al. (Charles Scribner's Sons, 1969), 6.

83 *"We met in Berkeley":* United States Atomic Energy Commission, *In the Matter of J. Robert Oppenheimer: Transcript of Hearing Before Personnel Security Board and Texts of Principal Documents and Letters* (MIT Press, 1971).

83 *"We had an adventurous time":* Ibid.
83 *"I remember a most interesting":* Ibid.

Creating the Manhattan Engineer District

87 *"When Styer first":* Vannevar Bush, interview by Eric Hodgins, 1964, MIT Libraries, https://dome.mit.edu/handle/1721.3/190108.

89 *"The thing could've":* James B. Conant, interview by Stephane Groueff, October 11, 1965, Voices of the Manhattan Project, Atomic Heritage Foundation, https://ahf.nuclearmuseum.org/voices/oral-histories/james-b-conants-interview/.

91 *"He was decisive":* Joseph Volpe, "War and Peace in the Nuclear Age," interview by WGBH, March 3, 1986, https://web.archive.org/web/20240619035001/https://openvault.wgbh.org/catalog/V_BBB91989C3FB4F1FB0F19A8F02530985.

Three Big Decisions

96 *"I might well have":* United States Atomic Energy Commission, *In the Matter of J. Robert Oppenheimer: Transcript of Hearing Before Personnel Security Board and Texts of Principal Documents and Letters* (MIT Press, 1971).

96 *"Groves took the":* Vannevar Bush, interview by Eric Hodgins, 1964, MIT Libraries, https://dome.mit.edu/handle/1721.3/190108.

97 *"We began to notice":* United States Atomic Energy Commission, *In the Matter of J. Robert Oppenheimer*.

98 *"We had originally planned":* Ibid.

98 *"Colonel Dudley said":* Edwin McMillan, "Edwin McMillan's Lecture," uploaded September 12, 2022, Voices of the Manhattan Project, Atomic Heritage Foundation, https://ahf.nuclearmuseum.org/voices/oral-histories/edwin-mcmillans-lecture/. Note: Dudley was promoted from major to lieutenant colonel on November 5, 1942, in the midst of the hunt for Los Alamos, so for clarity's sake I refer to him as lieutenant colonel, since that's how his colleagues from Los Alamos mostly recall him.

100 *"The Ranch School":* Stirling Auchincloss Colgate, interview by Cynthia C. Kelly, November 16, 2005, Voices of the Manhattan Project, Atomic Heritage Foundation, https://ahf.nuclearmuseum.org/voices/oral-histories/stirling-auchincloss-colgates-interview/.

101 *"About December that year":* Edward Teller, *Memoirs: A Twentieth-Century Journey in Science and Politics* (Basic Books, 2002), 166.

102 *"They did permit":* Sharon Snyder, "December 1942 War Department Letter Spelled the End for Los Alamos Ranch School," *Los Almost Daily Post*, January 25, 2019, https://ladailypost.com/december-1942-war-department-letter-spelled-the-end-for-los-alamos-ranch-school/.

102 *"Oppenheimer gave a":* Stirling Auchincloss Colgate, interview by Cynthia C. Kelly.

102 *"Gradually, Nichols and":* James C. Marshall, interview by Stephane Groueff, November 4, 1965, Voices of the Manhattan Project, Atomic Heritage Foundation, https://ahf.nuclearmuseum.org/voices/oral-histories/colonel-james-c-marshalls-interview/.

103 *"Our reaction at":* Walter S. Carpenter, interview by Stephane Groueff, January 25, 1965, Voices of the Manhattan Project, Atomic Heritage Foundation, https://ahf.nuclearmuseum.org/voices/oral-histories/walter-s-carpenters-interview/.

104 *"There was no":* Gordon Goodman, "History Lessons from du Pont for the Successful Development of Future Public-Private Partnerships in Fusion Enterprises," IAEA Fusion Enterprises Workshop, June 13–15, 2018, Santa Fe, New Mexico, https://nucleus.iaea.org/sites/fusionportal/Shared%20Documents/Enterprises/2018/Presentations/13.06/Goodman.pdf.

104 *"I had my doubts":* Crawford H. Greenewalt, "DuPont's Crawford H. Greenewalt," Atomic Heritage Foundation, posted May 30, 2008, YouTube, 00:06:57, https://www.youtube.com/watch?v=eB8SZqghxvU&list=PL8B75F9553F4961D1&index=3.

104 *"Boy—that bunch":* Norman Hilberry, interview by Stephane Groueff, March 7, 1965, Voices of the Manhattan Project, Atomic Heritage Foundation, https://ahf.nuclearmuseum.org/voices/oral-histories/norman-hilberrys-interview-1965-part-3/.

Making the Pile

109 *"As well as measuring":* Albert Wattenberg, "December 2, 1942: The Event and the People," *Bulletin of the Atomic Scientists* 38, no. 10 (1982): 22–32.

112 *"The colonel confirmed his credentials":* Charles Pellegrino, *The Last Train from Hiroshima: The Survivors Look Back* (Henry Holt, 2010) 343.

113 *"We had planned":* Ibid.

115 *"From the middle":* Ibid.

117 *"About eight weeks":* Ibid.

Chain Reaction

119 *"On December 2":* Albert Wattenberg, "December 2, 1942: The Event and the People," *Bulletin of the Atomic Scientists* 38, no. 10 (1982): 22–32.

120 *"The rest of us":* Ibid.

120 *"The most important":* Ibid.

120 *"Fermi periodically read":* Ibid.

121 *"It was 11:30 am":* Ibid.

121 *"Why he picked me":* This and other Greenewalt quotes from Crawford Greenewalt, interview by Stephane Groueff, September 12, 1965, Voices of the Manhattan Project, Atomic Heritage Foundation, https://ahf.nuclearmuseum.org/voices/oral-histories/crawford-greenewalts-interview/.

122 *"Herb Anderson, Bill":* Wattenberg, "December 2, 1942: The Event and the People," 22–32.

123 *"We had several different":* Ibid.

123 *"The trace on":* Ibid.

124 *"The radiation and":* Ibid.

125 *"It worked":* Crawford H. Greenewalt, "DuPont's Crawford H. Greenewalt," Atomic Heritage Foundation, posted May 30, 2008, YouTube, 00:06:57, https://www.youtube.com/watch?v=eB8SZqghxvU&list=PL8B75F9553F4961D1&index=3.

125 *"After all the others":* Wattenberg, "December 2, 1942: The Event and the People," 22–32.

Los Alamos: Project Y

168 *"Nobody was supposed":* Robert F. Bacher, interview by Mary Terrall, June–August 1981, February 1983, Archives of the California Institute of Technology, Pasadena, California, https://oralhistories.library.caltech.edu/93/1/OH_Bacher_R.pdf.

169 *"We started out the job":* United States Atomic Energy Commission, *In the Matter of J. Robert Oppenheimer: Transcript of Hearing Before Personnel Security Board and Texts of Principal Documents and Letters* (MIT Press, 1971).

170 *"It was mostly":* Robert F. Bacher, interview by Mary Terrall.

170 *"The object of the project":* Robert Serber, *The Los Alamos Primer*, 1943 (University of California Press, 1992).

170 *"My directive was to lose":* United States Atomic Energy Commission, *In the Matter of J. Robert Oppenheimer*.

Los Alamos: Working on the Mesa

178 *"We had to get away":* Richard Rhodes, *The Making of the Atomic Bomb* (Simon & Schuster, 1986), 483.

178 *"The stay in Stockholm":* Ibid., 484.

178 *"The Royal Air Force":* Ibid.

178 *"The pilot realized":* Ibid., 485.

178 *"Once in England and recovered":* Ibid.

182 *"When there were parties":* United States Atomic Energy Commission, *In the Matter of J. Robert Oppenheimer: Transcript of Hearing Before Personnel Security Board and Texts of Principal Documents and Letters* (MIT Press, 1971).

182 *"I think it must":* Ibid.
184 *"Naturally I am prejudiced":* Ibid.
184 *"He knew and understood":* Rhodes, *The Making of the Atomic Bomb*, 570.
184 *"I consider Dr. Oppenheimer's":* United States Atomic Energy Commission, *In the Matter of J. Robert Oppenheimer: Transcript of Hearing Before Personnel Security Board and Texts of Principal Documents and Letters* (MIT Press, 1971)

Life on Bathtub Row

194 *"I was supposed":* Louis Hempelmann, interview by Martin Sherwin, August 10, 1983, Voices of the Manhattan Project, Atomic Heritage Foundation, https://ahf.nuclearmuseum.org/voices/oral-histories/louis-hempelmann-interview-part-1/.
194 *"Louie Hempelmann, who":* Henry L. Barnett, interview by Joseph Dancis, July–November 1996, Oral History Project, Pediatric History Center, American Academy of Pediatrics, https://downloads.aap.org/AAP/Gartner%20Pediatric%20History/Barnett.pdf.

Los Alamos: Designing the Bomb

207 *"It was such a":* This and subsequent Robert Christy quotes from Robert F. Christy, interview by Sara Lippincott, June 1994, Archives of the California Institute of Technology, Pasadena, California, https://oralhistories.library.caltech.edu/129/1/OH_Christy_R.pdf.
207 *"There seemed to":* Robert F. Bacher, interview by Mary Terrall, June–August 1981, February 1983, Archives of the California Institute of Technology, Pasadena, California, https://oralhistories.library.caltech.edu/93/1/OH_Bacher_R.pdf.
210 *"Von Neumann was":* Nicholas C. Metropolis, interview by William Aspray, May 29, 1987, Charles Babbage Institute, The Center for the History of Information Processing, University of Minnesota, Minneapolis, https://conservancy.umn.edu/server/api/core/bitstreams/0febae83-9953-48aa-b626-8637433d52de/content.

Hanford: Life in a Construction Camp

218 *just preparing the vast site:* Paul Ham, *Hiroshima Nagasaki: The Real Story of the Atomic Bombings and Their Aftermath* (HarperCollins, 2011), 125.

Hanford: Making Plutonium En Masse

228 *But there is an argument:* Steve Olson, *The Apocalypse Factory: Plutonium and the Making of the Atomic Age* (Norton, 2020), 2–3.

Hanford: The B Reactor

238 *"This was the first big reactor":* S. L. Sanger, *Working on the Bomb: An Oral History of WWII Hanford* (Portland State University, 1995), 161.
238 *"Something happened":* Ibid.

Boeing's Bomber

247 *The B-29 "Superfortress" was a giant:* James M. Scott, *Black Snow: Curtis LeMay, the Firebombing of Tokyo, and the Road to the Atomic Bomb* (W. W. Norton, 2022), 5, 22.
248 *"The B-29 airplane":* Charles Marshall and Lindsey Silvester, *The Global Twentieth: An Anthology of the 20th AF in WWII* (Global Press, 1988), 38.
249 *"Two of the very":* Ibid., 14.
249 *"It was so large and complicated":* Scott, *Black Snow*, 20.
249 *"Hap took the chances":* Ibid.
249 *"Shortly after Eddie's":* Ibid., 35.
251 *"This airplane has more bugs":* Ibid., 65.
251 *"As many bugs":* Ibid., 119.
252 *"Eglin Field had":* Paul Tibbets, interview by Dawn Letson, February 24, 1997, Women Airforce Service Pilots (WASP) Oral History Project, Texas Woman's University.
253 *"The way they handled":* Dorothea Johnson Moorman, Oral History Interview, October 24, 1976, WASP Oral History Project, Texas Woman's University.
253 *"The colonel said":* Ibid.
253 *"They were dumbfounded": Fly Girls: Breaking Barriers in the Skies*, dir. Laurel Ladevich, WGBH, 1999, https://www.pbs.org/wgbh/americanexperience/films/flygirls/#cast_and_crew.
253 *"From that day":* Ibid.
254 *"In mid-summer 1943":* Marshall and Silvester, *The Global Twentieth*, 23.
254 *"On 15 June 1944":* Ibid., 51.
254 *"Hell is on us":* James M. Scott, *Black Snow: Curtis LeMay, the Firebombing of Tokyo, and the Road to the Atomic Bomb* (W. W. Norton, 2022), 144.

Code Name Silverplate

256 *"One day [in September 1944]":* Studs Terkel, "One Hell of a Big Bang," *The Guardian*, August 6, 2002, https://www.theguardian.com/world/2002/aug/06/nuclear.japan.
256 *"General Ent laid out":* Ibid.

Training the 509th

271 *"I took the airplane":* Studs Terkel, "One Hell of a Big Bang," *The Guardian*, August 6, 2002, https://www.theguardian.com/world/2002/aug/06/nuclear.japan.

Spring 1945

282 *"When the world":* J. Robert Oppenheimer, "Remarks at Memorial Service for President Franklin Roosevelt, Los Alamos, April 15, 1945," in *Robert Oppenheimer: Letters and Recollection*, eds. Alice Kimball Smith and Charles Weiner (Stanford University Press, 1995), 288.

100 Tons of TNT

286 *"Why I chose":* J. Robert Oppenheimer, Letter to Leslie Groves, October 20, 1962, University Archives, https://www.universityarchives.com/auction-lot/oppenheimer-fantastic-tls-to-leslie-groves-re-at_AD94B89B68.

289 *"This is a solemn":* Harry S. Truman, "Announcing the Surrender of Germany," May 8, 1945, Miller Center, University of Virginia, https://millercenter.org/the-presidency/presidential-speeches/may-8-1945-announcing-surrender-germany.

Selecting the Targets

293 *"I watched block after block": Case Studies in Strategic Bombardment*, R. Cargill Hall, Ed. (Government Printing Office, 1998), 319, https://apps.dtic.mil/sti/pdfs/ADA443291.pdf.

293 *"When the bombers started":* This and subsequent quotes from Tsuchikura are from Martin Caidin, *Torch to the Enemy: The Fire Raid on Tokyo* (Bantam, 1960), 170-174.

293 *"Everywhere I looked":* James M. Scott, *Black Snow: Curtis LeMay, the Firebombing of Tokyo, and the Road to the Atomic Bomb* (W. W. Norton, 2022), 213.

293 *"The fire seemed like a wave":* Ibid., 226.

294 *"As far as the eye could see":* Ibid., 221.

294 *"I not only saw Tokyo":* Ibid.

294 *"The entire river surface was black":* Richard B. Frank, *Downfall: The End of the Imperial Japanese Empire* (Random House, 1999), 15.

295 *"The 9 March fire-bomb raid":* Gene Gurney, *Journey of the Giants: The Story of the B-29 "Superfort"—The Weapon That Won the War in the Pacific* (Coward-McCann, 1961), 309.

295 *"Tokyo has been reduced":* Scott, *Black Snow*, 265.

295 *"The best psychological warfare":* Hastings, *Retribution*, 281.

296 *All told, sixty-six Japanese cities:* Ibid., 318.
296 *"We must not get soft":* Scott, *Black Snow*, 198.
296 *"If we lose":* Ibid., 170.
297 *"The experts felt":* Lauris Norstad, oral history interview by Robert Jordan, December 1987, OH-558, Dwight D. Eisenhower Presidential Library, Abilene, Kans.
299 *"Although it was":* Henry Lewis Stimson, "The Decision to Use the Atomic Bomb," *Harper's*, February 1947, https://harpers.org/archive/1947/02/the-decision-to-use-the-atomic-bomb/.

The Interim Committee

301 *For every four tons:* Hastings, *Retribution*, 53, 133; caloric intake and oil from Ham, *Hiroshima Nagasaki*, 32, 134.
301 *the fight for Okinawa in late June:* Richard B. Frank, *Downfall: The End of the Imperial Japanese Empire* (Random House, 1999), 71.
303 *Although the scientists:* Aide-memoire of conversation between the president and the prime minister at Hyde Park, "Tube Alloys," September 18, 1944, Significant Documents Collection, Box 1, FDR-66, Franklin D. Roosevelt Presidential Library & Museum, available at http://www.fdrlibrary.marist.edu/_resources/images/atomic/atomic_03.pdf.
305 *"The decision was pretty":* Vannevar Bush, interview by Eric Hodgins, February 5, 1965, MIT Libraries, https://dome.mit.edu/handle/1721.3/190114.
305 *"On June 1":* Henry Lewis Stimson, "The Decision to Use the Atomic Bomb," *Harper's*, February 1947, https://harpers.org/archive/1947/02/the-decision-to-use-the-atomic-bomb/.
306 *"We had just":* George C. Marshall, interview by Forrest C. Pogue, February 15, 1957, Forrest C. Pogue Interview Tapes, The George C. Marshall Foundation, https://www.marshallfoundation.org/wp-content/uploads/2014/05/Marshall_Interview_Tape16.pdf.
306 *"That was also":* Lauris Norstad, oral history interview by Robert Jordan.
307 *"Our troops have the right view"*: Paul Ham, *Hiroshima Nagasaki: The Real Story of the Atomic Bombings and Their Aftermath* (HarperCollins, 2011), 13.
307 *"American fighting men"*: Richard Rhodes, *The Making of the Atomic Bomb* (Simon & Schuster, 1986), 597.
307 *"They are the bravest people"*: John Masters, *The Road Past Mandalay* (Harper and Bros., 1961), 155.
307 *"The entire population of Japan":* Stanley Weintraub, *The Last Great Victory: The End of World War II, July/August 1945* (Dutton, 1995), 205.
308 *"If we could defeat the enemy":* Frank, *Downfall*, 196.
308 *"We had to end":* George C. Marshall, interview by Forrest C. Pogue.
308 *"There never was any":* Vannevar Bush, interview by Eric Hodgins.

Trinity

316 *"It was like being at the bottom"*: This and subsequent Joan Hinton quotes from Ruth H. Howes and Caroline L. Herzenberg, *Their Day in the Sun: Women of the Manhattan Project* (Temple University Press, 1999), 56.

321 *"We knew the world":* J. Robert Oppenheimer, "Now I Am Become Death . . . ," Atomic Archive, accessed March 13, 2025, https://www.atomicarchive.com/media/videos/oppenheimer.html.

322 *"Some people claim":* Virginia Grant, "The Trinity Test," July 6, 2020, https://web.archive.org/web/20241204185041/https://www.lanl.gov/media/publications/national-security-science/2020-summer/the-trinity-test.

324 *Oppenheimer's own copy: The Bhagavad-gita*, trans. Arthur W. Ryder (University of Chicago Press, 1929), https://shreevatsa.net/ryder/1929-gita/Ryder-BG.pdf.

Potsdam with Truman

327 *"General Groves' special":* Department of the Army Files, "No. 1305 The Commanding General, Manhattan District Project (Groves) to the Secretary of War (Stimson)," July 18, 1945, https://history.state.gov/historicaldocuments/frus1945Berlinv02/d1305.

328 *"Up to this moment":* Winston S. Churchill, *The Second World War, Volume 6: Triumph and Tragedy* (Houghton Mifflin, 1948), 551–53.

328 *"Now all this nightmare":* Ibid., 552.

At Tinian

337 *"One time an armed guard":* Charles Marshall and Lindsey Silvester, *The Global Twentieth: An Anthology of the 20th AF in WWII, Vol. III* (Global Press, 1988), 40.

Moving the Bomb

341 *By war's end:* Bob Drury and Tom Clavin, *Halsey's Typhoon: The True Story of a Fighting Admiral, an Epic Storm, and an Untold Rescue* (Grove Press, 2007), 51.

341 *"The ferocity of the ground fighting":* George C. Marshall, *The Winning of the War in Europe and the Pacific: Biennial Report of the Chief of Staff of the United States Army 1943–1945, to the Secretary of War* (War Department / Simon & Schuster, 1945).

344 *"My group ran the":* Frank Tarkington, Digital Collections of the National World War II Museum, accessed March 13, 2025, https://www.ww2online.org/view/frank-tarkington#prewar-life.

347 *"We would have to":* Richard Goldstein, "Adrian Marks, 81, War Pilot Who Led Rescue of 56, Is Dead," *New York Times*, March 15, 1998, https://www.nytimes.com/1998/03/15/us/adrian-marks-81-war-pilot-who-led-rescue-of-56-is-dead.html.

The Day Before

351 *"You knew it was":* Dutch Van Kirk, "My True Course," July 2012, Wings & Things Guest Lecture Series, National Museum of the United States Air Force, https://www.nationalmuseum.af.mil/Portals/7/documents/transcripts/my_true_course_transcript.pdf.

352 *"Captain [William "Deak"]":* Ray Gallagher, interview by Joseph Papalia, uploaded September 12, 2022, Voices of the Manhattan Project, Atomic Heritage Foundation, https://ahf.nuclearmuseum.org/voices/oral-histories/ray-gallaghers-accounts-hiroshima-and-nagasaki-missions/.

Code Name Centerboard

360 *"Almighty Father, who":* William L. Laurence, *Dawn Over Zero: The Story of the Atomic Bomb* (Knopf, 1946), 208.

368 *"It's one of the":* Theodore Van Kirk, interview by the Georgia World War II Oral History Project, 2007, PBS, https://ny.pbslearningmedia.org/resource/2f7fea8a-2309-4bb3-80f1-f0f04cc5ff17/theodore-van-kirk-major-army-air-corps/.

371 *"What all of us":* Ray Gallagher, interview by Joseph Papalia.

372 *"Everything was burning":* Paul Ham, *Hiroshima Nagasaki: The Real Story of the Atomic Bombings and Their Aftermath* (HarperCollins, 2011), 297.

372 *"My God, what":* Paul W. Tibbets, with Clair C. Stebbins and Harry Franken, *The Tibbets Story* (Stein & Day, 2009), 226.

373 *"It was a terrific":* Laurence, *Dawn Over Zero*, 219.

Ground Zero in Hiroshima

377 *"The bombs' six-hundred-meter":* M.G. Sheftall, *Hiroshima: The Last Witnesses* (Dutton, 2024), 85.

377 *"August 6th began":* This and subsequent Siemes quotes are pulled from "Atomic Bomb on Hiroshima [—] Eyewitness Account of P. Siemes," n.d. [Translated from the German by Averill A. Liebow, 27 September 1945], https://nsarchive.gwu.edu/document/30506-document-25-atomic-bomb-hiroshima-eyewitness-account-p-siemes-nd-translated-germa.

383 *"I just could not understand":* Robert Jay Lifton, *Death in Life: Survivors of Hiroshima* (Random House, 1967), 22–23.

383 *A later official count:* Richard B. Frank, *Downfall: The End of the Imperial Japanese Empire* (Random House, 1999), 286.
386 *"The city was afire":* William L. Laurence, *Dawn Over Zero: The Story of the Atomic Bomb* (Knopf, 1946), 208, 252.

Landing at Tinian

393 *"It kept changing":* William L. Laurence, *Dawn Over Zero: The Story of the Atomic Bomb* (Knopf, 1946), 219.
394 *"I had a strong conviction":* Paul W. Tibbets, *Flight of the Enola Gay* (Buckeye Aviation Book Co., 1989), 229.

Hiroshima Burning

406 *"I was with one of the first relief":* Nakaichi Nakamura in *Hibakusha: Survivors of Hiroshima and Nagasaki (trans. Gaynor Sekimori)* (Kosei Publishing Co., 1986), 78.

Reaction to the Bomb

410 *"We received our first":* Walter Cronkite, *A Reporter's Life* (Random House, 1996), 124.
411 *"In war—particularly this war":* Hanson W. Baldwin, "The Atomic Weapon," *The New York Times*, August 7, 1945, 10.
413 *"I certainly do recall":* S. L. Sanger, *Working on the Bomb: An Oral History of WWII Hanford* (Portland State University, 1995), 163.
414 *"I was a member of":* Walter S. Carpenter, interview by Stephane Groueff, January 25, 1965, Voices of the Manhattan Project, Atomic Heritage Foundation, https://ahf.nuclearmuseum.org/voices/oral-histories/walter-s-carpenters-interview/.

Mission #16

432 *"It doesn't take much":* Frederick L. Ashworth, *An Autobiography* (American Veterans Center, May 2001), 182, accessed via the American Veterans Center, https://americanveteranscenter.org/wp-content/uploads/2016/02/VADM-Frederick-Ashworth-Autobio_Part2.pdf.
435 *"Again no success":* Ibid.
437 *"Captain Beahan, the":* Ibid., 101.
438 *"The evidence of these":* Ibid.
439 *"For a second was":* Merle Miller and Abe Spitzer, *We Dropped the A-Bomb* (Verdun Press, 2015), Kindle.

Ground Zero at Nagasaki

443 *"Near the center":* Masao Shiotsuki, *Doctor of Nagasaki: "My First Assignment was Mercy Killing"* (Kōsei Publishing Co., 1989), 8.

445 *"As the relief squad":* Ibid., 58

447 *"I reported to the director":* Richard Lloyd Parry, "The Luckiest or Unluckiest Man in the World? Tsutomu Yamaguchi, Double A-Bomb Victim," *The Times* (London), March 25, 2009, https://web.archive.org/web/20140921181444/https:/blogs.thetimes.co.uk/section/asia-exile/20579/the-luckiest-or-unluckiest-man-in-the-world-tsutomu-yamaguchi-double-a-bomb-victim/.

448 *"On August 9, the devil's":* Charles Pellegrino, *The Last Train from Hiroshima: The Survivors Look Back* (Henry Holt, 2010) 273.

449 *The atomic bomb exploded:* Joseph Quinn, "The British POWs of Hiroshima and Nagasaki, 1945," The National Archives (UK), September 4, 2020, https://blog.nationalarchives.gov.uk/the-british-pows-of-hiroshima-and-nagasaki-1945/.

450 *"I was with a work party":* Hugh V. Clarke, *Last Stop Nagasaki!* (Unwin Hyman, 1984), 96.

V-J Day

466 *"The destruction at":* George C. Marshall, interview by Forrest C. Pogue, February 15, 1957, Forrest C. Pogue Interview Tapes, The George C. Marshall Foundation, https://www.marshallfoundation.org/wp-content/uploads/2014/05/Marshall_Interview_Tape16.pdf.

466 *"Permit me to respectfully suggest":* Ham, *Hiroshima Nagasaki*, 379. Footnote on same page is Hastings, *Retribution*, 507.

467 *"The Supreme War Council":* Richard B. Frank, *Downfall: The End of the Imperial Japanese Empire* (Random House, 1999), 347.

467 *"I have given serious thought":* There is no verbatim transcript of the final imperial discussions, but the emperor's remarks were re-created as best as possible—"meticulous[ly]" even, in the words of Frank, *Downfall*, 295—by Robert Butow in his book, *Japan's Decision to Surrender* (Stanford University Press, 1954), 175–76, based on surviving records and testimony.

469 *"Thinking of the people dying":* Frank, *Downfall*, 19.

471 *"It wasn't until":* Merle Miller and Abe Spitzer, *We Dropped the A-Bomb* (Verdun Press, 2015), Kindle.

474 *"During the week when":* United States Atomic Energy Commission, *In the Matter of J. Robert Oppenheimer: Transcript of Hearing Before Personnel Security Board and Texts of Principal Documents and Letters* (MIT Press, 1971).

474 *"Under a brilliant New Mexico sky":* Richard Rhodes, *The Making of the Atomic Bomb* (Simon & Schuster, 1986), 758.

475 *"I could have died":* Mark McDonald, "Tsutomu Yamaguchi, Survivor of 2 Atomic Blasts, Dies at 93," *New York Times*, January 6, 2010, https://www.nytimes.com/2010/01/07/world/asia/07yamaguchi.html.

The Sickness

480 *"There were no medicines":* Paul Ham, Hiroshima *Nagasaki: The Real Story of the Atomic Bombings and Their Aftermath* (HarperCollins, 2011), 419.

481 *"One of the greatest":* Masao Shiotsuki, *Doctor of Nagasaki: "My First Assignment was Mercy Killing"* (Kōsei Publishing Co., 1989), 11.

Epilogue

483 *"That the atomic bomb":* Leslie Nakashima, "Hiroshima as I Saw It," *United Press International*, August 27, 1945, https://www.upi.com/Archives/1945/08/27/Hiroshima-as-I-saw-it/8051438702501/.

484 *On Friday, August 31, 1945:* Associated Press, "Japanese Reports Doubted," *New York Times*, August 31, 1945, 4, https://timesmachine.nytimes.com/timesmachine/1945/08/31/88287747.html?pageNumber=4.

484 *"Japanese reports of":* Leslie Nakashima, "Hiroshima Gone, Newsman Finds; City Vanished Under Single Blow of Atom Bomb, He Says After Tour of Area Dumfounded by Destruction Damage Extends for Miles," *New York Times*, August 31, 1945, 4, https://www.nytimes.com/1945/08/31/archives/hiroshima-gone-newsman-finds-city-vanished-under-single-blow-of.html.

486 *"The Japanese claim that":* William L. Laurence, "U.S. Atom Bomb Site Belies Tokyo Tales," *New York Times*, September 12, 1945, 1, 4, https://timesmachine.nytimes.com/timesmachine/1945/09/12/306097342.pdf?pdf_redirect=true&ip=0.

486 *"As one of":* Masao Shiotsuki, *Doctor of Nagasaki: "My First Assignment was Mercy Killing"* (Kōsei Publishing Co., 1989), 12.

487 *"When headlines say":* Lewis Gannett, "Books and Things," *New York Herald Tribune*, August 29, 1946, 23.

490 *"Her eyes were shining":* This and following quote from Masahiro from Pellegrino, *The Last Train from Hiroshima*, 294, 291.

494 *"We established Nihon":* Nihon Hidankyo, Nobel Lecture, December 10, 2024, https://www.nobelprize.org/prizes/peace/2024/nihon-hidankyo/lecture/.

494 *"We did this job":* J. Robert Oppenheimer, "Speech to the Association of Los Alamos Scientists, November 2, 1945," in *Robert Oppenheimer: Letters and Recollection*, eds. Alice Kimball Smith and Charles Weiner, 317.

495 *"I have been asked again":* S. L. Sanger, *Working on the Bomb: An Oral History of WWII Hanford* (Portland State University, 1995), 217.

497 *"I do not know":* There have been many slightly different versions of this Einstein quote circulated over the years. This version is best approximated by an interview he gave the magazine *Liberal Judaism*, "Einstein at 70," with Alfred Werner (April–May 1949), 12. See also Alice Celaprice, *The Ultimate Quotable Einstein* (Princeton University Press, 2011), 280.

INDEX

Page numbers in *italics* refer to photographs and maps.

IMAGE CREDITS

Interior

Author's Note—National Archives, NAID #414401105
Foreword: Dawn at Trinity—U.S. Department of Energy, Historian's Office.
Particles Unseen—Wikimedia Commons
Darkness Falls on Europe—National Archives, NAID #162124785
Fleeing Fascism—American Institute of Physics Emilio Segrè Visual Archives, Wheeler Collection
Adjusting to the New World—*March of Time*, "Atomic Power" episode, Getty Images/Universal History Archive
The M.A.U.D. Committee—New York Times Paris Bureau Collection, National Archives NAID #541917
December 7, 1941—U.S. Naval History and Heritage Command Photograph, NH 50930
Setting Up the Met Lab—Photo from Lawrence Berkeley National Laboratory; © 2010 The Regents of the University of California, Lawrence Berkeley National Laboratory
FDR's OK—U.S. Department of Energy, Historian's Office.
Creating the Manhattan Engineer District—American Institute of Physics Emilio Segrè Visual Archives
Three Big Decisions—U.S. Department of Energy, Historian's Office.
Making the Pile—U.S. Department of Energy, Historian's Office.
Chain Reaction—U.S. Department of Energy, Historian's Office.
Oak Ridge: Creating the Clinton Engineer Works—U.S. Department of Energy, Historian's Office.
Oak Ridge: Y-12—Photo by Ed Westcott, U.S. Department of Energy, Historian's Office.

Oak Ridge: Living Inside the Gates—U.S. Department of Energy, Historian's Office.

Oak Ridge: Making U-235—U.S. Department of Energy, Historian's Office.

Los Alamos: Project Y—U.S. Department of Energy, Historian's Office.

Los Alamos: Working on the Mesa—U.S. Department of Energy, Historian's Office.

Life on Bathtub Row—U.S. Department of Energy, Historian's Office.

Oak Ridge: Glimpsing Plutonium—U.S. Department of Energy, Historian's Office.

Los Alamos: Designing the Bomb—U.S. Department of Energy, Historian's Office.

Hanford: Life in a Construction Camp—U.S. Department of Energy, Historian's Office.

Hanford: Making Plutonium en Masse—U.S. Department of Energy, Historian's Office.

Hanford: The B Reactor—U.S. Department of Energy, Historian's Office.

Boeing's Bomber—Special Collections and University Archives at Texas Woman's University

Code Name Silverplate—U.S. Air Force Number 59470AC, National Archives NAID #204995289

Training the 509th—Photo from Historic American Buildings Survey, UT-125 (#ut0288), Library of Congress

Spring 1945—Lead photo: White House Photo, National Archives NAID #291414349. Interior Truman swearing-in: White House Photo, National Archives NAID #289577644

100 Tons of TNT—U.S. Department of Energy, Historian's Office.

Selecting the Targets—U.S. Air Force Number 58408AC, National Archives NAID #204834836

The Interim Committee—National Archives NAID #213260234

Trinity—U.S. Department of Energy, Historian's Office.

Potsdam with Truman—U.S. Army Signal Corps, National Archives, NAID #348307613

At Tinian—U.S. Air Force Number 69657AC, National Archives, NAID #204976340

Moving the Bomb—Department of the Navy, Bureau of Ships photo, National Archives NAID #496082657

The Day Before—Lead Photo: War Department. Office of the Chief of Engineers. Manhattan Engineer District., National Archives NAID #76048570. Interior *Enola Gay* crew photo: US Air Force Reference Number: 58206AC, National Archives, NAID #204972595

Code Name Centerboard—US Air Force Reference Number: 69655AC, National Archives NAID #204974377

Ground Zero in Hiroshima—Lead photo: U.S. Air Force Number 60604AC, National Archives NAID #204836181. Interior photo by Yoshito Matsushige.

Landing at Tinian—Lead Photo: U.S. Air Force Number A59476AC, National Archives NAID #204972490. Interior Tibbets photo: U.S. Air Force Number B59473AC, National Archives NAID #204972586

Hiroshima Burning—National Archives NAID #22345674

Reaction to the Bomb—U.S. Department of Energy, Historian's Office.

The Day After in Hiroshima—National Archives NAID #414401105

Mission #16—U.S. Department of Energy, Historian's Office.

Ground Zero at Nagasaki—Photo by Yōsuke Yamahata, National Archives NAID #558581

The Return of Bockscar—U.S. Air Force Number 69680AC, National Archives NAID #204836906

Afterward in Nagasaki—Photo by Joe O'Donnell, United States Information Agency

V-J Day—Photo by Ed Westcott, U.S. Department of Energy, Historian's Office.

The Sickness—Photo by Shunkichi Kikuchi

Epilogue—National Archives NAID #350290443

Photo Insert 1

1 Wikimedia Commons

2 Fermilab, U.S. Department of Energy

3 Photo by Donald Cooksey, National Archives NAID #

4 Photograph by Donald Cooksey, National Archives NAID #7664945

5 National Archives NAID #558594
6 Photo by Laura Gilpin, "Los Alamos School, School and Patrol Groups," May 1933, copyright 1979, Item #P1979.235.66 located at the and used by permission of the Amon Carter Museum of American Art, Fort Worth, Texas.
7 Photo # apf3-00232, Hanna Holborn Gray Special Collections Research Center, University of Chicago Library
8 U.S. Department of Energy, Historian's Office.
9 U.S. Department of Energy, Historian's Office.
10 U.S. Department of Energy, Historian's Office.
11 U.S. Department of Energy, Historian's Office.
12 American Institute of Physics Emilio Segrè Visual Archives.
13 U.S. Department of Energy, Historian's Office.
14–31 Los Alamos National Laboratory
32 US Air Force Reference Number: B56138AC, National Archives NAID #205000605
33 U.S. Air Force Number 85180AC, National Archives NAID #204837506

Photo Insert 2

1 Photo by Jack W. Aeby, U.S. Department of Energy, Historian's Office.
2 Los Alamos Scientific Laboratory, National Archives NAID #348341916
3 War Department, Office of the Chief of Engineers, Manhattan Engineer District, National Archives, NAID #519397
4 Los Alamos National Laboratory Archive
5 U.S. Air Force photo
6 U.S. Strategic Bombing Survey, National Archives NAID #540225
7 U.S. Strategic Bombing Survey, National Archives NAID #540226
8 US Air Force records, National Archives NAID #148728174
9 U.S. Strategic Bombing Survey, National Archives NAID #22345677
10 U.S. Air Force Number K6014, National Archives NAID #205001904
11 US Air Force Photo 080715-F-1234S-006
12 Photo by Yōsuke Yamahata
13 Photo by Gonichi Kimura, National Archives NAID #519686
14 U.S. Air Force Number 60589AC, National Archives NAID #204836172
15 National Archives NAID #519384

16 Photo by Hajime Miyatake

17 Photo by Yōsuke Yamahata

18 War Department, Office of the Chief of Engineers, Manhattan Engineer District, National Archives NAID #280957391

19 Photo by Eric Long and Mark Avino, Smithsonian National Air and Space Museum (NASM 98-15873).

ABOUT THE AUTHOR

GARRETT M. GRAFF has spent two decades covering politics, technology, and national security. The former editor of *POLITICO Magazine* and longtime WIRED and CNN contributor, he writes the popular *Doomsday Scenario* newsletter and hosts the Edward R. Murrow Award–winning podcast *Long Shadow*. He is the author of ten books, including the #1 national bestseller *The Only Plane in the Sky* and the *New York Times* bestsellers *When the Sea Came Alive* and *Watergate*, which was a finalist for the Pulitzer Prize in History.